Best wishes.

Pamela Blevin

16 May 2009

Ivor Gurney & Marion Scott

This dual biography of Ivor Gurney and Marion Scott tells the dramatic story of two geniuses who met at the Royal College of Music in 1911 and formed an unlikely partnership that illuminated and enriched the musical and literary worlds in which they moved. Gurney's poetry and songs have taken their place as 'part of the inheritance of England'. Scott, Gurney's strongest advocate, emerges from his shadow for the first time. Her own remarkable achievements as a pioneering music critic, musicologist, advocate of contemporary music and women musicians place her among the most influential and respected women of her generation.

Based on original research, this is the first biography of Gurney since 1978 and the only biography of Scott. It offers new, in-depth perspectives on Gurney's attempts to create music and poetry while struggling to overcome the bipolar illness that eventually derailed his genius, and restores Marion Scott's rightful place in music history.

PAMELA BLEVINS, a former journalist and public relations consultant, is managing editor of *The Maud Powell Signature*, a magazine about women in classical music. She has published widely on British composers and poets.

Ivor Gurney
&
Marion Scott

Song of Pain and Beauty

Pamela Blevins

THE BOYDELL PRESS

First published 2008
The Boydell Press, Woodbridge

ISBN 978-1-84383-421-2

The Boydell Press is an imprint of Boydell & Brewer Ltd
PO Box 9, Woodbridge, Suffolk IP12 3DF, UK
and of Boydell & Brewer Inc.
668 Mt Hope Avenue, Rochester, NY 14620, USA
website: www.boydellandbrewer.com

A CIP record for this book is available
from the British Library

The publisher has no responsibility for the continued existence or accuracy of URLs for external or third-party internet websites referred to in this book, and does not guarantee that any content on such websites is, or will remain, accurate or appropriate

This publication is printed on acid-free paper

Designed and typeset in Adobe Warnock Pro by
David Roberts, Pershore, Worcestershire

Printed in Great Britain by
CPI Antony Rowe, Chippenham, Wiltshire

Dedicated to David Goodland, Patsy Murray,
Jill Robinson, Karen Shaffer
and to the memory of Mae Lindsay (1903–2005)

Contents

List of Illustrations   viii

Preface   x

Acknowledgements   xiii

Abbreviations   xvii

Poem: 'Song of Pain and Beauty'   xviii

PART I   *For various reasons, I don't think the whole story of Gurney's life, friends, misfortunes will ever be known.*   – Gerald Finzi

Prologue   2

1   London, 1911   3

2   A Clash of Wills   19

3   An Island of Serenity   29

4   Friendship and Poetry   40

PART II   *For after all, it is the artist's life which binds together the things of his creating, and neither of them is quite intelligible without the other.*   – Marion Scott

5   The Gurney Family   50

6   Golden Days   60

7   A Lad's Love   68

8   The First Breakdown   77

9   The Lost Year   84

PART III   *On our right? That's the road to Ypres. The less said about that road the better: no one goes down it for choice – it's British now.*   – Mary Borden

10   The Experiment   92

11   A Partnership   99

12   The Dirty Business of War   110

13   Blighty   120

14   'Love has come to bind me fast'   131

15   'You would rather know me dead'   148

16   An Uncertain Course   165

PART IV *What's madness but nobility of soul / At odds with circumstance?*
                                              – Theodore Roethke

17 A New Mastery 180

18 The Tide of Darkness 196

19 'There is dreadful hell within me' 206

20 Asylum – 'The soul halts here' 215

21 The Last Chance 222

22 'A fantastic mix-up' 238

23 Bitter Troubles and Suffering 253

24 'In time to come' 264

    Epilogue 283

APPENDIX 1 Ivor Gurney's Published Music 296

APPENDIX 2 Ivor Gurney's Published Writings 300

APPENDIX 3 Ivor Gurney – A Select Discography 302

APPENDIX 4 Marion Scott's Writings – A Select List 306

APPENDIX 5 Marion Scott's Unpublished Compositions –
            A Select List 309

    Bibliography 311

    Index 321

Illustrations

Between pages 110 and 111

1 Marion Scott in 1911 (Marion Scott Collection, The Royal College of Music, London)
2 Henry Prince (Photograph Courtesy Peabody Essex Museum, Salem, Massachusetts)
3 Sydney Charles Scott (S. Hardy Prince Collection)
4 The Scott home (Permission Audrey Hammond)
5 Ernest Farrar (Adrian Officer Collection)
6 Members of the Society of Women Musicians (Marion Scott Collection, The Royal College of Music, London)
7 Sir Charles Villiers Stanford (Maud Powell Society for Music and Education, Brevard, North Carolina)
8 An early view of the Royal College of Music (Maud Powell Society for Music and Education)
9 Ivor Gurney at the RCM (Permission of the Trustees of the Ivor Gurney Estate)
10 Herbert Howells (Paul Spicer: Private Collection)
11 Sydney Shimmin (The College Archives of The Cheltenham Ladies College)
12 Herbert Howells and Arthur Benjamin (Paul Spicer: Private Collection)
13 Ethel Voynich and family (Courtesy Dr Desmond MacHale, University College Cork, Ireland)
14 The Cotswolds near Painswick Beacon (Author's photograph)
15 Florence Gurney (Permission of the Trustees of the Ivor Gurney Estate)
16 David Gurney (Permission of the Trustees of the Ivor Gurney Estate)
17 Florence Gurney loved nature (Permission of the Trustees of the Ivor Gurney Estate)
18 Florence Gurney and her son Ronald (Permission of the Trustees of the Ivor Gurney Estate)
19 Winifred Gurney (Permission of the Trustees of the Ivor Gurney Estate)
20 Winifred in the early 1950s (Permission of the Trustees of the Ivor Gurney Estate)
21 Dorothy Gurney (Permission of the Trustees of the Ivor Gurney Estate)
22 Gurney in his early teens (Permission of the Trustees of the Ivor Gurney Estate)
23, 24 Ronald Gurney (Permission of the Trustees of the Ivor Gurney Estate)
25 Gloucester Cathedral (Author's Collection)

26 Frederick F. W. Harvey (Permission of the Trustees of the Ivor Gurney Estate)

27 The Reverend Alfred Cheesman (Permission of the Trustees of the Ivor Gurney Estate)

28 Westgate Street, Gloucester (Author's Collection)

Between pages 206 and 207

29 Private Ivor Gurney (Soldiers of the Gloucestershire Museum)

30 Gurney and Herbert Howells (Permission of the Trustees of the Ivor Gurney Estate)

31 Arthur Benjamin (Paul Spicer: Private Collection)

32 Gurney at bayonet practice (Soldiers of the Gloucestershire Museum)

33 Gurney at Rouen (Permission of the Trustees of the Ivor Gurney Estate)

34 Gurney in November 1917 (Permission of the Trustees of the Ivor Gurney Estate)

35 Volunteer Nurse Annie Drummond (Peggy Ann McKay Carter)

36 VAD Drummond with patients (Peggy Ann McKay Carter)

37 Ward 24, Bangour Hospital (Author's photograph)

38 Annie Drummond with her parents (Peggy Ann McKay Carter)

39 The Reverend T. Ratcliffe Barnett (Author's Collection)

40 The canteen at the Edinburgh War Hospital (West Lothian Libraries)

41 Annie Drummond after the war (Peggy Ann McKay Carter)

42 Gurney in 1920 (Permission of the Trustees of the Ivor Gurney Estate)

43 Marion Scott at the age of 45 (Marion Scott Collection, The Royal College of Music, London)

44, 45 Ivor Gurney portraits (Permission of the Trustees of the Ivor Gurney Estate)

46 Gerald Finzi (Gift of Joy Finzi)

47 Edmund Blunden (Margi Blunden)

48 John W. Haines (Pippa Bush)

49 Annie Drummond on her wedding day (Peggy Ann McKay Carter)

50 Gurney inscription to Drummond (Peggy Ann McKay Carter)

51 Gurney holding dog (Permission of the Trustees of the Ivor Gurney Estate)

52, 53 Gurney in the asylum (The Ivor Gurney Archive)

54 Gurney reading (Permission of the Trustees of the Ivor Gurney Estate)

55 Florence Gurney in old age (Permission of the Trustees of the Ivor Gurney Estate)

56 Gurney at Dover Beach (Permission of the Trustees of the Ivor Gurney Estate)

57 Gurney's grave (Permission of the Trustees of the Ivor Gurney Estate)

58, 59, 60 Marion Scott portraits (Author's Collection, gift of Joan Chissell)

Preface

$\mathcal{W}$RITING A BIOGRAPHY is an adventure, one that locks a writer in a long-term relationship with her subject, or in my case, two subjects: Ivor Gurney and Marion Scott. It's a bit like marriage – a commitment with its good times and bad, joys and sorrows, frustrations and rewards. Few writers realize at the outset just how complex and demanding a relationship it will be or where it will lead. I certainly didn't!

When I first encountered Gurney in 1983, I never thought that one day I would write his life. At the time my only interest in him was his connection with composer Gerald Finzi and that's really how it all began. In 1982 I had founded the Finzi Society of America to promote wider interest in Finzi's music and life in the United States and Canada. The following year I wrote a brief article about Gurney and Finzi for my newsletter. I didn't think much more about Gurney after that because I was so focused on Finzi. To me Gurney was little more than a footnote and Marion Scott was like a leaf on the wind, seen one minute then blown away and forgotten!

Then in 1984 I attended the Summer Weekend of English Music, a Finzi event held at Oxford, where I met Joy Finzi for the first time. Over dinner one night, my life was about to change in ways I could not imagine. Joy had read my article and started talking about Gurney and his family without any prompting from me. She told me about the work she and Gerald had done to preserve Gurney's legacy and a little about some of the people involved. I don't remember any of the details because they faded into the background when she launched into a description of the tailor's shop run by Gurney's brother Ronald in Gloucester. With her artist's eye for detail and her poet's sensibility for atmosphere, she described how the opening and closing of the door sent a breeze into the shop's dark interior that lifted the corners of bolts of cloth to give them the illusion of 'bats fluttering about'. It was an image I would never forget. I felt an odd chill on that warm summer evening.

After our first meeting, Joy and I corresponded regularly and I would see her when I visited England. Inevitably she would turn to Gurney in her letters and in conversation. We never discussed Finzi. Was I being directed to look more deeply at Gurney, I began to wonder?

I decided that perhaps there was more to him than I realized, so I reread Michael Hurd's biography, bought P. J. Kavanagh's excellent edition of Gurney's poetry, found a few recordings (LPs in those days) and enjoyed getting to know Gurney better. It might have remained that way – Gurney as someone I simply enjoyed – had a friend and I not started working on a small project about the poets, artists and composers of World War I. That's when Gurney really took hold of me, but the more I read the more I realized that I was asking questions for which I could find no answers. Who was Marion Scott? Who was Annie Drummond? Had Gurney been shell-shocked? Was he really schizophrenic? – I had known a schizophrenic woman quite well, and Gurney seemed nothing like her. I decided that I must search for answers myself.

When I was in England in the summer of 1988, Joy Finzi insisted on taking me on her own tour of 'Gurney Country'. We set off on a dismal wet and windy September morning, coincidentally the 32nd anniversary of Gerald Finzi's death. As we headed west the rain stopped, leaving the landscape cloaked in a lingering white mist. I could see only hints of what lay in the shrouded distances. When we neared Gloucestershire, the sun broke through almost as if on cue. With Joy as my guide, I saw for the first time Ivor Gurney's Gloucestershire: the Cotswolds, Birdlip Hill, the city of Gloucester with its cathedral so central to Gurney's early life, and finally at the end of the day, the parish church of St Matthew at Twigworth, where Joy, tired by now, sent me off alone in search of Gurney's grave in the over-grown cemetery. I remember well the abandonment and neglect that then pervaded the church building, bordering on eerie with its cold stone façade and unkempt grounds. I felt unsettled. It was not a place of comfort.

Outside the church grounds I saw sheep grazing in a field and beyond that the pale blue line of the Cotswolds. Then I turned and saw May Hill with its distinctive cap of trees and I felt that Gurney was at least lying between the hills he loved. The grave itself was overgrown with grass and weeds, the marker pitted from the weather and covered with lichen.* It was not what Marion Scott had in mind when she wrote to Gerald Finzi, 'there is something tranquillising now in the thought of him lying at peace in Twigworth Churchyard' in 'an oak coffin lined with elm and cushioned with white satin', after a burial that 'befitted a poet'. Joy Finzi's tour had come to a bittersweet climax. When we reached the motorway, rainbows began arching over the landscape. Sometimes we seemed to drive into them. They were all around us. Marion Scott, a metaphysician, would have interpreted them as a 'sign'. Maybe they were, I don't know. By the time we returned to Joy's home, I knew that Ivor Gurney was going to be in my life for some time.

I became a detective, first searching the Gurney archive thanks to a fellowship from the English Speaking Union of Boston and then digging for clues and information in London at the Royal College of Music, in Edinburgh and Armadale, Scotland, and in Boston, Wellesley and Salem, Massachusetts. There have been many high points in my quest: discovering Marion Scott's diary and four chapters of her unpublished memoir as well as her writings; meeting Marion's goddaughter Margaret Brockway; talking to Marion's niece Audrey Priestman; finding S. Hardy Prince, the historian for the American side of Marion's family; tracking down Annie Nelson Drummond and having many conversations with her daughter Peggy Ann and others who knew Annie; visiting Annie's home in Scotland and seeing the grounds of the former Edinburgh War Hospital where she and Ivor Gurney met; discussing Gurney's bipolar illness with Dr Kay Redfield

---

* The original marker collapsed, as Gurney's mother Florence feared it might, and is now on view inside the church. A new marker stands in its place and the grave is well maintained.

Jamison; finding Don Ray, an American pioneer in Gurney scholarship, and carrying on a lively correspondence with him until his unexpected death; receiving newly discovered images of Gurney and his family from Anthony Boden and, best of all, making new friends along the way.

There were some minor frustrations: not being able to find many photographs of the Scott family and of Marion Scott because, as her niece told me, 'if she didn't like the way she looked in a photograph, it disappeared'; not being able to locate any images of Margaret and Emily Hunt who were so important in Gurney's early life. Of course there were times along the way when I did not want to go on because I felt overwhelmed by such a huge task but inevitably a new piece of information would land in my lap and my momentary lapse would be forgotten in my excitement.

My original plan was to write a biography about Gurney as a composer and poet but as I got to know him better I came to believe that his life was his greatest creation. His music and poetry are threads that run through my text but it is his troubled and tragic life that stitches all the pieces together. As Marion Scott wrote: 'For after all, it is the artist's life which binds together the things of his creating, and neither of them is quite intelligible without the other.' I have chosen to focus on the life and will leave it to others to delve more deeply into his music and poetry.

In the early days of my writing I kept encountering roadblocks and I wondered why. I had done my research. I had a lot of new information and different perspectives. I had a sense of purpose and direction but something seemed to be missing. Then I realized what it was: Marion Scott.

For all that Gurney suffered and for all the disappointment that dogged his life, there was always one constant in it that he could rely upon – Marion Scott. When they met at the Royal College of Music in 1911, she was young and vibrant and possessed a poetic pre-Raphaelite beauty. It wasn't long before the two became friends. This friendship would endure through years marred by war and his illness, factors that indeed served only to strengthen and deepen their union, to bind them closer together. Over time each became dependent upon the other and on the support, love and mutual nurturing that was at the core of their relationship.

Marion Scott was no mere leaf on the wind. I saw sides to her that had never been explored or written about, sides that were essential in understanding why she laboured for Gurney with such devotion and often at great physical and emotional cost to her. Her life beyond her work for Gurney was rich, full and rewarding. Marion was, like her American ancestors, a pioneer and visionary adventurer who opened new fields to women; a gifted writer and musician; a romantic and metaphysician, an organizer and shrewd promoter. Those sides of her would remain hidden unless I brought her out of Gurney's shadow and into her own light. Her own remarkable life became as important to me as Gurney's and I realized that any biography of Ivor Gurney coming from me must also include Marion Scott because she was, in fact, his partner. To separate them would only tell part of the 'Song of Pain and Beauty' that bound them together.

Pamela Blevins
Brevard, North Carolina

Acknowledgements

No BOOK is written alone. Many individuals helped me bring the story of Ivor Gurney and Marion Scott to the printed page.

In a way the stage was set many years ago when I was still in high school in the United States. In those days, the early 1960s, music appreciation was still taught as a major subject along with English, mathematics, history, languages and science. I was fortunate that my teacher was Mae Lindsay, a visionary educator who made music and its creators come alive against a backdrop of history. From her I learned about possibilities, about the importance of connections and how music can be used to teach all other subjects. Mae Lindsay set me on the path that ultimately led me to write about Ivor Gurney and Marion Scott. Sadly she died in March 2005 at the age of 102 before she could hold the finished book in her hands.

When I began my career in journalism, I was fortunate to work under Patsy Murray, a fine writer and demanding editor who asked nothing of me that she was not willing to do herself. She set a high standard of excellence that I have tried to maintain throughout my writing career.

The late Joy Finzi was the catalyst for this work. From the time we first met in 1984, she seemed to be guiding me to look at Gurney's life. Although Gerald Finzi was my primary interest then, Joy kept steering me in Gurney's direction.

I owe a great debt to three friends: David Goodland, Jill Robinson and Karen Shaffer. David shared his own extensive research on Gurney as well as his insights in many conversations and letters over the years since our first meeting at Gloucester Cathedral in 1989. He became a partner in the evolution of this book, someone I could always rely on for help and encouragement. He also 'cracked the whip', so to speak, to keep me working, focused and on track. 'Keep writing', he told me time and again when I'd falter. His careful reading of each chapter and his suggestions not only improved the book but helped give it shape and make it stronger.

Jill Robinson's encyclopaedic knowledge of Gurney proved invaluable. Any time I found myself wondering where a line of poetry came from or where I had seen a reference no matter how obscure, I simply called Jill, who provided an immediate answer. She generously shared her own research and perceptions and played devil's advocate to help me sort through the complexities of Gurney's life.

Karen Shaffer played many roles. Acting as a sounding board, she listened patiently as I talked *endlessly* about Gurney and Scott throughout the writing of the book. Her clear lawyer's mind and persistent questioning, which at times made me feel like a witness on the stand, helped me keep my writing focused and my approach objective and balanced. She demanded precision, honesty and fairness of me. Her thoughtful editing of the initial drafts made the revisions easier. She guided me to deeper insights and understanding of Gurney, Scott and others who were involved in their story. As a biographer herself, she understood and shared the joy and difficulties I experienced in writing about Gurney and Scott.

Peggy Ann McKay Carter, Annie Drummond's daughter, shared memories of her mother and the details of her life with me and generously gave me the photographs and copies of the documents that appear in this book. The late Isabella Watson of Armadale, Scotland, who lived in the house that Annie's family built, knew the Drummonds and provided me information that was unknown even to Peggy Ann and that would otherwise have been lost.

Sydney Hardy Prince, Marion Scott's American cousin, her father's namesake and the Prince family historian, shared years of research with me that traced the family back to 1639 in what was then the New World. He kindly provided me with a rare photograph of Scott's father Sydney Scott and a letter from Scott's mother Annie Prince Scott as well as leads to other important information.

Margaret Brockway, Marion Scott's goddaughter, invited me to her home to talk about her 'Aunt Marion' and to share details about life in the Scott household. The late Audrey Priestman, Marion Scott's niece, the most direct link with Marion, gave me personal information about her aunt and about the family that ultimately led me to Sydney Hardy Prince.

Linda Hart became my right hand helping me fill in some of the gaps in my research at the Gurney Archive when I could not return to England myself. Her support, encouragement and enthusiasm throughout the long process of producing this book also helped keep me on track.

My quest for information took me to many places in journeys made possible thanks to email and the Internet.

I want to thank the following individuals:

In Australia – Dr Barbara Garlick.

In Canada – Dr Evelyn Harden, who so generously gave me copies of her research on the Whistler and Prince families in St Petersburg.

In England – Martin Anderson, Paul Andrews, Robert Barnett, the late John Bishop, Anthony and Anne Boden, Kathleen Boothman (Cheltenham Ladies College), Ian Bown, Angela Bromley-Martin, Julie Cheesman, the late Joan Chissell, Andrew Cook for kindly sharing his enlightening research on Ethel and Wilfrid Voynich, P. R. Evans (Archivist, Gloucester), the late Howard Ferguson, Christopher and Hilary Finzi, Councillor Janet Grigg, Wendy French, the late Ursula Howells, Helen F. Keen (County Archivist, Surrey History Centre), Paul Kelman, Philip Lancaster, Dr William Marshall, Dr Gary Midgley, Sally Minogue, Robert Moreland, J. Paul Northall, Adrian Officer, Lynn Parker, Francine Payne, Bruce Phillips, the late Donald Roberts, Peter Shimmin, Paul Spicer, David and Ann Tolley, Ian Venables, Brian Wheeler, the late Ursula Vaughan Williams. Special thanks to Audrey Hammond for providing me with a copy of the ink and watercolour painting of the Scotts' home which she painted in 2004 for Mrs Jean Cran, a classicist and teacher who had lived in the house for many years. And to Rolf Jordan for his fine work in restoring various photographs in the book and for locating others for me.

The Gurney Archive was, of course, an invaluable resource. I thank Penny Ely (former Trustee), Graham Baker, Anthony Boden, John Phillips, Ian Venables. The Royal College of Music: Christopher Bornet, and Peter Horton, who led me to Marion Scott treasures that enabled me to expand on Marion's life in ways I didn't think possible when I began the book.

In Ireland – Dr Desmond MacHale, University College Cork, for sharing his research on Ethel Voynich and her remarkable family, and Carol Quinn, Archivist at Cork for providing me with leads and with photographs of Mrs Voynich.

In Scotland – the late Janet Barnett, daughter of the Reverend T. Ratcliffe Barnett, Andrew Bethune (Edinburgh Central Library), Isobel and Derek Bilsland, M. Sybil Cavanagh (Local Collection Historian, West Lothian), Alistair McKay, Donald A. D. MacLeod (Consultant Surgeon, West Lothian NHS Trust St John's Hospital at Howden), Mrs E. A. Munro, the Reverend Ian G. Scott (Greenbank Church, Edinburgh). Special thanks to Jo Leighton who made so much possible during my visits to Edinburgh, particularly our tour of the Edinburgh War Hospital grounds that became more of an adventure than we anticipated!

In South Africa – C. M. Blight at the Cory Library for Historical Research at Grahamstown.

In the United States – Maria Foltz Baylock, Rachel Canada (Manuscripts Department, University of North Carolina, Chapel Hill), Charles S. Carriker, the late Gary Clark, Dr Joseph Corbo, Natalya Fishman (Morton Grove Public Library, Illinois), Dr Paula Gillett, Mary Hogan, Dr Kay Redfield Jamison (Johns Hopkins School of Medicine), the late Dr Harald N. Johnson, Stephan McKeown, Linda Merrill (Associate Curator of American Art, Freer Gallery, Washington, DC), Patsy Murray, Colonel Edward Raymond, Jacqueline L. Robinson, Nora Sirbaugh, Ilene Sterns, Phyllis Sullivan, Susan Szpak (Salem, Massachusetts Public Library), Charlotte Tibbetts, Lillian Wentworth (Thayer Academy, Braintree, Massachusetts), Janet S. White. The Peabody Essex Museum, Salem, Massachusetts: Mrs G. M. Ayers and Jane E. Ward. The staff at the Office of Vital Statistics, Boston, Massachusetts, the Library of Congress Music Division and Periodicals Division and Robin Rausch, Washington, DC. Special thanks to Marc Pachter, Linda Lear, Kitty Kelley and all the members of the Washington, DC Biography Group for a decade of insight, sharing and knowledge about the art of biography.

Grants: The English Speaking Union Boston Branch, Traveling Fellowship. The Thanks Be To Grandmother Winifred Foundation, Wainscott, New York.

Gurney scholarship is a co-operative venture with different individuals laying foundations for others to build upon to bring Ivor Gurney's legacy to a wider public. I owe a large debt of gratitude to Dr R. K. R. Thornton for his painstaking work in compiling Gurney's letters for publication – more than 400 letters written between 1912 and 1922. Without this important volume, my task would have been much more difficult, time consuming and certainly more costly because I would have had to take up temporary residence in England in order to have access to the letters.

I must acknowledge the work of the composer and educator Don B. Ray, who sadly passed away in April 2005. Mr Ray's early research into Gurney's life began in 1950 at a time when Marion Scott, members of Gurney's family and his friends were still living. Mr Ray's pioneering research marked the first concentrated effort to gather the facts of Gurney's life and laid a foundation for those of us who came after him. And I must acknowledge the late Dr Pauline Alderman, Mr Ray's department chairman at the University of Southern California, who brought Gurney to his attention. I extend my gratitude to Dr Charles Moore, another American pioneer in Gurney scholarship, who catalogued Gurney's songs and who introduced American audiences to Gurney's music in the early 1960s.

Dr George Walter, P. J. Kavanagh and again Dr Thornton for their work on Gurney's poetry. The late Michael Hurd's groundbreaking biography, written at a time when the Gurney papers in the Archive were disorganized and it was difficult to work with them. Anthony Boden and Sylvie Price for spending two years organizing the Gurney Archive, making it so accessible and, in the process, ensuring the preservation of Gurney's legacy.

A special thanks to readers David Goodland, Rolf Jordan, Sally Minogue, Karen Shaffer, Nora Sirbaugh and Ian Venables who took the time to read the text carefully and make invaluable suggestions.

And finally, I acknowledge Marion Margaret Scott for her love and devotion to Ivor Gurney.

The author and publishers are grateful to all the institutions and persons listed for permission to reproduce the materials in which they hold copyright. Every effort has been made to trace copyright holders; apologies are offered for any omission, and the publishers will be pleased to add any necessary acknowledgement in subsequent editions.

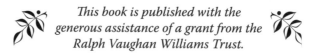

This book is published with the generous assistance of a grant from the Ralph Vaughan Williams Trust.

Abbreviations

CL	Ivor Gurney, *Collected Letters*, ed. R. K. R. Thornton (Ashington: MidNAG; Manchester: Carcanet, 1991)*
CP	*Collected Poems of Ivor Gurney*, ed. P. J. Kavanagh (Oxford: Oxford University Press, 1982)
DBR	Don Brandon Ray
DBR, IG	Don Brandon Ray, *Ivor Gurney (1890–1937): His Life and Works* (MA thesis: California State University at Long Beach, 1980)
ELV	Ethel Voynich
FG	Florence Gurney
FWH	F. W. Harvey
GA	Gurney Archive
GF	Gerald Finzi
HH	Herbert Howells
IG	Ivor Gurney
JF	Joy Finzi
JWH	John W. Haines
KD	Kathleen Dale
KE	Katharine Eggar
MMM	M. Muir Mackenzie
MMS	Marion Scott
MSC	Marion Scott Collection, Royal College of Music
OIG	Michael Hurd, *The Ordeal of Ivor Gurney* (Oxford: Oxford University Press, 1978)
RCM	Royal College of Music
RD	Randolph Davis
RG	Ronald Gurney
SGS	Sydney Gordon Shimmin
SWM	Society of Women Musicians
WG	Winifred Gurney

* I have followed Dr Thornton's codes for dating in the *Collected Letters*: (E) editorial note on a letter; (G) Ivor Gurney; (KT) Kelsey Thornton; (O) *The Ordeal of Ivor Gurney*; (P) Postmark; (PB) Pamela Blevins; (S) Marion Scott; (W) George Walter.

Song of Pain and Beauty

(To M. M. S.)

O may these days of pain,
  These wasted-seeming days,
Somewhere reflower again
  With scent and savour of praise.
Draw out of memory all bitterness
  Of night with Thy sun's rays.

And strengthen Thou in me
  The love of men here found,
And eager charity,
  That, out of difficult ground,
Spring like flowers in barren deserts, or
  Like light, or a lovely sound.

A simpler heart than mine
  Might have seen beauty clear
Where I could see no sign
  Of Thee, but only fear.
Strengthen me, make me to see Thy beauty always
  In every happening here.

IVOR GURNEY
In Trenches, March 1917

Part I

For various reasons, I don't think the whole story of Gurney's life, friends, misfortunes will ever be known.

– Gerald Finzi, 26 May 1940

Prologue

O N 18 FEBRUARY 1911 Marion Scott clipped a brief notice from *The Times* of London. She wrote the date across the top and added it to a substantial collection of articles that chronicled important events in her life. But this article was different; it did not mention her. It simply announced the recipients of the 'free Open Scholarships' to the Royal College of Music, where she worked. She had not saved such a notice before. Yet on that winter day, Marion Scott had no way of knowing that one person mentioned in *The Times* would become entwined in her life and change it forever – a young composition scholar from Gloucester, Ivor Gurney.

CHAPTER 1

London, 1911

*T*O NEWCOMERS at the Royal College of Music like Ivor Gurney, Marion Scott's petite stature, soft voice and quiet demeanour gave the impression of fragility. In 1911, at the age of thirty-four, she was, however, a tough, pragmatic, strong-willed and visionary woman who possessed steel-like courage tempered by a personal magnetism that drew both men and women to her. She was a natural leader, still young enough to be idealistic but mature enough to know how to channel her idealism into practical schemes that benefited many people.

In addition to music, Scott's gifts included poetry, writing, teaching, historical research and strong organizational, promotional and entrepreneurial skills, the latter inherited from several generations of her adventurous American ancestors. She possessed an acute analytical mind and a strong aptitude for mathematics and design that prompted one friend to declare that 'engineering might have been her choice of profession had she been a man'.[1] She was also a skilled photographer.

Born in 1877, Marion Scott was a young woman at the right time. Women were stirring public sentiment and challenging the social order as they raised their voices in pursuit of equality. They had already made minor gains in England when in 1869 unmarried women householders were granted the right to vote in local elections. The same year, John Stuart Mill published *The Subjection of Women*, which argued for the equal treatment of women under law. This forward-looking book became a centrepiece for the worldwide women's movement. Other men joined him in supporting the cause of women and working for their rights. In 1879 radical barrister Richard Pankhurst and his wife Emmeline became activists for women's suffrage and for married women's property rights. Eventually Emmeline rose to become a powerful militant feminist and founder of The Women's Social and Political Union. In 1884 the Married Women's Property Act gave women the right to keep all personal and real property instead of relinquishing it to their husbands. By 1894 married women had won the right to vote in local elections but were still forbidden to vote in national elections.

The suffrage movement was gaining strength as it found support in progressive thinkers and generous activists like Marion's parents, Sydney and Annie Scott. Both were deeply committed to various reform movements, including temperance and women's suffrage, taking a particular interest in the plight of women and children in all strata of society. They were outspoken advocates for better treatment of the servant class and set an example for others to follow. They paid their domestic staff well, gave them generous paid holiday leave amounting to three weeks a year, and treated them with respect.

During her teenage years, Marion regularly accompanied her parents to temperance and suffrage meetings. She was introduced early to the practice of men and women working co-operatively to achieve common goals, an approach she employed throughout her life to win support for the advancement of women in music.

The Scotts' liberal attitude extended to education. 'Like the ancient Greeks my parents decided I should learn dancing and music ahead of other subjects', Marion revealed in an unpublished memoir. 'I was accordingly entered as an infant pupil in the Dancing Class held weekly by a Miss Louisa Pears at the Crystal Palace School of Art'.[2] The Crystal Palace became central to Marion's childhood.

Located on Sydenham Hill about a half mile from the Scotts' home on The Avenue (now Dulwich Wood Road), Gipsy Hill, the Palace was a monument to Victorian imagination and excess. Originally in Hyde Park, the building was dismantled, reassembled and enlarged to stand on 200 acres eight miles south of London, where 'town and country met'. The massive glass structure with its high-ceilinged nave and long north and south transepts was the world's first theme park, the forerunner of today's world's fairs. Its courts, gardens and grounds were filled with an eclectic mix of art, history, modern exhibitions, live animals, re-creations of the past, music festivals, band concerts, cycling races (later Marion became an ardent fan of the sport), cricket, food, fireworks; in short a gamut of events, activities and pleasures to appeal to all ages, all tastes. The Crystal Palace opened in all its pristine splendour at Sydenham in 1854, a 'fairy palace' of 'clean glass flashing diamond-wise under sunlight'.

To the young Marion Scott, it was a map of the world, a window into history and a vast stage for music. By the time she was old enough to appreciate it, 'the fairy brightness had been veiled beneath years of London dust' but it had not lost any of its power to enchant and seduce a curious, imaginative child like Marion. She thrived on the adventure it offered. When her dance class concluded for the day, Marion always begged her mother to take her through the courts, for

> In a moment we could plunge into Italy of the Renaissance, and find ourselves face to face with the sculptured masterpieces – in life size and first rate replicas – of the works of Michael Angelo, Torrigiani, Donatello and the rest. They made a powerful impression on me; though too small to understand them, I obtained a photographic appreciation of their beauty. Or we could ... enter the court which reproduced a room in the Alhambra – the splendours of colour and patterning covering the walls glowing in a perpetual mystery of the dim light ...

From the exotic Moorish world, Marion and her mother journeyed to ancient Greece and Rome, where 'the faces of Augustus, Antinous and the Dying Gladiator became more familiar to me than our own local postman'. And from there to ancient Egypt where a statue of the great Rameses mesmerized her and where she studied the frescoes in which 'Osiris, Isis, Horus, Pharoahs, Priests, Cats and Slaves, and offerings figured in endless intricacy'.

Perhaps more than anything, the mythological statues of the Venus de Milo, Apollo and Perseus lit young Marion's curiosity and fired her imagination. They also gave her a rare taste of adult censorship. When she was ten years old she went to stay with an aunt. Finding a copy of *Smith's Classical Dictionary* in her bookcase, Marion 'had a beatific time browsing over it, till my occupation was discovered, and the book confiscated as totally unsuitable for a little girl', she recalled. 'In point of fact I was too young to be depraved by it! The immoral doings of pagan deities slid by me more meaninglessly than the proverbial water off a duck's back.' Marion's aunt was perhaps more cautious than her own parents.

For Marion and her younger sisters, Stella and Freda, 'History lived as something encountered, not as something learnt.' They were so intrigued and enchanted by what they saw that they begged their parents to allow them 'to be instructed in the ancient world to explain what we could not fathom from frescoes and busts'. The Scotts agreed, and enrolled Marion in a class on Greek history taught in French, which she labelled an early 'bribe' that moved her toward her interest in languages.

It was at the Crystal Palace, among the beautiful plants, towering ferns and palms, moist scents, statuary, music, the alluring Alhambra Court and the light filtering through the panes of glass, that Marion Scott encountered the first dissonant notes of her childhood – Victorian abuse of animals. As part of their daily routine on the way to her class, Marion and her mother passed through the transept where the Handel Festival Orchestra played and where the names of the composer's works were frescoed in enormous letters around the top of the stage. Marion walked along, spelling the names out to herself – *Esther, Israel in Egypt, Acis and Galatea* among them – before they passed down to the north nave and arrived at the fountain at the end where she heard screams and cries and saw

> parrots and cockatoos chained to their perches like uneasy genji. They were reputed to be very fierce, and I cannot wonder if they were. Their lives must have been miserable. Flapping and screeching, they struggled at the ends of their chains, teased by passers by, and tormented by captivity. Why were Victorians so stupidly cruel to birds?

She and her mother never lingered by the monkey house where they were assailed by 'frightful' smells and 'intensely active' animals leaping about in their prison. Nor did they stop in the aquarium with its dank air and fish swimming in 'melancholy tanks' or care to see the bear pit or the crocodiles all living in captivity so alien to their natural environments. Even as a child, Marion sensed the animals' rage, particularly in the crocodiles as they 'lay blinking their weary but unchangeably wicked eyes at the entire human race'. On one occasion, Marion watched in horror as a bear attacked a man during a circus performance, savagely mauling him. Only the quick action of Herbert Godfrey, the bandmaster, who rushed at the bear and beat it with a bar, saved the man.

During a performance of the Bach Concerto in D for two violins, the Scotts wondered if some of the animals might be about to take just revenge on the humans who imprisoned them. The concert was in progress when the distinctive sounds of lions and tigers demanding their supper intruded. Their demands grew so loud that the Scotts and everyone else wondered, 'Had the lions escaped? If so, what, or who, would they eat?' After that Marion could never hear the Bach Double without seeing the two violinists on the stage, 'pale of face, glancing nervously over their shoulders, but sticking gamely to their job, their heavenly strains in the Adagio, mingling with the most hellish growls off scenes'. She much preferred the annual domestic cat shows.

As Marion grew older, music became the main attraction at the Crystal Palace. She heard her first opera there, a 'boring' work whose title she forgot, that nonetheless left her with a vivid memory of the tenor Charles Hedmondt. Years later when she heard him in the first English 'Ring' under Hans Richter at Covent Garden, she understood why he had so impressed her as a child: 'He was that rare combination of a singer, a musician and a forceful actor in one'.

When Marion was about twelve years old, she heard Schubert's C Major Symphony for the first time in a performance conducted by Sir August Manns at the three o'clock Saturday Concerts. It was a defining moment in her life. '[I] came away almost reeling under the revelation, with my eyes dazzled with golden light and my head ringing for twenty-four hours afterwards with the finale.'[3] After that, she attended Crystal Palace concerts nearly every Saturday and on week days when she was able, making her way up the 'cocoa-matted aisle of the Centre Transept' to hear 'Pacific rollers of sound' wash over her.[4] Her recollection of these concerts was vivid from the sight of individuals in the orchestra and audience fainting in the stifling summer heat in the greenhouse-like atmosphere to August Manns 'looking like a miniature of himself at that distance' with 'his florid complexion, fierce moustache, massive white hair, velvet coat, flower in buttonhole, and light kid gloves'.[5]

Marion first became acquainted with choruses of Handel's *Messiah* as they 'spread out' over her neighbourhood from the open casements of the Palace, enabling the Scotts to hear the music in their own garden. On occasion the music coming from the Palace posed a dilemma for young Marion. She could often hear a variety of music from her home, night and day, particularly from the North Tower Garden band concerts. 'The Military Band was one of the regular amenities of the Crystal Palace', she recalled, continuing:

> The evening session always ended loyally with 'God Save the Queen'. As these North Tower Garden performances were audible for a half a mile or more around, we heard a good deal of them in our home in the Avenue. This sometimes posed me with a pretty problem. From very tender years I had been taught to stand for the National Anthem. When my bedtime advanced to an hour that synchronized with the close of the Band Concert, I found myself in a dilemma. Should a praying child spring from its knees and stand to attention till the Sovereign had been saved, or should it address itself unmoved to Heaven?[6]

The Handel Festivals, the Saturday concerts, the organ recitals, the band concerts, all made a profound impression on Marion Scott. 'For myself no words can express what I owe to them nor how intensely I loved the music I heard performed at them.'[7]

Marion was a precocious child. She began piano lessons early and made excellent progress. However, she found her teacher unimaginative, uninspiring and ultimately very boring. Marion resented her staid approach of introducing music chronologically, much preferring to learn music that interested her, be it Mozart, her childhood favourite, or the work of living composers. Her teacher would have none of it.

Eventually, Marion abandoned the piano for the violin. She knew immediately that not only had she found her natural instrument, she had found a 'faithful friend'. Like her father, Marion was attuned to the metaphysical world, even in her youth, and she believed that her violin possessed a soul. When she caressed its strings with her bow and felt them vibrate beneath her fingers, she believed that she was awakening her violin's 'fourfold voices', which revealed knowledge and 'secrets deep' that brought her 'close to Heaven's door'.[8] Her gift as a violinist was so impressive and promising that her father purchased a fine Guadagnini violin for her.

As she approached her teenage years, Marion set a goal to study violin and composition at the Royal College of Music. To gain practical experience, she performed in public at every opportunity. Her first documented solo appearance dates from 21 March 1893, when she was fifteen years old. She participated in a dinner hour concert, arranged by her father, at the City Temple Hall, and shared the stage with another violinist and two singers. Marion played a *Gipsy Rondo* by an unnamed composer, probably Haydn. She was constantly learning and absorbing new solo violin music, including the Grieg Violin Sonata in E, the Intermezzo from Mascagni's *Cavalleria rusticana*, Edward German's *Bolero* and Sarasate's *Ziegeunerweisen*.

At the same time she experienced a different discipline as an orchestra player in the Reverend E. H. Moberly's Ladies' String Orchestra when it gave concerts in London. As a member of the orchestra she performed a variety of traditional music by Bach, Handel, and Schubert; and new music by such composers as Antonin Dvořák, Johann Svendsen, and Alexander Glazunov.

Moberly, the son of the Bishop of Salisbury and a well-known choral-orchestral conductor, produced oratorio performances on a festival scale in Salisbury. In 1891 he formed an orchestra of nearly 100 'ladies' from Wiltshire and Hampshire, which in 1892 began annual visits to London, where talented young women like Marion Scott occasionally joined them. Moberly was a crusader. A man ahead of his time, he had the courage to risk forming an all-woman orchestra and the vision to present new music, often programming 'far more than the average of compositions new to England'.[9] The ninety women, who dressed in white for each performance, were joined by four or five men in the double bass section.

Moberly and his ladies met with acclaim. Their concerts were hailed for the 'intelligence', 'spirit of industry' and 'welcome precision and almost masculine vigour' that marked each performance. A critic for the *Evening*

Post informed readers that Moberly's orchestra gave a concert at St James's Hall

> made up of material which should now and for ever remove all reproach upon lady violinists, because the chief of all the weaknesses of lady performers upon stringed instruments namely, the want of power of tone, was conspicuous by its absence. The playing of the orchestra was remarkable in more senses than one, and the united efforts of all concerned served to form an epoch in the history of female violin playing.[10]

In her mid-teens Marion was an active member of the Upper Norwood Total Abstinence Society along with her parents. The elder Scotts were leaders in the organization, which boasted a membership of 1,100 and a treasury that sometimes carried a balance of £100, which emptied quickly to fulfil the society's mission. Typically, the meetings consisted of prayers, lectures and refreshments, but time was always given over to musical programmes. Marion was a regularly featured artist who knew how to select music that pleased her audience. She was an electric, appealing soloist with the ability to excite such enthusiasm among listeners that, according to newspaper accounts, she was often rewarded with a standing ovation and demands for encores.

From the age of fifteen Marion Scott understood the value of publicity and learned how to use it to benefit herself and others. She might be petite, soft spoken and fragile in appearance, but she was neither timid nor lacking in initiative or courage. She took full advantage of the free publicity and exposure newspapers offered, and used the medium effectively as a promotional tool. If she were giving a solo recital or playing in a chamber ensemble, she made certain that the newspapers were informed.

By the time Marion entered the Royal College of Music in 1896 at the age of nineteen, both the musical and poetic muses had taken hold of her as they would later take hold of Ivor Gurney. She wrote verse and ballads marked by lingering vestiges of the romantic view of life. Her poetry revealed a young woman full of optimism and enthusiasm, who was not repressed by the constraints of Victorian morality. She expressed her determination to enjoy life and make the best of it. 'Let life be long, or life be brief, I'll live it utterly', she wrote in 'Fragments from The Marquis Gorham's Song'.[11] If she encountered 'both joy and grief' in her life, she vowed to 'face them straight'. Marion's character in this poem admits that he has a restless spirit and cannot, by his nature, stay in one place for long. He has to move on, to roam just as Marion would later do as she juggled several careers at once. Her verse is marked by a strong visual imagination and mystical sensibilities, but it is derivative and very much a product of its time.

At the RCM, Marion studied violin with Fernández Arbós (1863–1939), piano with Marmaduke Barton (1865–1938), and composition with Walford Davies (1869–1941), and later became one of the first female composition pupils of the formidable Charles Villiers Stanford (1852–1924). She attained a Grade V, the highest, in violin, harmony and counterpoint, and a Grade IV in composition, but only a Class C for piano.

She seemed most comfortable composing songs, preferring the texts of Robert Louis Stevenson above others. 'Under the wide and starry sky' is the text for her *Requiem*, and she used nine Stevenson poems from *A Child's Garden of Verses* in a suite for voice and piano composed for her young niece Audrey Lovibond. Her other vocal works include 'Falmouth Town' for tenor and piano with words adapted by W. E. Henley; 'Golden Slumber' for contralto and piano, a setting of Thomas Dekker; 'The Autumn Day is Fading'; 'The Bells of Forrabury'; 'To Sleep'; 'The Tide Rises, The Tide Falls'. Among the poets she set were Bliss Carman, Gwenith Gwyn, Henry Newbolt, Alice Meynell, Austin Dobson, and Christina Rossetti. Some of her incomplete songs appear to be settings of her own poetry.

In addition to songs with piano, Marion was among the earliest British composers to set verse with string quartet and chamber orchestra. Not all her efforts went smoothly. On the manuscript of a student composition, an unaccompanied vocal quartet titled 'For the Lord will not fail his people', one of her teachers, either Stanford or Davies, wrote: 'Not very illuminating subjects either of these. You ought to make your voices climb about and cross one another more. They move too much in blocks. The individual parts are dull.' [12]

Even as a student, Marion was in demand as a performer, a demand that she created in part by making herself known outside the walls of the college. She arranged concerts, generated publicity for herself and others, travelled, attended meetings and worked for the various organizations to which she belonged.[13] She also enjoyed a wide circle of friends and socialized regularly. She attained her ARCM (Associate of the Royal College of Music) in violin in April 1900 and continued course work on and off until March 1903 when she ended her student affiliation with the College.

Throughout her life Marion maintained a punishing schedule, which is all the more remarkable because she was often in ill health even when she was young. In addition to her studies and her participation in the college orchestra, she served as the Secretary of the Library, created by violinist Helen Egerton for female students in 1901. Through her association with Egerton Marion first met Emily Daymond, who had invited the two women to her Eastbourne home. On a winter's afternoon they sat around the fire in Daymond's study discussing the creation of a student union. Nothing came of it until later, when Daymond, the first English woman to earn a doctorate in music (at Oxford), joined the teaching staff at the RCM. She and Scott developed an enduring friendship.

In 1901 Marion realized her dream of performing at the Crystal Palace when she participated in a chamber music concert featuring works by Schumann, Brahms, Schubert, Tchaikovsky and her contemporary, William Hurlstone. She played in the Schumann Quintet in E flat with Fanny Davies at the piano.

As a young violinist and aspiring composer in the early twentieth century, Marion Scott had few female role models: Lady Hallé, the Moravian-born Wilhelmina Neruda (1838–1911), and the American virtuosa Maud Powell (1867–1920). Powell, who first appeared in London in 1883 and 1884, was based there from 1898 through 1905.

Although more women had ventured into composition, the majority were generally regarded as miniaturists who were best known for their songs and piano pieces. However, some women were composing large-scale works which were given public performances, winning both critical and public acclaim: from the Continent, Clara Schumann (1819–96), Augusta Holmès (1847–1903), and Cécile Chaminade (1857–1944), and, in England, Rosalind Frances Ellicott (1857–1924), Ethel Smyth (1858–1944), Mary J. A. Wurm (1860–1938), and Dora Bright (1863–1951). Wurm, born of German parents in Southampton, preceded Marion Scott as one of Stanford's earliest female pupils.[14] Singers later included Marion's songs in their recitals.

From early childhood, Marion Scott was strong willed, independent and ambitious. Sydney and Annie Scott had wisely encouraged their daughters to participate in the shifting social climate through the family's commitment to social reform. They strongly believed that women were equal to men in all fields, and allowed their children unparalleled freedom and opportunities. Thus, Marion and her sisters entered the twentieth century full of optimism and confidence and with the knowledge that they were as capable as their male contemporaries of attaining success, achieving their goals and becoming pioneers whose contributions influenced and changed lives. Marion Scott had no fear of failure and never hesitated to explore unknown regions, initiate new projects and bring them to fruition. In order to bring about change, create opportunity, and improve life for herself and others, she willingly took risks that paralysed less intrepid individuals.

Although she possessed a romantic sensibility and was inclined toward traditional modes of expression in her own poetry and musical composition, Marion was anything but conservative in thought and action. She did not dismiss ideas because they were new, nor did she ridicule daring trends in music and literature because they failed to appeal to her personally. No matter what she thought or how she felt about the burgeoning movements in art, music and literature that were filtering into England in the first decade of the twentieth century, she remained steadfast in her belief that 'time alone' would be their judge.

With her taste for the new, she understood the importance of promoting contemporary music. As a teenager, she had championed modern music. After college she became an established professional violinist who enjoyed playing in orchestras, where she occasionally served as leader under conductors including Sir Hubert Parry, Sir Charles Villiers Stanford, Sir Walter Parratt, Gustav Holst and Samuel Coleridge-Taylor. However, Marion much preferred the independence and freedom of performing solo or in chamber ensembles.

After a hiatus of three years, Marion returned to the RCM in 1906 to found the Royal College of Music Student Union along with Emily Daymond and Aubrey Aitken Crawshaw. In her position as Secretary, she was responsible for managing the Union and all of its activities.

During her first meeting with Marion in 1901, Daymond realized that the younger woman was a willing and able worker with the diplomatic skills essential for winning favour for new ideas. After they established the RCM Union, they turned their attention to creating a Loan Fund as a service of the Union. They soon had a battle on their hands when RCM director Sir Hubert Parry and others opposed the idea, claiming it was too risky and that the money borrowed would never be repaid. 'You must drop it, Emily, you must drop it', Daymond was told.[15] The two women devised a strategy. They decided that Daymond should write to Charles Morley, the leading member of the Executive Committee of the RCM. Her eloquent letter convinced Morley that the fund was a good idea and prompted him to contribute the substantial sum of £100 to start it. Influenced by Morley's participation and support of the fund, Parry capitulated and the women quietly accepted their victory.

In 1908 Marion formed the Marion Scott Quartet, mainly to introduce British music to London audiences. Her quartet, with equal numbers of both sexes, consisted of Ivor James, cello, Sybil Maturin, viola, Herbert Kinze, second violin, and Scott, first violin, with William H. Harris joining them when a pianist was needed.[16] Their programmes at Aeolian Hall featured new works by her teacher Charles Villiers Stanford, James Friskin, Frank Bridge, Walford Davies, C. Hubert Parry, William Hurlstone and others along with occasional early music by Arne and Purcell.

In her programming Scott did not limit her selections solely to string quartets, but featured trios, quintets, songs, and works for vocal quartets with soloists to provide musical diversity for audiences. When she was not on stage herself, she was busy organizing concerts of contemporary music, primarily chamber works, to showcase young composers. She published articles about music in various London area newspapers, tackling topics such as salaries for women music teachers and music as a profession for women. Marion dealt with realities and did not attempt to glorify conditions:

> Professional life is a really hard struggle, which has been made infinitely worse by the crowds of unsuitable or badly trained people, who rush in, prove unfit and end either by taking starvation fees or posts as lady-helps and nursery governesses.[17]

She cautioned that often the only jobs open to women musicians were as teachers:

> String players will also find their safest openings in teaching, either in schools or privately, while to this they can add concert, ensemble, and orchestral work. There is usually more scope in these latter directions for viola players and 'cellists than violinists, and with orchestral work it must be remembered that all the best engagements are filled by men, with the exception of the harpists in some orchestras.[18]

1911 was a year of professional success for Marion Scott. In addition to her job at the RCM Union, her busy performing schedule and her writing, she earned extra income lecturing regularly on diverse topics including folk music from England, Scotland, Ireland and Wales, medieval and church music, early composers, Elizabethan and Tudor music, the evolution of English music, and the 'Renaissance of English Music and its leaders in the latter half of the 19th century'. She enlivened her talks by illustrating them with musical examples presented by her friends William Harris or Harold Darke at the piano, vocalists Gladys Hislop and Louis Godfrey, with herself on the violin.

Marion's promotional literature reveals that she also offered courses on technical subjects: composition, harmony, counterpoint, musical form, analysis and orchestration. She boasted references from England's musical élite: Sir Charles Villiers Stanford, Sir Hubert Parry, Percy Buck, Sir Walter Parratt, and H. Walford Davies. She usually spoke at venues where controversy and liberal ideas routinely held centre stage and audiences were open to new ideas and experiences. She appeared frequently at the Sydenham Ladies' Political and Literary Debating Society or the liberal Pioneer Club at Piccadilly, where debate focused on social issues that mirrored her own thinking, including 'That every man and woman should have a vote'. She made certain that newspapers published notices of her lectures and that, on occasion, they sent a reporter to cover them.

By 1911 Marion had drawn her friends Gertrude Eaton (1861–?) and Katharine Eggar (1874–1961) into her plans to establish the Society of Women Musicians, an organization Scott had conceived to provide women composers, performers and writers on music with the opportunity to come together to learn, discuss and share in musical matters. She and Eaton had discussed their strategy and drafted their agenda earlier that year while on a spring holiday in the New Forest.

In Eaton and Eggar, Scott found compatible partners who were willing to work with unflagging commitment to match her own. Eaton had trained as a singer in Italy, and from 1894 to 1897 studied at the Royal College of Music, where she met Scott. Eaton was the editor of the *Royal Society of Music Magazine* and a voice teacher who was also an active worker in prison reform and in other movements that benefited women and children. Eggar had studied piano in Berlin and Brussels, and composition with Frederick Corder at the Royal Academy of Music. She had composed a number of chamber works, including a piano quintet and string quartet as well as songs.

As the women envisioned the society, it would promote a sense of co-operation among women in different fields of music, provide performance opportunities and advice and would even help women with the practical business aspects of their work. Professional women – performers, teachers, conductors, composers – paid 15s 6d for a subscription fee while non-professional women paid £1 6s to join. Marion's solicitor father Sydney C. Scott drew up a constitution and rules for governing the organization.[19] Marion produced a full-sized book for keeping minutes and an equally large account ledger to record the SWM's financial transactions. The organization would be professional in every way.

Before the society was even launched, the women had their critics who were quick to accuse them of exclusivity, aggression and politics, but they were ready for them. The founding women and their Provisional Council made it clear that the society would have no political agenda, and that it would be open to men. Although she was well aware of the inequities suffered by women in male-dominated society, Marion Scott was never antagonistic toward men. 'She always expected and received their support, and had a completely natural attitude ... no one had more devoted men friends', Katharine Eggar later recalled.[20]

As dues-paying associate members at 5 shillings a year, men were invited to attend debates, performances and meetings, and, as the organization broadened even more, to have their music performed at SWM concerts. Chamber music promoter Walter W. Cobbett (1847–1937), a successful businessman, amateur musician and founder of the Cobbett Prize, was the first benefactor of the organization. Composer-teacher Thomas Dunhill (1877–1946) was the first associate member.[21] Cobbett and Dunhill were among twenty male associates to join in the first year. Thus the SWM operated on an agenda of equality, its leaders believing that their purpose was best served by including, rather than excluding men. Scott, the force behind this open philosophy, achieved her goals through a combination of 'the ladylikeness of a Liza Lehmann and the fighting nerve of an Ethel Smyth' who had become a militant Suffragette.[22]

'We were then in the thick of the Women's Suffrage battle and anything determinedly feminine was suspect', Eggar explained. 'Facetiousness about "the ladies" had to be endured, and nice men hardly liked to hear their [female] relations refer to themselves and their friends as *Women*.'[23] Even women, conditioned to a subservient role, were fearful and reluctant to take charge of their own lives when opportunity presented itself.

At the time, 'No one ever dreamed of a woman critic: no one had ever heard of a woman musicologist', Eggar observed, noting of the woman composer, 'There she was, without a past, with a hesitating present, and no future.'[24] Women could not blame these conditions entirely on men. 'The attitude of women musicians to each other was on the whole selfish', Eggar acknowledged. 'Musicians were not as awakened as women in other professions, and badly needed a jolt in their egotistical outlook.' Marion Scott provided the jolt while bearing the brunt of dissent from within the ranks. 'She took the long view of the Society's role in musical life and never wavered in her belief in its necessity. In this determination to do something for her fellow-women musicians, Marion was ahead of her contemporaries', Eggar declared.[25]

The women held their first meeting on 11 July 1911, at the Women's Institute, 92 Victoria Street. More than 150 crowded into the room and immediately joined the new organization. Others, including Lady Elgar, violinist May Harrison and singer Agnes Nicholls (Mrs Hamilton Harty), were among those sending regrets that they were unable to attend owing to previous commitments. News of the event had spread rapidly when Scott's promotional skills resulted in the publication of more than a dozen articles in newspapers and magazines including the *Evening Standard* and *St James Gazette* (a two-part feature), *Daily Telegraph*, *Musical Times*, *Musical Courier*, *Music Student*, *Musical Standard*, *Musical News* and a five-column feature article in the *New York Times*.

Scott and Eggar collaborated on the speech that Eggar, the temporary chairman of the SWM and its designated public voice, delivered at the inaugural event. 'We want women with brains, but with hearts behind their brains', Eggar declared in her rallying call to the assembled women. 'To some this idea of sex exclusiveness is distasteful. There is a suggestion that it has a political significance. We wish the society to have none whatever. We intend it to be a great factor in the development of Art, and we feel that that is a basis broad enough to admit of all variety of political opinion.'[26]

With women all around them challenging convention, it was time for musicians to do the same. Eggar urged the women not to be content with 'unquestioning acceptance of convention or submission to abuses in music and musical doings', which often denied them equality in 'the monster of commercialism that rules the musical world.' The days when women in music were doomed to a silent destiny were over.

'Here writers and performers will be able to meet and measure their art in co-operation', Eggar declared. 'New lights will flash ... the joy of first hearing her composition will infuse courage and vitality into the toil of the musical author. Work done in the study will be no dumb phantom, but a living vital creation.' The audience cheered. The women were triumphant. At the heart of this visionary new enterprise stood Marion Scott. Women in music could finally believe in themselves and in a future. They had found strength, courage and hope in their unity. Their energy was electric. In the first year, with composer-singer Liza Lehmann (1862–1918) serving as president, the SWM membership explored a number of topics: piano technique, French lyric diction, Indian music, Polish folk songs, brass instruments and the Music Copyright Bill. They launched the annual Composer's Conference, formed a choir and closed out their first year with a comfortable bank balance.[27]

The next year and subsequent years were even more productive. The women formed an orchestra and added an Advisory Section to help young or inexperienced musicians with their professional careers. They began their popular private and public concerts and a series of Bach chamber concerts and inaugurated Composers' Trial Meetings, which offered women an opportunity to submit their compositions for criticism. They started a library and formed an educational committee.

By mid-1911 Scott's reputation as a musician and visionary leader was deemed 'too well known to need comment', according to an anonymous writer covering the first meeting of the SWM for the *Musical Times*. Marion Scott and Katharine Eggar formed a writing partnership and published a series of articles about women in chamber music for the Chamber Music Supplement of the *Music Student*.[28] Marion continued to champion contemporary British music through her own performances or by arranging concerts, including popular 'At Home' recitals held at her parents' elegant London home. From all appearances, Marion was a capable woman in control of her life who turned everything she did into a success. But her public image and the accolades she received were in sharp contrast to the disappointments and self-perceived failures that clouded her personal life.

At the time she was winning professional acclaim, Marion Scott was struggling to overcome a personal crisis, one of many that would darken her own life throughout the years. Ernest Farrar, the man she loved, had announced his engagement to another woman. Farrar, a composer, pianist and organist, had come to the Royal College of Music on an open scholarship, arriving in 1905 at the age of twenty. Like Scott, he had been born in the Lewisham borough of London, where his father the Reverend Charles Druce Farrar was Curate of St Mary's Church. Both Scott and Farrar were born in July, but he was eight years younger.[29] The Farrars moved to Micklefield in Yorkshire, when Ernest, the middle of three children, was two years old, so it is not likely that the Scotts and Farrars were acquainted. As a highly regarded composition student of Sir Charles Stanford, Farrar soon began to attract attention, winning prestigious prizes and securing performances of his music. During this time he was a member of The Beloved Vagabonds Club, founded by Audrey Alston.[30] Members were allowed into the exclusive club by invitation only. They met several times a term in a studio at Holland Park to perform music and socialize. Marion Scott was also a member.

Farrar, a handsome, reserved man, won a high place in Marion's favour although it is not possible to determine exactly how or when their friendship began. However, by 1909 they were appearing together in recitals. On 9 August Marion joined Farrar at Micklefield for an evening organ and violin recital at the local St Mary's Church. The programme was particularly demanding for Farrar, who played solo organ works by Reger, Brahms, Schumann, and Franck, and accompanied Scott in her performances of Bach's 'Sonata in A' and Mendelssohn's 'Andante from Concerto'.[31]

On 18 November 1910 Marion journeyed north to South Shields, where Farrar was living and working as organist and choirmaster at St Hilda's Church. With the assistance of the choirboys from St Hilda's, they presented another challenging programme at the Victoria Assembly Hall, featuring the first public performance of two movements of Farrar's *Celtic Suite* for violin and piano along with contemporary works by Parry, Edward German, Cecil Sharp and Walford Davies. Farrar dedicated the first movement of the *Celtic Suite*, 'Dalua', to Marion, who had given him technical advice on writing the violin part.[32] An anonymous critic for the *Shields Gazette* observed that the *Celtic Suite* was 'written with a fine sense of the weird and dramatic' and that Scott and Farrar 'very cleverly and faithfully emphasized the characteristics of each movement' with Marion showing 'wonderful mastery' of the solo violin passages. The work was based on Celtic stories by Fiona Macleod; in it Farrar composed each movement as 'complete in itself ... representing a succession of episodes under their emotional and atmospheric aspects'.[33] Farrar's dedications of earlier works to Esmé Tulloch in 1908 and 1909 and to others indicate that he was in the habit of dedicating his music to the women in his life.

Dalua is a character from Macleod's verse drama *The Immortal Hour*, first published in 1900, which later became the basis for Rutland Boughton's popular opera of the same name. Stories involving the shadowy worlds of Celtic mysticism, mortal and immortal planes, spirits, other-worldly dimensions, dreams and visions held great appeal for Marion, who was deeply immersed in metaphysics.

The last appearance of the Scott–Farrar duo occurred on the evening of Tuesday 17 January 1911, at Marion's home at 92 Westbourne Terrace,

Hyde Park, in a programme that featured Harold Darke, Beatrice Dunn, Clive Carey and William Harris. Scott and Farrar played the *Celtic Suite* once again; this performance included the last movement, 'Eily', which was unfinished at the time of the November recital. Farrar dedicated 'Eily' to Olive Mason.

Shortly after this performance, perhaps even that night, Farrar told Marion about his engagement to Olive, whom he had met at St Hilda's. The news was a shock, an unexpected blow. Marion was so devastated and angered by Farrar's rejection of her that she cut him out of her life and never spoke to him again. 'Anger never flames more swiftly than when love burns beneath', she once wrote.[34] The passage of time and change of circumstances later reduced her pain and disappointment. 'It is a strange thing, but in some subtle way this evening, I felt as if Ernest Farrar had come in thought and resumed the old footing of friendship', she wrote in her journal after his death in 1918. 'This is the first time I have ever felt this to be the case since that January years ago – 1911– when he became engaged.'[35]

The arrival of Ivor Gurney at the Royal College of Music in the spring of 1911 began to provide a welcome distraction from her misery at the loss of Farrar. Gurney left no account of his first impressions of Marion Scott, but she left a revealing one of him. Ivor's 'uncommon', somewhat dishevelled appearance and the 'look of latent force in him' were enough to make her take notice of him, right down to the extraordinary colour in his eyes – 'hazel, grey, green and agate … denoting genius' – as he passed her in a corridor at the RCM.[36]

By the time of this first sighting in May 1911, Marion had already heard talk about a remarkable new student from Gloucester rumoured to possess the gifts of another Schubert. She seemed to know instinctively who he was the moment she saw him, and was finally able to put a face with the name she had seen in *The Times* article. Two weeks passed before she met him officially, when he walked into her office at the RCM to join the student Union and introduced himself as Ivor B. Gurney.

NOTES

1 Hester Stansfeld Prior, 'Marion Scott as Fellow Student and Friend', in Society of Woman Musicians, *Commemoration of Marion Scott* (programme book, 25–6 June 1954), p. 7.

2 MMS, 'The Crystal Palace', from *The Home of All Our Mortal Dream*, an unpublished memoir, MSC. Marion Scott's memories and descriptions of the Crystal Palace that follow are from this memoir.

3 KD, 'Memories of Marion Scott', *Music and Letters*, vol. 35, no. 3 (July 1954), p. 238.

4 KD, 'Marion Scott as Music Critic and Letter Writer', in Society of Woman Musicians, *Commemoration of Marion Scott* (programme book, 25–6 June 1954), p. 12.

5 MMS, 'Grand Old Concerts', *The Observer*, 12 June 1932.

6 MMS, *The Home of All Our Mortal Dream*, pp. 13–14.

7 Ibid., p. 16.

8 MMS, from her poem 'To my Violin', early 1890s, MSC.

9 Unsigned, *The Times*, 23 May 1894.

10 Anonymous critic, *The Evening Post*, 13 May 1893.

11 'Fragments from The Marquis Gorham's Song', MSC.

12 All of Scott's music manuscripts are in the RCM. She was proud that Dr Ernest Walker (1870–1949), a composer and scholar, could still quote a phrase from her piano trio that he had heard only once some 30 years earlier.

13 In 1899, Scott was a member of the RCM orchestra when it participated in a farewell concert given by Madame Emma Albani before her South African tour. In 1904, Ivor Gurney, then a chorister at Gloucester Cathedral, would be called upon to sing with Madame Albani, filling in for a singer who was indisposed.

14 Rebecca Clarke (1886–1979) is often cited as Stanford's first female pupil, but this is erroneous. Marion Scott, Mary Wurm (1860–1938) and Katherine Ramsay, later the Duchess of Athol, all preceded Clarke as Stanford's pupils by many years. Clarke began her studies with Stanford in 1907, 11 years after Scott had begun hers.

15 MMS, 'Obituary: Emily Rosa Daymond', *RCM Magazine*, vol. 46, no. 1 (February 1950), pp. 25–6. Daymond was born at Framlingham, Suffolk, on 11 July 1866. She entered the RCM as a Foundation Scholar on 7 May 1883, when the College first opened, studying with Ernst Pauer (piano), Richard Gompertz (violin), Dr Frederick Bridge (harmony and counterpoint) and Dr Hubert Parry. Parry liked Daymond and affectionately referred to her as 'Em'ly'. She called him 'Pedagogue'. She completed her studies at the RCM, passed her examinations for the bachelor of music degree at Oxford in 1896 and for her doctor of music in 1901. It took Oxford another 20 years to allow women to hold the degrees they had won. In addition to her teaching, Daymond conducted choirs, lectured and made a study of troubadour music. She was a keen sportswoman. Toward the end of her life, she learnt Bach's *Well-Tempered Clavier* by heart so she would have them with her when she was blind. Daymond died on 10 October 1949.

16 Sir William Harris (1883–1973), organist, composer and teacher. In 1899, he attended the RCM on an organ scholarship. He and Marion Scott performed together and formed a life-long friendship. In 1918, she became the godmother of his daughter, Margaret (Brockway).

17 MMS, 'Music as a Profession', *Daily Express*, 1909 (no date), pp. 1–2. Scott either wrote or contributed to a book titled *Work for Women*, which sold for one penny and was available from all bookstalls and newsagents.

18 Ibid.

19 Sydney Scott donated his services to the SWM until his death in 1936.

20 KE, 'Marion Scott as Founder of the Society of Women Musicians', in Society of Woman Musicians, *Commemoration of Marion Scott* (programme book, 25–6 June 1954), p. 4.

21 Walter Willson Cobbett (1847–1937) was the founder and chairman of the successful Scandinavia Belting, Ltd. A fine violinist who had his own quartet, he championed chamber music and commissioned chamber works by British composers, and established the Cobbett Medal for services to chamber music in 1924. He was the editor of the *Cyclopaedic Survey of Chamber Music*, first published in 1929. Thomas Dunhill (1877–1946), composer, writer and teacher, was, like Marion Scott, a student of Sir Charles Stanford at the RCM, where they met.

22 KE, 'Marion Scott as Founder of the Society of Women Musicians', p. 5.

23 Ibid.

24 Ibid.

25 Ibid. (June 1954).

26 Subsequent quotes from Eggar's inaugural speech are taken from the SWM promotional material appearing in a number of publications between July and October 1911.

27 Among the first women associated with the SWM were May Mukle, Lucie Johnstone, Florence MacNaughton, Mabel Saumarez Smith, Ethel Smyth, Maud Valerie White and Ethel Barns. The organization disbanded in 1972. Other early presidents were Dr Emily Daymond, French pianist-composer Cécile Chaminade and then Eggar (1914–15), Scott (1915–16) and Eaton (1916–17).

28 Eggar later became a literary critic and spent over 30 years researching the life and times of Edward de Vere, 17th Earl of Oxford, whom she believed was the real author of Shakespeare's works. She planned to publish her writings but died before her book was completed. Marion Scott would have disagreed with Eggar and others seeking to attribute Shakespeare's work to different writers. 'Why in the name of wonder any one should think that only the highest social position can produce genius – in short that Bacon wrote Shakespeare – is incomprehensible. The evidence, if any, is in the other direction', Scott wrote in her 1934 biography of Beethoven.

29 Farrar was born on 7 July 1885. Marion Scott was born on 16 July 1877.

30 Alston became the viola teacher of composer Benjamin Britten.

31 Only a few programmes from their recitals are extant.

32 Farrar biographer Adrian Officer in a letter to the author, 1991.

33 *The Shields Gazette*, 19 November 1910. Fiona Macleod was the pseudonym of novelist William Sharp (1855–1905), who belonged to an esoteric group that included Frederick Bligh Bond, who excavated Glastonbury Abbey, composer John Foulds and Fould's wife Maud McCarthy, violinist, singer and a protégée of spiritualist Annie Besant. When Sharp admitted publicly that he was Fiona MacLeod, a scandal ensued. Marion Scott was a follower of the esoteric and her father, Sydney Scott, studied psychic phenomena with the purpose of debunking or finding rational explanations for such events.

34 MMS, *Beethoven*, The Master Musicians (London: J. M. Dent & Sons, 1934), p. 29.

35 MMS, Journal, GA. In a letter to Edmund Blunden (23 August 1953, Gurney Archive), composer Gerald Finzi wrote that it was from Ernest Farrar, his teacher, that he first heard of Marion Scott. Farrar told Finzi that Marion was known to have had love affairs.

36 MMS, 'Ivor Gurney: The Man', *Music and Letters*, vol. 19, no. 1 (January 1938), p. 3.

CHAPTER 2

A Clash of Wills

*I*VOR GURNEY was charming, irresistible and brimming with a contagious, unbridled enthusiasm when he swept into the Royal College of
Music in 1911. His early compositions, untamed, ecstatic and lyrical, had
been born as he walked beneath the ever-changing West Country skies
where 'the earth entered into my making and into my blood'.[1] His was a fresh,
vital and exciting talent, reminiscent of Schubert, that had impressed no
less respected musicians than Sir Charles Stanford, Dr Walford Davies, Dr
Charles Wood and Sir Hubert Parry enough to award him an open scholarship to the RCM worth £40 a year. On seeing Gurney for the first time, the
awestruck Parry is reported to have whispered 'By God! It *is* Schubert!'[2]
The young scholar had much to live up to, indeed perhaps too much.

Twenty-year-old Gurney was riding a wave of self-confidence and pride
when he arrived in London full of dreams. His energy was electric. It was
impossible not to notice him no matter what he did. Everything about him
was different and highly individual, almost as if he were creating a character for a novel and parading him to see how the public reacted before he
wrote the next chapter. Athletic and fit at five feet nine inches tall, with
deep-set piercing eyes, wavy brown hair and a long firm jaw, he cut a striking figure. When Marion Scott, who appreciated individuality more than
most, first saw Ivor in the crowded corridor, his attire was hardly what she
expected to see: a 'thick, dark blue Severn pilot's coat, more suggestive of
an out-of-door life than the composition lesson ... for which he was clearly
bound'.[3]

Ivor craved attention and thrived on it. Dressing as he did, whether it
was a conscious effort or carelessness, was just one way of ensuring that
he stood out from his peers. And for a while he did, both as a promising,
highly gifted student and for his winning personality. He was popular, sincerely interested in the work being done by his fellow students, and generous in his praise of it. He enjoyed seeing his friends succeed and shared
their joy when they did.

At this juncture in his life he was a scattered, immature artist. Musical
ideas welled up in him and spilled out, confused, urgent, and, as his friend
Herbert Howells observed, 'strewn with signs of struggle in the making'.[4]
Unlike the gifted Howells, who joined him at the RCM in 1912, Gurney
did not have the patience or temperament to harness his ideas. They had
met as teenagers when both were pupils of Dr Herbert Brewer, organist
and Master of the Choristers at Gloucester Cathedral. Howells, two years
younger, became one of Ivor's closest friends.

Like Gurney, Howells yearned to experience the greater world that lay
beyond what he termed 'provincial' Gloucester. Both Ivor and Herbert
came from homes where money was tight and both realized their good
fortune in possessing musical talent. They believed that if they applied

themselves to their art, fame and fortune awaited them in London and beyond. Like Gurney, Howells did not find his studies with Herbert Brewer illuminating or particularly helpful. He eventually quit and spent a year composing on his own, influenced by the music he heard around him. In 1910 Gurney and Howells had attended the première of Ralph Vaughan Williams' *Fantasia on a Theme by Thomas Tallis* at the Gloucester Three Choirs Festival. After the performance they wandered the streets all night, so great was their excitement. They knew that they had heard something important and that they had been present at a defining moment in music history.

For young men like Gurney and Howells, London in the early years of the twentieth century was an exciting place to be. The seeds of modernism being sown throughout Europe were blowing across the Channel to England. New voices in music, literature, art and drama were emerging everywhere. Old conventions were crumbling against the rush of new ideas. The atmosphere was charged with tension as people expressed a collective dissatisfaction with social, economic and political conditions. Even women had turned militant to win the right to vote.

Artists, poets, and composers, always the conduits of change, were the first to sense this vast shift in human consciousness and their works soon began to reflect the unsettled temper of a changing world. The traditional artistic values of splendour, pathos, sentimentality and sensuality did not fit the mood of these turbulent times. The ideal of beauty was seen as a mask, an illusion that distracted people from the harsh realities of life and the struggles of the common man and woman. To portray life as idyllic was a fraud.

Culture was now defined by a series of 'isms' piled one on top of another, overlapping, interwoven, individual, short-lived, violent, bland, quick to burst into life, some quick to die, some to endure: Cubism, Realism, Expressionism, Imagism, Fauvism, Symbolism, Modernism, Futurism, Vorticism.

Music was becoming harsh, cold and abstract, its rhythms more in time with machines than with the soul. Stravinsky's *Firebird* (1910) and *Petrushka* (1910–11) were just warm-up exercises for *The Rite of Spring* (1913) with its wild, aggressive rhythms and their 'dark undertones of violence and dread', melodies 'designed to frighten' and harmonies 'to disrupt the mind'.[5] By the time Schoenberg's lush symphonic cantata *Gurrelieder* had been received by a cheering audience in 1913, he had abandoned tonality and turned his back on Romanticism.

In London, concert goers could feast on the more traditional musical fare of Edward Elgar, Granville Bantock, Alexander Mackenzie, Hubert Parry, Charles Stanford and the choral epics of Samuel Coleridge-Taylor, or they could take a bold leap into the world of modernism, both British and European. H. Balfour Gardiner introduced new British music by Arnold Bax, Gustav Holst, Cyril Scott, Frederick Delius, Percy Grainger and others at his Queens Hall concerts. Even more daring were the Promenade Concerts of Henry Wood featuring the music of the Rumanians George Enesco, the thirteen-year-old Austrian *Wunderkind* Erich Wolfgang

Korngold, Arnold Schoenberg, Maurice Ravel, Claude Debussy, Igor Stravinsky, Gustav Mahler, and orchestral works by women including Dora Bright, Amy Horrocks, and Poldowski (Irena Wieniawska).

This then was the musical world eddying around Ivor Gurney in London. It was a world both appealing to Ivor and at odds with him, a juxtaposition of conflicting thoughts, feelings and ideals. His instincts were modern and defiant; his mind open, restless and inquiring; his actions reckless and callow, but part of him remained sheltered within the safe confines of tradition.

At the RCM Ivor and Herbert were joined in friendship by a young Australian pianist and composer, Arthur Benjamin, 'Benjee' to his friends. Born in Sydney on 18 September 1893, he spent his formative years in Brisbane. A brilliant pianist blessed with perfect pitch, he was hailed as a child prodigy. His gifts had come to the attention of the teacher and composer Thomas Dunhill, who had met Benjamin during a visit to Australia and encouraged him to study in England.

In 1911 Benjamin left Australia to study harmony and counterpoint with Dunhill and piano with Frederic Cliffe, whose wife was related to Benjamin's father. He spent his first summer in London as a regular attendee at Henry Wood's Promenade Concerts where he 'acquired a nodding acquaintance with the orchestral repertory' by attending nearly sixty concerts in the series.[6] Although he had not composed music for some time, he began to feel the urge again. Then, prompted by Cliffe, he decided to compete for the RCM open scholarship in composition in 1912.

Benjamin first encountered Howells at the college during their presentations to the scholarship examining board. As Benjamin entered a small waiting room filled with other student candidates, Herbert was entering the examining room. 'The College rooms being far from sound-proof, we distinctly heard a violin sonata being played by the composer and a brilliant violin student who had been pressed into service – none other (unless memory betrays me) than Eugene Goossens', recalled Benjamin. He and the other students 'looked at one another ruefully, shrugged our shoulders and decided we might as well go home, so amazing, for a youngster of Howells's age, was the quality of the music that seeped through to us.'[7] Benjamin recognized in Howells the same force and genius that Marion Scott had observed in Gurney that set him apart.

'I at once introduced myself to Howells – slight and small, young-looking even for his age, with a beautiful head – asked him about himself and suggested a luncheon together', Benjamin wrote years later. The two young men (Herbert was nineteen, Arthur, eighteen) were joined by Herbert's mother, Elizabeth. Always sensitive to the feelings of others, Benjamin was quick to observe Howells' anxiety about the outcome of the examinations. His future was riding on the results. Later in the day the scholarship candidates had to set Byron's 'She walks in Beauty' and complete the scherzo of a string quartet. To his 'amazement' Benjamin, who had done his 'poor best', was awarded one of the scholarships, while the other one went to Howells.[8]

Gurney had been a student at the RCM for a year by the time both

Benjamin and Howells joined him as pupils of Charles Stanford. Benjamin was comparatively secure financially, generous, gregarious, and comfortable with being homosexual in an era when being so was dangerous. The three young men shared their love of music. They attended many concerts together, including another Ralph Vaughan Williams revelation, the London première of his *Sea Symphony*, an experience that left them breathless with excitement and joy. They talked about their own work, exchanged ideas, and they confided in each other.

Gurney, Howells and Benjamin presented a study in contrasts. All three were attractive, but Gurney made a markedly different impression, one that spoke of inner turmoil, distraction and indifference. While Howells and Benjamin appeared tidy and appropriate in dress and manner, Gurney often appeared rumpled. At times his flamboyant, theatrical behaviour embarrassed those in his presence and left an impression of an immature, high-strung young man who was out of control.

Howells and Benjamin got along well with their studies, participating in college events and socializing on the outside. Herbert was working on large-scale compositions, including chamber music, instrumental works, choral music, an orchestral suite and a piano concerto.[9] Concertos, symphonies, tone poems, choral works and opera were fashionable when Gurney, Howells and Benjamin arrived in London. Mahler's Symphony no. 9 and *Das Lied von der Erde*, the Sibelius Symphony no. 4, Rachmaninov's Piano Concerto no. 3, Schoenberg's *Five Orchestral Pieces* and operas by Richard Strauss had crossed the Channel, giving London audiences a taste of what the future held.

Ivor had grand plans in keeping with the musical fashion of the day. He announced that he was going to write an opera based on John Millington Synge's *Riders to the Sea*, a cycle of operas based on Yeats' short plays and a music drama about Simon de Montfort, the fourteenth-century revolutionary.

By this time he had run directly into an obstacle: his composition teacher, Sir Charles Villiers Stanford. A temperamental man who demanded order and perfection from his students, Stanford did not tolerate poor work habits, slovenliness and chaos, crimes of which Ivor was guilty in abundance. In his teacher, Ivor encountered an unyielding force who would neither pamper nor praise him and who spared him no mercy when he presented poor or inadequate work. Accustomed as he was to adulation, criticism was something new for Ivor, and he did not take it well. Although Stanford might appear to be just the man he needed to teach him and bring discipline to his work, Ivor could not overlook what he saw as his abrasive ways and conservatism. The relationship was adversarial, one of fire and water, in which Stanford's inflexible adherence to rules threatened to extinguish Gurney's flame.

Born in Dublin in 1852, Charles Stanford had left his native land in 1870 to begin building a distinguished career as a composer and composition teacher. The only child of talented amateur musicians who nurtured their son's gifts, he studied various musical instruments, but his strongest talent seemed to lie in composition. His career in music was marked by success from the beginning. In 1870 he obtained a choral scholarship to Queen's College, Cambridge, and in 1871, a classical scholarship as well. His love of choral music prompted him to undertake the leadership of the Cambridge Musical Society and the Cambridge Amateur Vocal Guild, both all-male organizations until he combined them and boldly opened the society to women. At Cambridge, he won recognition as a composer and conductor, and was privileged to be awarded periodic leave between 1874 and 1876 to study in Germany.

From 1878 on, the year he married Jane 'Jennie' Wetton, the list of Stanford's achievements continued to grow and many honours came his way.[10] At the age of thirty-five he was elected Professor of Music at Cambridge University, and when the Royal College of Music opened in 1883 he was appointed there as professor of composition and orchestral playing. He held four honorary doctorates and was knighted in 1902. As busy as he was teaching, conducting, and writing books, Stanford, like Gustav Mahler, often had to wait for holidays to work uninterrupted on his music.[11] He was a prolific composer, writing operas, symphonies, rhapsodies, sacred and secular choral works, songs, chamber music, instrumental pieces for the piano and for organ. He assigned 177 opus numbers to his compositions. Although performances of his compositions were well received by the public and critics, interest in his music had begun to fade by the time Gurney met him in 1911. Debussy, Strauss, Mahler, Stravinsky and Schoenberg were capturing the public's imagination. The rise of modern music, with its experimental sounds and defiance of rules, threatened Stanford's adherence to a more traditional mode of composition and expression. He refused to compromise his art to keep pace with the times. He made no effort to hide his resentment, likening the abstractions and diversity of new music to 'unhealthy mud-ponds from which his ugly ducklings [pupils] quacked at him.'[12]

As a composition student of Stanford and a violinist performing under his direction in the RCM orchestra before the turn of the twentieth century, Marion Scott knew a different, more open-minded and daring Charles Stanford. 'People who only knew him latterly have levelled reproach that he was unsympathetic to modern compositions', she recalled. 'His choice of works for the College orchestra goes far to refute this. During the time he was in his prime he kept abreast of all new ideas, and I distinctly recollect his playing Elgar and Strauss while it still required courage to do so.'[13]

Stanford possessed a highly creative mind overflowing with ideas that he spilled onto paper with a confident urgency, usually in ink, without having made any preliminary sketches. Yet in his later years he dwelt in a self-imposed isolation, keeping away from the stimulation others sought and found in artistic circles. He had few friends among other composers with whom he could discuss his ideas. He did not get along with his colleague Hubert Parry and had a contentious relationship with Edward Elgar, despite having been one of the first conductors to acknowledge Elgar's genius and perform his music. Ironically, Stanford's relationship with Elgar worsened when Elgar openly championed Richard Strauss. Stanford found companionship in the younger, more traditional composer Arthur

Somervell, with whom he retreated to the stodgy comfort of his clubs, the Saville and the Athenaeum. Stanford cloistered himself from contemporary trends like a medieval monk, and expected his pupils to do the same, but 'ugly ducklings' like Ivor Gurney resented his archaic attitude and instinctively rebelled. Unlike Marion Scott, Gurney knew Stanford only in his later years, and could not see the bold, forward vision that had been the making of a teacher whom some considered unrivalled in Europe.

Like Stanford, Ivor could not get his ideas down on paper fast enough, but there was a significant difference. Where Stanford took a single idea and developed it fully, Gurney often tried to work on all of his ideas simultaneously, flying off in half a dozen different directions, heedless of the effect such undisciplined behaviour had on his work. The 'cool beauty of music's science' that Stanford laid before his students was lost on Gurney. He balked at order and rules, and simply could not abide the discipline that Stanford demanded. It ran counter to his nature.

Clashes between the untameable and wilful Gurney and the authoritarian Stanford were inevitable. Ivor was not one to hold his temper, not even when facing so formidable and respected a figure. While other students were intimidated and dared not challenge the great master's pronouncements, Ivor not only stood his ground but was capable of giving back as good as he got from Stanford.

In one recorded incident, Stanford made some changes in a song of which Ivor was particularly proud. Gurney was furious and told Stanford, 'I see you've jiggered the whole thing.' Herbert Howells, one of two other students in the room at the time, sat 'shivering' in anticipation of what would happen next. Stanford, his Irish temper flaring, grabbed Gurney by the scruff of the neck and 'shoved him out the door'. According to Howells, Stanford then leaned against the door and said, 'I love the boy more each time!'[14]

No student, with the possible exception of his favourite Howells, escaped Stanford's prejudices, rules, explosions, impatience, dismissals, inflexibility, pointed and caustic criticism. Even Vaughan Williams, who had studied earlier with Stanford, found his dismissive rudeness and small-minded attitude toward anything new in music difficult to endure. 'Damnably ugly, my boy. Why do you write such things?' became Stanford's predictable reaction to the original works Vaughan Williams brought to his lessons. Yet Vaughan Williams found that Stanford's 'deeds were better than his words – later he introduced my work to the Leeds Festival thus giving me my first opportunity of a performance under those imposing conditions'.[15] Vaughan Williams came to feel that 'Stanford was a great teacher, but I believe I was unteachable.'[16]

Like many influential teachers, Stanford's stern posturing was a part of his method, even if it did seem unreasonable at times. Although the majority of his students and peers believed that beneath his tough exterior there dwelt a great-hearted friend, a man of considerable wit, or – as Vaughan Williams acknowledged – a man with a 'loving, powerful and enthralling mind', Ivor seemed to have difficulty fathoming this side of Stanford.[17]

Marion Scott had witnessed the 'Celtic fires' that were part of Stanford's nature, but she believed that he was essentially a kind but demanding man who set high standards. He asked nothing of others that he was not prepared to do himself. 'What he demanded was not so much loyalty to himself as loyalty to his ideals', Marion observed. 'Stanford was unsparing, enthusiastic, almost ruthless in the thoroughness of his preparations and rehearsals', and in every aspect of his work.[18] He brought dignity to the college orchestra and regarded the musicians as his 'children'. He took great pride in its appearance, demanded punctuality and did not tolerate insubordination. Marion recalled the times when Stanford grew 'ashy white' with anger, but remembered also that he could convey his authority calmly and with dignity.

'His rule was rather autocratic, like that of Romans in Britain, but in his discipline there was something that made for strength and thought in the pupils', Scott said.[19] However, if he made a mistake or accused a student of an infraction of his rules and was challenged or proved wrong, he was quick to apologize. Sometimes his severe façade collapsed and he even laughed at himself.

His humour often saved the day. When his pupil Samuel Coleridge-Taylor proudly presented him with the score of his new Symphony in B, Stanford immediately spilled his cup of tea all over the manuscript. With the young composer on the verge of tears as he surveyed the sopping brown mess, Stanford quipped, 'Why it isn't a symphony in B, it's a symphony in T, me boy!' And, according to Scott, who witnessed the scene, 'Coleridge-Taylor positively laughed.'[20]

Stanford was a man of distressing prejudices that he himself often contradicted through his behaviour. Ivor, the most tolerant of men, could not abide certain of his teacher's attitudes and actions. He was not alone. In a revealing portrait of Stanford, Arthur Benjamin wrote that 'Musically (and not only musically) he certainly was a bigot' who dismissed modern music and experimentation, but he possessed prejudices beyond music.[21]

'He was bigoted in his dislikes – in his antipathy towards Elgar and still more towards Debussy and Ravel', Benjamin recalled years later. 'He would speak of the Frenchmen's "eunuch music". Yet he included their works in college programmes.'[22] Benjamin wondered if 'Stanford was a man born out of his right time?', adding his own observation that if Stanford had been born in 'some other age he might have been a truly great composer. Again and again in his music there is unmistakable inspiration, though only in small forms did he achieve sheer masterpieces.'[23]

In behaviour surely inappropriate for a teacher, Stanford talked about some of his students with other students, sometimes speaking disapprovingly of them. He made scathing pronouncements against Jews that found their way into the classroom. Benjamin, who was Jewish, reported being incredulous the first time he became a victim of Stanford's bigotry. 'You Jews can't write long tunes. Always two-bar and four-bar phrases, repeated!', he once railed at Benjamin, telling him pointedly that Wagner's masterly handling of short leitmotifs 'was due entirely to the fact that he was half-Jewish.' To which he added that 'You had only to see him to know his father was a Jew!' Yet Stanford loved Wagner's music. Stanford even told Herbert Howells, a very close friend of Benjamin, 'I don't know why I like that boy Benjamin. He's a Jew, you know!'[24] However, Stanford did not tolerate prejudice in his students. When he overheard a pupil spouting racial insults at Coleridge-Taylor, who had an African father, he took Coleridge-Taylor aside and told him he had more talent in his little finger than the other student had in his whole body. Many years later in 1950, when recalling the insults Stanford hurled at him, Benjamin excused his teacher's behaviour by claiming 'that there was no malice in this kink of his' which was 'shown by his being consistently sympathetic with me. Never did he skimp one of my lessons.'[25]

Although Stanford's students feared him, most claimed real affection and respect for him. As Herbert Howells later wrote, 'For [Stanford's] students, learning at his feet was a blending of Paradise and Purgatory, Heaven and Hell.'[26] For Ivor the experience seemed to be Purgatory and, at times, Hell. For Stanford, the experience of teaching Gurney was equally frustrating and disappointing, for he believed that Gurney possessed the greatest potential of all his pupils, including Vaughan Williams, Holst, John Ireland, Howells and many others. But Stanford saw that Ivor's potential was in jeopardy from the start, and declared to Howells that Gurney was 'the least teachable' of his pupils.[27]

Stanford found pleasure in teaching and took pride in the achievements of his students. On one occasion he told a friend, '[Y]ou must come upstairs: I want to show you my aureole', and taking him to his teaching room at the RCM, he pointed to photographs of his pupils hung around the walls. 'There', he said gesturing to them, 'that's my aureole.'[28]

Gurney seemed unable to resolve his hostile feelings toward Stanford. Yet he sought his teacher's approval of his work, and never stopped questing after it. Stanford had become like the parent a child can never please. '[W]hat a lot I have to learn and how long it will take me to learn to write one good sonata movement; to satisfy C.V.S.', he later acknowledged to Marion Scott.[29] Ivor, so accustomed to praise and in need of it, was bereft when it was seemingly withheld even from someone who evoked such ambivalent, hostile and contradictory feelings in him.

Ivor Gurney belonged very much to the modern world, while to him, Stanford was a relic of another age. What Ivor in his inexperience, pride and youth could not see was how much he needed the discipline and order of a Charles Stanford to help shape him as an artist. But Gurney, with his 'invincible independence of thought and action', continued to go his own way.[30]

Gurney was as full of himself and his dreams as ever, but in actual fact he was producing very little accomplished music at this point in his life: a string quartet, a theme and variations for piano, a violin sonata, a March in B Flat for orchestra, a string trio, the usual student exercises and a smattering of songs in which his individual voice was beginning to emerge. His manuscripts were disorganized and chaotic – mirrors, it might seem at first glance, of the turmoil of the genius simmering inside him. But there was more at work within the young Ivor Gurney than the struggle of emerging genius. No one knew then that he was already suffering from the bipolar illness that would dominate his life.

Gurney watched Howells rapidly advance to become the star composition student at the RCM while he struggled to shape and focus his ideas, plodding along on his own, resenting Stanford's discipline and feeling trapped by the rules that were the very making of Howells' early success. Yet Ivor took pride in his friend's achievements, encouraged him and showed none of the petty jealousies that so often flourish when creative young people find their work laid bare for judgement by peers and teachers. He does not appear to have considered music a competitive art, but at times he could be uncharacteristically tight-lipped about his own work.

Although Ivor was out-going with his close friends like Howells and Benjamin, he appeared distant and uncommunicative with others. Composer Arthur Bliss, a fellow student, recalled Gurney at this time as a 'strange fellow' who would never engage him in conversation about his music. If Bliss chanced to meet Gurney in a corridor, he would ask him about his latest work, but Gurney would say, 'Nothing, absolutely nothing.'[31]

NOTES

1 IG, 'To Gloucestershire', *Collected Poems*, ed. P. J. Kavanagh (Oxford: Oxford University Press, 1984), p. 260.

2 Harry Plunket Greene, 'Ivor Gurney: The Man', *Music and Letters*, vol. 19, no. 1 (January 1938), p. 2. In a letter written to A. J. A. Parrott in 1966, Gurney's elder sister, Winifred, attempted to connect her brother directly to Schubert, claiming that her grandfather, William Gurney, born in 1820 on the Isle of Wight, was the illegitimate son of 'Priscilla, the 7th daughter of John Gurney (a "woolstrapler and banker of Norwich"), and Franz Schubert'. Winifred was guilty of wishful thinking. Schubert never visited England. The family she refers to might have been her ancestors, but there was a Priscilla in another Gurney line in the same area, cousins of the John Gurney family.

3 MMS, 'Ivor Gurney: The Man', *Music and Letters*, vol. 19, no. 1 (January 1938), p. 3.

4 HH, 'Ivor Gurney: The Musician', *Music and Letters*, vol. 19, no. 1 (January 1938), p. 13.

5 David Tame, *The Secret Power of Music* (Rochester, VT: Destiny Books, 1984), p. 96.

6 Arthur Benjamin, 'A Student in Kensington', *Music and Letters*, vol. 31, no. 3 (July 1950), p. 198.

7 Ibid.

8 Ibid.

9 Charles Stanford conducted the first performance of Howells' Piano Concerto in C minor at Queen's Hall on 10 July 1914 with Arthur Benjamin as pianist. Howells dedicated the composition to Benjamin.

10 The Stanfords had two children, Guy and Geraldine, who died in the 1950s.

11 Stanford's books include a short biography of Brahms, *History of Music* (with Cecil Forsyth), *Interludes, Studies and Memories, Pages from an Unwritten Diary, Musical Composition*.

12 Harry Plunket Greene quoted in Peter J. Pirie, *The English Musical Renaissance, Twentieth Century British Composers & Their Work* (New York: St Martin's Press, 1980), p. 37.

13 MMS, 'Charles Stanford and the R.C.M. Orchestra', manuscript article, MSC.

14 Conversation between Herbert Howells, artist Richard Walker and Howells' pupil Robert Spearing on 1 April 1971, quoted in Christopher Palmer, *Herbert Howells: A Centenary Celebration* (London: Thames Publishing, 1992), pp. 352–3.

15 Quoted in Ursula Vaughan Williams, *R.V.W.: A Biography of Ralph Vaughan Williams* (Oxford: Oxford University Press, 1964), p. 45.

16 Ibid., p. 44.

17 Ibid.

18 MMS, 'Charles Stanford and the R.C.M. Orchestra'.

19 Ibid.

20 Scott quoted in Harry Plunket Greene, *Charles Villiers Stanford* (London: Edward Arnold, 1935), p. 113.

21 Benjamin, 'A Student in Kensington', p. 201.

22 Ibid.

23 Ibid. (In 'The Future of Irish Music', an unsigned piece appearing in the *Christian Science Monitor*, 13 April 1925, dateline Dublin, the writer observed: 'When Sir Charles Stanford wrote anything free of the Irish atmosphere, his music failed, but when he utilized an Irish melody or a fragment of one, the transformation was so great as to place him among the great composers.')

24 Ibid., pp. 202–3.

25 Ibid.

26 HH, 'Charles Villiers Stanford (1852–1924): An Address at his Centenary', *Proceedings of the Royal Music Association*, vol. 80 (1952–3), pp. 19–30.

27 HH, 'Ivor Gurney: The Musician', p. 14. Gurney was teachable and certainly did learn but in his own way. Apparently Stanford felt that Ivor was unresponsive to his teaching methods and thus labelled him 'unteachable'.

28 MMS, 'Stanford: Parratt: Bridge', manuscript article, MSC.

29 IG to MMS, 23 February 1917, *CL*, p. 217.

30 MMS, 'Ivor Gurney: The Man', p. 4.

31 Arthur Bliss, quoted in Palmer, *Herbert Howells: A Centenary Celebration*, p. 372.

CHAPTER 3

An Island of Serenity

*I*F HE WAS taciturn and distant in the presence of his fellow students, Ivor was quite the opposite around his new friend Marion Scott. As secretary of the bustling RCM Union, she was an important, influential and highly respected figure at the college, facts that would not have escaped his notice. The door to her office was always open, and the Union, guided by her zeal, energy and vision, offered a variety of programmes ranging from teas and dinners to intimate recitals and major concerts, all of which were essential to student life.

Marion and her parents, Annie and Sydney Scott, frequently opened their elegant home at 92 Westbourne Terrace for the At Homes that had become a college tradition by the time Gurney was a student. To guests, Westbourne Terrace seemed to belong to another world, an island of serenity anchored in the midst of a noisy, crowded city. For many, including Gurney, it became a second home.

The Scott residence was unlike anything in Ivor's experience. It occupied five floors in a gleaming white Edwardian row sheltered from the main avenue by a natural barrier of trees. Columns that supported a narrow, wrought iron terrace framed the front entrance. The comfortable, light, airy family rooms were decorated to reflect the personal taste of the Scotts rather than to impress visitors. Two grand pianos dominated the huge formal drawing room, where the Scotts held parties, teas and recitals. Music always held centre stage in the Scott home.[1] Marion's bedroom was on the top floor.

As one of Marion's favoured acquaintances at the College, Ivor became a regular visitor to the Scott home. The exterior elegance of the dwelling, its gardens and the formality of some of its rooms stood in sharp contrast to the bustling lifestyles and diversity of its occupants. The Scotts were a very close family. They were also wealthy, liberal and adventurous. In addition to Marion and her parents, the household included Marion's younger sister Stella, their niece Audrey and her widowed father George Francis Lovibond, who was a young solicitor in Mr Scott's law office, domestic help, and the family cats, usually numbering two or three.

Audrey Lovibond was the child of the youngest Scott daughter Freda, who had died at the age of twenty-four from complications following her baby's birth in 1909. Stella and Marion reared the child as their own daughter, sharing the responsibilities of motherhood.[2] Stella was in charge of running the Scott household for her parents, a considerable task that she performed with an efficiency reflecting the business sense she had inherited from her mother's side of the family. Stella was tall, slim and handsome, and, like her mother, a formidable woman.

Ivor first met the family in 1911 when Audrey was a two-year-old toddler and very much the centre of attention. It was clear to him that Marion took her unplanned role of motherhood very seriously. He understood the importance of her influence in Audrey's life and highly praised the way she nurtured the child's interests, which included an early passion for language. He enjoyed watching Audrey 'grow up ... seeing what her smile grows to be'. He told Marion: 'Some day she ought to do some individual work for she has eyes and forehead enough and character, which under your careful training, ought to produce something worth having ...'[3]

The Scott home sometimes resembled a cosmopolitan hotel, so varied were the people who visited. Gurney might encounter Mrs Scott's American and Russian relatives and friends who stayed for extended periods. He might also find himself in company with a variety of other guests who were temporarily down on their luck or in need of the Scotts' care until they could recover from whatever blow life had dealt them. Ivor was quick to observe the gulf of difference between Marion's parents and his own.

The backgrounds of Annie and Sydney Scott were rooted in diversity, so it was natural that they would expose their children to a variety of experiences and philosophies and introduce them to people from all walks of life. There was nothing staid or predictable about the Scotts. They were unconventional parents whose lenient attitude towards their three daughters must have shocked their Victorian contemporaries. Mrs Scott, a free-spirited American who had been born and reared in St Petersburg, Russia, had little regard for rules and traditional education. She believed firmly that the education of her children was best left to tutors, frequent European holidays and abundant free time for them to day-dream and explore the imaginary worlds of childhood. The Scotts were committed to nurturing, rather than controlling, the interests of their daughters, even if, as in Marion's case, it was a tendency to spend considerable time reading detective novels, an activity most Victorian parents would have scorned. They had reared their children in a positive, can-do, try-it atmosphere, imposing few limits on them. However, their expectations were high. Above all else, Marion, Stella and Freda were taught to respect other people whatever their situation in life. The Scotts instilled in them a sense of fairness, compassion, duty, and a social conscience that would serve Marion well throughout her life.

At the time Ivor met Sydney Charles Scott, he was a well-known and highly respected figure in the legal world and a partner in the firm of Scott, Bell & Company. Sydney Scott and his twin brother Edward were born in 1849 in London 'in an old house almost under the shadow of Saint Paul's'.[4] His father William was a solicitor originally from Woolwich, and his mother was Mercy Scott from Surrey. Sydney and Edward had an older brother, Herbert. The Scotts moved from King Street, where the boys were born, to Ludgate Hill in the 1850s and then to Dulwich in the 1860s. Young Sydney followed in his father's footsteps, pursuing a career in law. He was a gifted scholar in his youth and qualified as a solicitor before he was actually old enough to practise. He was admitted to the bar at age twenty-three. His knowledge of the law was encyclopaedic, but his interests were far ranging, encompassing music, literature, social issues, history, and the occult.

In his youth he was an avid cricket player and remained a fan of the game throughout his life.

A gifted amateur pianist, Sydney Scott had studied with Walter Bache, a pupil of Liszt who became professor of piano at the Royal Academy of Music. As a young man he had worked with Bache to gain wider recognition for Liszt's music in England. Away from the demands of his legal work, Mr Scott devoted evenings and Sunday afternoons to a regimen of piano practice. He was the accompanist for a double quartet of amateur singers who performed a wide range of challenging music from *Don Giovanni* to the *St Matthew Passion*. For a number of years, starting around 1892, he served as Marion's regular accompanist. Their joint appearances at a variety of venues in London and in Scarborough, where Mrs Scott had family, were given in support of charities. Father and daughter were a successful violin–piano duo. Newspaper reporters covering these events described Mr Scott as a most efficient accompanist, while his daughter was routinely singled out for high praise.

Beyond his practical achievements in music, law, business and social reform, Mr Scott had become an active member of the Society for Psychical Research in 1884. His long association with this organization was consistent with his metaphysical philosophy, his interest in esoteric practices and in the investigations of the spiritualist movement, then in its infancy in Britain. He volunteered to incorporate the Society in 1894, subsequently serving as its vice-president and as a member of its finance committee. He handled a variety of legal matters for the organization, and 'unsparingly placed time, trouble, sagacious judgment, and professional knowledge at our disposal without any charge on our funds', as one of Mr Scott's associates at the Society recalled.[5]

Arthur Conan Doyle, who had published his first Sherlock Holmes story *A Study in Scarlet* in 1887, was also a member. A friend of Sydney Scott, he was a welcome guest in the Scott home, where his conversation impressed young Marion as much as his detective stories. Many years later, she recalled 'once hearing Sir Arthur Conan Doyle complain, with rueful humour, that he had intended Sherlock Holmes to be an embodiment of pure intellect – an icy character without human ties or emotion. Instead, Holmes insisted on playing the violin and developed artistic tendencies.'[6]

As members of the Society for Psychical Research, Scott, Doyle and others were often called upon to investigate paranormal occurrences. Mr Scott was a man who believed in possibilities and was open minded about the occult, but he also was sceptical of the increasing number of alleged paranormal incidents being reported throughout England and on the Continent. He was a careful, thoughtful investigator who worked with the tenacity and skill of a detective to expose the fraudulent tricks perpetrated by phoney mediums, charlatans and others who claimed to have special powers.

In the late summer of 1894 Mr Scott, Conan Doyle and Frank Podmore, another member of the Society, were asked to investigate a 'haunted house' in Dorset. A Colonel Elmore, who shared the home with his wife and thirty-five-year-old daughter, had summoned the three men. Not wanting to appear foolish or to upset his family by telling them he had brought in 'ghost hunters', Elmore requested that Doyle, Scott and Podmore pretend that they had served with him in the second Afghan War. The situation in the Colonel's home had the mysterious elements of a Sherlock Holmes story, complete with someone moaning in pain, pathetic weeping that disturbed the sleeping household, the sound of chains dragging across the bare floors, and for the benefit of the investigators, the appearance of a ghostly white figure. The family dogs would not go near certain rooms, and some of the servants were so frightened that they had fled to find employment elsewhere. On their second night in the house, the investigators easily captured the 'ghost', the Colonel's daughter. When they threatened to expose her activities to her father, she promised to stop. Marion, her sisters and her mother were delighted when Mr Scott's ghost-hunting adventure was later immortalized in an episode of Conan Doyle's *The Hound of the Baskervilles*.[7]

Ivor Gurney was at ease with Mr Scott and enjoyed his company, but he sometimes found Marion's mother intimidating, which made him uncomfortable. She was an independent, strong-willed woman whose unusual childhood and ancestry had endowed her with drive, fortitude and vision unusual in women of her day. No one among Ivor's acquaintances and friends could lay claim to the singular heritage that Annie Prince Scott possessed. Time spent in her company was akin to having a living guide conduct a personal tour through American and Russian history so colourful and exciting were her lineage and the achievements of her ancestors. Few children had mothers like Annie Scott.

She was a member of an old Salem, Massachusetts, family of adventurers, explorers and entrepreneurs. The family had been a mainstay of the Salem community from the time the earliest Prince left England in the 1620s to settle in the untamed New World. Their vision, daring, and business acumen played a major role in ushering in the resplendent Golden Age of Sail that brought fame and wealth to Salem and made it the foremost shipping centre of the Colonies for decades. The family's earliest misfortune contributed to Salem's sobriquet, 'Witch City', and the shame associated with that dark period in American history. Their later imprudent behaviour helped spread the scourge of slavery in the southern states. They made fortunes and lost fortunes but they never let failure stop them. They simply started over again.[8]

Marion's mother was born Annie Ropes Prince in St Petersburg in 1853, the second of seven children. Her father George Prince had lived and worked there since 1838, having arrived at the age of sixteen to apprentice in William Ropes & Company, a Boston, Massachusetts-based family mercantile business managed by Prince cousins. By the age of twenty-one, Prince, with his cousin, was managing the firm and a fleet of supercargo ships that criss-crossed the seven seas. In 1850 he married Marion Amelia Hall, a cousin of his business partner and a member of a wealthy Scarborough family.

George Prince had instilled his deep love of Russia and its people in his children. It is likely that his daughter Annie Prince would have stayed in St Petersburg, where some of her siblings chose to live, had she not met an ambitious young solicitor named Sydney Scott on one of her visits to England. They were married at the British and American Chapel in St Petersburg on 14 September 1876. Annie was twenty-three, her husband, twenty-seven.

They returned to London and settled at 66 Longton Grove in Lewisham, where their first child, Marion Margaret, was born on 16 July 1877. At the time, the Scotts had two servants: Sarah Fuller, their cook, and Agnes Monk, Marion's nurse. Marion's sisters Stella Christine Millett and Freda Millicent were born in 1881 and 1884. Marion's earliest memory recalled 'a purple lilac bush against a blue sky, a grove of pink chestnut trees in blossom, and a road out between the fields'.[9] Here her 'infant feet ploughed lightly through sand' as she picked London wildflowers, white clover, pink persicaria, scarlet pimpernel, to gather into a posy for her mother on Sunday mornings.[10] From Lewisham, the Scotts moved to an elegant Victorian house at 28 The Avenue, Gipsy Hill, Upper Norwood, 'the inner rim of the Thames basin' within sight of London when the weather was clear.[11] From this vantage point Marion saw a foreground of trees and houses, the far towers of Westminster and following the line of river that appeared like a 'floating band of delicate mist', she saw the spires of Wren's churches, the great dome of St Paul's and the Inns of Court, where her father went daily. If her eyes scanned farther east she saw the Tower Bridge, a reminder to her that London was a maritime city. More distantly she glimpsed the heights of Highgate, Hampstead and beyond to Harrow Church. She regarded this panorama as 'one of the noblest views in the world'. Marion remembered, too, the obscuring mists that turned London into 'a pillar of cloud' and the nights when it became 'a pillar of fire' lit by the 'glow of its innumerable lights ... mirrored on the cloud, till that quarter of dark heaven was suffused with orange light'. Marion viewed all of this from her bedroom, looking 'with awe at these wavering northern lights', listening for the 'deep hum-note on the horizon' which gradually emerged on her hearing as silence fell all around, 'that sound which was the sound of London, mysterious as "the murmur of the outer Infinite" or of the sea night under toned by the ground swell'.

As liberal as her parents were, young Marion still found the Victorian Age 'a little suffocating' for her, 'the ardently artistic small creature whom it cradled'. Yet she realized she was living in a 'remarkable' time and place, one where 'terror had practically been eliminated from the scheme of things; science held a position in the world comparable to that of duty in the moral one; freedom was so assured that one might travel almost anywhere in Europe without a passport'. To Marion and her sisters their childhood world seemed so settled and peaceful that they 'concluded with some regret [that] history had come to an end'. When their mother read aloud Jules Verne's *Twenty-Thousand Leagues Under the Sea*, the Scott girls classed it as 'pure fairy tale' and for their 'strongest asseveration of impossibility' said 'You might as well try to fly'.

Marion discovered poetry at an early age and pursued it with a passion that her parents nurtured along with her musical studies. Writing came easily to her, as it did to all members of her family. Her first published efforts appeared in a magazine she created for distribution among her young friends. Her sensitivity to words found expression in her own teen-age verse with its imagery of 'pale moon, wan stars ... trailing wreaths of mists and damp', ' ... storm-tears of the rain' and 'The vapour vallum of her cheerless camp'.[12]

Among Marion's other recollections were those of summer mornings when her father took Mrs Scott and the children to the Temple Church at the Inns of Court. As with the Crystal Palace, Marion's strongest attraction to the Temple Church was the music, but she was drawn also to the 'dark mystery' of the Round Church, its 'iron restlessness' and the romance of the Knights Templar in their 'uneasy sleep'.[13] She felt 'A heavenly George Herbertish tenderness and tranquillity', on those Sundays when they jour-neyed to the Temple Church via an old Chatham and Dover train, emerg-ing at St Paul's station. From there they walked along Fleet Street or the Embankment until they reached the 'grandly sombre portico' of the church. Once inside, they did not linger in the 'warrior world' of the Round Church, but were ushered to the choir, where the family separated, Mr Scott joining the men in the centre while Mrs Scott and her daughters sat in the high pews at the side. Occasionally, when the church was crowded, the Scott females sat in chairs in the aisles where, during prayers, Marion enjoyed studying the tiles on the floor. However, she preferred the side pews 'with their carved ends, high-backed narrow seats, breast level book rest, stacked with solid leather volumes edge to edge, and the hinge-dropped lit-tle kneelers below for one's comfort during devotions'. A tiny child, Marion saw nothing but pews, books, roof and pulpit when she sat or knelt, but when she stood she was able to survey the whole scene, taking in details of light, colour, and atmosphere like an artist storing visual impressions for a future canvas. She paid little attention to the sermons. In the silence of prayers or when the preacher was speaking, she tuned her ears instead to the music of chirping sparrows as it drifted through the open windows. 'Whether the sermons to which I listened were without spiritual wings, or whether I was insensitive to words, I hardly know, but today I cannot recall a single thing said in the pulpit by the Master or the Reader', she admitted many years later. 'Yet I would have travelled more miles and sat through many more sermons than I did to hear [the music].' She particularly loved the tones of the organ which 'stood to other organs in the same relation as a perfect Stradivarius to other violins', making it 'almost as sensitive as a string quartet'.

The young Temple Church organist, H. Walford Davies, who later became Marion's teacher and friend, mightily impressed her with his 'magnificent command of rhythm and phrasing that gave his playing its superlative quality':

> When in the mood to play, Walford Davies would interpret Bach's D minor Toccata and Fugue with an almost terrifying grandeur. It might not have been – indeed it hardly would have been – orthodox

Bach, but it had something Michael Angelesque and Miltonic that was unforgettable.

Also unforgettable to Marion were the yearly performances of Bach's *St Matthew Passion* with organ. It was during one of these performances that for a moment Marion 'stepped from Time into Eternity and had a glimpse of its nature'. To her the experience was 'as if round a rock one passed from a tearing wind straight into infinite calm. ... That silence beyond music was the loveliest thing I ever heard at the Temple.'

Marion, Stella and Freda were born into a life of privilege. Although young, their father was a highly successful solicitor who by the age of thirty-one was able to afford an expensive home at Gipsy Hill. Their mother, whose family had made fortunes, had independent means. She adorned their home with personal treasures from Russia, including opal bowls and a frosted silver tea set.

The Scott children grew up in a world of nannies, servants and private tutors. Their beloved cook, Gillie, prepared meals for them. All of their clothing was made for them by dressmakers or by Mrs Scott using only the best fabrics. They shopped for other items on Bond Street or at the Army and Navy Stores. Sydney Scott's father lived nearby. A 'martinet with his own children', the elder Mr Scott was as malleable as clay with his challenging granddaughters and doted on them. Marion was the artist – sensitive, observant and outgoing. Stella, the tomboy, was masterful and practical. Freda, shy with a lisp, was temperamental and given to emotional outbursts guaranteed to be 'vivid' and exasperating to adults.

The Scotts were comfortable in company with Lords and Ladies, writers, musicians, generals, politicians and businessmen. They moved in rarefied circles but recognized the inequities of the class system and worked to change them. They instilled in their children a deep love and respect for their Queen and their country, which stayed with Marion and Stella throughout their lives. Marion enjoyed several brushes with the Royal Family.

On one occasion, Lady Montgomery Moore, a friend of the Scotts, invited young Marion to join her on a visit to one of Queen Victoria's drawing rooms at Buckingham Palace to see the Ladies at the Palace before they entered the Throne Room. They made the journey by train and arrived at the Palace in a four-wheeled cab. Marion remembered the afternoon in vivid detail: the crimson velvet pile carpet and white walls; the spring sunshine that threw the Ladies into 'jewel-like radiance', the mass of 'sweeping trains, flashing like gems, [their] feathers and veils'. As the women put the final touches to their feathers and frocks, Marion 'divined a flutter, a nervousness among them' that she never fully understood until she saw Queen Victoria herself on one of her last public appearances in London. Then a student at the Royal College of Music, Marion stood on Exhibition Road on a grey March day waiting for the Queen to pass by:

> At last, showing as little pomp as any Sovereign ... came the open landau, and for an instant I gazed close at the Majesty of England. A little old lady, all in black, wearing a simple black bonnet. ... But the

ineffable dignity of her bearing, the extraordinary concentration in her look of the supreme powers of a great leader ... as she acknowledged [the] acclamations, could never be adequately described by anyone.

In that one instant Queen Victoria made such an impact on Marion that years later when recalling the episode she could still experience 'the force of it.'

When the Queen died on 22 January 1901, the Scotts and their staff went into mourning with the rest of the nation. Mr Scott provided money to purchase black for his wife, daughters, and servants, and Mrs Scott and Marion set off to the Army and Navy Stores. They arrived early to find the place 'heaving with people ... everywhere women were trying on garments and assistants were scuttling round'. They dived into the throng. Later, under a 'dark and sullen sky', they walked back to a half-deserted Victoria Station where they boarded their train. As they sat waiting for it to move, Marion looked idly across some vacant platforms where she

suddenly saw a train of saloon coaches sliding in, the coal on the engine's tender covered with whitewash. A Royal train! It drew to a standstill. A small group of officials gathered near the door of the central coach opposite. The door opened, all hats were doffed. Out of the doorway stepped King Edward VII – his first entry into London as King of England. Upon him was a look of supreme dignity.

Marion Scott considered herself a Londoner first and English second. 'We know our city as sailors know the sea', she observed in her memoir.

We divine its currents of emotions as Thames pilots sense their channels when bringing in great ships; and we experience an utter contentment when in the City itself that I can only liken to the contentment of seagulls swinging up and down on sea-waves; riding the surface of an immense energy with utter restfulness. ... Probably [other] Londoners like myself can no more recall the first sight of London than their first sight of their fathers and mothers. London was simply there, and their awareness of it grew with themselves.

Marion believed that London had a soul, which 'as with a living person shone out unaware'. She first experienced that soul when, as a girl of seventeen, she was returning home from her first ball, 'tired, happy with little white kid shoes, danced dusty and dirty'. As she and her parents were driving over Westminster Bridge in the magical brightness of a June sunrise:

It was the view and hour of which Wordsworth wrote, though his green fields had gone, the towering temples and palaces were there, flooded with a tide of sunlight as full as the high water of the river. Westminster Abbey, the Houses of Parliament, rose out of the quiet streets, daffodil and blue, casting their shadows, like the laying of a benediction. ... Everything, it seemed, that London _is_ was in that view.

In keeping with their social activism, the Scotts were among the first to join the newly formed Distressed Gentlefolks Aid Association in 1897 to help 'gentlefolk who had come to dire poverty'. Mrs Scott served as membership secretary, and Sydney Scott helped raise money to lend to those in need. The indifference of society towards women suffering from financial difficulties was often a theme of meetings. One member complained that public charities would not help 'any woman whose husband was alive, even though he was a helpless invalid'. The message was clear: such once-wealthy women now fallen on hard times would have to sort out their problems on their own. For Marion this harsh indifference was intolerable. She would work throughout her life to change public attitudes towards women, not just in music but in society at large. As an adult she never turned anyone away who sought her help, a trait that would benefit Ivor Gurney much later.

Shortly after the turn of the twentieth century, the Scotts moved house to 92 Westbourne Terrace, which was more central for Mr Scott's business, Marion's burgeoning career and the busy social lives of his daughters. Marion was now a regular on the London concert circuit, often appearing with her RCM friend William Harris in benefit performances. She participated in chamber music concerts featuring music so new that the musicians had to work directly from the composers' manuscripts.

In 1905 Marion published her first, and only, collection of poetry, *Violin Verses*, which garnered eight extant reviews in newspapers in England, Scotland and Ireland.[14] Marion used her promotional skills wisely and well to draw attention to the slim thirty-five-page volume. The reviews, published between 23 June and 25 August, ranged from a few lines in *The Times Literary Supplement* to lengthy notices in the *Musical News* and in *The Strad*. Critics were varied in their opinions of this small achievement. A writer for the *Glasgow Evening News* found the verses to be 'of very unequal merit, and it seems to us the author has done herself unnecessary injustice by limiting her choice of theme to subjects immediately connected with violins'.[15] He found that some poems were 'much below the author's highest level', while 'Her best is, however, verse of excellent quality'.[16] Other critics praised her ability to 'bring to the surface the true poetry' of the violin,[17] her 'chaste and beautiful' language, and her 'noble, refined, and inspiring' thoughts.[18] The book enjoyed a modest success.

After Ivor Gurney read *Violin Verses*, he told Scott that her collection had 'sincerity, directness, power; its only fault is too many adjectives. For a book on one subject it is surprisingly successful; on which success please accept my congratulations. You ought to have written more, done far better work than this, since', he observed. 'It seems a pity that with all the new verse and new technique you have not stuck at it; but the desire to help other people has proved too strong ...'[19]

As she approached her thirtieth birthday in 1907, Marion Scott was searching for a direction in her full and active life. She had friends. She had not married. Men sought her companionship, but she could be possessive of them. She harboured a jealous streak that produced a smouldering, sometimes vindictive anger. Marion was successful in her musical endeavours and was building several careers. She was on the verge of becoming a musical pioneer by forming her own string quartet.[20] She was intelligent and persuasive. She was daring and witty. She was well educated yet never stopped searching for knowledge. She had an innate understanding of business and knew how to organize people. She had money, looks and charm. She did not need to work for a living.

If she chose, Marion could stay at home to devote herself solely to writing verse and music, but she took criticism of her creative work seriously. She accepted that she would never be more than an average poet or composer, and understood that her energies were best directed elsewhere. But where? Like many multi-talented individuals, she was not satisfied with a single pursuit, and had to try everything that came her way to see what suited her best. She had more choices than most people because she had so many interests and talents. It would take another twenty years for her to find that direction, one that led her down two avenues – music scholarship and music criticism. But even then she would continue to explore new paths. As her friend Herbert Howells observed: 'No one knowing Marion Scott could have found in her any sign of a comfortable formula of life, or a set approach to complexities of modern conditions, or anything negative; least of all any narrowing of the spheres of interest. ... As for the scope of her interests, this grew and was extended with the passage of time.' [21]

Perhaps the most profound driving force in Marion Scott's life was her 'powerfully active principle of friendship', which knew no bounds of class or convention.[22] Her friendship was a valued gift, given freely, and one that would benefit many individuals, but most particularly Ivor Gurney, who became one of Marion Scott's young protégés.

NOTES

1 Westbourne Terrace is located near Paddington Station. The Scotts' former home has been converted into apartments.

2 Freda Scott married George Francis Lovibond of Bridgwater on 19 October 1907 at Holy Trinity Church, Paddington. Scott's friend Katharine Eggar also took on the task of mothering her brother's son and daughter.

3 Later, when Audrey was eight and nine years old, she occasionally wrote letters to Gurney, as did all members of the Scott family. Audrey's precocious understanding of language and the imaginative way in which she used words impressed Gurney. She had a fondness for making up her own version of phonetic Elizabethan English. Audrey's early love of words led to her successful theatrical career as a teacher of speech and drama. The child Audrey was the 'Lady' in Herbert Howells' first string quartet, *Lady Audrey's Suite*, composed in 1915. According to Marion, 'The four movements form a series of fanciful pictures about the little girl whose name it bears and whose charming chatter of fairies and golliwogs gave the central impetus for the music'. (From a Scott manuscript, MSC.)

4 MMS, *The Home of All Our Mortal Dream*, unpublished memoir, MSC.

5 'W.H.S', quoted in the *Journal of the Society for Psychical Research*, October 1936, in a tribute to Mr Scott after his death in September. Mr Scott was also the legal adviser to Herbert Spencer's trustees and served in the same capacity with the Society of Women Musicians from its inception in 1911.

6 MMS, 'A Dictionary of Chamber Music', *Music and Letters*, vol. 10, no. 4 (October 1929), p. 363.

7 Conan Doyle turned the character of the daughter into the wife of the servant whose brother is an escaped murderer living on the moors.

8 Henry Prince (1764–1846), Marion Scott's early American ancestor, was a sea captain and adventurer who opened new trade routes to the Philippines and Zanzibar, and helped establish the 'Golden Age of Sail' in Salem. Sarah Osborne, a relative through marriage, was one of the first women arrested in the Salem witch hunts of 1692. For a detailed account of the Prince family, see Pamela Blevins, 'Marion Scott's American Heritage', *Ivor Gurney Society Journal*, vol. 11 (2005).

9 MMS, *The Home of All Our Mortal Dream*.

10 Ibid. Subsequent quotes in this section are taken from the Scott memoir.

11 The Scotts' home still stands today and retains its elegance.

12 MMS, 'The Outer World, and my Poor Mind', early 1890s, MSC.

13 MMS, *The Home of All Our Mortal Dream*. Subsequent quotes in the following section are from this source.

14 *Violin Verses* was published by The Walter Scott Publishing Company in June 1905. It sold for 2 shillings.

15 *Glasgow Evening News*, 29 June 1905, MSC.

16 Ibid.

17 W. W. Cobbett, *Musical News*, 22 July 1905, MSC.

18 John Broadhouse, *The Strad*, July 1905, MSC.

19 IG to MMS, 21 March 1919 (S), *CL*, pp. 476–7.

20 Before Marion Scott formed the Marion Scott Quartet in 1908, only a few other women in England had dared so bold a venture: Emily Shimmer formed a quartet in 1888; Jessie Grimson in 1901; Marie Molto in 1903; Edith Robinson in 1905, and Norah Clench in 1907.

21 HH, 'Marion Margaret Scott, 1877–1953', *Music and Letters*, vol. 35, no. 2 (April 1954), pp. 134–5.

22 Ibid., p. 134.

CHAPTER 4

Friendship and Poetry

*T*HE FRIENDSHIP between Ivor Gurney and Marion Scott developed rapidly. Within months of their first meeting in her office in 1911, he was sufficiently at ease with her to assume attitudes that were relaxed, direct, self-centred, and laced with humour. Any inhibitions he might exhibit before other friends and acquaintances in London melted away in her presence.

To a young man like Ivor coming from provincial Gloucester, Marion embodied the cosmopolitan diversity of London. In her, he found a woman to listen to him, to share his enthusiasms and to encourage his dreams. But more importantly, he encountered a woman whose keen intellect, poetic sensibility and thorough musical knowledge stimulated him. He could not help being drawn to her. Marion fed Ivor's need for attention, and he fulfilled her enjoyment of being in the company of gifted young men whom she could nurture and help, and with whom she sometimes found romance.

Initially, Scott observed in Gurney a student 'still very much a boy in his alternative bursts of shyness and self-reliance'.[1] But she also discovered that the young man before her possessed an all-consuming intellectual vitality, was exceptionally well read, and made a brilliant and provocative conversationalist, qualities she found irresistible and challenging.

In the early stages of their friendship, Marion took the lead, providing Ivor with concert tickets, inviting him to her home to participate in musical evenings and corresponding with him when he was at home in Gloucester. He perceived that she had taken a serious interest in him and was eager to help him. He was flattered, and, like any young man infatuated with a woman, he wanted to impress her.

For his part, Ivor eagerly accepted her invitations, shared his excitement about his music, the concerts he attended and the books he was reading. His earliest extant letters to her, written in 1912, depict a busy, confident young man full of himself and the half-mocking notion that he was a 'genius'. He had heard the word enough in reference to himself to believe that he was indeed a genius. Few letters exist from this period because Ivor saw Marion regularly.

By 1913 the tone of his correspondence changed from rather light-hearted comments to more serious matters, largely confidences about his health, which, despite his youth and athletic physique, was already giving him trouble, notably his digestive system and his nerves. He was pushing himself hard in his studies, composing new music and developing a deepening interest in writing poetry.

Poetry was very much in the air. Ivor was already enamoured of Yeats, Belloc and W. H. Davies, but many new names were rising above the horizon. Some like Ezra Pound were developing distinctly new voices in poetry, while others like Wilfred Gibson and Rupert Brooke were exploring the terrain of traditional forms and writing verse with popular appeal. While composers experimented with sound, poets experimented with language, some writing chaotic verse laden with symbolism and nightmarish imagery. Across the Atlantic Ocean a young American named Thomas Stearns Eliot had begun reinventing poetry with 'The Love Song of J. Alfred Prufrock', four 'Preludes', 'Suite Clownesque I–IV', and 'Rhapsody on a Windy Night'. Eliot's literary mosaics would later explode poetic convention and topple tradition, drawing poetry into the vortex of the modern age.

Ivor's boyhood friend Frederick W. ['Will'] Harvey, newly qualified as a solicitor in Gloucester, was writing poetry and influencing his younger friend to follow his lead. Ivor felt that his own poem 'The Irish Sea', from about 1913, was good enough to send to Hilaire Belloc's literary journal *The Eye Witness*. Although it was rejected, Gurney was proud of this effort and gave a copy to Scott with 'diffidence'. She found it 'very young', but reflecting 'an indefinable quality of vision which seemed to promise the unfolding of a gift'.[2]

At this stage in his life, Gurney was experimenting with words and with the rhythms of language, but it would be years before he made a stylistic leap into originality. Marion along with Will Harvey and John Haines, another Gloucestershire friend, became sounding boards for Ivor's poetic efforts.

In the meantime, London provided Gurney with many opportunities to meet and mingle with poets, including perhaps a venture to Harold Monro's Poetry Bookshop, which opened officially on 8 January 1913. Located near the edge of Bloomsbury in a neighbourhood variously described as 'unsavoury' and a 'murderous slum', the shop was a literary oasis tucked in among pubs and decaying buildings. The interior breathed a peaceful atmosphere of intimacy and domesticity enhanced by a warm coal fire in the winter, the soft light of oil lamps or candles (since in the early days there was no electricity in the building), and the presence of a cat and dogs. The oak furniture was 'massive but finely proportioned' and the space was filled with bookshelves, settees and tables covered with copies of literary reviews.[3]

Under the banner of the Poetry Bookshop, Monro had agreed to publish the first edition of Edward Marsh's and Rupert Brooke's *Georgian Poetry, 1911–1912* in December 1912, featuring 'the best recent verse, chiefly by the younger poets' including Lascelles Abercrombie, W. H. Davies, Brooke, Walter de la Mare, D. H. Lawrence and others.[4] Although Brooke thought that Marsh had selected 'too many rotters' in the first anthology, the book proved so popular that it was in its third edition by February and had sold 9,000 copies by the end of the year.

The Poetry Bookshop was the centre of poetic life in London. Each week, on Tuesday and Thursday at 5:30 or 6:00 p.m., poets gave informal readings from their works. Given his increasing interest in poetry, Gurney would have been attracted to such a gathering. Whether or not he actually attended the readings is not documented, but his enthusiasm for poetry was contagious enough that Arthur Benjamin later credited Gurney and

Herbert Howells with introducing him 'into the sacred groves of English poetry' which led him into a productive spell of song.[5]

By early 1913 Gurney regarded Benjamin as a man of the world and placed him alongside Marion Scott as his trusted confidant. He felt at ease with Benjamin and enjoyed his companionship. On walks about London with his new friend, Gurney, oblivious of passers-by, shouted the poetry of Shakespeare and W. H. Davies or sang folk songs at the top of his voice, actions that must have been somewhat embarrassing to Gurney's companion and bewildering to people on the street.

While Gurney was living in seedy quarters in Fulham, Benjamin lived comfortably in Bayswater. Aware of how little money both Gurney and Howells possessed, he entertained them at his lodgings and occasionally invited them to join him at the Café Royal, a favourite haunt of celebrities of the art world like Augustus John and the sculptor Jacob Epstein.

Gurney was consuming books at an incredible rate, reading everything from novels, poetry and drama to criticism, biography, and memoirs. His occasional forays into popular books included the equivalent of today's self-help books, one in particular on exercising 'for health's sake'. He had opinions about everything he read. He was critical of Hardy's *Tess of the d'Urbervilles* – '[T]he characters talk like handbooks ...' – and pronounced *Jude the Obscure* 'Grimy nonsense', but Hardy's poetic drama *The Dynasts* he found 'colossally good'.[6]

In August he reported to Marion Scott that he had 'actually condescended to read a lady-novelist. Mrs. Voynich.' He had made his way through her 1910 novel *An Interrupted Friendship*, which he found 'without form and void, but not uninteresting ...' to *The Gadfly*, her highly successful 1897 suspense novel. '[I] read it very carefully up to the capture of Felix, and read the rest in 15 minutes. Why ever did she lose grip in that way? Why did – – ? Why did – – ? Would – – – – ? It is the kind of thing one would write in cold grey dawns after a substantial breakfast of cold beef steak pie and porter', he wrote to Scott. 'But it really does strike me as an awfully fine book, in spite of the characters being non-attractive and a little puzzling.'[7]

At the time he wrote these comments, Gurney might not have been aware of how well Scott knew Ethel Voynich personally or that they had even been collaborators on a theatrical production in Manchester five years earlier. He was soon to learn that Mrs Voynich, who became one of his valued friends and an intellectual sparring partner, was no ordinary woman. By the time Ivor met Ethel Voynich she was nearly fifty years old, working with her husband Wilfrid in his rare bookshop in Soho and composing music. Her arduous route to London had taken her from Ireland to Germany, Poland and Russia. Along the way she met adventure and danger. She counted spies, revolutionaries and murderers among her close friends.

Born in Ireland in 1864, Ethel Boole was the youngest child of the eminent mathematician George Boole (1815–64), who died six months after her birth, and Mary Everest Boole (1832–1916), a visionary but eccentric woman whose books on teaching mathematics to children were milestones in education. The Booles, like the Scotts, were an exceptional family.[8]

Ethel's sister Alicia (1860–1940) inherited her father's gift for mathematics. Although Alicia had little education, no training in mathematics and worked as a secretary, she nonetheless made important discoveries in the field of geometry. Another Boole daughter, Lucy (1862–1905), possessed great scientific talent that led her into the field of chemistry. She became a lecturer and demonstrator at the London School of Medicine for Women and was, it is believed, the first woman Professor of Chemistry at the Royal Free Hospital in London. Ethel's sister Margaret ('Maggie') Taylor (1858–1935) later became another of Ivor's confidantes.

After the death of George Boole the family fell into dire poverty, forcing his widow to place her children in the care of various relatives. Ethel went to live with a sadistic uncle who locked her in her room, threatened to put chemicals in her mouth and forced her to play the piano for him for hours on end. Upon returning home to her mother, Ethel suffered a nervous breakdown. She was ten years old. While the misery she endured in childhood left its scars, it also prepared her for the dramatic life she pursued in her twenties.

When she received a small legacy at the age of eighteen, Ethel went to Berlin, where she studied music at the Hochschule für Musik. Her teachers included Philipp Spitta, the famous authority on Bach. She studied piano and developed her talent for composition. In Berlin she became deeply interested in the revolutionary causes of Russia and Central Europe. She began a friendship with Sergei Kravchinski (1852–95), a Russian revolutionary known as 'Stepniak' who had fled to England after murdering the chief of the Tzarist secret police. Stepniak taught Ethel Russian. His revelations about the plight of the Russian people under Tzarist rule prompted her to move to St Petersburg in 1887, where she embarked on a life of adventure, danger and intrigue. Initially she worked as a governess, tutor and music teacher, but she soon cast aside this safe occupation to work tirelessly as an activist helping peasants and revolutionaries. She called herself Lily in those days and defined herself as a Revolutionary Nihilist.

Ironically, while *en route* to St Petersburg, she stopped in Warsaw. There her future husband Wilfrid Michael Voynich saw her standing in the square outside the Citadel, where he was imprisoned for his revolutionary activities. He was later sent to Siberia but escaped, making his way to England via Mongolia, China and Germany, a journey that took a year. In London he met Ethel and recognized her. He joined Ethel and Stepniak working for their Society of Friends of Russian Freedom, printing and sending to Russia revolutionary literature and forbidden books. With other dissidents they formed the Russian Free Press Fund.

By 1895 Ethel and Wilfrid Voynich were living together, seemingly as husband and wife. She had adopted his name earlier. She now identified herself as E. L. V., the moniker by which Gurney, Marion Scott and others knew her. The Voyniches did not marry until 1902, and then perhaps only to insure the success of Voynich's application for citizenship in 1904.[9]

Ethel turned her attention to translating both classical and modern Russian writers, as well as Ukrainian and Russian folk songs into English. Her first book, as Ethel Voynich, was *Stories from Garshin* that appeared in

1893. It was followed, in 1895, by *The Humour of Russia*, one of a series of books on humour from a dozen nations.[10] She had already written several short stories and was working on her first novel, *The Gadfly*. In between the publication of her two books, Ethel made a clandestine visit to L'Vov in the Ukraine to organize the smuggling of illegal publications into Russia. After she returned to England, Stepniak was killed in a rail accident in December 1895.

Sometime later, the Voyniches met another Russian exile, Sigmund Rosenblum, who eventually became known as Sidney Reilly. History would remember him as Reilly, Ace of Spies. According to legend, he and Ethel ran away to Italy where they carried on a passionate affair. After he opened his heart and told her the details of his background and adventures, he supposedly abandoned her in Florence. She returned to Wilfrid Voynich and began writing *The Gadfly* inspired by Reilly's life.[11]

That's the legend. The facts tell a different story. Reilly was not who or what he claimed to be. He manufactured the details of his early life to explain much later (1918/19) how he was recruited to British Intelligence. The story of Arthur Burton, the main character in *The Gadfly*, was actually the basis for the creation of the fictitious Sidney Reilly rather than the reverse. Reilly also dipped into Ethel Voynich's 1910 novel *An Interrupted Friendship* to borrow more ideas in plotting his own fictionalized version of his life.[12] Ethel had actually conceived the idea for *The Gadfly* in 1885/6, when Reilly was only about eleven or twelve years old, and had started writing the story in 1889. Her novel was nearly completed by the time she met Reilly.[13]

Some sources claim that the Voyniches ceased their revolutionary activities after Stepniak's death. Again the facts tell a different story. Wilfred was, in fact, playing a more covert role in the Society of Friends of Russian Freedom. He began dealing in rare books and manuscripts, a seemingly innocuous profession; however, his London bookshop, where Gurney undoubtedly spent time, was a front for smuggling the society's books and propaganda into Russia and for raising and laundering revolutionary funds. Both British and Russian authorities were aware of Voynich's operation because someone close to him, possibly Reilly, had betrayed him. Apparently neither the British nor the Russians acted on the information and Ethel continued to travel abroad regularly, serving as a courier for the organization.

Eventually the Voyniches ceased their revolutionary activities. Ethel turned her energy to writing full time, producing three more novels before Ivor Gurney met her: *Jack Raymond* (1901), *Olive Latham* (1904) and *An Interrupted Friendship* (1910). Elkins Mathews published her translations of Shevchenko and Lermontov in 1911. At some point in their marriage, the Voyniches unofficially adopted a daughter, Winifred Eisenhardt, who later became Winifred Gaye.[14]

Through his friendship with Mrs Voynich, Ivor came to know and develop a close bond with her sister Maggie Taylor. Maggie was the artist in the Boole family. She had studied art and had married one of her teachers, Edward Taylor, a landscape painter who made a living designing and painting decorations for large public rooms on passenger liners. They settled among other artists living in St John's Wood, where they reared their two sons, Julian, who became a physician, and Geoffrey, who became one of the most important and influential mathematical physicists of the twentieth century. Ivor was a welcome guest and occasional lodger in Maggie Taylor's home. Gurney's RCM friend Sydney Shimmin was also close to both Mrs Voynich and the Taylors. Marion Scott, Ethel Voynich and Maggie Taylor are examples of the kinds of women Gurney attracted and in whom he found the intellectual, creative and daring companionship he sought.

Voynich and Scott had known each other long before Gurney met either of them. Because the English-speaking community in St Petersburg was relatively small, there is every possibility that Ethel knew members of Scott's family and had been encouraged to make herself known to Marion's parents after she returned to England. Given Annie Scott's close ties to Russia and her advocacy of social reform, she might well have supported the Society of Friends of Russian Freedom and the Russian Free Press Fund. Mrs Scott had many relatives living in Russia and her nieces and nephews were all Russian citizens. Ethel Voynich and Marion Scott also shared a common interest in music. Ethel was a member of the Society of Woman Musicians.

In 1908 she and Scott had collaborated with actress Janet Achurch in a stage rendering of Lermontov's dramatic poem *The Song of Kalashnikov* in Manchester. Ethel translated the lyrics from the original Russian. Marion arranged Russian folk songs never before heard in England as an off-stage accompaniment performed by her own string quartet.

At this time in his life, Ivor Gurney possessed a great deal of charm which, coupled with his good looks, made him a most attractive young man. While some of his peers found it difficult to engage him in conversation and others looked upon him as being unsophisticated, Ivor stood out from his contemporaries through the magnetic power of his personality, his consummate intelligence and unconventional behaviour. Others were learning what Marion knew instinctively: that he possessed a tremendous force within him that begged attention and expression. He was not the kind of man capable of blending unnoticed into a crowd. Both men and women found him attractive and companionable, no one more so than Marion Scott.

The significant role Marion Scott played in Ivor Gurney's life has never been examined fully, while her feelings for him and her motivations have been sheltered in safe non-sexual terms – 'motherly', 'friend and mentor' and 'guardian'. Composer Gerald Finzi, whose laudable efforts to promote Gurney were frustrated years later by Marion's inability to let go of Gurney's manuscripts, did more than anyone to marginalize her place in Ivor's life. So great was Finzi's annoyance with Scott that he resorted to calling her names – 'mulish old maid' and a 'fragile fool' – creating an unflattering picture of her as an unattractive, repressed, aging woman.[15] Unfortunately this tarnished image is the one that stuck, masking from view the passionate young woman with a lively sense of humour and keen sense of fun who fell in love with Ivor Gurney.[16] The romantic element in the relationship between Ivor and Marion has generally been dismissed largely because of the thirteen-year difference in their ages, her social standing, the erroneous assumption that Gurney had no interest in sex, and that, as an older woman, Scott naturally assumed a protective mothering role in his life.[17]

While societal prejudices have occasionally kept older women and their younger lovers apart, this has not always been the case. Constance de la Cherois-Crommelin was eleven years older than her husband John Masefield, the Poet Laureate. Composer Josef Rheinberger married the poet Fanny von Hoffnaass, who was seventeen years his senior. Brahms was thirteen years younger than his beloved Clara Schumann. Edward Elgar was nine years younger than his wife, Alice. History abounds with other examples.

When Marion Scott and Ivor Gurney met, she was only thirty-three years old; he was twenty. It is unlikely that Gurney had any idea how old she was, or that he cared. What was important to him was the simple fact that she was interested in him, his work and his dreams. Marion was aware of his age, but age was never an obstacle in her romantic life. She preferred the company of the attractive, talented young men she easily gathered around her.

For his part, Ivor was eager to introduce her to his world, share it with her and have her participate in it with him. He wanted to spend time with her. It is not surprising to find sexual undercurrents running through some of Ivor's letters to Marion.

Writing to Marion from his bed – 'I am (if I may say so) in bed a-writing this?' He invited her and her sister Stella to visit Gloucester so he could take them sailing.[18] He felt she might benefit, as he had, from being active in the open air. 'What you want is sailing, I am sure. And if you came here I would give it to you. Could you manage it? You and your sister in distress? [I] don't suppose you'll come, *but why stay in Bridgewater* [*sic*]? [C]ome to Framilode, Fretherne, Elmore, Arlingham Saul!'[19] When Scott did not reply, he wrote expressing concern that nothing in his letter 'offended you. If recommending that you stay at Framilode was a liberty in your eyes, I am again sorry ...' In this letter he draws her attention to his body, describing his physical activities of barge loading and haymaking that create an image of a powerful, attractive and virile young man. '[I] can lift a ½ cwt weight with either hand above my head, which is probably more than any other R.C.M.-er can do.'[20]

Despite her frequent bouts of ill health and seemingly fragile appearance, Marion Scott was surprisingly strong and no stranger to physical activity. She appreciated Ivor's comments on his impressive strength and understood the value of exercise and hard labour. She would not have hesitated to sail or walk Gloucester ways with him. As a frequent traveller to Switzerland, Marion was not the kind of woman to be content simply gazing at the splendid views from the terrace of a chalet. She was a vigorous, agile walker who particularly loved mountains and the challenge of hiking in them.

At this stage in her life, Marion Scott was impressing people with her achievements, her leadership ability and her vision, but she was not as confident and self-assured as she appeared to be. Although she was financially secure and highly successful for a woman in her day, she was troubled by occasional bouts of insecurity and self-doubt as she explored new paths in her life. Over the next decade, however, as her own great gifts came into focus, she turned much of her energy to help shape the genius of Ivor Gurney and promote his music and poetry. According to Winifred Gurney, Marion Scott regarded Ivor as her 'sacred trust'.[21]

Marion sensed a fragility and emotional hunger in him that troubled her. She saw that he was sailing turbulent waters without an anchor. Eventually she began her own quest into his background to try to understand the young man who had swept into her life.

NOTES

1 MMS, 'Ivor Gurney: The Man', *Music and Letters*, vol. 19, no. 1 (January 1938), p. 3.

2 MMS, 'Recollections of Ivor Gurney', *Monthly Musical Record*, vol. 68, no. 794 (February 1938), pp. 41–6.

3 Joy Grant, *Harold Monro and the Poetry Bookshop* (Berkeley: University of California Press, 1967), pp. 60–6.

4 Ibid., p. 92.

5 Arthur Benjamin, 'A Student in Kensington', *Music and Letters*, vol. 31, no. 3 (July 1950), p. 204.

6 IG to FWH, early June 1913 (KT), p. 4; 17 August 1913 (KT), *CL*, p. 7.

7 IG to MMS, 31 August 1913 (O), *CL*, pp. 8–9.

8 Mary Everest Boole was the niece of Sir George Everest, the Surveyor-General of India after whom Mount Everest is named.

9 Information provided to the author by Andrew Cook, author of *Ace of Spies: The True Story of Sidney Reilly* (Stroud: Tempus, 2004).

10 In his 1985 biography of Voynich's father George Boole, author Desmond MacHale observes, 'Russian humour of the Victorian era is unlikely to provoke much laughter nowadays', and notes that Voynich's book has become a collectors' item.

11 Correspondence between Andrew Cook and the author, 10 July 2004. According to Mr Cook, it is not likely that Ethel Voynich had an affair with Reilly, since 'anecdotal family sources indicate that Ethel's sexual preferences may well have precluded a romantic attachment to Rosenblum [Reilly], or indeed any other man, come to that' (Cook, *Ace of Spies*, p. 37).

12 Robin Bruce Lockhart, whose father Sir Robert Bruce Lockhart had worked with Reilly, wrote about the alleged affair in his book, *Reilly: Ace of Spies* (London: Hodder & Soughton, 1967, revised 1984). An article by Tibor Szamuely, based on Lockhart's account, appeared in *The Spectator* in June 1968. Boris Polevoy, a journalist who visited Mrs Voynich in New York, and Eugenia Taratuta, who published a 1960 biography of Ethel Voynich in Russian, denied the story, but later claimed it was true. However, they also believed the fabricated story of Reilly's early background.

13 *The Gadfly* was published first in New York in June 1897 and then in England in September. Fearing that the book's anti-clerical, political and love themes, along with its graphic depictions of brutality and death, might trouble Victorian minds and unleash harsh criticism, the publisher, Heinemann, decided to test reaction by bringing the book out first in the United States.

14 In her will, Mrs Voynich made Mrs Gaye her secondary heir in the event that her primary heir Anne M. Nill predeceased her. Mrs Voynich states in the will that Mrs Gaye 'who

though not legally adopted by me has always been considered by me as a daughter'. Mrs Gaye had at least one son and was living in Somerset in 1992.

15 Finzi made these comments in different letters to his friend Howard Ferguson. Some writers on Gurney still rely on Finzi's depiction of Marion Scott and perpetuate this false image.

16 In a letter to Don B. Ray on 13 February 1951, Winifred Gurney wrote: '[P]erhaps Miss M. Scott is afraid of a biography because she was in love with Ivor definitely … if Ivor was in love with Miss Scott he stuck rigidly to his own opinions …' GA.

17 Michael Hurd observed that 'One is led to the conclusion that sex simply did not enter Gurney's calculations in any shape or form'. *OIG*, p. 44.

18 IG to MMS, May 1913, quoted in *OIG*, p. 44.

19 IG to MMS, no date, quoted in *OIG*, p. 44.

20 Ibid.

21 WG to DBR, 23 April 1951, GA.

Part II

For after all, it is the artist's life which binds together the things of his creating, and neither of them is quite intelligible without the other.

– Marion Scott, 1938

CHAPTER 5

The Gurney Family

*M*ARION SCOTT began gathering information about Ivor Gurney in a 'scrappy way'. She concluded that 'his childhood was not a happy one, observing that 'he seldom seemed to like to refer to it, at least that was the impression I gained'.[1] In Ivor she discerned characteristics that often made her think that 'he had a great deal of a Norman Baron in his make up. He had a tremendous pride, a swiftness to anger, a lavishness of generosity – when he had anything to be generous with – and his very bearing at times had in it something of a Norman pride and a sort of eagle-like power'.[2]

It would be some years before Scott made her first journey to Gloucester where she finally met Gurney's family and his friends. What she learned reinforced her early impressions. She wasted no time in forming insightful and largely unflattering opinions of each of the Gurneys as she probed deeply to define qualities in Ivor that she felt made him different from his parents and siblings and, in her mind, superior to them. With her eye focused on Gurney's future, Scott was already cultivating images of him for posterity.

Marion developed a close relationship with Ivor's friend Margaret Hunt, and became friends with other members of the Gloucester community who knew, understood and respected the young Gurney. She easily won the trust of his father David, a mild-mannered tailor, but other members of the family were far less attractive to her. In fact, David Gurney was the only member of Gurney's family whom Marion genuinely liked. 'He seemed to me to be gentle and slightly puzzled by life in general and his eldest son in particular', she observed. 'He was a very nice man, and I know that Ivor was very deeply attached to him. His father, I think, at least came the closest to understanding him of anyone in the family.'[3]

Ivor's mother, Florence, presented a sharp contrast to her easy-going husband. While Marion learned from Emily Hunt, Margaret's older sister, that David Gurney came from 'good Gloucestershire peasant stock', she was at a loss to determine 'precisely what the family was that [Florence Lugg Gurney] sprang from. She was so unusual in her whole way of thinking as to seem almost a "borderline" case at times. She worried inveterately … seemed to bear a continual grudge against life', Scott wrote many years after meeting the Gurney family.[4]

Marion was brutal and not entirely fair in her assessment of Florence, observing that she possessed a character 'as hard as flint with an easy surface sentimentality, and so far as I could gauge her, she did not only not love anyone, but was probably incapable of feeling anything like real love.' Yet Marion was correct when she observed that it was from Florence that Ivor inherited his 'strange power of placing ideas in unusual juxtapositions' but with a great difference. 'With him it was genius, and with her it was almost foolishness.'[5]

In the early years, Marion had little to say about Ivor's siblings, but after subsequent experiences with them, she was highly critical of Ronald and Winifred. She found Ronald to be an odious man who harboured a 'violent prejudice against the arts and a supreme contempt for Ivor's writings'[6] Marion considered Gurney's elder sister Winifred, a nurse, to be abrasive and very much 'her mother's daughter'[7] Only Gurney's younger sister, Dorothy, then a teenager, escaped unscathed by Scott's criticism.[8]

The discord Marion observed first hand in Gurney's family convinced her that his childhood had indeed been unhappy. But she saw, too, that Ivor had managed to insulate himself from the conflict. As a sensitive and gifted child, he sought to protect himself from the tension and discord in his home by escaping into a world of his own making where he could find shelter. This inner world was not limited solely to his imagination and dreams. His outgoing personality drove him to surround himself with sympathetic friends who understood, nurtured and encouraged him. It was clear to Marion Scott that Ivor Bertie Gurney knew how to take care of himself.[9]

Born on 28 August 1890 at 3 Queen Street in a dwelling that sat above undiscovered (at that time) ancient Roman ruins, Ivor was the second of four surviving children. His sister Winifred had been born in 1886. When Ivor was two years old, the family of four moved to larger quarters, a dreary two-story building on nearby Barton Street that served as both a tailor's shop and living space and remained the family home for thirty years. Ronald was born in 1894, and Dorothy, in 1900.[10]

On 24 September 1890 Florence and David Gurney dutifully brought Ivor to nearby All Saints' Church, where they had met, to have him baptized. Since they had not made any previous arrangements to have friends stand in as their son's godparents, the young curate of the church, Alfred Hunter Cheesman, became, by default, his godfather.[11] He would become a central and highly influential figure in Ivor's early life.

Ivor was a difficult, strong-willed child whose relationship with his equally temperamental mother was combative. Other members of the family perceived him as precocious, rebellious and stubborn. By the time he was six, Ivor was spending little time with his family. He took to wandering down to the nearby Gloucester docks to dream of adventure in distant lands or to roaming the peaceful hills and valleys of the Cotswolds, where he found solace and joy in Nature. The gentle lapping sounds of the River Severn in its quiet moods and the rhythms of walking dulled the memory of family arguments and discord.

Life could not have been easy for Florence Gurney, rearing children, keeping house and working with her husband in his business. Her job was made particularly difficult having to deal with an unruly child like Ivor whose contentious relationship with his brother Ronald caused much disharmony in the household.

Born at Bisley near Stroud in 1860, Florence was one of eight children of William Lugg, a house decorator, and Mary Dutton. Before she married

David Gurney, Florence worked as a dressmaker and lived at home with her parents, an elder sister, three younger siblings and a nephew. Her mother and sisters were all employed as dressmakers.

There can be little doubt that Florence was in control of the Gurney household. Her erratic behaviour intimidated her husband and children, making them anxious and wary because they never knew what would trigger her outbursts of temper or prompt her nagging. She was a good, caring, loving mother when her children were young but her behaviour was, like Ivor's, as varied as the wind.

David Gurney's children portrayed him as the one calming presence in the family. According to Winifred, 'happiness revolved around Father', but she claimed 'he was not allowed to give us as much love as he had for us …' [12] David was born at Maisemore in 1862, the youngest of seven sons of William Gurney, a builder and carpenter, and Mary Hawkins. Apprenticed to a tailor in Wimborne, he settled in Gloucester at the age of nineteen and lived with his elder brother John, a bricklayer, his wife and three children at 2 Charles Street. One brother, William, settled in Cheltenham, where he worked as a waiter, while David's other brothers settled in Gloucester, where they became independent businessmen following their father's trade.

David was a moderately successful tailor who achieved working-class respectability for his family, but he was not a particularly ambitious man. He did what was necessary and what was expected of him. He provided for his family, but Florence desired more. She was disappointed that he was not more ambitious. In her opinion, he spent too much time at football matches, on the bowling green or visiting with his friends, time that could be put to better use broadening his business horizons and earning more money. Yet David Gurney tried to relieve some of Florence's burden. He was the first to rise to chop wood and light the morning fire. According to Winifred, he was a better cook than his wife. Occasionally the Gurneys were able to afford domestic help.

As adults, Ronald and Winifred remembered their father with far more affection than they bestowed on Florence. 'My father was by far the more home-loving, affectionate parent, and he was our favourite', Winifred recalled. [13] He was the favoured parent in their eyes because he was adept at sidestepping conflict and they did not see him as the source of tension. The children related to him because, in some ways, he was one of them.

From the perspective of adulthood, Ivor believed that David Gurney's 'past dreams' were 'all broken' and he believed that his father had willed him '[T]o say what he had never / Been able to say or sing'. [14] The same held true for Florence, but no one recognized it in her. David had contributed to instilling a love of nature and beauty in his wayward son. But the elder Gurney seemed impotent in the face of his wife's mercurial moods.

Although Winifred and Ronald had little good to say about Florence, Ivor by contrast wrote or said very little about her or any other member of his family. He left no written record of complaints about Florence's treatment of him or his siblings. Judging from her letters, Florence took pride in Ivor's achievements and did her best to provide opportunities for him and her other children. If read carefully, Florence's own words cast doubt on the image of her as a cold woman who was incapable of feeling or giving love. Because she had difficulty expressing her feelings does not mean that she was devoid of them.

Florence might have had difficulty relating to her children, but she never forgot the details of their lives. The pride that she took in Ivor and the love that she felt for him are apparent in her own rambling, unpunctuated letters written to Marion Scott during the 1920s and 30s. These letters reveal a breathless energy and exude a sense of her being overwhelmed and in complete disarray, as if she cannot collect her thoughts or express herself in a coherent manner. Florence lays herself bare at times, expressing guilt, self-deprecation, helplessness and a fearfulness that goes beyond reason. Yet the letters hint of a woman with a sensitive nature and the eye of a keen observer, whose own vision and use of words leaned towards the poetic. She describes Ivor's hair as 'straight and silver', the hair of her other children as 'gold' and recalls a scene from her past in which garden tools and diggers 'shone like silver'.[15]

In a letter to Marion Scott, Florence once described how the words 'it is better to travel hopefully than to arrive' on a pulpit reminded her of life's disappointments. 'I had been looking forward to hearing the Band in the Park and oh I was disappointed twas music without a soul so that is how it is through life the very thing we look forward to so much is bitter.'[16]

Nature excited Florence just as it did Ivor. Winifred recalled that her mother would 'go into raptures over a beautiful sunset', while a niece recalled seeing Florence go 'into ecstasies over a flower'.[17] Florence was more sensitive than anyone realized and possessed an artistic temperament that craved expression. But she was imprisoned by circumstances, and saw no way of communicating her own poetic and musical sides. She had grown up in a household crowded with seven siblings, and once again in married life she was jammed into small quarters with four children of her own. Surrounded by people all of her life, she had known little but hardship and work. Her behaviour and attitudes speak of a woman consumed by disappointment, battling frustration, and looking for scapegoats in those closest to her, those she felt were responsible for her misery – her children and her husband. Florence undoubtedly felt that there was never enough of anything – time, money, space, quiet, freedom.

Most of the memories of the Gurney children centred on what they perceived as her inability to be warm and loving, her constant nagging, and her abrasive manner, dating primarily from their teenage years when Florence was in her forties and early fifties. With her children beginning to need their mother less and seeking their own independence, Florence Gurney probably no longer felt needed or loved. Her spirit soured. She resorted to nagging and appeared spiteful, selfish, mean and emotionally barren, but she had not always acted that way.

Winifred recalled that her mother 'possessed us as babies' and 'certainly did her best to bring us up well', caring thoroughly for their material needs.[18] Despite Winifred's and Ronald's emphasis on unpleasant memories, life in the Gurney household had not been wholly miserable nor was Florence always difficult. She could be tender and understanding when she knew she needed to be.

Although family members clashed, they shared common interests. Florence, Ivor and Ronald shared a love of reading although David Gurney and Winifred did not. For a short time Ronald, who was 'not without ear and tune' learned to play the violin 'a little'.[19] When Ivor and Ronald were little boys, they were given small garden plots in the back garden at 3 Barton Road. They planted seeds. When Ivor's plants began to appear, he pulled them up 'to see how the roots were growing'.[20] Other bright spots included frequent outings in the countryside, visits to David's mother in Maisemore, even walks with Florence.

When Ivor was six, Florence and David purchased a piano that had to be hoisted up from the street and brought in through a second story window, making the already crowded quarters even more congested. But the loss of space was a sacrifice Florence was willing to make to bring music into her home. Winifred was the first Gurney child to take piano lessons with a retired woman who lived next door. Florence had received some piano instruction and could sing. She claimed a strong musical background in her family, writing 'There was quite 4 musical families interlaced with us' and recalling that her mother 'sang nicely and was always singing Scotch songs and English Irish and Welsh'. Her father was an alto in the Bisley Choir 'but he didn't sing at home'. She also singled out her grandfather and her uncle as being musical but dismissed the Gurneys, saying they 'hadn't a note of music in them', which was not true.[21] Although David Gurney never studied music, he had been a fine singer as a boy. According to Winifred, 'an influential lady', who had heard him singing at the church in Maisemore, wanted to send him to the Cathedral at her expense but his parents refused.[22] David's maternal grandfather was a well-known boy alto, and Ivor's cousin Joseph was an organist at All Saints' Church. Another relative named Ronald was also an organist.

Around the time the piano arrived at the Gurney home, Ivor began attending Sunday School at All Saints' Church, where he encountered his godfather Alfred Cheesman more frequently. Cheesman began to take more than a casual interest in his godson.[23] As a latter-day Renaissance man with a deep love of poetry, literature and history, he was able and willing to provide the boy with an exciting range of intellectual experiences and education far exceeding what he received at the National School, which he attended. As Ivor grew older, Cheesman opened his extensive library to him and taught him the art of declaiming poetry, which, according to Marion Scott, nurtured Gurney's 'remarkable sense of word-setting'.[24] Together they read English literature, journeying from the Elizabethans and the Romantics to modern writers, including Rudyard Kipling, whom Cheesman had met. He provided his godson with a sanctuary away from his chaotic home, encouraged his dreams and over the years did everything in his power to turn those dreams into reality for Ivor. The young Gurney came to rely on Cheesman for approval, affection and the thrill of discovering new adventures in literature. Soon he was spending less time at home and more in Cheesman's company at his home on Derby Road.

When Ivor first knew him, Alfred Cheesman was in his early thirties, an attractive man of slender build and a finely chiselled face. It was generally known around Gloucester that he 'had a liking for lads of all ages', a fact that seems to have been accepted quietly without overt judgement or condemnation by the citizens.[25] Cheesman made no attempt to hide his preference from the public and walked openly about the city with an adored boy by his side. From all accounts, the interest he took in these boys and teenagers was unsullied, and one of a man who served as mentor, guide and confidant to those whom he befriended. He was known for helping his young friends find jobs, lending them money to start their own businesses and even raising money to further their educations. Ivor Gurney became one of his most pampered and indulged boys.

Alfred Hunter Cheesman was christened on 15 January 1865 at Bosham, a thriving oyster and shipbuilding port near Chichester. The Cheesman family were well known in the village. They had served as the Coroners of the Hundred and Manor of Bosham and Lay Rectors of the Chancery of the church. The family lived in Rectory House, known as Strange Hall today, with the Rectory Farm adjacent.

Alfred's father, also Alfred, was born on 22 May 1823. He and his first wife Caroline Louisa Halsted, born in 1825, had two daughters, Augusta, born in 1851, and Leonora, three years later. Caroline died around Christmas 1858, leaving her husband a widower at the age of thirty-five with two young children to rear. He took as his second wife the young Elizabeth Amelia Hunter, born in 1843, and still a teenager when she married Cheesman. They had three children, Charles Christopher Barwell, 1862, Alfred Hunter and Mabel Elizabeth, 1869.

The senior Alfred owned the Bosham Brickworks and Pottery from 1867 until his death in 1886, when its operation was taken over by his executors and managed by Robert Honnson. It closed during World War I. Alfred's widow continued to live at the Rectory House for many years until she moved to Twigworth to share the vicarage with her son, Alfred, who, by then, was serving at St Matthew's Church.

For an inquisitive, intelligent, history-loving boy like Alfred Cheesman, Bosham was an ideal place to spend his formative years. Fragments of England's Roman history are woven into the fibre of the community, a fact Cheesman shared with Ivor, who loved the Roman culture that was part of Gloucester's past. The Emperor Vespasian is believed to have had a residence in Bosham between AD 69 and 79. The present-day church was built on the site of a Roman basilica. Roman bricks are incorporated in its walls, while the remains of Roman pillars form the bases of the Saxon chancel arch. Bosham is depicted in the Bayeux Tapestry, and it was from its harbour that Harold II, the last Saxon king of England, set out in 1064 to settle his claim to the English throne with William of Normandy. Old photographs capture the colourful world of Cheesman's childhood when fishing boats, schooners and barges lined the quay, and the community was a mainstay of the nation's oyster industry.

Alfred received his basic education at nearby Chichester. He pursued his religious studies at Worcester College, Oxford, formerly the site of

Gloucester College for Benedictine monks, founded in 1283. He earned his bachelor's degree in 1888 and his master's degree in 1892. He was created deacon in 1888 and the following year he was ordained as a priest in the diocese of Gloucester and Bristol. Cheesman was first appointed curate at All Saints' Church, Gloucester, which drew its parishioners from the shopkeepers and artisan population of the east end of the city near the River Twyver. This included the Gurney family who lived only a few blocks from the church.

Although Cheesman was known for his enthusiasm and devotion to his work, he held only two clerical posts in his fifty-three-year career, the second as vicar at St Matthew's Church, Twigworth. He was the editor of the Gloucester *Diocesan Kalendar* from 1900 to 1927, and during the Great War he was an honorary chaplain in France. Secure and content in Gloucester, he was not driven by ambition to rise in the church hierarchy. In 1925 he was named an honorary Canon of Gloucester Cathedral.[26]

Alfred Cheesman was well loved by his parishioners at St Matthew's, who regarded him as a 'great man, very tactful and exceedingly discreet.'[27] 'To be in Canon Cheesman's company was always an education and an inspiration. His ready wit ... together with his profound knowledge of history ... [and] one of Nature's real gentlemen, made him at all times a most delightful companion', recalled an anonymous contributor writing in the St Matthew parish magazine.[28] Cheesman was known as a compassionate man who never stepped away when something out of the ordinary was asked of him and he had a gift for 'always saying just the right word and doing the right thing'.[29]

At Cheesman's suggestion, Ivor became a probationer in the All Saints' choir, a position that provided him with basic knowledge of music through sight-reading and part-singing. Two years later, when Ivor was ten, Cheesman encouraged him to compete for a place in the Gloucester Cathedral Choir, which he won in 1900. As a chorister, Ivor attended the King's School, where he received both a general and musical education. It was a prestigious position that Florence felt brought honour to the family. She was proud of her son, too proud perhaps, because Ronald began to feel resentment towards Ivor. He thought, not without justification, that his parents favoured his brother and that they were ready to sacrifice everything for him at Ronald's expense. Winifred shared Ronald's feelings. The brothers developed an antagonistic relationship that followed them into adulthood. This ongoing conflict fed more tension and only served to drive Ivor further away from any contact with his family.

Ivor began spending even more time walking in the countryside, visiting with friends and participating in school and choir activities. He wanted to do only what he wanted to do, not what was expected of him. 'Any routine irked him', Marion Scott recalled later.[30] He was clearly a rebellious child who was making his own way through life with little parental supervision or guidance. As his resentment of his family deepened, he became 'pompous and scornful' of them and they, in turn, viewed him with hostility, thinking that he felt he was too good to associate with them.[31]

With his independent undisciplined behaviour and contrary attitude anchored in place in childhood, Ivor continued to develop patterns that would later make it difficult, if not impossible, for him to follow rules, rein in his wild enthusiasms or focus on one project at a time. Trouble began when Sir Herbert Brewer, organist and director of the Cathedral Choir, insisted that Ivor study piano, basic theory, counterpoint, and harmony with another member of the staff, organist Charles Deavin. Brewer believed that the choirboys should learn an instrument to enhance their understanding and appreciation of music. While Ivor was enthusiastic and eager, he was also a typical boy who resented the time practice took away from his other activities.

With her sensitivity towards music, Florence was quick to observe that Ivor was rushing through his lessons as quickly as he could in order to escape to the outdoors. Fearing that he was in danger of jeopardizing his future at the Cathedral, something she knew was important for him and that she herself relished, she fixed a set amount of time for Ivor to sit at the piano, hoping to make practice more effective.

When Ivor continued to scramble through his assignments, filling the remaining time improvising and dreaming, Florence determined not to give in, but she knew that if she were demanding, he would rebel against her. She avoided his defiance by prodding him gently, guiding him slowly and patiently to practise his assignments with care and with his full attention. Her strategy worked because Ivor advanced musically, once becoming a momentary celebrity when he filled in without notice for an indisposed singer.[32]

Florence was proud of Ivor's achievements even though, paradoxically, she was jealous of his friendships outside the family, undoubtedly because she saw them taking her son away from her. Possessive and suspicious by nature, she felt that Ivor was spending too much time with people who were filling him with high-blown ideas.

Winifred remembered that Ivor was 'kindly disposed' to his mother as a child, but as he grew older they often clashed.[33] Ivor had a 'terrible temper', as did Florence. Ronald said that when Ivor was an adult he would hardly get in the house 'before his nerves and Mother's collide'.[34] The clashes between Florence and Ivor were not rooted so much in differences as they were in the similarities of two people of like temperament, each seeing in the other an unsettling self-reflection. Ivor was in fact deeply attached to his mother. Indeed, when Ivor Gurney later stood on the threshold of the darkest period of his life, his first concern was for the well-being of his mother.

The portrait of Florence as a woman incapable of feeling love or expressing it is drawn largely from the memories and impressions of Winifred and Ronald Gurney. They were jealous of Ivor, and harboured bitterness against their mother for what they felt were the sacrifices she forced other family members to make so that Ivor could study music. They sensed that Ivor was his mother's favourite given the lengths she went to ensure his success. Their memories of life in the Gurney household and of their mother and Ivor must be considered with a degree of caution. Clearly Florence and David Gurney did their best to provide for their children.

Petty jealousies, lack of communication, simmering resentments, clashing personalities and shattered dreams fuelled the current of anger and hostility that made members of the Gurney household tense, combative and embittered. No single family member was solely responsible for the turmoil.

Although soured by the circumstances of her childhood, Winifred understood better than anyone, in part, what went wrong. 'If we could only have broken down this terrible barrier and had a round table conference, we would have been a happier and more united family.' But Winifred found that 'obstinacy and determination was so practised amongst us, I think, that we developed unbreakable control, because our emotions were so strong. There was always the desire to clear matters up and let bygones be bygones, but as we were all stiff and unbending, we couldn't do it.' [35]

NOTES

1 MMS, Notes, MSC.

2 Ibid.

3 Ibid. Although Scott believed that David Gurney understood his son, it was David who told Marion Scott, 'I wish to heaven the boy had never gone to the cathedral choir school, but his mother would have it – she was full of ambition' (MMS, Notes, MSC).

4 Ibid.

5 Ibid.

6 Ibid.

7 Ibid.

8 Dorothy later moved to Australia, where she reared her own family.

9 When Scott first met Gurney and asked him what the 'B' stood for he replied 'disgustedly "My mother gave it to me".' Scott said she found out later that Mrs Gurney had given him the name Ivor Bertie 'out of social ambition, because at that time the Bertie family were very leading people in Gloucestershire, and Ivor Guest was particularly well-known. Mrs Gurney therefore gave her eldest son a name as near the Hon. Ivor Guest as she could, which in itself, is an indication of her extraordinary desire for social advancement', Scott wrote (MMS, Notes).

10 Florence Gurney had lost a son between the births of Winifred and Ivor.

11 The Reverend Herbert Foster, vicar of All Saints' Church, was also present, and served as Gurney's other godparent.

12 WG, quoted in *OIG*, p. 11.

13 Ibid.

14 IG, 'Petersburg', quoted in *OIG*, p. 12.

15 FG to MMS, no date, GA.

16 FG to MMS, 22 August 1927, GA.

17 WG, quoted in *OIG*, p. 11, and an unnamed niece quoted in William Trethowan, 'Ivor Gurney's Mental Illness', *Music and Letters*, vol. 62, nos. 3–4 (July/October 1981), p. 307.

18 WG, 'Memories of my Brother' (1951), GA.

19 WG to DBR, 29 November 1950, GA.

20 MMS, Notes.

21 FG to MMS, no date but after 1937, GA. All letters written by Florence Gurney quoted in this book appear as she wrote them. They have not been edited or corrected.

22 WG to DBR, 'Memories of my Brother', GA.

23 In a letter written to Marion Scott on 19 April 1937, Cheesman claimed that he did not 'remember anything much of him till he was 8-years old' when Ivor became a probationer to the Choir at All Saints.

24 MMS, 'Ivor Gurney, The Man', *Music and Letters*, vol. 19, no. 1 (January 1938), p. 3.

25 Reminiscences of Gloucester resident quoted in *OIG*, p. 10. According to Winifred Gurney, Cheesman had a 'very intimate friend' in Frederick Saxty, and was 'often in his company' (letter to DBR, 13 February 1951, GA). On occasion Ivor Gurney composed songs under the pseudonym Frederick Saxby.

26 All Saints' Church still stands not far from the park where, in Gurney's youth, sheep grazed around the bandstand. But the chorus of hymns and the humble prayers that once filled the Sunday morning air are no longer heard. The church was closed for many years but has been completely restored and is now a Chinese Cultural Centre. By contrast, St Matthew's Church, Twigworth, is working to present a new image to its parishioners after years of declining attendance.

27 Unsigned tribute in *St Matthew Parish Magazine*, July 1941.

28 Ibid.

29 Ibid.

30 MMS, Notes.

31 WG to DBR, 25 May 1951, GA.

32 Ivor sang with Madame Emma Albani in Mendelssohn's *Elijah* when one of the three angels failed to materialize for the performance. He performed 'Lift thine eyes' without a rehearsal.

33 WG to DBR, 25 May 1951, GA.

34 RG to MMS, 13 May 1919, GA.

35 WG to DBR, 25 May 1951, GA.

CHAPTER 6

Golden Days

*H*OME WAS NOT the only place where Ivor Gurney found discipline lacking. The demands on him as a chorister at the Cathedral and student at the King's School were neither all-consuming nor difficult. He had plenty of time to drift and dream his way through the days. While some early acquaintances described Ivor as seeming to live in a world of his own, he was not a shy, lonely, withdrawn child or teenager. He was naturally gregarious. Among his mates, Ivor was decisive and daring while older people found him charming and engaging. Marion Scott discovered that he was 'not an angel but a very human boy'.[1] He was very physical, participating aggressively in sports and taking great pride in his prowess in cricket and football: 'Centre-forward for King's School', '2nd best batting average' and '3rd best bowling', he declared.[2]

Selective in making friends, Ivor chose to spend his time with companions like Will Harvey and Herbert Howells, who shared his love of books, music and the Gloucestershire countryside. He did not squander time that could be put to better use playing music, reading, walking or sailing his small boat, the *Dorothy*, with Harvey on the Severn.[3] If his fellow students and neighbourhood children found him different, remote and 'strange in manner', it is because they did not understand that Gurney was an artist in the making who was exploring an inner landscape they could not see.[4]

The assistant Cathedral organist Samuel Underwood found that Ivor had an unusual sense of 'justice and fairness' in one so young. '[O]n one occasion when I had reprimanded a boy for some misdemeanour or other, Gurney came to me after the rehearsal and said, "Please sir, I don't think you were quite fair with that boy this morning." He was probably right and I have never forgotten the incident', Underwood recalled.[5]

When Ivor left the Cathedral Choir and King's School in 1906, he became an articled pupil of Dr Herbert Brewer. Brewer considered Ivor an ordinary boy, although he once admitted to David Gurney that he would have been happy to have composed a certain piece Ivor had recently completed.[6] Despite his own considerable musical gifts and his contributions to the musical progress of his native Gloucester, Brewer did little to nurture and inspire the budding musician in Ivor Gurney. Dr Brewer had been a chorister and as a gifted organist had held various organ appointments from the age of sixteen. By the time he was twenty, he had been elected organist of Bristol Cathedral. He returned to Gloucester in 1896 as the Cathedral's choirmaster and organist, a post he held until his death in 1928.

Brewer's most significant contributions to the artistic life of the city revolved around his work on the triennial Three Choirs Festival, the oldest surviving music festival in Europe, dating from the early eighteenth century. He was willing to stride into the twentieth century by programming new music, including the first performance of Ralph Vaughan Williams's

Fantasia on a Theme of Thomas Tallis that had impressed Gurney and Howells so profoundly. Brewer himself was a capable composer whose works displayed a thoughtful musicianship but perhaps too little passion.

Ivor's studies with Brewer were disappointing. Marion Scott felt that under his casual and indifferent tutelage, Gurney had merely become 'a practical if unpredictable musician'.[7] Ivor's friend Margaret Hunt was more severe in her appraisal, calling Brewer 'neurotic and utterly selfish and interested in his own concerns'. According to Hunt, he 'never did anything to help either of his clever pupils [Howells and Gurney] and did not wish them to go to London'.[8] Howells called Brewer 'an entertaining dwarf', a comment which prompted Scott to label him 'a dwarfed soul of the deepest dye' and to observe, 'How future musical historians will pillory him!!'[9] Even Gurney's sister Winifred claimed that Brewer gave Ivor 'little or no encouragement [and] did not appear to praise or do anything to help him ...'[10]

Ivor later told Marion that he would have done better if Brewer had been more of a disciplinarian. 'I would go to his house at the time fixed for my lesson', Gurney explained, 'and then Brewer would send me into the city to buy birdseed for his bird, or some other errand, and then when I got back he would say there really wasn't time for a lesson as he must go to the Cathedral, and I would only get half a lesson or else he told me to come on some other day.'[11] 'Ivor himself realized he had needed strict discipline over his studies', Scott observed.[12]

The 'impulse' to compose first came to Gurney while engrossed in reading Shakespeare as he 'minded' his father's shop, according to Scott.[13] He was only fourteen years old and began testing the waters of a new art, producing piano pieces and songs that hinted at a talent searching for direction. Several songs survive from this early period, including two settings of Kipling and one from the Song of Solomon, but it would be another few years before his emerging gift would begin to take shape and find a direction.

In the meantime, he was taking more calculated steps towards his independence, separating himself further from his home. His family rarely saw him and when they did, they claimed that Ivor was rude and indifferent to them and their friends. Winifred was often stung by his superior attitude. 'If I had friends [in], he just walked in and out of the home taking no notice of them at all', she recalled.[14]

In 1905 Ivor had decided to prepare for the examination to become an associate member of the Royal College of Music of Organists (ARCO), a professional organization. He passed later in the year. As it became increasingly apparent that Ivor was on the path to a career in music, his godfather Alfred Cheesman stepped in to help. He secured an organist's post for him at Whitminster, near Gloucester. Ivor did not stay there long before he left to take another position at Hempsted. According to Cheesman, Ivor 'was rather wanting in tact' and gave 'offence by being rather too outspoken – sometimes even to vicars' wives' which might account for the short duration of his employment at these churches.[15] He fared better at the Mariner's Church in the Gloucester docklands, which ministered to sailors in a less rigid, grittier environment, one more suited to Gurney's wayward temperament. According to some accounts, Ivor was appointed assistant organist at Gloucester Cathedral in 1906 to replace Samuel Underwood who had taken a new post.[16]

The money he earned bought Ivor independence, which he flaunted with an air of superiority before Ronald, who was working in their father's tailor's shop. Ivor's attitude and enviable financial position fuelled Ronald's resentment. Now that he was working, Ivor was able to contribute some money to the family but he indulged himself, too, buying books, music, the *Dorothy*, even a fine German edition of the Beethoven piano sonatas. Ronald became even more jealous and bitter towards his older brother. He was fully aware that his parents were paying term fees for Ivor's studies with Brewer while he worked without pay in his father's shop. No one seemed interested in Ronald's dream of studying to become a doctor.

During his frequent excursions away from home, Ivor could usually be found sailing the *Dorothy*, sleeping out under the stars when weather permitted, or visiting with Will Harvey, the Hunt sisters or with his godfather, Alfred Cheesman. In them, he found kindred spirits, individuals who understood and shared his love of music, books and nature. To his family, Ivor was a stranger who 'did not seem to belong to us', someone who 'simply called on us briefly, and left again without a word', Winifred said.[17] The problem, according to composer Gerald Finzi, was that Gurney was 'a radiant mind ... born amongst sterile, unimaginative minds'.[18]

In his friend Frederick William 'Will' Harvey, Ivor encountered an imaginative mind and spirit equal to his own. Both teenagers had been aware of each other during their days at the King's School, where Harvey had been a pupil from 1897 to 1902, but their friendship did not begin until 1908 after a chance encounter on a tram.

Will, born in 1888, was two years older than Ivor. He had already begun to study law with a Gloucester solicitor in 1906. He was not an ideal candidate for a career in law. At heart he was a poet with a marked inclination to daydream that did not fit the lacklustre routine of a solicitor's office. He often slipped away from the office to wander about the countryside and the city, his poet's eye and sensibilities taking in the beauty of the Cotswold Hills and the River Severn and the sights and sounds of colourful Gloucester, its docks, markets and history. Will possessed considerable charm, a strong independent streak, erratic discipline, a love of walking, nature, beauty, music and poetry, and a fine singing voice that Ivor considered one of the best drawing-room voices in the county. He wore spectacles and paid little attention to his personal appearance. Indeed, Will Harvey had much in common with Ivor Gurney, and it wasn't long before the new friends were inseparable.

Ivor and Will wandered the countryside together, absorbing the glories of the Gloucestershire landscape and the River Severn, discussing poetry and sharing their delight in books and music. One day after a ten-mile walk, the two friends settled in the Harveys' music room. 'O joy of dear companionship! Golden curves of Beethoven matching the fire of pear wood burning in the grate with no calm glow blinking embers but in a golden torment of fantastic flame', Will recalled of those idyllic days with Ivor. 'Peace was in that hour. Faith binding loveliness ... Hinted glory, – glimpses of Heaven'.[19] Winifred Gurney observed that the two young men were 'twin intellects ... perfectly in harmony'.[20]

Ivor was a frequent and welcome visitor to the Harvey home. He had an open invitation to play Mrs Harvey's grand piano. He shared meals with the family and participated in their outings. Here in the 'creeper covered house' in company with the Harveys, he found a peaceful haven, a shelter from 'the wind and storm' of his own home.[21]

If life in Gurney's household was tense and chaotic, life in Will Harvey's family was casual, calm, loving and full of good cheer, just what Ivor needed. The five Harvey children, four boys and a girl, and a niece of Mrs Harvey, had been reared in the large Georgian farmhouse, The Redlands. Set back from the main road in Minsterworth, it was four miles from Gloucester. There were meadows and orchards in which to play. The Severn flowed nearby. As a boy Will, like Ivor, was drawn to the river and became a keen observer of life along its banks. He came to know it in all of its unpredictable and, at times, violent moods.

From an early age the Harvey children were encouraged to play games outdoors and explore the countryside on horseback. Their father, Howard, a popular man and a highly regarded horse dealer, bred draught horses for brewers' drays as well as farm horses and pit ponies for the mines in the nearby Forest of Dean. He possessed a good sense of humour and was generous, giving friends food produced on his farm and welcoming tramps when they came to his door asking for a handout. Unlike David Gurney, who was not an authority figure, Howard Harvey was a man in charge in his household.

Will's mother Matilda was the opposite of Florence Gurney. She was a tall, striking woman with a profile like a figure in an ancient Roman relief.[22] Florence, with her features delicate and pretty in her younger days, already looked haggard. Where Florence was abrasive and cutting with her children, Matilda was gentle, sympathetic and encouraging. Domestic peace and order were important to her, and her home reflected the good taste of a cultured but unaffected woman. Her sensitivity and artistic talents, particularly in music, were stated quietly and with dignity while the artistic gifts that Florence undoubtedly possessed were never harnessed and floated away aimlessly like leaves on the wind. Unlike Florence, Matilda felt secure and content. She drew real pleasure from life and from helping others. Her kindness earned her the sobriquet 'The Walking Angel of Minsterworth' from the community's poor.[23]

Matilda had other advantages that eluded Florence. Her home was large and spacious enough to accommodate her family comfortably. She also had domestic help, a cook, washerwoman and live-in maid as well as additional assistance from her unmarried sister Kate Waters, who lived with the family. And her children adored her, particularly Will, who turned to her for advice, guidance and approval until her death in 1943.

Will's interest in poetry came to him early thanks in large part to the wise choice Matilda Harvey made when she hired a Miss Whitehead to be his governess. The scholarly daughter of a local vicar, Miss Whitehead loved literature and made it come alive for young Will. She introduced him to her favourites, Shelley and Browning. Will returned her enthusiasm by memorizing some of their poetry. At the age of seven he could recite Shelley's 'To a Skylark' by heart, and by the time he was eight years old he knew Browning's 300-line verse story, 'The Pied Piper of Hamelin'. Will had also begun to write his own poetry, pieces in which the eight-year-old child imitated the American Henry Wadsworth Longfellow.

Will's interest in the arts was not limited to literature. His mother had introduced him to music and taught him to play the piano. He became a competent pianist, but his natural musical gift lay in singing, a fact that prompted his parents to send him to the King's School in Gloucester in 1897. Ivor Gurney arrived in 1900, but Will left in 1902 to attend the Rossall School on the Lancashire coast, giving the boys little chance to become acquainted.

By the time their friendship began in 1908, Will was already describing Gloucestershire in verse. The idea of writing poetry appealed to Gurney, who was content then simply to be at Will's side walking the countryside, living and breathing poetry with him, gathering and storing impressions of the sky, light, the Severn, the weather, the Harvey home, the city, the mark of ancient Rome on Gloucestershire and Nature in all her moods, subjects that would later appear in his poems.

In Gloucester, Ivor also enjoyed a close friendship with a promising young composer, Herbert Howells.[24] The youngest of eight children, Howells was born on 17 October 1892, at Lydney, 20 miles down the River Severn from Gloucester. His father Oliver was a builder-plumber-decorator whose business had gone bankrupt. Although money was short in the household, goodwill, enthusiasm and passion for the arts and the mysteries of the universe were abundant. Oliver Howells loved music and possessed an artist's sensibility, traits he passed on to his children, who pursued successful careers in fields ranging from music for Herbert and his elder sister Florence, to art, science, business and education for the other siblings. The senior Howells played the organ dreadfully, in his gifted son's opinion, but he instilled a deep appreciation of music in Herbert. He often took the boy to hear organs and choirs in great churches in England and at nearby Gloucester Cathedral. The 'immemorial sound of voices' and the multifaceted voice of the organ seeped into his imagination and blood and later emerged as a distinctive force in his own music.[25]

Marion Scott, who was close to Howells throughout her life, observed that both his Celtic heritage and Gloucestershire were strong influences in his music. 'He came naturally by an inheritance of beauty, hill, sky, cloud, river, "blossomy plain"', she wrote. '[A]ll these things are Gloucestershire and behind them one glimpses the successions of centuries flowing down from the mists of Celtic times in an almost unruffled and ever-widening intellectual tide. Many races mingled their strains in the making of England', she continued. 'Gloucestershire is a microcosm of the whole [but] the Romans left here a deeper mark'.[26]

Scott further reported that 'two learned authorities on ethnography

– quite unknown to each other – singled out Herbert Howells and his brother as perfect types of Italian Celts'. Howells told Scott that the sound of Latin moved him 'in an extraordinary and unaccountable way' and that he composed to Latin with a freedom he hardly ever felt with English.[27] She connected 'the highly finished design' of some of Howells's music with Celtic art, noting that 'when heard or seen upon the pages [it] raises an insistent sense of its kinship with the designs of Celtic art'.[28]

Of the three young men, Will, from a comfortable background, seemed more complacent, almost indifferent, about his future, and would remain in Gloucester, stuck in a career at odds with his independent spirit and his artistic yearnings. So deeply did Will respect his mother and seek her approval that he seemed always to acquiesce to her, never defying her or summoning the courage to take full charge of his own life. Eventually Ivor became annoyed that Will seemed paralysed at times, unable to move forward unless his 'confounded family' gave him 'their August approval'.[29] Growing up pampered in a carefree environment where there is little or no conflict can deprive an artist of the one element that he needs to create – tension. Although the conflicts in their homes were different, both Gurney and Howells had routinely experienced tension from early childhood and each was driven to escape it. Will was more content and felt no need to get away.

While Gurney and Howells seemed to understand instinctively the importance of spending time with influential men and women who might help them advance their careers, Harvey put little effort into cultivating relationships with other poets. He did enjoy a friendship with John W. Haines, a Gloucester solicitor, botanist and poet thirteen years his senior. Haines, who cultivated friendships with literary men, often met with Gurney and Harvey to discuss music and literature. But it was Ivor, not Will the budding poet, who sought Haines out not only for the pleasure of his company but also for his connections in the world of poetry, connections that later included the poets who would live and work at nearby Dymock. Although it was only a few miles from the Harvey home, there is no evidence that Will took advantage of Haines' friendship with the Dymock poets or that he had any interest in becoming a member of their small community, a move that might have spared him some future unhappiness and disappointment.

Will suffered miserably when editors rejected his poems for reasons he could not fathom. He once went so far as to write to Lascelles Abercrombie, one of the Dymock poets, asking for his advice. It is not known if he sent the letter, but somehow Abercrombie knew about Harvey, a fact that is made clear in a letter Ivor wrote to Will in the summer of 1913: 'Did I tell you that Haines had seen Abercrombie? Who asked Haines whether he knew one named Harvey, who showed great promise.'[30]

Ivor was generous and sincere in his praise and support of his friends and their work. 'Don't think your poetic gift will not develop because you have to be at the office most of the day', Ivor wrote. 'I do not believe it. There are too many examples to the contrary.'[31] Ivor was truly happy when Will, ''Erbert' and other friends were recognized or achieved success with their work even when he might have felt neglected himself. Initially, he did not feel he was in competition with them, nor they with him.

Harvey and Howells shared the poetry and music they were writing with Gurney as he shared his work with them. Eventually they acknowledged each other and their friendship in original work they created. Herbert composed a tender, poetic portrait of Gurney marked 'Lament' in his early orchestral piece *The Bs* that also features musical portraits of Arthur Benjamin and others, as well as one of Howells himself.[32] Howells dedicated his Piano Quartet in A minor 'to the hill at Chosen and Ivor Gurney who knows it'. When Howells showed the work-in-progress to Marion Scott in 1916, she told him, 'The first movement laid a strong spell on me ...'[33] Later she would say that this movement captured perfectly her image of Ivor Gurney striding on Chosen Hill. Howells also orchestrated two of Gurney's songs, 'In Flanders' and 'By a Bierside'. He set two of Harvey's poems – 'Carol', which became the choral anthem 'Sing Lullaby', and a song setting titled 'Goddess of Night'.

Years later, Will recalled his friendship with Ivor in poems such as the 'Ballade of River Sailing' and 'To Ivor Gurney' and he included Gurney in the dedication of his post-war book *Comrades in Captivity, A Record of Life in Seven German Prison Camps*. For his part, Gurney was generous with dedications of his poems and music to both Howells and Harvey, also writing verse that recalled his friendship with Will in poems like 'The Farm', 'Afterglow' and 'To F.W.H.' He dedicated two drinking songs to Will: 'Wessex Drinking Song' and 'Captain Stratton's Fancy', which, during the 1914 war, Harvey sang in prison camps to the delight of his fellow captives. Ivor also paid Will the honour of setting seven of his poems, including 'In Flanders' and the walking song 'Cranham Woods'. Early in his career as a poet, Gurney approached Howells occasionally with his poems, suggesting that he set them to music. Howells never did.

Ivor was the first to break away from his idyllic friendships with Will and Herbert when he left Gloucester in 1911 to study at the Royal College of Music. Howells, eager to follow Gurney to London and to study with Charles Stanford, won a scholarship to the RCM and joined Ivor there in 1912. After failing his first law examination, Harvey finally qualified as a solicitor the same year, met his future wife and converted to Catholicism. He had no apparent desire to join his friends in London, preferring to live quietly in Gloucestershire where he was content to play cricket and capture the beauty around him in verse.

Gurney remained friends with Harvey and Howells, but the intensity and joy of his golden days with each of them between 1908 and 1913 would never be recaptured.

NOTES

1 MMS, Notes, MSC.

2 IG to MMS, 26 October 1917 (P), *CL*, p. 358.

3 Some sources claim that Gurney and Harvey purchased the boat together for £5. In his poem 'Ballade of River Sailing', Harvey wrote 'We got her for a five pound note/ At

second-hand'. Gurney's sister Dorothy remembered the purchase of the boat differently. In a letter to Don B. Ray, Dorothy claimed that Ivor bought the boat 'through the aid of Mr. Harris' (the lock keeper at Framilode on the Severn) in 1907, the first summer Gurney stayed with the Harrises. If we accept 1908 as the accurate date when Gurney and Harvey first met, then Harvey could not have purchased the boat with Gurney. In any case, Dorothy expressed doubts that Ivor ever paid the full £5 to the former owner.

4 William Trethowan, 'Ivor Gurney's Mental Illness', *Music and Letters*, vol. 62, nos. 3–4 (July/October 1981), p. 301. Trethowan was writing about Ethel Gurney's impressions of her brother-in-law.

5 Samuel Underwood to DBR, 29 December 1950, GA.

6 DBR, *IG*, p. 15.

7 MMS, Notes.

8 Margaret Hunt to MMS, 8 May 1917, GA.

9 MMS to HH, 24 April 1917, MSC.

10 WG to DBR, December 1950, GA.

11 MMS, notes to DBR on the first draft of his Gurney biography, 1952, GA.

12 DBR, *IG*, p. 8.

13 MMS, 'Ivor Gurney: The Man', *Music and Letters*, vol. 19, no. 1 (January 1938), p. 4.

14 WG to DBR, 25 May 1951, GA.

15 Alfred Cheesman to MMS, 19 April 1937, GA.

16 Both Marion Scott and Winifred Gurney claimed that Gurney was appointed assistant organist at the Cathedral, but no records have been found to support this assertion. According to Don B. Ray, Brewer is said to have recommended Gurney for the post. See DBR, *IG*, p. 12. Michael Hurd in *OIG* wrote that 'such a post did not exist in those days', p. 23.

17 WG to DBR, 21 May 1951.

18 GF to MMS, 1 January 1938, GA.

19 Frances Townsend, *The Laureate of Gloucestershire: The Life and Work of F. W. Harvey* (Bristol: Redcliffe Press, 1988), quoting from Will Harvey's scrapbook, pp. 17–18.

20 WG to DBR, December 1950, GA.

21 IG, 'The Farm', *War's Embers*, reprinted in *Severn & Somme and War's Embers*, ed. R. K. R. Thornton (Ashington: MidNAG; Manchester: Carcanet, 1987), p. 57.

22 According to Gurney, Mrs Harvey was Welsh, which might account for her Mediterranean appearance. Or like Howells, she might have been an 'Italian Celt'.

23 Townsend, *Laureate of Gloucestershire*, p. 11.

24 Harvey and Howells did not meet until March 1919.

25 Christopher Palmer, *Herbert Howells: A Centenary Celebration* (London: Thames Publishing, 1992), p. 12.

26 MMS, 'Introduction: Herbert Howells', manuscript 'revised by Ivor Gurney', MSC.

27 Ibid.

28 Ibid.

29 IG to FWH, early 1914 (KT), *CL*, p. 10.

30 IG to FWH, 17 August 1913 (KT), *CL*, p. 6.

31 IG to FWH, *c.* early 1914 (KT), *CL*, p. 10.

32 *The Bs* contains Howells's portraits of himself, 'Bublum'; Gurney 'Bartholomew'; Arthur Bliss 'Blissy'; Frances Warren 'Bunny', and Arthur Benjamin 'Benjee'. The recording is available on Chandos, *Howells: Orchestral Works*, vol. 2, CHAN 9557.

33 Palmer, *Herbert Howells: A Centenary Celebration*, p. 434.

CHAPTER 7

A Lad's Love

*M*ANY OF THE behavioural patterns that characterized Ivor Gurney were evident before he became a teenager. Looking back through the corridors of time, he was able to recall with clarity certain events that marked his development and set the tone for his future. In his poem 'What's In Time', written during a later period when memory brought forth an unbroken flow of truthfulness about his past, he describes his 'strange coming to personality'; 'the mother leaving' and his resulting 'insurrection and desire to be one's own and free'; 'The birth of creation in the heart, the touch of poetry', and the 'raining steel and furious fire' of war.[1] These memories hint at only a fraction of the complex circumstances, behavioural traits, hereditary factors and events that shaped Gurney and set him on an erratic course.

As a teenager, Ivor was driven by chaotic forces that spun him through cycles of moods and behaviours. These ranged from indifference, discontent, introspection, lethargy and an affliction he labelled 'sloth' to periods of turmoil, impatience, daring and intense productivity when he experienced surging rounds of energy marked by sleeplessness, restlessness and euphoria. The seeds of his bipolar illness had already taken root. He was never in one place for long and was always in motion, either walking in the countryside by himself, exploring the docklands, or visiting with friends.

As the Reverend Alfred Cheesman began to spend more time with Ivor at All Saints' Church, he perceived the turmoil in his young godson's life. He realized that the boy needed the stability he was prepared to offer through gentle discipline, stimulating companionship, intellectual challenges and, above all else, patience and kindness. A sensitive, poetic man, Cheesman recognized further that Ivor possessed gifts in words and music that needed to be developed, shaped and nurtured. As Gurney's godfather, he was in a position to assume certain responsibilities to help Ivor, and he started to act as an attentive surrogate parent. Where David and Florence Gurney failed to meet the needs of their wayward and difficult son, Alfred Cheesman might succeed.

When Ivor Gurney was in his mid-teens, Cheesman introduced him to Emily and Margaret Hunt. He could not have made a wiser choice. Both women were cultured musicians who had taught at a girls' school in the vicinity of Grahamstown, South Africa, prior to the Boer War (1899–1902). Emily played the piano and Margaret, the violin. According to Marion Scott, the Hunts were half-sisters, Emily being 'considerably older' than Margaret, who was born in 1875. They had settled at 54 Wellington Street around 1900 with Margaret's mother Annie. Their well-appointed dwelling stood among a row of solid buildings not far from the cramped quarters the Gurneys occupied above David Gurney's tailor's shop on Barton Street. Although they were financially comfortable in part from the income they had earned in South Africa, the Hunt sisters continued to teach and at various times after Annie Hunt's death in 1907, they took in lodgers.

Alfred Cheesman had met Emily and Margaret at All Saints' Church but their friendship extended beyond the church. They shared a mutual interest in literature, an enthusiasm that Cheesman was successfully cultivating in young Ivor, a voracious reader. Cheesman relied on the lure of the Hunts' extensive library to get Ivor to visit the sisters and in the process benefit from their 'feminine influence'.[2]

From 1905 on, Emily and Margaret Hunt graciously opened their home to Ivor Gurney. When he crossed the threshold of 54 Wellington Street, he entered a world markedly different from that of 19 Barton Street. Here in company with the genteel Hunt sisters, there were no disturbing distractions from customers in his father's shop, no disruptions caused by arguments between him and his mother or Ronald. Turmoil and tension were absent. Forewarned of Ivor's erratic behaviour, his indifference to time and lack of discipline, the Hunts laid down rules from the beginning as part of their willing assignment to smooth his rough edges. In the beginning months of their friendship, Ivor understood that he could not just drop in at midnight for a visit, but as time passed, Emily and Margaret Hunt relaxed their rules and Ivor became a welcome fixture in their home.

He usually arrived in the afternoon and often stayed well into the evening, likely spending part of nearly every day, particularly in winter, in their company. He followed the same intensive routine with Cheesman from 1905 until he left Gloucester to attend the Royal College of Music. When his friendship with Will Harvey deepened, Ivor divided his time among the three households. It is no wonder that his family rarely saw him and that his mother grew increasingly jealous of his friends. She felt, not without some justification, that she was losing him to them. The more Ivor was away from 19 Barton Street, the more Florence Gurney demanded of him. Her desperate behaviour only made matters worse, driving Ivor further away from his family straight into the sympathetic and protective arms of the Hunts and the Reverend Cheesman.

Margaret and Emily provided Ivor with everything he desired – music, books, conversation, affection and a quiet place to work. A Bechstein piano dominated their music room. They possessed music in abundance for Ivor to discover, read through and play. The Hunts introduced him to chamber works and German *Lieder* to which he was not exposed at the Cathedral. After an evening of lively discussion about history, a newspaper article they had all seen, or an author he was reading, Ivor played the piano, often choosing Bach and Beethoven but turning increasingly to his own works.

Margaret, small and fragile with dark hair, 'azure' eyes and a musical voice, was fifteen years older than Ivor. She became his favourite. In the early days of their friendship, he turned to her for the nurturing and inspiration he needed to fill the cravings of his artist's soul.

The desire to compose had already awakened in Gurney 'outwelling from the good soil' of his beloved Gloucestershire, which he sought to immortalize in his music, and later in his poetry.[3] By 1908 he was composing seriously and within a year had produced his distinctive piano nocturnes in A flat and in B major, as well as numerous extant works for solo piano and for violin and piano. In addition, he was setting to music the poems of Yeats, Henley, Stevenson, Bridges and others. The titles of Gurney's instrumental works reveal the romantic and poetic nature of their young composer – 'Song of the Summer Woods', 'Wind in the Wood', 'In August', 'Romance', 'Revery'. Music poured out of Ivor. To keep up with the flow, he worked rapidly and intensely, often through the night, establishing early on a pattern that remained with him throughout his creative life.

His passion for music consumed him with a fire that Margaret Hunt willingly stoked. From the beginning of their friendship she encouraged him in his work and in his dreams and he discovered that a 'new spirit moved him'.[4] He was aware of the unconditional faith Margaret had in him. That knowledge inspired him to push himself even harder. He started calling her 'Madge'. As a developing artist, he needed the audience Madge provided. Nearly everything he wrote, he wrote with her in mind. Music bonded their friendship.

After a visit with the Hunts, his 'soul full of air', he wandered out into the nearby country, along Severn lanes, through woods and meadows, alert, his senses wide open as the artist in him absorbed the light, colours, sounds and atmosphere of his beloved Gloucestershire landscape.[5] 'I got them all into my music', he wrote.[6] After walking for hours, he might return home and work through the night composing until dawn broke his reverie. Then he rushed back to Wellington Street eager to share his new composition with Madge.

From childhood throughout his life, Ivor attracted people who were willing to care for him, make sacrifices for him and help him. He was careful to guard these friendships. Margaret Hunt's faith in Ivor and her belief that he would one day be a great man inspired him, drove him on and gave him a purpose and a reason to create his art. Both Hunt sisters eagerly fed Ivor Gurney's ego, but it was Madge who fed his soul. She became his muse.

While her support and inspiration appeared untrammelled to Ivor, Madge had every reason to worry about his future. She had known from the beginning of their friendship that his mercurial behaviour was cause for concern and tried repeatedly to do what she could to stave off 'the old lethargy' that came over him periodically, derailed his work and flagged his spirit.[7] She recognized the danger in his moods and in his destructive behaviour. She worried what effect they might have on his work and indeed on his life. 'Ivor must always struggle hard for expression', she observed to Marion Scott. 'We know him so well of course and have seen him in so many moods and the joy of life and creation is so marked, while the reaction goes deeper than with anyone I have ever seen.'[8] At times Madge was profoundly aware of Ivor's troubles, and worried about him, while at other times she appeared almost naïve in dismissing his serious complaints about his neurasthenia or nerves as being a flight of 'nostalgia' and nothing more.[9]

When he left Gloucester to attend the Royal College of Music, Ivor carried Madge with him in his heart, distance posing no barrier because the spirit of 'love can carry across a hundred miles'.[10] While he was in London, they exchanged many letters. When he returned to Gloucester for his summer holidays, he spent part of his time vacationing with the Hunts at Portway, where he found inspiration in 'Great black shadows, white violets, intensely blue sky, and a sun like wine to the soul' and contentment in being in company with Madge and Emily.[11] 'I could only sing for joy, and cry in my heart with pure happiness', he exclaimed to Will Harvey.[12]

In the early years of the twentieth century Ivor Gurney was a developing artist, awakening to the world around him, sensitive to its beauties, excited by the limitless possibilities before him and sheltered by the love and understanding of Margaret Hunt. Yet the forces that would dramatically alter his life were slowly coming into play.

The intensity of his friendship with Margaret Hunt was surpassed by his relationship with Alfred Cheesman. In fact, between 1905 and 1911, Ivor called on Cheesman at least 2,000 times at his home at 17 Derby Road. Ivor's sister Winifred observed that after Ivor 'became attached' to Cheesman and 'practically lived with him', he had 'less time to devote to others'.[13] Indeed, in a letter written to Marion Scott in 1917, Cheesman told her that 'For many years [Ivor] nearly lived with me'.[14] Ivor dutifully marked his almost daily visits in Cheesman's own diary and Cheesman annotated these entries with his notes on what Ivor said and did. He found the boy 'not always easy' but observed that he always 'showed me much affection'.[15]

In another letter to Scott, written when Cheesman was an old man, he recounted with obvious delight the story of Ivor's promise to bring him a book, S. R. Crockett's *Lad's Love*. But when the day came, Ivor had, typically, forgotten the book and said, 'I haven't brought you a *Lad's Love* – at least, not the book.'[16] *Lad's Love* is a Victorian romance. It is also the name of a flower.

With the support and encouragement of the Hunt sisters and Cheesman, Ivor gained confidence and set his mind on his future. When he decided in 1907 that he wanted to study music at Durham University, he relied on Cheesman to coach him for the matriculation examination. Later, when Ivor sat for the exam, which he passed, Cheesman, not his own parents, accompanied him to Durham. While in the city, Cheesman, in a characteristic act of kindness, arranged for Ivor to play the cathedral organ. They returned home leisurely via York, Lincoln, Norwich, Ely and Cambridge on a journey that introduced the teenaged Gurney to the world beyond the confines of Gloucestershire. According to Cheesman, he and Gurney had 'been together to many parts of England' over the years.[17]

In his teens Ivor became increasingly indifferent to his appearance and developed irregular eating habits. Unkempt and uncombed, Ivor often dressed in rumpled or inappropriate clothing. Although these exterior traits remained with him throughout his life, he was, by contrast, fastidious about personal hygiene and became obsessively so as the years passed. Florence Gurney, a proud woman who did her best to keep her children well dressed and neat, tried unsuccessfully to get Ivor to pay attention to his appearance. He either ignored her pleas or reacted even more defiantly, igniting more battles between mother and son.

While such indifference to appearance is not uncommon among

pubescent boys, other aspects of Ivor's behaviour were cause for concern, and hinted at more serious problems. As he grew older, his disharmony with himself, his body and his environment increased to the point where he acted in ways that jeopardized his health and, at times, endangered his life. He was daring, bold and reckless, as if set on a path of self-destruction, always testing his limits and those of others. According to Marion Scott, Ivor 'was not a tame specimen' and 'great natural forces were his playfellows'.[18] He 'adored violent exercise, exulted in storms, and sailed with a daring near to madness'.[19] He was a powerful athlete whose habit of walking had pushed his capacity for sustained physical activity to a high level. He became a tough, aggressive participant in schoolboy sports and so self-centred that he 'seemed to think he could beat the other side on his own'.[20]

Ivor manned his boat *Dorothy* without any regard for his safety or the safety of his passengers. One day, behaving recklessly on the dangerous Severn, he nearly capsized the boat. He terrified Ronald, his passenger, and a bystander who was watching from shore. He narrowly escaped drowning on another occasion. Once while out hunting game birds with his father's sporting rifle, he accidentally shot himself in either the wrist or foot.[21]

Ivor flirted with more than external physical danger. His eating habits were abnormal and reflected his frightening disregard for good nutrition and regular meals. Winifred observed that he neglected himself 'by going almost without food and then eating ravenously'.[22] If the recollections of his friends are accurate, Ivor ate virtually no foods containing protein, which, among other functions, aids digestion. His poor eating habits were not only damaging his digestive system but also jeopardizing the functions of his entire body and creating chemical imbalances. Ivor actually had an unhealthy obsession with food, a condition created by something deeper than poverty or forgetfulness as his friend Arthur Benjamin assumed.

Gurney consumed large quantities of sweets, which gave him a rush of sugar, a 'sugar high', that would elevate his mood and make him hyperactive. Devoid of any nutritional value, the sweets gave him a false feeling of fullness, which soon wore off, leaving him craving more. He would gorge on cakes, apples, and butter as one might eat ice cream, and devour odd assortments of food thrown together. This strange pattern of eating did not provide him with the nutritional balance that his body needed to function normally. Ill-nourished, Ivor suffered from serious vitamin and mineral deficiencies.[23] While dental problems (his overbite and adjustments made to improve it) might account for some of his erratic eating habits, his behaviour around food, starving himself and then gorging on unsuitable combinations, suggests a deeper cause than difficulty in chewing. He began to suffer from digestive trouble that would eventually interfere with his work and studies. He labelled his condition 'dyspepsia' (indigestion).

Ivor had been a reasonably healthy child who contracted typical childhood illnesses, including chronic bronchitis and unspecified ear trouble. His poor eyesight was detected in his early teens and corrected with spectacles. His teeth 'grew projecting out', according to his mother. Some effort was made at 'pulling them in' by extracting other teeth that were crowding his mouth.[24] The resulting row of uneven teeth left him with a poor bite which Florence felt made matters worse for her son.

Ivor pushed his capacity to function on very little sleep. 'But night to labour, To work, read, walk night through', he wrote of the pattern of his early years that continued into his adulthood.[25] As a teenager, he preferred to walk into the countryside after an evening with the Hunt sisters instead of returning home. Thrilled by the sights and sounds of nature and absorbed in his own thoughts, he might work through the night composing music. During the warmer months he sometimes slept outdoors under the stars in fields, or on Chosen Hill, or wherever he happened to be when sleep finally overtook him.

The teenaged Ivor Gurney was living a very full life, one in which there was little time for rest or relaxation. His days were brimming with activity between school, his music lessons, reading, his walks, his visits with friends, his own attempts at composition and his part-time work as an organist. However, he had already entered into the destructive habit of working to exhaustion until he was forced to stop and rest. He came to view the need to rest as a defect in his character. Yet what he regarded guiltily as 'sloth' in himself was more likely a state of depleted mental and physical energy induced by his poor nutrition, irregular sleep, obsessive work habits, digestive problems and illness. He was experiencing an emotional behavioural pattern of extremes ranging from euphoric highs to despairing lows, with little level ground in the middle on which to stand firmly.

Although his behaviour was erratic and worrisome, his appearance unkempt, and certain of his actions obsessive, Ivor was neither shy nor timid. He was a strong-willed, self-assured and independent young man who knew what he wanted in life and set about getting it. In this regard he had a great advantage over Will Harvey, whose submissive behaviour and sense of duty, particularly towards his mother, compromised his dreams and his art. Ivor Gurney felt little obligation to anyone but himself.

As much as he loved Gloucestershire and the inspiration he drew from the surrounding countryside, he knew that his opportunities for education and a career there were limited. During the Three Choirs Festival at Gloucester in 1910, Gurney made the acquaintance of William 'Billy' Reed, a violinist, Edward Elgar's friend and the new conductor of the Festival Orchestra. Ivor had ample confidence in himself and in his abilities to approach Reed during a rehearsal break to show him some of his violin compositions. Reed was impressed enough to encourage the young composer to apply for an open composition scholarship at the Royal College of Music in London, where he taught. He promised his support.

Forty candidates had applied for the two scholarships. In the late autumn of 1911 Gurney was called to London to face a formidable committee of examiners, men of great importance in music: Sir Hubert Parry, Sir H. Walford Davies, Dr Charles Wood and Sir Charles Villiers Stanford. Although Ivor was aware that he had made an impression on the committee, he did not learn the results of their decision for some weeks.

When word finally came that he had won a scholarship worth £40 a year, his godfather Alfred Cheesman worked quietly to bring about a minor miracle. He approached Ivor's friends, including the Harveys, the Hunt sisters and Ivor's own Aunt Marie, and raised an additional £40 to provide Ivor with enough extra money to enable him to live modestly but comfortably in London. Ivor left Gloucester in April 1911 to begin his studies at the Royal College of Music, the extra money tucked gratefully in his pocket.

Once settled in London, he was quickly caught up in his busy student life, but his social life was one-sided. Although he was an engaging conversationalist, attractive and charming, he appears to have had little experience with women beyond his idealized love for Margaret Hunt and his new infatuation with Marion Scott. Both women were considerably older than he. Naïve and self-centred in his relationships with women, he used his music and poetry to attract their attention and keep it focused on him. The women in his life filled his need for approval, nurturing and intellectual stimulation.

The extent of Ivor's sexual experience by the time he arrived in London is unknown. Surely by the age of twenty-one he had desires and the usual drives of a young male, but how much of his sexual energy found release remains open to speculation. As a teenager he enjoyed the love of Margaret Hunt. Marion Scott's abiding affection for Gurney deepened over time, but we know nothing of a physical relationship between them.

As a chorister at the Cathedral and student at an all-boys' school, he typically had had little opportunity during his teenaged years to develop relationships with girls his own age. He had spent most of his time with Will Harvey, Herbert Howells, Alfred Cheesman and the Hunt sisters.

Ivor moved in broader social circles in London. In addition to concerts in the city, he attended recitals at Marion Scott's home and participated in more casual RCM student gatherings. Despite his forays into mixed society, Ivor mentioned no female students or women companions, nor did he hint at any love interest in his slim correspondence from this time.

Ivor was most comfortable with his male companions – Howells, Harvey, Shimmin and Benjamin – friendships built initially on shared intellectual interests. He was openly affectionate with Will Harvey, whom he deeply loved. They were kindred spirits. In Will, Ivor saw a reflection of himself – the same nervous energy alternating with periods of introspection, self-absorption and discontent; the same carelessness about his appearance and 'an idealism that could not be contented with realities'.[26] It was Harvey who had ignited the poetic flame in Gurney. Their affection for each other grew with shared walks, boating adventures on the Severn, books, music, intimate conversation, and love of Gloucestershire.

Ivor kept a photo of Will on his piano in his London lodgings. Later, he told Marion Scott, 'I do not look ever for a closer bond ... if I have the good fortune ever to meet with such another, he has a golden memory to contend with.'[27] In his poem 'After-glow', dedicated to Will, Ivor painted a vivid picture of two souls acting as one, consumed by the fire of youthful discovery heightened by shared intimacy and joy. Recalling a sunset they had watched together, Ivor wrote:

The elms with arms of love wrapped us in shade
Who watched the ecstatic West with one desire,
One soul unrapt; and still another fire
Consumed us, and our joy yet greater made:
That Bach should sing for us, mix us in one
The joy of firelight and the sunken sun.[28]

Revelling in male companionship, Ivor regarded the male body as an object of beauty and strength. He admired men who possessed powerful physiques, and made no secret of it. From about 1913 on he was obsessive about developing his own physical strength and building his body through vigorous daily exercise.

At college, Ivor busied himself with his studies and kept steady company with Howells and Benjamin. Benjamin enjoyed Ivor's companionship and admired his gifts. However, he regarded Ivor as 'unworldly and even rustic'. Benjamin felt a stronger physical attraction to the stylish, gifted and practical Howells. His friendship with Gurney was complicated by the fact that he never could be sure how Ivor would act in public. Gurney's dishevelled appearance and odd mannerisms, perhaps amusing when they were alone, might prove awkward in certain social circles. There was, as Marion Scott had detected earlier, something still very boyish and immature about Ivor.

In later years Benjamin, Gurney's trusted confidant, disclosed his belief that Ivor was homosexual but didn't recognize it.[29] But Herbert Howells, himself the object of Benjamin's youthful affection, was appalled at the suggestion, and claimed that Gurney 'would have died first'.[30] As a homosexual, Benjamin was particularly sensitive to detecting the same trait in others. He possessed insights into Gurney and an understanding of his later behaviour that could only have come from astute observation and from Ivor's confidences, which he steadfastly refused to divulge.

During the time the friendship between Gurney and Benjamin was developing, homosexuals inhabited a secret, closed underworld. They were criminals in the eye of the law, sinners in the eye of the church, 'inverts' to physicians, and outcasts in an intolerant hypocritical society too timid to emerge from behind the thick curtain of Victorian morality. The spectre of the scandalous Oscar Wilde trial, his public disgrace and imprisonment in 1895 had ignited widespread public condemnation of homosexuals.

It was dangerous to be homosexual. Most homosexual men, fearing persecution and prosecution, hid their true identities. They dwelt in quiet isolation or moved between two different worlds: one a charade in which they repressed their natural tendencies and pretended to live according to the rules of social respectability; the other, a twilight world of secret rendezvous, rent boys and fleeting assignations that left them vulnerable to blackmail. Young men like Ivor Gurney and so many others were reared to believe that homosexual love was wrong, a sin that could only bring shame upon a man and his family.

While Ivor could express his tender feelings for Will Harvey in verse and admire the strong physiques of other men, he might have believed it wrong to engage in physical activity any more intimate than draping his arm around his friend's shoulder as they walked. How much Gurney's own questions about his sexuality played a role in what was to come is not known.

NOTES

1 IG, 'What's In Time', *CP*, p. 246.

2 MMS, Notes, MSC.

3 IG, 'On a Memory', *OIG*, p. 147.

4 Ibid.

5 IG, 'The First Violets', *Best Poems*, p. 45.

6 Ibid.

7 Margaret Hunt to MMS, 18 June 1917, GA.

8 Margaret Hunt to MMS, 8 May 1917, GA.

9 Ibid.

10 IG, 'On a Memory', *OIG*, p. 147.

11 IG to FWH, August 1913, *CL*, pp. 7–8.

12 Ibid.

13 WG to DBR, 29 November 1950, GA.

14 Alfred Cheesman to MMS, 13 April 1917, GA.

15 Ibid.

16 Ibid.

17 Cheesman to MMS, 13 April 1917, GA.

18 MMS, Notes, MSC.

19 Ibid.

20 Ibid.

21 Dorothy Gurney remembered that Ivor had shot himself in the foot, while Winifred Gurney recalled that he had shot himself in the wrist.

22 WG to DBR, 16 April 1951, GA.

23 Consultations with Dr Harald N. Johnson, Scituate, Massachusetts.

24 FG to MMS, no date, GA.

25 IG, 'Chance to Work', *CP*, p. 266.

26 IG to MMS, 24 August 1916 (P), *CL*, p. 138.

27 Ibid., pp. 137–8.

28 Gurney wrote 'After-glow' in January 1917 while Harvey was a prisoner of war in Germany. It was published in *Severn and Somme*, p. 47; Thornton edition, p. 39.

29 Benjamin made this observation around 1955 in a casual conversation with Michael Hurd, who refers to it on p. 197 and in a footnote on p. 224 in *OIG*.

30 Ibid. Herbert Howells quoted on p. 197.

CHAPTER 8

The First Breakdown

*I*N THE SPRING of 1913 Ivor Gurney suffered a nervous breakdown in London. He was twenty-two years old and still a student at the Royal College of Music. 'My brain, heart, nerves, and physique are certified sound, but ... I am overworked and quite run down', he explained in a letter to Marion Scott.[1] There is no official documentation of his illness. Few letters from this period survive so it is difficult to determine exactly when Ivor suffered this collapse, but he was showing signs of both physical and mental problems as early as January. He was so depressed and 'sick of everything' that he had even dropped his usual defences against criticism of his work. 'I will allow anyone to say anything against my Scherzo, my slow Movement even, which shows to what depths I have descended', he admitted to Marion in February.[2] While he made some effort to keep the tone of this letter light and conversational, he could not hide the fact that he had been very ill.

Ivor told Marion that he had 'crawled' out of bed to attend the London première of Ralph Vaughan Williams' Sea Symphony on 4 February, and asked her if she had heard it. Either the excitement of the performance had fogged his memory or he was so ill that he had completely forgotten that he, along with Herbert Howells and Arthur Benjamin, had met Marion in the vestibule of Queen's Hall that night! She later recalled that the three young men were 'almost speechless from the shock of joy the music had given them, and all trying to talk at once ...'[3] Despite the thrill of the music, Ivor only had enough energy to return to his quarters at Fulham, where he spent another three days in bed before he felt well enough to return to the college. As his depression deepened, he isolated himself throughout much of the spring.

Finally, sometime in early June, he consulted a Doctor Harper on Threadneedle Street, who gave him orders for 'Homeward Bound' as Ivor called it.[4] He returned to Gloucestershire. Instead of staying with his parents or recuperating with the Hunt sisters or Alfred Cheesman, he chose to spend part of the time with his friends the Harrises at Lock House in Framilode. Ivor had known the Harris family since 1907, when he had spent much of the summer with them. Gurney's sister Dorothy remembered that earlier time as an 'especially happy' one.[5] Both she and Florence Gurney had visited Ivor at Framilode with Dorothy making the journey on her bicycle while her mother travelled by riverboat.

Ivor felt at ease with the Harrises and observed in the lock keeper attributes that he respected: his dedication to work that seemed to have no beginning or end; his ability to be a friend to all men, be they 'coalmen, farmers, fishermen'; his love of nature and of a good time at the pub; his knowledge born of experience; his intelligence and physical strength.[6]

Harris was a 'tall lean man' with a face 'lit with bright bird-eyes', whose movements, as he worked reminded Ivor of the 'up-and-down' motions of a marionette. He saw in his friend a practical working man who moved through his day as a poet might, observing, absorbing, contemplating and gathering impressions of everything that surrounded him. 'His knowledge transcend[ed] books' and he seemed to be an expert on subjects ranging from wasp-exterminating and bird-stuffing to boat-building, the habits of wild animals and the signs of the weather. He also possessed a prodigious memory full of 'old country tales ... Yarns of both sea and land' which he told in 'rough fine speech'. What Ivor learned from books, Harris knew from living. 'There was nothing he did not know', Ivor claimed. Ivor left a striking word painting of Harris sitting 'in the deep chimney-corner' seen in 'Shadow and bright flare' looking 'saturnine and lean; / Clouded with smoke, wrapped round with cloak of thought ...' 'I'll travel for many a year [and never] find / A winter-night companion more to my mind', he recalled later. In his need to get away from the chaos of London and the emotional turmoil that was making him ill, Ivor knew instinctively that time spent with the Harrises at Framilode would be a balm for him.

Once away from London, Ivor threw himself into hard physical labour and turned also to sailing and walking, activities that became his own means of combating the effects of his mood swings throughout his life. When his obsessive mental activity overwhelmed him, he shifted his attention from his mind to his body and became a physical force. Gurney was incapable of ceasing all activity. Part of him was always in motion. Although he had toughened his body impressively during his break at Framilode, built his stamina and boasted of his great strength, he admitted to Marion Scott that he had 'a pretty bad time of it for the first six weeks, and then an increasingly better time of it'.[7]

In July Gurney returned to Gloucester, staying with his parents, and ful-filling plans outlined earlier to Will Harvey to sail beneath the blue sky, 'taking risks in pure glory of soul and joy of heart and yelling and quoting and singing and hauling at the sheet ... and breaking my arm with holding the tiller'.[8] He read books at a rapid rate: Hardy's monumental *The Dynasts*; Belloc's *On Something*; Shaw's *Mrs Warren's Profession*; Chesterton's *The Victorian Age in Literature*, and a biography of Beethoven among them. He made an effort to write poetry.

Gurney's health, both physical and mental, might have been improving somewhat in his eyes, but he was far from well. His chief complaints were attacks of 'the Blues', 'a dry-up of thought', a brain that 'won't move', and poor digestion.[9] He made light of his troubles in couplets he sent to Will Harvey:

> My tears are near the top, and welly,
> Because the devil's in my belly.
> Oh, may I find some potent pill
> To turn him out, or make Him ill.[10]

It is difficult to determine how much time Ivor and Will spent together in the summer of 1913. Harvey, who had been ill and also suffering from depression, had undergone surgery to remove an infected gland from his neck. While in hospital he had fallen in love with one of his nurses, Sarah Anne Kane. Between his recovery, his new romance, cricket and his law work, Will had less time to participate in Ivor's sailing adventures and elver fishing or to accompany him on his long walks.

Herbert Howells and Arthur Benjamin joined Ivor for a brief holiday, walking in the Forest of Dean and along the Severn and Wye rivers. But they did not linger in Gloucester, because Benjamin, smitten with Howells, had invited him on a holiday to Switzerland, Herbert's first trip abroad. At nineteen, Benjamin was already widely travelled. He shared his resources and goodwill with his friends. Herbert was the direct beneficiary of his generosity while Ivor, who considered Benjamin his confidant, remained in Gloucestershire struggling to regain his health.

Yet Ivor was not without companions. He enjoyed a brief holiday with the Hunt sisters at Portway. Sydney Shimmin, his friend from the Royal College of Music, spent part of the late summer in Gloucestershire. Ivor took great pride in showing off his physical prowess to the 'gentle Sidney' [*sic*] who watched Gurney 'splice the mainbrace or cleat the halliards or in other ways bemuse the bourgeois!' [11] At the invitation of Jill and Daisy Levetus, friends of Marion Scott and Ethel Voynich, Ivor and Sydney travelled to Southwold to holiday with them from 15 to 25 September.

Ivor returned to London after this break and resumed his studies at the RCM. He was still on the mend and found the city 'worse than ever to bear' especially after the 'Blue river and golden sand, and blue black hills' of the Severn and the Cotswolds.[12]

Although the cause of Ivor's 1913 breakdown is generally laid to 'overwork', his creative output in the early months of that year and in 1912 was comparatively slim. His studies, assignments and college rehearsals occupied much of his time. However, Howells, Benjamin and other students were equally challenged, yet managed to be productive, remarkably so in Howells' case. Ivor had been working on several compositions, including a string quartet in A minor, a string trio in G major, a violin sonata and some songs. In the string quartet, composer Michael Hurd, Gurney's early biographer, notes that Gurney's 'fingerprints are much in evidence: intricate cross rhythms, subtle enharmonic changes ... sudden wrenches into the unexpected, flexible, rather wayward melodic lines ...' and 'the tendency to let the line degenerate into a mere scrabble of buzzing semiquavers that leads nowhere in particular'.[13]

Ivor's music actually reflected the chaotic disposition and confused state of his mind that derailed his ability to focus on his work. Keeping up was difficult if not overwhelming. The imposition of regimen simply annoyed and frustrated him, often sparking anger and rebellion. His efforts were further defeated by his compulsion to follow his own erratic direction unlike Howells who followed a more prescribed path.

In a letter to Marion Scott written in the early summer of 1913, Ivor had related that upon being told (by whom he does not say) that he was 'quite able to work', he found that in reality all he could do was 'stare at blank paper till I was sick at heart!' [14] He told her that he was looking forward to 'two months abstention from music' and included a brief commentary that summed up his feelings:

> I'm glad
> I've got to hate it.
> Music, that is.[15]

In August, Ivor felt more optimistic about his music and reported to Will Harvey that he had both a violin sonata and a setting of 'Trafalgar' from *The Dynasts* 'in my head'.[16] He was also writing verse. By the time he returned to London after his Southwold holiday, he had completed the song 'The Night of Trafalgar', which he was eager to show to Marion. His long summer holiday, the calming time spent with the Harrises at Framilode, his outdoor activities – sailing, walking, hard physical labour – as well as reading, spending time with Harvey, Shimmin, Howells and Benjamin and enjoying a seaside holiday all contributed to restoring his health to some degree.

However, Ivor Gurney had an incurable, undiagnosed illness. He would never be free of the shifting moods and the stomach problems that had troubled him throughout his mid-to-late teenage years into adulthood. His mood swings and ill health had always been a concern of Margaret Hunt, who remarked that Ivor often appeared 'to waste time and his health seems always to interfere with steady work'.[17]

The creative process was especially difficult for Ivor when he aimed too high. It must have been frustrating for one so brimming with grand ideas to have to work his way slowly, even methodically, through a complex process in order to obtain results. He seemed disappointed that works did not blaze into full-blown glory once he had conceived them.

Ivor had admitted to his friend Maggie Taylor, Ethel Voynich's elder sister, that he couldn't compose 'anything but short things – songs', and that he couldn't 'do anything sustained yet. ... The reason he gave was delightfully Gurneyesque', Mrs Taylor observed. 'He can write – or has written – some songs as good as Schuberts [*sic*], but Schubert has done it, and no one can go beyond him with songs. So Ivor's songs are not a new thing for the world.'[18]

Both Ivor and his friends always seemed to be searching for excuses to explain his perceived, although not necessarily real, shortcomings. While his friends blamed periods of 'lethargy' that descended on him for holding him back from making a real step in music, he blamed his health. He believed that if he could recover, he would be able to compose large-scale compositions.

Composing songs came to him with far less effort than it took him to conceive and work out the parts of larger compositions. Although Ivor was not a jealous man and always one to wish his friends well in their endeavours and, indeed, to help them when he could, he surely must have felt that his difficulty in composing large works was indicative of some inadequacy, some flaw in his make-up.

Howells was working on a piano concerto and his suite for orchestra *The Bs*, with its musical portrait of Gurney.[19] He had copyrighted a work for unison voices and orchestra, and had composed a mass, a motet for double choir, several chamber works (including variations for eleven solo instruments) along with piano pieces and a number of songs. His *Mass in the Dorian Mode*, a first-term exercise composed for Stanford, was soon thereafter performed at Westminster Cathedral. Howells had begun to write essays which would win him the RCM Director's History Essay Prize six times between 1913 and 1916 and lead him to write music criticism and articles for publication as early as 1915. Benjamin had proved himself a highly capable musician when he appeared as the soloist in the première performance of Howells' Piano Concerto no. 1 in C minor with Sir Charles Stanford conducting at the Queen's Hall in July 1914. Benjamin had also begun to shape the musical ideas that would lead him to compose operas and become a successful film composer.[20]

While Howells and others at the RCM were blazing a trail of youthful achievement and success, Ivor appeared to be lost in attempts to compose music that was beyond his reach, producing performance manuscripts that were in a state of confusion or illegible. Herbert recalled 'piano preludes thick with untamed chords; violin sonatas strewn with ecstatic crises ... an essay for orchestra that strained a chaotic technique to breaking point'.[21] Ivor spent hours discussing his plans or the books he had been reading and how he might turn literature like Yeats' plays into music. He tried to appear worldly like the urbane Benjamin. He had started to smoke a pipe, an affectation perhaps inspired by his friendship with Mr Harris. He consumed vast quantities of tea but still ate poorly.

People who were close to Ivor knew that his erratic behaviour was cause for concern, but no one realized that Ivor was already in the early stages of a serious mood disorder, or bipolar illness, that would only get worse. No matter what he tried to do to help himself when he felt the symptoms taking hold of him, Ivor Gurney would never be able to tame this illness or be well enough to compose the 'big' works that filled his dreams. He would never be able to lead a normal life and have a successful career like his fellow students at the RCM, Howells, Benjamin, Arthur Bliss, the Goossens brothers.

In 1913 no one knew how bleak Ivor's future was. There was little understanding of bipolar illness in the early years of the twentieth century when it was often confused with schizophrenia. Tragically, there were no drugs to control the symptoms and many victims, no longer able to function in society, were institutionalized. The onset of Ivor's illness was slow, with signs of it appearing in his early teens. His lethargy or 'sloth', apathy and confusion, inability to think or concentrate, unevenness and decrease in the quantity and quality of his productivity, carelessness, indifference to his surroundings and appearance were all symptoms of depression. In this state he appeared withdrawn, indifferent, self-absorbed and 'dreamy'. He berated himself for his bad habits, his failures, his slowness, or any number of self-perceived deficiencies.

As his black mood passed like a cloud lifting from the landscape, he was flooded with energy. His mood became expansive. He switched from being a brooding introvert to a gregarious extrovert. His confidence and self-esteem were restored and he became cocky, arrogant and vain. In this manic state he thought he was invincible. He was impulsive and rash, undertaking daredevil physical activity that put him in danger such as sailing the *Dorothy* recklessly or accidentally shooting himself. When his mood was soaring, he had no regard for propriety, and might make a spectacle of himself in public by shouting verse or singing at the top of his lungs, drawing the attention of bewildered passers-by. He acted like a sponge, absorbing everything around him and firing it back in a flood of monologues that left his listeners breathless and unable to take it all in. His physical and mental energy were overwhelming, almost out of control, and his creativity greatly heightened. At these times, Ivor was so full of himself that he felt his work and his opinions of it were above reproach, and he became angry when an authority like Stanford challenged him. His anger might result in him striking another person.[22]

Ivor threw himself into his work with such fervour that he forgot about sleeping and eating and seemed able to survive on a bare minimum of both. Then with his candle burning at both ends, the string drawn as tightly as possible, he would begin to come down from his high and stumble back into the darkness.

NOTES

1 IG to MMS, Summer 1913 (KT), *CL*, p. 3.

2 IG to MMS, February 1913 (KT), *CL*, p. 2.

3 MMS, Notes, GA.

4 IG to MMS, June 1913 (PB), *CL*, p. 3. Date previously listed as May 1913.

5 Dorothy Gurney memories in DBR, *IG*, p. 16.

6 Gurney's observations on Mr Harris are in his poem, 'The Lock Keeper', in *CP*, pp. 103–6, and in an earlier version in *War's Embers* (see Thornton edition, p. 99). All quotes are taken from these two sources.

7 IG to MMS, August or September 1913 (PB), *CL*, p. 6.

8 IG to FWH, early June 1913 (KT), *CL*, p. 4.

9 Ibid.

10 IG to FWH, 17 August 1913 (KT), *CL*, p. 7.

11 IG to MMS, quoted in *OIG*, p. 44.

12 IG to MMS, quoted in *OIG*, p. 45.

13 Michael Hurd, *OIG*, p. 36. Hurd was unwittingly describing the characteristics of Gurney's emerging illness.

14 IG to MMS, Summer 1913 (KT), *CL*, p. 3.

15 IG to MMS, June 1913 (PB), *CL*, p. 3.

16 IG to FWH, 17 August 1913 (KT), *CL*, p. 7.

17 Margaret Hunt to MMS, 8 May 1917, GA.

18 Margaret 'Maggie' Taylor to MMS, 26 October 1915, GA.

19 *Suite for Orchestra: The Bs* was first performed in February 1919.

20 Benjamin's early film successes included Alfred Hitchcock's 1934 classic spy mystery *The Man Who Knew Too Much*, which features his *Storm Clouds Cantata* in a long, tense sequence filmed at the Royal Albert Hall. The film was remade in 1956, starring Doris Day and James Stewart and featured Benjamin's cantata again. Benjamin is visible as an extra in the audience during the performance of the cantata.

21 HH, 'Ivor Gurney: The Musician', *Music and Letters*, vol. 19, no. 1 (January 1938), p. 13. See also Christopher Palmer, *Herbert Howells: A Centenary Celebration* (London: Thames Publishing, 1992), p. 267.

22 MMS, Notes. Scott recounts Herbert Howells telling her of an incident where Gurney struck another boy and broke his spectacles. She had also witnessed Gurney's 'hawk-like swiftness' of anger.

CHAPTER 9

The Lost Year

1914 IS THE LOST YEAR in Ivor Gurney's life. Few facts about his movements are known or documented. An absence of correspondence with Marion Scott indicates that he spent most of the year in London. Only two known letters from this period survive: one to Will Harvey and one to John Haines.

After his creative dry spell, physical illnesses and breakdown in 1913, Ivor dived headlong into the new year with renewed energy and purpose. In mid-January he was among 184 students taking the ARCO examination, and was one of only twenty who passed. He won the Frank J. Sawyer Prize for second-highest marks for tests at the organ, suggesting that he was highly accomplished on the instrument due in large part to his early training in Gloucester and practical experience playing in churches.

Ivor was still complaining about his indigestion but felt that his condition was improving and that he would be well by 'Midsummer!!!!'[1] Despite being confined to a dreary lodging in London with no nearby countryside to explore, he kept fit by exercising daily using J. P. Muller's *My System: 15 minutes' work a day for health's sake*. His 'abstention from music' had ended. He was composing again but with a command and originality that even he found surprising.

'Willy, Willy, I have done 5 of the most delightful and beautiful songs you ever cast your beaming eyes upon', he wrote to Will Harvey in early 1914. 'They are all Elizabethan – the words – and blister my kidneys, bisurate my magnesia if the music is not as English, as joyful, as tender as any lyric of all that noble host.'[2] The songs were his *Five Elizabethan Songs*, or as he affectionately nicknamed them, the 'Elizas'. Ivor knew that he had achieved a significant advance in his work.

'Technique all right, and as to word setting–models', he wrote. 'How did such an undigested clod as I make them? That, Willy, I cannot say. But there they are – 'Five Songs' for Mezzo Soprano – 2 flutes, 2 clarinets, a harp and two bassoons.'[3] He set a new standard for English art song in which words and music became one. In one breath of genius, Ivor equalled the song achievements of his teacher Charles Stanford as well as those of other notable composers of the day, including Sir Hubert Parry, Sir Edward Elgar, John Ireland, Roger Quilter and even Ralph Vaughan Williams.

Unlike these older men, Ivor did not rely on tradition to shape the form and power of his music. The 'Elizas' were the result of an instinctive response, not one dictated by rules, but by something that welled up from deep inside Gurney and poured out. He had broken away from what he perceived as the shackles of Stanford's discipline to compose five songs that became archetypes for a new generation of composers looking to the future and no longer willing to hold onto the past. The songs are suffused with feeling, ranging from sensual to melancholic to joyful.

According to Marion Scott, Ivor had drafted 'Orpheus' (Shakespeare) and 'Under the Greenwood Tree' (Shakespeare) in Gloucester and had composed 'Sleep' (Fletcher), 'Spring' (Thomas Nashe) and 'Tears' (anonymous but possibly Fletcher) in 'the Fulham slums'.[4] Although Gurney did not date the manuscripts, the songs appear to have been completed in early 1914.

Marion recalled that 'he knew when he composed the "Elizas" that they were jolly good, and he never rested till he made me see them'.[5] She realized at once that with the composition of these songs, Ivor Gurney had stepped into the realm of genius. Marion later described 'Sleep' as 'distinctive and magical' and as expressing 'extraordinary beauty and pathos'.[6] The 'Elizas' were a turning point for Marion as well as for Ivor. She now stood ready to nurture and promote his musical gift in any way she could. She became his unflagging champion.

'[Y]ou have done some songs which will take their place as part of the inheritance of England', Scott wrote. 'They have the vital beauty, the vital truth that gives life. ... God has given you that rare gift – He has given you genius instead of the talent which is meted out to most people ... your compositions ... will blaze into splendid music which will bring the light of joy to scores of human folk', she predicted. 'Already you hold a great power over the wells of emotion in music.'[7]

When Ivor wrote to Will about the 'Elizas' and his ARCO success, he was feeling the 'sacred hunger for Spring that nourishes the fire in you' and included a bar from his song 'Spring'.[8] By the time the longed-for season with all its uplifting promise had arrived, Ivor was edging towards depression and suffering from exhaustion and stomach trouble. During one brief holiday in Gloucester, he had made plans to visit with John Haines but wrote instead to apologize for missing the appointment and failing to send word. '[I] was sincerely sorry to miss the walk and talk, even though my bloody-bloody head is thick and my naughty-naughty inside fractious', he wrote to Haines.[9]

John Wilton Haines became another of Ivor's confidants, along with Harvey, Benjamin, Marion Scott, Margaret Hunt and Maggie Taylor. Gurney probably met Haines through Alfred Cheesman around 1910, although Haines himself claimed incorrectly that he came to know Gurney in 1914.[10] Like Cheesman, Haines possessed an extensive library that he opened to Ivor, but he offered other compelling attractions: he was regarded as the friend of many poets, an excellent conversationalist, a naturalist and dedicated walker.

Born in 1875, Haines was a member of an established Gloucester family in the legal and medical professions. Away from his duties as a solicitor in the firm of Haines and Summer, he was a respected authority on botany and a collector of first editions of contemporary poets. By contacting authors personally to request books, he established many enduring friendships. Occasionally his poet friends called on him to render legal services, but more likely they turned to him for information about the Gloucester landscape, particularly its flowers, to ensure accuracy in their descriptions of the local topography.

Literature was central to Haines' life. As a student at Cheltenham College, he had won the Irdell Prize for Literature twice. He wrote poetry. In 1921 he published his only volume, *Poems*, which won Ivor's forthright appraisal, 'Your book is better at its best than I could have thought ... An unpretentious half successful book ...' [11]

Jack Haines counted among his friends the literary critic and biographer Edward Thomas, who was soon testing poetic waters; the American poet Robert Frost, who was living with his family in Dymock in 1914, as well as John Freeman, W. H. Davies, Walter de la Mare, Lascelles Abercrombie, John Drinkwater and Will Harvey, who eventually worked in Haines's law office. Ivor and Will often visited Haines. During the war when Ivor was away from Gloucester, Haines corresponded regularly with him.

While Alfred Cheesman laid the foundation for Ivor's early education in poetry, John Haines built on it. He introduced Ivor to a host of poets, including Edward Thomas and Gerard Manley Hopkins, whose work had an influence on Ivor's later writing. [12]

Haines described Gurney as 'the most dynamic creature I ever met' and considered him a genius. [13] In the early days of their friendship Haines saw Ivor as 'a remarkable figure, tall, handsome, powerful, crammed with vitality, excessively opinionated and somewhat violent in his critical views. His eyes flashed with excitement in argument and a very good memory made him a very effective conversationalist, then and later', Haines recalled. [14] He recognized and understood Gurney's 'fierce individualism which has always made him a rebel, though a rebel who hates being a rebel and worships the order and discipline he finds so incompatible with his nature.' [15]

Although Haines was actively involved with the Dymock Poets and had talked to Ivor about them and their work, there is no record that Gurney himself had ventured to the Dymock area during the summer of 1914 or earlier. His first documented visit dates from the spring of 1916 when, as a soldier on his last leave before shipping to France, he chanced to go there. He was riding his bicycle and after stopping by a pub to quaff 'a foaming beaker of gingerbeer', he turned off to Ryton where Wilfrid Gibson and Lascelles Abercrombie lived. [16]

'Then a wandering thought became firm', he wrote to Marion Scott. 'I would go see their houses.' After asking directions, he came to The Gallows, where the Abercrombies lived. 'I stood hesitating for long with my eyes fixed on its white front; made up my mind, went up and knocked', he continued. He was greeted by Catherine Abercrombie, whose husband was away, working in an ammunition factory in Liverpool. Gurney spent six 'very full hours of joy' with Mrs Abercrombie, played with her children, wheeled a pram and 'talked of books and music ... the genius of the place; all set in blue of the sky, green of the fields and leaves, and that red, that red of the soil.' [17]

Many years later in a 1956 BBC radio interview, Catherine Abercrombie recalled her meeting with Ivor differently. She claimed she was in a field playing with her children when 'A youth in khaki came walking towards us, asking if I could direct him to Lascelles Abercrombie's cottage, as he wanted to see it, and him, if possible.' Gurney's recollection of the event is more likely to be accurate, since he told Marion Scott about it shortly after he had met Mrs Abercrombie.

In 1914, however, Ivor was apparently content to learn about contemporary poets working in the Gloucester area through Jack Haines rather than to seek them out himself. Had he ventured to Dymock in the summer of 1914, he might have met Abercrombie, Gibson, Edward Thomas, Robert Frost and Rupert Brooke. At this time Gurney was a fledgling poet, having written only a handful of poems. Music consumed nearly all of his energy. He had produced the five landmark Elizabethan songs and was working on seven other songs, including 'The Twa Corbies' and his rollicking setting of John Masefield's 'Captain Stratton's Fancy', also known as 'The Old Bold Mate', which he finished in 1917. The possibilities in both arts were beginning to stretch before him while growing tensions between Great Britain and Germany were accelerating talk of war.

By 1914 Marion Scott was gradually moving away from performance and focusing on her new career as a writer. She was a contributor to a number of music publications, including *The Music Student*, where her by-line began appearing regularly after 1911. In May 1914 Scott and Katharine Eggar, now serving her term as president of the Society of Women Musicians, journeyed to Leipzig, Germany to attend the International Exhibition for the Book Industry and Graphic Art. At first glance, the event might seem an unlikely venue for women interested in music, but it contained musical treasures in abundance. Housed in a spacious building designed by Emilie Winkelmann called 'Das Haus der Frau', the exhibition featured a Women's Section with one room devoted solely to women's work in music from the seventeenth to the early twentieth centuries.

The scope of the exhibition and the spirit of unity it represented impressed Scott and Eggar, who described it as 'an event of conspicuous importance'.[18] In addition to manuscripts and printed scores, the collection included books, paintings, photographs and sculpture that captured images of women composers and performers in Europe, Britain and America: Clara Schumann, Jenny Lind, Pauline Viardot-Garcia, Fanny Hensel and Amy Beach among them. Contemporary British women figured prominently in the exhibition with music by Eggar, Liza Lehmann, Ethel Smyth, Majory Kennedy-Fraser and others attracting attention.[19]

Scott and Eggar were impressed by the number of string quartets represented, but as composers of chamber music themselves they observed that this particular collection 'might have been larger still but for the fact that the authorities in charge specially asked for *printed works*, or duplicates, as they very naturally did not wish to incur the care of original manuscripts. Any woman who has attempted to publish chamber music, except at her own expense, knows only too well how difficult, almost hopeless, the conditions are, though perhaps they are less prohibitive in Germany than elsewhere.'[20]

After touring the exhibitions, women could retire to the adjacent Tea Room, where, besides the conventional menu of tea and coffee, they could listen to weekly performances by women whose compositions were on

view in the Music Room. For many these informal concerts were the high-
light of the exhibition because they brought women's music to life.

During her holiday in Switzerland in July, Marion wrote about the exhibition for *The Music Student* and sent her article by post to England. She
would not see the article again for many weeks. On 4 August England
declared war on Germany, and Scott was forced to cut short her holiday.
Before leaving Switzerland, she reluctantly destroyed all the material she
had gathered at the International Exhibition, including the catalogue and
her notes. She anticipated the kind of reception she might receive if cus-
toms officials in France, the first stop on her journey home, opened her lug-
gage and found it full of items written in German. When her article finally
arrived in England some two months after she posted it, Scott and Eggar
were unwilling to let war win over art.

'[T]he question arose what should be done with it. Things German are
not acceptable now', Scott observed in her prefatory note. 'Yet it seemed to
me my paper might possess a certain antiquarian interest.' They convinced
the editor of *The Music Student* that it must be published because the content 'described a state of affairs gone for ever, swept away as utterly as if
centuries instead of weeks intervened', Scott lamented.[21]

Ivor Gurney's whereabouts when war was declared are unknown.
According to Scott, he 'promptly volunteered' but was rejected 'on account
of his eyesight'.[22] She places him in London for the remainder of 1914 finishing out his term at the RCM. In the autumn he had taken a new post as
organist at Christ Church at High Wycombe, a town in Buckinghamshire.
Marion might have played a role in this appointment, possibly having
learned of the job through her RCM friend, the organist William Harris.

Ivor journeyed from London to High Wycombe on the weekends, and
soon made the acquaintance of Edward Chapman, the churchwarden.
Chapman took an interest in Ivor and opened his home to him each weekend, ensuring that the young organist had companionship and comfort. Mr
Chapman, an employee of the Great Western Railway, and his wife Matilda
were the parents of four children: Catherine (Kitty) at seventeen, the eldest,
followed by Winifred (Winnie), Arthur and Marjorie (Micky). Ivor fitted
easily into the routine of the household. His kindly presence, his sense of
fun, his music and his poetry readings made a lasting impression on the
children.

Although he appeared to be relaxed and content as he sat with the
Chapmans in the evening before the fire smoking his pipe and talking, he
was still wrestling with his mood swings and stomach trouble. He had
been ill again in September, causing concern for Herbert Howells, who
remarked a few weeks later in a letter to his future wife, Dorothy Dawe,
that he had seen Gurney 'who looks about the same: I think he is mend-
ing.' [23] Ivor was still riding an emotional roller coaster, his moods rising and
falling, seemingly locked into a pattern mirroring what he experienced in
1913 and spawning physical illness.

Shortly after becoming the weekend guest of the Chapmans, Ivor asked
Edward Chapman for permission to marry his seventeen-year-old daughter Kitty. The request has an air of unreality about it and reflects Gurney's

lack of social skills, common sense and consideration for others. He was twenty-four years old, a student attending college on a £40-a-year scholarship. He had never held a steady, long-term job. The income he earned as a part-time organist at High Wycombe was negligible. As 1914 drew to a close, he had no prospects for regular work and no means to support a wife and a family. Under such circumstances, to ask for the hand of a young woman in marriage whom he barely knew was a rash act.

Further, Ivor had already shown marked signs of emotional instability and self-centeredness; though these might not have been apparent to the Chapmans at this time, they would have turned Kitty Chapman into Ivor's caretaker and supporter instead of an equal partner. She would have had to serve him from beginning to end, riding his moods, and perhaps feeling neglected when he was indifferent or incapable of maintaining sexual relations with her. Edward Chapman wisely, but gently, refused Ivor's request, telling him that Kitty was too young to become engaged. Even Kitty felt that she was not ready for such a deep and responsible commitment.[24] It is also possible that Gurney sought marriage thinking he might find shelter from the plague of internal storms that fractured his sense of well-being.

With the exceptions of Margaret Hunt and Marion Scott, Ivor did not sustain lasting relationships with women. Margaret was his muse. His relationship with Marion was built more along intellectual lines, spiritual affinity and on a mutual love and appreciation of music and poetry. Marion's attention to Ivor and her willingness to nurture and help him fed his ego while it created a dependency on her that lasted throughout his life.

Ivor was a man who needed help from others to give him a sense of direction and guide him. Although he was of an independent nature in matters of his art, in matters of day-to-day living and business, he was impractical, scattered, contrary and, at times, often blind to the needs of those around him. Clearly, he was not prepared in any way for marriage and the responsibilities it entailed when he asked for Kitty Chapman's hand.

As 1914 drew to a close, Ivor began to think once again about joining the army. The war on the Western Front had escalated dramatically by the beginning of the new year and the army had relaxed its fitness requirements. When Ivor volunteered for duty in February, his poor eyesight was no longer enough to keep him from serving England. On the ninth day of the month, he traded in his civilian clothes and became Private Ivor Gurney, number 3895, in the 5th Gloucester Reserve Battalion.

NOTES

1 IG to FWH, early 1914 (KT), *CL*, p. 10. Dr R. K. R. Thornton dated this letter on the basis that Gurney mentions passing his ARCO examination at the RCM 17 and 24 January 1914. Prior to Dr Thornton's dating, the letter was believed to have been written in the summer of 1912 because it was found in an envelope postmarked 5 July 1912.

2 Ibid.

3 Ibid.

4 MMS, Notes, MSC.

5 MMS, 'Ivor Gurney: The Man', *Music and Letters*, vol. 19, no. 1 (January 1938), p. 3.

6 MMS, 'Ivor Gurney', *Grove's Dictionary of Music and Musicians*, Supplementary Volume (New York: The Macmillan Company, 1940), p. 260.

7 MMS, drafts of letters to IG written in 1918, GA.

8 IG to FWH, early 1914 (KT), *CL*, p. 10.

9 IG to JWH, Spring 1914 (KT), *CL*, p. 11.

10 In a letter to Don B. Ray on 19 March, 1951, Haines claimed 'I met Gurney in 1914'. Penny Ely, former Trustee of the Gurney Archive, dated the meeting between Gurney and Haines as 1910, with the Reverend Alfred Cheesman introducing them. See *Ivor Gurney Society Journal*, vol. 1, no. 1 (1995), p. 59.

11 IG to JWH, July 1921 (received by Haines on the 16th), *CL*, p. 520. That same month, Haines gave an inscribed copy of his book to Marion Scott.

12 In her notes at the RCM, Marion Scott wrote that Gurney was 'specially influenced by Edward Thomas and Gerard Manley Hopkins'.

13 JWH, 'An Hour with Books, Mr. Ivor Gurney A Gloucestershire Poet', *Gloucester Journal*, 5 January 1935.

14 JWH to DBR, 19 March 1951, GA.

15 JWH, 'An Hour with Books'.

16 IG to MMS, 25 April 1916 (Hurd transcript), *CL*, p. 79.

17 Ibid.

18 MMS and KE, 'Women Musicians and the Leipzig Exhibition', *Music Student*, November 1914, p. 29. This account is the only one known to exist in English.

19 Scott and Eggar referred to the American composer Amy Beach (1867–1944) by her given first name, not by her married name, Mrs H. H. A. Beach, as she was usually known.

20 MMS and KE, 'Women Musicians and the Leipzig Exhibition'.

21 Ibid.

22 MMS, 'Ivor Gurney: The Man', p. 4.

23 Quoted in Christopher Palmer, *Herbert Howells: A Centenary Celebration* (London: Thames Publishing, 1992), p. 63.

24 *Stars in a Dark Night: The Letters of Ivor Gurney to the Chapman Family, 1914–1919*, ed. Anthony Boden (Gloucester: Alan Sutton Publishing, 1986), p. 12.

Part III

On our right? That's the road to Ypres. The less said about that road the better: no one goes down it for choice – it's British now.

– Mary Borden, *The Forbidden Zone*

CHAPTER 10

The Experiment

$\mathcal{F}$OR IVOR GURNEY, military service was an 'experiment' undertaken not so much out of patriotic duty as out of the need for self-preservation and to escape, if only temporarily, from increasing emotional disturbances he could neither control nor understand. He believed that in the hard, disciplined army life with its demands for order, routine and attention to detail, he might find some stability and perhaps come away with his fragile mental and physical health restored. 'I joined to cure my belly!!' he told Herbert Howells.[1] In a letter written to Ethel Voynich shortly after he became a soldier, Ivor implies that he had contemplated suicide during his breakdown in 1913. 'It is indeed a better way to die; with these men, in such a cause; than the end which seemed near me and was so desirable only just over two years ago', he admitted to Voynich.[2] He wrote optimistically to Will Harvey, who wrestled with his own moods and conflicts, which Gurney recognized and understood: 'Let's hope it'll do the trick for both of us, and make us so strong, so happy, so sure of ourselves, so crowded with fruitful memories of joy that we may be able to live in towns or earn our living at some drudgery and yet create whole and pure joy for others.'[3] Ivor knew, however, that the fulfilment of such hopes was 'a far cry' for him.[4]

In the early months of his training in England, Ivor's experiment seemed to be working. He claimed to be in 'a very much happier frame of mind' than he had been for four years, and believed that his health was improving very slowly.[5] Despite the rigorous training he was undergoing, he told friends that although he was 'always tired', he was experiencing 'healthy' fatigue, not 'nervous exhaustion'.[6] He told Marion Scott that 'fatigue from body brings rest to the soul–not so mental fatigue.'[7]

Perhaps for the first time in his life Ivor Gurney was eating regular meals and a more balanced diet. Although he declared that the food was 'scant and coarse' and the bread 'fit for museums', he ate three times a day and his diet included meat, something he rarely ate prior to joining the army.[8] Hours of physical exertion each day increased his hunger for nourishing food and he began to spend half his money buying extra food, chiefly meat.

While Ivor presented a cheerful, optimistic outlook to his friends, he found aspects of military life distasteful. 'They are mad as hatters here', he told Howells, who was exempted from service due to illness.[9]

Ivor had been undergoing rigorous training that began each day when shrill reveille shattered the morning calm at five o'clock. The long days were filled with marches that sometimes covered 20 miles, bayonet practice, rifle practice, mock night battles, instruction in handling grenades and mortars, how to build trenches and the mundane – polishing buttons and boots, brushing his clothes. He reported that on one occasion he walked nine miles with a 50–60-pound pack on his back. The soldiers learnt Morse Code and the correct way to apply field dressings on the wounded. They stood in snow and freezing cold enduring long inspections by Members of Parliament or representatives of the Army General Staff. They slept in a small hut on bare boards, their bodies covered only by damp blankets.

When he was able to steal time for himself, Ivor read, wrote long letters to his friends and played bridge and chess with his Army mates. One night he attended a weekly debate at camp in Essex only because he had promised a friend. He joined in the debate on 'Ghosts', talking 'mostly against my convictions, a contrary attitude', he told Sydney Shimmin.[10] Ivor argued so convincingly on the topic that not only did he reduce the meeting to 'perspiring silence', he was elected to be on the debating committee![11] He enjoyed the challenge and intellectual stimulation of debating and continued to debate on a variety of topics, once becoming the Leader of the Opposition against a Socialist Government. Ivor also found some relief from the boredom of Army life when he was recruited in August to play the baryton, 'a kind of brass cornet' in the 2nd/5th Battalion Gloucester Regimental Band. 'Fancy getting an interesting job in the noble profession of Arms', he wrote to Scott, adding that it was 'a soft job usually, but not on the march'.[12]

For the most part, army life was a series of 'long blanks of tedium', broken only by work at boring tasks or exhausting exercise.[13] 'The aim of training troops is to make them as tired as possible without teaching them anything', he wrote Howells. 'Take em for a route march, stand em on their heads, muck about with em in any fashion so long as they get tired and sick of soldiering.'[14] Despite these complaints, so common to the soldier, the artist in Gurney was alive and alert to the sensations, sights and sounds in his new world. The language in his letters is poetic, his descriptions vivid, his observations keen, his arguments and discussions about books, music and ideas philosophical, searching and profound.

In a letter to Ethel Voynich, he welcomes a 'good healthy quarrel, on literary matters especially' as 'pleasing to my still unquiet mind'.[15] He spars with her on the merits of John Milton and Bach: 'Milton is one of the great men not worth crossing the streets to speak to. Bach was worth a hungry pilgrimage to see', he wrote. He tells her that 'Hardy's sins are chiefly the result of a narrow spiritual outlook, or dryness of the soul.' He rails against Hardy's characters 'as essentially uninteresting in themselves' and finds his prose 'often that of the leading article, or the magazine writer – desiccated and non-committal'.[16]

An article appearing in the *Saturday Westminster* on poet Walter de la Mare's 'confession of Faith' prompted Ivor to share his own opinion on faith with Marion. For a man reared in the Church of England, Ivor's views were surprisingly individual and realistic, not what one would expect from someone nurtured on religious doctrine. He informed her that he 'hates all formal ceremonies and Churches' and that 'my master in all these things is Wordsworth, and my place of worship his'. Ivor believed that 'the important thing to remember now is that there are no problems now that were not

equally urgent two years or 2000 years ago. A Faith which needs recon-
struction now will need it often again maybe. ... People who find their Faith
shocked by this war, do not need a stronger faith only, but a different one,
without blinkers'. To Gurney, the question of faith was summed up in the
last line of Bach's A flat Prelude, where he observed 'you will find a complete and compendious summary of all necessary belief'.[17] He confessed to
Marion that prayer was of no use to him.

Ivor was acutely aware of the world around him. He soaked it up. Writing
to Marion as winter began to shrug off its cloak on Salisbury Plain where he
was in training, he observed, '[T]he first violet has not yet arrived, whereas
the woods must be happy-eyed with them at home – in Gloucestershire
where Spring sends greetings before other less happy counties have forgotten Winter and the snow'.[18] He wrote poetically of '[W]inter when
the trees are naked, and frost binds all moist things with iron, and breath
goes strangely up in vapour'.[19] When he was stationed at Essex, he found
it a 'grey unuseful unbeautiful waste' where 'there are no sunsets, and no
colour; no mystery in woods, no sense of other-worldliness'.[20]

As Ivor watched 100 men go off to the Front, he caught the spirit and
excitement of the send off and tossed it back to Marion Scott. 'The cheering was immense, overwhelming, cataractic', he wrote to her. 'The only
things that can give you an idea of that sound are either elemental sounds
like the war of winds and waves or the greatest moment in music – the end
of the development in the 1st movement of the Choral Symphony. Like the
creative word of God.'[21]

He enjoyed the companionship and diverse backgrounds of his fellow
soldiers, finding much to admire in men like Fred Bennett, 'a delightful
creature. A Great broadchested heavy chap', a Morris dancer, who played
hymn tunes on his trombone during training.[22] To Gurney, Bennett was
'chock full of immense tolerance and good humour and easy to get on with'.
He admired Bennett's 'great simplicity' and told Marion Scott, '[I] hope to
be like him some day. So strong in himself, set fast on strong foundations.
Not likely to be troubled with neurasthenia'. He found another soldier, Tim
Godding, to be 'one of the most original people in all of this regiment', a man
of humour whose use of words led Ivor to describe him as 'a Shakespearian
character'.[23] When Ivor transferred from Company D to Company B, he
reluctantly left Godding behind.

Ivor's army mates were rough hewn and earthy and swore frightfully,
but he found them to be 'good men inside, and full of things for such as I
to imitate'.[24] While he appreciated and envied certain physical and emotional strengths in them, which he felt were lacking in himself, he had little
in common intellectually with fellow soldiers like Fred Bennett. He was
lonely and isolated in his new life. '[O]ur talk is rough, a dialect telling of
days in the open air and no books', he told Marion.[25]

Ivor's closest friend during training and in the early months in France
was Basil Cridland. Before joining the army, Cridland had worked as an
analyst at the Stevens Jam factory in Gloucester. He possessed an intelligence and spirit of adventure that appealed to Ivor. He introduced his new
friend in letters to Marion Scott, John Haines, Edward Chapman, Howells

and Mrs Voynich. He mentioned him more than other soldiers in his company, singling him out as his steady companion. With Cridland by his side, Ivor ventured away from the dull routines of camp life in Salisbury and Essex. They eagerly explored the countryside around Salisbury, venturing into Salisbury itself where Ivor's 'town pride' was jolted when he found the town and surroundings to be more impressive than Gloucester but the cathedral 'not so fine'.[26] Ivor thought highly enough of Cridland that he wanted him to share in any good fortune that might befall Ivor himself. When Edward Chapman attempted to contact a 'miracle-working gent' who might have been able to recall Gurney 'like Orpheus, from Hell' and bring an end to his military service by placing him in a railway job, Ivor Gurney mentioned that Cridland, too, would be delighted to get a position.[27] However, nothing came of Chapman's efforts.

When the two soldiers reached France at the end of May 1916, they remained together. Both spoke the language well enough 'to get what we want' from the natives, and it is likely that Cridland and Gurney used their linguistic skills to make deals on purchases of bread, coffee and beer.[28] They also enjoyed occasional visits to villages where they were allowed to go where they pleased. They sat in cafés drinking coffee, beer and wine, listening carefully to the talk around them so they could become more fluent in French.[29]

Ivor was with Cridland on their first night in the trenches when 'at the beginning of afterglow', they crawled into a signallers dugout 'lit by a candle, and so met four of the most delightful young men that could be met anywhere'. They were Welsh, and Ivor, fearing initially that they would be a 'rough type', was surprised to find that they were educated and sensitive and 'unlike some men out here, they didn't try to frighten us with horrible details ...'[30] Ivor was enchanted by his 'handsome' new friends and so excited by their intelligent conversation that he had no sleep for thirty-six hours. '[T]here was too much to be said, asked, and experienced . ... It was one of the notable evenings of my life', he told Marion.[31] He must have felt like a thirsty traveller who stumbles on an oasis in the desert. 'We talked of Welsh Folksong, of George Borrow, of Burns, of the RCM; of – yes – of Oscar Wilde, Omar Khayyam, Shakespeare and of the war', Ivor wrote to his friend Catherine Abercrombie.[32] While the men talked they were aware that only some 300 yards away snipers were continually firing, and a distant rumble of guns 'reminded us of the reason we were foregathered'. The Welshmen sang 'David of the White Rock', the 'Slumber Song' and their own folksongs in 'sweet natural voices'. But like a traveller at an oasis, Gurney lingered as long as he could before he had to move on and participate in the demanding business of war.[33]

Once Gurney crossed the English Channel and landed in France, he found war 'damned interesting' and told Marion Scott that it would be 'hard indeed to be deprived of all this artists [*sic*] material now'.[34] He felt that he was more able to shut introspection out of his mind as he became 'saner and more engaged with outside things'.[35] His experience with the Welsh soldiers did more than fulfil his need for conversation with men who thought as he did; it profoundly moved the artist in him. 'We were standing outside our dugout cleaning mess tins, when a cuckoo sounded its call from the shattered wood at the back', he told Mrs Abercrombie. 'What could I think of but Framilode, Minsterworth, Cranham, and the old haunts of home. This Welshman turned to me passionately. "Listen to that damned bird," he said. "All through that bombardment in the pauses I could hear that infernal silly 'Cuckoo, Cuckoo' sounding while Owen was lying in my arms covered with blood. How shall I ever listen again ...?" He broke off, and I became aware of shame at the unholy joy that filled my artist's mind', Gurney admitted.[36]

Although Gurney declared that he was ready 'if necessary to die for England', he felt it would be a waste. 'I do not see the necessity; it being only a hard fast system which has sent so much of the flower of England's artists to risk death, and a wrong materialistic system; rightly or wrongly I consider myself able to do work which will do honour to England. Such is my patriotism, and I believe it to be the right kind', he explained to Marion.[37]

Even before he arrived in France and while he was in England training at Essex and Salisbury, the conditions in which Ivor found himself had already touched the poet in him. Lonely and cut off from ideas, intellectual stimulation and the inspiration of country walks and friends who shared his interests, he soon immersed himself in the world of words. Of all his friends, he drew Marion Scott in with him more completely and devotedly than anyone else, forming a bond that resulted in one of the most unusual literary collaborations in history.

Throughout the war, Ivor wrote hundreds of letters to his friends at home, but many of them, like the letters to the Hunt sisters, are lost while others, like a small collection of letters to Herbert Howells, have been discovered. The letters that Ivor's friends wrote to him were, of necessity, left behind on the battlefields of France, swallowed in the mud of Passchendaele or abandoned in a trench or used as toilet paper. A few letters to him from Marion survive, as do letters about Ivor that were exchanged among Howells, Haines, the Hunts, Alfred Cheesman, Will Harvey and Florence Gurney, who corresponded with Marion Scott.

Ivor established different relationships with the recipients of his letters. Some were light-hearted, as were those to the Chapman children. Letters to Howells, Sydney Shimmin and Jack Haines were chatty, often humorous discussions of the war, music, poetry, the RCM, mutual friends, and occasionally topics that he could not share with Marion like his romance with a nurse later in the war. A third category of letters was more searching, analytical, challenging and intimate, and contained Ivor's unrestrained 'soul out-pourings'. A few of these letters were addressed to Ethel Voynich but the vast majority of them were written to Marion Scott.

Ivor could be a demanding, self-centred correspondent who expected his friends to be as diligent as he in carrying on wide-ranging, in-depth discourses in their letters. Only Marion seemed up to the task. She had already sensed that Ivor was no ordinary man in 1911 and began saving his first brief letters to her as early as 1912. He, too, came to realize the importance of his correspondence when he wrote to her expressing relief that she was out of danger after one of her illnesses and thus 'able to resume that correspondance [sic] which is inevitably fated some day to be the joy and wonder of my biographers.'[38] But writing to Marion was based on more than this seeming vanity. Ivor felt that she alone understood what he needed and could give it to him. 'My friendships are mostly queer ones, and this is queer, but believe me, a very valued one. You have given me just what I needed, and what none other of my friends could supply to keep me in touch with things which are my life; and the actuality of which is almost altogether denied me', he told Marion.[39] Her letters, arriving in distinctive green envelopes, obviously meant a great deal to him, stimulated his imagination, inspired him, informed him, touched his senses and fired him with enthusiasm. 'Your letters interest me very much', he told her.[40] He respected Marion's intellect, her sensitivity and her advice, but most of all he trusted her as he trusted no one else. Ivor felt at ease with her and free to say what was on his mind.

The tenor of their relationship was about to change dramatically. As the weeks stretched into months, Ivor became increasingly dependent on her, and she became dependent on him. Together they formed a singular, unspoken partnership that remained in place for the rest of their lives.

NOTES

1 IG to HH, June 1915 (KT), *CL*, p. 27.

2 IG to ELV, February 1915 (KT), *CL*, p. 14.

3 IG to FWH, February 1915, *CL*, p. 12.

4 Ibid.

5 IG to HH, 8 April 1915 (P), *CL*, p. 17.

6 IG to the Chapman family, 9 March 1915 (P), *CL*, p. 16.

7 IG to MMS, 9 May 1915 (P), *CL*, p. 19.

8 IG to HH, 8 April 1915 (P), p. 17, and to MMS, 3 August 1915 (P), p. 29.

9 IG to HH, June 1915 (KT), *CL*, p. 27. Howells suffered from Grave's disease, a serious thyroid condition that affected his heart. Diagnosed in 1915, he was given six months to live. However, he underwent experimental treatment for his condition, enduring injections of radium into his neck twice a week for two years. He was the first person to undergo this treatment. Despite a poor prognosis, Howells enjoyed a very long life, living to the age of 90.

10 IG to SGS, November 1915 (KT), *CL*, p. 59.

11 Ibid.

12 IG to MMS, September 1915 (S), *CL*, p. 36.

13 IG to MMS, 22 March 1916 (P), *CL*, p. 74.

14 IG to HH, June 1915 (KT), *CL*, p. 27.

15 IG to ELV, September 1915 (E), *CL*, p. 57.

16 IG to ELV, late September 1915 (KT), *CL*, p. 40–1.

17 IG to MMS, September 1915 (S), *CL*, p. 35.

18 IG to MMS, 22 March 1916 (P), *CL*, p. 75.

19 IG to MMS, October 1915 (KT), *CL*, p. 51.

20 Ibid., p. 50.

21 IG to MMS, 28 June 1915 (P), *CL*, p. 25.

22 IG to MMS, 15 September 1915 (S), *CL*, p. 37.

23 IG to ELV, April 1916 (E), *CL*, p. 77.

24 IG to HH, February 1916 (KT), *CL*, p. 72.

25 IG to MMS, 9 May 1915 (P), *CL*, p. 19.

26 IG to JWH, around 2 May 1916 (KT), *CL*, p. 82.

27 IG to Edward Chapman, October 1916 (KT), *CL*, p. 49.

28 IG to ELV, June 1916 (KT), *CL*, p. 90.

29 Although Gurney did not mention Basil Cridland in his letters after the summer of 1916, they remained friends. Cridland visited Gurney in Gloucester in October 1918, after Gurney had been discharged from the Army.

30 IG to Catherine Abercrombie, June 1916 (KT), *CL*, p. 91.

31 IG to MMS, 7 June 1916 (P), *CL*, p. 86.

32 IG to Abercrombie, June 1916 (KT), *CL*, p. 91.

33 The encounter with the Welsh soldiers impressed Gurney so profoundly that he wrote about it to Marion Scott, Ethel Voynich, Catherine Abercrombie, the Chapman family and Herbert Howells.

34 IG to MMS, 7 June 1916, *CL*, p. 87.

35 Ibid.

36 IG to Abercrombie, June 1916 (KT), *CL*, p. 91.

37 IG to MMS, 27 July 1917 (P), *CL*, p. 288.

38 IG to MMS, 16 August 1916 (O), *CL*, p. 132.

39 IG to MMS, 2 April 1917 (G), *CL*, p. 240.

40 IG to MMS, 17 May 1916, *CL*, p. 84.

CHAPTER 11

A Partnership

*A*FTER JOINING THE ARMY, Ivor Gurney again began thinking seriously about writing poetry. In a letter written to Marion on 9 May 1915 from his training camp at Chelmsford, Essex, Ivor, acting with uncharacteristic shyness, included a sonnet inspired by the famous sonnets of Rupert Brooke whom they had been discussing.[1] Initially Ivor believed that Brooke 'has left us a legacy of two sonnets which outshine by far anything yet written on this upheaval. They are as beautiful as music. They are so beautiful that at last one forgets that the words are there and is taken up into ecstasy just as in music.'[2]

By August, Gurney was feeling differently about Brooke's contribution. 'The Sonnet of R.B. you sent me I do not like', he informed Marion.[3] 'It seems that Rupert Brooke would not have improved with age, would not have broadened, his manner has become a mannerism, both in rhythm and diction. Great poets, great creators are not much influenced by immediate events; those must sink in to the very foundations and be absorbed', he observed. 'Rupert Brooke soaked it in quickly and gave it out with great ease ... but what of 1920?'[4] Coincidentally Ivor mailed the letter containing his sonnet 'To the Poet Before Battle' on 3 August, which would have been Brooke's twenty-eighth birthday.

Like Brooke when he wrote his sonnets, Ivor had not experienced war when he composed his first war poem, an idealistic and patriotic effort that echoes Brooke's sentimentality. Although Ivor claimed to have 'no great opinion of it', he was eager to learn what Marion Scott thought of his poem.[5] He even acknowledged to Ethel Voynich that it was with 'bashfulness and blushes' that he had sent this poem to Marion.[6] Within a month he had posted three more poems to her. In addition to writing sonnets, he had begun to write a ballad of the Cotswolds, an exercise he found 'very grateful and comforting to the mind'.[7] Impressed with Ivor's verse and seeing an opportunity to encourage him in his new venture, Marion secured publication of 'To the Poet Before Battle' and 'Afterwards' in the Christmas Term 1915 issue of the *Royal College of Music Magazine*. He was delighted and started to send poems regularly to her, marking the tentative beginning of the collaboration between Ivor Gurney and Marion Scott.

Marion now commented frankly on Ivor's poems as he had requested. Sometimes he found her suggestions valid and made changes, while at other times he argued against them, explaining his reasons to her. By October 1916 Ivor informed Marion he had it 'in my mind to write 15 or 20 more, and chiefly of local interest, make a book and call it "Songs from the Second-Fifth".'[8]

In the early days of writing with Marion's encouragement, Ivor practised his craft, drawing on what he saw around him, what he imagined war to be like and what he recalled of his native Gloucestershire. But it wasn't until he reached France and found himself in the thick of battle that, according to Marion, his poetic 'genius suddenly flowered'.[9] 'It may be that those strange conditions [at the Front], where life and death burned at their fiercest, were for him a sort of no man's land of the spirit in which his mind moved clair-voyantly', Scott observed many years later. 'From then onward the poems ... came to him freely.'[10] Nearly every letter to Marion contained a poem, and by the winter of 1916/17, the two friends were deeply immersed in their col-laboration on what was destined to become Ivor's first book, *Severn and Somme*.

Although the initial title of the collection was *Songs from the Second-Fifth* in honour of his regiment, Ivor soon realized that it would not work, since there was so little about his regiment in the book. He considered other titles, *Remembered Beauty*, *Songs Before Dawn*, *Songs in Exile* and *Strange Service*, before settling on *Severn and Somme*. ' "Strange Service" is a very exact description of the feeling that made the book; it would sell better as "Severn and Somme" perhaps but that is your business ...', he observed.[11] Marion continued to refer to the work-in-progress as *Strange Service*.

The project was jeopardized more than once. Marion had not been well during the latter part of 1915, and her problems continued throughout most of 1916, as letters from Ivor attest. A broken blood vessel, a severe cold, exhaustion and an attack of nerves blamed on overwork plagued her during 1915. Her illnesses in 1916 were severe and life threatening, yet she managed to continue her correspondence with Ivor, keeping her letters full of news, topics of interest, comments on his poetry, and encourage-ment.

Marion's first illness in 1916 struck in April. She showed no signs of being unwell when she wrote to Howells on 5 April. She had completed an article titled 'Words for Music' and was happily engrossed in her study of Arthur Bliss's String Quartet in A Major, which Howells had lent to her. She had also begun work on a piece to commemorate com-poser William Sterndale Bennett in his centenary year and provided Howells with an amusing and telling picture of her approach to musical analysis:

> With much delay and difficulty, I have borrowed all the necessary scores, and study the *Sestett* by spreading out the part on the music room floor thus
>
> | 1st violin | Viola | 2nd Cello |
> |------------|-------|-----------|
> | 2nd violin | 1st Cello | Double-bass |
>
> while I kneel in front clutching the piano part, and try to reconstruct the score in my mind. The family say I look as if I were performing some Hindu rite of worship!! Poor S.B. – I fear I feel rather far from it at times when he makes one of his point blank modulations on a weak-beat! – a trick of his I find very wearisome.[12]

She fell ill soon after writing this letter. Her condition was serious enough for Gurney to observe to Howells that it was 'a near squeak this time apparently, although he does not mention the nature of her illness.[13] In July she had the mumps, an infectious childhood disease that is a very painful and serious condition in adults, and can affect the pancreas and the reproductive organs, causing sterility. Marion became dangerously ill for the second time that year in August, from complications of the mumps. While she lay near death in London, Ivor was beginning to find his own poetic voice on the battlefields of France.

'Your news is a very bad surprise, and I was very sorry to get it—more sorry than I can say', Ivor wrote to Marion's mother, Annie Scott, who had already lost her youngest daughter Freda in 1908.[14] '[I] hope the news is better now, and that Miss Marion is well out of danger. But what can be said, if this is not so? We have not been real friends for very long, but since I have been in France, her letters have been one of my looked for pleasures. If these came no more, there must be a distinct gap; not to be filled up', he said.[15]

Indeed, if Marion Scott had died at this early stage of her deepening friendship with Gurney, several months before their literary collaboration reached full bloom, it is likely that his poetic voice would have been diminished or perhaps not have taken flight at all. Marion had become his lifeline to the world beyond the dirt, danger and death of the emasculated battlefields of France where he now resided. She was his first audience and his most important one, and he addressed his poems to her. Her encouragement, enthusiasm and support motivated him to continue writing. Without Scott, Gurney might have turned to John Haines for help, but it is unlikely that their poetic collaboration would have been as intense or productive as the one he had with Marion. Haines supported poets and was a practical businessman, but he would not have nurtured and encouraged Gurney with the same patience, devotion and, most significantly, such unconditional love as Scott.

By late August Marion was showing signs of recovery from her near-fatal illness, but she was still weak. It was not until she had surgery in September for an unknown condition that she began to improve. As soon as she was able, Marion, accompanied by her mother and her sister Stella, settled in a leased house at Hindhead, Surrey. No sooner had they arrived than Stella suffered an attack of appendicitis, a condition so serious that she was not told the gravity of her illness. Mrs Scott, who had spent the summer worrying about Marion, not knowing if she was going to live or die, now feared for Stella's life. They had to extend their stay because Stella could not be moved. By the middle of October her crisis had passed, and the Scotts rejoined Mr Scott at 92 Westbourne Terrace.

Marion enjoyed a short run of better health, but 1917 found her suffering again from a series of illnesses that began in February with influenza, which left her weak and bedridden. She had a bout of rubella in the spring, and in April endured an attack of colitis, which she claimed was caused by the maize in the war bread. In July she endured another unnamed illness. It appears that she again had surgery in September as she had in the previous year. This time Marion's doctor removed, in Ivor's words, 'a radical defect'.[16] Although it is difficult to ascertain the exact nature of Marion's various illnesses, she did suffer from intestinal disorders throughout her life, possibly due to serious injuries suffered when she was thrown from a hansom cab in her youth.[17]

Despite her disabilities and frequent confinements, Scott was remarkably productive and active in 1915, 1916 and 1917. She maintained a very high level of steady correspondence with Ivor, continued to work at the RCM, guided the fortunes of the Society of Women Musicians, performed occasionally, conducted research, wrote articles and cared for ailing friends, including Sydney Shimmin, who stayed with the Scotts during one of his illnesses.[18]

As she approached forty, Marion Scott was entering a transitional stage in her own life. She was focusing more on music scholarship and writing a book, quite possibly *History of British Music, 1848–1900*, which she eventually completed but never published.[19] Although she was an aggressive, self-assured woman, Marion was not immune to bouts of self-doubt, ebbing confidence and insecurity. She made an effort to write poetry and compose music again but she seemed uncertain about her abilities and at different times turned to Ivor for advice. She confided her doubts and fears to Gurney, who, in a complete reversal of roles, reassured her and became her strength. 'Life will begin to widen itself for you soon, with the violin and your book; let but the winter be but kind and you should be finely set up by May ...', he wrote to her. 'When Peace comes, all the air now full of uneasiness and hate will sweeten; when Europe is sick it is not strange that a spirit like yours should be affected.'[20] Ivor cautioned Marion that she must 'have mastery of yourself, or perish' and acknowledged that they were very much alike in that 'There is the same uncertainty with us two, for instance – the same aching thought; whether we shall get the chance to use the rewards of patience. Please do not accuse yourself of uselessness', he admonished her. 'At least not at any rate to me, who have so much to thank you for. ... If there were no MMS [Marion Margaret Scott] it would be necessary to invent one.'[21]

As supportive as he was of Scott, Gurney did not praise her work just to make her feel good. She expected him to be honest with her and he was always as truthful and direct with her as she was with him. Having seen only her songs, he was non-committal about her music. 'About your work I am going to be simply honest. I don't know what to say, and that's true', he wrote to her in January 1918. 'Should you go on writing? Well, I care only for Music of strong individuality; Bach, Beethoven, and Herbert Howells and Vaughan Williams. It is the same with verse – I care only to hear what I cannot do myself; I like what is beyond me.'[22]

Marion regarded herself as a contributor to the body of English music rather than as an innovator, which prompted Ivor to observe, 'But as to the use of making a body of *English* music there is no doubt, whether it has genius or not; but I, who am paralysed by doubt, before writing as to whether it is worth while or no, cannot be expected to give advice.'[23] Later he worried that she might have found his comments discouraging, and hoped that she was not 'affected in any way by my non-committal attitude as to your future work. It is that I do not feel myself competent to judge.

If you cannot make up your own mind, Time and the drift of circumstances may decide for you, Dear Friend.'[24]

In one of her earliest published lectures, 'Contemporary British War-Poetry, Music, and Patriotism', Marion's topic was largely inspired by her perspectives on Ivor's artistic experiences in war.[25] Gurney's rare gifts for both music and poetry were at the heart of the address that she presented, in her role as president, to members of the Society of Women Musicians on 2 December 1916. Scott built a case for poetry and music as the two arts that are indispensable at all times but especially when a nation is at war.

Marion recalled that when war broke out, 'many people wondered what would become of art' and that there seemed to be 'no place for it in a world of such gigantic horrors and unchained forces'. She observed that many people 'even thought that all Art should be put aside, as a frivolity unsuited to the dignity of Armageddon'. While some still believed that art had no place during war, 'we musicians have never believed it (we never will!), and the men of the Navy and Army have more than supported our view'. Scott told her audience that despite 'battling with enemies such as man never met before, facing hardships past imagination, enduring such trials as seem superhuman, they have done another very wonderful thing: they have brought a fresh spring of life into English poetry and music! It is those very Arts which have glowed into fuller life during the war', she wrote with Ivor's burgeoning achievements under duress of battle in mind.[26]

Marion took the opportunity to introduce Ivor's poem 'To Certain Comrades' to her audience of 'the foremost women in London', and commented on its 'haunting beauty' and 'nobility of thought and expression'.[27] She related his trench experience with the Welsh soldiers 'who so enraptured the newcomers by their music that they had not the time to feel as – well, as new battalions might very reasonably feel when they first come under fire!' She refers again to Ivor but without naming him when she notes that 'A certain amount of composition is even done at the Front itself' and that 'few things are more moving nowadays than the sight of these manuscripts, which come home from the trenches, stained with mud, scribbled in pencil and marked by the censor.'[28]

By the time Marion gave her lecture, she had seen Ivor's setting of John Masefield's 'By a Bierside' that 'came to birth in a disused Trench Mortar emplacement' in the summer of 1916, with Gurney recalling the poem from memory.[29] To her, Ivor's manuscripts were 'human documents bearing witness that the soul of Man is greater than all material devastation and horror, and that music is a thing immortal – some wonderful spiritual stream, which, like the River of Life, proceeds from the Throne of God'.[30]

Scott sent Gurney a copy of the lecture when it was published. He commented that the 'whole address is very interesting ... and must have given great pleasure' but he did not refrain from being critical. He told her that he did not have a 'very high opinion' of the other two poems she quoted – 'England' by Geoffrey Howard, a lieutenant in the Royal Fusiliers, whose poetry appeared in at least five anthologies published up to 1930, and 'Before Action' by William Noel (W. N.) Hodgson, a lieutenant in the Devon Regiment whose book *Verse and Prose in Peace and War* went into three editions, while his poetry now appears in some twenty anthologies. Hodgson, who also wrote under the pseudonym of Edward Melbourne, was awarded the Military Cross in 1915 but later died in the Battle of the Somme. Gurney found Howard's poem 'so empty', commenting that 'the man uses words without feeling their meaning'. He thought Hodgson's poem 'slightly precious' but decided that it was 'likable and memorable'.[31] Gurney was annoyed that Scott had omitted two words from 'To Certain Comrades' but was quick to tell her that the omissions did not spoil the poem 'for anyone can see something has been dropped'. Scott quoted 'Then Death with you, honoured, and swift, / And so – Not Die'. The poem actually reads, 'Then death with you, honoured, and swift, and high; / And so – not die'.[32]

Although Scott's lecture 'Contemporary British War-Poetry, Music, and Patriotism' is not a true collaboration with both parties actively participating in its creation, it serves as an example of how Ivor and Marion influenced each other in their work. In this case, Marion's topic was inspired by Ivor's accomplishments as a poet and composer who managed to practise both arts while fighting in a war. Ivor had shared his experiences with Marion and she drew on them to create an independent work of her own.

Despite her own efforts at original writing, Marion often devoted more time to Ivor's poetry and music than to her own creative endeavours. The years of her personal sacrifices for him had begun. She believed in Ivor's genius and was determined to help him gain the recognition and rewards she felt he deserved. In addition to introducing his work to the Society of Women Musicians and securing the first publication of his poetry in the *Royal College of Music Magazine*, she saw to it that four more poems appeared in the magazine: 'To Certain Comrades' (Midsummer Term issue, 1916); 'Song of Pain and Beauty', which was dedicated to Marion Scott (Midsummer Term issue, 1917); and 'Ypres' and 'After Music' (Easter Term issue, 1918).

In the autumn of 1916 Marion, acting as Ivor's 'literary representative', showed some of his poetry to E. B. (Edward Bolland) Osborn, a critic for the *Morning Post*, who was preparing an anthology of 'war poems, for the most part written in the field of action', to be called *The Muse in Arms*. When this volume was published in 1917, it contained four of Gurney's poems: 'Strange Service', 'To the Poet before Battle', 'To Certain Comrades' and 'Afterwards'.[33]

While Ivor was in France, both Marion and Herbert Howells secured performances of his songs at the RCM and at Aeolian Hall in London as well as in venues at Oxford and Reading. In June 1916 Herbert arranged a performance of Ivor's 'The Twa Corbies' at the RCM in a concert that featured Herbert's own string quartet, *Lady Audrey's Suite*, inspired by and composed for Marion's niece Audrey Lovibond.[34] Ivor did not know that his song had been performed until Marion sent him the programme. He was pleasantly surprised. Shortly thereafter, under the auspices of the Society of Women Musicians, Marion arranged the first performance of Ivor's *Five Elizabethan Songs* at the RCM.

Marion held the 'Elizas', Ivor's name for them, in very high esteem. She was particularly fond of 'Sleep', which she found to be 'of extraordinary beauty and pathos'.[35] In the spring of 1916, when the war was threatening London and 'monstrous Zeppelin moths' were floating dangerously in the skies above the city, Marion, fearing that her house might be destroyed, gave the full score of the 'Elizas' to Howells for safekeeping in the country where he was staying at Churchdown in Gloucestershire.[36] After a frightening night when 'Paddington was plunged into darkness' and fire engines moved 'ominously' through the streets while the Scotts stood by for hours anticipating an emergency, she wrote Howells that she was 'devoutly glad that the full score … was safe in Gloucestershire with you'.[37]

During the winter of 1916/17 Herbert completed orchestrations of 'By a Bierside' and 'In Flanders' that were performed at the RCM in mid-March with Ivor's former teacher Sir Charles Stanford conducting. Ivor told Marion that Howells had the 'absolute yea-or-nay-say' on the orchestration of 'By a Bierside'.[38] However, the soloist, 'Mr. Taylor', took liberties in his interpretation of 'By a Bierside', which Marion reported to Ivor, who was not pleased.

'But Mr Taylor seems remarkably like a dam-fool; it was good of you to wrestle with him, but difficult to convince a man who held such "movie" views on the "Bierside" ending', Ivor replied. 'The first part of the song is of course a rhapsody on beauty, full of grief but not bitter, until the unreason of death closes the thought of loveliness, that Death unmakes', he explained. 'Then the heart grows bitter with the weight of grief and revelation of the impermanence of things – Justice and Strength turning to a poet's theme. But, anger being futile, the mind turns to the old strangeness of the soul's wandering apart from the body, and to what tremendous mysteries! And the dimly apprehended sense of such before us all overpowers the singer, who is lost in the glory of the adventure of Death. But that's all summed up by asking what the foremizzentopmast did I write "ff" [for] if it were as this Taylor man suggests.' [39]

Between June 1916 and December 1917 Ivor's war songs were featured in six known recitals or concerts. By the end of 1917 the tenor Gervase Elwes had featured Gurney's 'Sleep' in a recital at Aeolian Hall that also included songs by Ralph Vaughan Williams, Frank Bridge and Colin Taylor, and performances by the London String Quartet of four Bach airs and the Mozart String Quartet in G major.[40] Ivor was pleased that a critic for the *Sunday Times* had singled out 'Sleep' for mention. 'Many interesting novelties were introduced – too many for notice, although mention must be made of two songs by Mr Frank Bridge, "Where she lies asleep" and "Love went a-riding"; "Sleep" by Mr. Ivor Gurney, and "A Pastoral" by Mr. Colin Taylor.' [41]

In addition to promoting Ivor's poetry and music, Marion concerned herself with his personal comfort and intellectual needs. With other members of her family, she began sending him everything from *café au lait* and lemonade crystals to tobacco, bread, chocolate and 'insect preventer' as well as newspapers, books, music manuscript paper and notebooks in which he could write down his poems. He enjoyed other gifts from home, including equally thoughtful and useful presents from the Chapman family and the

Hunt sisters. Typically, Ivor generously shared his bounty with his friends in the trenches who came to regard Marion as their 'Fairy Godmother'.[42]

As time passed, Ivor grew less shy of making requests of her, particularly for books or individual poems. In one letter to Scott written on 27 July 1916, he asked for inexpensive editions of Keats, Shelley, Browning, Tennyson and Walt Whitman 'if you can', as well as manuscript paper.[43] When the parcels arrived within a few days, Ivor was quick to respond, telling her that he recognized what they must have cost in money. Her gifts gave him 'considerable' pleasure. 'The reason I dared to ask for all these things is … that it has been impossible to get these things ourselves, in the towns and villages. As for our canteen, the only thing one is certain of getting, is boot-polish, and perhaps bachelors buttons. This is an apology for having asked for so much', he wrote.[44]

As he had with Masefield's 'By a Bierside', he asked her to send Laurence Binyon's poem, 'To the Fallen', because 'I might have a shot at that, though not easy to make a song of'. Earlier Gurney had mentioned 'To the Fallen', which he called 'noble', to Herbert Howells, John Haines and Ethel Voynich. He asked Howells if he had heard Elgar's setting of it, saying, 'I envy any man who can set that properly'.[45] Gurney told Haines that 'To the Fallen' 'runs continually through my head out here' and told him that it 'delights me ever more and more'.[46] When he asked Marion Scott for a copy of the poem, she sent it to him immediately. He responded, 'The Binyon poem is too long, too big, I fear, for any setting I could give it, but perhaps, perhaps …'[47] Later when he had begun to feel 'some stirrings in me', Gurney lost the poem and asked Scott to send him another copy![48] In this era long before the advent of photocopy machines, Marion either wrote out in her own hand or typed all the individual poems Ivor requested.

At other times, Marion simply sent him copies of poems she thought might interest him. In one of his many light-hearted moments, Ivor, writing a list of items he would like, tells Marion that 'a piano would also be acceptable, but not insisted upon'.[49]

'Whack! there goes another mosquito', he begins a letter to Matilda Chapman.[50] As guns go off around him while he is writing to Marion Scott, 'Crrunch!' and a few minutes later, 'Another Crunch. O sound of Fear. Unpleasing to a soldier's ear.'[51] In considering alternative approaches the Germans might take in battle, he observes, 'Supposing instead of a strafe, they played [Strauss's] Heldenleben [A Hero's Life] at us …' He once jokingly asked Scott to send him a copy of a 'Walford Davies work to protect my bosom …'[52] When Marion Scott complained to him that she could not sleep, he wrote back suggesting that she read, 'Dr. Johnson's work, or Addison's, which are nearly as bad.'[53]

Beneath the humour, serious currents ran through Ivor's letters to Marion. He was a soldier at war, acutely aware of how close to death he was each day as he had a few close calls himself and watched his comrades fall. After one round of combat in the trenches, he wrote a long letter to Marion in June 1916, sharing his feelings about war and his place in it. He felt detached from the war, that he had no emotional connection with it and that fighting in it just happened to be what he was doing at a given time. 'I wake up with a start from my dreams of books and music and home, and I am – here, in this!' He felt like 'a cinematograph shadow moving among dittoes'.[54]

Considering himself strong and tough, Ivor boasted to Marion 'that in a hand to hand fight I shall be damned dangerous to tackle'. He claimed to have little fear, partly, he said, 'because I am more or less fatalistic; partly because my training in self-control, not yet finished, has been hard enough. Partly because I possess an ingrained sense of humour.'[55] A skilled marksman, he did not lack courage in battle. Shortly after arriving at the Front, he informed Scott that he was nearly recommended for a 'D.C.M. [Distinguished Conduct Medal] or something or other' but he failed to tell her why.[56]

Although Ivor complained occasionally about the drudgery of army life, calling it an 'awful life for an artist', he was actually finding that the 'queer' experience of war nourished his artist's spirit and opened all of his senses to the world around him.[57] Nothing escaped him and he turned much of what he saw and heard into precise miniatures in music and words, fragments that might be remembered and one day pieced together to form an image in a poem or the wandering accompaniment in a song. Images became music to him.

'High up in the air like harmless gnats British aeroplanes are sailing … in their circles lovely little balls of white fleece … They go round and come back to the accompaniment of thumps like a soft tap on the bass drum when distant, or a loud tap on timpani when near', he observed.[58] He contrasted the disruptive chaotic noise of a trench mortar with the pulsing voice of a cuckoo, and described hearing a shell go down the chromatic scale. 'The machine gunners manage to make their job interesting by playing tunes on their guns.'[59]

Even in the midst of battle, Ivor's fine ear was tuned to the pitches and rhythms of war. With his poet's eye, he saw his fellow soldiers, the enemy and the landscape as actors in a drama on a vast outdoor stage.

> Someday all this experience may be crystallized and glorified in me; and men shall learn by chance fragments in a string quartett [*sic*] or a symphony, what thoughts haunted the minds of men who watched the darkness grimly in desolate places. Who learnt by the denial how full and wide a thing Joy may be, forming dreams of noble lives when nothing noble but their own nobility … was seen to be. Who kept ever the memory of their home and friends to strengthen them, and walked in pleasant places in faithful dreams. And how one man longed to be working to celebrate them in music and verse worthy of the high theme, but did not bargain with God, since it is best to accept one's Fate when that is clearly seen.[60]

Ivor looked at his war experience as 'a means to an end'. '[I]t is better to live a grey life in mud and danger, so long as one uses it', he observed to Marion.[61] Once Ivor began to make art out of war, he wanted to be able to go on drawing freely from this deep well of images, sounds and ideas. But he knew he was always living on the edge, that the line between life and death was indistinguishable on the battlefield. He was frightened but he did not fear death. What troubled him more than losing his life was '[T]he thought of leaving all I have to say unsaid.'[62]

NOTES

1 Brooke died from blood poisoning *en route* to Gallipoli on 23 April 1915.

2 IG to MMS, 9 May 1915 (P), *CL*, p. 19.

3 IG to MMS, 3 August 1915, *CL*, p. 29.

4 Ibid.

5 IG to ELV, 12 August 1915 (KT), *CL*, p. 32.

6 Ibid.

7 IG to MMS, September 1915 (S), *CL*, p. 36.

8 IG to MMS, 19 October 1916 (P), *CL*, p. 157.

9 MMS, 'Recollections of Ivor Gurney', p. 43.

10 Ibid., p. 40.

11 IG to MMS, 27 July 1916 (P), *CL*, p. 288.

12 MMS to HH, 5 April 1916, MSC. Scott published the Sterndale Bennett article in *Music Student*, October 1916, pp. 11–12. In addition to the Sestett in F sharp minor, she discussed the Chamber Trio in A major and the Sonata for Piano and Cello in A.

13 IG to HH, 2 May 1916 (P), *CL*, p. 81.

14 IG to Annie Prince Scott, August 1916 (KT), *CL*, p. 131.

15 Ibid.

16 IG to MMS, 12 September 1917, *CL*, p. 325.

17 Not only was Scott seriously ill during this time, but Gurney's friend Ethel Voynich suffered from various complaints as well, including whooping cough. Illness seemed to go in cycles in the Scott household. As soon as Marion seemed recovered, her sister Stella or one or both of her parents would fall ill. As an adult, Marion Scott was prone to childhood illnesses which, in addition to the mumps when she was 39, included measles when she was 36. Gurney commented that the war diet was probably the cause for so much illness in his friends at home! He was right in part. I think that Scott probably suffered from chronic colitis or diverticulitis.

18 In a letter to Herbert Howells written on 24 April 1917, shortly after her own bout of colitis, Scott reported that 'Sydney is progressing fairly well, but has had two violent attacks of sickness and pain which have exhausted him a good deal.'

19 By early 1917, she had completed one chapter of her book and by the spring, the book was, in Gurney's words, 'tugging at the leash.' However, her illnesses and other distractions slowed her progress at the time but she resumed work later and completed the brief book. Her typed manuscript is at the RCM.

20 IG to MMS, 16 April 1916 (O), *CL*, p. 133.

21 Ibid.

22 IG to MMS, 11 January 1918 (P), *CL*, p. 392.

23 Ibid.

24 IG to MMS, 3 February 1918 (P), *CL*, p. 403.

25 Marion Scott's 'Contemporary British War-Poetry, Music, and Patriotism' was originally published in *Musical Times*, vol. 58, no. 889 (1 March 1917), pp. 120–3. It was reprinted in the *Ivor Gurney Society Journal*, vol. 2 (1996), pp. 76–86, with an introduction by Anthony Boden, pp. 73–5.

26 Ibid.

27 Ibid.

28 Ibid.

29 IG to MMS, 16 April 1916 (O), *CL*, p. 133.

30 Scott, 'Contemporary British War-Poetry, Music, and Patriotism'.

31 IG to MMS, 23 March 1917 (P), *CL*, pp. 229–30.

32 Ibid.

33 *The Muse in Arms: A Collection of War Poems, for the most part written in the field of action, by Seamen, Solders and Flying Men who are serving, or have served in the Great War*, ed. E. B. Osborn (London: John Murray, 1917). The anthology also includes six poems by Will Harvey.

34 The suite was first performed at a concert at the RCM in June 1916.

35 MMS, 'Ivor (Bertie) Gurney', *Grove's Dictionary of Music and Musicians: Supplementary Volume*, ed. H. C. Colles (New York, 1944), p. 260.

36 MMS to HH, 5 April 1916, MSC.

37 Ibid.

38 IG to MMS, 19 January 1917 (G), *CL*, p. 194.

39 IG to MMS, 1 April 1917 (G), *CL*, p. 238.

40 Colin Taylor (1881–1973) is not to be confused with the problematic singer Mr Taylor. Colin Taylor, a composer and piano teacher, was also the music master of writer-composer Peter Warlock (Philip Heseltine) at Eton.

41 *Sunday Times*, 9 December 1917, p. 4.

42 IG to MMS, 1 August 1916 (G), *CL*, p. 129.

43 IG to MMS, 27 July 1916 (P), *CL*, pp. 124–6.

44 IG to MMS, 1 August 1916 (G), *CL*, pp. 127–8.

45 IG to HH, 21 June 1916 (P), *CL*, p. 96.

46 IG to JWH, 22 June 1916 (KT), *CL*, p. 107.

47 IG to MMS, 25 October 1916 (G), *CL*, p. 159.

48 IG to MMS, 7 January 1917 (P), *CL*, p. 181. Gurney's poem 'To Certain Comrades' was originally titled 'To the Fallen'. He never set Binyon's 'To the Fallen'.

49 IG to MMS, 5 July 1916 (KT), *CL*, p. 115.

50 IG to Matilda Chapman, July 1916 (G), *CL*, p. 122.

51 IG to MMS, 27 July 1916 (P), *CL*, p. 124. Gurney is rephrasing a line from 'When daisies pied …' in Shakespeare's *Love's Labours Lost*.

52 IG to MMS, 17 July 1916 (G), *CL*, p. 120.

53 IG to MMS, 16 August 1916 (O), *CL*, p. 133.

54 Ibid.

55 IG to MMS, 21(?) June 1916 (KT), *CL*, p. 101.

56 IG to MMS, 22 June 1916 (KT), *CL*, p. 103.

57 IG to ELV, June 1916 (KT), *CL*, p. 90.

58 IG to MMS, 21 (?) June 1916 (KT), p. 100.

59 IG to MMS, 27 July 1916 (P), *CL*, p. 125.

60 IG to MMS, 9 December 1916 (G), *CL*, p. 171.

61 Ibid.

62 IG to MMS, 16 June 1915 (P), *CL*, p. 21.

CHAPTER 12

The Dirty Business of War

B Y THE END OF March 1917, Private Ivor Gurney of the 2nd/5th Gloucesters had been in France just over ten months. He had first entered a real, but unused, trench at Riez Bailleul on 29 May 1916 for final instruction in warfare. Two days later he was 'bang in the front seats', experiencing his first strafe.[1] Although he personally saw no one wounded then and described the bombardment as 'nothing but noise and apprehension', eight of his fellow soldiers were killed within a single week.[2] In fact, by the war's end more than one-third of the men who had crossed the English Channel on the HMT 861 with Ivor would die in France.

Real war, as Ivor experienced it, was not the idealized sentimentality of Rupert Brooke's verse. It was harsh, uncompromising, uncomfortable, filthy and deadly. '[A] whiz-bang missed me and a tin of Maconachie (my dinner) by ten yards; a shower of dirt no more', he informed Marion Scott. '10 high explosives were sailing over the signaller dugout where I was in front of it. A foot would have made a considerable difference to us I think. They burst 30 yards behind.'[3] These weapons often hit their human targets, blowing men to pieces. Ivor was lucky. Others were not. A childhood friend died within a month of arriving in France, and two new friends whom he had hoped to meet after the war were also killed.[4] His respected platoon officer Lieutenant Cole died too, and Company A of the Gloucesters were massacred when, thanks to a tactical error, they ventured into No-Man's-Land. Another admired friend came up 'a cropper' in battle and was hospitalized suffering from 'a breakdown'.[5]

By June, Ivor was sharing the terror of war with Catherine Abercrombie. Perhaps because he did not have a strong emotional bond with her, he wrote with a graphic directness he did not employ in his letters to Marion Scott, Ethel Voynich and other friends, whom he seemed to be protecting from the worst of his experiences. He admitted to Mrs Abercrombie that during a surprise attack on his company he was 'filled with fear' as he crouched in a fire bay with other men waiting for 'instant destruction'.[6] The men were the targets of 'shells, rifle grenades, trench-mortar-bombs, aerial torpedoes, what not' that fell on them. Gurney, his powers of observation keen and his poetic senses alert despite the danger, described how 'out of silence there sprang the rattle of machine guns, which increased to a hell of a sound; like devils raging blasphemy in a great wind; or fretting spiteful fiends of the sea. (This is the worst of war sounds I have yet heard).'[7] He tuned his ear to the underlying voice of war: 'The sound of shells not far above one, and dropping, is exactly like the ripple of water from the bows of a little sailing boat moving say at 3 knots or 4 maybe. Or sometimes the larger ones sound like the quick intake of a huge breath of pain.'[8] The misery of Army life gripped Gurney. He told Mrs Abercrombie that he was mired in a 'rotten existence' and that 'no one outside will ever know the

Marion Margaret Scott (1877–1953) in 1911, the year she founded the Society of Women Musicians and met Ivor Gurney. Although petite and soft-spoken, she was a tough, strong-willed natural leader who knew how to channel her vision and idealism into practical schemes that benefited many people.

Henry Prince I (1764–1846), Marion Scott's American ancestor. Sea captain, adventurer, entrepreneur who dealt in cinnamon, hemp and slaves, he was among the men who ushered in the Golden Age of Sail in Salem, Massachusetts.

Sydney Charles Scott (1849–1936), a solicitor and gifted pianist, had studied with Walter Bache, a pupil of Liszt. He worked with Bache to gain wider recognition for Liszt's music in England. Scott was Marion's early accompanist.

The Scott home at 28 The Avenue (now Dulwich Wood Avenue), Gipsy Hill, located a half mile from the Crystal Palace, which became central to Marion's childhood. Marion viewed the panorama of London from her bedroom window where she often watched it become a 'pillar of fire' as the 'glow of its innumerable lights mirrored on the clouds' suffused the dark heaven with orange light.

Ernest Farrar (1885–1918), composer, pianist, organist, served as Marion's performing partner from 1909 to 1911. He dedicated music to her and sought her advice when writing violin parts. After he announced his engagement to another woman, Scott never again spoke to him.

Members of the Society of Women Musicians at their first council meeting in 1911. From left to right: Julia Cook Watson, Lucie Johnstone (who composed as 'Lewis Carey'), Gertrude Eaton (co-founder), Marion Scott (founder), Liza Lehmann (president), Katharine Eggar (co-founder), A. B. Darnell and Florence MacNaughten. The organization was open to men, who were able to join as associate members.

Sir Charles Villiers Stanford (1852–1924). Marion Scott was one of his first female students. Ivor Gurney was one of his most rebellious and challenging pupils. 'What [Stanford] demanded was not so much loyalty to himself as loyalty to his ideals', Scott observed.

An early view of the Royal College of Music.

Ivor Gurney at the Royal College of Music. When Marion Scott first noticed him in a corridor at the college he was wearing a 'thick, dark blue Severn pilot's coat, more suggestive of an outdoor life than the composition lesson ... for which he was clearly bound'. Scott was struck by the 'look of latent force in him' as he passed by her. Two weeks later he walked into her office at the Student Union and introduced himself as Ivor B. Gurney. Their friendship began.

Herbert Howells (1892–1983), one of Gurney's most valued friends. He joined Ivor at the RCM in 1912 and also enjoyed a deep friendship with Marion Scott.

Sydney Shimmin (1891–1968), a close friend of Gurney, Scott and Ethel Voynich. He taught at the Cheltenham Ladies College from 1921 to 1958.

12

Herbert Howells and Arthur Benjamin with Katherine Waterhouse and an unidentified woman, possibly Howells' wife Dorothy. Benjamin, an Australian, met Gurney and Howells at the RCM. He recognized the same force of genius in Howells that Marion Scott had detected in Gurney. Benjamin became one of Ivor's trusted confidants.

Ivor Gurney attracted strong-willed, independent, intellectual woman like Ethel Voynich (standing second from the left) as his friends. E.L.V. (1864–1960), as she was known, was also a friend of Marion Scott, who had collaborated with her on a stage production in Manchester in 1908. Voynich was a novelist, composer and translator. Prior to meeting Gurney and Scott, she had lived a life of adventure and daring as a revolutionary working in causes for the Russian people. Today she is best known as the author of The Gadfly. Her father was the mathematician George Boole. Voynich is second from the left in this family photograph. To her right is her sister Margaret ('Maggie') Taylor, another of Gurney's confidantes with whom he sometimes lodged. With them are their sisters Alicia Stott, a mathematician, Lucy Boole, a chemist, Mary Ellen Hinton, a writer. Maggie has her hand on the shoulder of her son Julian, who became a physician. He is next to his brother Geoffrey, one of the most important physicists of the twentieth century. The sisters' mother, Mary Everest Boole, a mathematician and educator, is holding Mary Stott, and next to her is Leonard Stott. George Hinton is seated. Geoffrey Taylor would later help rescue Gurney when he became trapped by the incoming tide while on a Cornish holiday with Mrs Voynich.

The Cotswolds near Painswick Beacon. Gurney knew his local landscape well and captured it in both his poetry and music.

> The Cotswolds stand out eastward as if never
> A curve of them the hand of time might change,
> Beauty sleeps more confidently for ever ...
>
> ('Above Ashleworth')

Florence Lugg Gurney (1860–1945). A seamstress, she worked with husband David in his tailor's business. Sensitive and poetic, she experienced mercurial moods like her son Ivor. Marion Scott believed that Ivor inherited his 'strange power of placing ideas in unusual juxtapositions' from her.

David Gurney (1862–1919), regarded by his children as the 'more home-loving, affectionate parent' (Winifred Gurney). Marion Scott found him to be 'gentle and slightly puzzled by life and his eldest son in particular'. Ivor believed that his father had willed him 'to say what he had never / Been able to say or sing'. The same held true of his mother but no one recognized these qualities in her.

Florence Gurney loved nature and maintained a small garden at the rear of her home. She encouraged Ivor and his younger brother Ronald to cultivate their own gardens. According to Winifred Gurney, her mother 'possessed us as babies' and 'certainly did her best to bring us up well'.

Florence Gurney with her son Ronald. She had five pregnancies and lost one child who was born between Winifred, the eldest, and Ivor.

Winifred Gurney (1886–1984), front centre, as a nurse trainee. She had previously been a teacher. During the war she served as a volunteer nurse in Gloucester while her brothers were overseas.

In the early 1950s Winifred carried on an extensive correspondence with an American student Don Ray. Her letters recall details of her family and of Ivor that might otherwise have been lost.

Dorothy Gurney (1900–1982), the youngest Gurney sibling. She emigrated to Australia early, married and reared her family there.

Ivor Gurney in his early teens with friends. His sister Winfred recalled that he was 'kindly disposed' towards their mother, but as he grew older they often clashed.

A dapper Ronald Gurney (1894–1971) in India. After his father's death in 1919 he became the head of the Gurney family, a role he took seriously.

Gloucester Cathedral and the River Severn were central to Ivor Gurney's life. As a child he roamed the river valley, the hills and the city waterfront.

Frederick W. (F. W.) Harvey (1888–1957). After Ivor met Harvey, a budding poet, in 1908, the two became inseparable friends. Harvey and Gurney wandered the countryside together, absorbing the glories of Gloucestershire. Later Gurney would set Harvey's poetry.

The Reverend Alfred H. Cheesman (1865–1941) took seriously his role as Ivor's godfather. A latter-day Renaissance man with a deep love of poetry, literature and history, he provided Ivor with a broad range of intellectual experience, opened his extensive library to him and taught him to declaim poetry. He introduced Ivor to the Hunt sisters, Emily and Margaret.

Busy Westgate Street, Gloucester, as it was in Ivor Gurney's early years. Ivor often purchased books from the Wallace Harris shop there.

daily humiliation that fills the bitter souls of all who hate the Army as I and my friends do. Iron in the soul.'[9]

In August 1916 the emotional cruelty of the war hit Gurney, striking him a terrible blow. His friend Will Harvey was reported missing after he had gone on patrol. Gurney presumed the worst. 'F.W.H. is almost certainly dead, and with him my deepest friendship ...', he wrote to Herbert Howells.[10] Ivor admitted that he had not spent much time with Will over the preceding two years, but he felt somewhat comforted that they had met accidentally the morning Harvey went out alone on patrol. Will had lent Ivor his own pocket edition of Robert Bridge's *Spirit of Man*, 'Mine for always I suppose now.'[11]

During this particularly black period Gurney was trapped in limbo, not knowing for certain the fate of his friend, but fearing the worst. He was alone and isolated from the personal contact of friends and even family whom he needed to help him through this agonizing time. Letters were his only emotional outlet. In writing to Howells, Scott and Ethel Voynich, Gurney did not begin, as one might expect, with the awful news of Will's disappearance, even though it must have torn him apart. Instead he wrote routinely about other topics and chatted quite normally as if nothing unusual had happened in his life. Then, abruptly, he introduced the story of Will's disappearance. Gurney needed the cushion of other thoughts to steel him before he could write about Harvey.

He mourned what he perceived as the 'unworthy ending for so fine a spirit, who should have died, if his destiny were to die in this horrible anonymous war, hot in the battle, in some hopeless-brave attack.'[12] He deserved a hero's death, not a sniper's bullet. Gurney paid tribute to his friend in terms that reveal a profound insight into Harvey's character and a clear understanding and unconditional acceptance of his kindred spirit. He described Will as restless, introspective, brave, generous, and kind, the possessor of 'all the gifts save only serenity' which left him 'full of unsatisfied longings.'[13] '[I]f the Fates send that I live to a great age and attain fulness [*sic*] of days and honour, nothing can alter my memory of him or the evenings we spent together at Minsterworth', Gurney explained to Scott. 'My thoughts of Bach and all firelit frosty evenings will be full of him, and the perfectest evening of Autumn will but recall him the more vividly to my memory. He is my friend, and nothing can alter that ...'[14]

Over the ensuing weeks he referred occasionally to Harvey, 'remembering with an ache what Glostershire [*sic*] is in such a season as September, and with whom I usually spent the best of it – with Will Harvey.'[15] Then, in October, Ivor rejoiced with the news that Will was not dead; he was being held a prisoner of war in a German camp. 'Yes, FWH, is well, but hungry. Tray bong [very good]! No more to be said, except – since I am freed from supposing him to be na pooh [dead], I have only to worry about not being na poohed myself, in order to meet him again.'[16]

Eventually, Gurney expressed his early anguish and later relief in his poetry. In the nostalgic 'Afterglow' in *Severn and Somme*, he recounted the joy, laughter and close bond of their youth mingled with their rapture over nature. He recalled happy memories with the Harvey family in 'The

Farm', acknowledged the publication of Will's 'A Gloucestershire Lad' in the 1917 poem 'To F. W. H', and dealt optimistically with Will's imprisonment in Germany in 'Ypres-Minsterworth'.[17]

Gurney was able to communicate with Harvey in the POW camp, which brought him comfort. He eventually sent Will a copy of his song 'Captain Stratton's Fancy' ('The Old Bold Mate'). Harvey, to whom the song was dedicated, in turn introduced it to his fellow prisoners and he wrote to Gurney 'everywhere it has been a great success'. 'Do you want to make a lot of money? If so, publish "The Old Bold Mate" either in a set of drinking songs or by itself. And stick out for a royalty.' He told Gurney that the song had become 'a household thing' at Crefeld, where he was being held, and that he had to write out dozens of copies for his fellow inmates. 'By this means it will be known all over Scotland, Wales, Ireland, Canada, Argentina, etc. within a few years of peace and you ought to reap what grain is forthcoming', Harvey continued. 'Your best things will not pay you very well I expect, but this jolly piece of fooling should make you a fortune.' [18]

Physical and emotional hardships were constant companions of the soldiers. Ivor was able to survive both reasonably well because he was physically strong and he had the ability to find solace from emotional stress through writing. No matter what devices soldiers used to protect themselves from the adversity they encountered daily, war remained an unnatural way to live.

In addition to his fellow soldiers, Ivor's trench companions included disease-spreading rats and mice, lice, which infested him badly, and flies that fed on human waste and dead bodies and then landed on the men and their food. Hygiene was non-existent. Men at war cannot change their clothes and bathe every day. '[I] don't shave, and ... Don't wash over often', Ivor admitted to Marion.[19] They often went days on end wearing the same stinking uniform stained with sweat, urine, faeces, vomit, all that nature discharges involuntarily when men are terrified and cannot control their bodily functions – an unavoidable condition of war rarely, if ever, mentioned in poetry and novels or depicted in war films.

The weather presented its own misery. In the hot and sultry summer months, the men were burdened by rough, heavy, scratchy clothing. In the cold, raw, wet winter, they lived outdoors in sleet, snow, ice and wind, piling on layer upon layer of clothing in a vain effort to keep out the cold. Soldiers were not permitted to wear their long, warm greatcoats into battle. In a word, the weather was 'execrable', according to Ivor. 'The cocoa dregs freeze in the mess tins' and 'Tis cold ... my oil-sheet is over my legs', he informed Marion at different times. Or 'the cold upset my belly and other parts'. The rains, when they came, turned the land into a churning mass of mud that sometimes drowned men unfortunate enough to slip from duck boards into the 'nasty yellow' mire. Trying to protect himself from the mud, Ivor wrapped 'horrid looking sandbags' around his legs, which made him look more like a 'scarecrow' than a soldier.[20]

Food in the trenches where they needed it most was 'skimpy' and poor. Sometimes the men reported waiting more than twelve hours for their water supply to be replenished. Ivor, a heavy smoker of cigarettes, cigars and a pipe, found Army tobacco foul. Marion's father, Sydney Scott, started sending him parcels containing quality tobacco, which Ivor shared with his mates. Food and money were more serious concerns for him. The soldiers were paid 5 francs a week, but paydays came irregularly. Everyone was broke. Paper, which was his lifeline, was very dear, and cost him one-fifth of his weekly income. 'O never was writing paper so dear ... I'll write no more ... Partly because of the huge price of bearable writing paper ...', he explained to his friend Catherine Abercrombie.[21]

In the trenches the men were lucky to get a third of a loaf of dry Army bread in their rations along with dry bully beef, hard tack biscuits and greasy stews. With Army food in short supply, soldiers bought what they could from the French, particularly coffee, beer and bread. They much preferred the great round slabs of soft moist French bread available from farmers or in the cafés, or *estaminets*, in villages. Ivor observed that most soldiers thought the French were thieves who charged outrageous prices for items they knew the soldiers were desperate to have. But for each 'thief' there were many more individuals who treated the soldiers with kindness, generosity and compassion in the face of their own personal hardship.

After days or even weeks at the Front, the men were sent to a farm or village to rest, sate their various appetites, and scrape away the wastes of war that caked their bodies and minds. In such a setting the war might seem miles away, instead of being fought, as it often was, just across the fields. Most men experienced a complete reversal of mood and found it easy to fall quickly into a new routine, a different rhythm, to put the war out of mind and live in the moment. To poet Siegfried Sassoon, being out of the trenches was like being born again.

The men much preferred to be billeted in a village where they could participate in a semblance of normal life again. La Gorgue on the marshy meadows of the River Lys, was such a place. Ivor first saw it in the summer of 1916. In peacetime La Gorgue was a cotton-manufacturing town where cotton was spun in long, low sheds running down toward the river. During war these same sheds, operating from 7 a.m. to 7 p.m., became bathhouses for the soldiers, cleansing as many as 1,000 men a day. After time in the trenches, a bath was the soldier's first priority. Clean, lice-free clothing was the second. If they were lucky, the men would be paid and could set off to enjoy all that La Gorgue had to offer: entertainment in the form of two cinemas, a theatre, a canteen where they relished comforting meals of eggs, chips and coffee, a YMCA, a reading room, many cafés where beer and wine mixed with camaraderie and brothels. The desire for women was as great as the desire for good food.

In his letters Ivor reveals very little about his activities on rest. He was much more open and fluent about the hardships of living in trenches with rats, dealing with low rations and fear while mourning the lives of 'beautiful youth wasted in the tragic tomfoolery of war'.[22] In general, being on rest drew little attention on the home front. War artists did not spend time painting scenes of men and women relaxing and enjoying rounds of drinks together in cafés. They concentrated on scenes of British-inflicted destruction of the enemy, British victory, the suffering of men, their heroism and their companionship at the Front. Graphic photographs of dead and dying soldiers were censored.[23] Since few photographs depicting men enjoying a good time on leave seem to exist, it is not unreasonable to speculate that they suffered a similar fate. If photographs of men on leave are published even today, they generally show them in convivial situations with no women visible. By contrast, photos of soldiers billeted in relative isolation on the less desirable farms where they endured discomfort in crowded tents pitched in fields are easier to find, as they were published more routinely. Rest was necessary, but it was not a dramatic or heroic aspect of war. With so many thousands of men dying each day, it was incongruous and insensitive to present images of men in uniform drinking, smiling, kissing and embracing women. After all, war was very serious business. To depict it any other way was considered irresponsible.

In one of his letters Ivor claimed that 'resting is a tiring business', but otherwise he was very close-mouthed about what he did on leave. While he says little in his letters, he drops hints of his activities in a few of his poems – 'The Estaminet', 'Robecq Again', 'On Rest', 'The Battalion is Now On Rest'. The events described appear sanitized, as if to assure readers of the soldiers' respectability.

'The Estaminet' describes a crowd of men drinking and telling stories but repeatedly drawing the conversation back to the topic of greatest interest – girls 'Vain, jolly, ugly, fair / Standoffish, foolish flighty ...', girls who offered 'kisses not a few'. After the night's revelry has ended, the men leave the estaminet in silence, 'slinking / Straight homeward(?), into bed(?)'.[24]

In 'La Gorgues', written after the war in 1919, Ivor describes a house which

> The kindest woman kept, and an unending string
> Of privates as wasps to sugar went in and out.[25]

The woman is portrayed as a miracle worker who provides comfort, peace, warmth and food to the grateful soldiers. But the image of a house so popular that it attracts men as 'wasps to sugar' suggests that men might find more than an innocent *café au lait*, beer and bread at this establishment.

Whether Gurney frequented brothels like his fellow soldiers is not known. He was not about to write of his sexual experiences in letters to Marion Scott, the Hunt sisters, Ethel Voynich or other friends. If such letters did exist, it is likely that well-meaning individuals seeking to protect and purify Ivor's image destroyed them upon receipt or later. We cannot pretend that Ivor was not a sexual being or that he would shy away from enjoying sexual pleasure. He patronized cafés, drank beer, enjoyed the company of the French people. He admired the courage of the French women.

Marion instinctively feared losing Ivor to another woman, an experience she had suffered with Ernest Farrar. As the war progressed and the danger heightened, her feelings for Ivor grew even deeper as they exchanged letters, worked together and shared their thoughts and fears. A stronger intimacy and dependency had developed between them. Every day Marion awoke knowing that word might come telling her that Ivor was dead.

The thought of losing him was unbearable to her. Her constant anxiety weakened her already fragile condition, making her even more vulnerable to the illnesses, largely digestive, that plagued her during 1916 and 1917. It is telling that once Ivor was finally out of danger, Marion seemed less troubled by health matters.

After Ivor sent her the poem 'To an Unknown Lady' in late December 1916, she wrote immediately to ask him who the 'lady' was. She might have hoped he was referring to her but more likely she suspected that he was writing about a woman he had met in France. This possibility upset her fragile sense of security. Marion's anger flared when her possessive streak was aroused. Ivor would eventually learn how vituperative Marion could be when she felt betrayed or hurt by a man. He was quick to assure her that such a lady did not exist. 'O, the Unknown Lady is really unknown. She's but a figment or a dream of passion', he explained.[26] Although Ivor claimed the woman was a product of his imagination, certain passages are unusually passionate for Gurney:

> Your careless-tender speaking, tender and low …
> We wasted thoughts of love in laughter clear …
> But in me now a burning impulse rages
> To praise our love in words like flaming gold,
> Molten and live forever …[27]

Whether this poem is truly a reflection of Ivor's dream, as he claimed, or a reality remained his secret. However, it is not difficult to see why his intensity worried Marion and caused her to wonder if he had fallen in love with another woman.

While Ivor was sending verse home to Marion from the battlefields and billets of France, she had begun to write her own poems, embracing the theme of war on the home front. Even though she and hundreds of other women who wrote about war were not experiencing battle first hand, they were as much victims of the conflict as the men in the trenches. War exempts no one. 'War is waged by men only, but it is not possible to wage it upon men only', Helena Swanwick, a feminist and pacifist, observed in 1915. 'All wars are and must be waged upon women … as well as upon men.'[28] Yet the poetry written by women during and after the war was, until the 1990s, largely overlooked or dismissed as irrelevant. Men went 'forth into battle with pulse that throbs for strife'.[29] Men knew the 'joy of action, the zeal and thrill of life' while the women stayed behind to keep the home fires burning.[30] In reality, women endured a different kind of suffering, and fought their own private wars on battlefields strewn with emotion – fear, anger, longing, compassion, grief, and perhaps worst of all, uncertainty that bred the constant anxiety Marion experienced each day Ivor was at the Front. Most British women did not witness the actual physical carnage of shattered, dismembered and bloodied bodies, but they lived with the despair, agony and sorrow wrought by death. As mothers, wives, fiancées, sisters, children and friends, they mourned the loss of men they loved.

For many women on the home front, poetry became a means of coping with war and unleashing their feelings in a society that did not encourage women to express themselves. Marion Scott could not remain silent, and turned to her old friend poetry. She cast her war experience in a sentimental and spiritual mould, contrasting, as Ivor did, the light and dark of her world. In her poems England is a haven, a shelter from the storms of war, where an 'exquisite spring' lights the land with an 'ethereal beauty'.[31] It is an idyllic place of 'vast calm waves of curving hill', with 'serenities around' until she gazes eastward across the horizon where, in the muted distance across the Channel, 'War's tides ebb and flow'.[32] She writes of innocence corrupted by war:

> You went out there to kill ...
> Out there you heard the thunder
>   And goblin-screeching shell,
> Endured the grave-like trenches,
>   Lived through a thousand hells.[33]

She assembled a small selection of her own war poems under the title of *Songs of the Five*.[34] Although the collection was never published, she signed the title page 'one of the "other" five, Marion M. Scott'. She did not identify her fellow writers, presumably referring to a group of friends who were actively writing at the same time. It seems likely that Marion and her friends intended to publish an anthology of their poetry. Her poems date from about the spring of 1916 to 1918 and reflect an emotional restraint. While poets like the American-born Mary Borden, who adopted England as her home, wrote searing anti-war poems that pre-date the poetry of Wilfred Owen and Siegfried Sassoon, Scott never lashed out against the war. She mourned its effect on England and on the men and women whose lives would never be the same in its aftermath. There is no scathing anger or bitterness in her poems, just sadness and flickers of optimism that the 'blinding showers' of war would be replaced one day by 'celestial calm'.[35]

Like Ivor, Marion found solace and hope in England's landscape. 'It is lovely to be in the country now, and it is the great spaces and great silences which are the most restful things of all', she observed in one of her war letters written at Hindhead.[36] 'In beautiful country it is beauty interpreting a still more beautiful spirit which one loves ... one gets the feeling that the lovely Earth possesses some secret – which we never quite discover in full – a secret of peace founded on some understanding of the things which only seem tragedy to us. But perhaps the Earth has always had it – perhaps she discovered it long ago'.[37]

Marion had little time to turn her thoughts, feelings and observations into poetry. She was too busy dealing with the increasing number of Ivor's poems coming to her from France while writing to him almost daily. Her letters to Ivor were not dashed off in haste but were carefully thought out and drafted, as was all of her correspondence. Marion was writing other friends as well, including Sydney Shimmin, Herbert Howells and, later in the war, to friends of Ivor's in Gloucestershire. She and her sister were rearing their niece Audrey, now eight years old. Marion was working at the RCM, leading the Society of Women Musicians as its president, organizing concerts and other events, lecturing and working on a book. She was copying entire poems that Ivor requested, negotiating with E. B. Osborn to include four of Ivor's poems in the anthology *The Muse in Arms*, even shopping to buy various items for him, all while coping with the serious illnesses that continued to plague her.[38]

In addition to reading Ivor's poetry and making suggestions, Marion was also trying to find a publisher for him. She had been successful getting his poems into the RCM magazine, edited by her friend Thomas Dunhill. She turned to Dunhill for help when, in February 1917, Ivor began to push for the publication of his book. 'The number of things mounts up – it is over twenty now', he had reminded Marion in January.[39] He suggested she approach Sidgwick & Jackson, his first choice as a possible publisher, noting 'They do print well, and good stuff', or Elkins Mathews, his second choice. 'If these publishers cannot sell, then none can', he observed.[40] With his connections at Sidgwick & Jackson, Dunhill was the perfect man to open doors for Ivor.[41]

As the editorial task of shaping the volume progressed via post, the pressing business of war continued unabated for Ivor. He managed to be remarkably productive under the worst of conditions. 'Song of Pain and Beauty' came into being with a 'Frosted finger, written lying on soaked sandbags' according to a note on a typed copy of the poem.[42] The day he composed 'By a Bierside' in a 'disused Trench Mortar emplacement', he also wrote the poem 'Strange Service'.[43]

Despite appalling conditions, Ivor's creative flame continued to burn brightly. Few soldiers at the Front were as busy as Ivor Gurney. He was writing poetry, composing songs, reading books, going through the editing process on his proposed volume of verse, carrying on written conversations with Marion Scott and other friends on a wide range of topics, all while fighting a war. While his fellow soldiers rested, Gurney stayed awake, observing them and sometimes turning what he saw into a poem. Art was everywhere and he could not resist it.

In March 1917, when Ivor was on rest after the longest time he had experienced in the trenches, two of the five songs he composed in France, 'By a Bierside' and 'In Flanders', were performed in London in versions orchestrated by Herbert Howells. No other soldier of Ivor's acquaintance could boast such an achievement.

Ivor was experiencing a familiar pattern of behaviour. His excess of activity indicates that he was in one of his manic cycles, though it was not as severe or overwhelming as past episodes had been. It did not interfere with his ability to carry out his duties, which he did admirably, nor did he plunge into his usual deep post-manic depression when he began to slow down a little at the beginning of 1917. The depression that did creep up on him took the form of introspection instead of physical collapse and illness. War was too demanding, too physical, and it didn't allow much time or space for the kind of depression into which Ivor was capable of sinking. He had to be alert every waking moment that he was in the trenches. His life and the lives of others depended on it.

Ivor was aware of his moods and how they affected his behaviour, and was frank about them with Marion. 'My Hamlet mind revolves its usual course – From the desire to set, to – the being too lazy to set, to – Self Castigation, to – the Beastly Bother of Setting, to – Half Disgust, to – Carelessness, to – Will it be Elation?' he explained to Scott.[44]

Ivor also began to express more concern for Marion and her health. He acknowledged how much she was sacrificing for him. 'Your three letters were a great pleasure to receive; they seem to keep me in touch with the things I love, and what I hope to be. Occasionally the heart in me almost dies with the strain of endurance, and the long waits and the work in the mud; then it is your letters are as stars in the night or blinks of sunlight – promises of blue', he wrote with gratitude to Scott.[45]

Ivor was growing tired of war, and watched with envy as some of the men were taken out of the line 'almost weeping for exhaustion and sheer misery' as they were carried away for treatment. 'Why do not I fall ill? God knows! The soul in me is sick with disgust, and hospital now would be a good stroke of business', he admitted to Scott.[46] In four weeks, Ivor would get his wish.

NOTES

1 IG to MMS, 7 June 1916 (P), *CL*, pp. 86–7.

2 Ibid.

3 Ibid.

4 These friends were probably Private E. Skillern and Private J. Hall, who were remembered by Gurney in his poem 'To Certain Comrades' dedicated to 'E. S. and J. H.', published in *Severn and Somme*.

5 IG to MMS, 29 June 1916 (G), *CL*, p. 111.

6 IG to Catherine Abercrombie, June 1916, reproduced in Jeff Cooper, 'Ivor Gurney and the Abercrombies', *Ivor Gurney Society Journal*, vol. 9 (2003), p. 8.

7 Ibid.

8 Ibid.

9 Ibid.

10 IG to HH, 24 August 1916 (KT), *CL*, p. 136.

11 IG to ELV, written on his birthday, 28 August 1916 (G), *CL*, p. 140.

12 IG to HH, 24 August 1916 (KT), *CL*, p. 136.

13 Ibid.

14 IG to MMS, 24 August 1916 (G), *CL*, p. 138.

15 IG to MMS, 13 September 1916 (P), *CL*, p. 145.

16 IG to HH, 30 October 1916 (P), *CL*, p. 161.

17 'The Farm', 'To F. W. H.' and 'Ypres-Minsterworth' were published in *War's Embers*.

18 From Frances Townsend, *The Laureate of Gloucestershire: The Life and Work of F. W. Harvey* (Bristol: Redcliffe Press, 1988), p. 42. 'Captain Stratton's Fancy' was published in 1920.

19 IG to MMS, 29 June 1916 (G), *CL*, p. 110.

20 Various letters to Scott, February 1917, *CL*.

21 IG to Catherine Abercrombie, June 1916 (KT), *CL*, p. 92.

22 IG to MMS, 25 March 1917 (G), *CL*, p. 234.

23 In 1932 a graphic book containing 'war's gruesome glories' was published by Brewer, Warren & Putnam of New York. Compiled by Frederick A. Barber, *The Horror of It* leaves nothing to the imagination. 'Here are pictures that tell the true story of war as words

cannot tell it', Barber wrote in his acknowledgements. 'Even more gruesome photographs could be shown – some are too horrible to print – but these will serve their purpose if they convey to the youth of our nation a realization of war in its true colours.' The book depicts men in death, some in pieces, and others who survived to endure a life of suffering from horrific wounds, particularly facial mutilation.

24 'The Estaminet', *Severn & Somme*, pp. 40–2; Thornton edition, pp. 34–6.

25 'La Gorgues' was among the poems Gurney had selected for his post-war collection *Rewards of Wonder: Poems of Cotswold, France, London*, which was not published until 2000, by MidNAG/Carcanet, edited by George Walter, pp. 64–5. 'La Gorgue' is the correct spelling but Gurney added an 's' to the name.

26 IG to MMS, 7 January 1917 (P), *CL*, p. 181. In another letter written in July, he asked Scott if he had marked a dedication on 'To an Unknown Lady'. 'I do not remember, but, for its title's sake, it must not be dedicated at all.' (27 July 1917, *CL*, p. 289.)

27 Gurney, 'To an unknown Lady', *Severn & Somme*, p. 35; Thornton edition, pp. 31–2.

28 Helena Swanwick, from *Women and War* (1915), quoted in Nosheen Khan, *Women's Poetry of the First World War* (Lexington: University Press of Kentucky, 1988), p. 2.

29 Grace Mary Golden, *Backgrounds* (Oxford: Blackwell, 1917), quoted in Khan, *Women's Poetry of the First World War*, p. 1.

30 Ibid.

31 MMS, 'Spring on Hindhead', MSC.

32 MMS, 'Spring on Hindhead II', MSC.

33 MMS, 'The Hospital Patient', MSC.

34 MMS, manuscript, MSC.

35 MMS, 'Hymn Before Dawn', MSC.

36 MMS to HH, 24 May 1916, MSC.

37 Ibid.

38 *The Muse in Arms* was published in 1917 by John Murray. Scott was acknowledged as Gurney's 'literary representative'.

39 IG to MMS, 18 January 1917 (P), *CL*, p. 189.

40 IG to MMS, 5 March 1917 (P), *CL*, p. 221.

41 Scott's friendship with Thomas Dunhill (1877–1946) dated back to their early RCM days when they were both students of Charles Stanford. They remained friends until his death. Scott, ever the promoter, was always eager to win publicity for Dunhill's music and wrote about him at every opportunity. The 24 January 1920 issue of the Boston-based *Christian Science Monitor* featured a long study of Dunhill written by Scott, who served as the newspaper's 'Special Correspondent' in London. She also wrote the entry on Dunhill in W. W. Cobbett's *Cyclopedic Survey of Chamber Music*, published in 1929. Dunhill was regarded as an authority on chamber music, and was the first recipient of the Cobbett Chamber Music Medal in 1924. In 1913 Dunhill published a standard work, *Chamber Music: A Treatise for Students*.

42 The poem is in the Gurney Archive, see *Severn and Somme*, p. 52; Thornton edition, p. 42. Gurney was 'rather proud' of 'Song of Pain and Beauty', which he dedicated to Marion Scott.

43 IG to MMS, 16 August 1916 (O), *CL*, p. 133.

44 IG to MMS, 11 January 1917 (G), *CL*, p. 184.

45 IG to MMS, 10 March 1917 (G), *CL*, p. 232.

46 IG to MMS, 7 March 1917 (G), *CL*, p. 221.

CHAPTER 13

Blighty

*T*HE WINTER OF 1916–17 was severe, unrelenting, freezing. Ivor described himself as a 'lump of panged ice' in the hellish cold that assailed the men day and night.[1] The wind blew 'gales of icy needles'.[2] Few winters had been so bad. The expatriate American writer Mildred Aldrich, who experienced war first hand at her home on a hilltop above the Marne, declared that 'Not since 1899 have I seen such cold as this in France'.[3] In January 1917 the temperature skated back and forth between 6° below zero centigrade and a bone-chilling minus 13°. The French fields had frozen solid shortly after the turn of the new year and the snow that fell promised to stay on.

While officers at the Front quaffed rum and whisky to keep out the cold, ordinary combat soldiers like Gurney were lucky if they could find a fire to thaw the ice in their water bottles, much less experience even a momentary rush of comfort and warmth from any source. Yet for some soldiers the frozen waste was preferable, less dangerous and somehow friendlier than the oozing, heaving mud that sucked men and horses to their deaths and swallowed tanks and ambulances into its seemingly bottomless depths.

Mary Borden, another expatriate American, lived with the mud for four years. As the founder-director of a mobile hospital that moved through 'the forbidden zone', a strip of land immediately behind the line of fire, Borden occupied a battlefield of her own, one strewn with mangled bodies and soaked with blood. She was as close to war as a woman could be, and like Gurney, she was acutely aware of every detail in the surreal landscape of war. She understood mud:

> This is the hymn of mud – the obscene, the
>   filthy, the putrid,
> The vast liquid grave of our armies.
> It has drowned our men.
> Its monstrous distended belly reeks with the
>   undigested dead ...[4]

By February the business of war was all consuming. As Ivor edged closer to the Somme, he feared that 'there will be little writing till this tyranny be overpast'.[5] Yet with the ground beneath his feet trembling with violent explosions, his fingers frozen, bullets and shells whizzing past him, his belly empty, and the atmosphere heavy with the stench of death, Ivor did not let war's tyranny stop the flow of his words. Although he could never be certain when he would have time to write, within a month he had sent Marion Scott nine new poems, including one of his most famous, 'The Ballad of the Three Spectres'. They continued the editing process.

In early March, confident that a publisher would be found, Ivor wrote the preface to his growing volume of poetry, *Severn and Somme*. Around the same time, he also composed one of his finest songs, 'Only the Wanderer', a setting of a poem he had written in January at Caulaincourt, where, in an attempt to find some respite from the vicious cold, Gurney opted to spend the night in a mausoleum of a ruined chateau. He and his fellow soldiers were fully aware that by doing so they risked being blown to bits by German booby traps.

By March, conditions for the men in Ivor's regiment had deteriorated. They spent three weeks in the line under almost constant fire, yet the one item that sustained them, food, was in dangerously short supply. The General Staff, confused by the rerouting of troops, had failed to deliver provisions to the men at the Front. Even Marion's generous parcels containing bread, biscuits, cake, and other delights were slow in reaching Ivor. Although he tried to diminish the seriousness of the food deprivation in his letters to her, Ivor was as 'weak as a rabbit'. The lack of nourishment made him bad tempered and upset his digestive system.[6] Nothing grew in such a barren waste of emasculated trees and frosted mud, and the soldiers were not likely to find edible game of any kind. In the minds of generals, the fact that rations were virtually non-existent was no excuse to stop fighting. The war must go on. The starving men must still work like beasts of burden. Later, Ivor would tell Marion just how much he had really suffered from the want of food and how the men were ordered to perform tasks such as hard marching and digging when they barely had the strength to put one foot in front of the other or lift a shovel.

In spite of his suffering, or perhaps because of it, Ivor continued collecting his 'ill-gained' wealth of artist's material spawned by war. 'When the war is over shall I ever write as voluminously again? I doubt it ...', he mused.[7] On another occasion, after referring to a soldier from the 7th Gloucesters who had been wounded at Gallipoli, he wrote Marion, 'I don't think it will be ever possible to tell you much about these people, but they are all part of me, stored up in the novelist part, and an influence to fulfil my music with humanity.'[8] As novelist Edith Wharton observed in 1915, '[O]ne of the most detestable things about war [is] that everything connected with it, except death and the ruin that results, is such a heightening of life, so visually stimulating and absorbing'.[9]

In a letter to Marion begun on 2 April 1917, Ivor was waiting to go 'over the top' at Vermand. 'This place is quite pretty, very pretty; and this morning I saw, at first dawn, one mystical star hanging over a line of black wood on the sky-line; surely one of the most beautiful things on earth ... O that the Nice Blighty might come soon!'[10] The next day he rejoiced when he saw 'daisies ... poking their heads out here and there – without steel helmets! O the Spring, the Spring! Come late or early, you must give hope ever to the dwellers in the house of flesh.'[11]

On 6 April the United States declared war on Germany. The next night, Good Friday, Ivor Gurney was shot. He sank to the ground, his right arm 'blazing with bright ardour of pain'.[12] In the first minutes after the bullet tore through his upper arm, Ivor feared he might be so badly injured that his wound meant 'The end of music' for him. At first he couldn't move his arm, but slowly, as the initial trauma passed, he began to feel motion returning. Stretcher-bearers bound the wound 'In the darkness whitely' and carried him to safety as a barrage of German machine gun fire sprayed the hillside.[13] He was evacuated the next day to the hospital at the 55th Infantry Base Depot at Rouen.[14]

Marion learned the news when she received a standard, Army-issue postcard written by Ivor, dated 11 April 1917. He had listed her as his 'next-of-kin'. A few days later, he wrote his first letter to Marion since the incident, informing her that he was wounded 'but not badly; perhaps not badly enough'. He claimed that his arm 'hurt badly for half an hour, but now hurts not at all', noting that there was 'no real damage ... not enough to please me ... I write with my perforated arm, so you see not much is wrong'. His dreams of Blighty soon vanished.[15]

Although he knew he would be sent back to the Front, Ivor at first welcomed the respite from war that his injury provided. He was suffering from battle fatigue and understandably felt 'illused'. But as the long, idle days passed, Ivor grew increasingly bored in hospital. There was little to read and he had no money for books. He did not feel like playing the piano in the recreation room because it was 'a mixed pleasure to play from memory things which the hearers do not care for'.[16] 'As for verse', he wrote to Marion, 'we have been altogether too harried for me to get any calm, and anyhow I seem to have run dry'. He was disgusted and felt 'sterilised' by his circumstances. 'Why cannot I not write now? Don't know, but I believe after this long frowst [frost] ... the line will give me beaucoup ideas'.[17]

While the trauma of months of action at the Front and the fact that he had been wounded would surely cause depression, the timing of this particular 'dry' stretch for Ivor coincides with the seasonal pattern of highs and lows and subsequent depression characteristic of his past behaviour. The winter months had been full and intense. Then, as spring approached, he reached his saturation point and began to come down from his high. He berated himself for this period of lethargy as if it were a defect. Nothing seemed to be moving in his brain. He did not understand that even Ivor Gurney needed to stop occasionally and rest.

Two weeks after his hospitalization, Gurney was allowed short leave, and made his way into Rouen. He went to the cathedral 'and stayed awhile in the perfect peace there. It was so still and beautiful that Bach's music mingled with the sunlight and bathed my mind with peace ...'[18] On another visit to Rouen he had his photograph taken, and sent a copy to Scott. She must have been horrified by his appearance. He looked gaunt and lifeless. His eyes, usually alive and intense, were weary and diminished in their dark hollow of puffy skin. His gaze was vacant, the empty gaze of battle fatigue. His uniform was badly rumpled and his greatcoat hung on him. He described his appearance as 'doleful'.

While Ivor was in hospital at Rouen, Marion was enduring her bout with rubella, which he described as 'queer and inconvenient'.[19] Shortly thereafter, she was suffering from the colitis brought on by a reaction to the poor food that even wealthy Londoners had to eat. Ivor observed that her 'bedroom life must be terrible in these blue and momentous days' of spring.[20] As ill as she had been that winter and spring, she was still very responsive to all of Ivor's requests. She worked diligently on his poems, contacted publishers, sent him the books and other publications he requested, and kept up her end of the correspondence. When he happened to mention that he might try setting Housman's *A Shropshire Lad*, no sooner was the letter in Marion's hand than she sent him a copy of the book along with manuscript paper so he could begin. But he wasn't ready.

Thanks to Marion, Ivor was able to keep up with current poetry in the *Poetry Review* and *The Times Literary Supplement*, while another friend sent him a copy of *Soldier Poets*, in which he found 'precious little of value' but much of interest, singling out Julian Grenfell's 'Into Battle' as the best.[21] He had also heard of 'a man named Sassoon' and remembered having seen 'quite good stuff' by him.[22]

Ivor was beginning to chafe for some action on his own poetry. 'Please rush my book into print as soon as possible', he urged Marion on 30 April.[23] Then, a couple of weeks later when the tedium of lazing about, washing clothes and playing chess was weighing on him, he announced that he was to begin training again, 'a good thing; you get frightfully slack doing nothing'.[24]

By 18 May he was back with his battalion and assigned a new number, 241281. They were training and marching toward Arras, where poet Edward Thomas had died in April, the same weekend Ivor had been shot. Gurney was talking again about Blighty, hoping for the kind of wound that would result in a large pension for him. He rambled on about living off the money and tramping about England alone. A lifestyle full of freedom was preferable, he claimed, to being a church organist and wearing a 'boiled shirt'.[25] Now that he was no longer idle, his outlook was improving and his mind seemed to be clearing. Six days later, he sent Scott a long poem, 'Spring 1917 Rouen'.[26]

Meanwhile in England, Will Harvey's book *Gloucestershire Friends* was published by Sidgwick & Jackson, the same publishers that Thomas Dunhill, as a favour to Marion, had approached about Gurney's *Severn and Somme*. The Scott family was working its way through its usual cycle of illnesses. Stella Scott was spending time away from home involved in war work, leaving Marion to take more responsibility for the care of their young niece, Audrey. Mr Scott was ill with laryngitis while Mrs Scott was suffering from the fatigue of caring for everyone with little help. Sydney Shimmin was seriously ill again with appendicitis amidst several relapses of flu. Herbert Howells was still suffering from his thyroid condition. He had become engaged to marry Dorothy Dawe, a singer he had begun to court while he was engaged to another woman.[27]

On the surface, Ivor appeared pleased for Howells but privately he wrestled with mixed feelings, which he sometimes found difficult to suppress. His inability to keep up with Howells' achievements at the RCM had lent an edge to their friendship. Then too, Gurney's admiration for his friend was tempered by disappointment as he sensed that Howells might not have the courage to live up to his gifts. Gurney once confided in his friend John Haines: 'Oh, Howells will just get married & that will be the end of him, and a Dr of music which is what he is best fitted for.'[28] By his standards,

Gurney thought Howells should be as willing as he to put his art and himself above all else.

Gurney's ambivalence is evident in a curious letter written to Howells in May 1917. Offering his congratulations on the engagement, Gurney asks, 'But why don't you write to me? Your letters are as light in the darkness or as a third of a loaf of bread instead of a quarter, up the line. And you must have other news.' [29] Then he writes somewhat sarcastically: 'And look here; I have totally forgotten whether I dedicated "By a Bierside" to you. If so, it is hereby reft away from you and given to Miss Scott. If I had given it to you, old man, please don't mind: Miss S. seems glad to have it and you can write your own masterpieces dedicated to yourself. And she has been as good as gold about everything.' [30]

Later, in the autumn, Ivor wrote to Herbert in a similar vein: 'This is a sad shock for you, bear up, my man. There is nothing dedicated to you in *Severn and Somme*. Why? Because there were too many friends to whom I wished to dedicate, and all took away from the prime dedication. Miss Scott in consideration of her faithful service has two; Will Harvey has two more which directly refer to him ... I hope you won't mind and will understand.' [31] In the letter, he continues in a joking vein as if to temper the blow he has just struck. At times Ivor's attitude towards Herbert reduced Howells, if only temporarily, to the status of a verbal punching bag. There is no evidence that he treated his other friends this way.

In the end, the plan to include separate dedications for each poem was scrapped, but Ivor did mention Howells appreciatively in his preface. The book was dedicated solely to his muse, Margaret Hunt, whose spirit Gurney carried with him to France, where it 'shone in me as light on water' and her letters 'made bright patches of love' for him in that desolate landscape. [32]

In his preface, Ivor acknowledged the friends he treasured when he wrote: '[U]nder that single name [Margaret Hunt] and sign of homage and affection, I would desire such readers as come to me to add also ... my father and mother; F. W. Harvey ... Miss Marion Scott, the Vicar of Twigworth ... Herbert Howells (and this is not the last time you will hear of him) ...' [33]

What must Ivor have truly felt to find himself trapped in France, sacrificing his career, and putting his life on the line every day, while Howells, exempted from service, remained in London, safe and free to compose music, enjoy a social life, earn money and pursue success? Yet a few weeks after writing to Howells about 'By a Bierside', Ivor's resentment turned to compassion upon learning that Herbert's poor health had forced him to give up his enviable post as assistant organist at Salisbury Cathedral. Howells was facing his own death sentence after his Grave's disease diagnosis.

Howells was not the only target of Gurney's growing resentment and frustration with his lengthening war service. In letters to Marion, Ivor could not resist tossing off the occasional stinging commentary against Stanford:

> I tell you should we return to the R.C.M., it will not do for Sir CVS to act as python to our rabbits. We live in holes, but only for protection

against Heavy Artillery, and his calibre I fear is not as huge as other more modern calibres.[34]

On another occasion, after receiving a letter from Stanford, Gurney, who flippantly referred to him as 'Dear Old Charlie', told Scott that the letter was 'nice' and 'jolly' but 'illegible'. He complained that one of Stanford's remarks 'was such as only a superannuated civilian could write – he wished he were out here. Marvellous experience, etc. Perfect civvy blither, which may be true, but chiefly is the product of ignorance, not nobility'.[35] Gurney felt that his experience dealing with 'Sergeant majors and other lovable but eccentric people' would give him 'the ability to wangle through his disfavour, if there be any'.[36]

Gurney had no idea how much Stanford himself was suffering on the emotional battlefield of the war being fought by so many at the home front. For Stanford and his wife, the war years were a lonely, frightening time. Stanford suffered badly from anxiety that reduced him to a 'bundle of nerves'.[37] His doctor insisted that he sleep outside the City at Windsor, but allowed him to return to London only by day. During this difficult time, Stanford 'began to show signs of the trouble which eventually brought about his death. Whether this was due to the air raids or not one cannot say; but it must have been so in the opinion of his doctor ...'[38]

Stanford's son Guy served in the Devonshire Regiment. He was at the Front when he suffered acute appendicitis and was sent home. Stanford's daughter Geraldine served in a private hospital in Surrey and in France before serving at Lady Forbes-Leith's Private Hospital at Torquay. The war, with all its uncertainty and danger, diminished Stanford, a fact that seems to have eluded Gurney as he continued his verbal assaults in letters to Scott.

As spring drifted into summer, Ivor began to feel ideas stirring in him. He was eager to finish *Severn and Somme* to, as he put it, 'get the thing off my chest, and my chest out of Khaki'.[39] He longed to return to England 'To hear strings again, strings that can tear the heart out of any mystery. To ramble round second-hand bookstalls, begriming one's eager hands ... To see grey stone and Cotswold gardens ... To be continually drinking tea and playing Bach of evenings. To be free and interested ...'[40]

He sent more poems to Marion and informed her that 'In my head is "On Wenlock Edge" waiting to be written ...'[41] He remained sensitive to the beauty around him and savoured it. 'We are ... in a charming village [Buire au Bois], where there are roses, roses, roses; honeysuckle not fifty yards from me, cheaper drinks, orchards, little hills ... and houses tinted white, or pink or pale blue; very charming against the green, the continual leafage of French village'.[42] But on some days, when the reality of war laid heavily upon him, he found it 'hard to live a fine life in surroundings like this; not impossible, but nearly so for myself; who need intellectual work to steady me ... And since Music and books and my friends are not this life, therefore Life itself lacks the vital impulse and natural joy'.[43]

Ivor had become his platoon's best marksman. On 15 July he learned that he was to be transferred to the 184th Machine Gun Company. This order came as 'rather a wrench' to Ivor, who had made 'many good friends' who showed 'real regret' that he was leaving them.[44] His disappointment was soon tempered. Within 30 minutes of learning that he had been transferred, he received a telegram that would change his life. It was from Marion Scott, and read simply, 'Sidgwick will publish your book'.[45] The months of waiting were over. Their partnership had given birth to a literary offspring. Gurney referred to *Severn and Somme* as Marion's 'foster child carefully reared and baptised by you'.[46]

'Never was I so flabbergasted to get anything Postal as that telegram', he wrote to Scott a few days later. 'Who could it be from, and what was it about? Its being French in form put me off, the flimsy blue after our larger yellow. Well, S and J had not made the Great Refusal. I take this as an omen'.[47] Thomas Dunhill and Marion Scott had come through for him and Ivor was appreciative. '[T]o return to my book. I hope you will triumph and get joy therefrom, since you had done all the dirty work. I doubt that it would have been written but for you'.[48]

As Ivor's battalion headed for Ypres in Flanders, the business of book publishing played a sweet harmony to the dissonance of war. When Marion sent Ivor the terms of his contract, he was pleased, but suggested that she could negotiate a better deal 'since publishers are our lawful prey and natural enemies'.[49] As it stood, he would earn 10 per cent on all copies sold after the first 500 and up to 2,000. His royalties increased to 15 per cent from 2,000 to 10,000 copies and to 25 per cent if sales went above 10,000.

Gurney told Scott that he did not write the book for money, but that it was 'chiefly an occupation and mind exercise' to free himself from the circumstances of his existence in France, cold feet, lice and fear. However, with publication at hand, he began to see his situation differently. '[I] really do not see why the book should not pay, though I do not expect any very laudatory reviews in the *Times* etc. You have won the preliminary skirmishes anyhow'.[50] As the days passed, he acknowledged to Marion that 'Yes, I think with you that Sidgwick and Jackson have treated us very well, and you have no need to chivvy them very much more. ... It is surely a good omen for sales (and reviews) that a firm like Sidgwick's has closed quickly with the book and offered good terms?'[51]

Ivor was eager to share his success with Herbert Howells and Sydney Shimmin, but as was his habit when relating important news, he buried it in the middle of his letters. To Howells, he wrote, 'Well, you must know that Miss Scott and myself have passed the first most dangerous channel with my book, and soon I hope will be bearing strongly out to sea with Publication ...'[52] To Shimmin: 'You have heard perhaps of my Tome, now accepted by the high and mighty Sidgwick and Jackson. They will fork out too bless 'em'.[53]

As the business end of publishing took final form, Ivor wrote to Marion telling her not to send anything for him to sign, because 'You have full power over all matters of business connected with *Severn and Somme* ... trouble not the master'.[54] But that simple statement was not enough. In handing over his business affairs to Marion, Ivor had created a legal problem. Always cautious, Marion turned to her solicitor father to determine how best to protect the interests of everyone concerned. Mr Scott advised Ivor to send a letter directly to Sidgwick & Jackson, stating clearly that he had given Marion Scott 'full authority to do whatever she may please to do in regard to *Severn and Somme*. ... And so I wash my hands of all business arrangements while I am in France'.[55] He also listed his permanent address as 'c/o Miss Scott, 92 Westbourne Terrace, Hyde Park, London w2'.[56]

By the end of July the weather in France had turned nasty. The rains fell. The earth churned with thick mud. The air was chilled. 'Tonight I saw small birds settled together on a telegraph wire, and that was surely enough sign of Autumn, "that leads on Winter and confounds him quite," and us; but this Winter will be better than last', he prophesied.[57] As Ivor waited to return to the line, he received unexpected, disturbing news from home. Sydney Shimmin's younger sister, Mona, who was one of Ivor's correspondents, had apparently suffered a nervous breakdown and committed suicide. Shortly before he received this news, he had asked after Mona since he had not heard from her in a while. '[W]ho could have expected anything of the kind?', he wrote to Shimmin. 'I suppose her breakdown was due to overwork, and if so she has truly died for England as any the most brave soldier in the line.'[58] Ivor lived with death every day in France and could even talk dispassionately about witnessing the death of a German pilot who was shot down and whose body landed 'not 30 yards from me. The only exciting, really thrilling thing I have seen in France.'[59] Yet he found it 'Strange to hear of Death from England.'[60]

As August edged closer to September, Ivor was growing discouraged, disillusioned and lonely. The ruins of war made the country look like 'the last Hell of desolation'. He longed to 'wake up tomorrow to find it all a dream, myself in London just before teatime, making ready to visit you ... there is stuff enough in me to talk for ages. ... Yarns that I think would strike you pink, and petrify your ear', he wrote to Scott.[61] He looked forward to the day when he and Marion could play Beethoven's 'Kreutzer' sonata 'most stormfully'. He was 'sick of being away from all my friends'.[62] He was sick of living in what he called 'slum' conditions.

In his new job as a machine gunner Ivor faced grave danger. He got caught in a barrage of German shells and reported to Marion that he was hit twice by shrapnel, 'once on the blessed old tin hat, (dent and scar) and one on the belt (no mark)'.[63] He was nearly shot by a sniper, but as a machine gunner he could put some distance between himself and the men he was being paid to kill. He no longer had to consider the horrible screams of Germans he might run through with his bayonet. 'I have never really reconciled myself to the thought of sticking a man', he admitted to Marion.[64] He had experienced his first gas attack. He was angry. His letters to Marion became more graphic than they had been. He was no longer going to spare her from the real horror of war as he knew it.

'[I]t is not fit for men to be here – in this tormented dry-fevered marsh where men die and are left to rot because of snipers and the callousness that War breeds ... Why does this war of spirit take on such dread forms of ugliness, and why should a high triumph be signified by a body shattered, black, stinking; avoided by day, stumbled over by night ... What consolation can be given me as I look upon and endure it? [G]od should have done better for us than this ...' He was hoping again for Blighty, this time a wound that would put him out of action. 'O if it were but a small hole in the leg!' [65]

When Ivor's Blighty finally came, he was not even aware of it. Writing to Scott on 12 September, he reported that his throat was 'still sore from gas; ... as if I had had catarrh, but only an occasional explosion of coughing is left now'.[66] He assumed that his exposure to gas had been mild and 'no worse than a bad cold'.[67] He foresaw 'No luck' for Blighty, but he was wrong.

By the 17th he was out of the line, resting and content to have a break. He used the time to correct the proofs of *Severn and Somme* that had arrived the day before he 'went sick'. He made light of his condition, but the effects of the gas on his system worsened, and by 22 September Ivor was 'steaming down the loveliest river in the world, in the loveliest weather'. The River Seine, Ivor's route to freedom, struck him as 'one splendid Symphony, the greatest I have ever seen'. At last he had his Blighty. He was able to joke with Scott that he would soon be telling her all about himself and analysing his emotions 'till you are bored stiff'.[68]

But as he looked around him, he was keenly aware that none of his fellow soldiers appeared well. Even though they were heading back to the shores of England and safety, Gurney observed: 'There was not any more jollity than if it were merely Another Move. The iron had entered their souls, and they were still fast bound; unable to realize what tremendous changes of life had come to them for a while.' [69]

NOTES

1 IG, 'The Retreat', *CP*, p. 262.

2 IG to MMS, 14 February 1917 (P), *CL*, p. 211.

3 Mildred Aldrich, *On the Edge of the War Zone* (Boston, MA: Small Maynard & Company, 1917). Aldrich (1853–1928), who was from Massachusetts, settled in France in 1898. She wrote best-selling accounts of her war experiences beginning with her classic *A Hilltop on the Marne*, which was a series of letters to her friends Gertrude Stein and Alice B. Toklas. In 1922 the French government awarded Aldrich the Medal of the Legion of Honour, stating that her books helped 'to sway American opinion toward entrance into World War One'. Aldrich, who was never financially secure, donated most of the income from her books to aid the families of French soldiers killed or maimed in the war.

4 Mary Borden, 'The Song of the Mud', *The Forbidden Zone* (Garden City, NY: Doubleday, Doran, 1929). Borden (1886–1968) was born in Chicago and educated at Vassar College, but settled in England after her first marriage prior to the war. During World War I she established a mobile hospital using her own money, and spent the entire war in France directing its operation in an area known as *The Forbidden Zone*. The French government awarded her the Croix de Guerre and she was named a member of the Legion of Honour for her service during World War I. After the war Borden became a controversial figure whose best-selling novels challenged conventional views of marriage and religion.

5 IG to MMS, 17 February 1917 (P), *CL*, p. 201.

6 'The Retreat', *CP*, p. 264.

7 IG to MMS, 10 March 1917 (G), *CL*, p. 223.

8 IG to MMS, 26 March 1917 (G), *CL*, p. 235.

9 Edith Wharton, 'In the North', *Fighting France* (New York: Charles Scribner & Sons, 1918).

10 IG to MMS, 2 April 1917 (G), *CL*, pp. 239–40.

11 Ibid.

12 'The Retreat', *CP*, p. 265.

13 Ibid.

14 The poet Edward Thomas, whose poetry Gurney admired and would later set to music, was killed at Arras on 9 April.

15 IG to MMS, 14 April 1917, *CL*, p. 242.

16 IG to MMS, 21 April 1917 (P), *CL*, p. 246.

17 IG to MMS, 4 May 1917 (P), *CL*, p. 251.

18 IG to SGS, 24 April 1917 (P), *CL*, p. 247.

19 IG to MMS, 30 April 1917 (P), *CL*, p. 248.

20 IG to MMS, 4 May 1917 (P), p. 251.

21 Julian Grenfell (1888–1915) was a professional soldier who wrote, 'I *adore* war', likening it to a 'big picnic' and claiming that 'One loves one's fellow-man so much more when one is bent on killing him.' Grenfell was killed in May 1915.

22 IG to MMS, 4 May 1917 (P), p. 251.

23 IG to MMS, 30 April 1917 (P), p. 249.

24 IG to MMS, 4 May 1917 (P), p. 252.

25 IG to MMS, 18 May 1917 (G), *CL*, p. 262.

26 Although 'Spring. Rouen, May 1917' was included in *Severn and Somme* and a critic singled it out for praise, Gurney was not pleased with it. 'Why the Ruddy Hades did I write "Spring 1917"? Why, O why did I, did I write ...' he groaned in a letter to Marion Scott. See *Severn and Somme*, pp. 53–6; Thornton edition, pp. 42–5.

27 Howells was engaged to Kathleen Smale, who was to become the mother of actress Deborah Kerr. Howells was not a monogamous husband and had numerous love affairs throughout his long life (Paul Spicer, *Herbert Howells* (Bridgend: Seren, 1998)).

28 John Haines quoted in a letter from Gerald Finzi to composer Robin Milford, in Stephen Banfield, *Gerald Finzi: An English Composer* (London: Faber & Faber, 1997), p. 64.

29 IG to HH, 18(?) May 1917 (KT), *CL*, p. 260.

30 Ibid.

31 IG to HH, autumn 1917 (PB), *CL*, pp. 344–5.

32 IG, 'On a Memory', *OIG*, p. 148.

33 IG, Preface, *Severn and Somme*, 1917.

34 IG to MMS, 24 August 1916 (P), *CL*, p. 138.

35 IG to MMS, 17 August 1917 (P), *CL*, p. 300.

36 IG to MMS, 11 February 1918 (P), *CL*, p. 403.

37 Harry Plunket Greene, *Charles Villiers Stanford* (London: Edward Arnold, 1935), p. 269.

38 Ibid.

39 IG to MMS, 4 June 1917 (P), *CL*, p. 268.

40 IG to MMS, 25 June 1917 (G), *CL*, p. 275.

41 IG to MMS, 11 June 1917 (G), *CL*, p. 272.

42 IG to MMS, 25 June 1917 (G), *CL*, p. 275.

43 IG to MMS, 1 July 1917 (G), *CL*, p. 277.

44 IG to MMS, 15 July 1917 (KT), *CL*, p. 284.

45 MSS to IG, telegram, GA.

46 IG to MMS, 27 November 1917 (P), *CL*, p. 374.

47 IG to MMS, 27 July 1917, *CL*, p. 285.

48 Ibid.

49 IG to MMS, 27 July 1917 (P), *CL*, p. 287.

50 Ibid.

51 IG to MMS, around 27 July 1917, *CL*, p. 291.

52 IG to HH, 31 July 1917 (P), *CL*, p. 292.

53 IG to SGS, 31 July 1917 (KT), *CL*, p. 292.

54 IG to MMS, 3 August 1917 (P), *CL*, p. 295.

55 IG to Sidgwick & Jackson, around 8 August 1917, *CL*, p. 298. Gurney sent the letter to Scott with his letter to her of 8 August 1917 (G), *CL*, p. 299.

56 Ibid.

57 IG to MMS, 8 August 1917 (G), *CL*, p. 299. Gurney wrote two letters to Scott on this date.

58 IG to SGS, 14 August 1917 (P), *CL*, p. 300.

59 IG to MMS, around 23 August 1917, *CL*, p. 309.

60 IG to MMS, 14 August 1917 (P), *CL*, p. 300.

61 IG to MMS, 23 August 1917 (P), *CL*, p. 307.

62 IG to MMS, no date but enclosed with letter of 23 August 1917, *CL*, pp. 307–9.

63 IG to MMS, 24 August 1917 (G), *CL*, p. 310.

64 IG to MMS, 22 July 1917 (P), p. 285.

65 IG to MMS, early September 1917 (KT), *CL*, pp. 320–1.

66 IG to MMS, 12 September 1917 (G), *CL*, pp. 325–6.

67 IG to MMS, 17 September 1917 (KT), *CL*, p. 326.

68 IG to MMS, 22 September 1917 (G), *CL*, pp. 328–9.

69 IG to MMS, 26 September 1917 (G), *CL*, p. 330.

CHAPTER 14

'Love has come to bind me fast'

*T*HE TRAIN carrying sick and wounded soldiers from the battlefields of France via Southampton pulled into the railway siding at the Edinburgh War Hospital, Bangour, in the early morning hours of 23 September 1917. Private Ivor Gurney, too ill to walk, was carried on a stretcher to a warm, well-lit reception area, where he was evaluated and processed along with the 150 to 250 other men who had arrived on the same train. He was then moved to a waiting ambulance and driven through the darkness to a hill on the western edge of the grounds, where attendants carried him directly to his bed in Ward 24.

Before leaving France with his 'Blighty', Ivor had been given the option of choosing a hospital in one of six districts in Great Britain, which included Gloucester and ranged from 'Bristol, Cardiff, Birmingham and somewhere to the East.'[1] Claiming he knew that getting into hospital in England 'was practically a fluke', he selected Bangour. 'I wished to see Scotland, Edinburgh in particular, so why not?'[2] But Ivor had a more devious reason behind his decision: he did not want family and friends to visit him. He knew that the long distance from London and Gloucester and the 'fearfully high' railway fares would deter people from making the journey.[3] He had no way of knowing that he had selected one of the finest military hospitals in all of Britain.

The Edinburgh War Hospital, which opened officially on 12 June 1915 with 100 patients, had moved rapidly into the forefront of medical advances, particularly in orthopaedic surgery, bone grafting, nerve suturing, tendon transplants, radiology, amputations and in the treatment of serious diseases, including malaria, dysentery and black water fever. Prior to being pressed into service as a war hospital, the facility was known as the Bangour Village Hospital, a centre for the compassionate care of the 'mentally insane'. The visionary founders felt patients could 'best be provided for by isolating them in the country where they would benefit from the peace, solitude and fresh air while at the same time being more easily occupied labouring on the land'.[4]

When it opened in 1906, Bangour, meaning 'the hill of wild goats', was set on 200 acres of woodland between 500 and 750 feet up the south side of the Bathgate Hills. The land was once the home of the poet William Hamilton (1704–54). The hospital was a model of its kind, where the goal of the doctors, nurses and staff was to provide 'a bright, cheerful effect' to ensure that the patients had 'liberty and freedom of action'.[5] Bangour Village was remarkable in many ways. Every consideration was given to the comfort and care of patients, their families and staff. The mentally ill were treated with respect and compassion. The use of force, strait jackets and other restraints was strictly forbidden, and there were no padded cells, bolts on the doors or shutters on the windows. Patients enjoyed an unusual degree of freedom and were encouraged but not forced to work in the various hospital facilities or at jobs such as needlework. Fresh air, light, space, cleanliness, the inclusion of plants and the careful choice of colours provided bright, cheerful and pleasant living space for patients. Staff were encouraged and advised 'for their health's sake to get away from their surroundings when off duty and to mix with their friends in the outside world ...'[6] Bangour boasted its own private railway line, the 'Wee Bangour Express', with cheap fares for the convenience of patients' families and the staff. It had its own power generating station and reservoir with a capacity of over 16 million gallons of water. The water was so pure and soft that it only needed to be passed through a series of sand filters before it could be used in the hospital. The reservoir was stocked with trout. In addition, Bangour had several farms, a dairy, bakery, laundry, nursery and recreation hall, all on site. As both an asylum and in its role as a war hospital, Bangour acquired a reputation as 'a haven of peace'. By the time Ivor arrived, the facility was accommodating nearly 3,000 men in light, airy buildings called 'villas' or in tents known as 'marquees' which were set up on the grounds for the care of those less seriously ill when villas reached full capacity. Black soldiers were not segregated from white, and were treated equally.

In addition to benefiting from the best medical care, the soldiers at Bangour enjoyed other advantages. Ensuring the personal comfort of the men and providing for their needs was of paramount importance. Patients were well fed and ate better than the majority of the civilian population. The hospital ran a self-sufficient farm, which ensured that the men were served fresh vegetables and milk along with beef, pork, and bacon. They also enjoyed a weekly Friday treat of fresh haddock and chips. All meals were prepared by a large staff in the central kitchen and delivered hot on horse-drawn carts. Each ward also had its own small kitchen, where the kettle was on the boil around the clock. The soldiers were supplied with writing paper, postcards and postage stamps thanks to Mrs John Keay, the wife of the commanding officer, who solicited these items from the nearby community of Dechmont. The men enjoyed picnics on the peaceful grounds as well as frequent ward parties, music, lectures and other entertainments. Plants, flowers and even small trees from the hospital's nursery and gardens further brightened their quarters.

After sixteen months at the Front living in extreme filth, sleeping on the cold, wet ground, and inhaling the stench of death, Bangour hit Ivor like a ray of summer sunshine. He was clean, lice-free, and sleeping between 'sheets white and smooth'. Within twenty-four hours of his arrival, he was up and about and even spent two hours playing the piano. He fell immediately into hospital routines and was calmed by the 'noises domestic' and the 'flurries and scurries' of the nurses and volunteers as they went about their demanding work.[7] 'With quiet tread, with softly smiling faces / The nurses move like music through the room', Gurney later wrote in his poem 'Hospital Pictures – Ladies of Charity'.[8]

Ward 24 was a medical accommodation where victims of German gas or those suffering from malaria, dysentery and other illnesses were treated. 'Our shifts were so long that we all had to be resident; hours did not matter', recalled Effie Day, a volunteer nurse in Ward 24. 'If an ambulance train came in we were all there until every single patient was cared for.' [9] Ward 24, dubbed the 'Ragtime Ward', had a contagious, lively, upbeat spirit all its own that made it the envy of Bangour. Everyone worked together, not just nurses and doctors. Patients who were not confined to bed were encouraged to help serve meals and perform other small but time-consuming tasks which freed the sisters and VADs for nursing.

Bangour had the soothing effect of a holiday retreat on Ivor and the other soldiers, but the enforced idleness soon began to wear on him as it had done when he was hospitalized in Rouen. After only a few days in hospital he was impatient and restless. '[S]taying in bed makes me unfit in no time – a bundle of oppressed nerves', he informed Marion Scott.[10] 'Now and here, in this light clean room, there is nothing for me but the old feeling of inefficiency, sadly wasted time, still buried talents, and a sense of shame at my continual grumbles where others are content.' [11] He was suffering from 'fatheadedness and unfitness and indigestion from doing nothing and eating too much.'[12]

Finally freed from the heavy hand of the censor, Ivor shared some of his experiences with Marion, drawing her a detailed verbal road map of his travels in France. At times, he was not even sure where he had been; the places blurred one into another in his steady march along the Front. His revelations were disturbing to Marion. She wanted to hold onto her image of Ivor as a romantic figure, who, by virtue of being a poet and composer, possessed more sensitive character traits than his fellow soldiers and would not sink as low as other men. But Scott was a realist. She knew that war was a sordid business that turned respectable men into animals, even if only temporarily. She understood reality better than most and had certainly sensed, against her will, that Ivor was indeed no different from any other man thrust into war. If she only suspected this to be true of him from a foul and offensive smelling souvenir he once sent to her, she now had proof in his own words.[13]

The base reality was that Ivor Gurney, the sensitive and gentle poet-composer, had killed other men, scavenged their rotting mutilated bodies, stolen from them without a pang of guilt and then expressed regret that he was not able to steal more. Men took what they could use and carry – food, revolvers, watches, rings, badges, compasses, books, papers. Ivor confided in Marion that after one battle he had spent an hour taking tea and sugar from dead men. He called this activity 'salvaging'.[14] 'O the souvenirs I might have had! But only officers have any real good chance of souvenirs, since only they can get them off', he wrote, adding that officers could make themselves 'rich with booty'. But low ranking combat soldiers like Ivor who 'could not carry [their plunder] very well, and had no place to store things and hardly a leave' often left a scene empty-handed. 'You see, if one finds something interesting, it may be a hot corner, and how is one to carry it, for the haversack is full. Suppose one gets it out the line, then one must wait for leave, or a friend's leave. And if a wound comes all your stuff is lost', he explained as coolly as if he were describing an unsuccessful shopping expedition.

'The A.S.C. do well, for they have room to store. R.T. officers, with Real Homes. Brass Hats can get what they would. Only the poor fool who goes over the top – and under the bottom – seems to be without anything at all', he wrote. Ivor's biggest regret seems not to have been that he had stolen from the dead, or even that he had killed other men, but that while on training near the Front he and other men had 'trampled down crops and crops enough to make you sick. But what cared Brass-hats for all-day-light labour gone to ruin?' Ivor had detached himself temporarily from his humanity, his means of coping with the grim reality all around him. But away from the battlefield and safe at Bangour, he wrote too about what the combat soldier truly valued. 'It is only fair to say that ... with bare life, warmth, and food, he must be counted rich ... [He] doesn't care a ha'penny obscenity about souvenirs save in his leg or arm; marketable, magic-carpet-like, transmuting talismans as they are.' The talismans were the bullet and shrapnel wounds, mustard gas and illness that brought a soldier his 'Blighty', his ticket to life.

In another letter he explained the slang of war to Marion, keeping the vocabulary far more decorous than it was in the trenches, where cursing was 'frequently foul', expected, accepted, companionable and often the only way to react to danger, horror and death. The strongest word he uses in his discourse is 'Hell', but he invites Marion to fill in the blanks: 'The Germans, in anger, are referred to as "them — bastards".'[15] Although he wrote more openly and honestly to Marion about army life, he never again referred to his own sordid activities in extant letters.

Life in Ward 24 began to brighten for Ivor during his second week at Bangour. He made new friends, noticed a 'charming and tender' volunteer nurse, Annie Nelson Drummond, and met the Reverend Doctor T. Ratcliffe Barnett, chaplain at the Edinburgh War Hospital and a Presbyterian minister in the Free Church of Scotland.[16]

Ivor first encountered Barnett on the evening of 3 October when he attended the chaplain's impressive lecture on Adam Smith. After two and a half years in the army cut off from his friends and the world of ideas, Ivor was starved for intellectual stimulation, and both the lecture and the man who presented it thrilled him. 'I could have sat all night', he wrote to Marion the next day. 'He had a slip of paper with subjects for the next ten weeks, and O but I wished him to use them all – to start with Adam Smith and go on to Nelson!'[17] Within a few days, Ivor made himself known to Barnett and they established a stimulating friendship. Barnett was no ordinary minister, a fact that Ivor detected immediately, noting that his chaplain was '[A] Truth-teller, Lecturer on English Literature, Mountaineer, Lover of Men, Music, and Books.'[18] But there was much more to this dynamic middle-aged man with his 'eyes that can look you through ... a fine head with a Roman nose defiant at the fore ... A great man to finish with whose aim at present is to set men at ease when they talk to him.'[19]

Thomas Ratcliffe Barnett, the son of James Barnett and Janet Ratcliffe, was born at Kilbarchan, a weaving centre in Renfrewshire, on 23 December 1868. Educated at John Neilson's Institution at Paisley, the University of Glasgow and the United Presbyterian College, Edinburgh, he was ordained on 20 October 1899 and inducted to Fala, Blackshiels in the Lammermoor Hills.[20] He married Margaret 'Maggie' Muirhead Forrest in 1900 and they had two daughters, Margaret and Janet.[21]

In 1914 Reverend Ratcliffe Barnett was called to Greenbank Church in the Morningside section of Edinburgh, where he began a highly successful ministry. He drew young people to the parish, swelled the congregation of fewer than 300 members to 850 and during his long tenure raised thousands of pounds to build a new church. However, the outbreak of war cast a shadow over Barnett's plans for his parish. Soon members of the church were dying in France. His monthly messages in the church publication *Leaflet* reveal how deeply the war and the suffering of the men and women at the Front affected him. In the summer of 1916, at the age of forty-eight, he decided to join them, and spent three months serving at a YMCA hospital hut at Étretat, France. As a result of this sobering and heart-rending experience, he volunteered to act as chaplain at the Edinburgh War Hospital, some 16 miles west of his parish. In addition to conducting Sunday services, Barnett spent Wednesdays meeting with the patients and ended the day with a lecture, usually on English literature, at 6 p.m.

When Gurney met him, Barnett was already an established author and newspaper columnist with seven popular books to his credit. Between 1913 and 1915 alone, he published *Reminiscences of Old Scots Folk*, *The Winds of Dawn*, and *The Makers of the Kirk* and would go on to write another ten books before his death in 1946. Like Gurney, Barnett loved nature and walking. A keen observer, he was essentially a travel writer. The majority of his books deal with his impressions of different places in Scotland, the people who inhabited them and their history. Barnett's books reveal him as a humorist, poet, artist and above all, a mystic who understood and respected Celtic legends and beliefs. He was an avid beekeeper and golfer, but most importantly to Ivor, Barnett was also an accomplished musician, who played the violin and the bagpipes in public. His books occasionally contained one or two of his poems as well as beautifully drawn and sometimes whimsical maps complete with sea monsters, spouting whales and ships. His metaphysical viewpoint is reflected throughout his books in observations such as 'Mountains always speak with a mystic voice to those who love them. But that voice can only be heard by those who climb and it is heard best by those who climb alone. You must woo Nature in solitude and silence if you would enter into her secrets.' Marion Scott was also a metaphysician who shared Barnett's beliefs and vision and who sought solace in mountains. They never met.[22]

Barnett had learned of Ivor's 'literary dealings' and gave him a copy of *Reminiscences of Old Scots Folk*, which he inscribed 'My House an Ever Open Door to You.' The inscription refers to an experience Barnett had in Galloway. In his essay 'The Hidden Sanctuary' he writes of hearing about a church 'among the trees' where it was 'the desire of the minister that the door of the church should never be closed.' [23] He was well aware that the Presbyterian church was commonly known as 'the religion with the closed door'. Churches were only open on Sunday for public worship and closed the other six days of the week, thus limiting access. He could not believe that the door of the little church in Galloway stood open all night so he set out at night to see for himself.

'There was a touch of frost in the September air ... [as] down the road I wandered to the gate and up the pitchy avenue under stilly trees', he wrote. Beyond the gleam of graves, he saw the church and groped his way to it in the dark, passing his fingers along the wall until he found the door. It was standing wide open and he could find no means to close it. 'Wayfaring men ... might slip in here to sleep, to make a vow, or to pray', he wrote. 'After all, was it not their Father's House? Who then dare close the door? I looked at the stars quivering above the graves and wondered what God thought of our narrow ways. Then I went into the pitch dark church and made my vow. From that day to this the door of another church has been open every day of the year.'

Ivor made a lasting impression on Barnett and was probably one of the few men the clergyman met at the hospital who shared so many of his own interests and had such wide knowledge. Later, Barnett invited Ivor to play the piano for officers at the Edinburgh War Hospital. He performed an ambitious programme of Beethoven, Bach and Chopin, and was pleased to report to Marion that the officers 'listened beautifully', while 'Mr. Barnett ... listened in a pure ecstasy.' [24] Ivor had copied out 'By a Bierside' for Barnett, who insisted that Ivor sing it for him along with 'The Folly of Being Comforted'. The evening was a great success.

Gurney had informed Marion Scott that Mr Barnett was going to try to arrange an outing for him in Edinburgh, 'a complete tour of everything that can be packed into a short stay'. He mentioned to Scott that Barnett was a 'great friend of Lord Guthrie who owns the R.L.S. [Robert Louis Stevenson] house' at Swanston. Lord Guthrie had taken an interest in another young poet Wilfred Owen, who was then hospitalized at Craiglockhart in Edinburgh. Swanston and Morningside, where Reverend Barnett lived and where his church was located, are all within a short distance of each other. Arthur Brock, Owen's doctor at Craiglockhart had introduced Owen to Lord Charles Guthrie. Guthrie, a judge, historian and friend of Robert Louis Stevenson, liked Wilfred immediately and was so impressed by the young soldier that he talked him into helping him do some historical research in the Edinburgh libraries. Owen was far from enthusiastic about the assignment and felt he had fallen into 'a trap.' [25]

Ivor longed to visit Edinburgh but his physical condition was serious enough that doctors kept him confined to his ward and the grounds. He was on a light diet, weak and not up to making the train journey to the city. Even the simple task of wiping cutlery and plates after a meal tired him. He was disappointed when Barnett left for a week, but he had made other friends – a sailor he identified only as Nielson and T. Evans, a Welsh miner. Both men were the strong, rugged type that Ivor found attractive, men who laboured hard and told tales of their adventures.

Nielson, 'brave as a lion' and 'tender-hearted as a child', impressed Ivor with his stories of Norway, Iceland and the Shetland Islands and of the men who lived with the sea. He found Nielson's 'wrinkled wise face and deep eyes ... lovely to look at' and claimed that they gave him 'strength'.

Through Nielson's talk 'ran ever the old charm of moving salt green water, and the pictures of fearless sailors taking their chance'. When Nielson was discharged from hospital, Ivor did not ask for his address, believing it 'wiser, since he is there in my mind as clear as life ...' [26] For Ivor, Nielson was a man's man, hardy, strong, invincible.

Ivor's interest in Private T. Evans took on a different hue. Although Evans made his living as a miner, Ivor felt he deserved a better fate. He defined him as a 'Welsh singer' who should give his 'service to the muse'. If Ivor saw Nielson as an external force of brawn and grit, he detected a 'primal fire' and a 'restless spirit' in Evans and believed that his musical gifts should be developed.[27] Ivor became solicitous and protective of Evans. As he often did when he needed help or had a mission, he turned to Marion Scott, asking her to assist Evans upon his return home to London.[28] Ivor explained to Marion that Evans was 'horribly depressed, what with sickness of mind and body'.[29] He asked her to invite Evans to visit with her and requested that she give him concert tickets so that he might hear serious music and be fuelled to cultivate more knowledge of it. 'You will not often get a chance of doing so much good so easily as in this instance', he claimed.[30] While at Bangour, Ivor wrote a poem about Evans, 'The Miner'. He had great faith in Evans' ability and the two remained friends at least until the end of the war when Evans visited Ivor in another hospital. Both Nielson and Evans took their places with Will Harvey to stand among Ivor's exalted 'golden people'.

Of all the people Ivor met at the Edinburgh War Hospital, VAD nurse Annie Nelson Drummond made the most dramatic and lasting impression on him. She touched his heart and captured his imagination in a way that no other woman had been able to do, not even Margaret Hunt. Their friendship began in early October. How it started is not known, but by Ivor's second week at the hospital, Annie was keenly aware that he was both a poet and a musician. A kind, determined and resourceful woman, Annie had the sensibilities of an artist tempered by her practical Scots upbringing. She played the piano competently and was searching for a way to express her own great love of beauty and nature when Ivor walked into her life.[31] She had never met a man like him, a talented, romantic figure who lifted her out of the routines of daily life and stirred her own imagination.

When they met, Annie Drummond was a month away from her thirtieth birthday. She had, in Ivor's words, 'a pretty figure, pretty hair, fine eyes, pretty hands and arms and walk. A charming voice, pretty ears, a resolute little mouth'. Yet the qualities that struck him first were her 'beautiful simplicity ... the fundamental sweet first-thing one gets in Bach, not to be described, only treasured'; 'her guarded flame' and 'a mask on her face more impenetrable than on any other woman I have seen.' [32] As their friendship grew, her mask dissolved in Ivor's presence. She, in turn, awakened new feelings in him and infused him with a happiness he had not experienced before. 'I forgot my body walking with her; a thing that has not happened since ... when? I really don't know', he confided to Herbert Howells.[33]

Annie Drummond came from the same trade background as Ivor, and had been reared in a household dominated by strong, resourceful women. Both of her grandmothers were skilled and prosperous businesswomen who were regarded with esteem in the community. The eldest of five children, Annie was born on 9 November 1887 at Armadale, a small village anchored on a barren, wind-swept landscape in West Lothian. Her father, Robert, was a coal miner who worked the pits north of Armadale. Her mother, Margaret Boyd Drummond, inherited her family's enterprising nature and ran her own flourishing millinery business. In 1896 Annie's grandmother Boyd, a successful draper, created excitement in the village when she had a building constructed on West Main Street that was large enough for two dwellings and a shop. No woman in Armadale had ever done anything quite so bold.[34]

Annie, her parents and brothers lived in the house on the east end of the building. An aunt and uncle occupied the centre dwelling, and her grandmother's shop occupied the west end. With a busy mother working long hours and her father often gone for days, the care of her four younger brothers, George, Robert, Alexander and John, became Annie's responsibility.[35] As they grew older, she had more time for herself and eventually began to study nursing. When war broke out, she interrupted her formal studies to join the Scottish Red Cross Territorial Brigade. She completed courses offered by the Red Cross in advanced nursing and eventually volunteered to serve at the Edinburgh War Hospital six miles from her home.

Nurses and volunteers were discouraged from having relationships with the men in their care, though it was nearly impossible to police them. They had to be circumspect and proper while on duty, but what they did on their own time was their own business. Annie Drummond became Ivor's secret, a mystery woman whose identity he hid in cryptic names, 'The Princess', 'Puck' and 'Hawthornden'.[36] He was very selective about whom he told of his romance, sharing his joy with Herbert Howells, Will Harvey, Ethel Voynich and Maggie Taylor, but making every effort to keep knowledge of it from Marion Scott.

Ivor was not ready to sacrifice his intense, highly dependent spiritual connection and business relationship with 'Miss Scott' for a more earth-bound physical relationship with Nurse Drummond. He needed Marion too much. Like others, he had probably heard the rumours and stories about her bitterness when Ernest Farrar betrayed her love for him. Ivor wanted to avoid a similar icy and permanent end to his friendship with Scott. He wrote to her as he had before, revealing nothing to arouse her suspicions beyond his references to 'a certain sister' to whom he had lent his copy of Harvey's *Gloucestershire Friends*.[37]

Meanwhile, in his correspondence with Marion, he praised and complimented her. He told her she was 'wonderful', let her know how much he valued her opinion of his music and his poetry and how her writing on so many diverse topics made him 'desire very much to go into certain things once more'. He continued to pour out his feelings. Looking at his war experience, he asked, 'How shall formal religion console me? It is only Music that will comfort the heart – mine does already, and when more dross is burnt out of me, perhaps then I shall see Beauty clearly in every-thing. Yet O, that this purification should come by war! Obscene and purely dreadful.'[38]

Ivor wrote new poems and sent them to Marion. He composed a song, 'The Folly of Being Comforted', a 'setting of those wistful magical words of Yeats'.[39] He told her that the lines ' "O she had not these ways / When all the wild summer was in her gaze" ... will raise your hair'.[40] But he didn't tell her what moved him to write it. By the time he composed the song, Ivor had begun to feel the stirring of an emotion new to him, the awakening of love with its transcendent joy.

At the end of October, with his discharge from the Edinburgh War Hospital imminent, Ivor wrote to Marion, telling her that he planned to begin his leave between postings with a visit to her. His next assignment would be to Seaton Delaval, a pit village in Northumberland, where he was to train in a signalling course. He would be returning to France. Still his new posting meant separation from Annie Drummond. Discharged on the morning of 5 November 1917, Ivor first made his way to Edinburgh, where he finally fulfilled his desire to see this great northern city, possibly in com-pany with Ratcliffe Barnett. Ivor later gave him a copy of Severn and Somme inscribed 'To that Bon Chaplain and Good Friend T. Ratcliffe Barnett, this Highly Expensive Book from Ivor Gurney, December 1917, Seaton Delaval'. Barnett treasured the book and kept in it a photograph of Ivor, as well as newspaper clippings documenting Gurney's life after he left Edinburgh.[41]

During his leave, Ivor visited with friends and family in London, High Wycombe and Gloucester. He was pleased to see Howells and Arthur Benjamin, now a gunner with the Royal Flying Corps. He spent time with the Hunt sisters, Mrs Voynich and her sister Maggie Taylor and her family, and with the Harveys. He stayed with the Scotts in London and with the Chapman family at High Wycombe but something happened to mar each of these visits. Ivor found no fault with Marion, her sister Stella or with Mr Scott, but Annie Scott upset him, as did Matilda Chapman. He did not indicate the cause of the trouble but hinted his own behaviour might have caused 'an upheaval ... occasionally'.[42] He felt that he would never be invited to stay with the Scotts again and that if he were, he would not accept the invitation. The cause of friction between Ivor and Mrs Scott had no effect on his relationship with Marion.

Those who knew Mrs Scott recalled her as a formidable woman. Ivor's arrival disrupted her household more than she could tolerate at the time. Mrs Scott was already overburdened by family illnesses, the revolving-door presence of multiple guests, coping with war shortages and her wor-ries about the fate of her siblings, nieces and nephews who were Russian citizens caught up in the Revolution. Ivor was not an easy man at the best of times, and it is likely that he simply tried Mrs Scott's patience to the breaking point.

In mid-November Severn and Somme was published to favourable reviews, particularly in The Times and the Morning Post. Ivor was pleased to read in the Telegraph he had 'the authentic voice of the true poet'.[43] His friends did not send him a copy of the 'rather savage and very stupid' review of his book in the *Gloucester Journal*. The anonymous critic was blunt and had come down on Gurney 'like a ton of bricks'.[44]

> I am not disposed to be severe, especially as most of these verses were composed in the trenches; but it must be said, for Mr. Gurney's benefit, that he fails very frequently, unnecessarily I feel sure, both in rhythm and metre. These pieces are verses rather than poetry ... I deal with the real matter – is our author possessed of ideas and can he express them in poetical terms? Mr. Gurney is unequal, and some-times falls to limping prose; the pictorial word, the novel emblem, the representative tones of Nature, sounding in Gloucester if not in Flanders, are caught only too seldom.[45]

John Haines came immediately to Ivor's defence:

> Mr. Gurney has, as it is obvious to anyone who has studied mod-ern English poetry, read and practised it pretty thoroughly, for the influence of Rupert Brooke, and to a lesser degree of Messrs. A. E. Housman and W. H. Davies, is obvious. I am quite aware that Mr. Gurney's rhythms and metres are not those of Miss Ella Wheeler Wilcox or Mr. John Oxenham; but they exist, they are his own, and they are in most cases appropriate and beautiful ... [read-ers] will find in this little book ... poetry that is vivid, gracious and memorable.[46]

Walter de la Mare, who later took a personal interest in Gurney, added his voice to the praise:

> The paramount effect on the mind after reading these new poems is a sense of supreme abundance. One has ascended to the top, as it were, of some old Gloucestershire church tower and surveyed in a wide circuit all that lies beneath it.[47]

By 17 November Ivor was settled at Seaton Delaval and missing Annie Drummond. 'Not yet has any letter come from the Princess to me, but still I feel that all is well, and feel that our hearts are conscious one of the other; which brings a kind of serenity after the heat', he declared to Howells.[48] Seven days later, he had still not received an anticipated letter from Nurse Drummond, as he noted surreptitiously in a list of dedications for his new poems sent to Marion Scott, including one 'To Puck, if she will write'.[49] By the 19th the anticipated letter had arrived, for he wrote again to Marion, asking her to alter the dedication simply 'To Puck'.

Gurney spent December in 'artistic exile' at his bleak new post close by the North Sea. He was miserable in this 'freezing, ugly, uncomfortable Hell of a Hole'.[50] He didn't feel like reading and complained of being dried up creatively with all his 'strength being taken up by endurance' and observed, echoing the words of Robert Louis Stevenson, 'I am constipated in the brains'.[51]

It is unlikely that he saw Annie Drummond, but their correspondence continued. By early January Ivor was looking forward to spending a week-end leave with her in Edinburgh. In a letter written to Howells around this time, Ivor hinted that Annie was growing restless and was beginning to doubt his intentions. Parts of this letter are missing, apparently nibbled by mice, so important details are missing. However, Gurney told Howells that '[She tes]ted me with a pretty severe test. I said, if she wanted me to I would [c]ome and see her'.[52]

The weekend was 'just perfectly and radiantly All Right. I have reached Port and am safe', he later wrote to Howells, adding, 'I only wish and wish you could see her and know her at once. You and Harvey. ... but it was a hot pain leaving her. We had a glorious but bitterly cold Sunday evening. A snowy but intimate Monday evening. For the first time in ages I felt Joy in me; a clear fountain of music and light. By God, I forgot I had a body – and you know what height of living *that* meant to me.'[53] Thoughts of marriage, perhaps prompted by Howells' own engagement, were clearly on Ivor's mind. He wrote of getting Annie to settle down and make 'a solid rock foundation for me to build on – a home and a tower of light'.[54] He seemed confident that she would be willing to provide him with the stability and love he needed, but he failed to mention what he might provide for her.

Ivor cautioned Howells not to tell anyone he had gone to Edinburgh and Bangour because 'it will need explanation I am not ready to give yet, and of course my people will want to know why I did not go home – but a week-end leave is so short'.[55] It is possible that during their weekend together, they discussed marriage. Ivor wrote a new poem for Annie, 'My heart makes song on lonely roads / To comfort me while you're away ...'[56] He swore his younger sister, Dorothy, to secrecy when he asked her to have his cap badge dipped in gold and made into a brooch for Annie. Howells, Harvey, Maggie Taylor and Ethel Voynich knew about Annie. Marion Scott did not. However, years later, she acknowledged that Ivor and Annie had indeed been engaged.[57]

Ivor returned to his duties at Seaton Delaval and continued to write poetry, gaining 'happiness and health and power over my mind and external things; and gain this not only by desire but because One Other is giving me such gifts as I may desire'.[58] He had made plans to see Annie again but had to postpone their meeting when he lost a ten pound note, nearly all the money he had. In an attempt to make light of the loss, he told Herbert Howells 'I came here to save money' – 'here' being the Newcastle General Hospital, where he had been sent with stomach trouble 'caused by gas'.[59] He was soon transferred to Brancepeth Castle, a convalescent facility, in Durham.

Bad news dovetailed into good news. While Ivor was coping with worries about his father, who had undergone cancer surgery and needed a second operation 'to make things shipshape', he learned that the first edition of *Severn and Somme* had sold out.[60]

He was eager to see Annie, but remained stuck in hospital, relying on her letters to cheer him. Again he shared his joy with Howells: 'I feel certain-sure for both of us', he wrote in reference to Howells' engagement to Dorothy Dawe and his own promising relationship with Annie. Her words made him feel as if she were there with him 'whispering most comforting things these last few days, and I have walked in my loveliest most beloved path with her, drawing free glad breath from that sweet South Western Air.'[61] He had composed a love song for her, 'Song of Silence', a setting of his own words:

> Oh my darling, how shall I give you thanks enough
> for any song ...
> All the thoughts of wonder crowding my adoring
> heart today ...[62]

His spirits were soaring. Then, suddenly, Annie Drummond was gone from his life. The break came in March, perhaps around the spring equinox. The first hint comes in a letter to Scott postmarked 22 March 1918, when he quotes Romain Rolland: 'Mozart could not compose save in the presence of the one he loved', and later that he could not play either. 'It is so with me. I take no delight in playing, walking, reading, existing by myself; and how many years is it I have been lonely now? My work is chiefly a Stunt at present, and done to preserve self-respect chiefly.'[63]

Only Ivor and Annie knew why she ended the relationship, and what words or letters were exchanged between them. The reason died with them. However, as a trained nurse, Annie had undoubtedly begun to see that Ivor Gurney was an undependable, unstable young man, facts she might not have been willing to allow herself to admit earlier. She knew what it was to dream, but she knew, too, that living in a dream was not the way to build a life together. The prospect probably frightened this practical, down-to-earth woman. There was simply no ideal time to end the relationship without hurting Ivor. The longer they continued to see each other, the more difficult parting would be. She had to act. Ivor was devastated.

After the break with Annie Drummond, Gurney's precarious emotional state deteriorated dramatically. It was spring again, the time when he usually fell into a cycle of depression. He was angry, bitter, sombre and detached, often referring to himself in the third person. He complained of an irregular heartbeat, a sign that he was suffering from anxiety as well as depression.

'You know how a neurasthenic has to drive himself, though he feels nervy and his heart bumps in a disturbing but purely nervous fashion?', he wrote to Marion from Durham. 'Well, Ivor Gurney determined to drive himself. His heart certainly did not feel right, but that was imagination and he must go on ...' with the war despite never feeling well, and suffering from 'continual digestive and general nervous trouble.'[64] He raged bitterly about his treatment at the hands of Army doctors who, he claimed, found him fit for duty and sent him back to work when he was ill. 'Surely a prostitute's job is cleanly compared to doctors who allow this and mark "Debility" on a case sheet', forcing a man to leave the hospital and 'go on til he drops again? That's what they have done for me.' He was determined to do nothing more strenuous than clerical work and '*never* march again.'[65] He was 'furiously angry at being treated as I have by people who will never run any chance of danger.'[66]

As he had done during other bouts of severe depression, Ivor heaped abuse on himself for what he perceived as his failures and for his mental 'impotence'. He complained to Marion that he was 'getting weaker and fuzzier in the head without knowing why'. He labelled himself a coward. He slipped into despair deeper than any he had previously experienced. He mused about getting a 'Board [certification of his condition] and then a chance for discharge'.[67]

Then, he dropped a bombshell on Marion. He claimed to have developed supernatural powers that enabled him to communicate with the spirit of Beethoven and to talk – without benefit of a telephone – directly to his father who was many miles away. 'And yesterday I felt and talked to (I am serious) the spirit of Beethoven. No there is no exclamation mark behind that, because such a statement is past ordinary ways of expressing surprise. But you know how sceptical I was of any such thing before', he explained to Marion.[68] 'It means I have reached higher than ever before – in spite of the dirt and coarseness and selfishness of so much of me.' Mysteriously, he adds: 'Something happened the day before which considerably lessened this and lightened my gloom. What it was I shall not tell you, but it was the strangest and most terrible spiritual adventure', he declared. Gurney explained that he was playing the slow movement of the D major sonata when he felt

> the presence of a wise friendly spirit; it was Old Ludwig all right. When I had finished he said 'Yes, but there's a better thing than that' and turned me to the 1st movement of the latest A flat Sonata – a beauty (I did not know it before). There was a lot more: Bach was there but does not care for me. Schumann also, but my love for him is not so great. Beethoven said among other things he was fond of me, and that in nature I was like himself as a young man. That I should probably not write anything really big and good; for I had started late and had much to do with myself spiritually, with much to learn. Still he said that he himself was not much more developed at my age (spiritually) and at the end – when I had shown my willingness to be resigned to God's will and to try first of all to do my best, he allowed me (somehow) to hope more much more. It depends on the degree of spiritual height I can attain – so I was somehow led to gather. There! What would the doctors say to *that*? A Ticket certainly, for insanity. No, it is the beginning of a new life, a new vision.[69]

Ivor shared this news with Marion because he trusted her and believed that she, of all his friends, would understand. He was confident that she would not react hysterically or dismiss his claims. He told her he was 'as sane as ever – only different ... Don't think I am cracked. No you won't'.[70] He had been around the Scott household enough to know that they were open-minded people with experience in the occult. Marion was a highly intuitive metaphysician. Her father studied the paranormal and sought logical explanations of strange, mysterious, otherworldly events.

For all her exploration and understanding of the supernatural, Marion knew, however, that Ivor Gurney had crossed over the line of reason. His behaviour was delusional and indicative that something was seriously wrong with him. She was frightened yet she appears to have said little about the incident. She must have written a carefully considered, reassuring response to his claim because he wrote back, addressing her as his 'Dear and True Friend', telling her that her letter had given him 'great pleasure'.[71] She had not betrayed to him any sense of her own escalating fears about his worrisome mental state.[72]

The flood of letters that had been the hallmark of their friendship had begun to taper off in January 1918, when Ivor was happily occupied with his thoughts of Annie Drummond and his dreams of their future together. By April, his letters to Marion and everyone else were not only infrequent, they were noticeably different in tone. He was no longer so full of himself, so concerned with Ivor Gurney. He was curiously resigned, grateful, almost humble, and made uncharacteristically solicitous comments to Marion and Herbert Howells about their activities and work. He admitted to Howells that he had suffered a nervous breakdown and blamed it on working too much. He wrote wistfully of the past that he had shared with Howells and with Sydney Shimmin, and seemed to be mourning what could never be again. 'Ah, if only the past were to do again with new eyes! ... Ah, would it were all over Erb and we foregathered once again in the old College tearoom. When it's all over Erb; when it's all over', he wrote to Howells.[73]

In April, after a short leave spent in Gloucester, Ivor returned briefly to Newcastle General Hospital before returning to duty at Seaton Delaval. He made only a passing reference to Annie Drummond and said nothing about their relationship beyond a vague reference that she was 'flourishing still in the North Countree'.[74] He told Howells that he was still 'crocky from my heart and a nervous breakdown from working too much at Brancepeth Castle'.[75]

On 8 May he was back in hospital, this time at Lord Derby's War Hospital, a 3,300-bed facility, in Warrington. Prior to being pressed into service during the war, Lord Derby's was known by a much different and more ominous name, Winwick Asylum. Opened in 1902 on 206 acres of flat, characterless land five miles north of Warrington, Winwick was Dickensian in comparison with the far more advanced, attractive and compassionate facility at Bangour.[76] It was the worst possible choice for Ivor, who was tortured by the gnawing reality that he was mentally unstable. He had not recovered from the nervous breakdown he suffered in March and he now saw first hand what his future might be if he could not bring his 'neurasthenia' under control. He was desperate and terrified.

Everything had caught up with Ivor Gurney. His world was falling apart and he was helpless to do anything about it. He had spent sixteen months in France fighting in a brutal, gruesome war. He had been wounded and gassed and was still suffering the after-effects of the gas and residual battle fatigue. He was worried about the failing health of his father and of his friend Margaret Hunt. He was fearful and uncertain about his own future after the war and was plagued by doubts about his abilities as a musician and poet. He was deeply wounded and humiliated by the failure of his relationship with Annie Drummond. He was troubled by the uncertainty of his self-diagnosed 'neurasthenia' which seemed to be growing worse. The fragile thread that linked Ivor Gurney to sanity was always stretched to the breaking point but now, in the face of all his worries, doubts, disappointments and failures, it finally snapped. He saw only one avenue open to escape from his despair.

NOTES

1 IG to MMS, 1 October 1917 (P), *CL*, p. 337.

2 Ibid.

3 Ibid.

4 W. F. Hendrie and D. A. D. Macleod, *The Bangour Story: A History of Bangour Village and General Hospitals* (Edinburgh: Mercat Press, 1992).

5 Ibid.

6 Ibid.

7 IG to MMS, 26 September 1916 (G), *CL*, p. 329.

8 IG, 'Hospital Pictures – Ladies of Charity', published in *War's Embers*; Thornton edition, pp. 80–1.

9 Effie Day, quoted in Hendrie and Macleod, *Bangour Story*, p. 23.

10 IG to MMS, 1 October 1917 (P), *CL*, p. 336.

11 Ibid.

12 IG to MMS, 1 October 1917 (P), *CL*, p. 337. Two of Gurney's letters to Scott were postmarked 1 October.

13 The item was a fragment of a notebook.

14 IG to MMS, 29 September 1917 (P), *CL*, pp. 334–5. All subsequent quotes about Gurney's 'salvaging' are taken from this letter.

15 IG to MMS, 4 October 1917 (P), *CL*, p. 341. Heavy-handed censors in both England and the United States made sure that the foul language and obscenities of war were softened or excised before they ever reached the reading public, an action that compromised the writer's intent and the truthfulness of the story. The American novelist John Dos Passos was accused of using 'the common language of the degenerate' when he employed the actual speech of enlisted men in his 1921 novel *Three Soldiers*. He was told to revise these passages or cut them, or his book would not be published. Dos Passos apparently discarded his original draft of the book.

16 IG to HH, January 1918 (KT), *CL*, p. 394.

17 IG to MMS, 4 October 1917 (P), *CL*, p. 339.

18 IG to MMS, 8 October 1917 (KT), *CL*, p. 345.

19 Ibid.

20 Like many people living in the Lammermoor Hills region, Ratcliffe Barnett was intrigued by Lady John Scott, composer of 'Annie Laurie', who had been born and reared at Spottiswoode on the other side of the hills. Her name and her exploits were legendary. Barnett devoted part of his essay 'Home of My Heart' in his book *Scottish Pilgrimage in the Land of Lost Content* to this 'little Scots gentlewoman ... full of music and poetry'.

21 Janet Barnett worked as her father's driver. She died in an Edinburgh nursing home in 2001 at the age of 96. Her sister, Margaret, a teacher, died in 1992 at the age of 91. Mrs Barnett died in 1952.

22 *Reminiscences of Old Scots Folk*, published by T. N. Foulis in 1913, is a particularly fine edition. Bound between warm brown boards with gold embossing on the cover and printed on high-quality paper, it contains ten colour plates of paintings by R. Gemmell Hutchison, RSA.

23 T. Ratcliffe Barnett, 'The Hidden Sanctuary', *Scottish Pilgrimage in the Land of Lost Content* (Edinburgh: John Grant Bookseller, 1944), pp. 85–8. Subsequent quotes about the Hidden Sanctuary are taken from this source.

24 IG to MMS, 31 October 1917 (P), *CL*, p. 360.

25 It's worth speculating that had Gurney been able to obtain leave, Barnett might have taken him to meet Lord Guthrie, who might have invited Owen as well.

26 IG to MMS, 12 October 1917 (P), *CL*, p. 347.

27 IG, 'The Miner' included with other poems mailed to Scott on 24 November 1917, *CL*, p. 372. The poem was published in *War's Embers*; Thornton edition, p. 83.

28 Evans lived at 40 Harold Street in Upper Norwood, which was just around the corner from Gipsy Hill, where Marion Scott had spent her childhood.

29 IG to MMS, 26 December 1917 (P), *CL*, p. 385.

30 Ibid.

31 Author conversations and correspondence with Peggy Ann McKay Carter, Annie Drummond's daughter.

32 IG to HH, January 1918 (KT), *CL*, p. 395.

33 Ibid.

34 The solid stone structure still stands today on one of the main streets of Armadale. It is divided as it was in Annie Drummond's day into two separate living quarters with a shop. Today the low hills covered with grass and wildflowers roll north in the direction of the old coalfields. Annie would have seen a different picture – a village that no longer exists, two churches, fields and a forest. Remarkably, the shop, which is a beauty parlour today, remains little changed. Now, as in 1896, it overlooks the street, and a small workroom in the rear looks out onto fields and a few houses. The double-entry door with glass panels is the same. The wood-panelled walls have been refinished to their original rich colour, which was blackened by years of coal smoke from the fireplace in the room.

35 Annie's brother George settled in Princeton, New Jersey. John was a chemist, and Robert was an engineer. Alexander, the youngest, died in 1943 when he was accidentally gassed by a defective heater while he slept.

36 'Puck' refers to Rudyard Kipling's 'Puck of Pook's Hill'. 'Hawthornden' refers to Drummond of Hawthornden.

37 Among the books Gurney lent to Drummond were W. W. Gibson's *Friends*, possibly the copy Marion Scott had sent to him, Belloc's *The Path to Rome*, and an unnamed book by Rose Macauley.

38 IG to MMS, 31 October 1917 (P), *CL*, p. 361.

39 Ibid.

40 Ibid.

41 Barnett's copy of *Severn and Somme* was later purchased by James Jaffe, a bookseller in Pennsylvania. The articles Barnett saved include an obituary from the *Dispatch* of 28 December 1937, 'Ivor Gurney Dead: Musician's Tragedy of Unfulfilled Promise', along with a number of other newspaper clippings laid in, and 'An English Schubert?' from the *Radio Times*, 15 July 1938, pasted to four sheets of heavy paper, as well as Hubert Fitchew's 'Maurice Ravel and Ivor Gurney' from the Sunday *Times*, 2 January 1938. Janet Barnett told the author that she recalled meeting one soldier in particular who came to the Barnett home. He was impressive enough that more than 80 years later she still recalled meeting him. She did not remember his name, but it is possible that the man was Ivor Gurney, given the personal interest her father had taken in him.

42 IG to SGS, November 1917 (KT), *CL*, p. 365.

43 Quoted in IG, *Severn & Somme and War's Embers*, ed. Thornton, p. 114.

44 IG to MMS, 12 December 1917 (G), *CL*, p. 377.

45 'A Local Response to Severn & Somme', *Ivor Gurney Society Journal*, vol. 3 (1997), pp. 75–8, reproduces the review from the *Gloucester Journal*, appearing on 1 December 1917.

46 Ibid. The Haines response is also reproduced.

47 Walter de la Mare, *The Times*, 28 December 1937.

48 IG to HH, 17 November 1917 (P), *CL*, p. 367.

49 IG to MMS, 24 November 1917 (P), *CL*, p. 373.

50 IG to MMS, 10 January 1918 (KT), *CL*, p. 391.

51 IG to MMS, 23 December 1917 (KT), *CL*, p. 384.

52 IG to HH, January 1918 (KT), *CL*, p. 396.

53 IG to HH, around 16 January 1918 (G), *CL*, p. 396. This letter was enclosed with one dated 16 January 1918.

54 Ibid.

55 Ibid.

56 Gurney sent an early version of the poem titled 'Song' to Will Harvey with the notation, 'You know whom that's meant for'; see *CL*, p. 400. An altered version was published in *CP*, p. 54.

57 In comments sent to Don B. Ray in 1952, Marion Scott stated, 'This nurse seems to have played fast and loose with Ivor, got engaged to him, then broke it off and refused ever to write in answer to his letters.' See DBR, *IG*, p. 47. The cap badge was not found among Annie Drummond McKay's possessions after her death in 1959.

58 IG to FWH, February 1918 (KT), *CL*, p. 399.

59 IG to HH, 25 February 1918 (P), *CL*, p. 407.

60 IG to MMS, 25 February 1918 (P), *CL*, p. 405.

61 IG to HH, 12 March 1918 (P), *CL*, p. 409.

62 'Song of Silence' is one of *Five Songs* dating from this period. The others are 'Thou Didst Delight my Eyes', also possibly written for Annie Drummond, 'The Cherry Tree', 'Red Roses' and 'The White Cascade'. Richard Carder published 'Song of Silence' in his article 'Long Shadows Fall: A Study of Ivor Gurney's Songs to his Own Poems', *British Music Society Journal*, vol. 15 (1993). 'Song of Silence' and 'Red Roses' are available on the SOMM recording, *Severn & Somme*.

63 IG to MMS, 22 March 1918 (P), *CL*, p. 415.

64 IG to MMS, 26 March 1918 (S), *CL*, p. 416.

65 Ibid., p. 417.

66 IG to MMS, 28 March 1918 (G), *CL*, p. 418.

67 Ibid.

68 Ibid.

69 Ibid.

70 Ibid.

71 IG to MMS, 5 April 1918 (G), *CL*, p. 420.

72 Scott wrote to Don B. Ray that Gurney 'developed delusions in March 1918'.

73 IG to HH, 22 April 1918 (P), *CL*, p. 423.

74 Ibid.

75 IG to HH, 7 May 1918 (P), *CL*, p. 424.

76 The buildings at Winwick were demolished in 1998 to clear the land for executive housing.

CHAPTER 15

'You would rather know me dead'

*W*HAT STARTED as a routine day in the Scott household quickly unravelled after the morning post arrived on Thursday, 20 June 1918. Marion was pleased to find a slim envelope from Ivor Gurney among the assorted pieces of mail addressed to family members. The voluminous correspondence that had poured out of him in France had diminished to an uncharacteristic trickle of only five known letters since April. She knew he had suffered a breakdown and that his serious condition had prompted his transfer from Newcastle General Hospital to Lord Derby's War Hospital at Warrington in early May.

As the weeks passed, Marion continued to write faithfully to Ivor, giving him encouragement, praising his achievements and consoling him. She sent him flowers, books and articles from newspapers and journals that she thought would interest him. Knowing that Ivor was despondent and severely depressed, she sat down on 19 June, the day before his note arrived, to draft a sensitive, reassuring letter in which she attempted to assuage his deepening belief that he was a failure as a musician and poet. She was well aware that when he took stock of his achievements and compared them to those of Herbert Howells, he felt, as he admitted to her, 'shame and despair with so little done'.[1]

'It is abundantly true that in both music and poetry you have the real thing – you <u>are</u> a poet, you <u>are</u> a composer', Marion wrote. 'Ivor, it is the <u>quality</u> of work which is what counts in the end, and though you feel yourself that you have accomplished little as yet compared to what you hope to do, you have done some songs which will take their place as part of the inheritance of England', she declared. 'They have the vital beauty, the vital truth that gives life. ... God has given you a rare gift – He has given you genius instead of the talent which is meted out to most people – and I suppose that in nearly every case genius gives to its possessor as much pain as joy.'

'Your genius does not let you take an easy rest especially in these years when it is for the most part pent up in you by circumstances, instead of having the congenial surroundings and constant opportunities which have fallen Herbert's lot the greater part of his career', she continued. 'You say so little of the weary time of illness, and make light of it, but Heaven knows it must be hard enough to pull along week after week as you have done, fighting your way back to strength. Perhaps only people who have had months of illness themselves can appreciate the dreariness of the continual struggle.'[2] Marion knew only too well from her own illnesses just how long and dreary that struggle could be.

Only a few days earlier she had written to Howells expressing her mounting concern for all of her friends, including Ivor, each on 'their own Via Dolorosa', struggling with 'the hardness meted out to them by life'.[3]

But nothing could have prepared her for the shocking revelation in Ivor's letter. When she slit open the envelope, she found that it contained two small pieces of paper, one addressed to Sir Hubert Parry, the other to her. Hers read:

> My Dear Friend
>
> This is a good-bye letter, and written because I am afraid of slipping down and becoming a mere wreck – and I know you would rather know me dead than mad, and my only regret is that my Father will lose my allotment.
>
> Thank you most gratefully for all your kindness, dear Miss Scott. Your book is in my kit bag which will be sent home, and thank you so much for it – at Brancepeth I read it a lot.
>
> Goodbye with best wishes from one who owes you a lot.
>
> May God reward you and forgive me.
>
> > Ivor Gurney[4]

Ivor asked Marion to deliver the second letter to Sir Hubert, which read 'I am committing suicide partly because I am afraid of madness and punishment and partly because my friends would rather know me dead than mad.'[5] Scott and Parry were not the only ones to receive suicide notes. Ivor sent six in all to people he cared for and whom he believed cared about him, individuals he knew would try to rescue him: his father, Scott, Howells, Parry, Will Harvey, and Margaret Hunt. Only Scott responded immediately. Although terrified by the suicide threat, Marion acted calmly without a moment's hesitation, fully aware that any delay on her part could be fatal. 'I got in touch at once by telephone with the hospital at Warrington, also with the police in my effort to avert a tragedy', she recalled many years later. 'That afternoon [actually the next day] my mother and I went off to Warrington and got there (trains were few and took a long time over such a considerable distance at that stage of the War) too late to see Ivor that night but did so the next morning at the hospital.'[6]

Upon returning from Warrington, she wrote to Howells insisting that he come to see her 'for an hour's talk please: and until I have seen you and been able to talk with you I would rather you did not mention this to anyone – not even mention that I want specially to have a talk with you this week. My mother and I went to Warrington on Friday, and I saw Ivor on Saturday morning and again in the afternoon, before mother and I had to return to London', Marion explained to Herbert. 'The Gurneys will know by now that I have seen Ivor, for I wrote to them yesterday. He made enquiries about you, and was full of solicitude for you. But I will tell you about the visit when I see you. ... I found Ivor looking better than I feared', she reported.[7]

Upon arriving at Warrington, Marion learned that Ivor had planned to drown himself in a canal. He had 'lost courage' and eventually hospital attendants found him sitting unharmed by the water.[8] While Marion and Mrs Scott were rushing to Warrington, hospital officials were sending telegrams to inform her that Gurney was 'quite safe and under special supervision.[9] These communications were waiting for her when she arrived back in London.

Meanwhile, Ivor's sister Dorothy wrote to Marion on 23 June 1918, informing her that all the suicide notes had been destroyed. Only those to Scott and Parry were preserved. The fact that Ivor sent a suicide note to Will Harvey underscores his irrational state of mind. It would have been impossible for Harvey to intervene in any way since he was still in a German prisoner of war camp.

Neither Scott nor Howells left any written account detailing what they discussed in their private meeting about Ivor. But one thing is certain – Marion had seen for herself that Lord Derby's War Hospital was the wrong place for someone as fragile as Ivor. Visiting Gurney later, John Haines affirmed the Scotts' revulsion: 'Warrington is the most detestable place I have ever spent six hours in, without exception, and the place would drive me mad, despite my lack of genius, in a very few weeks. How Gurney must dislike it I can well imagine.' [10]

Marion and Annie Scott were appalled by conditions at Lord Derby's although they never specified openly what so upset each of them. Whatever it was, they returned to London determined to get him away from the facility. Marion wasted no time. She consulted with Haines, who suggested a hospital in Cardiff, not far from an area 'most beautiful with grand hills,' which surely would have appealed to Ivor. Haines advised Marion to keep Ivor away from Gloucester 'until he is better than now: the father is too delicate and the mother too nervy.' [11]

In July an unexpected offer of help came from M. Muir Mackenzie, an eminent member of the legal profession and a friend of both Scott's father and of Sir Hubert Parry, who had alerted him about Ivor's situation and the conditions at Lord Derby's. Mackenzie suggested that he and Marion might try to get Ivor into Kings Weston, a convalescent hospital catering to soldiers suffering from shell shock and war neuroses. His wife's cousin, Philip Napier Miles, had opened the facility on his vast estate near Bristol and managed it with his wife and her sisters. Mackenzie thought Kings Weston was ideal for Gurney.

Napier Miles, born in 1865, was a musician and composer who had studied with Parry and had set verse by poets Ivor admired, among them John Freeman. He was active in bringing the new music of Ralph Vaughan Williams, Gustav Holst and others to the public through the choral concerts and other venues he organized. Not only had Mackenzie taken into consideration the intellectual and musical stimulation Ivor would find at Kings Weston, he saw another equally important aspect of the facility. It was located on a triangle of land embraced by the Severn and Avon rivers, and would have been a perfect place for Ivor to walk and be close to the restorative power of nature that meant so much to him. Mackenzie was confident that Napier Miles would welcome Gurney 'for his own sake and on our recommendation.' [12]

By the time Ivor's case was presented to Kings Weston, however, he had been away from the battlefield for ten months. Surely any signs of serious shell shock would have been present in the weeks and months immediately after his return to Britain, but Ivor displayed none of the obvious symptoms of this affliction. It was only after his breakdown in the spring of 1918 that doctors at Lord Derby's, seeking to explain Ivor's erratic behaviour, came up with a diagnosis of 'Nervous breakdown from deferred shell shock'.[13]

Although eager to have Ivor at Kings Weston, Mrs Napier Miles expressed doubts from the beginning. She was concerned that Gurney was a ' mental case', and told Scott and Mackenzie that the authorities did not allow Kings Weston to take such cases.[14] Mackenzie then recommended that Ivor be sent first to Napsbury War Hospital at St Albans to become 'more conva-lescent' which might diminish his symptoms and make it possible for him to be allowed to go to Kings Weston.[15] Parry concurred, but Mrs Napier Miles anticipated problems with that arrangement. She doubted that military officials would permit Ivor to make two transfers, one from Lord Derby's to Napsbury, and then a second from Napsbury to Kings Weston. However, she made it clear that no matter what was wrong with Ivor – mental illness or war neurosis – she was confident they could help him. 'I do wish Gurney could come here at once as we should, I know, be able to give him all sorts of things we know he could not get in a _real_ hospital and we should be so proud and glad to do it', Mrs Napier Miles wrote to Mackenzie.[16] The reluc-tance to accept him outright at Kings Weston strongly suggests that army doctors saw a deeper, more entrenched problem at the root of his trouble than shell shock.

Few doctors could be absolutely certain what was wrong with some of the soldiers who were hospitalized during the war with mental and emo-tional symptoms. Dr Thomas W. Salmon, a Major in the Medical Officers Reserve Corps and Director of the National Committee for Mental Hygiene in the United States, visited English hospitals and studied these men. In his opinion, 'it was by no means rare for a soldier with shell-shock to be mis-takenly categorized as being insane, or for an insane soldier to be thought to have shell-shock'.[17]

Men who suffered from shell shock displayed, for the most part, obvi-ous physical symptoms, including a stammer, deafness, paralysis in one or more limbs, sometimes blindness. They trembled violently. They fidgeted and complained of tingling in their limbs, palpitations and breathlessness. They complained of headaches and indigestion. Their faces were drawn, set in a chronic frown with a wrinkled forehead, and mirrored a range of nervous mannerisms like blinking and grimacing. These men had night-mares and dreaded sleep. They suffered from depression marked by feel-ings of hopelessness and shame at what they sometimes perceived as their own cowardice and incompetence. In the more advanced cases, men suf-fered total paralysis, curvature of the spine, deaf-mutism, violent hysteria, incontinence and hallucinations. Some believed that they were still in the trenches and relived the horrors of their experiences.

Ivor was severely depressed in 1918. He suffered from palpitations, expressed feelings of hopelessness, felt incompetent, had experienced hal-lucinations in his encounter with the spirit of Beethoven, suffered from indigestion and berated himself for his failures and felt shame. Perhaps the fact that at this particular time he did not want to return to France instilled in him the notion that he was a coward even though he had been a dependable and courageous soldier. But, with the exception of hallucinations, these few symptoms and behaviours associated with shell shock were not new to Gurney. They had been present in varying degrees since his teenage years and were characteristic of his undiagnosed bipolar illness. Ivor had none of the physical symptoms that mark a shell-shock victim. Later he would acknowledge that he had lied on the application for his Army pension when he gave 'after shell shock' as the reason for his needing a pension. It was, he admitted, a 'false' declaration.[18]

Ivor knew that something was seriously wrong with him. He defined it as 'neurasthenia'. This term fit his notion that he suffered nervous debility or exhaustion caused by 'overwork' or prolonged mental strain. It was an explanation that seemed to make sense to him. He worked hard and then he collapsed. The pattern was all too familiar.

Gurney had used the term 'neurasthenic' to describe himself. He thought this term defined his trouble in 1913 when he suffered his first nervous breakdown, and now again in 1918 as he reassessed his condition. He had written to Will Harvey's mother, Matilda, telling her that he had suffered a nervous breakdown and admitted that he believed his mind was 'slightly unhinged'.[19] An official at Lord Derby's War Hospital, Warrington, had written to David Gurney, Ivor's father, telling him that Gurney claimed he was hearing 'imaginary voices which urge him to commit suicide'.[20]

Ivor feared he was slipping closer to the edge of insanity and had even told the doctors he wanted to be admitted to an asylum. He knew instinctively what needed to be done for him, but military doctors were dealing with thousands of mentally confused young men and didn't act upon Ivor's cry for help. After his suicide attempt, however, doctors placed him under 'special supervision in order to provide for his safety'.[21]

Marion's visit had a calming effect on Ivor even though he admitted that it made him 'feel very ashamed'.[22] He had sent out a plea for help, and she responded in person when no member of his family bothered to make the journey. That must have been a disappointment to him but not a surprise. He had come to rely heavily on Marion, and she had not let him down. She never would. Her relationship with Ivor was about to change dramatically as she suddenly found herself thrust into the role in his life that she would maintain for the rest of his life and her own – that of his guardian and caretaker. From this point on when there was trouble with Ivor, everyone would turn to Marion Scott to act and find solutions.

Marion made the arrangements to have Ivor transferred to the Middlesex War Hospital, Napsbury, St Albans. On 24 July 1918 he left the gloom and anguish of the 'awful No 5 Down West Ward' at Warrington, where he had existed in misery and despair since early May.' [23] Freed from Lord Derby's, Ivor wrote to Marion, '[T]his [letter] is finished hurrying South on the train to Knapsbury [*sic*] War Hospital, St Albans, which your good offices I think has done for me.' [24]

Toward the latter part of July, while arrangements were being finalized to move Gurney, Marion made her first visit to Gloucestershire in company with her parents. Mr Scott's presence with them was unusual.

He rarely travelled with his wife and daughters on holidays but usually joined them later when he could get away from his busy law practice.[25] On the occasion of her first visit to Gloucester, an anxious Marion felt it necessary and prudent to have her legal adviser nearby since she had no idea what she might encounter in her dealings with Gurney's parents. Now that she was finally going to meet them, she was determined to discuss Ivor's situation and his future and in the process gain some sense of how, or if, they planned to help him.

She found they were concerned about Ivor but seemed paralysed by the prospect of taking responsibility for him and making any decisions about his care. The Gurneys were consumed by their own problems and they were frightened. David Gurney was recovering from cancer surgery and facing another operation. He was simply too ill to take any action on behalf of his son. He wanted someone to tell him what to do, or better yet, remove from him the worry and responsibility of taking care of Ivor. Ronald had been wounded in the war and was back home as the result of a compassionate discharge which enabled him to take over his father's business during Mr Gurney's long illness. Ronald had enough on his mind without adding Ivor to his list of responsibilities. Florence Gurney's nerves were on edge. In Marion's opinion, she was acting strangely. She was hardly capable of helping.

It was clear to Marion that unless she took responsibility for Ivor, no one else was capable or interested. The only member of the Gurney family who rallied for Ivor was his younger sister Dorothy. The rest of the Gurneys seemed to think that if they ignored the problem it might go away or resolve itself. Marion disagreed. She had already been in regular communication with John Haines and the Hunt sisters, and now turned to them to determine what action they might take collectively and independently to help and protect Ivor. At least Haines and the Hunts understood the problems and were ready to offer what assistance they could.

Ivor was thrilled that Marion had finally made her way to Gloucestershire. He was pleased with the impression she had made on his friends and even on his family. By this time he was feeling better. The tone of his letters was more cheerful. He had begun to look forward to participating in life again, engaging in simple pleasures like playing music and being with friends. He reported to Marion that 'Dorothy fell in love with you at first sight, and wrote a jolly letter about your visit; she is a first rate sister, and I am proud of her.' Emily and Margaret Hunt 'were delighted with your visit, and say it was like a visitor from another world "in our backwater" but say you looked rather tired. ... Mr. Haines has not written, but I shall expect a letter soon full of book-talk he has had with you, for any contact with a booklover such as you, would necessarily set him going; talking at top speed doubtless.'[26] During Marion's visit to Gloucester, Haines introduced her to the Cathedral and dined with her and her parents. Ivor probably did not realize that Marion's trip to Gloucestershire was not taken entirely for pleasure as he assumed but rather to take steps to help him.

Marion Scott had more on her mind than Ivor Gurney, but as usual she dedicated massive amounts of time and energy to him while trying to do her own work, maintaining a busy schedule of commitments including writing assignments and lectures, all while helping other friends, particularly Howells. In many ways, Marion was as devoted to Herbert as she was to Ivor, and worked tirelessly to guide his career, find opportunities for him, secure performances, promote him and even serve as the sounding board for his new compositions. '[N]o unusual thing: everything I did, musically, was known by her', Howells acknowledged.[27] In addition to her worries about Ivor, Marion was concerned about Herbert's precarious health. He was frequently ill due to the thyroid condition that affected his heart. He was still undergoing experimental radium treatments that eventually became routine in treating certain thyroid illnesses. Howells endured this debilitating regimen twice a week for two years, dividing his time between London and his home in Lydney, where his mother cared for him.

Unlike Marion's letters to Ivor, which are, for the most part, lost, some to Howells have survived. They reveal a close relationship between the two built on mutual admiration, respect and trust. She worked closely with Herbert on the articles she wrote to promote him and his music. Typically she consulted Howells when she planned to write about his Piano Quartet in A minor, which he had dedicated 'To the Hill at Chosen and Ivor Gurney who knows it'. 'So I will do two articles on it, but before I write the "Music Student" one I want to ask you how much I may or may not tell of the Quartet's underlying ideas – of the Hill at Chosen at early morning and the wind, of the vast summer skies of the slow movement, of the wind of March dancing through the daffodils in the finale. And may I allude to the way in which the Quartet connected itself with important events in the lives of the Darkes? and would you rather I did not mention anything about I.B.G. and the dedication to him, or may I say that you were both friends in Gloucester Cathedral and College days?'[28]

Her admiration for Herbert's work seemed deeper, more heartfelt and intellectual than any she expressed for Ivor's music. While she believed that Ivor possessed gifts in both music and words, she did not work as hard to introduce his music to the kinds of audiences she sought for the prolific Howells or to individuals who could help him advance his career. In Ivor's case, she put more energy into promoting his poetry. She believed that Herbert had more potential and ultimately more promise to realize his musical gift than Ivor. It is not likely that Ivor fully understood the extent or depth of Scott's relationship with Howells or how much she actually did for him.

Marion's friendship with Howells and her writing about his music led her to develop 'a new way of analysis', that would serve her well as she embarked on her new career as the London music correspondent for the *Christian Science Monitor* in 1919. She told Howells, '[Y]our things must be written of with the poetic aspect continually in mind, in language which approximates as nearly to beautiful prose-poetic as can be achieved'.[29]

Marion and Herbert added collaboration to their friendship when he asked her to write a poem for a hymn tune he had composed. The request rattled and intimidated the usually self-assured Scott, and she admitted that she did not feel equal to the task. 'I have not been forgetting my promise to try and write words for that noble hymn tune of yours, and I have done one hymn, but am so dissatisfied with it that I will not enclose it with this, but will wait to send it until I have done another and also have revised No. 1, and then you shall have the two to choose from. The music is so perfect that I can't come near it in words', she explained to Howells.[30]

Absorbed as she was with her concerns about Ivor and her work for Herbert, Marion learned 'all in one breath' the alarming news that Captain Arthur Benjamin had been shot down over Germany in August, was missing and then turned up a prisoner of war in Germany like Will Harvey.[31] Benjamin had originally joined the infantry but developed a 'veritable ecstasy of delight in flying' and joined the Royal Flying Corps in which he was serving as a gunner when his plane was hit.[32] As Ivor had done when he learned that Will Harvey was missing, Herbert plunged into despair over the uncertain fate of his friend. He fell ill with tachycardia, an excessively rapid heart rate common in certain thyroid diseases that can be triggered by anxiety. Herbert had not yet recovered from the loss of his beloved friend, the violist and composer Francis Purcell Warren, who had died at the Battle of the Somme on 3 July 1916 at the age of twenty-one. 'I was sorry to learn ... that what I feared was the case – that those weeks of awful anxiety about Captain 'Benjie' had made you very ill', Marion consoled Howells. 'It is no wonder that such a terrible shock as you received should have made your heart worse for a time, but I do truly lament it and send you much sympathy and many hopes that you are feeling better again now.' Scott expressed her concern for Benjamin's mother and for Jeanne Curas, whom Scott identifies only as 'Pauvre petite' adding 'all this is bitterly hard for her.'[33] Surely Gurney must have known what had happened to Benjamin and, like Howells, would have been concerned, since Benjamin was one of his closest friends. However, none of Ivor's extant correspondence mentions the incident.

By August the tone of Ivor's letters to Marion and her own visits to him affirmed that his condition was improving steadily now that he was away from Warrington. '[A]nd St. Albans I like extremely – for its position on a hill and its own clean delightful self', he informed his friend John Haines.[34] Situated just north of London, the hospital was easier for Marion to visit. His only other visitor during his months at St Albans was his army friend Private Evans, whom he had met at the Edinburgh War Hospital. His parents, siblings, even Herbert Howells appear not to have made any effort to see him. 'Napsbury is incomparably better', Marion informed Herbert, telling him that on a recent visit she had found Ivor 'so much better, so much more vigorous'. Although he was 'cheery', Marion still had difficulty getting 'a laugh out of him. If I told him anything funny the laugh came, but slowly – as if he had almost forgotten what mirth was and were just remembering ... anyway Warrington was enough to crush all laughter out of a man.'[35]

In early September 1918 Ivor wrote Marion that he would be visiting with her in London, arriving by bus on Saturday, 14 September if an anticipated day-pass to leave the Middlesex War Hospital came through for him. It did. Marion was pleased when she saw Ivor, reporting to Howells that she found him 'still further improved in health'. However, she expressed concern that 'he is still absolutely set on the idea of going back to France and the Front. What troubles me', she confided, 'is the thought of what things are like in France now – worse than when he was there a year ago. If it was suffering then, it would be doubly so now. But perhaps one lays too much value on escaping pain and suffering – God knows everyone must go their own path, and it is not always the things of pain which are the things of regret afterwards when one looks back', she observed. 'Only – it does trouble me that Ivor is so set on France: he is better, and one does so want him to get quite well.' [36]

Ivor's outlook was a promising sign that he was indeed getting better and regaining a degree of balance in his life. His depression was lifting and he was engaged in writing both poetry and music. Marion's reassuring visits to him at Lord Derby's had been a balm for his spirit. Despite the dreadful conditions there, Ivor had begun to rally. Even there, he had turned his attention to music, working on a violin sonata and producing two new song settings of Edward Thomas's verse, 'The Penny Whistle' and 'Sowing'. In September at St Albans, he composed 'The County Mayo', a song Scott described as 'really superb'.[37] In fact she felt that all three of Ivor's new songs were 'first rate'.

He had also turned his mind to poetry, both writing it and discussing it. He was thinking about Edward Thomas, whom he admired. He was eager to learn what poets Robert Frost and John Freeman said about Thomas when they were in company with Haines. '[A] great deal would I give to have been a floating disembodied spirit in that company.'[38] As he had done in past years, he was slowly moving into a period of productivity. The cycle of his bipolar illness had turned another revolution.

Although he told John Haines that there was 'not much verse coming from me' and that his head was 'empty of beauty altogether', he had, by September, written many of the poems that would appear in his next book, *War's Embers*: 'Migrants', 'Twigworth Vicarage', 'Interval', 'To F.W.H.', 'Fire in the Dusk', 'That County', 'De Profundis', 'Ypres-Minsterworth', 'Solace of Men', 'Girl's Song', 'Hidden Tales', 'Omens', 'From the Window', 'The Poplar', 'Toussaints'.[39] He sent his verse to Haines and Scott, accepting criticism from both while encouraging Marion, 'Please like these; my new children, but you do like everything I do apparently; a too appreciative critic.'[40]

Ivor appeared to be acting rationally and was feeling well enough to be discussing his future and his conflicting feelings about devoting himself to poetry and/or music. 'Personally I should like to chuck verse altogether and make music alone, but the way is too difficult perhaps in the Army, and the two paths must be kept just at present', he explained to Haines.[41] Earlier Ivor had told Marion that 'my real groove lay in Nature and Music, whereas Pain and Protest forced the other book [*Severn and Somme*] into being'.[42] He speculated that 'When Sidgwick and Jackson have accepted ... this next book [*War's Embers*], I mean either to chuck verse or music until the war's over, and then Music, music hard.'[43]

In mid-September Ivor still believed that the war remained an obstacle between him and his art, and that he would soon find himself back in the thick of it. 'But meanwhile there's the War – the war.'[44] Around 21

September he was expressing concern to Marion that 'duty seems to point to the Army again'.[45]

Then unexpectedly, within a week, he was looking forward to his upcoming discharge. The Army had decided to release him, concluding that he was not fit for service or combat. Gurney's later pension documents confirmed that he was suffering from 'Manic Depressive Psychosis [bipolar illness] ... Aggravated by but not due to service'.[46] Marion visited him around 1 October and by Friday, 4 October, he was on his way to spending his first night of freedom from the army since February 1915 with Marion Scott and her family in London.

After his overnight with the Scotts, Ivor made his way to Gloucester for a reunion with his family and friends. His homecoming was bittersweet. He knew that Eric Harvey, Will's younger brother, had been killed in France at the end of September, and that Sir Hubert Parry was dying.[47] The Army had granted Ivor a small pension of 12 shillings a week. It became apparent immediately to all who came into contact with Ivor that he was not well. He was entering another period of turmoil, marked by erratic behaviour of manic intensity. He was about to throw the lives of everyone he knew into chaos.

Ivor had only been home for two days when John Haines began writing anxious letters to Marion about their friend's disturbing behaviour, including his 'ideas about voices'. On Saturday, the day he had arrived in Gloucester, he stopped by Haines' office and was behaving so strangely that Haines took him for a long walk 'for the whole afternoon; tired myself out and I hope him. He was much more normal and left me happy enough with plenty of books and less annoyance from his voices – I think', Haines informed Scott. He also expressed his concern to her about Ivor's 'shrunken appearance ... his quietness and humility'.[48] Ivor was talking about going away to sea, an idea he had brought home with him from St Albans.

A few days later, Marion received another troubling letter from Haines. Ivor had disappeared after claiming he was going to Lydney to see Howells, even though Howells was in Gloucester, a fact Haines believed Ivor knew. Although he felt that there was 'no special cause for anxiety', Haines walked from Newnham to Lydney looking for Gurney.[49] He failed to find him, but when he got back to Gloucester, he learned that Ivor had returned home after going to Newport to search unsuccessfully for a berth on a ship. The situation was clearly very serious to all involved, including the Gurneys, who even gave the police a photograph of Ivor together with his description. They were stunned by his behaviour and rendered nearly helpless as people who suffer a severe shock often are.

Ivor had gone first to Lydney but found no openings on any ships there. He then walked 23 miles to Newport, where he found a ship that would take him, but it would not be leaving for another week, which didn't suit him. He spent the night at Newport with a man he had met and from whom he borrowed money so he could return home. Ivor thought, rather belatedly, to write a postcard to his father informing him of his plans, but it arrived in Gloucester when he did.

'Ivor had taken his kitbag with him, and his everyday requirements and some books, so he was in earnest', his sister Dorothy reported to Marion. 'I must say he looks very much better than on Tuesday and he is quite collected and clear now, but he was very bad on Monday and Tuesday. The walk evidently did him good', Dorothy observed.[50]

Ivor, who was dwelling in a kind of mental oblivion, realized that he had made a 'hash of things', but didn't think he had done anything wrong, according to Dorothy. Herbert Howells, still in fragile health and very vulnerable to the slightest upset, was 'terribly' worried about Gurney.[51] He had stayed in Gloucester specifically to be with Ivor after his homecoming but Ivor forgot that he had made plans to meet him. Howells fretted so much over Ivor's disappearance that he fell ill.

In the meantime, Edward Chapman had come down from High Wycombe to visit Ivor, only to stumble into the midst of the chaos Ivor had created when he left home without telling anyone exactly what he planned to do. Chapman managed to talk Gurney out of the notion of going to sea, but then Ivor decided he wanted to work as a labourer at the docks. The well-meaning Chapman even went so far as to offer to adopt Ivor Gurney, by then a twenty-eight-year-old adult. Florence and David Gurney must surely have been hurt by the suggestion. Although they were confused and did not know how to handle Ivor, they loved their son and were not about to give him up to anyone.

Haines continued to send reports to Marion, who was growing increasingly concerned about Gurney's apparently worsening condition. 'I always seem to be writing contradictory letters to you about Ivor. The fact is I simply don't know what to make of him and he varies as the wind', Haines explained. 'On Friday he seriously alarmed me by his depression and the "possession" he appeared to be under by his voices.'[52]

Once again Haines went with Gurney on a long walk during which Ivor was 'perfectly happy and quite normal all the time ... He enjoyed the scenery, quoted poetry, and got as near to his old enthusiastic self as I have yet seen.'[53] These reassuring words brought some comfort to Scott, but Haines' description of Ivor's strange and obsessive behaviour over food must have thoroughly alarmed her. He would eat nothing and then gorge himself. 'His chief trouble is concerned with food. ... He asserts that if he gives way to the desire for food he is unable to stop. ... He declares that if he has lunch he invariably afterwards goes out and buys huge quantities of cakes and eats them and continues doing so as long as he has the money.'[54]

Ivor was ashamed of his behaviour around food and admitted as much to Haines, whom he trusted with some of his dark secrets. 'He is horribly afraid of losing moral sense and stealing or doing something of the kind to get food. It is pathetic', Haines wrote. 'He refuses food at home, later gets it out of the cupboard when his mother isn't looking and then comes and accuses himself to me as a thief.'[55] Haines suspected that Gurney was at times so desperate for food that he would sell his books to get money to buy cakes. He also believed that 'this craving for food is at the bottom of the trouble with him'.[56] He was partly right.

Ivor Gurney was suffering from an eating disorder that resembles *bulimia nervosa*. Symptoms of bulimia include episodes of intense eating, consuming large amounts of food in a short period of time, eating in secret and feeling a loss of self-control. Further, victims of bulimia indulge in various forms of purging such as self-induced vomiting, misuse of laxatives and enemas, fasting and excessive exercise. They also indulge in binge eating as Gurney did. It is not known whether he forced himself to vomit, but gorging binge episodes would certainly have caused him to regurgitate when he became too full. It is not known whether Ivor abused laxatives, though he did have a fixation with bowel functions and could be crude when writing about them.

In a note Gurney sent to Howells, he described an imaginary 'Mass Meeting of Dyspeptics' at Albert Hall where 'Sir Jeremy Flatulence and the Rt. Hon: Tare-an-Ounds Acidity MP will scarify enghast and sententifact the audience. None of regular bowel action need apply. As the phraseology will be unflinchingly exact, ladies are advised to apply rouge, and to hold tight with both hands at certain episodes not possible to omit. Signed Regularity Ejection P.C. President.'[57]

From some of his letters, it is clear that Ivor was obsessed with enemas and used them regularly.[58] He fasted and exercised excessively. Finally, like other individuals who suffer from eating disorders, Gurney felt self-disgust, embarrassment and guilt about his behaviour in connection with food.

His strange eating habits dated back to his years in Gloucester before he left home to study at the Royal College of Music in 1911. Haines theorized that the 1918 episodes were traceable to the Edinburgh War Hospital and thought it 'highly probable that Bangour has something to do with it ... I think it is from that quarter that he gets his spiritual catchwords and phraseology. I do not think he is in communication with the place now.' [59]

There is no evidence whatsoever that Gurney had any bad experiences at the Edinburgh War Hospital at Bangour or that he came under the influence of a religious fanatic who twisted his thinking and filled him with guilt. He was far too intelligent, strong willed and egotistical to succumb to the sort of brainwashing and guilt invoked by religious fanatics.[60] The only religious figure Ivor is known to have encountered at Bangour was the liberal and compassionate Reverend T. Ratcliffe Barnett, whom he greatly admired. Very much a freethinker, Barnett was not in the habit of thrusting his beliefs on others nor did he feel it necessary to intimidate them into believing as he did in order to be saved. Gurney held Barnett in high esteem.

Haines was incorrect in assuming that Ivor had ceased communication with Bangour. He maintained some correspondence with Barnett. Although his relationship with Annie Drummond had failed, he had communicated with her as late as September 1918 when he sent her a copy of *Poems of To-Day*, inscribed 'To Nurse Drummond With Thanks for joy and best wishes for all things to come From Ivor Gurney St. Albans.'[61]

By mid-October Ivor was well aware that his behaviour was cause for concern among his family and friends, and took it upon himself to get help. He wrote directly to Philip Napier Miles at Kings Weston, asking if he might be allowed to go there 'at once'. He admitted to Marion that he was not 'sure of my impulses' and that he was anxious not only to 'save myself, but also my father, who must be more worried by my being here, than there under care'.[62] Howells had told Marion of Ivor's plans and she sent her own letter to M. Muir Mackenzie, asking for his help. He responded with 'bad news … as Gurney is no longer in the Army he cannot be with patients in the Hospital'.[63]

Ivor's next step toward self-preservation led him to take a job at Quedgley Munitions Works in Gloucester, starting on 23 October. Marion learned this news indirectly, 'not from one of the Gurneys', who had not communicated with her for so long that she concluded that 'all the Gurneys must be down with influenza'. She had fallen ill herself as had other members of her family and Howells to whom she reported her head felt like 'the Lord Chancellor's Woolsack'.[64] Ivor's seemingly battered constitution was still strong enough to ward off the highly infectious Spanish influenza that was sickening and killing millions. He reported to her in a letter postmarked 2 November that 'I am better myself, after a fortnight's hauling of heavy things about the Munitions Works'.[65] He was referring to his mental state. Ripples of news that peace was in the offing signalled to him that his job would not last long. Knowing that he would have to find other work, he told Marion that 'I may be "going to sea" again, and this time less ignominiously I hope!' [66]

As he had done before he left Gloucester in 1911, Ivor was now dropping in on friends and often staying with them instead of returning home to his family. Some of these same friends, namely Margaret Hunt, Herbert Howells, John Haines and, occasionally, Dorothy Gurney, served discreetly as informants, keeping Marion apprised of Ivor's comings and goings.

Although Ivor was showing signs of improvement, Marion knew that he still needed care. When his efforts to get himself into Kings Weston failed, she began taking steps on her own to explore other possibilities for him. Before she fell ill with influenza, she had gone to the Headquarters of the Shell Shock Commission to get all the latest data about 'these new Homes of Recovery specially for men who have been discharged from the Army for shell shock and neurasthenia'.[67] She identified a London home and located doctors on Harley Street who specialized in the treatment of shell shock, which she believed was contributing to Ivor's condition. She even inquired about securing a pension for complete disability for Gurney but nothing came of it, nor did Ivor and his parents act on any of the information Marion had supplied about Homes for Recovery. Despite their worries over Ivor, the Gurneys' focus shifted to David Gurney when he appeared to have a relapse that might warrant further surgery. He did not require another operation, but one crisis after another seemed to be hitting the Gurneys.

In the meantime, Ivor's spirits lifted toward the end of October 1918, when he learned that Will Harvey had been released from the POW camp in Germany and was in Holland waiting to be sent home. He was also delighted to receive a royalty cheque from Sidgwick & Jackson via Marion for additional sales of *Severn and Somme*. Typical of his generosity, he told her that he was planning to use some of the money to buy a copy of Robert Bridge's anthology *Spirit of Man* for the Hunt sisters. He learned, too, that a second edition of *Severn and Somme* was going to be published and that Sidgwick & Jackson would bring out his new volume of poetry, *War's Embers*. Scott, in her ongoing role as Gurney's business manager, secured publication of three of his poems in *The Spectator*.[68] Ivor was working on a violin sonata and had produced a 'beautiful' slow movement according to Howells. Gurney had begun to emerge from his depression and despair.

On 10 November 1918, the eve of the Armistice, Marion Scott was in a reflective mood. For the first time in four years, the dark curtain, which had so often been drawn around her, was beginning to open. She knew that the world was now a different place and that the future was uncertain, yet she felt a lightness of spirit buoyed by the promise of Ivor's gradual recovery and the return to peace. She wrote to Herbert Howells:

> O what a time this is – [I] feel sometimes as if my heart were too small to carry such a flood of ideas and emotions – or no, that isn't quite the simile: I feel more as if I were a bit of seaweed on the Atlantic sea-floor near shore, with the immense tides passing over me. Other times I get a haunting sense of watching Europe like one of Hardy's 'Intelligences' in 'The Dynasts'. Again comes an odd sense of an ironic likeness between the last scene of a Harliquinade where everything falls down and all sorts of unexpected forms and fairies emerge from the debris – and the collapse of Central Europe. O, it's no good trying to talk about it all – it's too great.[69]

Instead she copied out her poem 'Waters of Comfort', written several months earlier, at a time when she was gazing into the future.

> Grey mist of rain, and just a stir in the leaves
> Where wet birds ruffle, and the fat mothers sleep;
> While heavy-headed roses over pools full deep
> Hang trancéd with the spell calm water weaves,
> The ancient spell that earth of care bereaves
> In some dream, life or death. Ah me! –
> Could tears weave such a glamour, sweet their fall
> Over the sorrowful world: we should see grief
> Mirror back comfort, pain glide to relief,
> Faithlessness to strong confidence that the call
> Of the future's no false music, but is all
> We longed for, and the thing our eyes shall see.[70]

She observed that 'things have such an odd way of working in spirals', and recalled how four years earlier the Scotts had 'hunted out all the clothes we could spare to give to the Belgian refugees'.[71] And now with peace less than twenty-four hours away, Marion and Stella Scott were thinking about the survivors of the brutal war once again as they went through all their possessions gathering 'nearly a trunk-full of frocks, hats & underclothes to send for the liberated Belgians'.[72]

The plight of the Belgians symbolized the strength of the human spirit to Marion, but it was the two friends she held dearest to her, Ivor Gurney and Herbert Howells, who symbolized the tenuous promise of the new life each faced in the aftermath of war. She told Howells, 'It makes me very happy that at this great time in the world's history, you and Ivor are both bringing into the world these beautiful things, which will live and go down to succeeding generations as flowers of the English spirit, fadeless and fragrant.'[73]

NOTES

1 IG to MMS, 10 June 1918 (P), *CL*, p. 429.

2 MMS to IG, draft of letter written 19 June 1918, GA.

3 MMS to HH, 9 June 1918, MSC. Scott used American dating on her letters.

4 IG to MMS 19 June 1918 (P), *CL*, p. 430. The book he refers to is probably her copy of *The Muse in Arms*. 'Brancepeth' refers to Brancepeth Castle, a convalescent depot where Gurney spent a short time in March after he had been treated for sickness from the gas he had inhaled in September.

5 IG to Sir Hubert Parry, GA.

6 MMS, notes to DBR, 1952. The passage of years had slightly altered Marion's memory of the time sequence. She and her mother actually left for Warrington on Friday, 21 June, a fact she reported to Herbert Howells in her letter of the 24th to him.

7 MMS to HH, 24 June 1918, RCM.

8 IG to MMS, 20 June 1918 (KT), *CL*, p. 431.

9 Telegram from the Matron at Warrington sent to Scott on 21 June 1918, GA. Another telegram sent the same day informed her: 'Matter in hand writing further'.

10 JWH to MMS, 1 July 1918, quoted in *OIG*, p. 125.

11 Ibid.

12 MMM to MMS, 11 July 1918, GA.

13 Dorothy Gurney to MMS, 20 June 1918, GA.

14 MMM to MMS, 17 July 1918, GA.

15 Ibid.

16 Mackenzie quoted Mrs Napier Miles in a letter to Scott dated 20 July 1918, GA.

17 Anthony Babington, *Shell Shock: A History of the Changing Attitudes to War Neurosis* (London: Leo Cooper, 1997), pp. 90–1.

18 IG to the London Metropolitan Police Force, written during his hospitalization at the City of London Mental Hospital, quoted in *OIG*, p. 3.

19 Gurney's sister Dorothy told Marion Scott about this correspondence in a letter dated 21 July 1918, GA.

20 Major Robertson to David Gurney, 22 June 1918, GA.

21 Telegram to MMS from Lord Derby's Hospital, 21 June 1918, GA.

22 IG to MMS, 23 July 1918, *CL*, p. 439.

23 MMS to HH, 23 August 1918, MSC.

24 IG to MMS, 23 July 1918, *CL*, p. 439.

25 Mr Scott was usually so busy that Marion once commented that having him at home for the best part of one week during the summer of 1918 was something of a 'little holiday' for the family. Even at the age of 68, Sydney Scott was working full time, doing volunteer work, and playing an active role in the Society for Psychical Research.

26 IG to MMS, 22 July 1918 (P), *CL*, p. 435.

27 Notes by Howells for his Piano Quartet in A minor, quoted in Christopher Palmer, *Herbert Howells: A Centenary Celebration* (London: Thames Publishing, 1992), p. 432.

28 MMS to HH, 23 August 1918, MSC. The Darkes were Harold and Dora, friends from the RCM. Harold Darke (1888–1976) was a composer, conductor and organist. The article

appeared as 'Herbert Howells' Piano Quartet, An Appreciation by Marion M. Scott', in *The Music Student*, November 1918, p. 92.

29 Ibid.

30 Ibid. There is no evidence among Howells' compositions that Scott ever completed the poem to his or her satisfaction.

31 MMS to HH, 24 August 1918, MSC.

32 Sir Hubert Parry to HH, 4 July 1918, quoted in Palmer, *Herbert Howells: A Centenary Celebration*, p. 20.

33 MMS to HH, 23 September 1918, MSC. The identity of Jeanne Curas and her relationship to Benjamin are unclear.

34 IG to JWH, 11 September 1918 (Haines), *CL*, p. 455.

35 MMS to HH, 23 August 1918, MSC.

36 MMS to HH, 23 September 1918, MSC.

37 'The County Mayo' is dedicated to Ethel Voynich's sister, Margaret 'Maggie' Taylor, and salutes her Irish heritage.

38 IG to JWH, 11 September 1918 (KT), *CL*, p. 460.

39 IG to JWH, 11 September 1918 (received by Haines), *CL*, p. 455.

40 IG to MMS, 21 September 1918 (KT), *CL*, p. 463.

41 IG to JWH, 11 September 1918 (KT), *CL*, p. 461.

42 IG to MMS, 12 March 1918 (P), *CL*, p. 412.

43 IG to JWH, 11 September 1918 (KT), *CL*, p. 461.

44 Ibid.

45 IG to MMS, 21 September 1918 (KT), *CL*, p. 463.

46 Ministry of Pensions form for disability, 29 January 1925, GA.

47 Parry died on 7 October 1918.

48 JWH to MMS, 6 October 1918, quoted in *OIG*, p. 128.

49 JWH to MMS, 10 October 1918, quoted in *OIG*, p. 129.

50 Dorothy IG to MMS, 10 October 1918, quoted in *OIG*, p. 129, GA.

51 Ibid. pp. 129–30.

52 JWH to MMS, 20 October 1918, quoted in *OIG*, p. 130.

53 Ibid.

54 Ibid.

55 Ibid.

56 Ibid.

57 IG to HH, R. K. R. Thornton, 'New Howells–Gurney Papers', *Ivor Gurney Society Journal*, vol. 1 (1995), p. 71.

58 For example see the asylum letter in *OIG*, p. 2.

59 JWH to MMS, 20 October 1918, quoted in *OIG*, p. 131.

60 In his biography, *OIG*, Michael Hurd, in searching for answers to explain Gurney's behaviour after the war, speculated: 'Did he perhaps dabble in spiritualism, or come under the influence of some kind of religious fanatic?' This question is footnoted with a reference to T. Ratcliffe Barnett and the copy of his book *Reminiscences of Old Scots Folk* with the inscription to Gurney: 'My House an Ever Open Door to You'. The source and meaning of these words are explained in Chapter 17.

61 This gift from Gurney was found hidden among Annie Drummond McKay's possessions after her death.

62 IG to MMS, 17 October 1918 (P), *CL*, pp. 465–6.

63 MMM to MMS, 21 October 1918, GA.

64 MMS to HH, 29 October 1918, MSC. Howells developed pneumonia. One by one the Scott household fell victim to the 'flu', with Annie Scott being hardest hit because 'she had to nurse so many of us more or less helpless ones simultaneously, and to add to the worry for her, the cook dashed off to nurse her sister'. The Scotts were more fortunate than many other families, who endured long suffering and death in the pandemic that eventually claimed an estimated 20 million lives. They recovered quickly.

65 IG to MMS, 2 November 1918 (P), *CL*, p. 467.

66 Ibid.

67 MMS to HH, 20 October 1918, MSC.

68 Between December 1918 and February 1919, *The Spectator* published 'The Battalion is Now "On Rest"', 'In a Ward' and 'The Volunteer'. His poem 'The Day of Victory: November 11th 1918' was published in the *Gloucester Journal* in January 1919.

69 MMS to HH, 10 November 1918, MSC.

70 'Waters of Comfort', MSC.

71 MMS to HH, 10 November 1918, MSC.

72 Ibid.

73 Ibid.

CHAPTER 16

An Uncertain Course

'THE DULL SKIES wept' in Gloucester the morning of 11 November 1918.[1] Ivor Gurney arrived at the Quedgley Munitions Works to begin another day's labour, but by 11 o'clock weapons and the men and women who manufactured them were no longer needed. The war had ended. Like millions of others in Britain, Ivor joined in the celebrations. He stood among the crowds jamming Gloucester's streets as 'Rain fell, miserably, miserably' and listened as the bells 'from square towers pealed Victory', but for Ivor, the Allied victory held 'no triumph'. Beneath the veneer of joy, the 'Joking, friendly-quarrelling, holiday making ... gay laughter ... common jovial noises', Gurney, the battered soldier, discerned 'a new spirit learnt of pain'.[2] The old world had ruptured, scattering seeds of discontent, uncertainty and change through every stratum of society. As the starless night descended on Gloucester and the rain-sodden flags hung forlorn and 'glory-bare', Ivor observed 'That strange assort of Life; / Sister, and lover, / Brother, child, wife, / Parent – each with his thought, careless or passioned / Of those who gave their frames of flesh' for the hollow victory they were celebrating.[3]

Ivor counted himself lucky. He had survived and in the process had proved himself to be a competent, dependable soldier. He had discovered his poetic voice and turned war into art. He had published a successful volume of poetry and was working on another collection. He had composed five significant songs in France, three of which had been performed in London. He had fallen in love, and, for a time, he managed to find some respite from the mental anguish that had tormented him before the war. He had been wounded but not badly. He had been gassed seriously enough to be invalided back to Britain and spared from having to face combat again.

The psychological turmoil and erratic behaviour that had marked his return to Gloucester in October seemed to subside as he fell into old routines and grew more accustomed to being among friends in familiar surroundings. Gloucester had once again provided the balm that soothed Ivor's despair. The nearly frantic letters from John Haines and Dorothy Gurney to Marion Scott expressing concern about Ivor had tapered off.

Gurney was relieved and grateful that, against the odds, his close friends Will Harvey, Arthur Benjamin and Sydney Shimmin had all survived the war and that they would soon be reunited. Ivor knew that none of them would ever be the same. They could never recapture the past they had shared, but at least they were all alive.

At the end of November he wrote a cheerful letter to Shimmin informing him that he would be returning to the Royal College of Music on his 1911 scholarship. 'Thank Goodness the War's over; thank Goodness there is a chance we'll all be back again soon moving our fingers over black and white. ... We'll sit in some inn parlour and chortle "Widdecombe Fair" together for joy of return, reunion, mere existence – Joie de vivre, as the linguists say.'[4]

Ivor continued to seek out his friends and spent increasing amounts of time with them. By early December Haines was able to report encouraging improvement in Gurney's state of mind and behaviour. Ivor was putting the finishing touches on his poems and had taken the time to go over them with Haines. He was working on a Violin Sonata in E flat major and had set 'Epitaph on an army of mercenaries' (Housman), 'The scribe' (de la Mare) and 'O happy wind' (W. H. Davies).

Shortly before Christmas Ivor travelled to Cornwall to enjoy a holiday in the company of Ethel Voynich and other members of her family. He wrote enthusiastically to Haines about this 'grey land of blue sea and frowning cliffs of might … dashing spray … clear stars … Armada clouds' where violets bloomed in December.[5] Several years later, the dramatic images of Cornwall that Ivor retained found their way into his poems 'Of the Sea' and 'Like Hebridean', but on this holiday, he turned his mind again to music, composing 'Desire in Spring', a setting of Francis Ledwidge's verse 'Twilight song'. In his letter to Haines, he failed to mention that his absorption in writing the song nearly led to him being trapped atop the rocks at Gurnard Head by the incoming tide. Mrs Voynich's nephew Geoffrey Taylor and Geoffrey's friend Adrian Boult rescued him. Before he left, Ivor thanked Mrs Voynich by giving her a manuscript copy of 'Desire in Spring'.[6]

Ivor returned to Gloucester on Monday, 30 December in time to celebrate the new year. Arthur Benjamin, newly returned to England from his imprisonment in Germany, was staying nearby in Lydney with Howells. The two young men spent their days together playing music and walking, perhaps occasionally including Ivor in their activities. Howells was ecstatic to be in Benjamin's company again after the traumatic and uncertain days in September when Benjamin's plane was shot down and he was reported missing. Despite his ongoing battle with illness and his distracting worries over Gurney and Benjamin, Howells continued to add new works to his growing list of compositions.[7]

While Ivor laboured over his verse and new compositions in Gloucester, Marion Scott was busy in London making plans to showcase the music of her friends in January. She was preparing a celebratory party to reunite Gurney, Howells and Benjamin with other friends from the Royal College of Music and to introduce them to important members of society, including Lady Olga Montagu. She invited violinist Sybil Eaton to play new violin works by Howells and Benjamin, and she asked pianist George Thalben-Ball to perform in Howells' 'Chosen Hill' piano quartet. She decided to wait until later in the year to introduce Ivor's violin sonata at a coterie party and chose instead to include a group of his songs on the programme.[8] Marion was eager to programme Howells' Violin Sonata in E major, which the composer had dedicated to Sybil Eaton; however, Eaton played his Four Pieces for Violin and Piano instead. Scott later told Howells of the impact the Violin Sonata in E major had on her: '[H]ow often that sonata has come into my thoughts since I heard it – the music has a quality which lasts in one's inner ear; perhaps in the way in which, after one has smelt violets or mignonette one keeps on thinking the perfume is still there, even after the flowers are out of one's normal radius of perception.'[9]

By mid-January Ivor was back in London with his books, clothing and works-in-progress, all indications that he planned to stay in the city and resume his studies at the RCM. He had arrived in the city without any preparation and immediately faced the daunting task of finding a place to live. After a 'heart breaking hunt for digs', he found temporary lodgings an impractical distance from the college on Sterndale Road in West Kensington.[10] It was a dingy place, as his quarters tended to be, and he lived there in what he described as 'bivvy' conditions.[11] He attended Marion's party on 18 January. The next day he joined Howells, Benjamin and two other friends for supper in Oxford Street after attending a concert featuring Herbert's music.

There is a gap of some six weeks in Ivor's correspondence, so his movements are difficult to trace with certainty, but he was steering a course directly into another episode of manic activity. While he worked on his new poems and struggled with his compositions, his new collection of poetry, *War's Embers*, was at Sidgwick & Jackson, who had, by this time, issued the second edition of *Severn and Somme*. Three of his poems had been published: 'In a Ward' and 'The Volunteer' in *The Spectator* and 'The Day of Victory' in the *Gloucester Journal*. Upon his arrival in London, he reported to Haines that his efforts at composition were going 'haltingly', but that he had roughed out one set of verses and had written half of another set.[12] His attendance at the RCM was erratic, if he attended at all. His waywardness only reinforced his brother Ronald's concern that Ivor was not yet fit to return to his studies. Within five weeks of leaving home for London, Ivor was back in Gloucester.

Meanwhile, Marion had begun working as the London music correspondent for the highly respected and influential *Christian Science Monitor*, an international newspaper published Monday through Saturday in Boston, Massachusetts. Mary Baker Eddy, the controversial founder of Christian Science, had established the *Monitor* in 1908. Prompted by Joseph Pulitzer's smear campaign against her in his *New York World*, at the age of eighty-seven, Mrs Eddy decided to publish her own independent newspaper, one not controlled by 'commercial and political monopolists' and one that pledged 'to injure no man, but to bless all mankind'. She believed that newspapers of the day were a 'hazard' because they injected readers with large doses of negativity and created an atmosphere of fear and anxiety that had an adverse effect on both mind and body. She chose to place her principles before dividends, and to publish a newspaper that was honest, fair and forthright; one that was rich in ideas and substance.[13] Pulitzer had accused Eddy of being incapable of managing her own affairs and convinced Eddy's sons to sue for control of her estate. A judge dismissed the case.

In Marion Scott's day as now, the *Monitor* set high standards and relied on first hand reports from correspondents stationed in countries throughout the world, not on wire services and other second-hand news sources. The *Monitor* featured a wide range of articles on its Music, Art, Theatre and Home Forum pages in Scott's day and well into the later years of the twentieth century. A reader might find reviews of books by Edward Shanks,

Edmund Blunden, John Drinkwater and Edward Thomas, under the title 'Our Poets' or articles and essays about William Langland, Thomas Hardy, Mary Webb, W. H. Davies, W. H. Hudson, Samuel Johnson and even one on 'Bishop Percy's "Reliques" and Popular Ballads' as well as pieces about 'Skylarks and Poets', 'London in the Nineties – Some Famous Book Shops', and 'The Shepherd with the Poets'. The *Monitor* featured poetry in every edition, often including works by British poets such as Walter de la Mare, Robert Bridges and Vita Sackville-West among others. It was the first American publication to print excerpts from two of Ivor Gurney's poems, 'Firelight' on 22 May 1918 and 'Song at Morning', on 28 May 1918, both from *Severn and Somme*. The *Monitor* offered many articles about people and places, history, theatre, dance, and later, as technology progressed, articles about radio and aviation became staples of the newspaper. Eventually other critics including Bernard van Dieren, Walter Schrenk, Emile Vuillermoz, José Subira, Winthrop P. Tyron and W. H. Haddon Squire were featured on the music pages along with Marion Scott.

Although not a Christian Scientist herself, Marion was well aware of Mrs Eddy, whose metaphysical philosophies and ideals were compatible with her own. Mrs Eddy had died in 1910 but her legacy was still alive and thriving on the pages of her newspaper when Marion signed on as London music critic. She became the first English woman to write music criticism for a newspaper based in the United States and one of only a few women critics writing anywhere. Her earliest documented contributions appeared on 4 January 1919, a feature article reporting on the 'Musical Situation in Italy' and 'English Notes' containing eleven short notices and reviews. In one of her brief commentaries, Marion praised a Frank Bridge setting for voice and orchestra of Rupert Brooke's 'Blow Out, You Bugles'. She called it a work of 'considerable beauty' which enabled the soloist, tenor Gervase Elwes, to fully realize the 'dignity and nobility of the music'.[14]

Marion was already in the process of writing a two-part article about the Royal College of Music that would be published in May, and she was working on a long profile of Herbert Howells that would appear on 14 June. She had begun research for an in-depth feature entitled the 'Gloucestershire Group', which included Gurney, Howells, F. W. Harvey, and John Haines among other composers and poets whose roots were sunk deep in Gloucestershire earth.[15] Scott rarely received a by-line for her criticism and feature articles in the *Christian Science Monitor*, a standard practice at the time. She was known only as 'Special Music Correspondent'. Occasionally her initials, M.M.S., appeared at the end of a piece. Later, in the 1920s, her full name appeared occasionally. She submitted her copy to the *Christian Science Monitor's* European News Office at 2 Adelphi Terrace in London.

As January drifted into February, the Scott household was once again beset with illness. Marion endured the 'ghoulish' extraction of a tooth that caused her face to swell painfully and left her unable to eat. Sydney Scott and little Audrey were both ill with heavy colds. To add to the misery, the entire family watched with grave concern the mounting hostilities in Russia in the aftermath of the Bolshevik Revolution of 1917. While most members of the Prince family remained in St Petersburg or crossed the border to nearby Finland, Marion's cousin Eugene and his English wife, Elizabeth, had fled Russia for the United States. Their whereabouts were unknown for weeks. Fearing for their safety, the family were later relieved to learn that they had made a safe passage across the Atlantic.[16] A long visit from Annie Scott's elder sister Emily Prince provided a pleasant diversion for the family. Haines reported to Gurney that he met Miss Prince and enjoyed her company.

By the last week of February, Ivor was in Gloucester, relieved to be away from the 'grey waste of London'.[17] He sent the corrected proofs of *War's Embers* back to Marion, and continued to write new poems. Will Harvey had returned to his family home, The Redlands, at Minsterworth. Ivor all but moved in with the Harveys, placing an extra burden on the household. Will was grieving for his brothers, Eric, who was killed in France, and for Bernard, who died in 1914, aged nineteen, in a motorcycle accident near the family home. Will himself was weak and ill with jaundice contracted in the prison camp. Gurney and Harvey swapped stories of their war experiences. Harvey reiterated for Gurney the tremendous popularity Ivor's drinking song 'Captain Stratton's Fancy' had enjoyed among his fellow prisoners of war. 'What shoals of prisoners have heard it F.W.H. says can hardly be counted', Ivor wrote proudly to Marion.[18]

As the two men renewed their friendship, they began collaborating on a forthcoming poetry recital they planned to present at nearby Stroud. Ivor set three of Will's poems to make up a cycle called a *Gloucestershire Lad*. He had already composed 'In Flanders' in France, and had nearly completed 'The Horses'. A few weeks later, Will recited his poetry, illustrated by Ivor's songs. Ivor played accompaniment and told Marion that the evening, somewhat enhanced by champagne and gin, 'went off very satisfactorily' despite Harvey's physical weakness.[19]

Haines, still monitoring Gurney's behaviour, wrote to tell Marion that Ivor was 'wonderfully normal and well ... and appears to be composing both verse and music with the same extraordinary rapidity still'.[20] Haines thought that Gurney was well, but he was, in fact, cycling into a manic state.

Although Ivor was happy to be in company again with Harvey and Howells, he was growing increasingly concerned about the health of both his father and his beloved friend Margaret Hunt. David Gurney had terminal cancer and was deteriorating rapidly. 'Poor old chap he is very sick, very much in pain, and a soon end is best', Ivor wrote to Marion, thanking her for sending a thoughtful letter to his father.[21]

Margaret, never a robust woman, suffered from a heart condition and was greatly weakened when she contracted a serious case of influenza in February. Ivor watched helplessly for several days as she drifted closer towards 'the ill thing', her death, which came on 3 March 1919.[22] Although he revealed little emotion to his family and friends, Ivor was devastated. Haines reported to Marion that Ivor had seemed little affected by Margaret's passing and observed that Ivor felt 'it was a happy release for her, since she was in considerable pain'.[23] He seemed to absorb this deep loss and went on with his work, throwing himself into it at a fevered pitch. But Ivor was affected, deeply. Margaret had been his muse, she had nurtured him and loved him and he had loved her.

Without Margaret, the house at 54 Wellington Street felt empty to Ivor, yet it remained his sanctuary. He still visited Emily regularly, working there as he had always done and would continue to do until he left Gloucester permanently in 1922. Instead of visiting Margaret's grave he preferred to remember her in ways he thought more fitting: he 'walked in quiet places that she loved, or on hill roads far from crowds or noise ...'[24] Looking back later, measuring his life through the perspective of time, he declared that Margaret had 'ruled my Making' as an artist through her 'goodness and true grace'.[25] 'My work was meant for her', he acknowledged.[26] Without her, there would forever be a void in his life.[27] To make matters worse, Ivor's idyll with Will was interrupted when Will returned briefly to fulfil a military obligation at Seaton Delaval before his official release from the army.

By mid-March Ivor reported to Marion that he had completed the first movement of his Violin Sonata in E flat and was working on the violin part of the slow movement as well as the finishing touches to the 'authoritative version' of 'In Flanders'.[28] He declared that he was restless. His energy level was clearly running at high speed for he also talked about sketches of ' "A Gloucestershire Rhapsody", a Symphony, 3 songs needing correction, Two writing out. ... There is the Mass too! Of course there's the Quartett [sic – Gurney habitually spelled quartet with two t's at the end] ... a short Violin piece half done'.[29] He was particularly pleased with his song 'Cathleen ni Houlihan', a setting of Yeats, 'which will knock you flat', he boasted to Marion.[30]

Ivor was so proud of 'Cathleen ni Houlihan' that he sent it to Marion, who played it for Howells in London. In May, when Howells was in Gloucester with his fiancée, Dorothy Dawe, the three went for a walk on Robinswood Hill. Ivor reported to Marion that he 'started [singing] "Kathleen" [sic] to [Howells] but he said that you had already played it over to him'.[31] Ivor must have felt slighted and hurt by the rebuff but he said nothing. Earlier, in March, he and Howells had met for lunch in Gloucester at which time Gurney had given him a copy of *War's Embers* written out in Marion Scott's hand. Howells noted in his diary for that day that Ivor wrote out a copy of his 'lovely poem *The Crocus Ring*' and gave it to Herbert, asking him to set it to music.[32] But Howells never set any of Gurney's poetry despite Ivor's prompting.

When Ivor asked Marion to find a publisher for his *Gloucestershire Lad* cycle, she approached Winthrop Rogers. He did not accept the cycle, deciding instead to publish 'Sleep'. While Ivor was composing music, he was also writing poetry, sending his latest efforts off to Marion as he had done during the war. She dutifully offered suggestions and had the poems typed.

The spring of 1919 was cold and wet. Usually at this time of year Ivor experienced signs of depression, but he was revolving through a cycle of intense productivity instead. He filled his days and nights working, socializing and wandering in the Gloucestershire countryside. He had contacted poet Lascelles Abercrombie in nearby Dymock and reported to Marion that Abercrombie was going to try to secure a concert of his music in the North. Ivor spent little time with his family, even though his father was in great pain and failing rapidly. He made no mention of his godfather, Alfred Cheesman, but went around daily to Emily Hunt's where he felt most welcome and comfortable to write poetry and compose. He visited regularly with Haines and practically lived with the Harveys. His letters to Marion were breathless. He was sleeping little and eating poorly. His mood was elevated, his senses were heightened to every nuance of nature. '[B]ut O April's a disagreeable lady this year, after the bad example of March. ... Trees only just beginning to bud in Mid April, in Gloucestershire! Shocking!' 33 But even in dismal weather, Ivor found beauty. 'Yesterday brought me that rare sight – the ground end of a rainbow. I could see the hedges through it – a wonderful sight. Under Crickley, it was, under the Roman camp – such a ridge, such a sky, such a rainbow, and (afterwards) such a sweeping scud of storm – a wonderful glittering curtain of rain sweeping across the valley.' 34

Ivor must have recognized that he was over-extending himself and felt the frenzy in his behaviour, because in April he turned again to rigorous physical activity, his usual antidote for mental strain. He took a job as a labourer at 5/– a week at Dryhill Farm in Shurdington, a village between Gloucester and Cheltenham, where he was 'set to learn the farm business, to become sane and glad for life'.35 The location of the farm suited Ivor. 'A place of thorn, oak, ash, elm, clear streams, a 500-feet-up place where one gets a sight of the Severn Sea, May Hill and on clear days of the Welsh Hills, by looking out of a window merely or wandering out of a gate ... the good earth and winds, sun and stars must restore me to some semblance of the old bodily sick but spiritually sound me ... time will show whether this will be worthwhile to me', he observed to Scott.36 Ivor's vivid description of the countryside prompted Marion to consider taking a holiday at the farm, where they welcomed paying guests, but in the end she went to Lichfield with her sister and mother. As with all of Ivor's subsequent attempts to succeed at an ordinary job, this one failed. Although he managed to amuse the farmer, he was hopelessly impractical when it came to learning the rudiments of farming.37 According to Marion Scott, Ivor 'could never do things except in his own way'.38

In his increasingly unsettled state, he was casting about for a direction. He asked Marion if she thought the RCM would take him back at the half term. A few weeks later, in early May, Ivor made his decision: he would resume his studies. He asked Marion if she could find him a grant for a good piano, all that he desired upon his return to London.

On 10 May, the day after Ivor posted this request, his father died. David Gurney was fifty-seven years old and had suffered from cancer for more than a year. In the end he suffocated, according to Ronald Gurney. Ivor was with the Harveys at Minsterworth when the news reached him. He returned home on the day of his father's funeral, carrying a bunch of flowers, and wearing a bandage to cover a boil on his neck. He was unusually subdued. 'To my great surprise he allowed me to dress the boil and brush his clothes. At no other time would he allow this; and after the funeral he went straight to the piano and played Chopin's Funeral March', his sister Winifred recalled.[39]

Ronald Gurney informed Marion of his father's death and used the letter to convey his mounting concerns about Ivor, asking her if it were true that the RCM had asked him to come back to the college. 'I don't honestly think that he is fit – but personally I think that the evil of his returning is less than the evil of remaining in this atmosphere and is worth the risk', Ronald observed.[40] The 'atmosphere' was created by the constant tension between Ivor and his mother. 'When I get a chance I'm going to give him a rattling good talking to and doubtless 3/4 of it will be disregarded', he added.[41] If Ronald had that talk with his brother, Ivor ignored it. If Ivor wrote to Marion about his father's passing, the letter has been lost.

A few days after the funeral, Ivor was back in London, lodging with Maggie Taylor and her family in St John's Wood and looking forward to Marion's return from her brief holiday in Lichfield. He seemed to be in good humour, and his correspondence and activity give no hint of grief. He was eager to meet with Marion to discuss his new compositions and poetry, the works-in-progress that had occupied him since he left London in February. Marion's two-part feature on the Royal College of Music had just been published in the *Christian Science Monitor* and Gurney, Howells and Haines were eagerly anticipating her series on Gloucestershire poets and composers.[42]

War's Embers, dedicated to Marion Scott, was published in May 1919. Critics had expected more from Gurney in his second volume. *The Times Literary Supplement* called his verse 'good journalism' but declared that it was 'not poetry'. The *Birmingham Journal* claimed Gurney had 'no sense of the witchery of words' and recommended that he study Shakespeare. Even Will Harvey, writing for the *Gloucester Journal*, had to admit that while there was 'not a bad poem in the book', Gurney's verse displayed 'a certain lack of polish, and occasional signs of hasty workmanship'.[43] Ivor seems not to have been upset by the less than laudatory reviews. He was amused by one from the *Aberdeen Daily Journal* in which the critic assumed that Ivor had voyaged in the ss *Aberdonian* merely because one of his poems bore the title 'Aberdonian'.

Ivor was not in London long before he was on the move again, this time to a farm in the village of Leigh, near Reigate, Surrey. He stayed with a couple named Nicholson and described Mrs Nicholson only as 'the authoress' and Mr Nicholson as 'a great chap most noble to behold ... and able to trace his descent from Norse time'.[44] Ivor's reason for being at Leigh is not clear. Usually when he went to a farm, it was to stave off the encroaching demons of his illness by engaging in hard physical labour. This time, however, he appears to have been a guest who enjoyed 'delightful rooms and garden, very kind people, a piano, books enough'.[45] In this pleasant environment, he worked on both his music and poetry, reporting to Marion that he finished the slow movement of his Violin Sonata in E flat and that 'There are also two songs (Sappho) and 3 piano Preludes. One finished. One sketched, and a third in writing. One or two new poems are also done ...'[46]

He was also the beneficiary of an unnamed individual who gave him the substantial sum of £50.

After three years in the Army, including sixteen harrowing months at the Front, where he was shot and gassed, a failed romance, a nervous breakdown, a suicide threat, extended hospitalizations and an erratic recovery period after his Army discharge, Ivor Gurney finally seemed to be drawing the pieces of his life together. During 1919 he began to take advantage of the important personal connections of his friends in an effort to win the attention and support of influential people like John Masefield. Performances of his music were winning praise. An anonymous critic writing in *The Times* after a concert featuring 'In Flanders' and 'By a Bierside' declared that the songs 'have an austere simplicity of expression, which is arresting' and went on to exclaim that if 'they are a sample of music from the War we may look forward to something big'.[47]

Ivor had agreed to return in September to his pre-war organist's post at Christ Church in High Wycombe where his friends the Chapmans lived. The job would begin in September and carried an annual salary of £60.

Although he was as full of himself as ever, Ivor showed more interest in his friends and their activities, asking questions and commenting on their replies. He was solicitous of Marion and her family. He was enjoying his time with Maggie Taylor and her artist husband Edward whose studio was in their home at 30 Clifton Hill. He happily engaged in discussions with Haines about Edward Thomas and was working on a setting of Thomas's 'Digging' ('Today I think only with scents').[48] 'E.T. grows more dear to me as the days pass', he told Haines.[49]

Ivor was stepping out into society too, mingling with the musical and literary élite. In early July he and Howells attended a formal affair at the Trocadero as guests of the Society of English Singers and found themselves in company with Sir Charles and Lady Stanford; the singer Agnes Nicholls and her husband, composer-conductor Hamilton Harty; pianists Harold Samuel and Fanny Davies, violinist Sybil Eaton and conductor Sir Henry Wood, among others. During a discussion on English song, Ivor, masterful and passionate, stood up and recited Edward Thomas's poem 'Words', which begins

> Out of us all
> That make rhymes
> Will you choose
> Sometimes –
> As the winds use
> A crack in the wall
> Or a drain,
> Their joy or their pain
> To whistle through –
> Choose me,
> You English words? [50]

It was a spontaneous but brilliant move on Ivor's part, one that summed up the effect of words on both the poet and composer, and focused audience attention on him. 'I shall never forget Gurney's extraordinary entry into [the discussion]', Howells recalled. 'He stood up and recited a poem by the late Edward Thomas (*The Word* [*sic*], which was written at John Haines's house), and promptly sat down again. He was in great form.'[51]

However, it was Howells, as usual, who walked away with the prize of the evening, an introduction to Sir Henry Wood. Sir Henry, clearly impressed by the young composer, and perhaps having read Marion's feature in the *Christian Science Monitor*, invited Herbert to conduct *Puck's Minuet*, a 1917 work, at the coming season of Promenade Concerts at Queen's Hall. He also asked Howells to conduct a 'bigger' work later for his Symphony Concerts. Although Ivor apparently made no important connections that night, he was pleased that he had captured the audience with his recitation, and was so high on his personal success that he walked around London the next day still dressed in his evening clothes.

While Herbert was immersed completely in music, Ivor continued to juggle composition and poetry simultaneously as if they were one art, the rhythms and cadences of words intertwined in his mind with the rhythms and cadences of music. In a letter written to Marion in late July 1919, he shifted back and forth between music and poetry, both arts clearly driving and consuming his creative energies. He enclosed thirteen new poems, or 'variegated ... masterpieces' as he called them. As usual he sought Marion's comments and approval. In the same letter he informed her that he was working on song settings of Bliss Carman's Sappho translations. Then he mentioned visiting a London bookshop where he encountered the poet Edward Shanks and got involved in a discussion about a poetry prize. In the next breath he switched back to music talking about Alexander Scriabin and John Ireland and his own violin sonata which seemed to be causing him trouble – 'I suppose, having started it, I must go on.' The letter ended with references to his new poems and to *War's Embers*.[52]

At this point in his life Ivor was in an artistic limbo, productive but not soaring like Howells. His music was coming slowly, and the larger forms continued to elude him. His poetry was neither fresh nor distinguished at a time when experimentation was coming to the fore. Some of his verse was trite, some of it so cumbersome that the effect of good lines and images was diminished or lost as in 'High St – Charing Cross', a poem written in London in June:

> Theres that within the breeze
> Stirring my hair,
> That says of flowers and trees
> Fine things to hear
> Of floors grass pavemented, untainted stream
> In the heart hidden of longing; the honey of dream.[53]

Many of Ivor's new poems reflected signs of the hasty workmanship that Will Harvey had observed in his review of *War's Embers*. Ivor's impatience and lack of focus were apparent in his work, but as he admitted, '[O]ne wants always not the moment's task.'[54] He continued submitting his poems to magazines and journals – *The Spectator*, *The Athenaeum* and *Harpers*

Magazine – but editors returned them unpublished. When Ivor learned that John Squire, editor of *The Spectator*, thought him 'one of the best men below the horizon', Gurney asked the obvious question as to 'why he had rejected so much lately'.[55]

Ivor returned to Gloucester in August and enjoyed a visit from Sydney Shimmin, who was still unwell from the various ailments that had assailed him for many months. However, the two friends visited Portway, Cranham, Birdlip, Crickley – places Gurney loved – and they spent time with Emily Hunt. Ivor later joined Haines on a walking tour of Wales. By early September he was living at 51 Queens Road, High Wycombe, and commuting to the RCM.

Gurney's personal experience was a world apart from that of his fellow students, most of whom were much younger and still enjoying youthful innocence and wonder of discovery. He was a twenty-nine-year-old man, a published poet and composer and an organist who had fought in a war. His life so far, with its drama, excitement, romance and challenges to survive, was more the stuff of novels than of the day-to-day life of a college student. Yet in spite of the responsibilities he faced as a soldier, the injuries, hardships and losses he had endured, and his modest success as a poet, he was, for all his experience, still drifting without an anchor, searching for his place in the world. College provided a safe haven for him, another temporary shelter along the uncertain course he was navigating.

NOTES

1 IG, 'The Day of Victory', *War's Embers*; Thornton edition, pp. 92–4.

2 Ibid.

3 Ibid.

4 IG to SGS, 30 November 1918 (G), *CL*, pp. 468–9.

5 IG to JWH, 26 December 1918 (G), *CL*, pp. 469–70.

6 Ethel Voynich visited Cornwall periodically with her mother's relatives before she emigrated to the United States, settling in New York City in 1921. Her 1946 book *Put off thy Shoes* was set in Cornwall. Many years later, in 1938, after Gurney's death, Voynich completed a motet that she and Gurney had discussed during the Cornish holiday. Ethel Voynich kept the copy of 'Desire in Spring' among her music manuscripts. It is in the E. L. Voynich Collection at the Library of Congress, Washington, DC.

7 By the end of 1919 Howells' list stood at 32, including a piano concerto, orchestral songs, orchestral music, choral works, songs and organ pieces.

8 Sybil Eaton was once the object of composer Gerald Finzi's youthful affection. She became a lifelong friend and admirer of Howells. George Thalben-Ball (1896–1987) was an organist and composer and, like Benjamin, an Australian.

9 MMS to HH, 12 February 1919, MSC.

10 IG to JWH, 16 January 1919 (P), *CL*, p. 471.

11 Ibid.

12 Ibid.

13 Although the *Monitor* is owned by a church, the Christian Science Church has never used the newspaper to promote a denominational doctrine. Ironically, the *Christian Science Monitor* has won more than half a dozen Pulitzer Prizes (founded by Joseph Pulitzer) for excellence in journalism.

14 Elwes had performed Gurney's song 'Sleep' at Aeolian Hall in London in December 1917.

15 The 'Gloucestershire Group' articles were subtitled 'The Home', 'The Poets', 'The Composers'. Gurney is mentioned in all three parts that were published on 26 July, 2 August and 9 August 1919.

16 Marion was close to Eugene Prince, who was six months older than Gurney, but towards the end of her life appears to have had a falling out with him that resulted in her revoking a bequest to him in her will.

17 IG to MMS, 25 and 26 February 1919 (S), *CL*, p. 472.

18 Ibid., p. 473.

19 IG to MMS, 11 March 1919 (KT), *CL*, p. 475.

20 JWH to MMS, 10 March 1919, *OIG*, pp. 132–3.

21 IG to MMS, 11 March 1919 (KT), *CL*, p. 475.

22 IG to MMS, 25 and 26 February 1919 (S), *CL*, p. 473.

23 JWH to MMS, 10 March 1919, *OIG*, p. 132.

24 IG, 'On a Memory', *OIG*, p. 148.

25 Ibid.

26 Ibid.

27 The 1974 edition of Edmund Blunden's *Poems of Ivor Gurney* included 'Robecq Again', Gurney's recollection of France. The Blunden version of the poem ends with the line, 'O Margaret, your music served me. I also made beauty'. Subsequent editions of Gurney's poems by other editors omit that line. It does not fit the poem and reads more like an outburst of emotion or memory than a part of the actual poem. There is no original manuscript of the poem. It is possible that Gurney wrote this line on the page as he was composing 'Robecq Again' and that a typist incorporated it into the text. The fact that Gurney perhaps 'doodled' this line on a work in progress implies that Margaret Hunt was often in his thoughts.

28 IG to MMS, 21 March 1919 (S), *CL*, p. 477.

29 Ibid. When Gerald Finzi worked on Gurney's music manuscripts he developed 'arbitrary markings' to denote them as being bad, indifferent, good or very good. Finzi cautioned that these markings 'need not be taken too seriously, but are a rough guide as to which should be looked at first, when considered for publication. He ranked the Violin Sonata in E flat as good. There are many parts of this work-in-progress at the Gurney Archive.

30 IG to MMS, 17 March 1919 (KT), *CL*, p. 476.

31 IG to MMS, 9 May 1919 (P), *CL*, p. 485.

32 Herbert Howells' diary entry, 15 March 1919, quoted in Christopher Palmer, *Herbert Howells: A Centenary Celebration* (London: Thames Publishing, 1992), p. 78.

33 IG to MMS, 15–16 April 1919 (S), *CL*, p. 480.

34 Ibid.

35 IG to MMS, 22 April 1919 (KT), *CL*, p. 481.

36 Ibid.

37 The farmer's daughter, Mrs Herring, in conversation with David Goodland. Gurney gave her a signed copy of *War's Embers*.

38 MMS, Notes, MSC.

39 WG, quoted in *OIG*, p. 133.

40 RG to MMS, 13 May 1919, GA.

41 Ibid.

42 Published 10 May and 17 May 1919.

43 FWH, 'Mr. Gurney's New Book', *Gloucester Journal*, 17 May 1917.

44 IG to JWH, 2 June 1919 (P), *CL*, p. 487. According to the Local Studies Index, electoral registers for the parish of Leigh 1919 and the local library catalogue, the only reference to

Nicholsons living in Leigh in 1919 were for Eric Pearson and Cecilia Nicholson dwelling at Leigh Place in the spring and autumn of that year. The only reference to a local writer is Phyllis Nicholson, author of several books including *Norney Rough* (1941) and *Country Bouquet* (1947). The publication dates are much later than 1919, which makes it unlikely that she was Gurney's 'authoress'. I have not been able to locate any books by Cecilia Nicholson, who was the Mrs Nicholson with whom Gurney stayed.

45 IG to MMS, mid-summer 1919 (PB), *CL*, p. 489.

46 Ibid.

47 *The Times*, 2 July 1919, quoted in R. K. R. Thornton and George Walter, *Ivor Gurney: Towards A Bibliography* (Ivor Gurney Society and the School of English at the University of Birmingham, 1996).

48 Gurney had already set or was working on Thomas's 'The Penny Whistle' and 'Lights Out', the title of Gurney's song cycle of Thomas's poems completed in 1926. Gurney set 15 of Thomas's poems to music, including the popular 'Adlestrop' in 1920.

49 IG to JWH, 22 June 1919 (P), *CL*, p. 488.

50 'Words', in *Poems by Edward Thomas (Edward Eastaway)* (London: Imperial War Museum, 1997), courtesy the late Myfanwy Thomas.

51 From a diary entry of HH dated 9 July 1919, quoted in Palmer, *Herbert Howells: A Centenary Celebration*.

52 The letter, which was not included in the *CL* because it was misplaced, and 'High St – Charing Cross' were published in George Walter, ' "My True Work Now" An Unpublished Ivor Gurney Letter', *Ivor Gurney Society Journal*, vol. 3 (1997).

53 Ibid.

54 Ibid.

55 IG to MMS, 10 October 1919 (P), *CL*, p. 497.

Part IV

What's madness but nobility of soul
At odds with circumstance?

— Theodore Roethke, 'In a Dark Time'

CHAPTER 17

A New Mastery

*T*HE SPECTRE OF WAR haunted the corridors and classrooms of the Royal College of Music when Ivor Gurney returned in the autumn of 1919 after a nearly five-year absence. The sun still glinted off the windows and filled the rooms with warmth and light but the atmosphere was sombre as if a fog had crept in and dampened its soul. The buoyant pre-war mood that had filled Gurney and his friends with joy, anticipation and hope for the future had been shattered.

For those like Marion Scott and Herbert Howells, who had stayed at the college throughout the war years, the changes were less perceptible and not as startling or dramatic as they would have been to someone who had not experienced their gradual evolution. Marion was a mainstay of the RCM and had used the college Union to help students and staff on active service maintain what they could of their musical interests and careers. Along with Harold Samuel, Harold Darke and Mabel Saumarez Smith, Scott worked diligently to help them find reliable individuals to fill the positions they had to vacate, teachers for their pupils, or representatives to collect their royalties and keep track of their business affairs. Union committee members and volunteers wrote supportive letters to RCM men and women and provided warm welcomes when they returned home on leave. They kept as much of the college tradition alive as they could, maintaining a schedule of concerts, recitals and social events for those still at the college.

A few students like Howells had been exempt from service and were able to continue composing and building their careers. This freedom gave them an edge over Gurney, Arthur Benjamin, Arthur Bliss and others who had to 'lay aside all they most loved in life for the cause of humanity'.[1]

Once away from the college and England, the men 'fought in every theatre of the war, faced the arctic cold of northern Russia, crossed burning deserts, endured the horrors of trench life on the Western Front, entered Jerusalem, served in monitors and battleships, raided Rhine towns by night, learnt the torment of German and Turkish prisons', Marion recalled. 'Nor were the girls less devoted: they nursed in hospital ships or ashore; they drove ambulances, they made munitions, they served canteens.'[2]

Even the RCM building was shaken by war. During an air raid, a shell case crashed through the roof of the concert hall, barely missing the organ, splintering the floor and landing in the examination room below. No one was in it at the time. However, the war's most lasting effect on the college was measured in the final tally of men who died – thirty-eight, including Ernest Farrar, George Butterworth and Howells' beloved friend Francis Purcell Warren.[3] 'But the war, in cutting its great mark across our times, has done music one valuable service', Marion had written in mid-1919. 'It has proved that art to be an essential element in communal life and not a mere accessory. An art which could go with men into the trenches, and illuminate their hardest hours, is no longer regarded as a social toy by the public, and there is abundant hope that music in Britain is coming into its own.'[4]

War was not the only contributor to the sombre atmosphere at the RCM. On 7 October, just a little more than a month before the Armistice, Sir Hubert Parry, the college director, succumbed to illness at the age of seventy. A man of great energy, enthusiasm and compassion, he was held in high regard. He was one of Gurney's champions. His passing was a blow to everyone and especially poignant coming so close to the war's end, denying him the opportunity to witness its outcome. Parry had ridden a wave of anxiety for the RCM men caught in the war's 'vortex of barbarism'. 'The thought of so many gifted boys being in danger ... is always present with me', he had written to Howells. 'This is what horrible senseless war means – and we can do nothing.' He had expressed particular concern for Ivor, observing that his 'case I feel to be quite a special martyrdom. His mind is so full of thoughts and feeling so far removed from crude barbarities that it seems almost monstrous.'[5]

Ivor's return to the RCM was bittersweet. Friends had died. Parry was no longer there to provide encouragement and support. However, some of the unpleasantness that had marred his pre-war student days was absent. The intractable Sir Charles Villiers Stanford, who had aged dramatically during the war, was more an object of Gurney's concern than an adversary. Both Stanford and Gurney had mellowed, one with age, the other with experience. Ivor's new composition teacher was Ralph Vaughan Williams, who had served in France and Greece as ambulance orderly in the 2/4th London Field Ambulance. Prior to his demobilization in February 1919 at the age of forty-six, he had held the post of Director of Music, First Army, British Expeditionary Forces in France. He and Gurney shared the common bond of knowing war first hand, even if from different perspectives.

Under the guidance of the less-demanding and more temperamentally compatible Vaughan Williams, Ivor might finally begin to find his way and move into the larger forms of music that had eluded him. But he was still as independent as ever. Vaughan Williams did not have the authoritarian personality and command needed to discipline someone as wayward as Ivor. No one did.

Initially Ivor seemed committed to his studies, even allowing their demands to cause him to miss a September reunion of 2nd/5th Battalion in Gloucester. He was taking courses in conducting, learning new piano works for performance and writing his own music, some of it nodding to Scriabin, one of the few modern composers who appealed to him.[6] According to Marion, Ivor 'investigated the fashionable new music with its spiky technique and harsh sounds ... His disappointment was overwhelming'. She believed that 'it was the absence of beauty which made him doubt the value of this new technique in composition and if it was not beautiful he could not bother with it'.[7]

During his early months at the RCM, Ivor began composing a symphony but nothing came of it. He made progress on another ambitious orchestral work, *A Gloucestershire Rhapsody*, which he completed in 1921.

He continued to compose songs and began the first of his extended vocal-instrumental works, *Ludlow and Teme*. Inspired by Vaughan Williams's 1909 song cycle *On Wenlock Edge*, settings of poems from A. E. Housman's *A Shropshire Lad*, Ivor had turned again to Housman, whose verse he had first set as early as 1907.[8] Between September and December 1919 he composed the seven songs that form *Ludlow and Teme*, the more assured and successful of his two song cycles for voice, piano and string quartet.

The Western Playland (and of Sorrow), a second song cycle on Housman's poetry, traced its beginnings to 1908, when Gurney had begun two songs, 'Loveliest of Trees' and 'Is my team ploughing'. He resumed working on the individual songs in 1918 and in February 1919 had sent 'Is my team ploughing' to Marion, telling her 'The rest shall follow as promised, but not just yet.'[9] Additional songs in *The Western Playland* were not forthcoming until 1921. This cycle, for baritone, piano and string quartet, is slightly more ambitious than *Ludlow and Teme* in the number of texts Gurney set – eight. However, it lacks the stride and lustre of *Ludlow and Teme*. *The Western Playland* was dedicated to 'Hawthornden', one of his secret names for Annie Nelson Drummond. Gurney's attempts at orchestral works, a *'Coronation' March* composed in 1910/11 for a competition and the *Gloucestershire Rhapsody*, remain in manuscript. Only his *War Elegy* has been published.[10]

Ivor was dividing his time between London and High Wycombe, where he lived in quarters near the railway station, a convenient location for his commute to the city. He rekindled his close friendship with the nearby Chapman family – Edward and Matilda and their now mature children, Kitty, Winnie, who had adored Ivor, Arthur and Marjorie.[11] He attended to his job as organist at Christ Church on Sundays and engaged in composing a set of Christmas carols for the coming holiday.[12] In his leisure time he enjoyed the homey atmosphere of the Chapman household and found the nearby 'delectable land' with its 'changing soils in the valley and a happy air of peace over all' a balm for his spirit after a day in the city.[13]

Although he was writing both poetry and music at a rapid rate, Gurney was finding music more difficult to harness. 'Lots of stuff in me apparently, but the devil's own job to get at it', he wrote to John Haines in September. Later he complained to Scott that '[S]omehow or other I cannot work'.[14] He was hinting too that his obsession with food was on him again, admitting that 'an appetite for cakes is an expensive thing' and complaining later that eating 'too much' was causing him to 'feel empty-heavy-headed'. He blamed a case of nerves for missing an engagement with Marion. He was becoming annoyed by the seeming lack of enthusiasm for his poetry. He complained to Haines that 'every single lousy editor has returned every single unfortunate one of my priceless productions. To say that comment is needless is weak – to say that comment is useless (save the most violent) is just, but unhelpful. Perhaps Masefield will help or give advice.'[15]

A personal meeting with John Masefield was in fact on the horizon. In June 1919 Stainer & Bell accepted Gurney's setting of Masefield's 'Captain Stratton's Fancy' ('The Old Bold Mate') and asked for 'particulars'. This request gave Gurney an opportunity to make himself known to Masefield.

However, he did not appear confident enough to approach Masefield directly, preferring to ask Haines if Lascelles Abercrombie might serve as a go-between and forward a letter to Masefield for him. By late August or early September, Masefield was aware of Gurney and impressed enough, possibly by *War's Embers*, to send Ivor 'the most delightful of letters' about his work, which Ivor promptly circulated among his friends. During this time, Gurney completed settings of Masefield's 'On the Downs' and 'Halt of the Legion'.

Gurney finally met Masefield on Saturday, 8 November, thanks to Will Harvey's initiative in writing to the older poet in October.[16] The afternoon proved to be a gathering of poets. Robert Bridges, Robert Nichols and Robert Graves, who was living in a cottage on the grounds with his wife Nancy, were also present. It is possible that Gurney already knew Graves, perhaps having met him as early as the late spring or early summer.[17] The lunchtime meeting with Masefield and his family was a success. Ivor reported to Haines that the poet was 'extremely nice, a boyish, quiet person with a manner friendly enough, and easy to get on with'.[18] Gurney and Harvey performed for the Masefields. Both believed that the poet did not think much of 'By a Bierside', but that 'Captain Stratton's Fancy', 'The Halt of the Legion' and 'On the Downs', all Gurney's settings of Masefield's poetry, pleased him. Masefield expressed admiration for *War's Embers*, calling it 'jolly good'. Ivor left with his spirits further buoyed, believing that Masefield 'wants me to go to Oxford on a grant'.[19] However, Ivor was not particularly taken by the appearance of Boar's Hill, expecting perhaps that a poet would choose to live in a more beautiful place. He declared that it was 'not pretty as *we* know prettiness but it isn't bad'.[20]

In the meantime, Ivor was beginning to move in London's literary circles. He had met poets Edward Shanks and W. J. Turner, and had made himself known to the influential Harold Monro at the Poetry Bookshop.[21] By early November he knew Shanks and Monro well enough to socialize with them. All three attended a recital featuring singer Steuart Wilson in a performance of Vaughan Williams's *On Wenlock Edge*.

Gurney was not shy about taking advantage of Haines' literary connections. When Ivor's request for permission to use Yeats' 'Cathleen ni Houlihan' went unanswered, he turned to Haines: 'Can you ... Stir up [Lascelles] Abercrombie to prod Yeats, or otherwise assist in this difficulty?'[22] Ivor was growing anxious because A. H. Fox Strangways, editor of *Music and Letters*, had accepted the song for publication in the quarterly journal.

As 1919 drew to a close, Ivor was standing on the threshold of the most productive and successful period of his artistic life, but the outward appearance that his life was under control masked the turmoil simmering inside him. The signs of his on-going struggle to maintain a balance were apparent to those who knew him well and to Ivor himself.

Matilda Chapman was among the first to express anxiety for Gurney, whom she saw frequently while he was living at High Wycombe. Writing to Marion Scott in February 1920, she observed that Ivor's behaviour had been 'very strange sometimes lately'.[23] She was concerned because he had left for Gloucester on foot the previous day, planning to walk the entire distance. Mrs Chapman speculated that his worrisome behaviour was the result of 'overwork'.[24] The causes were much deeper and more complex. Ivor probably did not feel he could confide in Matilda Chapman and tell her that he was miserable at High Wycombe, plagued as he was by inexplicable emotional unrest and self-doubt about his music and feeling trapped in a job that was leading him nowhere.[25] At the same time, it is likely that he had no real understanding of what was happening to him and therefore could offer no acceptable explanation for his behaviour.

Ivor did indeed walk toward Gloucester. He covered about 16 miles from High Wycombe to a village east of Oxford, probably Tiddington, where he boarded a train to the Cotswolds. Once there, he walked to Dryhill Farm near Crickley Hill, where he had stayed the previous April. While in the Gloucester area, he met with Howells, who saw clearly that Ivor's old restlessness had returned, prompting his need 'for open air farm work to refurbish his musical mind and give him "ideas"'.[26] Although Gurney's future looked promising as more opportunities came his way, he was of a mind 'to give up everything of a strictly professional life, in favour of work on a farm, from which he would hope for brief periods of absence for the purpose of going to London to hear a concert or two'.[27] Howells reported their meeting to Scott and told her that he had 'passed no definite opinion on the wisdom or folly of the scheme' but that he had advised Gurney 'to take counsel of you and others ere he did anything so drastic as the renunciation of professional life'. Howells also observed that Ivor's mood was more 'deep-seated than any ordinary mood'.[28]

Ivor planned to stay in Gloucester until after Easter, which fell on 4 April that year, but he was back in High Wycombe by mid-March in time to attend the première of *Ludlow and Teme* at Marion Scott's London home on the 19th. Marion titled the Friday night programme a 'Gloucestershire Evening', featuring music and poetry by Gurney, Howells and Will Harvey. As usual, she turned the event into an elegant affair. She invited the musical and social élite of London, highly placed individuals who might use their influence to help her three Gloucestershire friends advance their careers. Invitations had gone out in February to give people plenty of notice to attend. One of the first to reply was folk-song collector and writer Cecil Sharp, who told Scott he was 'very interested in Ivor Gurney's work'.[29] The Shanks sent their regrets. Aware perhaps of Ivor's erratic behaviour, Phillis Shanks, a musician, cautioned Marion, 'Don't let Mr. Gurney play the piano part himself!'[30] However, Gurney did accompany Harvey's performance of three of Gurney's songs – 'In Flanders', 'Severn Meadows' and 'Captain Stratton's Fancy'. Tenor Steuart Wilson sang *Ludlow and Teme* accompanied by the Philharmonic Quartet and George Thalben-Ball, pianist. When the audience, which included Sir Charles and Lady Stanford, Thomas Dunhill and Arthur Bliss, responded enthusiastically to his composition, the usually outgoing, confident Gurney was humbled. He had never heard such acclaim for his work. When he did not appear to take a bow, he was, according to Marion, 'sought and at length found, bashfully hiding behind the big bookcase at the far end of our back drawing-room'.[31]

The programme also featured two works by Howells: the first performance of his string quartet 'In Gloucestershire' and 'Procession' for piano with Howells as soloist. After the music concluded, the guests enjoyed a late supper.

In spite of his success that evening and the promise of more success through the publication of his music and poetry and performances of his songs, Ivor was still unsettled. He needed to be outdoors pushing himself physically to keep his mind and body from rebelling against him. He had no other means of control. In Ivor's day there were no drugs to treat mental illness or chemical imbalances in the human body. He knew he was at his best when he was outdoors, taxing his body. When he exercised, his system seemed to be more in balance.

Fortunately, Ivor had sensed instinctively that hard physical labour was essential in keeping his personal demons at bay. However, he would not have known the medical reasons why exercise seemed beneficial to him. In a way, he was a man ahead of his time. Exercise releases endorphins that elevate mood naturally for certain periods of time. Today we associate endorphins with what is known as the 'runner's high', an euphoric state. Current research suggests that endorphins provide a link between the well-being of our emotional states and the health of our immune systems.[32]

In his depressed state, Ivor was incapable of pushing away the mental clouds and usually sank deeply into despair. During these times, he suffered more from his habitual digestive problems and lapsed into lethargy. His natural defences against illness weakened as his mental state deteriorated. When he forced himself to exercise, he released endorphins. He began to feel better, and as he did, his difficulties usually lessened. However, as with any serious illness that goes untreated, the sufferer can only do so much to help himself. Without treatment, the condition will only worsen no matter how hard he fights against it.

By early 1920 Ivor was already losing his battle against his self-diagnosed 'neurasthenia' or, in fact, his bipolar illness. He knew that if he kept his mind and body active, he could stay afloat; but he knew, too, that he could not keep up such a demanding regimen. Yet he tried. Unfortunately, his rise from depression usually hurled him directly into a manic state, during which time he slept little, ate poorly, and was charged with uncontrollable energy.

Once back in High Wycombe, he resumed his organist post but set off immediately on what he described as 'two pilgrimages'.[33] At his first stop, a nearby inn, he met a Mr Ward, who had known Rupert Brooke, John Masefield and Steuart Wilson. Mr Ward, a 'farmer or some such man', told Ivor about the Pink and Lily, Brooke's favourite pub in the hills above Princes Risborough in the Chilterns. Ivor visited the pub at the end of March and saw the guest book that Brooke had signed twice. Then he signed it himself. He chatted with the owners, Mr and Mrs Tom Wheatley, who had operated the pub since 1900. They had known Brooke, who had already become the symbol of youth and innocence destroyed by war. According to Ivor, they liked Brooke 'extremely'. Ivor found the Wheatleys 'a nice old boy – and she a nice old girl'.[34] Rupert Brooke once recalled the publican differently, 'asleep rather tipsy' in the small room where he was writing a letter to his friend, the actress Cathleen Nesbitt.[35]

As Ivor wandered about the countryside unsettled and at odds with himself, his poetry and music were attracting attention in London. He would see the publication of his songs 'The Twa Corbies' in *Music and Letters* in March 1920; and later in the year 'Captain Stratton's Fancy' by Stainer & Bell; the *Five Elizabethan Songs* by Winthrop Rogers; 'Desire in Spring' in *The Chapbook*, and 'Carol of the Skiddaw Yowes' by Boosey & Company. His poems 'The Hooligan' and 'April 20th 1919' were published in the *RCM Magazine;* 'In a Ward' appeared in *Public Health Nurse*, an American publication, and 'Equal Mistress' and 'The Crocus Ring' were printed in *Music and Letters.*

Ivor was a study in contrasts: a popular man about town, keeping company with literary and music luminaries in London, but a near tramp when he was on his own. By late April, 'in a fit of not being able to stand it any longer', he decided to leave High Wycombe and his studies at the RCM.[36] He returned to Gloucester.

During his February visit to the Cotswolds, Ivor had found a cottage at Dryhill and returned to it thinking he might live there. It was an impractical notion. Ivor's retreat to Dryhill epitomizes his attempts to find a place where he fit in. The cottage was a derelict ruin, virtually uninhabitable, draughty and damp with holes in the floor and roof, the grounds overgrown with weeds. It was not the kind of dwelling a man in control of his life would find acceptable. In the end he realized the cottage was uninhabitable, and lodged in the farmhouse attic. Ivor admitted to Marion that he was 'a bit afraid' about his new venture, but told her he hoped 'to earn a little somehow.'[37] He had put his job and his on-again-off-again education on hold 'to find out what might be found out.'[38] If he failed to earn some income, he was prepared to work as a cinema pianist or attempt to go to sea. Typically, he had gone off in quest of the security that eluded him without a plan in mind. He could not think beyond the moment and never looked ahead realistically or practically at how he might devise a workable plan.

Despite his years in the army, where discipline was the order of the day, Ivor remained intractable, strong-willed and independent. However, his seeming waywardness, his unwillingness to conform, and his inability to find and hold a job were beyond his control. He was locked in a battle with an unseen, undefined enemy that was rapidly advancing. He moved in and out of the conflict raging in his mind, some days feeling in control but increasingly wanting only to flee to a safe haven where he might feel secure. Ivor was nearly thirty years old and the only steady job of any length that he had held up to this time was as a private in the army. It was a job he could not quit on a whim, to do so would be desertion, a crime. He had no choice but to stay with it.

Of all his friends, Ivor had shown the most promise and seemed marked for greatness, but now he was spinning around in circles going nowhere. He was still relying on friends and family to support him. He could not sustain himself on his small army pension and the negligible royalties trickling in from his two poetry books and the handful of songs that had been published. His was a precarious existence. He was always worried about money and what he could do to get it. By comparison, all of Ivor's friends were settling into careers, enjoying the security and success that eluded him. Howells was teaching composition at the Royal College of Music, while Ivor remained a student there. Further, Howells was acting as an Examiner to the Associated Board of Royal Schools of Music and preparing to take on the responsibility of marriage to Dorothy Dawe. Even though his spare time was limited, Howells continued to compose, primarily unison and part songs from which he received additional income.

Arthur Benjamin embarked on a promising career as a pianist and had returned to Australia to become professor of piano at the Conservatorium in Sydney. Sydney Shimmin was music master at Malvern College. Will Harvey was working as a solicitor and contemplating marriage. Marion Scott, encouraged by Ivor, had launched a successful career as a music critic. Ivor was merely limping along behind them searching for his own direction. He had a profession – he was an organist. But he was not able to work in the one position that might have brought him a steady income and a sense of security.

Because Ivor could not function within the normal bounds of a civilian employer's authority, an employer could not depend on Gurney to do the work for which he was hired. Howells recalled that one morning while Gurney was playing the organ at Gloucester Cathedral, he became so excited and distracted by the sunlight striking the east window that he suddenly announced 'God, I must go to Framilode!' He left and, according to Howells, he was gone for three days.[39] Ivor wanted only to compose music and write poetry. He regarded everything else as obstacles blocking his way. Ideally, he needed someone to take care of him as a child would be cared for, someone to give him lodgings, money for books, make sure he ate and slept and that he had abundant time to wander the countryside, free to think, dream, and create his art.

One family was in a position to provide this kind of care for Ivor – the Scotts. They were in the habit of taking friends into their home who needed help and allowing them to stay until they were on their feet again. They applied no pressure and asked for nothing in return. Sydney Shimmin usually lodged with the Scotts when he was ill and Ivor had, on occasion, stayed there too but only for brief periods. Mrs Scott would not have welcomed an extended intrusion of the disruptive Gurney no matter how strongly Marion might have pleaded his case. Mrs Scott could take Ivor only in small doses. All Marion could do at this point was give him money and try to advance his career through her own connections while keeping tabs on his wanderings through her contact with Howells and Haines. She could have set him up in an apartment or in a more suitable cottage, but even for the liberal Scott such action would have exceeded the bounds of propriety. She would have to let Ivor be on his own no matter what the outcome.

Marion's own life had become a whirlwind of activity since she had signed on as London music critic for the *Christian Science Monitor*.

She could ill afford too many distractions. Her demanding job was driven by deadlines. Required to attend as many as a dozen concerts and events a month, she wrote reviews ranging from a few paragraphs to in-depth critiques that filled several columns. She also submitted long feature articles that required her to act as a newspaper reporter, interviewing her subjects, undertaking additional research and occasionally travelling. In January 1920 alone, she published eight concert reviews, profiles on Thomas Dunhill and John Ireland, and the first of a two-part feature on the history of the British violin sonata.[40] Her articles and reviews usually appeared every Thursday and Saturday.

With Ivor seemingly safe in England, her wartime anxiety for him had lessened and her overall health had improved. She continued her work at the RCM Union, remained an active force in the Society of Women Musicians, served as a mentor to composers and performers, particularly Howells and Gurney, and attended to family matters. At the same time she was expanding her writing career to other publications, including *The Sackbut*, then edited by Philip Heseltine (Peter Warlock).[41]

As she did with the *Christian Science Monitor*, Marion used *The Sackbut* to benefit her friends Gurney and Howells by citing their songs as examples to illustrate a point. In a *Sackbut* article titled 'Poets' Touches', she wrote: 'Another instance of a melisma, employed to enhance by a poet's touch the meaning of a word, is to be found in a setting of Masefield's poem "By a Bierside," by Ivor Gurney.' Scott noted that

> The song is one which Parry himself admired greatly and considered the most tragic thing he knew in music. Towards the end of the poem the line occurs: *Death drives the lovely soul to wander under the sky.* This the composer has set to highly sensitised harmonies and on the word 'wander' the voice drifts down upon a long and tenderly lovely melodic melisma. This is word-painting of the finest type.[42]

Scott's article is a discourse on poetry and song. She wrote:

> [I]n vocal music, particularly in songs, poetry and music meet on equal terms, and a situation is created which unites 'the finest' attributes of both. The sense, the meaning, can be conveyed in words with crystalline clarity, at the same time that the vaster issues, which music alone has power to express, can be indicated. Finite and infinite sense are linked together. There are many means in music by which these 'Poets' Touches' can be achieved: by some subtle adaptation of form, some shade of harmony, some significant line of melody, by word-painting, even by silence. But it is no use to tabulate methods; as well as try to map cloudland since these Poets' touches are not realism, but idealism, and can never be taught. Unless a composer has them in his heart it is useless to hope he can acquire them by study. They are the outward and visible sign of some inward grace of truth of which he himself even may be only partially conscious.[43]

While Ivor was trying to find his way at Dryhill, composing songs and writing poetry, Marion was maintaining a hectic schedule that left her no time for an extended holiday in the summer of 1920. She covered major events in London including the Promenade Concerts, the Handel Festival, the British Music Society's first National Congress, and the Cobbett Music Competition. She journeyed to Cambridge to report on a performance of Milton's *Comus*, and reported on the Three Choirs Festival held at Worcester in August that year. She attended the wedding of Herbert Howells and Dorothy Dawe on 3 August and wrote about the musical aspect of the celebration for the *Monitor*. While it is likely that Ivor attended the wedding, there is no record that he did.[44] He was not one of the composers who contributed to the creation of a 'folk-song gift' for the couple. According to Marion, 'The gift takes the form of a collection of original tunes in the folk-song style with each composer having either contributed a new one or else sent a quotation from some work of his already written.' George Thalben-Ball 'wove these tunes, and certain other significant musical quotations, into what was nominally a Fantasia, but which, to people who can follow the language of music, was also an eloquent and moving oration upon the ideas of love and peace.' Howells was one of the contributors with his 'exquisite melody' known as 'The Chosen Hill Tune', which he had composed for Dorothy.[45]

Back in London by October, Ivor lodged at Earl's Court and nominally became a student again. He reported enthusiastically to Haines that Winthrop Rogers was willing to take more of his songs and that the first edition of some of the Elizabethan songs had sold out. The state of Ivor's finances was so poor that Rogers advanced him £20.

His isolation in the Cotswolds appears to have done Ivor some good. Photographs taken in 1920 show a confident, determined, well-nourished, healthy, intense Gurney, dressed neatly, his suit of good quality, brushed and not rumpled, a lock of wavy hair casually falling on his forehead. His letters were full of energy and good news tempered occasionally by references to the misery of living in London, in what he called a 'houses and drain-pipe streets life' devoid of the beauty of Gloucestershire.[46] His social calendar was full. He was associating with some of the brightest and most influential men of the day: J. C. Squire, editor of the *London Mercury*; Charles Scott-Moncrieff, translator of *Song of Roland, Beowulf* and Proust and friend of the late Wilfred Owen; Harold Monro, owner of the Poetry Bookshop and champion of poets; Winthrop Rogers, the publisher of Gurney's songs; poets Edmund Blunden, then the assistant editor of *The Athenaeum*, Walter de la Mare, Edward Shanks, Wilfrid W. Gibson; composer Armstrong Gibbs; singers Steuart Wilson and Gervase Elwes.[47] All took a sincere interest in Gurney and his work.

Ivor knew Blunden well enough by the autumn of 1920 to socialize with him. He was invited to Blunden's home and Ivor welcomed him to his own lodgings. Gurney described him as 'a very nice chap, and a devil for work'.[48] At the time, Blunden was working on his collection of the poems of John Clare (1793–1864). Years later Blunden recalled Gurney as a 'nomadic being entirely devoted to his poetry and music', a 'perfectly friendly and generous man' who was 'unlike London types, and brought something of country strength and directness with him'.[49] Like others who came into contact with Gurney, Blunden was astounded by the speed at which Ivor worked and by the fact that he could work anywhere, at any time, under any conditions. One evening Ivor went to Blunden's home for supper. Blunden left him alone while he went into the kitchen to finish preparing the meal. When he returned to the room, he found that Gurney had written one song and was half-way through another, which he finished during the meal.[50] Blunden sensed in Gurney 'the urgency of a new character among the poets, giving fresh and attractive emphasis to metres that were not in themselves revolutionary. The poet's nature could not but fling a rude strength into what in other hands might have been just easy melody.'[51] Such behaviour was typical of Ivor. As Marion Scott recalled, '[W]hen good ideas occur to him, nothing else counts – not even his own safety. In some men this might seem an affectation; with Gurney it is sheer absorption.'[52]

In November Ivor's financial worries lessened somewhat when he received a government grant of £120 a year, back-dated to September. With the prospect of his grant, his small army pension and the income from the sales of his music, Ivor might finally taste the sweetness of economic security. His music was being accepted for publication and performed. His poetry was finding its way into various publications and he was writing verse for a third book.

On 9 November tenor Steuart Wilson, pianist Anthony Bernard and the Philharmonic Quartet gave the London première of *Ludlow and Teme* at Aeolian Hall. Marion's review of the concert appeared in the *Christian Science Monitor* on Christmas Day 1920. Compositions featuring voice and string quartet, a form Scott herself had attempted years earlier, were a rarity at the time. According to Scott the result was 'so enjoyable that some people expressed surprise that a form of music they termed "an oddity" could be so satisfactory'.[53] Gurney was the star of the evening. American audiences learned this about *Ludlow and Teme*:

> There is a fine, clear, out-of-doors ring about the setting of 'When smoke stood up from Ludlow', and one could well imagine the tune upon the lips of any 'young yeoman' as he 'strode beside his team'; while the second song, 'Far in a western brookland', is a pure efflorescence in music of that poetry of the 'windless night time' alluded to by Housman, and expressed here by the composer with tender truth and beauty of melody. 'The lads in their hundreds' and 'On the idle hill of summer' are equally rich in imaginative qualities: also virile in style (as the words demand), while 'When I was one and twenty' is a good little thing in the folk style as one could wish to meet anywhere. The unexpected and fascinating run of the tune delighted the audience. 'The Lent Lily', with its beautiful melismatic passages, brought the cycle to a close, and the composer to the platform.[54]

A few weeks later, Gurney's *The Western Playland* was premièred at the RCM in a programme billed as a *Chamber Concert in Commemoration of the Share taken by Collegians in the War*. Also featured were works by Vaughan Williams, Bliss, Benjamin, Parry and Ernest Farrar.

The British Music Society included Gurney in its 1920 Annual, listing 'By a Bierside' and 'In Flanders' under orchestral works, along with two violin sonatas, 'A Shropshire Lad' for voice, piano and string quartet, two song cycles, sixteen individual songs and a piano prelude. Ivor's poetry was attracting the attention of men like Masefield, de la Mare and Robert Bridges. Fox Strangways, founder and editor of *Music and Letters*, regarded Gurney as one of the most promising men of his generation.

In 1920 alone, Ivor composed about sixty songs, including parts of *The Western Playland (and of Sorrow)*, 'The Boat is Chafing', 'An Epitaph', 'Nine of the Clock', 'Goodnight to the Meadow', 'The Latmian Shepherd', 'The Fields are Full', 'A Cradle Song', 'Black Stitchel', 'Blaweary', 'To Violets', parts of his Edward Thomas cycle *Lights Out*, 'Hawk and Buckle' and 'Most Holy Night'. He was pleased with the progress he was making on the songs but was finding his piano sonata and a *War Elegy* for orchestra 'a hard and futile grind'.[55]

Despite his difficulties in harnessing extended musical works, Ivor sailed into 1921 as if driven by a strong tailwind. The year stretching out ahead looked promising as both his poetry and music continued to attract attention. He seemed to be taking command of his career, and was no longer relying solely on Marion Scott and others to open doors for him.

On his own initiative, Gurney cultivated relationships with established literary and music figures who could benefit him. For instance, he made certain that the influential Walter de la Mare, A. E. Housman and Robert Bridges, England's Poet Laureate, were aware that he had set their verses. He wrote to Bridges asking for his permission to dedicate to him 'Since Thou O Fondest and Truest', which was soon to appear under the Boosey & Company imprint. He informed Bridges that he had set a number of his poems, and offered to lend him 'the only copies I have'.[56] Ivor continued to meet with Blunden, Shanks and others and also encountered the American poet John Gould Fletcher.

Ivor also attempted to capitalize on his friendship with Blunden, hoping that as the assistant editor of *The Athenaeum*, he might wield some influence in getting his poems published. Blunden kept one of Gurney's poetry manuscript books for three months, but in the end, he returned it without having made any attempt to seek a publisher for them.

In a slightly different venture, Ivor produced occasional essays on music for publication. Fox Strangways rejected one for *Music and Letters*, but at least two others found their way into print eventually, one in *The Times Literary Supplement* and another in *Musical Quarterly*.[57]

In the meantime, Ivor completed his *War Elegy* in time for its première at the Patron's Fund rehearsal at the RCM on 16 June 1921. The *Elegy* shared the programme with Thomas Dunhill's symphony, Hugh Bradford's *Fox-Trot* for twenty-six players, Eric Fogg's *The Golden Valley* and R. O. Morris' *Novelette* for orchestra. Scott, reviewing the concert in the *Monitor*, described the new works collectively as 'a hopeful crop of compositions', adding 'Though none was impeccable, the general level stood high, and their virtues were positive as well as negative'. She cited their sincerity, purpose and 'illumined' beauty in the positive column and noted that each had 'something distinctive about it, and all were different'.[58]

Marion was direct in her assessment of Ivor's composition:

> The first, a war elegy by Ivor Gurney, is comparatively short but produces an impression of great aims. The themes are heartfelt and sincere, their treatment is grave and sensitive, and the opening and closing sections of the work are eloquent. Toward the middle, the music loses its grip and wanders around rather than holds the direct onward flow. It will probably gain by being rewritten.[59]

Marion's description of the music losing its grip and wandering around rather than 'holding the direct onward flow' can also be read as a description of Ivor at this time in his life. From all appearances he was doing well but appearances belied the reality. Ivor was in trouble. March came and with it, he fell temporarily from view. In the previous months he had worked at his music and poetry with an intensity he could not sustain indefinitely. It was spring and as he had done in the past, Ivor tumbled into his annual cycle of depression. Following a safe and familiar pattern, he retreated to the restorative landscape of Gloucestershire. By April he was in Gloucester, living with his aunt Marie at Longford.

Ivor had been driven from London by his precarious financial situation, due in part to the delayed arrival of his government grant and his own careless management of his army pension and royalty money. He was reduced to accepting Marion's offer of £5 to see him through until his next pension payment or the grant arrived. The royalties from his books and music were not enough to sustain him, a fact his brother Ronald would use cruelly in the months ahead.

To compound Ivor's worries and feelings of inadequacy and failure, he had to face the fact that his friends were achieving all that was eluding him. They were leaving him behind. He felt increasingly alone. Will Harvey was established in his legal practice and had married Sarah Anne Kane at the end of April. Howells, also married, was going to South Africa for the summer in his new capacity as Examiner to the Associated Board of the Royal Schools of Music. With the exception of John Haines, his Gloucester friends were too involved with their own lives to spend as much time with him as they had done before.

Ivor was well aware that he was lagging behind as if stuck in mire. He had failed his exams at the RCM and did not qualify for the positions requiring a degree. His scholarship had run out. He failed to get into Edward Marsh's new edition of *Georgian Poets, 1920–1922*. Ivor felt desperate enough to send a song to poet/journalist Iolo Aneurin Williams, admitting 'I can not get my things published – or very slowly ... If you could get anyone to take it I should be very glad ...' [60] He continued to submit his poems and songs to publishers and journals with decreasing success. He was reduced to working occasionally as an ordinary labourer.

Ivor's letters to Marion Scott written over the next few months reveal the beginnings of his bleak trajectory into despair. He hinted that 'something is more wrong than formerly'. His 'neurasthenia' was upon him again and he was depressed. 'Have patience with a fool, and perhaps out of a pretty black welter something may emerge.' [61] He complained of a 'congested liver' and his difficulty in finding employment. He had turned to walking and labour to control his neurasthenia. 'A night walk brought me at dawn to Birdlip; I had done 6 hours digging that day, and am still sick. It is a beastly thing. And one feels such a great musician at that time! "If only I were well".' [62]

Gurney returned briefly to the High Wycombe area in July, but did not resume his organist post. Winnie Chapman recalled seeing Ivor one day and was so distressed by the look on his face that she asked him 'whatever is the matter?' [63] Ivor did not reply. Instead, his eyes filled with tears and he 'made a little gesture of hopelessness with his hand and walked quickly on without a word.' [64]

Ivor Gurney was losing control of his life, and he knew it.

NOTES

1 MMS, MSC, *Christian Science Monitor*, 17 May 1919.

2 Ibid.

3 The memorial dedicated to the 38 men who died was unveiled at the RCM on Armistice Day 1922.

4 MMS, *Christian Science Monitor*, 17 May 1919.

5 Hubert Parry to HH, 13 April 1917, quoted in Christopher Palmer, *Herbert Howells: A Centenary Celebration* (London: Thames Publishing, 1992), p. 19.

6 Upon hearing Igor Stravinsky's *Fireworks* at a Promenade Concert in October, Gurney pronounced it 'awfully good in its way' in a 10 October 1919 letter to MMS.

7 MMS, Notes, MSC.

8 Marion Scott had preceded both Gurney and Vaughan Williams in composing for voice and string quartet during her student days at the RCM. Examples of her work in this form include settings of Bernard Weller and Robert Bridges.

9 IG to MMS, 25 and 26 February 1919 (S), *CL*, p. 473. The *Western Playland* was published in 1926 by the Carnegie Collection of British Music.

10 Lichfield: Chosen Press, 2008. Michael Hurd observes of the *'Coronation' March*: 'It is not a work of any great importance, nor is it typical of Gurney's style, but it makes a brave attempt to be what an Elgarian march should be.' (*OIG*, p. 36).

11 Winnie possessed a lock of Gurney's hair and kept it in an envelope marked 'My Dearest Ivor's Curl'. (*Stars in a Dark Night: The Letters of Ivor Gurney to the Chapman Family, 1914–1919*, ed. Anthony Boden (Gloucester: Alan Sutton Publishing, 1986), p. 12.)

12 According to Winifred Gurney, Ivor received no credit or recognition from Christ Church for these compositions. They have not been found.

13 In a letter to Haines (11 November 1919), Gurney names Beaconsfield as one of the places he visited in his walks. When the American poet Robert Frost and his family first came to England in 1912, they lived at Beaconsfield. Later Frost settled for a time in Dymock, where he met Haines.

14 IG to MMS, 8 November 1919 (P), *CL*. Around this time, Gurney had been troubled again by a boil that seems to have caused him to feel unwell.

15 IG to JWH, 23 September 1919, *CL*, p. 495.

16 Masefield's note to Harvey is reproduced in *Stars in a Dark Night*, ed. Boden, p. 104.

17 In June 1918 Marion Scott had asked her friend Lady Mary Trefusis to give Gurney an introduction to Graves, who was then second in command at *The Spectator*. Scott thought it would be helpful for Gurney to meet him.

18 IG to JWH, around 10 November 1919, *CL*, p. 500. At the time of the meeting, Masefield was 41 years old. He was named England's Poet Laureate in 1930.

19 Masefield's poem 'A Memory of a Singer' is believed to recall his meeting with Gurney and Harvey. The poem was published in Masefield's *In Glad Thanksgiving* (London: Heinemann, 1966), p. 56. It also appears in Edmund Blunden's *Poems of Ivor Gurney, 1890–1937* in a slightly different version and titled 'Of One Who Sang His Poems' – the poem begins, 'Long since, after the weary war, you came, / You, with a friend, to see me, and to sing / Poems of yours ...'

20 IG to JWH, 11 November 1919, *CL*, p. 500.

21 In November 1919 Gurney set one of Shanks's poems, 'The Singer'. In 1920 he set Shanks's 'The Latmian Shepherd', 'Dover's Hill', 'The Fields are Full' and 'As I Lay in the Early Sun'. Shanks, two years younger than Gurney, was London born and Cambridge educated. Seven of his poems appeared in the 1918–19 edition of *Georgian Poets* published by Monro. Turner was an Australian, six years older than Gurney, who was represented with six poems in the 1916–17 *Georgian Poets* and with seven poems in the 1918–19 volume. Turner was also a music critic.

22 IG to JWH, 23 December 1919 (P), *CL*, p. 500.

23 Matilda Chapman to Marion Scott, 25 February 1920, GA.

24 Ibid.

25 On one of Gurney's visits to the Chapmans after he was released from the Edinburgh War Hospital, he appears to have had a run-in with Mrs Chapman as he had had with Marion Scott's mother. It is likely that both women lost patience with him. He might have felt less comfortable in Mrs Chapman's presence as a result and might not have been inclined to share confidences with her.

26 HH to MMS, 29 February 1920, GA.

27 Ibid.

28 Ibid.

29 Cecil Sharp to MMS, 1 March 1920, GA.

30 Phillis Shanks to MMS, 24 February 1920, GA.

31 MMS, 'Recollections of Ivor Gurney', *Monthly Musical Record*, vol. 68, no. 794 (February 1938), p. 42.

32 Endorphins were not identified until the mid-1970s. A rise in blood levels of endorphins is measurable after exercise. More recently, researchers have been investigating phenylethylamine (PEA), a natural stimulant produced by the body, as a factor in the 'runner's high'. Exercise increases PEA levels.

33 IG to JWH, 31 March 1920 (P), *CL*, p. 502.

34 Ibid. In a letter to Gurney, John Masefield admitted that he was not able to recognize 'Mr Ward' from the information Gurney supplied. Masefield explained that the man might have been a Ward who married the Masefield's maid to whom he had given some of his books. The poet also explained the origin of the pub's name: 'A Mr. Pink married a girl called Lily.' (Masefield's letter was published in R. K. R. Thornton, 'New Howells–Gurney Papers', *Ivor Gurney Society Journal*, vol. 1 (1995).)

35 Mike Read, *Forever England: The Life of Rupert Brooke* (Edinburgh: Mainstream Publishing, 1997), p. 181.

36 IG to MMS, 13 May 1920 (PB), *CL*, p. 503.

37 Ibid.

38 Ibid. The question of when Gurney wrote this letter has been raised, with some believing that it actually belongs to the period in 1919 when he was at Dryhill Farm. However, I believe the 1920 date is correct, because Gurney refers to his job at the church at High Wycombe. He was not employed at the church early in 1919 when he first went to Dryhill Farm. He began his organist duties in September 1919.

39 HH, quoted in *OIG*, p. 21.

40 In her 3 January 1920 review of Dorothea Webb's performance of 'Twilight Song' ('Desire in Spring') on 26 November 1919 at Aeolian Hall, Scott called the song 'a delicately lovely little thing of soft harmonic tints and perfectly managed word setting'.

41 In 1920 Winthrop Rogers reorganized his magazine, *The Organist and Choirmaster* to appeal to a more general audience and launched *The Sackbut*, which under Heseltine's hand published a substantial amount of controversial material between May 1920 and March 1921. Just when the publication seemed poised for success, Rogers, distressed by the sometimes 'contentious' contents, withdrew his financial support. J. Curwen & Sons took over as publishers and Heseltine was out of a job.

42 MMS, 'Poets' Touches', *The Sackbut*, June 1920, p. 77.

43 Ibid.

44 If he wrote letters between May and October, none has survived.

45 MMS (writing anonymously as the 'Special Music Correspondent'), 'Folk-Song Gift to Herbert Howells', *Christian Science Monitor*, 11 September 1920. Music by Charles Stanford, Dr R. R. Terry, Ralph Vaughan Williams, George Thalben-Ball, Gustav Holst, Hubert Parry, Rupert Erlbach and Howells made up the folk-song gift.

46 IG to JWH, 9 February 1921 (P), *CL*, p. 507.

47 In a letter to Edith Harvey in October 1920, Gurney praised Scott Moncrieff's translation of *Song of Roland* as 'magnificent … iron and ringing iron at that'. During the war, Scott Moncrieff, who had been severely wounded and invalided back to Britain, met Owen at the wedding of Robert Graves in January 1918 and fell in love with him. Scott Moncrieff was working at the War Office and tried to use his influence to keep Owen in England for the duration of the war but was not successful. He had tried to draw Owen's 'heart to me' but Owen rejected him. The story of the Owen-Scott Moncrieff relationship is covered in detail in Dominic Hibberd, *Owen the Poet* (Basingstoke: Macmillan, 1986) and *Wilfred Owen: The Last Year, 1917–1918* (London: Constable & Co., 1992).

48 IG to JWH, October 1920 (H), *CL*, p. 504.

49 Edmund Blunden to DBR, 29 August 1950, quoted in DBR, *IG*.

50 Recollection of Christopher Finzi of a conversation with Blunden.

51 Edmund Blunden, 'Ivor Gurney: The Poet', *Music and Letters*, vol. 19, no. 1 (January 1938), p. 11.

52 MMS, 'Ivor Gurney: The Man', *Music and Letters*, vol. 19, no. 1 (January 1938), p. 6.

53 MMS ('Special Music Correspondent'), 'Programs by the English Singers', *Christian Science Monitor*, 25 December 1920. On the same day, Scott's long discussion and detailed analysis (31 inches long) of Howells' string quartet 'In Gloucestershire' appeared in the newspaper.

54 Ibid.

55 IG to JWH, 6 November 1920 (P), *CL*, p. 506.

56 IG to Robert Bridges, 18 February 1921 (KT), *CL*, p. 508.

57 'Cotwolds Plays', a review of Six Plays by Florence Henrietta Darwin, appeared in *The Times Literary Supplement* on 23 March 1922, and 'Springs of Music' appeared in *Musical Quarterly*, vol. 8, no. 3 (July 1922), pp. 319–22. Another essay was written for *The Times Literary Supplement*, but I have not been able to locate it.

58 MMS ('Special Music Correspondent'), 'Recent Music in London Rehearsal', *Christian Science Monitor*, 16 July 1921.

59 Ibid. The *War Elegy* manuscript is in the RCM Library. It was not performed again until March 2003 in Gloucester. It was recorded in 2006 by Dutton Epoch, and included on the CD *The Spirit of England*.

60 IG to Iolo Aneurin Williams, 1921, *CL*, p. 514.

61 IG to MMS, June 1921 (KT), *CL*, p. 516.

62 IG to MMS, 19 April 1921 (P), *CL*, p. 511.

63 IG to MMS, 26 April 1921 (S), *CL*, p. 512.

64 *Stars in a Dark Night*, ed. Boden, p. 115.

CHAPTER 18

The Tide of Darkness

*I*VOR GURNEY moved through his adult life believing that he could not alter his destiny 'by one hair's breadth from its appointed course'.[1] He sensed intuitively that his creative life would be short. He raced through everything he did at remarkable speed, as if he were trying to out-run a competitor. At times his haste and his impatience compromised his artistry. He felt that his survival depended on gathering 'the whole strength of me' and required him to turn his senses into 'my willing servitors'.[2] Over the next year, he would need all of his strength and resources to control his escalating mood swings with their debilitating effects that were propelling him towards the edge of an abyss.

By the middle of 1921 Ivor was exhibiting signs of increasing turmoil. He was rapidly becoming incapable of the normal functioning and practical behaviour expected of a thirty-year-old man. However, most men his age were not suffering from an untreated, worsening bipolar condition. In the early part of the twentieth century, mental illness was a poorly understood, mistreated condition that carried a stigma of shame for its victims and their families. It was confusing, distressing and frustrating for those who watched helplessly as the illness progressed.

Marion Scott could see that Ivor's condition was worsening. The flood of music and verse that had poured out of Gurney in 1920 was ebbing. As his letter written to her in the early summer of 1921 reveals, Ivor's attention span had been reduced to rapid-fire staccato measures. He scattered his unfocused thoughts far and wide, dovetailing one into the other, layering one on top of another, paralleling different thoughts. His tone was rushed, breathless and rambling. He ran through a range of topics that included the composition of his string quartet, his work at hoeing and his night walking along with comments on Wagner, Brahms, Bach, Scriabine [Gurney's spelling], Vaughan Williams, John Ireland, Edward Thomas, classical Greek writers, contemporary literature and music, Shakespeare and the Elizabethans, Scott's problems with the Society of Women Musicians, his strong recommendation that she read Ben Jonson and his assessment that 'There is no new musical thought, or practically so.'[3] The letter contains about thirty names of composers and writers plus references to compositions, books, journals, and newspapers. Ivor blamed this 'long screed' to her on 'an angry stomach'.[4] The cause ran deeper.

Marion was away on holiday in France and Switzerland during part of the summer of 1921, but her concerns for Ivor remained uppermost in her mind. As she journeyed through France, passing Étaples, Amiens, Chaulnes, Nesle, Rheims, she was able to report to him that she had finally seen for herself the 'wreckage and harvest' of the war in which he had fought.[5] Despite all the destruction littering the countryside, the sight of beauty beginning to flower again and reclaim the land moved her deeply.

'You know so well what the devastation looked like that it seems almost futile of me to describe all this, except that I thought you would be interested to know that even in nearly three years they have not been able to restore a normal aspect to the land', she wrote.[6] The train passed through villages, some 'dreadfully mutilated', some 'utterly dead', others beginning to come to life again with rows of 'little low bungalows following the lines of what once were streets'. She saw Rheims 'with its shards of a cathedral ... ringed with ruins'. She found the landscape 'infinitely pathetic' with many 'blasted trees' still standing 'like gaunt crucifixes' yet she sensed amid the rubble and destruction 'a strange glow of the peace of accomplishment. Everywhere crops could be induced to grow, there they were – mile after mile of golden mantle spread above the tortured earth'.[7]

Then in the evening 'just as the sunlight became a level evening flood of gold pouring over the golden fields, we passed a station and I saw a name (washed faint by the rains of many winter storms) painted on the board ... I feel sure it was Caulaincourt', reported Marion, who knew it as one of the places Ivor had been. He first saw Caulaincourt in March 1917, shortly before his battalion moved on to Vermand, where he was wounded on 7 April. In his poem 'The Retreat' Ivor recalled Caulaincourt as a 'valley of grace ... gleaming with lit sapling water'.[8]

But the valley and village Marion saw had been transformed by war. 'There was hardly any village to speak of, most being in ruins, but the harvest stretched for miles to the horizon: it was as if the country were indeed reflowering again "With scent and savour of praise"', she wrote. 'I <u>longed</u> for you to be seeing it.' [9] The scene brought to her mind the lines from Ivor's poem, 'Song of Pain and Beauty', written in the trenches in March 1917 and dedicated to her:

> O may these days of pain,
> 　These wasted-seeming days,
> Somewhere reflower again
> 　With scent and savour of praise.
> Draw out of memory all bitterness
> 　Of night with Thy sun's rays.
>
> And strengthen Thou in me
> 　The love of men here found,
> And eager charity,
> 　That, out of difficult ground,
> Spring like flowers in barren deserts, or
> 　Like light, or a lovely sound.
>
> A simpler heart than mine
> 　Might have seen beauty clear
> Where I could see no sign
> 　Of Thee, but only fear.
> Strengthen me, make me to see Thy beauty always
> 　In every happening here.[10]

As Marion travelled along 'what had roughly been the battlefront', she continued to see for herself what Ivor had experienced. Yet always amidst the ruin, she found signs of hope. 'The French peasants I saw were magnificent. The fussiness and indifferent physique of former times had vanished (I am thinking of before the war) and now one sees splendidly poised, purposeful Mennonite calm, handsome women. I never admired the French so much as I do now', she wrote.[11] 'Dawn was very beautiful, with a low rosy flush in the east at the rim of the flat country: to the north the long dark wave line of the hills, and the morning star blazing goldenly in the upper sky ... it seemed to me one could feel the deep content of this land at being French once more.'[12]

Marion had reason to be full of hope. That same war, which had created four years of chaos and destroyed the lives of so many men, had conversely given women new freedom. She relished it. Freedom and opportunities for women were goals she had pursued all of her life by setting examples of independence in thought, action and behaviour. From the time she was a teenager, she had dared to strike out on her own to clear a path for other women to follow, but like all women, even the most courageous, she had been restricted by old constraints that were now falling by the wayside.

Even women's attire had changed dramatically as their roles became more flexible and varied. Now when Marion travelled, she was no longer encumbered by the heavy, high-collared, ankle-length dresses that had been the required social uniform of women prior to the war. She had more freedom of movement and this suited her as she faced the physical challenges of the Swiss Alps. If the war had opened life for women, it had also denied Scott opportunities to travel beyond the shores of England for nearly seven years. Her separation from her beloved Alps had created a deep spiritual gap in her life that she now sought to mend.

While in Switzerland in the summer of 1921, she turned her thoughts briefly from the uplifting 'immortality of Beauty' all around her to consider a more practical and serious matter – Ivor Gurney.[13] Scott knew that he was searching for employment and that his quest was not going well. With Ivor's behaviour becoming more erratic and his financial situation so precarious, Marion feared that another episode of despair might prompt him to threaten suicide as he had in June 1918.

Marion knew the danger signs. As always in her dealings with Ivor, she was sympathetic and understanding. 'These days have been dreadfully trying to you, and the difficulties of finding work such a constant worry', she wrote. 'How are you feeling as to health? Are you better? I do indeed hope things have brightened for you in every way, both health and prospects for a job.'[14] Short of inviting Ivor to lodge with her family, which was out of the question, Marion was doing all that she could for him. When she prepared a lecture on Herbert Howells to be presented to the British Music Society, she handed her copy over to Gurney, who revised it. It was a minor task but one that engaged him if only briefly.[15] It was not enough. Nothing that anyone could do was enough to help him steer a different course.

It must have been brutal for Ivor, a proud, resilient and gifted man, to find himself reduced to begging for help, acting deferentially, accepting handouts and taking odd jobs that were beneath his abilities or totally alien to his nature. Living on charity was 'most dreadful' for him.

Ivor's friends became concerned as word got around that he needed financial assistance. In an effort to help Gurney, Alexander Kaye Butterworth sent £25 to Marion in memory of his son George, who had died on the Somme. Charles Scott-Moncrieff expressed concerns about Ivor's material welfare: '[H]ave you any work: can I do anything ... None of these questions needs an answer – but I feel concerned about your material welfare.' He mistakenly surmised, 'Your spiritual welfare is all right.'[16]

Gurney's humiliation reached new lows at the close of 1921, when he was arrested while walking the docks at night in London's East End. He had letters on him from John Masefield, Robert Bridges and Sir Charles Stanford but no personal identification. The police assumed that he was a spy, and held him until his army discharge papers were produced. When he was not walking the city streets, he slept like a vagrant on the Thames Embankment or found cheap lodging. According to Marion Scott, he was nearly robbed one night while he slept outdoors. He was growing increasingly careless and impractical with money. Books were more important to him than food and shelter.

While Ivor was clearly trying to find a job and friends provided leads to employment, steady, income-producing work eluded him. 'I've written again to Bristol about the Gloucester vacancy ... Meanwhile has come an offer from a London Cinema show, and since the Civil Service post will not fall vacant till the middle or end of March I am glad to take that', he wrote to Edward Marsh at the end of 1921.[17] Marsh had entered Ivor's life through the intervention of Walter de la Mare. Marsh sent Gurney some 'Rupert money', income from the estate of the late Rupert Brooke, whose poetry books were selling in the thousands.

Ivor worked as a pianist in cinemas at Plumsted on the far east side of London and Bude in Cornwall, but both jobs were short-lived. 'Cinema posts are hard to get, fearful to retain, easy to lose', he told Marsh in another letter.[18] He sent some of his poems to Marsh and apologized that they were 'so ill-written', adding that he was 'sorry for the horrible state of some of it, but am pretty badly done nowadays'.[19] He also sent him '5 Songs of Rupert Brooke, 4 settings, of which I do not think very much, but they are probably better than those of most folk'. At the bottom of this letter he wrote a bizarre ending after his signature which suggests that he was experiencing episodes of irrational thinking. While his words might have made sense to him, others might find them vulgar, confusing and inappropriate: 'A man named Tourneur wrote "The duke's son's great concubine / A drab of state, a cloth o'silver slut / Who has her train borne up but lets her soul / Trail i' the dirt." ' [20]

If Gurney, the artist, was trying to impress the influential Marsh, he failed. Marsh was unsettled by Gurney's correspondence but sensing that something was wrong, he did not abandon him. He informed Ivor that he did not care for the poems but he never replied to the letter with the Brooke settings nor did he return the music.[21]

While Ivor's behaviour struck others as irresponsible, indifferent, immature, inappropriate, bewildering and annoying, it was beyond his control. Seriously ill and deteriorating rapidly, he was unable to do the most ordinary tasks and was incapable of grasping the idea of what it took to do any job properly. No one, not even Marion Scott, was aware of the inner demons that were haunting Ivor or how desperately he was fighting to hold onto his sanity.

By February 1922 Gurney was back at Longford on the edge of Gloucester, living with his Aunt Marie. He was taking odd jobs as they came his way, but mostly he spent his time writing poetry, working on his string quartet, trying to get *Ludlow and Teme* ready for the Carnegie Trust Collection competition, reading voluminously and visiting with friends. Yet he had fewer friends he could rely on for company. The support he had enjoyed in the past was dissipating. His Gloucester friends were absorbed in their own lives, work, families, and responsibilities, and had little time left over for the demanding Gurney who drained their energy.

He found that 'the long evenings of music-and-book talk' he had once enjoyed with Will Harvey 'seem to have vanished'.[22] The Harveys, now with a new-born daughter Eileen Anne, found Ivor's late night visits and piano playing disruptive and inconsiderate. Will was more comfortable with Ivor in the company of John Haines and W. (William) R. P. Kerr, another Gloucester friend and minor poet. Herbert Howells and his wife, Dorothy, were expecting their first child in September.[23]

Ivor's godfather, Alfred Cheesman, no longer welcomed him to stay at the Twigworth vicarage, claiming that he found his visits disruptive and his behaviour rude. For some reason Gurney removed his music from Cheesman's home. 'I once had a great deal of Ivor's music', Cheesman told Marion Scott, 'but one day he took it away', leaving his godfather with only two compositions.[24]

Ivor was unmarried and unemployed, and had no prospects on either count. He simply did not fit in comfortably with his old friends. They could never be certain how he might behave, nor did they know how to deal with him. His unpredictability created a level of discomfort and tension that made his presence difficult to accommodate except in small doses. Ivor's friends had changed and so had he, but with Gurney the changes were far removed from the normal progression of life for an adult man. To some who observed him, Ivor 'seemed like a man running a high temperature'.[25]

Despite the changes in his relationships, Gurney still had what we would today call 'a strong support system'. His friends believed in him, cared deeply about him and tried to help. Although Edward Marsh sensed that his efforts on Gurney's behalf might result in disaster, he was about to fulfil his promise to find a post for him. Ivor's former composition teacher, Charles Stanford, took it upon himself to send a copy of *Severn and Somme* to Poet Laureate Robert Bridges for his comments. Bridges detected the 'influence' of Gerard Manley Hopkins, whose poems Ivor had indeed read during the war.[26] The Poet Laureate preferred Gurney's later poems, indicating that he 'had found a worthier expression than was at his command before'. Bridges told Stanford that if Gurney should 'think of taking to writing poetry, he might wish to perfect his manner before he introduced himself to the public ... It is certainly in his power to write good poetry if he gave himself up to it.[27]

According to Marion, Ivor was 'stung by a comment of Bridges that his technique was rough'.[28] She believed that this observation pushed Ivor to study and 'experiment passionately, earnestly in the new poetical method'. She declared that his experiments resulted in 'a style of condensed, craggy terseness that shocked many critics'.[29]

He submitted a new collection of eighty poems to Sidgwick & Jackson, only to have it rejected. '[I]t won't do for publication ... it is far too long, and the process of selection is your business, not ours. But more important, I cannot help feeling that the poems are unfinished, uncorrected, unpolished as they are certainly unpunctuated', wrote Frank Sidgwick in a terse letter. 'The whole MS. is more like a poet's notebook than a volume of finished poems', Sidgwick concluded.[30]

Ivor reduced the selection to forty poems and resubmitted it. '[W]e are unable to see any improvement in it save for a slight reduction in the length. The whole thing wears, to us, a haphazard appearance', Sidgwick wrote, rejecting the book for a second time.[31] Ivor asked Edmund Blunden to 'send it on to Cobden Sanderson', adding 'I am an unsuccessful and angry poet writing to a successful poet who has already done things for him, but the Swan of Avon himself had occasionally had his wing plucked here, I think.'[32] Gurney believed that this post-war collection contained 'thundering good stuff ... beauty and a very good sense of form and no swank'.[33]

In the early summer of 1922 Ivor reported to Marion that he was hoeing wheat and 'consequently have a job'.[34] He told her to stop sending him an allowance and made the same request of Vaughan Williams. The weather was hot, but Ivor enjoyed being outdoors in the midst of nature that had always fed his spirit. As his friends faded into the background, Gloucestershire became his most constant and dependable companion and never let him down. He was as keenly observant as always and sensitive to the nuances of light, colour, atmosphere and the ever-changing sky that found their way into his verse. Even while working hard in the fields, he paused to record a mental snapshot of 'two meadows; and the cathedral shows, and a horse and plough are going in the next field; a lovely brown covered thing with noble furrows that come straight up at one'.[35] He made one last effort to obtain a musical post 'which of course I ought to have but have been unable in 4 whole months to obtain one'.[36] Nothing came of this attempt, and Ivor continued courting the favour of Edward Marsh, an effort that finally paid off.

By the end of June, thanks to the influence of Marsh and William Kerr, Gurney secured a post as a clerk in the Gloucester Income Tax Office. Accepting it was the worst move he could have made. No position was more degrading and alien to the freedom-loving Gurney than one that confined him indoors and reduced him to shuffling papers. While he might have felt a rush of relief that he was finally to be employed and earning a steady income, the idea of being confined must have caused him considerable distress and not a little despair. His freedom was compromised, yet he felt he had no other choice, particularly with his brother Ronald badgering him to behave like a responsible adult.

The tax office was located on the corner of College Court, then a shallow canyon of bland brick buildings with characterless storefronts darkened by shadows. Ivor had more to say about the building than his work. He described the location as 'not so bad for Taxes' and noted that there was 'a view across to Malvern from higher window looks, and an interesting view across good slate roofs and honest 18th Century brick'.[37] He did not describe his work, and told Marion only that he had 'cribbed' notebooks from the office for his own writing and received his second week's pay 'without outcry, so I suppose it is all right, but all things frighten me rather'.[38] In fact, he was terrified. It must have been agonizing for Ivor to climb the staircase each morning, breathe in the stale air, take his seat and shuffle papers while from the windows he could see the changing light and watch the 'great cloud-fleets' that he loved racing across the sky.[39] He was no longer in a position to succumb to nature's temptations and rush out the door to Framilode, Crickley, Chosen Hill or the Severn to revel in nature. He was a civil servant who now had to obey the discipline of the clock, not the prompting of his spirit. He was trapped and he had good reason to despair.

Little encouraging news came Ivor's way. He corrected proofs of *Ludlow and Teme* and his *Five Country Sketches (Children's Pieces)* from Stainer & Bell. The *Musical Quarterly* in the United States published his rambling essay, 'Springs of Music' in their July number.[40] Despite the ongoing efforts of Marion Scott, Walter de la Mare and others to keep Gurney in the public arena, there was little interest in either his poetry or music. The death of Winthrop Rogers, who had agreed to regular publication of Ivor's songs, was a major blow. Ivor had seen in Rogers' commitment a ray of hope and promise that might eventually help establish his reputation. When Rogers' daughter, Calista, tried to fulfil her father's commitment to Gurney, she found herself staring incomprehensibly at manuscripts that were in complete disarray and often indecipherable. She had no choice but to reject his music.

By early August Ivor's life was cracking and shattering all around him. He was depressed, angry, frustrated and lonely. Occasionally his frustration exploded into violence. Once he beat a dog.[41] He was on a self-imposed liquid diet, consuming massive amounts of tea, coffee, water and occasionally ale. He ate very little, avoiding meats and bread in particular, eating mainly fruit, salt and probably sweets instead. He was obsessed with cleanliness, beginning each day with a ritual that included washing his body, vigorous exercise and an enema. He walked and worked through the night and slept little, sometimes not sleeping at all for twenty-four hours or more. All the liquid he consumed served as a natural diuretic, while the fruit served as a natural laxative. Enemas cleared out what nature did not remove. He believed that through these rituals and through self-denial, he might purify his body and mind, but he could not function properly without food and proper nutrition. Ivor was slowly starving himself. He lost weight and grew weak, rundown and confused. He began to experience delusions, believing that evil forces were at work on him, and that he was being tormented by electricity and the wireless.[42] All of Gloucester was under 'Electrical Control'.[43]

When he walked into a Gloucester police station one day to demand a permit to carry a revolver, the officer on duty sensed that Ivor was troubled, and called his sister Winifred, who, as a nurse, recognized that her brother was ill and in danger. She tried to convince him to see a specialist but only managed to anger him even more. He was unable to work. His absences at the Tax Office increased to the point where they could no longer be tolerated. He was fired.

His understanding and patient Aunt Marie was drawn innocently into the vortex of Ivor's behaviour and found herself incapable of coping with him. As September neared, Ivor rarely stopped by her house, preferring to sleep in fields or wherever he was when weariness descended on him. During the first weekend in September 1922 he was photographed sitting on the front steps of Marie's house holding a dog. He is wearing a suit and tie, his tousled hair sweeps down across his forehead, his face wears a mask of anguish. That same weekend, 3,000 miles across the Atlantic Ocean in Wellesley, Massachusetts, Annie Nelson Drummond married James L. McKay, a Scottish carpenter from Forfar whom she had met at the Edinburgh War Hospital in 1919. Mercifully, Ivor knew nothing about the wedding of the woman he once dreamed of marrying.

Shortly after the photograph was taken, Ivor left his Aunt Marie to move in uninvited with his brother Ronald and Ronald's new wife, Ethel. His presence proved an ordeal for the couple. Ivor resented Ronald bitterly, and blamed him for forcing him to take the tax clerk post. He was determined to make his younger brother suffer and be as miserable as he was. He tracked mud into the house and then deliberately sat on a new chair. He refused to sleep and complained that he was being tortured by the 'wireless'. He locked himself in a room and would not let them enter, leaving them standing helpless by the door listening to his anguished screams. He became violent and threatened suicide, trying once to gas himself. He begged the police to protect him from the voices that were assaulting him.

Harold C. Terry, Ivor's doctor, was called in. He told Ronald and Ethel that nothing was wrong with Ivor 'organically' and that his delusions were 'a direct result of undernourishment'.[44] He believed that Ivor could be cured with six months of regular food and sleep. He prescribed sedatives, which Gurney gulped down all at once. Will Harvey, Arthur Benjamin, John Haines, Vaughan Williams and other friends were more deeply concerned about his refusal to eat than the doctor. They believed that '<u>something</u>' was behind it but they didn't know what. Harvey, speculating without evidence to support his theory, offered 'Devil Worship'.[45]

A Ministry of Pensions doctor also examined Gurney with the result that the Ministry indicated it would take responsibility either to cure him or to provide a disability pension for life. It was recommended that he be sent to a 'neurasthenic Convalescent Home' near Bristol but 'authorities', presumably the Ministry, advised that he not be 'certified insane for the present'.[46]

Meanwhile the Gurneys didn't know what to do. Winifred had tried to get Ivor to seek help, but failed. Florence Gurney was nearly hysterical and helpless. Ronald was angry, frustrated, confused and frightened. He had no understanding of Ivor's condition or sympathy for him. He believed Ivor was an irresponsible, undisciplined egotist who had stepped above his station, put on airs and ultimately brought his troubles on himself. Ronald was blind to the fact that his brother was critically ill. He thought that Ivor could be cured of his wayward self-serving behaviour through the imposition of iron discipline devoid of any leniency or compassion. Recalling this difficult time many years later, Ronald described Ivor as

> Totally and utterly selfish.
> A complete Egoist
> An utter egotist
> A mental bully – totally intolerant[47]

With his patience withering and his anxiety level climbing daily, Ronald felt he had no choice but to turn to the authorities for help. He invited a doctor and a magistrate to his home to observe Ivor. According to Ethel Gurney, Ivor appeared normal when they arrived and they felt they could not take any action against him. Then Ronald suggested they go into another room and pretend to read a newspaper. Within seconds, Ivor joined them and said to one of the men, again according to Ethel Gurney, 'I say old sport. You don't happen to have a revolver on you, do you? I want to shoot myself.'[48] What they experienced in that very brief encounter apparently was enough to convince them that Ivor Gurney was dangerous to himself and possibly to others. They recommended committal.

NOTES

1 IG, 'Acquiescence', *Severn and Somme*, p. 32; Thornton edition, p. 30.

2 Ibid.

3 IG to MMS, June 1921 (KT), *CL*, pp. 515–18. Scott was usually very receptive to Gurney's suggestions, and did indeed take his advice about Ben Jonson.

4 Ibid.

5 MMS to IG, 30 July 1921, GA.

6 Ibid.

7 Ibid.

8 IG, *CP*, p. 262.

9 MMS to IG, 30 July 1921, GA.

10 *Severn and Somme*, p. 52; Thornton edition, p. 42. Gurney was 'rather proud' of 'Song of Pain and Beauty', which he wrote with 'Frosted finger ... lying on soaked sandbags' (*CL*, p. 233).

11 MMS to IG, 30 July 1921, GA.

12 Ibid.

13 MMS, Journal, GA.

14 MMS to IG, 30 July 1921, GA.

15 Across the top of the typed manuscript at the RCM, Marion Scott wrote: 'This copy was corrected by M. M. S. and revised by Ivor Gurney'.

16 Charles Scott Moncrieff to IG, 14 October 1921, quoted in *OIG*, p. 142.

17 IG to Edward Marsh, December 1921 (KT), *CL*, p. 522.

18 IG to Marsh, December 1921, *CL*, p. 523.

19 IG to Marsh, early 1922 (KT), *CL*, p. 524. Gurney's carelessness at this time also prompted him to apologize to Edward Shanks' wife for sending her a 'smudgy' copy of 'The Fields are Full' (see *CL*, p. 526).

20 IG to Marsh, no date, early 1922, *CL*, pp. 526–7 – quoting 'The Revenger's Tragedy'.

21 Marsh's biographer Christopher Hassall found the songs in 1959 and handed them over to Oxford University Press. They remain in manuscript at the GA but were performed on 10 May 2003 in Worcester by Paul Martyn West (tenor) and Nigel Foster (piano).

22 IG to MMS, 9–10 April 1922 (S), *CL*, p. 530.

23 Ursula Mary Howells was born on 17 September 1922. She died in 2005.

24 Alfred H. Cheesman to MMS, 19 April 1937, GA.

25 Unattributed quote from 'a friend' of Gurney's, in Christopher Hassall, *Edward Marsh, Patron of the Arts: A Biography* (London: Longmans, Green & Co., 1959), p. 491.

26 Robert Bridges to Sir Charles Stanford, 18 March 1922, quoted in *OIG*, pp. 142, 143.

27 MMS, Notes, MSC.

28 Ibid.

29 Ibid.

30 Frank Sidgwick to IG, 9 May 1922, quoted in *80 Poems or So*, ed. George Walter and R. K. R. Thornton (Ashington: MidNAG; Manchester: Carcanet, 1997), pp. 4–5.

31 Sidgwick to IG, summer 1922, quoted in *80 Poems or So*, p. 5. The originals of these letters are at the Bodleian Library, Oxford.

32 IG to Blunden, mid-July 1922 (KT), *CL*, p. 539.

33 Ibid., p. 539. *80 Poems or So* was published in 1997.

34 IG to MMS, May/June 1922 (KT), *CL*, p. 533.

35 Ibid., p. 534.

36 IG to Walter de la Mare, early June 1922 (GW), *CL*, p. 534.

37 IG to MMS, July 1922 (KT), *CL*, p. 540.

38 Ibid., p. 539.

39 'The Immortal Hour', *War's Embers*; Thornton edition, pp. 75–6.

40 Stainer & Bell purchased the *Five Country Sketches* but never published them. The five sketches are 'Minsterworth Reaches', 'Meredith', 'Longford Meadows', 'Poplars at the Sluice' and 'Wainload'.

41 Asylum letter quoted in *OIG*, pp. 2–3.

42 'Wireless' could have been the telegraph system Gurney knew during the war, not necessarily the radio.

43 IG asylum letter, undated, GA. Composer Robert Schumann, also a victim of bipolar illness, starved himself to death in an asylum.

44 FWH to MMS, 14 September 1922, GA.

45 Ibid.

46 RG to MMS, 14 September 1922, GA.

47 RG to DBR, 3 May 1951, GA.

48 Story quoted in P. J. Kavanagh, Introduction, *CP*, p. 9.

CHAPTER 19

'There is dreadful hell within me'

MARION SCOTT, the one person who might have saved Ivor Gurney from incarceration in an asylum, was on holiday in Switzerland when trouble escalated in Gloucester. Upon her return to London around 11 September 1922, she learned from Ralph Vaughan Williams that Ronald Gurney was preparing to have his brother declared insane.[1] In a matter of minutes the glimmerings of hope she had felt for Ivor earlier in the summer washed away in a flood of despair.

Marion was not prepared for this bad news, nor was she in any condition to deal with it directly. Rather than returning home refreshed and relaxed, she had arrived with a bad cold that sent her right to bed. The timing of events in Gloucester and her illness could not have been worse. She was scheduled to resume her demanding writing schedule for the *Christian Science Monitor* beginning with a Proms concert on the 15th. Instead she found herself drawn into a series of depressing exchanges with Ronald Gurney, Will Harvey, W. P. R. Kerr and Arthur Benjamin.

Harvey, who was responsible for protecting Gurney's legal interests, informed Marion that plans were under way to send him first to Ewell, the convalescent home near Bristol. If that did not work out, if Ivor were unhappy there or not improving, they would transfer him elsewhere. In the meantime, he was staying with Harvey, who believed, like Ronald, that Ivor would not be cured unless he was 'taken in hand'.[2] Harvey told Marion that he had warned Kerr to say nothing to the Gurneys about Marion's interest in the matter or her involvement as ' ... his people are as you know very queer'.[3] He advised her to wait until Ivor was at Ewell before trying to see him.

Marion had meanwhile heard from Ronald. She was incensed by the arrogant tone of the letter, particularly his opening salvo labelling Ivor an 'undeserving person'.[4] 'Personally I myself as you know have never been over sympathetic to him, as I have always been convinced that he was being handled in the wrong way', Ronald declared.[5] The 'wrong way' meant that Scott and Ivor's other friends had treated him with tolerance, patience, respect and kindness. Ronald let her know that he wanted Ivor's London friends to keep their distance and not become involved in the matter. 'Never again will I permit kind-but-lenient-and-letting-him-have-more-or-less-his-way-kind-of-people interfere', he told Marion, adding, 'I shall be glad if you will refrain from giving him anything but simple thoughts to think about'[hyphens added].[6] He made it clear that he intended to keep his family under control, and declared that they would 'do exactly as they are told'. He added a disclaimer which Scott did not believe: 'Please don't think I am directing that at London. The trouble is here, not there.'[7]

At the time he wrote this inflammatory letter, Ronald Gurney was only twenty-eight years old. He too had been wounded in the war and had

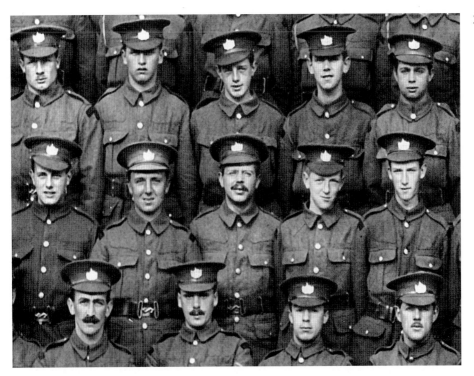

Private Ivor Gurney in the centre of the second row with the 2nd/5th Batallion, Gloucestershire Regiment. According to Marion Scott, he 'promptly volunteered' but was rejected 'on account of his eyesight'. By February, the army had relaxed its fitness requirements and Gurney traded his civilian clothes for a uniform.

Gurney and Howells in 1915. Howells, who suffered from a serious thyroid disorder, was exempt from service.

Arthur Benjamin became a gunner with the Royal Flying Corps. In August 1918 he was shot down and spent the remainder of the war in a prison camp writing music.

Gurney at bayonet practice. He is second from the right of the third rank, with glasses. He shipped to France in May 1916. At the Front his poetic genius flowered, and he and Marion Scott began collaborating on his first volume of verse, *Severn and Somme*. She acted as his editor, agent and business manager.

The face of war. Gurney photographed at Rouen, where he had been sent in April 1917 to recover from a shoulder wound. He sent the photograph to Marion Scott, calling it a 'doleful production'.

Rested and in love, Gurney appeared healthy in this November 1917 photograph taken about a month after his release from the Edinburgh War Hospital.

Volunteer Nurse Annie Nelson Drummond (1887–1959) served at the Edinburgh War Hospital. Gurney came into her care after he was gassed in September 1917. He was struck by her 'beautiful simplicity ... the fundamental sweet first-thing one gets in Bach, not to be described, only treasured'. Her 'guarded flame' ignited Gurney's love for her.

VAD Drummond, rear row, second nurse from the left, with soldiers in Ward 24. 'I forgot my body walking with her,' Gurney told Howells.

Ward 24, the 'Ragtime Ward', as it appeared in the late 1990s. Originally Bangour Village Hospital for the mentally ill, the facility was pressed into service as a military hospital in 1915 and rapidly moved into the forefront of medical advances and treatment.

Annie Drummond with her mother, Margaret, a successful businesswoman, her father, Robert, a miner, and her four younger brothers, whom she helped rear while her mother ran her millinery shop.

The Reverend T. Ratcliffe Barnett (1868–1946), a Presbyterian minister who served as hospital chaplain. A musician, poet, artist and writer, he and Gurney established a stimulating intellectual friendship.

The canteen at the Edinburgh War Hospital. The figure at the left front bears a resemblance to Gurney. Freed from the heavy hand of the censor, he shared some of his more graphic experiences with Scott, drawing her a detailed verbal map of his travels in France and discussing disturbing activities, including scavenging the bodies of dead Germans.

Annie Drummond after the war, shortly before she emigrated to the United States in 1921. In 1919 she had met James Livingstone McKay at the Edinburgh War Hospital. They became engaged and he left for America to find work as a carpenter in Wellesley, Massachusetts. Once he was established, she joined him there.

Ivor Gurney in 1920 at the height of his powers. After the war he worked in a white heat producing scores of poems and songs. His second volume of poetry *War's Embers*, dedicated to Marion Scott, was published in 1919. He kept company with literary and music luminaries in London. A. Fox Strangways, editor of *Music and Letters*, regarded him as one of the most promising men of his generation.

Marion Scott at the age of 45. An established music critic, she used her position as the London Correspondent for the international daily newspaper the *Christian Science Monitor* to introduce friends like Gurney, Howells and Thomas Dunhill to America. She also wrote for *The Observer*, the *Daily Telegraph* and a number of music journals. She became a respected authority on Haydn and wrote a classic biography of Beethoven.

44

45

Although Gurney appeared to be in control of his life after the war, his bipolar illness was beginning to take its toll on him. His friends grew concerned as word got around that he needed financial assistance. He could not hold a job. The flood of music and verse that had poured out of him in 1920 was ebbing.

Edmund Blunden (1896–1974) knew Gurney after the war. He recalled inviting Ivor to dine at his home. Blunden left him alone while he prepared the meal. When he returned, he saw that Ivor had written one song and was half-way through another that he finished during the meal.

Gerald Finzi (1901–56) and his wife Joy worked tirelessly to preserve and promote Gurney's legacy. Finzi first became aware of Marion Scott in 1923 when she organized a concert featuring one of his compositions. He approached her about Gurney in 1925.

John W. Haines (1876–1960), solicitor, botanist, poet and friend of poets, including Robert Frost and Edward Thomas. He took an interest in Gurney and became another of his trusted confidants.

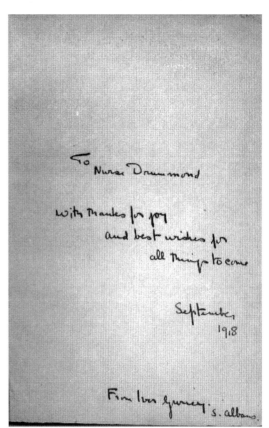

To Nurse Drummond

With thanks for joy
and best wishes for
all things to come

September
1918

From Ivor Gurney s. albans.

After their relationship ended, Ivor sent Annie a copy of *Poetry To-Day* inscribed to her. He never forgot Annie and continued to write music and poetry that he dedicated to her.

Annie Drummond on her wedding day in Wellesley Massachusetts, 4 September 1922. During the same weekend, Ivor Gurney, unaware of events 3,000 miles away, was photographed in front of his Aunt Marie's house. Within a few weeks he was committed to Barnwood House in Gloucester. He dedicated his song cycle the *Western Playland (and of Sorrow)* to Annie, and had Marion Scott send the printed score to her. Annie kept the score and the copy of *Poems of To-Day*. Her daughter found both after her mother's death. They were in a suitcase of 'treasured memories' found hidden in the back of a cupboard.

Throughout Gurney's confinement at Stone House, the City of London Mental Hospital, Marion Scott remained close to him, visiting, arranging day trips, consulting with doctors. She usually brought her camera with her on their outings to photograph Ivor, who was a somewhat camera-shy subject. He always had a book with him; if he didn't, Marion took him to a bookshop to buy one.

In 1934 Florence Gurney, shown *(right)* in her old age, grew alarmed about a bad cough Ivor had developed. Although she expressed her concerns and made it clear that she wanted her son returned to Gloucester, he remained at Stone House. With her own health deteriorating, she knew she could not continue making the long journey to London and feared that she would never see Ivor again.

One of the last known photographs of Ivor Gurney taken by Marion Scott during an outing to Dover on a day of 'racing wind and sun, the Channel full of moving colour'. Scott watched as Ivor shaded his eyes and stood still at the water's edge gazing 'long at the fields of France, hazy golden and blue across the water — his first and last sight of them since the war'.

Ivor Gurney died shortly before dawn on 26 December 1937. His grave at St Matthew's Church, Twigworth, rests between May Hill and the blue line of the Cotswolds that he loved. Marion Scott photographed his grave. The card with her wreath read 'in loving and unchanging memory of Ivor Gurney'.

Marion Scott in 1951, photographed by Joan Chissell. 'I remember her as a rather frail-looking, white-haired lady, very sensitive and soft-spoken, but with the keenest imaginable intelligence, and passionately-held convictions,' Miss Chissell recalled (letter to author, 13 June 1996).

returned home to take charge of his father's tailoring business when Mr Gurney fell ill. Ronald had been the head of the Gurney household since the death of his father in 1919. He took his responsibilities very seriously. He watched over his unstable mother, kept an eye on his sister Winifred, and managed to be the mainstay of support for himself, his wife, Ivor and his mother. He was attempting to impose some order on his chaotic family while he entered the dangerous, uncharted waters swirling around the dilemma of Ivor's care and his future. Ronald had endured a living hell trying to deal with Ivor's violent, threatening and dangerous behaviour in August and early September. He knew that once he placed his brother into care and became his legal guardian, he would be responsible for him although he was inexperienced in such matters. He was scared and had no one to rely upon but himself. Instead of asking for help, he pushed away the one person who was capable of giving it – Marion Scott.

Marion had never liked or warmed to Ronald. She regarded him as an artless, insensitive and pompous man who held Ivor and everything he did in contempt. For his part, Ronald resented Marion's influence over Ivor, her social position, her sophistication and her money. Although they had been in each other's company only in passing, the animosity between them was electric. Ironically, Ronald and other members of the Gurney family had, in the past, deferred to Marion's judgement and allowed her to take command of Ivor's life. They would expect her to do the same in the future, despite Ronald's legal position as his guardian. Marion did not accept Ronald's relative youth and inexperience as an excuse for his dismissive and patronizing attitude towards her. Instead of making overtures to him that might have comforted Ronald and encouraged him to act more reasonably towards Ivor, her temper flared. No one, least of all Ronald Gurney, was going to tell her how to treat Ivor or take control of Ivor's life without considering her ideas and concerns about his care. In her own mind, she believed that she knew far better than anyone what Ivor Gurney needed.

Marion heard from friends of Ivor's who were worried about the worsening situation in Gloucester. Arthur Benjamin, Gurney's confidant during the early RCM years, wrote an oblique letter that raises more questions than it answers:

> I think that psycho-analysis is the only cure for him; but that, of course, would mean entire confidence on Ivor's part, which is doubtful. I used to know a great deal about Ivor and on that knowledge – the details of which it is impossible for me to discuss with you – I think that psycho-analysis is the only chance.[8]

What secret was so dark that Benjamin refused to disclose it even though he suspected that the knowledge he possessed had a direct bearing on Ivor's condition? During the tumultuous year of 1913 when Ivor had suffered his first documented breakdown, Benjamin had come to know Ivor intimately. He believed that Gurney was, like himself, homosexual, and might have thought that Gurney's breakdown was related to his sexuality. Benjamin might have chosen to censor this 'knowledge' in order to protect his friend, since homosexuals were still the target of rampant hatred, arrest and prosecution.[9] Aside from his letter to Marion, Benjamin kept secret whatever Ivor confided in him.

Benjamin had other concerns. He did not believe it was a wise idea to send Gurney to Barnwood House because its 'name [as an asylum for the insane] is a byword to all Gloucester, and therefore to Gurney', he explained to Scott.[10]

Ivor's friend W. P. R. Kerr kept Marion apprised of the efforts to place Gurney in care. He informed her that Dr Terry believed that Ivor had been 'suffering from physical delusions for a long time' and that he planned to tell the medical superintendent at Ewell that Ivor 'was an exceptional person and of great talent'. Terry did not want Gurney certified as a 'lunatic' and did not want any treatment undertaken 'without consultation' with Ivor's friends.[11] Kerr informed Marion that Ivor was 'very much under Ronald's influence' and believed that Ronald's enforcement of strict rules such as demanding that Ivor go to bed and sleep for ten hours were 'doing him good already'.[12] But Kerr, like Gurney's other friends, did not understand the seriousness of his illness, and wrongly assumed that 'Nearly all his trouble arises from his own childishness, in refusing to sleep and eat normally. I believe myself that if he can be got into some institution where he is obliged to live sanely, he'll soon get sane.'[13] It was not that simple, nor was Ivor able to control his behaviour as easily as some of his friends assumed. On 28 September, six days after Kerr wrote this letter, Ivor Gurney was admitted to Barnwood House.

It was early October before Marion found time between assignments to take the train to Gloucester to visit Ivor at Barnwood. By this time, doctors had made their evaluation of Gurney's condition. 'He is under the delusion that persons whom he did not name, are constantly tormenting him through electrical influence, that they dominate him by this means, compel him to take food which he does not wish to take, preventing him from doing his work ... [T]hat he wishes to end his life by shooting himself or by poison', wrote James Grieg Soutar of Barnwood House in his report.[14] The diagnosis: 'Delusional Insanity (Systematic)'.[15]

When Marion finally saw Ivor, she 'found him not only suffering from delusions but <u>terribly thin and weak</u> as he had hardly eaten anything for six weeks. He was so weak from refusing to eat any food that when I saw him ... he could only just walk. It was a terribly sad time', she recalled.[16] Marion met with his doctors and heard their disturbing account of behaviours that they interpreted as clear indications of insanity.

Upon her return to London, Marion shared her observations with Ralph Vaughan Williams, her colleague at the RCM and Gurney's former teacher. Together they journeyed to Gloucester to see Ivor, and came away even more concerned about his physical decline. Fearing that he had not been properly examined and that he might be suffering from an undetected physical ailment, they insisted that Ronald permit a specialist to examine him and arranged for a Cheltenham doctor to see him. No known record of this examination or the results survives.

Ivor, knowing that Marion was trying to help him, and grateful for her kindness, wrote: 'One cried out of pain and another heard'.[17] His reports of Ronald's attitude and behaviour towards him only deepened Marion's resolve to take charge of Ivor's life. 'Yesterday Ronald came, but he doubted that the talk of my pain was more than electrical delusion. ... Ask Ronald to believe mere words and not his own opinion', he pleaded with Scott.[18]

Ivor wrote of his despair and desperation in a stream of poetry and heart-breaking letters to family, friends, the police, to anyone who might listen and 'rescue' him. He reminded Scott that during her visit she saw him 'less tormented than often'.[19] 'Rescue me while I am sane', he implored her.[20] 'Do not leave me here. I suffer', he begged his Gloucester friends John Haines and Will Harvey.[21] Writing to Vaughan Williams, Gurney protested that he did not want 'to be left here, where conditions are not such as one can get well in ...' He declared that he would do 'almost anything for freedom' because he did not want to be 'left here to rust into disuse'.[22]

Ivor knew what his incarceration meant. He had already experienced the sour taste of asylum life when he had been hospitalized at Lord Derby's War Hospital in Warrington following his breakdown in the spring of 1918. At that time, Lord Derby's reflected its grim pre-war history as Winwick Asylum. Since that episode, Ivor had been acutely aware that his self-defined 'neurasthenia' was getting worse. He knew that confinement in an asylum was a terrifying possibility for him, and he fought hard but unsuccessfully to save himself from succumbing to that fate. Barnwood House proved to be his worst nightmare come true.

> And I am merely crying and trembling in heart
> For Death, and cannot get it. And gone out is part
> Of sanity. And there is dreadful hell within me ...
> ... Gone out every bright thing from my mind.
> All lost that ever God himself designed ...[23]

Within a few weeks of his arrival at Barnwood House, Gurney escaped. He was soon returned to the facility, however. On 8 November he made a dramatic second escape when he hurled a large clock through a window, jumped through the jagged hole and scaled a high wall on his way to temporary freedom. He cut his hands so badly that he eventually gave himself up to the police. Ivor's determination to remain free was as enormous as the despair he felt on being locked up, a prisoner in an asylum. During his November escape from Barnwood House, he again contemplated suicide by drowning, throwing himself in front of a train or shooting himself. The staff kept a close watch on him to avoid further episodes.

By mid-November he was eating better and had improved physically. He occupied 'a good deal of his time in reading and writing and with his music', according to Arthur Townsend, superintendent of the facility.[24] Although Ivor appeared to be eating better, he was not eating normally. Townsend told Scott that Ivor was 'taking a good amount of food, though still not as much as I should like; the difficulty with regard to food is irregularity, he will miss a meal or two and then eat an abnormal amount at another meal'.[25] He was describing a pattern of eating that had been with Gurney for many years. Unfortunately, doctors in 1922 did not understand that Ivor was suffering from an eating disorder that caused vitamin and mineral deficiencies which exacerbated his mental instability. Doctors made no attempt to put him on a maintenance diet or to oversee his food intake.

On 23 November 1922 Townsend suggested that Marion try to place Ivor in the City of London Mental Hospital, explaining that he might be better off 'in some institution some distance from Gloucester, as being here is a constant source of anxiety to him ... I am sure his proximity to Gloucester creates a constant unrest in his mind'.[26] As Arthur Benjamin had pointed out to Marion, Ivor was afraid that someone in Gloucester might recognize him at Barnwood House, known locally as the 'lunatic asylum'. The issue of paying for his care had also surfaced. Townsend made it clear that the hospital 'Committee would do something for him ... but not maintain him permanently without payment'.[27] Ivor's mental state was not improving, and he might become an expensive liability.

The idea of removing Gurney from his native Gloucester did not meet with unanimous approval. His mother, Florence Gurney, who has been unjustly blamed for much of Ivor's trouble, did not want her son taken away from her, but she felt that she must agree to do what other, seemingly more sophisticated people thought best for him. A widow in her sixties, she did not have the physical strength or psychological stamina to cope with her son in her home, nor did she have money to pay for his care.

John Haines was 'exceedingly opposed' to Ivor's transfer to London. 'This is primarily a medical question and if the doctors consider removal likely to improve his health he should of course be moved; [but] unless they do, all other possible reason favours his staying', Haines informed Marion. 'I am certain that he will be better attended no where else and I do not believe that the local surroundings really affect him adversely. What he wants is freedom to get away ...'[28] Haines felt that it was important for Ivor to be near his friends and he also expressed concern about the financial burden that would fall to Marion since the London hospital cost more than Gurney's small Army pension of £2 a week paid. Money, however, was not a concern for Marion. Having Ivor near her was her priority.

Ronald continued haranguing Ivor and showed no sympathy for him. For once, Ronald had the upper hand. He was quick to remind Ivor that the royalties from his books and music were negligible – 'a total of £14 in 15 months' – and how much money Ronald had supplied to him.[29] 'My advice to you is not to shout so damned egotistically about your being a better man than me. You are only shouting at the very one you depend on', he reminded Ivor. 'If you were to forget for a while that you are such a wonderful man you might get well and, for a change, do something to prove it'. Ronald thought that by challenging Ivor, he could make his brother act like a normal, productive man. 'Personally I think you want your stubbornness broken at all costs, then you might think of others as well as yourself'.[30] Ivor was stung by his brother's comments and passed the letter on to Marion, whose reaction can only be imagined. She felt it more imperative than ever to move quickly to get Ivor away from his family.

Yet in his own plodding, abrasive way, Ronald was trying to help Ivor. He claimed that he understood 'the inner state of his mind' because he had the same temperament and nervous system. He implied that he had suffered similar emotional upheavals, claiming that he had 'travelled a long way down the same road that he has gone'.[31] Ronald did send Ivor money, and he made sure his brother had enough clothing and his books. He made it clear that he was willing to help Ivor if he would help himself. But Ronald was making unrealistic demands of a seriously ill man who was incapable of acting rationally.

Ivor's letters to Marion, to her father, to Dr Harper, his London physician during the RCM days, to the Gloucester police, to the Bishop of Gloucester and others leave no doubt that Ivor Gurney was desperately ill. He was under 'continual' wireless and electrical 'influence', and experiencing pain and delusions so intense and real to him that the only way he felt he could be free of the torment was to die. 'I cannot cut my throat on a window pane is all that is the matter. If I were dead it would be better. If alive could do good work. But I want death, as a compensation for so much pain', he wrote graphically to Scott.[32] He also informed her that he feared his friend Ethel Voynich was in danger because he had 'seen signs of her being tormented'.[33] Gurney was severely delusional, paranoid, irrational and in agony, yet he believed that he was 'saner and more innocent / Than many people walking in the open air'.[34]

In 1922 doctors had no drugs to control a patient's behaviour and the resulting psychotic episodes that are a natural progression of this illness when it is untreated. They had no drugs to lift patients out of the deep depression that follows a manic episode. Gurney was in a hopeless situation. 'If Hell ends tomorrow, I shall have had too much today', he wrote chillingly to his mother.[35]

In the meantime, the Scotts had already taken action to transfer Ivor from Barnwood House to the City of London Mental Hospital at Dartford, the facility suggested by Arthur Townsend. Sydney Scott, Marion's solicitor father, assured Ivor that 'active steps are being taken as you wish to change your residence & I feel this will be arranged very shortly'.[36]

But Gurney had to endure another month at Barnwood House, where

> All day nothing happens that is human ...
> And I am tormented, and life
> Is as easily shaken off in desire as a feather
> That I cannot write letters but in tangle,
> And there is nothing had of knowledge but
> A tangle of perplexities ...
> Why are things tied so in a knot? [37]

Marion was becoming increasingly alarmed by Ivor's references to means of committing suicide, which included slashing his throat with glass, shooting himself, taking poison, suffocating and drowning in mud or jumping from a bridge. The latter he felt would do the job more quickly than water. All of her old fears and uncertainty about Ivor had rushed back into her life with the force of a tidal wave. Every day brought new worries and no solutions. Like Ivor, she was forced to play a long waiting game as the paperwork for his transfer dragged through the bureaucracy.

Ivor, who had always relied on Marion, wrote heart-rending pleas to her to save him. 'I cannot stand much more', he told her.[38] The pressure on her was enormous from all sides. She was the one who was left to make all the arrangements. She was dealing with Ivor, with hospital authorities, with doctors, with Gurney's friends, with his difficult brother, with his confused mother. Marion knew that her desire to see Ivor moved was not welcomed by everyone. She was aware that he was going to become her responsibility since no one else seemed to know what to do or how to do it without her guidance. She felt herself sinking into depression.

Ronald's attitude didn't help matters. Writing to Marion on 16 December, he informed her that 'Dr Little, the assistant at Barnwood says that the Police Station business is perhaps gone too deep for cure', a reference to Ivor's earlier attempt to secure a revolver from the police so he could shoot himself.[39] Ronald complained that his mother was a 'menace' and that her visits to Barnwood House to see her son resulted in 'a heap of letters' from Ivor.[40] Ronald had reached the point where he wanted to be free of the constant stress and responsibility of having Ivor so nearby. He had given up. 'There is no hope at Barnwood', he told Marion.[41]

Two days later, when it appeared likely that Ivor would be sent to the City of London Mental Hospital, Ronald wrote to Marion: 'If you can get him on the Farm at Dartford [where the facility was located] that is the best possible thing. And tell them to work him till he is too tired to think. Treat him like a stubborn boy and not a cultured genius and I can assure you that will pull him up quicker than anything.' Ronald couldn't stop there, and his bitterness continued to flow. 'Kindness is wasted – try the other way – firmness with kindness out of sight. He is quite sane – only about five percent of kinks wrong. He suffers from inordinate self-thought and from the fact that the world does or has not seen what "a great man he is" and also he simply must have his way regardless.' [42]

Finally, less than a week before Christmas, word came that the transfer had been arranged. 'I feel sure it will be far better for Mr Gurney to be away from surroundings he knows so well ... sorry we have not been able to do more for Mr Gurney, he is such an extremely nice fellow and it is a most pathetic case', Townsend wrote to Scott on 20 December, the day before Ivor was scheduled to leave for London.[43] Ivor had just written another desperate plea to Marion, a one-line message: 'If I am left here any longer I shall go mad.' [44] The letter was posted on 21 December 1922, after he was already on his way to London.

At 7:30 on that day as the winter air chilled the grey morning, an automobile carrying Ivor Gurney and two attendants left the grounds of Barnwood House and turned right onto the old Roman road. He was leaving behind everything that was dear to him and that had shaped him as an artist and as a man. Ivor left no written account of what he felt or thought as he watched the places he knew and loved flash by, framed for an instant in the window glass: Cranham Woods, Shurdington where he had dreamed of living and writing in a crumbling cottage, Leckhampton Hill, the ancient Roman Villa, Witcombe, Birdlip, and finally the blue line of the Cotswolds receding and then disappearing from sight.

He never saw them again.

NOTES

1 Nearly 30 years later, Scott recalled the sequence of events leading to Gurney's incarceration differently than they in fact happened. In a note written in the early 1950s, she claimed she had returned home from Switzerland at the end of September and learned then that Gurney had been committed to Barnwood House. Gurney's admission to the asylum and the fact that he had been certified insane were not a surprise to Scott, as she implied in 1952. She knew what was going on as soon as she returned to London on 11 September. In correspondence with Don B. Ray, Scott wrote: ' … when I returned at the end of September 1922 I was horrified to hear of Gurney's relapse …' Gerald Finzi also claimed in a letter to Ray that Scott 'was horrified to find on return from a holiday abroad that he had been certified by his family and was in Barnwood Asylum …' See DBR, *IG*, p. 70.

2 FWH to MMS, 14 September 1922, GA.

3 Ibid.

4 RG to MMS, 14 September 1922, GA.

5 Ibid.

6 Ibid.

7 Ibid.

8 Arthur Benjamin to MMS, 15 September 1922, GA.

9 Benjamin was well aware that homosexuals were in a dangerous position after the passage of the Labouchère Amendment in 1885, a law that became known as the 'blackmailer's charter'. The amendment effectively made every form of male homosexuality a crime.

10 Benjamin to MMS, 15 September 1922, GA. Howells told Benjamin about Barnwood House being a byword for insanity.

11 W. P. R. Kerr to MMS, 15 September 1922, GA.

12 Kerr to MMS, 22 September 1922, GA.

13 Ibid.

14 Jas. Grieg Soutar, Barnwood House records, 28 September 1928, City of London Corporation Archives.

15 Gurney medical records, City of London Corporation Archives.

16 MMS, notes quoted in DBR, *IG*, p. 70.

17 IG to MMS, November 1922 (KT), *CL*, p. 546.

18 Ibid.

19 Ibid.

20 IG to MMS, November 1922 (KT), *CL*, p. 548.

21 IG to JWH and FWH, 4 November 1922 (P), *CL*, p. 542.

22 IG to Ralph Vaughan Williams, November 1922, *CL*, p. 543.

23 From 'To God', written at Barnwood House, *CP*, p. 156.

24 Arthur Townsend to MMS, 30 October 1922, GA.

25 Ibid.

26 Townsend to MMS, 23 November 1922, GA.

27 Townsend to MMS, 13 October 1922, GA.

28 JWH to MMS, 18 November 1922, GA.

29 RG to IG, 12 November 1922, quoted in *OIG*, p. 156.

30 Ibid.

31 RG, quoted in *OIG*, p. 157.

32 IG to MMS, December 1922 (KT), *CL*, p. 552.

33 Ibid. Scott told Voynich about Gurney's delusion. Voynich later referred to it as 'that dreadful fancy about the wireless … pitched on me'. She found the episode so upsetting

that she decided it 'was better that I should not see or write to him'. ELV to MMS, 13 January 1938, GA.

34 IG to Dr Harold Cairns Terry, November 1922 (KT), *CL*, p. 549. Terry was Gurney's Gloucester doctor whose surgery was at 14 Barton Street; his patients included many poor residents of the city.

35 IG to FG, undated letter, GA.

36 Sydney C. Scott to IG, 25 November 1922, GA.

37 IG to Dr Terry, November 1922 (KT), *CL*, p. 549.

38 IG to MMS, December 1922 (KT), *CL*, p. 551.

39 RG to MMS, 16 December 1922 (PB), GA.

40 Ibid.

41 Ibid.

42 RG to MMS, 18 December 1922, GA.

43 Townsend to MMS, 20 December 1922, GA.

44 IG to MMS, 21 December 1922, *CL*, p. 554.

CHAPTER 20

Asylum – 'The soul halts here'

*I*VOR GURNEY arrived at Stone House, The City of London Mental Hospital, Dartford, at 12:30 p.m. on 21 December 1922 to begin his torturous descent into Hell. He became patient number 6420 and faced a bleak future cut off from everything he treasured and loved – friends, conversation, ideas, walking, nature, beauty, music, Gloucestershire and most heart-rending, his freedom.

Marion Scott knew that tearing him away from his beloved Gloucestershire countryside and removing him from close contact with nature might hurt him deeply and even break his spirit. These painful realities were uppermost in her mind as she searched for a facility that could provide the care he needed and, at the same time, offer a natural environment in which he might maintain his contact with nature. She knew that he faced a long-term hospitalization and was well aware that he needed an advocate nearby to stay in touch with him and to deal directly with the doctors. It was clear to her that no one in his family was truly capable of shouldering that responsibility. Although some of his friends protested her taking him away from Gloucester, she was doubtful that they could be relied upon to oversee his care for the long term. She feared that their initial willingness to help would fade quickly as they went about the business of their own lives. They would become discouraged and soon come to resent Ivor as a burden.

Therefore it was essential that Marion find a situation amenable to her own ability to stay in touch with what was happening with him which meant going to see him as often as possible. That would have been impossible on a weekly basis if she had to travel great distances. She had to consider her own life too. She knew that by having him close to her, she could provide what others could not.

Arthur Townsend's recommendation of Stone House seemed to offer the best choice. Designed by James Burnstone Bunning and built by the Corporation of London, the City of London Lunatic Asylum had opened in 1866. By the time Ivor Gurney was admitted as a patient, Stone House was regarded as a leader in the care of the mentally ill, run by medical superintendents who were considered to be the best in their field. Nurses and other staff members underwent special training to care for the 800 patients housed within its walls. The standards set by its administration and its high percentage of private patients earned it a reputation for 'being like a gentlemen's club'. Each ward had a piano, gramophone and radio, and each week patients were treated to an evening of cinema and music.

The philosophy at Stone House was much the same as the philosophy at Bangour Village before it was pressed into service as the Edinburgh War Hospital, where Gurney was a medical patient in the autumn of 1917. Doctors at both facilities understood the importance of keeping patients active, particularly outdoors. In addition to its farm, which produced food for both the patients and staff, Stone House was near enough to the Thames that patients could walk along the riverbank.

Ivor's first week passed without incident. He was depressed and agitated, but he was co-operative. Doctors, aware of his previous suicide threats and attempts and his escapes from Barnwood House, placed him on 'parchment', or suicide watch, the day he arrived at Stone House. He submitted to a physical examination which revealed that he was in 'moderate' health, although doctors, reviewing previous medical records, noted that he had suffered an 'ulceration of the stomach some years earlier' and had been 'shell-shocked' during the war.[1]

Gurney was taken off suicide watch when he promised not to harm himself. Then on the morning of 4 January 1923, he cut his finger badly enough with a knife at breakfast to require two stitches. At first, doctors were alarmed, thinking that the injury was intentional, but they soon realized that it was the result of an accident.

Although Gurney knew that he was ill, he did not believe that he belonged in an asylum. He saw clearly what his imprisonment meant. In an early asylum poem, he wrote '[T]he soul halts here / Consumed with black fear'.[2] Gurney was a desperate man. He knew that any curtailment of his freedom to wander was inimical to his well-being.

On 6 January, two days after his accident with the knife, doctors allowed him out for an afternoon walk. He escaped. Authorities alerted Marion Scott via telegram, but Gurney avoided the Scotts. He visited instead with J. C. Squire, who apparently did nothing to raise an alarm. On his second day of freedom Ivor made his way to the home of Ralph Vaughan Williams and his wife Adeline in Cheyne Walk, Chelsea. Vaughan Williams had no choice but to telephone the authorities at Stone House. After he was taken from Vaughan Williams' home, arrangements were made to hold Gurney at the Workhouse Infirmary at Hounslow until he could be transported back to the asylum. Vaughan Williams felt like 'a murderer' when he turned Ivor in.[3]

Back at Stone House, Ivor's free spirit was once again confined in what to him were prison-like conditions. He suffered from anxiety and insomnia, prayed 'continually for death' and claimed he was harassed by 'wireless influence'.[4] He was given drugs to help him sleep, but doctors paid little attention to his other needs, including intellectual stimulation and exercise. They treated him cautiously, fearful for his safety should he escape again or attempt suicide.

From the start, Ivor proved to be a difficult patient. He was bitter, angry and defiant. However, it is unlikely that any asylum, no matter how good, would have been right for him. To the doctors and staff he was just another patient, a man believed to be suffering from 'delusional insanity' who was 'said to have been assistant organist in Gloucester Cathedral, and to have been a capable composer and an approved poet'.[5]

Once he was incarcerated at Stone House, Ivor was merely maintained, fed and given a bed and very basic health care. His mental illness was never properly diagnosed or treated, because there was no treatment. Like any untreated illness it grew worse with the passage of time. Little attention was paid to his diet, nor was any thought given to the possible connection between his poor eating habits and his mental state. Indeed, Adeline Vaughan Williams eventually complained that it was 'deplorable that the hospital does not take the trouble to see that Ivor gets fresh air and proper nourishment'[6]

Ivor's own means of controlling the more devastating effects of his mood swings – exercise and hard physical labour – were cut off by the confines of what he regarded as limited space in Stone House and lack of access, as he knew it, to the outdoors. Even if the doctors and staff did not appreciate or fully comprehend how gifted Gurney was, they did their best to try to please him by setting up a writing desk for him in the garden and allowing him to walk along the Thames. He eventually refused to go out in the grounds, which he regarded as 'a travesty' of the English countryside that was 'sacred to him'.[7] He told Marion that so long as he was in a mental hospital, he looked upon himself 'as one dead'.[8]

After two months in the asylum, he began to socialize minimally and was allowed occasionally to resume his old role as a cinema pianist for films shown to patients. Although he made a few friends among patients, he had nothing in common with them and was most content alone reading and working on new poems. 'The act of writing is a distraction in madness', he declared.[9]

At Stone House, Ivor told a new set of doctors that he was tormented by electricity. The 'Electrical Tricks' he described had grown 'very much worse since late August' but in looking back he could see that 'all his life he has been subjected to Electricity'. He claimed that when he was a student at the Royal College of Music 'he felt the same thing but did not realise it at the time'.[10]

Ivor's first documented encounter with 'electricity' actually dates from late 1917 or early 1918 when he was stationed at Seaton Delaval, Northumberland. In a small black notebook he kept at this time, he covered several pages with technical information about electricity and magnetism, presumably as part of his training in his signalling course. The material is straightforward and contains a few diagrams, definitions of terms, and brief explanations of how electricity and magnetism work. There is no suggestion whatsoever in Gurney's notes that this early introduction to electricity was anything but a learning experience.

Ivor attempted to explain the nature of his torment. He told doctors that he faced each day fearing the 'suffering' brought on him by electricity that was 'sent by certain persons' whom he did not wish to identify as it would 'incriminate certain people'. The electricity manifested itself 'chiefly in thought' and words were conveyed to him that were 'often threatening … obscene and sexual'. He claimed that he heard many kinds of voices and that he saw things when he was awake, faces he could recognize. He could not keep his mind on his work and complained of such pain in his head that he felt he would be better off dead. He tried to convince his doctors that he would do 'much better' if he were permitted to do farm work. They, in turn, regarded him as 'strange in manner' and were baffled by his condition.

But the physicians were not communicating directly with each other either. Their notes were contradictory. One doctor wrote that 'he takes food well,' while another reported that 'he occasionally refuses his food but so far has not had to be fed.'[11]

By June, Ivor was talking to no one and remained paranoid and delusional. Then, doctors decided to take radical action by inoculating him with 'a mild form of malaria'. Ronald Gurney gave his permission. The medical superintendent Dr R. H. Steen approached Marion Scott to apprise her of their plans 'in case you have any objection to offer.'[12]

The on-going trauma of dealing with Ivor tore Marion's heart. She was living on raw nerves and was skirting dangerously close to the edge of a nervous breakdown. She was apathetic and depressed, barely able to work, and was suffering from physical illnesses which she blamed on 'being sick ... in spirit'.[13] Recognizing how serious her own condition was, she had planned a restorative journey to Switzerland in July in company with Sydney Shimmin and Gertrude Eaton.[14] On the eve of her departure, she received the letter from Dr Steen informing her of the plans to treat Ivor with malaria. This news was more than she could bear, a final crushing blow in a series of ominous events.

'The world in general is not a very noble or inspiring place just now, and against this general background there was the particular problem of Ivor's insanity', she wrote in her journal. 'For months I had been dashing my thoughts and energies against the problem. Almost uselessly it seemed and my heart could only cry out in rebellion at the whole horrible torture of insanity, and revolt at the routine of acquiescence to which its continual sight has reduced physicians.'[15]

Marion left London on Thursday 26 July 1923, crossing the English Channel to France, where she and her companions boarded their train for Switzerland. This journey lacked the thrill of anticipation she usually felt upon visiting Switzerland. It might 'as well have been a trip to Siberia ... for I was too tired on starting to experience any spring of delight'. The next morning, when Marion awoke in her berth, she was in northern Switzerland. She gazed out the window. The gloomy 'London tints' that had added to the darkness of her days over the past months had been replaced by 'blue sky, compact green hills, houses, the early sun giving Sunday morning air to all' even though it was Friday. She watched the clouds lift off the mountains, rejoiced as the first snows came into view across the lake at Thun and savoured the colours of Alpine flowers glowing in fields below rock-edged flanks of mountains. 'So it is still here after all! So it really does exist', she said to herself. Then she wept, releasing the anguish, despair and sorrow locked inside her for months. Marion had been drawn to the Alps first as a child, encountering their drama and beauty on family holidays. For her, mountains were more than pinnacles of rock, snow and ice towering above pristine meadows. They were her connection to God, a balm for her spirit. She had always been attuned to the metaphysical world. Her spiritual life was bound to Nature, and it was in Nature that she sought answers, solace and guidance.

Her first days in Switzerland at Kandersteg in the Bernese Oberland were difficult. She described herself as 'uncomprehending most of the time', believing that the past year was tarnished by 'failure or barren accomplishments, or at best maintenance through hard struggle'. Dealing with Ivor, his family and physicians had taken a tremendous toll on her. Then on 30 July, as Marion and her companions entered the Zermatt Valley towards sunset, she suddenly felt like a 'pilgrim when his burden has rolled off. I saw why I had been sick', she recalled. 'It was as if God said to me, "No wonder you have been sick and felt your strength broken: what you have been trying to do is my work – no wonder it was beyond your strength".' She reached her turning point and from that moment she began to regain her health. 'I realized in a flash then why I had felt as if I were almost shattered at times. I saw too why I had got breathless and confused in heart. I had fallen out of step with the march of the universe', she acknowledged. 'Instead of keeping pace with the great rhythm of things, I was pattering alongside on my own.'

Marion's strength and resolve improved with each passing day. Although she often experienced poor health, she had the iron constitution of her ancestors and strong recuperative powers. Not content to sit comfortably in a lodge gazing out at the splendour of the Alps, she loved the challenge of hiking and climbing in them and exploring the valleys below. Fully immersed in mind, body and spirit, she became one with the mountains she loved.

Over the next month, Marion Scott relied on her metaphysical beliefs and her profound spirituality to lead her back to stable ground where she was able to find herself again. She spent many hours in company with the Alps, walking, observing and absorbing, trying to get 'onto their tuning' as she put it, borrowing 'a wireless simile'. She gave herself over to the power of the mountains, imbibing their wisdom and guidance. She regarded mountains as living, breathing entities, and singled out the Matterhorn as 'the most alive and individual of mountains … as much a creature of God's hand as an animal'. To her, it resembled 'some strange prehistoric entity – a monster from the time of creation when the morning stars sang together' to which she ascribed human behaviour: 'swift', 'unaccountable', 'vengeful', and 'noble … with the kindliness of chivalry lurking in it'.

One afternoon Marion watched a storm pass and then saw the valley fill with one cloud, 'smoothly impenetrable and seething, a sharp edge set between it and the sunshine as if penned in by an invisible wall'. The sight of the immense cloud reminded her of the time years earlier when she had been nearly killed in the hansom cab accident. 'It was an exact presentiment in matter of my mental image, but now I smiled to myself, knowing well that behind the cloud lay reality and beauty – everything there just as certainly as where we could see – and knowing the cloud to be only a transient condition', she wrote. 'It is like that with life and death. The natural world is full of beautiful analogies with the spiritual. Indeed I am inclined to think there is no sharp division, or antithesis between material and spiritual – more probably they are different bands in the same spectrum'.

That night it snowed, and the next morning 'All the summits were white, with a curious upward, outward gazing look about them. They fronted the eastern sun, their courage was crystalline, perfect, unencumbered. Courage was the message they had for me at last, and it was worth waiting for'. Marion and Shimmin set off on Les Chemin des Artistes and reached the top in brilliant sunlight with a great wind from Italy 'roaring against the rock face, pouring over the mountain tops' in a display of beauty so intense that it became sacramental for Marion. 'My impression of the day was that of the immortality of Beauty', she recalled. Shimmin was overwhelmed by the scene and felt sad. He told Marion that great beauty 'hurt' because it was 'too great a responsibility', one that composers 'shirked ... because it demanded too much from them'. He decided to leave her alone in her happiness and made his way down the 'road for artists' to their lodging. 'Presently rifts began to open below and beyond' providing glimpses of the lake at Zug in the valley below. 'I suppose knowledge of the next world is very like this view', Marion observed, 'just glimpses of great beauty caught through the rifts between sense and matter'.

She grew increasingly sensitive to the curative power of Nature, which had a narcotic effect on her. Each day brought a new revelation and awareness of what she must do. 'There was one beautiful evening when towards sunset, the stillness and beauty reached that point at which they become transparent, when through things seen, the things unseen appear. I think that in some way the great quiet and windlessness must be necessary before this can come about'. She recalled lines from Wordsworth's 'Intimations of Immortality':

> And sometimes in a season of calm weather
> Our souls have sight of that immortal sky
> Which brought us hither ...[16]

'No words can express that glimpsed joy ... it is clear [that] the unutterable beauty and goodness of that world spirit are lovelier, and more contenting than all the material world can give us. Beside it nothing else seems to count. ... I have glimpsed it before at rare times, but the certainty it engendered had faded', she admitted. 'These last months in England had blurred the vision, weakened my faith in it. Suddenly here it was again, clearer, more convincing than ever before. So strong was the impression that now I feel I know, even though I do not understand. And knowing that beautiful world lying behind the visible, I hope I shall have the necessary calmness to face the misery of Dartford'.[17]

NOTES

1 Medical records, GA. Ivor never suffered shell shock, although doctors treating him at Lord Derby's War Hospital in 1918 might have found in that diagnosis a convenient explanation for his nervous breakdown.

2 IG, 'There have been Anguishes', *CP*, p. 154.

3 Ursula Vaughan Williams, *R.V.W.: A Biography of Ralph Vaughan Williams* (Oxford: Oxford University Press, 1988), p. 216.

4 Medical records, GA.

5 Ibid.

6 Adeline Vaughan Williams to Scott, undated letter, GA. Mrs Vaughan Williams either did not date her letters or just wrote in the day and month, leaving off the year, so in some cases it is difficult to know when a letter was composed.

7 Helen Thomas, 'A Memoir of Ivor Gurney', *RCM Magazine*, vol. 56, no. 1 (December 1960), pp. 10–11.

8 MMS, 'Recollections of Ivor Gurney', *Monthly Musical Record*, vol. 68, no. 794 (February 1938), p. 43.

9 IG, Note, *CP*, p. 239. In his poem 'December 30th', Gurney wrote: 'It is the year's end, the winds are blasting, and I / Write to keep madness and black torture away …', *CP*, p. 200.

10 Medical records, GA.

11 All references in this paragraph are from the medical records.

12 R. H. Steen to MMS, 24 July 1923, GA.

13 MMS, Journal, GA.

14 Shimmin had also accompanied Scott to Switzerland in 1922.

15 MMS, Journal, GA. All subsequent quotations about Scott in Switzerland are taken from this source.

16 Scott was relying on memory and misquoted Wordsworth in her journal. The lines as written by Wordsworth read: 'Hence in a season of calm weather / Though inland far we be, / Our Souls have sight of that immortal sea / Which brought us hither …'

17 At the end of August, during her holiday in Switzerland, Scott visited Lake Como, an area that enchanted her. Years later, Michael Brockway, an artist and the husband of Scott's goddaughter, Margaret, was painting at Lake Como. One day he hiked to a remote location near Bellagio. When he opened his water tin, he found that it had leaked and was bone dry. He had no water for his watercolours so he substituted the one liquid he had with him – beer. Scott bought the painting and took great pleasure in owning a watercolour painted with beer instead of water.

CHAPTER 21

The Last Chance

W HILE MARION SCOTT was in Switzerland, doctors at Stone House began inoculating Ivor Gurney with malaria. By 18 August 1923 he was enduring 'daily paroxysms of malaria fever' that made him very ill and weak.[1] Malaria produced dangerously high fevers that triggered hallucinations, but physicians, believing that these fevers mentally 'cleansed' victims, were willing to take the risk. Although Gurney's medical records offer few details on how the illness affected him, individuals suffering from malaria typically experience flu-like symptoms that include shaking chills, headache, muscle aches, tiredness, nausea, vomiting and diarrhoea. There is no evidence that Ivor had any say in the decision to 'treat' him with an illness that made him so sick for weeks.

In the early years of the twentieth century, malaria was mainly used as a treatment for syphilis, but after the Great War, it was also used experimentally on soldiers believed to be suffering from shell shock and other war-related emotional disturbances and nervous conditions.[2] While it is possible that doctors, playing diagnostic roulette, might have thought Gurney was suffering from syphilis, it is highly unlikely. There is nothing in his history or in the medical records to indicate that he had ever contracted the disease.

When Ivor was admitted to the City of London Mental Hospital, his doctors were puzzled by his behaviour. They resorted to guesswork in dealing with his condition, partly because he became so uncooperative and partly because the physicians simply did not have the necessary knowledge or diagnostic skills to define his illness. Without any concrete medical evidence to support them, they assumed that he had suffered shell shock in France because the words had appeared on his previous medical records. 'Shell shock' became a catch-all diagnosis for ailments physicians could not otherwise identify or whose root cause eluded them. As Ivor's mental state deteriorated, the doctors were willing to try anything they thought might help him. There were no modern drugs then to alleviate or control his symptoms.

The malaria therapy continued for three weeks before physicians terminated it when they gave Ivor quinine. On 14 September Dr Steen wrote to Marion, informing her that Gurney's condition had 'not altered since his inoculation.'[3] Medical notes from October and November indicate that malaria 'had no beneficial effect mentally.'[4] The experiment had failed. It is possible that instead of having no effect on Gurney, the malaria further weakened or harmed him in ways the doctors did not observe. Individuals who experience extremely high fevers can suffer brain damage.

The spiritual insights and strength Marion had gained during her restorative holiday in Switzerland had prepared her for the discouraging news from Dr Steen. Instead of succumbing to depression, she was able to view the situation philosophically. 'In his Good Friday Music, [Wagner's *Parsifal*] touches a fineness of spiritual truth which I can never define but which always comforts me now when I think of Ivor's seemingly wrecked life', she wrote in her journal. 'Who knows beyond this madness and utter sensual confusion that cloud him may lie – must lie – sanity, tranquillity, purified perception and reconciliation to God.'[5]

Upon her return from Switzerland, Marion had plunged immediately into her work, covering musical events in London for the *Christian Science Monitor*. She organized a concert at the London Contemporary Centre in October, featuring the music of the young composer Gerald Finzi (1901–56), who would eventually play a major role in preserving Gurney's music and poetry.[6]

Before Marion had left for Switzerland she convinced Ronald Gurney to send her all of Ivor's music and poetry manuscripts in his possession. He complied without resistance. 'As I myself know nothing about music, I have packed everything on manuscript paper in his writing', he explained to Scott adding, 'I can assure you that anyone who sorts it out will have an unenviable job.'[7] By November she had all of Ivor's manuscripts in her possession. Further, Marion instructed hospital personnel to give her everything that he wrote: letters, music, poems, essays, and fragments of ideas on bits of paper. These she began storing in a trunk she kept in her bedroom.[8] With Ivor living under her watchful eye at nearby Dartford and with his music, poetry and letters stored safely with her, she had gained control of his life.

Ronald Gurney was relieved to let Marion take over the burden of responsibility for his brother. He continued to regard Ivor with contempt. 'Ivor is but reaping the punishment of his selfishness and stubbornness and he will have to endure it for the present on the least possible expenditure', he wrote to Marion.[9] Yet beneath his arrogant demeanour, contentious, abrasive attitude and bitterness towards his brother, which grew in part out of sibling rivalry, Ronald had a strong bond with Ivor. Deep down, he harboured admiration for his brother, but his practical nature, inflexibility and resentment were too entrenched to allow him to express it. Although Ronald claimed he knew nothing about music, he once succinctly described Ivor's torturous working process, declaring that he could always recognize Ivor's songs 'in the dark – unannounced. They're him – Ivor in torment ... They are not smooth – sort of jerked out of him in spasms.'[10]

As the days rolled towards Christmas, the joy of the season was tempered by the reports from Stone House. There was no change in Ivor's mental condition. The future looked bleak. Other disappointments taking root in the world outside the grey walls of the asylum would eventually turn Gurney more deeply into himself.

At first his friends Will Harvey, Arthur Benjamin, Sydney Shimmin and Herbert Howells tried to help him, but no matter how well intentioned, each proved incapable of dealing with Ivor's condition with courage, fortitude, self-sacrifice and love comparable to Marion Scott's.

Harvey, who had been as close to Ivor as anyone, grieved over his friend's fate but was helpless in the face of it. Once Ivor was in London, Will seems to have visited him rarely, if at all. He was practising law in Gloucester, writing poetry, rearing a family, and even playing cricket with Ronald Gurney. After his own experience as a prisoner of war, Will might have found it difficult or impossible to enter the prison-like facility where Gurney lived. Although Harvey remained in contact with Scott, he faded as a presence in Gurney's life.[11]

Sydney Shimmin had married and was serving as music master at Malvern College and teaching at Cheltenham Ladies College. When Shimmin was still in London and keeping company with Marion, he surely must have visited Ivor with her on occasion. However, once he left the city, there is no evidence that he continued to see his old friend at Stone House.[12]

After Ivor was transferred to the London asylum, Arthur Benjamin occasionally visited him with Marion. Benjamin participated in a recital at the asylum and accompanied a performance of two of Gurney's songs. However, he grew increasingly uncomfortable each time he saw Ivor. He finally admitted that he found time at Stone House too 'harrowing' and never returned to the asylum after Ivor once failed to recognize him.[13]

Herbert Howells found it very traumatic to visit Ivor at Dartford. According to Marion, he would not go to the asylum unless she took the lead in making all of the arrangements and then went with him. During the war and after, Marion tried to get Herbert to work with her when Ivor needed help or when decisions about his care needed to be made. Unfortunately, Howells was not emotionally equipped to be as helpful or as involved as she wished.[14] Marion was sensitive to Herbert's reluctance to see Ivor, so she resolved each time to make the visit 'as easy and pleasant as possible'.[15] Dealing with him was sometimes like dealing with a frightened child.

On one occasion, Marion tried three times to get Howells to see Ivor before she was successful. They finally agreed to meet at Charing Cross a few days before Christmas. Herbert was a bundle of nerves and full of excuses. First he told her that he needed to get back early because he had to attend a party. Then he claimed he was feeling ill and thought that he might be coming down with influenza. 'This rather dashed <u>my</u> program', Marion recorded in her journal, adding that neither was very cheerful for the rest of the afternoon.[16] The fact that it was a 'dull day ... with mists hanging all along the Thames' did nothing to raise their spirits. They arrived at Stone House shortly after two o'clock and found Ivor alone in the dining room, 'a bare place, with green distemper walls, a few steel etchings, common cane chairs, four long tables'. They settled in a corner with Ivor standing, Marion sitting, and Herbert 'perched on the edge of the table, his back to most of the room'. They talked mostly about poetry and music, 'but all felt pretty tragic', Marion observed. 'Ivor is so agonizingly sane in his insanity that he feels every thread of the suffering all the time.'

The horror of what Gurney witnessed every day as an inmate of the asylum disrupted their conversation. Other patients and visitors began to enter the room. 'Then the door opened again, and I saw Stephens, the attendant gravely helping a young wreck of a man in. He might have been twenty-five or so, and had evidently been in the war. He had lost one leg, some fingers on his left hand, he was totally blind, and he was insane. O my God – how can men make war', she exclaimed in her journal. Once the young man was seated, the attendant went out to bring in his visitors, a tall young man 'looking like a Naval officer' and an old man 'shaking with palsy and emotion', perhaps the patient's father or uncle. 'I shall never forget that group', Marion wrote. 'The sightless boy, at one side, the Naval man, talking quietly to him – perhaps purposely trying to give the old man time to control his voice – and the latter standing there crimson and trembling, his left hand clutched across his right wrist to still its shaking, his tongue protruding, his whole being convulsed with utter grief. Herbert wisely kept his back turned. Even I, accustomed to seeing tragedy there, nearly broke down.'

Seeing that Herbert was clearly upset, Marion cut short their visit. By the time they got to the station at Dartford for his 4:12 train, the 'blue winter dusk' had descended and lights were blazing. Marion chose not to return with Herbert as she piloted him to the train. 'Spent and sick at heart with distress', she needed time alone and sought comfort in a tearoom. While sitting there she thought about an old church a few doors away and felt 'a longing to go and sit there for a while. It would have been comforting so I went', she recalled. But she found the church locked. 'I might have guessed, so like the Church of England!'

She was miserable and walked back through the streets, encountering cheerful Christmas shoppers, as she slowly made her way to the station. 'From there I caught a glimpse of our after-sunset west – quiet, the old mystery and benediction lurking behind the visible. That was the first renewal of vision after the day's stress', she observed. 'There I was not shut out, and paced the station approach for a longish while lest I lost the tranquillity of that sight.' 'People thronged it everywhere', but Marion was too shattered to care that she was standing in full view of everyone, 'tears running visibly' down her cheeks. 'And then I saw a great pile of holly, all heaped and waiting to go by train for Christmas decorations. Druidical, immemorial in its origin I suppose, but now a symbol of the one Man who tried with his whole being to solve the enigma of sin and suffering, and who did mystically do so', she wrote. 'Then the train came and I went home.'

As Ivor's friends and family stopped playing active roles in his life, Marion Scott was left to shoulder the entire responsibility for him although the Gurneys retained legal guardianship. His mother continued to worry about him, communicating regularly with Marion about 'my dear Ivor'. The depth of her anguish and her concern for her son are apparent in letters in which she pours out her heart. 'I am wanting to hear about Ivor I suppose he is no better dear Miss Scott I keep wondering if now he isnt tortured whether he will get better in time such waves of anguish keep going over me I wish I could do something to make him better or that we could get him into a smaller place tis like a lot of cattle there he says it is hell poor old boy', Florence wrote to Marion in one of her rambling, unpunctuated letters.[17] On another occasion when an outside doctor was called in to help

Ivor, she wrote: 'I will go on my hands and knees to him if it will make [Ivor] better is it money dear Miss Scott that is stopping it would £20 be of any use?' [18]

Florence tried to see Ivor in London, but at times her life was 'so trying I cant save much money'.[19] Her visits inevitably distressed him for any number of reasons, some to do with the nature of his illness and some rooted in their personalities. Ultimately, she was left to feel that he did not care and that he did not want to see her. '[I] dont hear how he gets on he is so far off he will think I dont care anything about him ... I should like him to be where I could get at him better.' [20]

For his part, Ivor tried to keep in contact with friends and family. He wrote letters and sent copies of his poetry to them. Most of the disturbing letters he wrote appealing for help were never mailed, but occasionally one slipped through. Emily Hunt received one of his heart-breaking appeals for help in a package that contained some of his poetry. She 'broke down completely' when she read the enclosures.[21]

Ivor tried to contact Annie Nelson Drummond. He asked Marion to write to her in Scotland and to include some of his writing.[22] The reply from Annie's mother, Margaret, in 1924, brought disappointing news. Annie had emigrated to the United States in 1921 and was living in Wellesley, Massachusetts, with her husband. Ivor knew he would never see 'Nurse Drummond' or 'Puck' again. Marion, still jealous that Annie had captured Ivor's heart, was relieved. When Margaret Drummond's letter arrived, Marion, still smouldering over Gurney's affair with Drummond, could not resist the temptation to vent her anger. In distinctive red ink in the corner of the note, she wrote: 'This was the lively V.A.D. who played fast and loose with Ivor till she drove him to desperation in 1917 and 1918, who thereafter refused to have any communication with him – insane and poor. At Ivor's request I tried to get her to write, and sent her things by him. I wrote to her at this address, but never had a reply.' [23] In writing about Drummond later, Scott could only bring herself to call Annie 'a lovely girl and ambitious'.[24] She never reconciled herself to the fact that Ivor had become engaged to her.

Marion and Ivor's other women friends, including Ethel Voynich and her sister Maggie Taylor, also took a dim view of Annie Drummond and blamed her for his breakdown in March 1918. 'As for the Drummond girl, I don't suppose she ever arrived at an understanding of what she had done', Voynich observed many years later.[25]

By the time Marion wrote to her, Annie was happily married and, at the age of thirty-seven, the mother of a baby son, John. The past was behind her, and she felt it best for all concerned to leave it that way.[26] She did not reply to Marion's letter or respond to subsequent attempts to communicate with her, but she did keep the memory of her relationship with Ivor with her for the rest of her life.[27]

Outside of Marion's parents and her sister Stella, Ralph and Adeline Vaughan Williams were the only people Marion could rely on for support in her dealings with Gurney, his family and his physicians. They gave money regularly to help Marion pay the portion of Ivor's care not covered by his pension, but more importantly they visited him, monitored his condition and tried to find alternative care for him.

Walter de la Mare also tried to help. He did not visit Ivor, but remained in the background, explaining that he thought his presence at the asylum 'might be worse than useless'.[28] He donated money periodically, suggesting on one occasion when he sent money for a gift that 'it would be just as well not to let him know who it comes from, as that might worry him'.[29]

Friends, family and acquaintances simply did not know how to deal with Ivor's illness. Seeing him in an asylum made most of them extremely uncomfortable because they never knew what to expect from him. Their unfounded and, at times, selfish fears and lack of understanding denied him what he needed most and thrived upon – companionship and conversation which would have engaged his mind and given some purpose to his life. Instead, he was left alone to dwell with his own thoughts and wrestle with the demons that assailed him. He had no relief from their intrusion.

The official reports described him as 'mentally ... worse and he is very threatening at times', 'abusive and threatening and is considered dangerous', 'attempted to assault the medical superintendent', 'full of delusions', 'restless ... talks to himself', 'still tormented by wireless'. He suffered physical ailments: headaches, muscle pain which was probably rheumatism or cramps caused by vitamin and mineral deficiencies, a possible bladder or kidney infection, a rash on his legs, serious deterioration of his teeth and a condition the doctors described as 'evidently a scurvy', undoubtedly caused by poor nutrition.[30]

Yet Ivor, the man doctors described as 'mentally worse', was remarkably productive, working with breathless intensity to write some seven collections of poetry in 1924, revise old poems and compose new song settings. Seven of his earlier poems were published in the *London Mercury* in January. Events outside Stone House touched Gurney. Sir Charles Stanford had died on the morning of 29 March, twelve days after suffering a stroke. He was sixty-nine years old. In April Ivor wrote a short tribute to Sir Charles Stanford for the July issue of *Music and Letters*. Ivor had not forgotten his contentious relationship with his teacher, but wrote a restrained piece in which he lightly jabbed at Stanford's conservatism:

> He was a stiff master, though a very kind man; difficult to please, and most glad to be pleased. England will bury many in the Abbey and Westminster much less than he.
>
> By him the German influence was defeated, and yet had good learnt of it. He was a born poet, but had to overcome foreign form and influence. He wrote oratorio instead of string quartet, violin sonata, and such. When England is less foolish she will think more of him. Had he been wiser, he would have talked of Elizabethans at his lessons instead of the lesser string quartets of Beethoven, or the yet deader things that industry and not conscience got out of the German masters.
>
> As for his work in Irish folksong arrangements, so admirable, and his autobiographical books, still yet charming, the first will last long,

the second not long, but will amuse worthily. Only the fools will deny that he brought to them that Irish music, the best in the world, then, of known folksongs.[31]

Throughout the spring, summer and early autumn, Ivor was busy writing enough poems to fill at least seven poetry collections, which he sent to friends: *Dayspaces and Takings*; *Fatigues and Magnificences*; *La Flandre, and By-Norton*; *London seen Clear*; *Rewards of Wonder, Ridge Clay, Limestone*, and *Roman Gone East*. Another collection, *Out of June and October*, dates from around this time.[32] Only *Rewards of Wonder* is known to survive.[33] Ivor composed a handful of songs, which serve as a prelude to the outpouring of new music that was soon to come. He continued to write letters of appeal to friends, the police, doctors, the clergy, government officials, public figures, to anyone he thought might understand his plight and rescue him.

In November Ivor's song 'Lights Out' was published in the *Mercury*. J. C. Squire included 'Thoughts of New England', 'Smudgy Dawn' and 'Dawn' in the anthology *Second Selections from Modern Poets*.[34] Ivor worked on corrections to *Rewards of Wonder*. To make his task easier, Marion hired a typist to retype the carbon copy manuscript for him. At the end of the year, Ivor wrote again to Annie Drummond, a disconnected and jumbled letter telling her that he had written eight books of verse and informing her about his inclusion in the Squire publications. He complained about the mistakes in two of his poems in the anthology, a strong indication that he was alert, aware and able to concentrate. He mentioned new poems he had written and asked Drummond 'Would anybody in Scotland type for me?' He included a reference to 'Harvard and Yale' universities.[35] Ivor's handwriting had become very fluid with the letters flowing one into the other like waves. The effect is artful, and his writing, despite being difficult to read, imprints a mark of beauty on the page that resembles Arabic script. The letter to Drummond was not mailed.

In early 1925, aware that Annie had emigrated to America and was now married, Ivor's thoughts were full of her as he wrote a collection of poems titled *To Hawthornden*, one of his names for her.[36] This group of poems was followed by *The Book of Five Makings, Memories of Honour, Poems to the States, Six Poems of the North American States, Poems in Praise of Poets, The Book of Lives and Accusations, Poems of Gloucesters, Gloucester and of Virginia*, and *Pictures and Memories*. The quality of his writing was uneven but some fine and accomplished poems date from this period, among them 'Snow', 'Epitaph on a Young Child', 'It is near Toussaints', 'The Silent One', 'War Books', 'Song – I had a Girl's Fancies', 'The Mangel-bury' and 'The Poets of My Country'. At the same time that he was producing masses of poetry, much of it autobiographical, he was composing music, approximately fifty songs and 'an enormous amount of ... mainly chamber music' which Gerald Finzi later described as 'incoherent and completely useless'.[37]

Finzi had first learned of Gurney in 1921, when he heard Elsie Suddaby sing 'Sleep' in York, while listening in on her voice lesson with Ernest

Bairstow. The song made an indelible impression on him: '[O]ne can feel the incandescence in this song that tells of something burning too brightly to last, such as you see in the filament of an electric bulb before it burns out'.[38] By 1925 the twenty-four-year-old Finzi had approached Scott about preserving Gurney's legacy. It is likely their mutual friend the violinist Sybil Eaton had introduced Marion to Finzi and his music. But Finzi had heard about Marion Scott long before he had ever met her when, as a teenager, he was studying with Ernest Farrar at Harrogate. '[I]t was from him that I first heard of M.S. and in those days she was young, delightful and even said to have love affairs', he recalled later.[39] The first task Finzi undertook for Gurney was to help Marion edit Ivor's song cycle *The Western Playland (and of Sorrow)* for publication by the Carnegie Trust Collection of British Music in 1926. It marked the beginning of Finzi's long and often difficult relationship with Scott.

In the meantime, Marion felt heartened by the presence of Dr Randolph Davis, a young psychologist at Stone House, who was actually making progress with Gurney. He took an interest in his case and became 'a friend who really understood him'.[40] As a Canadian, Davis was likely aware of the revolutionary techniques and practices of Dr Richard M. Bucke (1837–1902), a pioneer in the study and understanding of mental illness. Bucke's major reforms humanized the treatment of the mentally ill and set new standards for their care in Canada in the late nineteenth century. Bucke spurned archaic methods such as restraints and the common barbaric practice of ovarian surgery on mentally ill women. He believed that patients regained their health better if they exercised regularly and were exposed to music and conversation. He encouraged doctors to interact with patients and forbade the use of the coercive and cruel techniques so prevalent then. He also believed that patients could be treated successfully away from the asylum at home or in a home-like environment.[41]

Dr Davis's personal approach in dealing with Ivor bore a striking resemblance to that of Dr Bucke. Davis believed that by establishing a relationship with Gurney, he could help him through what he called 'transference'. 'It is necessary that the patient like the psychologist in order that the patient be cured', he explained. 'Gurney might meet the finest psychologist in the world and if he did not like him no results would follow. This is the foundation of my influence on Gurney.'[42] He understood Ivor's need for exercise and the importance of the intellectual stimulation he enjoyed in conversation.

Marion liked Davis's sensible and compassionate approach and understood how it might benefit Ivor. She had always believed that Ivor might improve if he were in private care in a more natural and pleasant setting than an asylum. She knew that he needed human contact and was well aware that she was the only person who visited regularly and was capable of engaging his mind. She believed that Dr Davis was Ivor's saviour.

Davis took Gurney for long walks, talked with him but mostly listened, providing the platform his patient needed to express himself to another person. It was that simple. 'The great reason why I can do for Gurney what others cannot is because Gurney likes me, not because I particularly like him', Davis explained to Marion.[43] Indeed, Ivor progressed well during the time Davis worked with him.

Marion was encouraged by Dr Davis's success with Ivor, but Davis had problems of his own. For one, he was not happy at Stone House and in trouble there. Ambitious, outspoken and self-confident, he was eager to rise to the top in his profession but felt he had little future at the City of London Mental Hospital. His career was stalling and he was growing increasingly frustrated by the constraints he felt were imposed on him by his superiors. When Dr Navarra put an end to his walks with Ivor, citing concerns about suicide and fears that the unhappy Gurney might escape, Dr Davis reached his limit. He disagreed entirely with the order. By May 1925 he and his superiors were at increasing odds. He left Stone House under a cloud, creating a void in Ivor's life.

Marion despaired. Ivor had come to life under Davis's care. He seemed so different, happier, and more alert, and he was writing poetry and music again with fervour and commitment.[44] He had lost the one person he saw almost daily, who understood his needs and tried to ensure that they were met. Marion was struggling with this overwhelming turn of events when, in August, she received a letter from Davis who had contacted Ivor's publisher for her address.

'I have often wondered how he was progressing', Dr Davis explained.[45] With Ivor's future at stake, Marion regarded Davis's reappearance as a sign of hope. She socialized and corresponded with him. A plan to remove Ivor from Stone House and treat him privately began to take shape.

'Supposing I should offer to take charge of Mr. Gurney entirely for 3 months', Davis suggested. He was willing to 'give up any idea of practising' his profession during that period and asked Marion how much she might pay him.[46] Davis claimed that for his treatment to work successfully he must devote all of his time entirely to Ivor. That meant sharing quarters with him.

'It would certainly be the best way by far. And I feel quite sure that if I succeed in curing Mr. Gurney I will have spent 3 mos. to great advantage', he declared. 'And besides my being constantly with him will ensure every possible protection and every body's [sic] mind will be at rest.' [47] To that end he proposed taking rooms at 103 Camberwell Grove in a house owned by a Mrs Hay. She had a front drawing room with a piano which would be ideal for Ivor. Davis dismissed his own lodgings as unsuitable, describing his landlord as 'rather a queer chap' and a 'high strung erratic individual' with whom Ivor 'might not get on'.[48]

He encouraged Scott and Vaughan Williams to inspect Mrs Hay's rooms but cautioned them to say nothing to her about Ivor being in a mental hospital. He had already bent the truth, telling the landlady that Gurney had been hospitalized with stomach trouble, but he did so, he said, to protect Ivor. Mrs Hay was not averse to taking individuals like Gurney. She had done so in the past, but Davis, aware of Gurney's intelligence and sensitivity, claimed he did not want any slips that might upset him and abort the plan. 'If she knows she is sure to show by some act or other that she knows, no matter how careful she may be and you may be sure Mr. Gurney will notice immediately that she knows and it will interfere with Mr. Gurney's recovery and happiness.'[49]

On the surface, this manipulation of the truth might have seemed trivial and understandable given the circumstances, but it indicated that Davis was willing to lie, believing such deceit was justified by the higher aim he had in mind. His motives were not as pure as his correspondence suggests. To Davis, Ivor Gurney represented a potentially valuable asset in advancing his career. He knew that if he proved successful in 'curing' Gurney, he could publish his results and make a name for himself. But there was more. Davis was in debt and needed to repay an outstanding loan, an important fact he failed to mention to Marion. He also failed to mention that he had been dismissed from Stone House by his superiors, who suspected him of being an impostor.

However, Davis's motives were not entirely selfish. He was critical of conditions at the City of London Mental Hospital and concerned about their negative effect on Ivor. From his own experience there, he knew 'perfectly well that Mr. Gurney is not understood and that it is not right to keep him in a place which is only persecution to him. Should I have the least doubt as to whether I could put him squarely on his feet I should never attempt to try to help him for to fail in this would only do me harm. Understanding him, I know I can cure him', he wrote.[50] 'I remember so well the afternoon Gurney and I spent along the river and sitting on the grass in the roadside', he explained to Scott. 'It was the sympathy which he showed for things which I told him concerning my own experiences in different parts of the world which impressed me so profoundly with the fact that he was sane. Insane people invariably never show sympathetic interest in the experiences of others', he continued.[51]

'His sympathy and interest in experiences of which I told in my own life were so real, so thoroughly understanding', Davis observed. 'It showed his belief in himself as one who understood and that he was conscious of that understanding. Also it showed that his many months spent in the hospital had not dampened his spirits nor caused a permanent state of depression and lack of appreciation of his own worth. It is what a man thinks of himself that counts not so much what others think of him. Once a man loses faith in himself all is lost until he recovers that faith no matter what others may try to do for him', he concluded.[52] Davis intended to make sure that Ivor's faith in himself was not sucked out of him at Stone House.

He emphasized repeatedly to Marion that he was fully prepared to take the entire responsibility for Gurney, 'legally and otherwise ... at all times and in all ways'. '[S]hould any little complications arise, which I do not think will, as for example Mr. Gurney trying to run away and getting into the hands of the police, I would immediately be responsible.'[53]

Tough, demanding, shrewd and cautious, Marion wisely involved her solicitor father and Ralph Vaughan Williams in the plan. She and Vaughan Williams visited Mrs Hay to inspect the rooms. Although the house was pleasant, the front room cheerful and airy, there were problems. Marion was not keen on the idea of Ivor taking his meals with other lodgers, which was the routine. She did not know how Ivor might relate to other members

of the household and how they might relate to him. She found it unacceptable that Mrs Hay planned to use the drawing room at Christmas for a
large family party. To do so would displace Ivor.

'[I]t seems altogether as if there would be very little quiet or dependable comfort for you and Mr. Gurney and that while you would be thrown
a great deal with the Hays and their P.G.'s [paying guests] – who are of a
different stamp from you and Ivor Gurney – there would be few facilities
for him to see his own friends', she informed Davis.[54] He was not as concerned about the other lodgers as Scott was and told her so. He thought
that Mrs Hay was a 'critical' woman who would not rent to unsuitable individuals. The over-anxious Scott failed to consider an important fact she
knew about Ivor: that he related well to all people, not just to artists and
intellectuals.

Mrs Hay told Scott and Vaughan Williams that she had neither beds nor
a wardrobe to furnish the large front room as a bed-sitting room, but indicated to Marion that she would purchase beds and put a wardrobe outside
the door. Since the room had no gas meter, Mrs Hay tried to interest Scott
in letting one of the double bedrooms with the drawing room for a small
extra sum. But the only free bedroom was unacceptable. It was at the top
of the house, 'small, cold and stuffy'.[55]

Scott and Vaughan Williams agreed to pay Davis's £75 fee for three
months' treatment but they were not prepared to give him the entire sum
in advance as he insisted. They were willing to pay him £25 a month in
advance, no more. Further, Scott was concerned about 'the exact letter of
the English law relating to certified patients' being removed from a mental
hospital and placed with a person who is responsible for them, as Davis
would be.[56]

Marion wanted to be absolutely certain that Davis could get the consent of the authorities to take charge of Gurney. From the beginning, Davis
knew that Dr Navarra would object to allowing him to treat Ivor privately,
but he felt there were ways to overcome this obstacle, even though they
were illegal. In his desperation to make the plan work and collect his fee,
he tried to convince Scott and Vaughan Williams that their only option
was to remove Ivor secretly from the asylum. Vaughan Williams refused to
participate in what amounted to a plot to kidnap Ivor. Everything must be
done legally for the protection of all concerned.

'The matter is more complicated than it appeared', Marion warned
Davis.[57] 'It is illegal for the person who takes him to do so for gain. This
would have the effect that while morally you were not taking Mr. Gurney
for gain, technically it would place you in that position in the eye of the
law, and would render any contract void because it would not be legal', she
argued. 'This difficulty can be avoided if Mr. Gurney were transferred from
the Hospital to your single care at the request of the petitioner and under
and with the consent of the Board of Control.'[58] The plan was growing
more complex.

Davis sought to overcome the obstacles. He was firm in negotiating
with Mrs Hay. He let her know that under no circumstances was any room
but the drawing room acceptable and that he was unwilling to make any

concessions, even for her to use the room for her family party. After his convincing talk with Mrs Hay, she accepted his conditions, and even agreed to install a gas meter in the room.

On the issue of personal financial gain, Davis told Scott that the £75 'will not any more than pay expenses ... if there is anything left after 3 mos. of the £75 I will return it to those who give it. You may be sure if I wished to take him for gain I should never think of 75 pounds for 3 months [worth] all my time. It would be nearer 750 pounds.' [59] He was adamant that he be paid the full amount in advance and gave her until Friday morning, 4 December to decide.

Davis was offended and annoyed. 'Personally I think I have done a great deal in offering to help Mr. Gurney and have done so only because I understand him and feel that he can be helped. Otherwise I should never have considered the matter', he told Scott. [60]

Marion believed Davis was capable of helping Ivor and did not want to alienate him. She attempted to calm him, explaining that she could not meet his deadline because 'the decision does not rest with us but with Mr. Gurney's brother, and we should have to wait for his consent.' [61] She apologized for her comments about 'gain' and acknowledged that she realized £75 would do little more than cover his expenses. 'Please believe that we are genuinely concerned for your interests as well as those of Mr. Gurney', she assured him. [62]

But it was too late. Davis dropped a 'bombshell' on Marion in early December when he abruptly called an end to the plan. On the surface it might seem that he was annoyed with Scott and fed up with her caution and delays, but the truth is, Davis knew he could not make good on his promises. He had made grand plans that he could not implement. He had used the situation with Ivor to get his hands on money he needed to pay his debt. His deceit weighed on his conscience and he finally confessed to Marion.

'I have always felt that there is room at the top and my ambition will not let me rest until I get there. One cannot hold his mouth open and expect manna to drop into it', he wrote. [63] He knew he had to make his own success by any route open to him, but on this occasion he went off the track. He admitted to being 'humiliated' at having to explain his financial situation, but he liked Marion and felt she deserved the truth. He told her he had borrowed £75 from an acquaintance, even giving her his name and address, and that he needed to repay the money by January in order to maintain his credit and obtain further loans. He was also waiting for money to come to him from the sale of property in Canada. If he got the £75 in advance, he claimed, he could have paid his debt and then been able to borrow £200 to see him through his commitment with Ivor, by which time the money from Canada was expected to arrive.

'I did not want to state my financial position – none of us ever do', he admitted. 'I felt that your proposition was reasonable but dare not say so owing to the financial position in which I was placed, knowing that I could not very well go through with it had I agreed so to do. But I had to explain eventually and it is best because since your plans were reasonable and you were justified in getting a reasonable explanation as to why I could not accept them.' [64]

After he secured a position at the Bethlem Royal Hospital as a non-resident honorary clinical assistant, he wrote again to Scott expressing his concerns for Gurney and reaffirming his willingness to find a way to help him. When Marion told Davis that she planned to have a Harley Street psychiatrist see Gurney, he responded frankly. 'Seeing a patient but once is never sufficient for a doctor to understand a psychological case no matter who the specialist is and the specialist in this case will be of necessity influenced entirely by what the superintendent at Dartford says', he cautioned. He advised her simply to 'satisfy your own minds by all means'.[65] He offered a new option: transfer Gurney to Bethlem.

'I am just as interested in Gurney's ultimate return to a solid foundation as anyone can be. If I had my own home I should have opened it long ago', he wrote.[66] 'So I'll tell you what I will do and you can suit yourself. I am at the above hospital and will be for some time ... I might as well look after Gurney as anyone else. Fees at this hospital [are] 3–3–0 per wk. You might get it for less. Now, see the physician supt., tell him you heard I was at the hospital and of my influence on Gurney', he advised. 'Ask him if you send Gurney, will he permit Dr Davis to attend him and especially for me to take Gurney out for one or two hrs. each day for a stroll. This last is very necessary. They do let patients out on parole.' [67]

Davis's inclination to alter the truth emerged again. 'But you must on no account let the supt. think that I have suggested this to you. It will not be imposing on me in the least and it will be a pleasure for me. I will not, in fact could not, charge a penny for my services. I cannot do more. If you do not feel inclined to do this it is not necessary to answer', Davis concluded.[68]

After four months of trying to find ways to get Gurney into private treatment with Davis, Marion had had enough of him and his scheming. She gave up. She had failed to find a way to give Ivor a chance to return to society in such a way that he would have companionship, be protected, cared for and free 'just to write his music and poetry and be quietly happy'.[69] All hope for such an outcome vanished. Marion knew then that Ivor would never be released from Stone House. His future now lay in the hands of doctors who could do nothing for him.

NOTES

1 Medical records, GA.

2 Dr Julius Wagner-Jauregg (1857–1940), an Austrian psychiatrist, observed that patients in mental hospitals who had syphilis sometimes showed improvement in their conditions after they suffered high fevers during epidemics of typhoid, smallpox and other diseases. As early as 1887, Wagner-Jauregg believed that by infecting victims of syphilis with malaria, which produced spells of high fever, he could cure the physical and mental effects of the syphilis. However, it was considered too dangerous at the time because there was no cure for malaria and patients could die from the illness. In 1917, when quinine was found to be an effective cure for malaria, Dr Wager-Jauregg and his colleagues began infecting syphilitic patients with a mild form of malaria. Advocates of the cure claimed it worked in 85 per cent of those treated. Although Dr Wagner-Jauregg

won the Nobel Prize in medicine in 1927, the Nobel committee now regards the award as a mistake. Penicillin began replacing malaria as a treatment for syphilis in 1945.

3 Medical records, GA.

4 R. H. Steen to MMS, GA.

5 MMS, Journal, 21 September 1923, GA.

6 Finzi's *By Footpath and Stile*, a setting of six Thomas Hardy poems for baritone and string quartet, was premièred at the concert on 24 October 1923, with Sumner Austin, baritone, and the Charles Woodhouse String Quartet.

7 Letters from RG to MMS in June and November 1923, GA.

8 Scott never stopped collecting. Even before Gurney died, Scott 'possessed two or three trunks full of his autographs, music & poems', according to Howard Ferguson (letter to author 30 November 1989).

9 RG to MMS, 7 November 1923, GA.

10 RG to DBR, 3 May 1951, GA.

11 After Gurney was committed, Will Harvey maintained a friendship with Ronald Gurney. The two men were members of the Gloucester City Cricket Club. Ronald was team captain.

12 Shimmin married Elizabeth Margaret Whittington, who was known as 'Peggy'. Mrs Shimmin published two children's books, *First Year Stepping Stones* (Oxford University Press, 1932) and *The Story-Dancing Book for Less than Sevens* with Mary Day Lewis (Oxford University Press, 1948). With her husband she founded the Sydney and Peggy Shimmin Piano Prize.

13 Arthur Benjamin, 'A Student in Kensington', *Music and Letters*, vol. 31, no. 3 (July 1950), p. 204.

14 According to his daughter, Ursula, Herbert always returned from the asylum in a state of deep depression after visits in the 1930s.

15 MMS, Journal, 27 December 1923, GA.

16 Ibid. All subsequent quotations are taken from this section of Scott's Journal.

17 FG to MMS, 22 August 1927, GA.

18 FG to MMS, 12 December 1925, GA.

19 FG to MMS, undated, GA.

20 FG to MMS, 30 April 1926, GA.

21 Emily Hunt to MMS, 4 May 1923, GA.

22 Marion Scott had probably learned of Gurney's affair with Annie Drummond through Ethel Voynich or possibly from Sydney Shimmin after Ivor's 1918 breakdown.

23 Margaret Drummond to MMS, no date but sometime in 1924, GA.

24 MMS to DBR, Notes, 1952, GA.

25 ELV to MMS, 13 January 1938, GA.

26 Conversations between Peggy Ann McKay Carter and the author, 1991, 1992.

27 After Annie Drummond's death in 1959, her daughter Peggy Ann Carter found an old suitcase tucked in the back of a cupboard. When she opened it she found items she describes as her mother's 'treasured memories'. Among them were a copy of the printed score of *The Western Playland* (now in the author's possession) and a copy of *Poems of To-day* inscribed 'To Nurse Drummond, With thanks for joy and best wishes for all things to come, September 1918 From Ivor Gurney S. Albans'. The book was among the items Annie managed to save when many of her belongings were destroyed by a fire shortly after she arrived in the United States.

28 Walter de la Mare to MMS, 7 August 1925, GA.

29 Walter de la Mare to MMS, 14 March 1927, GA.

30 Medical Records, GA.

31 IG, 'Charles Villiers Stanford by Some of his Pupils', *Music and Letters*, vol. 5, no. 3 (July 1924), p. 200. Stanford died on 29 March 1924.

32 The only reference to it appears in some random notes made by Marion Scott at the RCM. *Out of June and October* was among the poems Scott lent to Ralph Vaughan Williams. It appears to be lost.

33 IG, *Rewards of Wonder*, ed. George Walter (Ashington: MidNAG; Manchester: Carcanet, 2000).

34 *Second Selections from Modern Poets*, made by J. C. Squire (London: Martin Secker, 1924).

35 IG to Annie Drummond, *c.* November 1924, GA.

36 Drummond sailed from Glasgow on the *Albania* on 21 May 1921, arriving in Boston on 29 May. She listed her occupation as 'Nurse' on her immigration documents.

37 GF, 1937 notes for a preface to the unpublished catalogue, quoted in DBR, *IG*, p. 162.

38 GF, quoted in Stephen Banfield, *Gerald Finzi: An English Composer* (London: Faber & Faber, 1997), p. 393.

39 GF to Edmund Blunden, 23 August 1953, GA.

40 RD to MMS, 3 August 1925, GA.

41 Richard Maurice Bucke was born in England in 1837 and emigrated to Canada with his parents a year later. He studied medicine at McGill University and began his medical practice in Ontario in 1864. In 1876 he was appointed superintendent of the Provincial Asylum for the Insane at Hamilton, Ontario, and in 1877 became superintendent of London, Ontario Hospital. He was a founder of Western University (London, Ontario), where he was also professor of mental and nervous diseases. He served as president of the Psychological Section of the British Medical Association and as president of the American Medico-Psychological Association. Bucke is best remembered today for his work on cosmic consciousness (the belief that certain individuals are gifted with the power of transcendent realization or illumination, which 'constitutes a definite advance in man's relation with the Infinite') and his deep friendship with Walt Whitman. Bucke wrote a biography of Whitman and became his literary executor.

42 RD to MMS, 16 January 1926, GA. Davis was also an advocate of the work of Dr Stoddard and recommended his book *The New Psychiatry*. The classical definition of transference is the unconscious repetition of the relationship patterns of the patient's past in the analytic situation.

43 Ibid.

44 At the time Dr Davis began working with Gurney in March 1925, Ivor was experiencing a manic phase of his illness and was producing masses of poetry and music.

45 RD to MMS, 3 August 1925, GA.

46 RD to MMS, 26 November 1925, GA.

47 Ibid.

48 Ibid.

49 RD to MMS, 27 November 1925, GA.

50 RD to MMS, 22 December 1925, GA. Given the nature of Gurney's illness, a chemical imbalance, Davis would not have been able to 'cure' him, but he might have made his life more comfortable, provided him with a nutritious diet and exercise, and perhaps enabled him to enjoy fewer severe episodes of his illness. Gurney needed drugs that had not yet been invented in order to control his illness. A cure for bipolar disorder has yet to be discovered and the exact causes of the illness are not fully known.

51 RD to MMS, 30 December 1925, GA.

52 Ibid.

53 RD to MMS, 30 November 1925, GA.

54 MMS to RD, 1 December 1925, GA.

55 Ibid.

56 Ibid.

57 Ibid.

58 Ibid.

59 RD to MMS, 22 December 1925, GA.

60 Ibid.

61 MMS to RD, 3 December 1925, GA.

62 Ibid.

63 RD to MMS, 30 December 1925, GA.

64 Ibid.

65 RD to MMS, 16 January 1925, GA.

66 Ibid.

67 Ibid.

68 Ibid. Davis was writing a two-volume book, *Emotions and Sanity* and *Emotions and Insanity*. I have not been able to determine if he published this work or learn what became of Dr Davis or whether he was indeed an impostor. If he was, he understood psychology well enough to be effective. He might have instinctively known what a patient needed or he might have had personal experience that enabled him to deal effectively with people like Gurney. One cannot ignore the parallels between his methods and those of Dr Richard Bucke. Bethlem Royal Hospital, where Davis worked, was the first asylum for the insane in England. In the seventeenth century it became something of a tourist attraction, with the public being allowed to watch the inmates as a form of cheap entertainment. This cruel practice continued until the early nineteenth century. Bethlem became best known by its nickname 'Bedlam'. The word eventually came into common usage to describe chaos and confusion. Ironically, the paths of Ivor Gurney and Randolph Davis crossed again in an abstract way when Gurney was honoured at the Imperial War Museum's war poets' exhibition, *Anthem for Doomed Youth* (2002–3). The central building of Bethlem Royal Hospital is now home to the Imperial War Museum. The other buildings of the complex were destroyed in 1936.

69 RG to MMS, 14 September 1922, GA.

CHAPTER 22

'A fantastic mix-up'

IN THE AFTERMATH of Dr Davis's departure, Ivor Gurney struggled to hold onto the fraying threads that tied him to sanity. He was suffering from anxiety and complaining of an irregular heartbeat as he had during his 1918 nervous breakdown. He submitted to a physical examination but doctors found nothing seriously wrong with him. Still believing that Ivor would benefit from outside help, Marion arranged for him to see the Harley Street psychiatrist, but nothing came of it.

Ivor continued to write poetry and had, at Marion's prompting, finished 'The Trumpet' to complete his setting of Edward Thomas's verse for the song cycle *Lights Out*, published early in 1926.[1] He completed his collection *Best Poems* in April 1926, the same month his song cycle *The Western Playland (and of Sorrow)* was published in the Carnegie Collection of British Music. This work for baritone, string quartet and piano was dedicated to 'Hawthornden' – Annie Drummond. At his request, Marion sent her a copy. Despite the dedication, Annie, now Mrs McKay, did not feel drawn to correspond with Ivor. Still, she was deeply moved and kept the music for the rest of her life.[2]

Ivor's doctors consistently portrayed him as 'very depressed', 'suffering from delusions', and noted that 'he imagines that his persecutors surround the hospital at night'. Their reports give no indications of the positive efforts Ivor was making to preserve his sanity.[3] Doctors failed to recognize valuable clues to his mental state by observing what he was actually doing – working with commitment, organizing his thoughts and focusing his mind and energy for long stretches during which he produced a remarkable number of poems.

Hospital authorities and staff knew Gurney was engrossed in writing because they saw him doing it. They also saw the results when they passed reams of manuscripts containing his poetry and music to Marion. The physicians ignored his creative work, probably dismissing it as nothing more than the incoherent scribbling of an insane man 'who talks to himself'. Paradoxically, when Ivor was dealing with what they considered 'the normal affairs of life' doctors found him 'quite sensible and coherent'.[4] One wonders what was meant by 'normal' and how often Ivor was permitted to experience what to him would be a normal life.

Ivor read voraciously, moving through literature from Plutarch to Hardy to Wilfred Owen. He once asked for a copy of Kipling in French. Words did not merely float aimlessly before his eyes; he retained what he read and could have discussed it had he been encouraged to do so. He was never without a book, even when he went on day trips with Marion. No physician after Dr Davis seemed to understand or care about the attempts Ivor was making to save himself. W. E. Anderson, who replaced Dr Davis as the Second Assistant Medical Officer, reported that when Ivor was 'induced to talk about music or poetry he tended to become rather more capable of coherent conversation', but no serious effort seems to have been made to engage Ivor regularly in such conversations.[5]

That Ivor was still capable of expressing himself coherently is evident in many of the poems he wrote between 1924 and 1926 and in a scattering that followed until about 1929. He began to write long autobiographical verse that helped him anchor his thoughts and enabled him to recreate his past with an honesty and clarity that sometimes eluded him in his earlier poems.

Ivor explored many topics in his asylum poems. When he wrote about the war, he was not writing as a man destroyed by war and reduced to reliving the experience over and over. He was writing as a poet whose freedom had been snatched from him, leaving him nothing in his present life that was worth translating into poetry. Cut off from the outside world, his only means of keeping in touch with reality was to recall the past. He could no longer walk the Cotswolds and the Severn plain where he might hear 'the flute call / Of my country's meadows',[6] feel 'The miles go sliding by under my steady feet',[7] or experience 'Glimmering dusk above the moist plough and the / Silence of trees' heaviness under low grey sky'.[8] Memory was all he had left and it provided the material he needed to keep himself alert, focused, thinking and active. The present held nothing for him but anguish, despair and loneliness.

Ivor's rage at being locked up was immense. His already quick and sometimes violent temper flared dangerously. He was 'hostile', 'obstinate' and abusive towards different attendants, some of whom he singled out as his tormentors. He screamed sexually explicit obscenities. He attempted to assault the medical superintendent. His behaviour frightened everyone. When doctors tried to give him a physical examination in 1926, he refused and told them that 'an examination of the floor or ceiling ... would be more to the point'.[9] When Marion and her father arranged to take Ivor to the theatre to see a performance at the Old Vic, doctors, fearing for his safety, suggested that she 'obtain a box ... as near the stage level as possible, so that there will be no risk of Mr. Gurney precipitating himself from a height'.[10]

For all his disturbing and frightening behaviour at Stone House, Ivor was quite a different man on those rare occasions when he was in company with visitors or out on a day trip with Marion. Adeline Vaughan Williams found him gentle. Marion often found him rational in conversation and always sensitive to his environment in ways that transcended the drabness of the asylum and called into question reports of his deteriorating mental condition. Marion visited him one summer's day when he had been ill for several weeks and confined to a bed in a dormitory ward. The bed was beneath the east window facing a solid wall across the room. When Scott arrived, he said, 'There was a beautiful dawn this morning.' She was surprised to hear this comment. ' "But how did you see it," I exclaimed. "O, I saw it in the mirror on the opposite wall" ', he told her.[11]

Marion remained optimistic that some means might be found to help Ivor, if not cure him. She was willing to try anything. In early 1927 Adeline Vaughan Williams suggested that they arrange for him to see H. M.

Lidderdale, a Christian Science healer who lived in Kensington. Marion agreed.

Lidderdale was clear from the beginning that it was 'not morally necessary and certainly most inadvisable' to tell hospital authorities that Gurney was undergoing Christian Science treatment based on prayer.[12] 'It is essentially a negation of what [Gurney's doctors] believe'. Lidderdale feared that the Superintendent 'could & quite possibly would object, out of sheer ignorance, and ... his knowledge of the fact that it was being applied would be a definite hindrance to its success because he would mentally oppose it', Lidderdale explained. 'I am quite sure that no one need ask leave of the Superintendent to pray for one of his patients, whom <u>he</u> has given up as "incurable"'. He believed that the only legitimate objection to treatment would be to one that might harm Ivor. 'It is not possible for C.S. treatment, which is simply the application of Truth and Love, to do that.'[13]

Ivor presented a challenge to Lidderdale, who sought to lead him to 'the infinite Divine Mind, in which all is happiness, freedom & joy'.[14] On some visits Lidderdale found him in good condition, clean-shaven, dressed in street clothes and 'less sunk in dreariness'.[15] His speech might be clear even though he rambled and claimed to be someone other than himself, like Walt Whitman. At other times, Ivor was argumentative, irritable and critical, associating Lidderdale with officials at the hospital whom he felt treated him badly. He did not like Lidderdale. When Lidderdale offered to take him for a drive, Ivor told him he could not take 'favours' from anyone but Marion Scott. She was the only person he trusted.

In spite of Gurney's difficult and erratic behaviour, the more time Lidderdale spent with him the less willing he was to accept the idea that Ivor was insane. 'It would undoubtedly help enormously to get him away from the atmosphere of hopelessness that there is there', he wrote frankly to Scott.[16] He could see that Ivor was being beaten down by his environment. Like Dr Davis, Lidderdale believed that Ivor was not getting the care and understanding he needed at Stone House. He was aware that the doctors had 'quite given up his case' and were acting as nothing more than his keepers. 'The patient never asked to be put under this doctor [Anderson, Davis's replacement], and we know that [Gurney's] interests, which are paramount, would best be served by removal from Stone [House], if that could legitimately be managed', he declared, echoing Dr Davis's opinion.[17] After three months of Lidderdale's 'secret' visits, Gurney showed no improvement, so Scott terminated the arrangement. Lidderdale understood.

The pressure on Marion was intense. She knew that Ivor did not belong in an asylum, but she was helpless now to remove him from Stone House. After three failed attempts to find outside help for Gurney, Scott had nowhere to turn. She had exhausted all hope. She had little choice but to convince herself that the treatment he received at Stone House was rendered with kindness that 'animated the whole staff from the Medical Superintendent downwards'. She found 'beyond praise ... the daily forbearance, courage and consideration shown by the male nurses in Gurney's ward'.[18] The reality was somewhere in the middle and raises doubts that Scott's decision to push for Gurney's transfer to the City of London Mental

Hospital was ultimately the right one for him. But it was a decision she had been called upon to make and one she had to live with.

Ivor's care at Stone House cost Scott £26 a quarter plus extras that she supplied: books, tobacco, clothing, paper, anything and everything that she felt he needed or that he asked for. His pension, along with donations from friends and money from Scott, paid for his hospital fees.[19]

The staff faced a formidable challenge in dealing with Gurney, who was unpredictable, wilful, rebellious, destructive and violent. It could not have been an easy task, but working with patients as difficult as Gurney should have been routine for them. He was not treated badly, but those closest to him did not think he was treated as well or as thoughtfully as he might have been. At times it appears that rather than try to help Ivor or try to control him, the staff were intimidated and simply left him alone. In the 1920s and 1930s a course of effective treatment for his illness was non-existent.

Ivor's physical health issues were troubling for doctors who were dealing with a patient who refused to let them touch him and who refused any medication. Beyond urinalyses, infrared treatments for rheumatism, and routine care for general ailments, little else was done for Ivor. No effort appears to have been made to ensure that he was well nourished or to improve his eating habits. He never should have developed an illness that resembled scurvy, an indication that he ate scant amounts of fruit and vegetables. His teeth were allowed to rot. No mention is made of any dental maintenance work being done to repair his defective teeth. Instead, they were pulled, as many as six at one time, eventually leaving him with no teeth in his top jaw and only seven on the bottom. From 1926 through 1936, Gurney underwent no recorded physical examinations, yet doctors noted: 'health is satisfactory', 'he is in moderately good health', 'enjoys satisfactory health', 'general health apparently only fair'.[20] How could they have known his physical condition without examining him? He was losing weight, yet doctors claimed he 'takes his food well'.[21]

Gurney's medical records are full of references to his delusions, hallucinations, paranoia and difficulty in communicating. He suffered severe psychotic episodes. After three and a half years at Stone House, he was claiming that he wrote the greater part of Shakespeare, Thackeray and Hilaire Belloc amongst others, and that Beethoven and Haydn never existed, he having composed all their music; 'that he "dug the River Thames in one night"'; that the instrument torturing him with electricity was 'an Othello'. His conversation was 'rambling and disjointed' and his speech more 'obscure' and 'at times completely incomprehensible'.[22]

When doctors were describing Ivor as delusional, speaking incomprehensibly and rambling, he was writing poetry with deliberation, clarity and form that flies in the face of their observations.

> Pebbles are beneath, but we stand softly
> On them, as on sand, and watch the lacy edge
> of the swift sea ...[23]

> Soft rain beats upon my windows
> Hardly hammering.

But by the great gusts guessed further off
Up by the bare moor and brambly headland
Heaven and earth make war ...[24]

Now the dust is on the road,
And the blue hills call to distances,
On my shoulders I take my fancies
And travel where good shows ...[25]
What did they expect of our toil and extreme

Hunger – the perfect drawing of a hearts dream?
Did they look for a book of wrought art's perfection,
Who promised no reading, nor praise, nor publication?
Out of the heart's sickness the spirit wrote ...[26]

Ivor's delusions and hallucinations were not constant. They were induced by defects in his brain chemistry and are a natural progression of an untreated bipolar disorder. The patient has little or no control over their occurrence, although Ivor previously had some success with physical exercise in keeping his moods from swinging too far up or too far down. He also tried on his own to keep his mind alert and engaged through his writing and reading. But it was one thing to read and write, and another to be able to share what he was doing with people who understood and were capable of responding. When he was suffering a manic episode, his mood was so elevated that no single person could keep up with him. But there was no one at Stone House to even try.

Gurney's poor nutrition exacerbated his condition. The body needs food to fuel its complex functions, but in the asylum, as he had done for much of his adult life, he ate poorly. One attendant expressed surprise when Ivor suddenly began eating meat, a food that supplies protein and should have been a regular part of his diet.

Marion Scott could not be at the hospital every day to talk to him, nor could the Vaughan Williamses. '[H]e gets no help at all for his mind from his surroundings', wrote Adeline Vaughan Williams after a visit. '[H]e also spoke of his loneliness "No one comes to see me". How I longed to take him away!'[27] Other visitors were rare, and Ivor was left alone. As his condition worsened and he had no outside stimulation; he detached himself from the world around him, insulating himself from it as best he could.

At the same time that Ivor was writing volumes of poetry, he attempted to compose music, but he found it difficult, if not impossible, to recapture the brilliance of his earlier songs. His new music often meandered without focus, and while there might be fragments of beauty tucked into a song, they were not developed. Gurney's last sustained period of intense creative activity ended around mid-1926, when he sailed off the edge into a depression from which he did not emerge.

Meanwhile, Marion continued to find publishers for his poetry and music although the task was growing more difficult. Unlike Herbert Howells and Arthur Benjamin, Gurney was producing little of value and was no longer an active and visible presence in public. Marion had to rely on his previous work to keep his name alive. Had she the time to read carefully and catalogue all that he wrote in the asylum, she would have discovered new poems and some music worthy of publication, but her busy life did not permit this luxury. In 1927 and 1928 only three of Gurney's poems were published.[28] His songs fared slightly better. Stainer & Bell published 'Star Talk', a setting of Robert Graves, in 1927, while Oxford University Press brought out five songs in 1928.[29] There were about five documented performances of his songs between 1923 and 1938. Gurney's voice had fallen silent and he was largely forgotten save for the glimmer of interest Marion managed to sustain.

Marion remained the most devoted of his friends, visiting him regularly and taking him to the theatre, to tea and for day trips in an automobile. These outings took their toll on her emotionally but she persisted even after she had found some measure of comfort in her friendship with the music critic Richard Capell.[30] She had met Capell around 1929 when he was the editor of the *Monthly Musical Record* and she was writing for an increasing number of publications, including *Music and Letters*. As was her habit when it came to her personal life, Marion kept the details of this relationship to herself, so little is known about it. The few clues she left imply that it extended beyond simple friendship. 'Late to sleep last night', Marion wrote in her journal in May 1930. 'In the small hours, perhaps between 1 and 2, I dreamt that I saw R.C. [Capell] standing by my side in a sort of patch of light that made him visible and left everything else dark. His face was white and bitter. He looked at me, laid his right hand on his breast and said, "Such as it is, it belongs to you".' [31]

Born in 1885 at Northampton as the eldest of nine children, Capell was a private man, a war hero and bachelor devoted to his mother. Like Marion, he revealed very little about himself and sidestepped conversation when it threatened to become intimate. In many ways, he was an ideal companion for her, and fit her preference in men. He was younger, daring and gifted, but beyond that they shared a love of humour, books, ideas, good conversation and music. Capell became an authority on Schubert; Scott on Haydn. Both possessed a strong literary talent, imagination, brilliant intellectual power, acuteness of perception and wide-ranging knowledge of many subjects. Each was fluent in French and German and shared an interest in new music, about which they wrote with insight, fairness and lucidity. Both were among the first to write about Gustav Holst. Scott began writing for the *Monthly Musical Record* in 1932 and eventually followed Capell to the *Daily Telegraph*, where he served as music critic from 1933 until his death in 1954. Marion's friendship with Capell lasted for many years.

As Ivor continued on his downward spiral in the asylum, Marion's life was becoming increasingly busy, rich and full of demands. She and her parents were devoting more time to their friendship with pianist Fanny Davies (1861–1934), who eventually lived with the family.[32] They had opened their home to her in the mid-1920s, and it was there that she sometimes taught her students, among them the young Kathleen Richards Dale, who eventually became Marion's assistant. Marion and Miss Davies had first met in 1901 when they performed in the Schumann Quintet in E flat at the Crystal

Palace, although Marion was already familiar with Davies from her recitals and concert appearances in London. Throughout the years they remained friends. Davies participated in programmes given by the Scotts and the Society of Women Musicians, and served a term as president of the organization. Marion often reviewed Davies' performances in the *Christian Science Monitor*. Both women shared an interest in contemporary British music and a commitment to bringing it to audiences. Marion described Davies as a pianist of glowing genius.[33] When Davies' health began to fail, the Scotts cared for her.

Amidst Marion's wide-ranging friendships, her work as a critic and at the RCM Union, her research, writing and lectures, her advocacy for women and contemporary music, and her active involvement with the Society of Women Musicians and other organizations, she boldly entered a new phase of her life. She turned her attention to musicology, a field traditionally off limits to women. In her lectures dating from 1910, her early feature articles for the *Christian Science Monitor*, and her substantial studies published in *Music and Letters* starting in 1925, Marion revealed her gift for daring and highly skilled detective work.[34] She approached her research as methodically and as carefully as an archaeologist who patiently removes layers of the past with a fine brush or small, delicate tool so as not to damage or overlook what lies hidden. She travelled extensively in France, Germany and Austria in her quest for original material, translating German and French sources when necessary. Her remarkable insight and instincts enabled her to make important connections between past and present and to inject clarity and vitality into her re-creations of earlier times that resonated with modern minds.

Marion began to work seriously as a musicologist in the late 1920s when she was just past her fiftieth year. Never one to resist a challenge, she had leapt at the suggestion made by Fox Strangways, editor of *Music and Letters*, that she attempt to sort out the 'muddled' chronology of Haydn's string quartets. She devised a process by which she checked and examined all known editions of Haydn's quartets and then collated them. This initial investigation led her to discover that the work presumed to be 'Opus One, Number One' of the string quartets had not always been the one in B flat, the official designee, but an early five-movement quartet in E flat. Haydn had relegated the youthful E flat to the divertimento section of his catalogue. Before Marion's detective work, it was believed that Haydn's quartets numbered eighty-three.

Marion discovered the work one winter afternoon in early 1930 at the Royal Academy of Music as she was conducting 'a systematic examination of four volumes containing eighteenth-century editions (in parts, not score) of Haydn's Quartets'.[35] Among them she found a copy of the 1765 edition by J. J. Hummel of Amsterdam of the six quartets forming the Opus 1. 'Beginning at No. 1 I saw something in E flat instead of B flat', she recalled. She was hardly surprised, because she had become 'inured to the confusion in the numberings', but when she found that the E flat Quartet was not to be found anywhere among the six in Opus 1 of her Thematic List, nor in Opus 2 or 3, she was bewildered. Marion then 'chased' the unknown E flat

Quartet through the entire thematic index without finding it. Her bewilderment turned to excitement as she realized she had found Haydn's 'real No. 1' quartet.[36]

'Haydn naturally cared little for compositions that represented him as an apprentice', she wrote, explaining that he had told his publisher that 'he wished his string quartets to be reckoned as beginning only after the first 18, since these early works did not embody the true principles of quartet form'.[37] Scott pursued the history of the E flat Quartet with care and commitment, and then prepared her edition of the quartet, which she dubbed the 'Lost Heir'. Oxford University Press published it in 1931. She also published 'A Study of the Complete Editions' in the July 1930 *Music and Letters* and a survey of Haydn's quartets, 'Haydn's "83" ', in the November 1930 issue of the same journal. To Scott, 'Haydn did not *invent* the string quartet; he *made* it – an infinitely higher achievement.'[38]

The London String Quartet performed the E flat Quartet on 3 October 1931. Marion's groundbreaking research and analyses of Franz Joseph Haydn's quartets were hailed as 'exemplary' and quickly established her reputation, bringing her international acclaim. Haydn scholars endorsed Scott's findings and newspapers throughout Great Britain, on the Continent and in the United States carried reports of her discovery. A *Times* writer observed that

> Miss Scott has used the same care in preparing her edition which she brought to the pursuit of her quest. She has not only recorded all the variants in the existing set of parts, but to her 'Preface' and her postscript she has added a 'Note on Performance' which performers must read. It deals chiefly with the interpretation of the 'Graces' and since almost every modern performance of eighteenth-century music exhibits ignorance or tastelessness in that matter, it is well to state the facts each time a work of that period is reprinted. Miss Scott seems to have thought of everything which could help to bring the 'lost heir' back to its rightful heritage, and she deserves the thanks of string players for enabling them to make the acquaintance of Haydn's firstborn.[39]

Haydn's life and music would occupy Marion Scott for the next twenty-five years, but she would make many intellectual side journeys during that quarter century.

Among the personal journeys Marion continued to make were her periodic visits to Ivor at Stone House. She was the only person who ever took him away from the asylum. The two were always in company with a nurse and an attendant who stayed in the background to ensure that Ivor would not escape or attempt suicide. By early 1929 Ivor Gurney was thirty-eight years old, his once-powerful physique no longer apparent in the gaunt man whose clothes hung on him like a scarecrow's. He stood ramrod straight and his wavy brown hair, now close-cropped, showed few traces of grey or a receding hairline. His face had thinned and lines creased the sides of his nearly toothless mouth, but he remained a striking man with aquiline features. Ivor's eyes behind spectacles still burned with alert, penetrating intensity and intelligence. Looking at him as Marion Scott so often did, it was difficult to believe that he was terrorized by hallucinations, tortured by 'electricity' and, at times, thought himself to be the author of Shakespeare's plays and the composer of Beethoven's music.

When Ivor was in Marion's company he was docile, pensive and acutely observant. He understood that he was not well and tried to learn why by asking her questions. Marion did her best. 'There are lots of questions I want to ask you', Gurney said to her during one of their outings. 'Can you answer them?' [40] When Marion said she would try, Ivor proceeded to ask her 'the puzzled, half indignant questions that wring one's heart. Why was he tortured thus, why was London doing this, or was Europe doing this, what was the cause. I could only say 'It springs from the same cause as a nightmare. It is best to think of it as a dreadful dream.' [41]

Marion's day trips with Ivor were traumatic for her, but she persisted because she understood how important they were to him and because she loved him. Only unconditional love could endure such a trial. It was a love she was incapable of relinquishing no matter how removed he might be from her both physically and emotionally.

Writing in her journal on 20 March 1929, Marion revealed that she had seen little of Ivor for several months. Cold weather with black fogs, a bout of influenza and work had kept her away from Stone House since November, an unusually long time. When she finally arrived at the facility on 4 March, Gurney asked her to take him for a drive so he might 'get out of the torture for an afternoon'. They arranged a date. Ten days later on Thursday, 14 March, Marion boarded a train that took her past a bleak landscape of bare, black trees, 'grass without green, rough like a moor pony's coat with rime on it ... stagnant ponds [with] a skim of ice' under cold leaden skies 'heavy with grey vapour'. A north-east wind was blowing so hard that the young hospital attendant who met her at the depot had thought she might not come.

Ivor, dressed in a grey pullover she had sent him and wearing a great coat from Arthur Benjamin, selected Rochester as their destination. They sat in the rear of the new Salon Austin recently purchased by the asylum. A male nurse and an attendant sat in the front seat, separated from their passengers by a sheet of glass. They drove first to Gravesend, stopping at the Promenade where they could see the 'great grey Thames [come] shouldering full tide against its shore and all that expanse of tossing water alive with ships'. The wind was blowing so hard that their eyes 'streamed'. The Promenade was bare of people save for a man huddled in a shelter. Ivor stood with his coat open, feeling the cold but he 'seemed so used to suffering that he never tried to protect himself from it'. Marion pulled his coat across his chest to protect him.

A row of buildings reminded Gurney of Ypres and 'set him off talking of it in the war; spinning thistledown tales, of times there that drifted hither and thither among fantastic ideas', Marion recalled. 'Ideas dance across him in a fantastic mix-up'. The day was full of ominous signs that belied the joy that was to come to Marion by day's end. On the road to Rochester, they passed an 'unutterably bleak' landscape of 'black trees, sullen solitary houses', encountered the first of three funerals they would see that afternoon, and watched a fire brigade fighting a blaze by a railway viaduct. When they finally arrived at Rochester Cathedral, it, too, seemed unwelcoming, 'dark with terrible windowless sockets against the sullen grey sky'. Yet it was impressive, appearing 'unnaturally high and majestic'. When Marion called out to Ivor telling him to look at the building, he glanced at it and replied 'Yes. It stands like King Lear'. 'That was a fine thing to say: a world of criticism and description in five words, a flash of the real Gurney genius', Marion observed. After a brief time in the cathedral, cut short by the distressing sound of hammering, they went to a second-hand bookshop and then for tea at the Gate House. Warmed now, they 'dived across the High Street', where Marion bought ground coffee for Ivor, who then asked if he could buy a Philips Atlas. They tried two bookshops without success. Ivor chose instead a copy of Shelley in the Augustan series of English poetry. It was time to return to Stone House.

The weather had worsened and the roads were nearly deserted 'as if the northeaster had blown away all but the folk of the soil'. Soon all they had before them was 'one empty stretch of grey', a winter mist having crept in to shut off all the long views. 'Civilization, except for the road, might have been gone a thousand years, or might still be a thousand years ahead. Things looked timeless, primeval', Marion recalled. When she thought she saw a patch of snow, Ivor, the observant countryman, corrected her by telling her it was chalk. They settled back into their seats and began sharing Shelley's poetry, which delighted Ivor. They read 'Ozymandias', 'A Lament' and 'Ode to the West Wind' but it was the 'Hymn to Intellectual Beauty' that most occupied them. Ivor moved his finger under the lines

> Like clouds in starlight widely spread,
> Like memory of music fled,
> Like aught that for its grace may be
> Dear, and yet dearer for its mystery ...

He moved on to the lines

> Or music by the night wind sent
> Through strings of some still instrument
> Or moonlight on a midnight stream
> Gives grave and truth to life's unquiet dream ...

Then he passed the volume to Marion and with his fingers still running under the lines he had her read aloud:

> I vowed that I would dedicate my powers
> To thee and thine: have I not kept the vow?

'Did he mean music or me?' Marion wondered. 'Both I think. Ivor the poet with his own poetry locked within him, unable to utter it, speaking through the words of another English poet. We were very happy'. This seemingly small gesture from Ivor spoke volumes to Marion. He had acknowledged and expressed his understanding of the bond that existed between them. Marion was elated and deeply moved.

She continued to see Ivor as often as possible. In September, on a clear day of 'racing wind and sun' when the Channel was 'full of moving colour', they went to Dover on one of their longer journeys.[42] She usually brought her camera with her to photograph Gurney surreptitiously when she could. He hated to be photographed, and Marion could only 'seize the moment' when he wasn't looking.[43] In her photos he nearly always had a book in his hands or was engaged in reading. At Dover, Marion captured a poignant image of Ivor, his back to her, his right hand shading his eyes, as he gazed across the Channel to the 'hazy golden and blue' form of France, where his poetic genius had flowered during a cruel war. Ironically, he had not seen the coast since he had watched it fade into similar haze from the boat carrying him back to England exactly twelve years earlier in September 1917. He savoured the view, sensing perhaps that he would never see it again.

By 1930 Ivor had written the last of his coherent, crafted and controlled poems. After eight years as an inmate at Stone House, his life in the asylum was a void. With the exception of Marion, he had no contact with the outside world. He could not go to the cinema, attend concerts, go on long rambling walks, linger at used bookstalls, eat in restaurants or socialize with friends who shared his interests. He could no longer control the rampaging symptoms that filled his mind with increasing delusions and paranoia and which disoriented and terrified him, ultimately derailing his genius. Although he continued to write 'poetry', the act was little more than an exercise to keep himself busy and apart from the degrading routines of the asylum which he held in great contempt. His last poem of any merit appears to have been 'The Wind', written sometime after March 1929:

> All night the fierce wind blew,–
> All night I knew
> Time, like a dark wind blowing
> All days, all lives, all memories
> Down empty endless skies – ...[44]

He signed it with the pseudonym 'Valentine Fane'.[45] The poems he continued to write were disjointed and incoherent, with words strung together without form or meaning. His letters, once a great joy to recipients, were now long, rambling affairs full of bewildering fragments of thoughts and ideas that scattered across his mind like leaves caught in a changing wind. He wrote as if some of his thoughts fell into a crevasse in his brain and he leaped over them without noticing they were missing: 'This is Franz Schubert's death day / and enough for Kent Reach to think of – whose chimneys smoke grandly, but Nature said "W. E. Henley Prague 1731 –" So light dies down – But after saying that Europe could not stand war for its thought, by 137 degrees ...'[46]

Ivor Gurney's free spirit was silenced. He became little more than another patient who was highly delusional, uncooperative, strong-willed and given to obsessive behaviour such as underlining every word in his books and hoarding rubbish. He still refused to allow doctors to examine him physically and was 'destructive ... very abusive and forceful in conversation'.[47] His keepers at Stone House found that he was growing 'dull and apathetic, dejected in his attitude, slow in his answers to questions' and that his memory was 'defective'. His statements were 'rambling and deluded'. Ivor told one doctor that 'Collins the International wrote Shakespeare's plays'.[48] He talked and muttered to himself and was restless. He wandered about interfering with other patients, and at times became aggressive, abusive and hostile towards the medical and nursing staff.

In her ongoing efforts to bring some joy to Ivor and to provide him with some contact with the outside world, in 1932 Marion contacted Helen Thomas, the widow of poet Edward Thomas, whose work Ivor admired and had set to music. She explained Gurney's situation and his passion for Edward's poetry, and asked Helen if she would visit him at Stone House. Marion told her that if she could 'face the ordeal of visiting him, she felt such indirect contact with Edward would mean more to him than we could imagine'.[49] Mrs Thomas was 'filled with pity' when she read Scott's description of Gurney, and agreed to visit him.

Upon arriving at the City of London Mental Hospital with Marion, Helen was struck immediately by its prison-like appearance and the number of doors that needed to be locked and unlocked before they were finally in Gurney's company. 'We were walking along a bare corridor when we were met by a tall gaunt dishevelled man clad in pyjamas and dressing gown … He gazed with an intense stare into my face and took me silently by the hand', Helen Thomas recalled. She had brought flowers which she handed to him and 'which he took with the same moving intensity and silence'. Then Ivor spoke: 'You are Helen, Edward's wife and Edward is dead.' Helen suggested that they talk about Edward. Ivor led her 'into a little cell-like bedroom where the only furniture was a bed and a chair. The windows were high up and barred and the walls bare and drab', she wrote in her account of the meeting.

Ivor commented on her hat and she sat by him on the bed talking about Edward and herself. Mrs Thomas found his 'talk was quite sane and lucid', although Ivor did make some delusional comments and told her 'They are getting at me through wireless'. Before Scott and Thomas left, Gurney took them into the common room and played the piano for the two women and 'a tragic circle of men' with '[h]opeless and aimless faces' who 'gazed vacantly and [their] restless hands fumbled or hung down lifelessly'. She saw no sign that the men were even aware of the music and she took pity on them all just sitting in a large room where 'there was not one beautiful thing for the patients to look at'.

Helen Thomas's visit was such a success that she returned again, bringing with her Edward's 'own well-used ordnance maps of Gloucestershire'. It proved to be a brilliant idea. Ivor spread out the maps and he and Mrs Thomas traced 'with our fingers the lanes and byways and villages of which Ivor Gurney knew every step and over which Edward had also walked … spotting a village or a track, a hill or a wood and seeing it all in his mind's eye, with flowers and trees, stiles and hedges, a mental vision sharper and more actual for his heightened intensity', she wrote. 'He trod, in a way we who were sane could not emulate, the lanes and fields he knew and loved so well, his guide being his finger tracing the way on the map … he had

Edward as his companion in this strange perambulation and he was utterly happy ...' Much to Ivor's delight and Marion's relief, Mrs Thomas continued her visits for several months.

In October Marion took him to visit with her friend Hester Stansfeld Prior at Eltham. Prior had left various music scores lying about 'as decoys'. After much coaxing Gurney suddenly picked up the score of Brahms' E minor symphony and 'played the slow movement with every lead given and no hesitation over the transposing instruments'. Prior and Scott were almost reduced to tears.[50]

Through Marion's continuing efforts, from 1930 to 1934, Ivor's poems appeared in four anthologies: *An Anthology of War Poems, Younger Poets of Today, The Mercury Book of Verse* and *Jewels of Song*. J. C. Squire published more than a dozen of his poems in the *London Mercury*. Nothing was heard of Gurney's music. More efforts were made to remove him from Stone House but they came to nothing. He continued to pray for death.

NOTES

1 Published by Stainer & Bell.

2 Conversation between Peggy Ann McKay Carter and the author, 1990 and 1991.

3 Medical Records, GA.

4 Ibid.

5 William Trethowan, 'Ivor Gurney's Mental Illness', vol. 62, nos.3–4 (July/October 1981), p. 304, paraphrasing a statement made by Dr Anderson.

6 IG, 'The Two', *CP*, p. 208.

7 IG, 'Walking Song', *CP*, p. 95.

8 IG, 'Glimmering Dusk', *CP*, p. 79.

9 Medical records, GA.

10 Dr Navarra to Marion Scott, 5 April 1926, GA.

11 MMS, 'Recollections of Ivor Gurney', *Monthly Musical Record*, vol. 68, no. 794 (February 1938), p. 46.

12 H. M. Lidderdale to MMS, 12 March 1927, GA.

13 Ibid. Scott found the philosophies of Christian Science worth exploring and attended services from time to time, but her frequent illnesses and need for medical care made her wary of giving herself over to the practice of Christian Science.

14 Lidderdale to MMS, 5 April 1927, GA.

15 Ibid.

16 Ibid.

17 Lidderdale to MMS, 12 March 1927, GA.

18 MMS, Notes, quoted in DBR, *IG*, p. 72.

19 I believe that Marion Scott's father Sydney Scott actually paid most of the bills for Gurney's care, if not all of them.

20 Medical records, various entries, GA.

21 Ibid.

22 Ibid.

23 IG, 'Sea Marge', *Everyman's Poetry: Ivor Gurney*, ed. George Walter (London: Everyman, 1996), p. 16.

24 IG, 'Soft Rain Beats upon my Windows', ibid., p. 97.

25 IG, 'The Peddlar's Song', ibid., p. 96.

26 IG, 'I Would not Rest', ibid., p. 97.

27 Adeline Vaughan Williams to MMS, quoted in *OIG*, pp. 166–7.

28 'Beethoven I wronged thee' in *Music and Letters*; 'To the Poet before Battle' in the anthology *Great Poems of the English Language: An Anthology of Verse in English from Chaucer to the moderns*, and 'Song of Pain and Beauty' in *Fiery Grains: Thoughts and Sayings for Some Occasions*. The first and second volumes of J. C. Squire's *Selections from Modern Poets* were reprinted in one edition in 1927 and contained Gurney's 'Dawn', 'To the Poet before Battle', 'Song of Pain and Beauty', 'Smudgy Dawn' and 'Thoughts of New England'.

29 'Desire in Spring' (Ledwidge), 'Walking Song' (Harvey), 'The Fields are Full' (Shanks), 'Severn Meadows' (Gurney) and 'The Twa Corbies' (Border ballad).

30 Capell studied at the Bedford Modern School, where he began his musical training. He studied cello privately in London and at Lille Conservatory. He recognized his limitations as a musician early and turned his attention to journalism. He was music critic of the London *Daily Mail* from 1911 to 1933 and of the *Daily Telegraph* from 1933 until his death in 1954. During the Great War he served in France, where he was awarded the Military Medal for gallantry at Vimy Ridge. While working his newspaper jobs, he also served as editor of the *Monthly Musical Record* and *Music and Letters*. During World War II he served as war correspondent for the *Telegraph* in France, the western Sahara and Greece. He wrote several books, including *Simiómata: a Greek Note-book* and *Schubert's Songs*, and translated into English songs of Wolf, Schubert, Schumann and Grieg and the libretto of Richard Strauss's opera *Friedenstag*.

31 MMS, Journal, 11 May 1930, GA.

32 Fanny Davies was born at Guernsey in 1861. She began her studies at Leipzig Conservatory in 1882, but the next year she moved on to the Frankfort Conservatory, where she studied for two years with Clara Schumann. Mme Schumann shaped the course of Davies' career, and Davies was one of the few pianists of her day to include Clara's music in her repertoire. Davies made her debut in England in 1886 at the Crystal Palace in a performance of Beethoven's Piano Concerto no. 4. She was an acclaimed interpreter of Brahms, whom she knew, and often performed music by Bohemian composers. In 1928 she recorded Robert Schumann's piano concerto.

33 MMS, 'The Society of Women Musicians', *Christian Science Monitor*, 14 August 1920.

34 Scott was always interested in musicology, as is indicated by some of her early lectures, which included 'Folk Songs of the Four Races – England, Scotland, Wales, Ireland', 'The Evolution of English Music' and 'English Music: The Inheritance of the Past'. She carried her interest to the pages of the *Christian Science Monitor* in feature articles such as her histories of British violin sonatas, folk song, English lutenist songwriters and the music of the Pilgrims. Her 1919 *Christian Science Monitor* article about music for the solo violin was the seed for her extended piece 'A Complaint of the Decay of Violin Solos' that appeared in *Music and Letters* in 1925. Scott had few equals among women in England working as musicologists. Across the Atlantic, Anne Shaw Faulkner, Marion Bauer (also a composer), Edith Lynnwood Winn, and Hazel Kinscella were early musicologists who found an outlet for their research in producing textbooks for children.

35 MMS, 'Preface', *Haydn, Opus 1, No. 1: Newly Edited after the Original Editions by M. M. Scott* (London: Oxford University Press, 1931).

36 Ibid.

37 MMS, 'Haydn's Opus Two and Opus Three', *Proceedings of the Royal Musical Association*, vol. 61 (1934–5), pp. 1–19 [paper given on 6 November 1934].

38 MMS, 'Preface', *Haydn, Opus 1, No. 1*.

39 Anonymous, 'Haydn's First Quartet: The "Lost Heir" Restored', *The Times*, 31 October 1931, p. 8.

40 MMS, Journal, 20 March 1929, GA.

41 Ibid. Subsequent quotations about this episode are taken from the entry for 20 March.

42 MMS, 'Recollections of Ivor Gurney', *Monthly Musical Record*, vol. 68, no. 794 (February 1938), p. 45.

43 MMS to GF, 7 February 1937, GA.

44 IG, 'The Wind', *CP*, pp. 220–1.

45 Gurney occasionally used pseudonyms, including Michael Flood and Frederick Saxby.

46 Fragment from an asylum letter written in 1933, quoted in *OIG*, p. 165. Joy Finzi, the widow of composer Gerald Finzi, burned an unknown number of Gurney's papers from the asylum years. These papers had come to the Finzis via a bequest in Marion Scott's will. Mrs Finzi destroyed them because she said they were incoherent and of no value.

47 Medical Records, GA.

48 Ibid.

49 Helen Thomas, with Myfanwy Thomas, 'Ivor Gurney', *Under Storm's Wing*, (Manchester: Carcanet, 1988), pp. 239–41. All subsequent quotations about this episode are taken from this source.

50 Hester Stansfeld Prior to MMS, 19 February 1938, GA.

CHAPTER 23

Bitter Troubles and Suffering

$\mathcal{B}$Y 1930 Marion Scott's multiple commitments had grown more demanding while the range of her interests continued to broaden. She and her sister Stella had guided their niece Audrey into adulthood and now watched with pride as the talented twenty-two-year-old woman stood poised on the threshold of her career in theatre. Young Audrey bore a striking physical resemblance to her Aunt Marion.

Marion remained the moving force behind the Society of Women Musicians, which had flourished under her leadership. She had steered the organization through a complex legal tangle to incorporation in 1930, a significant feat accomplished with the help of her solicitor father, who continued to donate his services to the organization. The Society now boasted two libraries for members at its 74 Grosvenor Street headquarters, where, at Marion's insistence, it continued to be run like a business. Members enjoyed regular concerts featuring contemporary music by both sexes, workshops dealing with the business and politics of music, social events, and an annual two-day 'Composers Conference' designed to provide women composers with the opportunity to meet with one another, share ideas and experiences and to offer mutual support.[1]

In 1930, when the women learned that the British Broadcasting Corporation had formed a symphony orchestra, they feared that women instrumentalists would be excluded. Marion devised a bold plan to open auditions to women and was determined that they would succeed. Instead of storming the BBC in the militant manner associated with earlier suffragettes, four Society of Women Musicians members, led by Scott, who understood the importance of first impressions, arrived at BBC headquarters fashionably attired. They approached Music Director Percy Pitt in his office with such calm, reasoned dignity and diplomacy that they won the day. From then on, all auditions were to be held behind screens to give women an equal chance to be judged on merit, not dismissed without a hearing because of the bias against their gender.

When Marion wasn't organizing others or playing an active role in the Society of Women Musicians or in one of the many other organizations in which she held membership, she was researching, writing, lecturing, travelling and taking care of Ivor as best she could. In her writing she approached new topics with insight, enthusiasm, and intelligence often laced with humour and enriched by her profound knowledge of literature, music and history. The Haydn biographer and musicologist Rosemary Hughes called Scott 'one of the great scholars of our day'.[2]

Marion presented her acclaimed paper on the young German composer Paul Hindemith (1895–1963) to the Royal Musical Association in April 1930 at a time when English audiences were finding it difficult to adjust to his modern sound. Outside of Germany he was known as 'the enfant terrible' of Europe.[3] Never one to dismiss anything new, Marion undertook the most comprehensive study of Hindemith in Britain up to that time. For her paper, Scott had researched Hindemith's life, all thirty-five years of it, and studied all of the music she discussed. She read the entire scores of three early atonal operas with librettos so daring that she doubted they would make it past the English censor. She observed that 'Paul Hindemith is an apostle of Atonality and Linear Counterpoint. But he is also a real person in music – a genuine composer who gives off music as a piece of radium throws off energy. That is what makes him interesting, and his music worthy of study.' [4] Scott found Hindemith 'too radically a musician to evade for ever the great emotions that go with genius. If they thaw the little piece of ice that lies in his artist's heart, the effect will be amazing', she said.[5]

In 1933 Marion resurrected the life, achievements and music of a forgotten woman composer, violinist and singer, Maddalena Lombardini (Madame Syrmen) (1745–1818) and introduced her to readers of *Music and Letters*. Her work on Lombardini came nearly fifty years before she became a topic for late twentieth-century scholars. 'Maddalena Lombardini was a minor character of eighteenth century music', Marion wrote. 'I have spent a long time composing paragraphs to show why minor characters are important. I have said they give the level of a period from which to measure the heights attained by the men of genius: I have said the minor musicians are often experimenters: I have even said Maddalena was a pioneer of the twentieth century women's movement! But really I am interested in her just because she insisted on "coming alive" in my imagination ...' [6]

Another composer who came alive in Marion's mind was Beethoven. She started working on his biography for J. M. Dent's Master Musicians series around 1931. She determined her approach early: 'I sternly conditioned myself into re-studying Beethoven and his music afresh from the beginning, in a chronological order ...' She found the experience 'enthralling' and along the way 'had to change some preconceived views' that 'heightened' her 'passionate absorption and excitement'.[7] Marion's research took her to Germany, where she encountered her subject first hand. She photographed Beethoven's world and read through little-known Beethoven letters from which she quoted in her book. She made her own translations of letters and books from the German and wrote about Beethoven from her deep insights as a metaphysician. She studied his scores and his sketch-books.

Scott brought a fresh approach and vitality to Beethoven's life and music. She was among the first scholars, if not the first, to suggest 'a possible strain in his heredity [that] has never been taken into account – a strain of Spanish blood'.[8] She detected 'distinct southern' features in portraits of him.

> From the moment the idea occurred to me, I saw it might account for some of the characteristics which neither the Flemish nor Rhenish strains in Beethoven quite explain; for example his tremendous pride, and anger quick as lightning. Records there are none in proof or disproof. My theory remains such and no more.[9]

Two years after her biography of Beethoven was published, Scott found support for her theory in Ernest Closson's *The Fleming in Beethoven* (English edition published in 1936). Closson wrote that Beethoven's 'swarthy complexion and coal black locks' had earned him the nickname 'the Spaniard' in his own family.[10] He discussed the influence of Spanish rule in the Netherlands and observed that 'This hereditary phenomenon is in fact generally spoken of in Antwerp as "Spanish blood".'[11]

Rather than accept the notion that Beethoven's mother was wanting as a parent and at fault for being unable to cope with her family, Scott drew on a contemporary report by the Society for the Prevention of Cruelty to Children to explain the Beethoven family dynamic. She wrote: '[W[here the neglect of a child is due to the laziness of the mother, the mother's apathy is due to the father's disregard of home and family'.[12]

Scott did not glorify Beethoven, the man. She was unsparing in her depiction of his slovenliness, referring to his living quarters as a 'home slum', and borrowing from another writer, observed that 'living with him would have been like living with a gorilla'.[13]

The more deeply she delved into Beethoven's music, the more clearly she saw into his inner life. For Scott music was a window into the soul of the composer whether she was dealing with Ivor Gurney, Hindemith, Vaughan Williams, Herbert Howells, Arnold Schoenberg, Haydn or Beethoven. She possessed an intuitive ability to grasp the essence of the man and his music, perhaps because she herself possessed a creative mind and an artist's soul.

Scott challenged the perceptions of musicologists who 'spent enormous labour in demonstrating from Beethoven's sketch-books how laboriously he built up his compositions, altering again and again almost up to the scriptural 70 times.'[14] She saw his creative process differently, agreeing with Ernest Newman, who saw Beethoven as

> the mere human instrument through which a vast musical design realized itself in all its marvellous logic ... that his mind did not proceed from the particular to the whole, but began, in some curious way, with the whole and then worked back to the particular ... not to find workable atoms out of which he could construct a musical edifice according to the conventions of symphonic form, but to reduce an already existing nebula, in which that edifice was implicit, to the atom, and then, by orderly arrangement of these atoms, to make the implicit explicit.[15]

Scott added her own view:

> I should like to suggest that a distinctive feature of ideas which float up from the unconscious into consciousness is their evanescence, and evanescence comparable to that of the rainbow. One minute they are so bright, it seems impossible they could perish; the next they have faded and may never be seen again. Beethoven's habit of sketching sprang from such a feeling.[16]

She explained that Beethoven had carried a sketch-book since childhood and that he always wrote down his first ideas. 'By such means not only will imagination be strengthened but one learns how to fix at the moment the most out-of-the-way ideas', Beethoven had written.[17] To Scott, Beethoven had explained in that sentence the

> fundamental purpose of his sketches ... The first sketch, tiny though it might be, was sufficient to anchor the metaphysical idea to the regions of material consciousness. Further, a close study of the processes by which Beethoven achieved his compositions strongly confirms the impression which many of his greatest works make of existing beyond the confines of this earth.[18]

In discussing Beethoven's late quartets, she observed that they 'are not the justification of modern music, but modern music has reached the point at which it justifies the quartets and proves Beethoven's genius to have been transcendental.'[19] Marion speculated that the late quartets in A minor, B flat major and C sharp minor 'might well symbolize body, soul and spirit' and that these quartets might 'stand for the threefold life of past, present and future. The A minor Quartet, retrospect; the B flat major, the present; the C sharp minor, the life of the world to come.'[20]

She saw his life in three distinct metaphysical stages:

> In the first, Beethoven saw the *material world* from the *material standpoint*; in the second, he saw the *material world* from the *spiritual standpoint*; in the third he saw the *spiritual world* from the *spiritual standpoint*.[21]

Describing Beethoven's poignant Heiligenstadt experience of 1802, Scott wrote:

> Beethoven had walked the meadows of Heiligenstadt, and his mind had roamed the Elysian fields of music before he passed into the crisis of his black sorrow. It was a veritable going down into the valley of the shadow of death. But just before the path had gone down, he had seen, as sometimes happens in mountain regions, across the near gulf and intervening ranges, a radiant vision of distant mountains on the horizon – he had seen Joy.[22]

In the summer of 1923, while in Switzerland, Marion Scott had also stood on the rim of her own black sorrow over Ivor Gurney. She had gone there seeking comfort and answers from her mountains. In a diary entry that year, she had described her catharsis, her own coming back to life, in much the same way that she chose to describe Beethoven's spiritual resurrection from the crushing realization that he was going deaf at the age of twenty-eight. She fully understood how Beethoven could find spiritual renewal and hope in the transcendent act of creation, enabling him to endure his 'wretched existence'. As Beethoven wrote: 'I would have put an end to my life, only art it was that withheld me.' Marion Scott found her own path to 'Joy' in her communion with Nature and in her belief that she, like Beethoven, 'could pass through tragedy to the greater knowledge beyond' material existence.[23] To Scott 'Beethoven *had* penetrated the veil and he looked back, insofar as any musician has ever done so, at the universe from God's side.'[24]

Marion Scott's 343-page illustrated volume appeared in 1934 to critical acclaim. *The Times Literary Supplement* praised her 'shrewd insight' and her ability to harmonize Beethoven's personality and music into a convincing portrait. 'Each part has been viewed in the light of her extensive knowledge of man and music – her familiarity, that is, with the whole Beethoven'.[25] Although the critic was reviewing four new editions in The Master Musicians series – Bach, Beethoven, Brahms and Haydn – he focused almost entirely on Scott's book, limiting his discussions of the other three books to a single paragraph.

Critic Rosemary Hughes praised Scott's 'associative power' and her 'perception of inner relationships' in making the book accessible to 'countless readers', enabling them to find 'their own groping and inarticulate thought brought into light and given form and clarity by one whose understanding was matched by her powers of expression'.[26] Sir Donald Tovey cited Scott's 'powers of vivid narrative and clarity akin to Beethoven's own' and praised her ability to deal with music in 'a manner it would be difficult to overpraise'.[27] A. H. Fox Strangways, writing for *The Observer*, declared that Scott's *Beethoven* was for 'student, scholar and taxi-driver' and that Scott's discussions of the music were 'short and pointed, graceful in expression, and original in thought'.[28] Marion Scott's *Beethoven* enjoyed popularity for five decades. It was reprinted at least a dozen times between 1937 and 1974.

After the success of *Beethoven*, Marion resigned her position as London music critic for the *Christian Science Monitor* in 1934 to devote herself more fully to scholarship, particularly her research on Haydn. However, she remained a regular contributor to *Music and Letters*, *Monthly Musical Record*, and *Musical Times*, and wrote occasional criticism for the *Daily Telegraph* and *The Observer*. Her life was productive, busy and ever changing as she sought and accepted new challenges.

Throughout the early 1930s Marion maintained her close contact with Ivor at Stone House, taking him for drives and spending time with him at the facility. It was clear to her that his condition had deteriorated badly yet she continued to see glimmers of Ivor's intelligence and sensitivity even though the physicians did not. He still refused physical examinations and his doctors observed that his health was 'indifferent'. His weight had dropped to 121 pounds, down from the 143 pounds noted on his admission papers. He suffered from rheumatism and was treated with infrared light. He refused to take any medications. He lost his sense of time. Day blended into night, night into day, one being no different from the other to him. He did not interact with staff or with other patients and in his paranoia he believed that someone was tampering with his food, possibly poisoning it.

Florence Gurney had grown alarmed about a bad cough her son had developed. She was troubled by the direct and unsparing comments doctors made to her about Ivor. She took them to heart and was wounded by them. She did not understand 'what it is my son does that hurts you?' [29] Doctors did not answer her directly, resorting instead to insensitive rhetoric, telling her that they were taking good care of him, thanks to people other than herself. 'You may rest assured that the above-named gentleman receives every care and treatment at this Hospital, and I consider that we ought to be deeply indebted to Dr Vaughan Williams and Miss Scott for the very great interest they take in him, so as to enable him to receive the benefits of the treatment which is given at this Hospital', wrote Dr Robinson, the Medical Superintendent.[30]

Florence wanted Ivor returned to Gloucester to Coney Hill Hospital, but her desire to have him back with her was dismissed or ignored. 'I think he would be better with something to do', she told them.[31] She was right. She also understood that it was wrong for the doctors to expect him to behave normally: 'when his brain is wrong you can't tell what it is they feel like', but she was willing to try.[32] Coney Hill was near her home. It offered a rural setting and had its own farm but on a much smaller scale than Bangour Village Hospital which had reverted back to its original function as an asylum in January 1922, after serving as the Edinburgh War Hospital.

Friends like Emily Hunt thought that returning Ivor to Gloucester would unsettle him and 'cruelly' revive all his 'longings to roam about his beloved Gloucestershire'. She naïvely assumed that the 'poor boy' was 'getting reconciled to Stone House' and was 'earning some privileges'. She had no idea how much he was suffering alone and cut off from the one place that always restored him when he was ill – Gloucestershire. She feared that if he were nearby, his mother would visit him regularly and felt that 'would be most undesirable' and do him 'immense harm' as she had 'always irritated him, got on his nerves'.[33] 'I hope I am not writing unkindly of the poor woman – she can't help her infirmities of course and I am sure she is most kind and well meaning but she is certainly not the kind of person to be often in contact with Ivor just now, if ever', Hunt observed.[34] Mrs Gurney, who suffered from osteoporosis, was growing old and feared that if Ivor were not returned to Gloucester she would never see him again. She could not go on making the long, exhausting journey from Gloucester to Stone House on the other side of London. No one seems to have considered her feelings in the matter. Ivor always came first.

Gerald Finzi had kept in contact with Marion and was aware that time was slipping away from Ivor. He approached her again in 1935 determined to rekindle awareness of Gurney. He interested Fox Strangways, editor of *Music and Letters*, in publishing a tribute to Ivor, featuring commentaries by Ralph Vaughan Williams, Herbert Howells, Marion Scott, Harry Plunket Greene, Walter de la Mare, Edmund Blunden and J. C. Squire. Publication was planned for October of that year.

In spite of Finzi's enthusiasm, it was difficult to co-ordinate efforts. Marion was distracted by her own commitments. The deadline passed and publication was delayed. Although Marion explained to Finzi that she had been 'desperately' rushed all spring and summer with 'incessant work' and had only a certain amount of time to devote to Gurney's affairs as well as visit him and deal with his doctors, Finzi took her explanations as hollow excuses and delaying tactics. He did not understand how busy she truly was. He lost patience with her and in his frustration resorted to inappropriate name-calling – 'Maid Marion', 'mulish old maid', 'fragile fool', 'Hermetic

Marion'.[35] In order to comply with Finzi's demands, Scott would have had to cease all activity and devote herself full time to reading, sorting and cataloguing the mass of Gurney's manuscripts of poetry, music and letters that now filled nearly three trunks in her home. It was an impossible task for one person, and not one she was emotionally prepared to undertake.

However, Marion was not the sole problem. A period of adjustment followed at *Music and Letters*, when Fox Strangways, then seventy-six years old, retired, and the editorship passed to Eric Blom. She told Ivor of plans for Finzi and Howells to visit. 'Finzi – doesn't he compose too?' Gurney had asked.[36] The meeting never took place. Herbert Howells' nine-year-old son Michael died unexpectedly in September 1935 from a virulent form of polio. Herbert was too grief-stricken to accompany Finzi to Stone House or to participate in the *Music and Letters* tribute. Marion, who was very close to Herbert, was devastated by the news of Michael's death, which came at a time when her elderly father was in failing health. In addition to the tribute in *Music and Letters*, Finzi began to plan for the publication of Gurney's songs by Oxford University Press, another project that required Marion's participation and made more demands on her already limited time.

Ivor's condition worsened. He was wasting away. He was losing weight dramatically and he was severely delusional. When Adeline Vaughan Williams suggested that he be allowed out of Stone House for a two-week visit to the country, the doctors refused, citing again their fear that he might commit suicide. They would no longer allow him to go out on day trips with Marion.

Marion took temporary leave from the pressures and worries mounting on her to enjoy the Silver Jubilee of King George V. 'Queen Victoria's Jubilee may have been a more resounding spectacle, but King George's was almost like a Thanksgiving sacrament between himself and his peoples', she observed. 'London flowered to its fullest splendour to welcome him'.[37] Marion's father, Sydney Scott, who at eighty-six was the oldest practising solicitor in the city, took Marion and her mother to see the decorations for the event.

> Mile after mile we drove along ways dazzling with masts, shields, flags, flowers, movement and colour, till we came to the square mile of the City itself which was perhaps the most powerful, as it was certainly one of the richest on earth. Wealth there of every sort; wealth of money, history, beauty, tradition and the proudest gold of liberty. In Cheapside on Ludgate Hill, everywhere we looked, flags and pennons, tossed in the tangle that caught the sunlight, and fascinated the eyes, making great vistas of colour beneath which crowds came and went, bright-faced, curious, festive.[38]

From the eve of Jubilee Day, London became 'unsleeping'. That night high in her bedroom at Westbourne Terrace, Marion listened as the strokes of Big Ben floated across Hyde Park. She was conscious of the moving millions as a 'great tide lifting quietly on its own strength, unflawed by wind or opposing currents ... breathing as tranquilly as a summer sea'.[39] All of this she could only tell Ivor Gurney, for he was not allowed out of Stone House to witness it himself.

Marion's happy outing with her father was one of the last they enjoyed together. Sydney Scott fell gravely ill during the summer of 1936, and after seven agonizing weeks of suffering, died on 18 September 1936. Marion had rarely left his bedside. After his death she was occupied with preparations for his funeral at Bridgwater and for the memorial service held at St Michael's, Cornhill, in the City of London on 25 September. Those present to honour his memory included Herbert and Dorothy Howells, Lady Olga Montagu, representatives from the Royal College of Music, the Society of Psychical Research and the Herbert Spencer Trust, and Mr Scott's many legal and business associates. William Harris, Marion's friend from her early RCM days and now organist at Windsor, composed 'Praise the Lord, O My Soul' in memory of Sydney Scott.

In the weeks after Mr Scott's death, Marion and Stella took charge of business matters and stayed close by their mother during this difficult period. Mr Scott left a substantial estate of £40,000, the house at 92 Westbourne Terrace and a Rolls Royce. Although Marion wrote the cheques, her father had been the main contributor to Ivor's care before his death. As his heir to a portion of the estate and with her own steady income, Marion knew she could always make her quarterly payments supporting Ivor. But her father's death prompted her concern about how Ivor's care would be paid for should she die before him. She wrote to Dr Robinson asking if there were any possibility of charitable funding to help pay for his care but the question was obviated by Gurney's deteriorating condition.

By November 1936 Ivor had grown too weak to resist a physical examination. Doctors detected no heart murmurs or enlargement, no aneurysm nor any abnormalities in his lungs or in his abdominal region. His remaining seven teeth were 'foul'. He complained of pain in his back and legs. Doctors continued to claim 'he takes his food well' yet he was losing weight dramatically.[40] When Marion went to see him at Christmas, he was in bed with back trouble. For a while she thought that the infra-red treatments he was receiving for his rheumatism might be ameliorating his mental condition. He was calm and observant, remarking to Marion 'what a lovely light in the sky' and then he pointed to 'the dove-gray in the east, visible through the windows opposite his bed.'[41]

Meanwhile the Finzis and their friend Howard Ferguson were sorting through Gurney's songs for publication. They found the task more difficult than they had anticipated, 'chiefly because there is comparatively little that one can really be sure is bad', Finzi reported to Scott.[42] 'Even the late 1925 asylum songs, though they get more and more involved (and at the same time more disintegrated, if you know what I mean) have a curious coherence about them somewhere, which makes it difficult to know if they are really over the border', he continued. Finzi felt that editing Gurney's music might be a great task requiring 'a neat mind [to] smooth away the queerness' while 'time and familiarity will probably show something not so mistaken, after all, about the queer and odd things'. He found Gurney's accompaniment 'very awkward sometimes' and noted the lack of dynamic markings on the scores.[43] He asked Marion to date the songs and supply the names of the poets whose texts Ivor had used.

Finzi devised a system of grouping the songs. By March 1937 he and Ferguson had selected an initial twenty-five, from which Vaughan Williams made the final selection for two volumes containing ten songs each. By August, Finzi learned that Hubert Foss at Oxford University Press had agreed to publish the collection to coincide with the *Music and Letters* tribute. He continued to complain about Marion, calling her 'possessive' and incompetent and faulting her for not doing tasks he regarded as simple. 'It is rather incredible when you realize everything was supposed to be ready for the cataloguing, sorted and in order two months ago', he ranted to Ferguson. 'But what can you expect from someone who hasn't "had time" to copy out those two little violin pieces you asked for nine months ago? I'm so polite to this fragile fool that I've not had the heart to remind her that I made the time to copy out 24 of his songs in a month.' [44]

For his part, Finzi had made little effort to consider what might be going on in Scott's life causing legitimate delays. By comparison to Marion, Finzi lived an easy life, one devoid of constant deadlines and multiple work and family commitments, which, in Marion's case, included caring for her elderly mother and preparing to move to a new home on Porchester Terrace. Finzi had his wife Joy to take care of his needs, while Marion had no one to look after hers. During the period when Finzi found her lax, she was working on revisions for a new edition of *Beethoven*, completing an article about Stradivari and violins, preparing a brief biography of Mendelssohn for Novello's *Great Musicians* series, delving more deeply into her research on Haydn, working on various articles for future publication, writing criticism, organizing events, judging competitions, lecturing, overseeing the operation of the Society of Women Musicians, working as an active member of the Critics Circle, the Music Board of the London Lyceum Club, the Music Section of the Forum Club, and watching Ivor Gurney slowly die.[45]

In 1937 Marion retired from the RCM Union to take a new position as editor of the *Royal College of Music Magazine*. She was sixty years old. Her health was not good. It slowed her down occasionally but it rarely stopped her. She suffered periodic bouts of influenza, anaemia and the ongoing intestinal trouble that had plagued her all her life. She was anxious and depressed about Ivor's hopeless situation. Marion's goddaughter Margaret Brockway recalled her often being ill and confined to a sofa or to bed during this time.

Finzi had time, a commodity that was in short supply in Marion's busy life. But there was more: Marion's deep emotional attachment to Ivor. She knew he was dying and it was impossible for her to give up the fragments of his tattered life that now filled several trunks in her bedroom. During the summer Marion found Ivor 'much weaker ... and really ill physically, as well as mentally'.[46] It was not until November that doctors discovered 'a massive right-sided pleural effusion together with physical signs of bilateral tuberculosis'.[47] Both lungs were inflamed and additional tests revealed tuberculosis in his faeces. X-rays confirmed that he was suffering from

Pulmonary Tuberculosis. On 20 November doctors aspirated 24 ounces of cloudy, straw-coloured fluid from his chest.

Six days later, Marion stopped by to see him. That evening upon returning home, she wrote a note to him:

> This evening the proofs of the January 'Music and Letters' arrived. I begged to have them for you – and I am sending them on at once so that you may have them tomorrow morning.
>
> Also as I went through Dartford on my way to the train I ordered some oranges and purple grapes and a couple of grapefruits to be sent to you tomorrow morning.
>
> I did not want to tire you with talking today, but it was good to have a sight of you, and as always, and more than ever, I honour your courage and fineness under bitter troubles and suffering.
>
> Dear Ivor.[48]

When the proofs arrived he was too weak to remove the paper around them. When told about the forthcoming publication of his songs he could only utter, 'It is too late.'[49] There was nothing anyone could do but wait.

In the early morning hours of 26 December 1937, Ivor Gurney, his once-athletic body now skeletal at less than 100 pounds, suffered a massive lung haemorrhage and suffocated on his own blood at 3:45 a.m. Two male nurses were his sole companions. He was forty-seven years old.

NOTES

1 The Composers Conference was usually held in the summer. The first day was devoted to papers given by women members and the second day was open to guests, including men. Gustav Holst, Herbert Howells and Arthur Bliss were among those who took part in these conferences.

2 Rosemary Hughes, 'Joseph Haydn (1732–1809)', in *Chamber Music*, ed. Alec Robertson (Harmondsworth: Penguin, 1957), p. 13.

3 MMS, 'Paul Hindemith: His Music and its Characteristics', *Proceedings of the Royal Musical Association*, vol. 56 (1929–30), pp. 91–108. Scott's father was also a member of the Association.

4 Ibid, p. 92.

5 Ibid, p. 105.

6 MMS, 'Maddalena Lombardini, Madame Syrmen', *Music and Letters*, vol. 14, no. 2 (1933), pp. 149–63.

7 MMS, *Beethoven*, The Master Musicians (London: J. M. Dent & Sons, 1934), p. v.

8 Ibid., p. 10.

9 Ibid.

10 Ibid.

11 Ibid.

12 Ibid., p. 18.

13 Ibid., p. 64.

14 Ibid., p. 122.

15 Ibid.

16 Ibid., p. 123.

17 Ibid.

18 Ibid.

19 Ibid., p. 263.

20 Ibid., p. 275.

21 Ibid., p. 79.

22 Ibid., p. 51. Scott virtually lifted her own language, thoughts and beliefs from the pages of her journal and applied them to Beethoven. See chapter 20.

23 Ibid., p. 49.

24 Ibid, p. 126.

25 Quoted on dust jacket of editions printed after 1934, taken from *The Times Literary Supplement*, 19 July 1934.

26 Rosemary Hughes, 'Marion Scott's Contribution to Musical Scholarship', *RCM Magazine*, May 1954, p. 40.

27 Ibid.

28 A. H. Fox Strangways, *The Observer*, 17 June 1934. Fox Strangways also revealed that Cuthbert Hadden, author of the volume on Haydn, had 'considerable help' from Scott.

29 FG, letter to City of London Mental Hospital, November 1933, GA.

30 W. Robinson to FG, 28 Nov 1933, GA.

31 FG, letter to City of London Mental Hospital, November 1933, GA.

32 Ibid.

33 Emily Hunt to MMS, 30 November 1929, GA.

34 Ibid.

35 GF, various letters between 1935 and 1937.

36 MMS to GF, 7 February 1937, GA.

37 MMS, 'London Itself', unpublished memoir, MSC.

38 Ibid.

39 Ibid.

40 Medical Records, GA.

41 MMS to GF, 8 January 1937, GA.

42 GF to MMS, 30 January 1937, GA. Composer Howard Ferguson (1908–99) was born in Belfast. He studied composition and conducting at the RCM and piano privately with his mentor Harold Samuel. Ferguson and Finzi met in 1926. They began corresponding regularly in 1927 when Ferguson was in the United States with Samuel. Once Ferguson returned to England, he and Finzi kept up their correspondence and their friendship, which lasted until Finzi's death in 1956. Ferguson worked closely with Gerald and Joy Finzi on the Gurney manuscripts. In 1960, he ceased composing and turned his attention to producing editions of keyboard music, among them works of William Croft, Henry Purcell, Schubert, Schumann, Brahms, Scarlatti and Mendelssohn.

43 Ibid.

44 GF to Howard Ferguson, 15 August 1937, GA.

45 In early 1937 Oxford University Press published a music book titled *The Band Book* by M. M. Scott. It contains 41 tunes for violins in unison, with piano accompaniment. The book was planned for use in violin classes and contains familiar and unfamiliar airs and British and foreign folk tunes. 'M. M. Scott' was 'Mary Margareta Scott', which seems likely to be a play on Marion's name – Marion Margaret Scott. Scott's clipping service had sent these reviews to Marion, which makes me think that it was indeed her work. The introduction was written by Armstrong Gibbs, another of Scott's RCM acquaintances.

46 MMS to GF, 9 July 1937, GA.

47 Medical records, GA.

48 MMS to IG, 26 November 1937, GA.

49 MMS to IG, GA.

CHAPTER 24

'In time to come'

W ITHIN FORTY-EIGHT HOURS, news of Ivor Gurney's death began appearing in newspapers throughout Great Britain, on the Continent and in the United States. Writing in the *Daily Telegraph*, Marion Scott's friend Richard Capell predicted that Gurney 'will live among the finest English song-writers', but he observed that his 'gifts did not include a great mastery of the larger forms, and those who know his unpublished instrumental works esteem them far less highly than the songs'.[1] An anonymous writer in *The Times* praised Gurney's 'Schubertian gift for melody' and his 'subtle feeling for the English language comparable to that of Hugo Wolf for the German'.[2]

The Gloucester *Citizen* announced his death in a story that dominated page 1 and featured the banner headline 'Death of Gloucester-born "Schubert"'. 'Gurney's life was a tragedy of unfulfilled promise, a fact which many of his friends attributed to his War experience ... the war had afflicted Gurney's imagination not less than his body. He failed to come to terms with life', the unsigned article reads. 'In 1921 the sensitive mind was so far from being able to distinguish between reality and sad illusion that retreat from the world became a necessity', the writer stated.[3]

In America the Associated Press wire service distributed a two-paragraph announcement to major newspapers across the nation, erroneously identifying Ivor as 'Ivor G. Gurney'. The prestigious *New York Times*, which drew its information directly from the London *Times*, allotted Ivor two bold headlines and nearly four column inches of space, asserting that he was 'incapacitated by service in France during the World War'.[4] The rival New York *Herald Tribune* also gave Ivor a double headline and an equal amount of space. The notice of his death appeared in nearly all of the Boston daily and evening newspapers, including the two that were read daily by Annie Drummond McKay and her husband.[5]

'The press has given him in his death more attention in a week than they gave his life in 47 years', Gerald Finzi observed.[6] He was annoyed, too, that people were claiming close associations with Gurney when, in fact, they had none; that they ' "were always amazed at his genius", that they visited him regularly when he was in the asylum, that they were best of friends, etc. etc. Even H. H. [Herbert Howells], who was a great friend of his in RCM days, but seldom went to the asylum in the latter years, now implies that he was a regular visitor.'[7] Howells went to see Ivor only when Marion Scott pressured him to do so, and always in her company.

Ivor's body, in an expensive coffin covered with a floral cross, was transported by cortège from Dartford to St Matthew's Church at Twigworth, just outside Gloucester, on Friday, 31 December 1937. Canon Alfred Hunter Cheesman, vicar and Gurney's godfather, met the procession at the gate. At three o'clock more than fifty mourners gathered inside the church, which still bore festive Christmas holly, for a brief service conducted by Canon Cheesman. Ill and unable to attend, Florence Gurney was denied the chance to be with her son one last time. The service opened with a reading of the 23rd Psalm and prayers.[8] Howells played Gurney's 'Sleep' and 'Severn Meadows' on the organ along with Elgar's 'Angel's Farewell', and a fourteenth-century French chanson that Ivor liked.

The Gloucester *Citizen* reported that Canon Cheesman paid 'an eloquent tribute' to his memory, recalling that for many years he and Ivor 'were on terms of greatest intimacy'. Cheesman noted that his godson had visited him 2,000 times in six years and that he never knew 'a more generous lad.' He told the congregation that he still treasured a book that Ivor had bought for him out of his first earnings.[9] 'He was so full of joy and beautiful things, because he loved beautiful music and poetry', said Cheesman, adding that Ivor's love of beauty included 'the Severn country, the distant hills, the fields, and streams and flowers'. He spoke of Ivor's years at the RCM and his war service, observing that he was 'one of war's embers' and that war had 'quenched the fire in him'.[10] Cheesman concluded the service with the last verse of Gray's 'Elegy written in a Country Church-yard' and added a final thought, 'After life's fitful gleam, he sleeps'. Howells closed the service with Sir Hubert Parry's 'Elegy'.[11]

Ivor's coffin was carried outside where, under cold grey skies, Canon Cheesman read the committal service. Marion Scott, in tears at the end, took several photographs of the flowers covering the grave. Her own wreath read, 'in loving and unchanging memory of Ivor Gurney'.[12] Mourners included his sister Winifred, brother Ronald with his wife Ethel, cousins, aunts and friends, among them Sydney Shimmin, Will Harvey, John Haines, his war-time companion Basil Cridland, members of the Chapman family, Gerald and Joy Finzi and Emily Hunt. Marion, the Finzis and the Vaughan Williamses, who were unable to attend, contributed towards paying the funeral expenses.

Marion was grateful for their help and support. 'You have done so many things for him that <u>thanks</u> seems a poor word to cover what is so much', she wrote to Finzi. 'At the last he did not speak to anyone, but just bore his pain alone. There is something tranquillising now in the thought of him lying at peace in Twigworth Churchyard, and I believe that all the details of his funeral were such as he would have approved', she continued. '[T]he inner shell of the coffin is of elm; and the coffin itself, as you saw, is of oak. He might have thought the white satin too costly, but I am thankful he was spared what befell Mozart, and was buried as befitted a poet.'[13]

Ironically, 1938 was a good year for Ivor Gurney. The *Music and Letters* Symposium and the two volumes of his songs published by Oxford University Press appeared in January.[14]

Marion wrote obituaries that were published in *The Listener*, the *Monthly Musical Record* and the *Royal College of Music Magazine* between February and July. She included two unpublished Gurney poems, 'Soft Rain' and 'Sonnet to J. S. Bach's Memory', in the Easter Term issue of the *RCM Magazine*. In February Howard Ferguson and violinist Isolde Menges performed *The Apple Orchard* in a London recital, and tenor Steuart Wilson performed seven Gurney songs in a BBC Midland radio broadcast. In April soprano Nancy Evans and pianist Hubert Foss made the first recordings ever of Gurney's music when they entered the Decca studios on Thames Street in London to record 'The Scribe', 'Nine of the Clock', 'All Night under the Moon', 'Blaweary', 'You are my Sky' and 'The Latmian Shepherd'.[15]

In July the BBC National Service broadcast four programmes devoted to Ivor's music, featuring Steuart Wilson, Arthur Benjamin, the Kutcher String Quartet, baritone Sinclair Logan and soprano Isobel Baillie.[16] Marion's announcement of the series, 'Four Special Recitals of Gurney's Songs', appeared in the 14 July 1938 issue of *The Listener* along with her obituary of Ivor. Writing the two-column article proved to be a difficult task for her, and she wrote a twenty-eight-page draft before she crafted the final wording. She discussed Ivor's music and his poetry. 'After the war, when the stir of fresh methods was in the air, Gurney investigated the new music with its spiky technique and harsh sounds and even spent six shillings for a work which was then much praised but never performed and forgotten today', Marion recalled. 'His disappointment in it was over-whelming ... Gurney cared nothing for fashion but everything for Truth and Beauty.' She thought that the new techniques in composition did not strike him as 'being either true or beautiful ... and if it was not beauti-ful he could not bother with it.'[17] She claimed that he experimented pas-sionately and earnestly in the new poetical methods, and named Edward Thomas, Gerard Manley Hopkins and the Georgian poets as influences. 'Unfortunately, various critics who enjoyed elegance, were excruciated by his later poems, and so it came about that his poetic modernism prevented a ready acceptance of his poems just as surely as his musical conservatism put him off the map of contemporary music.'[18]

Herbert Howells provided the BBC radio audience with an on-air intro-duction to Ivor. 'Gurney walking was Gurney composing ... His mind con-stantly sang, as it were, in response to the poem he was reading, or the scene he looked upon ... he worked with the extra authority of a man who was, in himself, a poet', Howells declared. 'This week you will hear Gurney's songs – songs of many kinds. You will hear none that took any note from the fashionable idioms of his day. You will hear the voice of a typical Englishman whose insight was deep and true. Of brilliant display there will be none. Instead, he will offer you a constant quiet-voiced Beauty.'[19]

Shortly after Ivor's death, Marion became the court-appointed admin-istrator of his estate. He had died intestate, leaving an unpaid debt of £143 19s 8d owed to her. Marion knew that Ronald and Florence Gurney were incapable of protecting Ivor's present and future interests and she feared, not without cause, that Ronald might destroy his manuscripts. She also knew that any royalties coming to them would likely be spent on themselves and not invested in preserving and publishing Ivor's music and poetry. She used the outstanding debt as leverage to gain legal control over Ivor's estate.

Marion arranged for the Gurneys to discuss the matter with Ernest Winterbotham, an associate of her late father, Ralph Vaughan Williams and herself to ensure that everything was done legally and with the full co-operation of the Gurneys. Both Ronald and Florence gave their consent, and on 26 February 1938 Marion was granted Letters of Administration enabling her to deal directly with Gurney's affairs. It was a wise strategy. She kept strict records of all accounts and paid income tax on royalties without ever taking any of the income to reimburse herself. Her purpose in gaining control of Ivor Gurney's estate was to 'nurse and foster the demand for future performances of [his] work ... and to secure the publication of more of his manuscripts'.[20]

After the initial flurry of publications, recordings and performances in 1938, interest in Gurney waned but never died. Musicians occasionally included his songs in their programmes. Soprano Joan Alexander performed 'Sleep' and 'Spring' on 1 November 1939, at the Scottish Academy of Music, Glasgow, prompting a critic for the Glasgow Herald to comment that 'The beauty of Ivor Gurney's two songs placed them among the finest of the programme'.[21] In May 1940 the BBC broadcast a fifteen-minute programme of his songs; Decca released a recording of The Apple Orchard by violinist Frederick Grinke and pianist Ivor Newton, and Oxford University Press published his Two Pieces for Violin and Piano: The Apple Orchard and Scherzo. In New York City, baritone Tom Emlyn Williams performed six unnamed Gurney songs at a Town Hall recital on 4 February 1940.

In the aftermath of Gurney's death, the Scott family was busy as usual. While Marion continued to work, her sister Stella still ran the household, which included herself, Marion, their mother, their niece Audrey, three maids, day help and the ever-present cats. Stella spent part of each day with Mrs Scott's younger sister Minnie Barham, who, at the age of eighty-four, now lived a few houses away on Porchester Terrace. Both elderly sisters were in failing health with Minnie's condition the source of 'constant anxiety' for the Scotts.[22] In July 1938 Marion and Stella hosted a garden party for Audrey, now thirty years old, who was off to spend the remainder of the summer visiting her father in South Africa.

While Audrey was away, Marion travelled alone to Devonshire, staying at Chagford, where she experienced 'the thunderstorm of the century', an unrelenting fury that raged for ten hours, cutting off the electric lights and knocking out telephone service.[23] Locals had never experienced such a powerful storm. From Chagford, Marion moved on to Two Bridges to an hotel anchored on the open moor, where she met a couple who took her on long drives over the moor. Marion and her new friends decided to go to Plymouth, the port of departure for the Pilgrims who sailed to the New World on the Mayflower in 1620. Marion set about photographing historic sites and the landscape, believing erroneously that one of her mother's ancestors, Priscilla Brewster, had sailed on the Mayflower.[24]

While Marion was away, Mrs Scott, always keenly interested in politics, was becoming 'much perturbed over European matters not without cause [with] so much trembling in the balance'.[25] She was an ardent supporter of King George and believed that 'we have a strong man in Chamberlain'. She was impressed by American Ambassador Joseph Kennedy, whom she considered 'a very good man'.[26] Meanwhile, the Scotts added their concern for Mrs Scott's wayward Russian-born nephew Eugene Prince to their list of anxieties. Eugene had disappeared again, as he had done during the Russian Revolution.[27] They believed he was somewhere in Europe and possibly in danger.

After Ivor's death Marion remained in regular contact with Florence Gurney, exchanging letters with her, sending her money and occasionally journeying to Gloucester to visit with her. Florence welcomed Scott into her life. As different as they were, they were bound together by their grief and love for Ivor. During the years Ivor was at Stone House, his mother became more trusting and less suspicious of Marion and her London ways. No one outside the family knew her son better or had done as much for him. 'How can I tell you how grateful I am to you for what you have done for Ivor ... what would he do without you', she had once written to Marion.[28] Florence felt she could talk to Marion and wrote to her openly and frankly about her son and her own concerns. She was respectful of Marion but not afraid to express her opinion when something upset her.

Shortly after Ivor's headstone was put into place, Florence wrote to Marion, worried that the fragile Cotswold stone was showing signs of deterioration in a matter of weeks. She predicted that it would only last about two years. Later she objected to proposed changes to the curb surrounding the grave. She expressed displeasure with a photograph of Ivor that Marion had sent: 'I don't like that photo I have hid it away it makes me grieve and it does no good that isnt how God made him ... I should have liked one of him in his coffin the dead look so lovely sometimes somebody said they wouldn't let anyone take a photo like that.'[29] Marion did not communicate with Ronald Gurney, preferring to distance herself from him.

She had devoted twenty-six years of her life to Ivor Gurney, the last fifteen being particularly difficult and painful for her. Her own health and work had suffered, but even in the face of overwhelming responsibilities, worries and commitments, she did not retreat to the safety of the sheltered life that her financial resources made possible. Throughout her life she had created her own opportunities, pursued them with vigour and as a result became a pioneering woman in the fields of musicology and music criticism. Others would follow her lead.

In 1938 Marion Scott was sixty-one years old and working at the pace of someone half her age. In fact, few women of her age and background were working at all since there were scant opportunities for them. Most had husbands to support them, and, if working, they were thinking about retirement. Not Marion. She did not slow down, and even as she grew older, she continued to plan new projects while working on two or three others at the same time. On these she needed help and was about to get it.

Towards the end of 1938, as the first anniversary of Gurney's death approached, Marion renewed her acquaintance with Kathleen Richards Dale, a slightly younger contemporary of Gurney, who was a composer, pianist, teacher and translator. Marion had first known Kathleen as a member of the Society of Women Musicians and later as a pupil of Fanny Davies when Davies gave lessons in the Scott home.[30] At the time of their meeting, Marion was writing music criticism for the *Daily Telegraph* and the *Musical Times*, articles for *The Listener*, the *Monthly Musical*

Record and other publications, preparing entries on Haydn and Gurney for the 1940 supplementary volume of *Grove's Dictionary of Music and Musicians*, editing the *RCM Magazine*, lecturing and pursuing her research on Haydn.[31]

'Possibly without realizing it, she needed an assistant to lend her a hand with some of the less specialized tasks', Dale recalled.[32] After locating rare editions of Haydn biographies for Marion as a gift, Kathleen became her 'scout' for early editions of his music. As a pianist she introduced Marion to Haydn's forty-nine piano sonatas, which Scott, as a violinist, had not yet explored. Not only did Kathleen play the Haydn sonatas but also sonatas by Domenico Scarlatti and C. P. E. Bach so Marion could compare them with Haydn's work. Dale found these sessions in the spring of 1939 'wonderful, though more than a little alarming, to play them to this learned authority, who sat beside me at the piano following the scores, noting similarities in styles between the sonatas and the orchestral and chamber music, and telling me of the circumstances in which some of the works were written.'[33] Marion and Kathleen felt great urgency to complete their sonata project because Hitler had begun his march across Europe and the threat of war loomed ominously.

In the meantime, Gerald Finzi continued to complain about Marion, who was, in his opinion, lagging behind on Gurney matters. He started applying pressure again, even calling on Vaughan Williams to 'have a talk with "The Maid"' to perhaps shame her into action. But Scott had other, more pressing concerns facing her. She and her sister Stella felt it imperative to get their eighty-six-year-old mother away from London before war broke out. As summer approached, they made arrangements to move to Bridgwater in Somerset, which meant taking personal possessions and most of the contents of their London home with them. For Marion this entailed packing not only her entire Gurney collection, but her books, music, and her valuable Haydn collection, which included all of her research, copies of his manuscript music that she had made in her own hand, the rare early editions, and items that once belonged to Haydn. The Scotts, some staff and their cats left London in August.

At the end of the month Marion wrote to Finzi. 'I have a quiet inner sense of thankfulness that my Father and Ivor cannot be hurt, and cannot suffer now from the material horrors of the world.'[34] It was difficult for Marion to be away from London. In late 1939 and early 1940 before the Blitz, she returned occasionally to do what work she could and to attend meetings and concerts. In February 1940 she attended a meeting at the Royal Musical Association to hear musicologist Karl Geiringer deliver his paper on Haydn's operas. When Marion participated in the discussion that followed his paper, Geiringer found himself happily in company with 'one of the foremost Haydn scholars of our time', a 'spirited' woman whose 'profound scholarship equalled her gift for making past times come to life and presenting Haydn as a very human and delightful person.' He admired her 'very thorough and intricate knowledge of the source-material as well as deep sympathy for the object of her research, free, however, from any tendency towards pedantry and excessive adulation … [she] showed us that a research-student can do outstanding work without losing his sense of humour'.[35]

Once bombs began falling on London in September 1940, Marion only occasionally ventured back to the city. In spite of the care she and Stella took in selecting their retreat, they found that Bridgwater was not immune to attacks, but it was safer than their home in London, which had been hit by bomb debris. On a midsummer day in 1941 Marion returned to the City to sign her will. London was sweltering 'beneath a bright haze in which hundreds of barrage balloons floated like silver fish in a shining sea, their noses south-east, their tails north-west in the light breeze'.[36] The haze she encountered was unnatural because 'the dust it held in solution [was] dust so impalpable that it hardly showed as grains, but stung acridly upon one's face and lips'. As Scott came into the City over London Bridge, she looked down the Thames, where

> the Tower and Tower Bridge heaved their familiar bulks against the sky, but ahead ... I hardly knew whether I was more moved by what had vanished or what remained. The stocky warehouses with their journeyman's faces were dead, many of Wren's Churches were gone, the sky-line had changed.

As she looked around, she noticed that the public clocks each told a different time, having stopped anywhere around the dial at the time of concussion. '[F]ew had survived to tell the time of their own destruction, only the empty frames remained'. She thought of her father as she made her way to Cheapside and to King Street where he had been born. She saw the 'towering ruin of the Guildhall ... the battered masonry of Bow Church, not gone, but gashed and disordered, with the familiar little figures knocked silly, and the church open to the street. I was glad my father had not lived to see this'. What gave her the 'sharpest pang of horror' was 'to smell that characteristic odour of an ancient church's interior from the <u>outside</u> ... The scent of Portland stone, pews, graves ...'

In her father's childhood neighbourhood, St Paul's 'rose more cliff-like than ever above the spent devastation of its eastern end ... Round the side traffic still followed, but the buses were now a thin red line, not a roaring torrent as of yore'. Above the southern front, high above the dome, 'the golden cross shone in the sunny air. It had become the symbolic rallying point of the world in the struggle against evil'.

She made her way through Watling Street, where houses on both sides of the street were nothing but 'shells and shards'. All was quiet, only a horse-drawn van moved slowly down the street. The few people she encountered 'had faces saddened by the continual contemplation of sorrow, and their backs bowed by its burden'. On the steps of a bombed office 'a boy sat whistling, his youth and cheerfulness accentuating the surrounding hush'. She had to tread carefully to avoid twisting her ankle in the bomb-pocks.

> My shoes were white with the dust of London's dead buildings, the aftermath from Hitler's Dance of Death. But here in the sunlit silence one could hardly remember Hitler; he merged into the distance of

history as an incident. But the devastation remained. I thought to myself 'This is at least the third time in two thousand years this thing has happened. When London was deserted by the Romans and savaged by the Saxons it lay desolate for decades. Along this very road wolves and rabbits ranged as they liked. London rose again. When the Great Fire [1666] swept from east to west the City was once more brought low; the citizens walked sadly through their beloved ruins as I do now. It rose again. This time the City has been wounded in a great cause, greater than the world has ever known. Better these ruins than the grandeurs of Paris, saved at the price of dishonour. "Resurgam"' [I shall rise again].

She paused. 'In the warmth and silence there welled up the old peace beneath, around and over me. Is it only something racial – the tranquillity of the sea-bird afloat on its remembered sea? Or was it something better – the benediction of God in the solitude?'

Marion returned to her 'involuntary exile' in Bridgwater, where she managed her duties as editor of the *RCM Magazine*, used her isolation to write a series of articles about Haydn and continued preparing her monumental catalogue of Haydn's work. She wrote long, colourful letters that often topped eight pages to her friends throughout England. 'She had an amazingly fertile pen', Kathleen Dale recalled. 'She wrote detailed accounts of her doings, leisurely descriptions of her surroundings, hair-raising tales as well as funny stories of bombings, quaint sayings of the local people and invariably something on musical subjects often with illustrations in musical notation.' [37] Marion also recounted dreams, wrote imaginary journeys into the musical past or recreated scenes and experiences from her adventures in the Swiss Alps. Recipients of her letters anticipated their arrival and delighted in their content.

Denied access to live concerts, Marion relished radio broadcasts and shared with friends her insights and responses to the new music she heard. After a 1941 performance of Shostakovich's 'Leningrad' symphony, Marion, with her strong connections to Russia, offered an insightful analysis of the long work in a letter to Dale.

> Had he written in the remote conditions of Peace he would, and could easily, have compressed the Symphony, but in War, as I know from Gurney's work, the work must be poured out as and when it can, or else it is quite likely not to be done at all … The size of Shostakovich's canvas for his tone-picture is very Russian. It seems to me in keeping with the vast tracts of that rolling, mysterious land, where the European plain runs right to the Ural mountains … The Russian mind moves in a world unlike our English one; *here*, empty space is almost unknown: there, the earth seems illimitable and man at once so little and so passionately conscious of his relationship to that vastness.[38]

Marion found the symphony 'queer' on the technical side, observing that it sounded as if it were 'nearly all melody, line and rhythm, with hardly any symphonic texture'. It made her think of 'an impressive frieze of music, executed in bold, undulating lines and curves'. In the music, she heard Shostakovich's 'mental membership to the new Russia' and believed that 'change' was one of the things he 'most desired to convey' in this vast musical canvas.[39]

Change was once again an element in Marion's life. Her sister Stella had married John Fahey in the spring of 1941, her first marriage coming at the age of sixty. On 15 August 1942 their mother, Annie Prince Scott, died and was buried in Bridgwater with her husband. The sisters were eager to return to war-torn London and with the passing of Mrs Scott were free to do so. They hauled all of their possessions back to the city, and Marion resettled herself in her damaged home on Porchester Terrace. She was willing to risk her safety to be near libraries again and to be able to resume her work as a critic, attending concerts instead of listening to them on the radio. She enjoyed reviewing new music, particularly controversial works by Schoenberg and Webern, writing about young composers, including Michael Tippett and Alan Rawsthorne, whose work intrigued her, or discussing Vaughan Williams' ventures into film music.

Marion remained in contact with Herbert Howells and with Gerald Finzi, who was serving in the Ministry of War Transport in London. Now in his early fifties, Howells was too old to serve in uniform, so he contributed to the war effort by being acting organist at St John's College, Cambridge, filling in for Robin Orr, who was on active duty in the Royal Air Force. Howells continued to fulfil his teaching commitments at the RCM and at St Paul's Girls' School and wrote broadcasts for BBC radio.

Little was happening for Ivor Gurney, but his name was still heard occasionally. Kathleen Ferrier and Isobel Baillie occasionally programmed a few of his songs in their recitals. His music was featured in a series of Boosey & Hawkes concerts in 1942. Tenor Eric Greene joined with the Zorian String Quartet for a performance of *Ludlow and Teme* on 20 October at St Patrick's Hall, Huddersfield. A critic writing for the *Huddersfield Examiner* found the work 'Ambitious and revealing a fresh, clear voice in British music'.[40] Gurney's poem 'The Fire Kindled' was published in the anthology *Landmarks: A Book of Topographical Verse for England and Wales*. In the summer of 1943 John Haines lent original manuscripts of Gurney's poems and compositions in his possession to the Gloucester City Library for an exhibition that also featured Edward Thomas.

Scott and Finzi were pleased when the publisher Felix Goodwin discovered manuscripts of fifteen songs that Gurney had submitted to the firm some twenty years earlier. They were returned to Marion. Finzi was still pressuring her to move forward on Gurney's poetry, but she was reluctant to let go of it and too distracted by her own work. When Joy Finzi volunteered to type out the poems, Marion let it be known that she preferred to put the task in the hands of her own typist. Eventually she did release some of the poems to Vaughan Williams, who hired a typist to do the job. Marion made a list of the poems she 'lent' to Vaughan Williams in a stenographer's notebook. The list includes one collection, *Out of June and October*, that appears to be lost. She made notes to herself about the method of selection to be used, the proposed collaborators and publisher, how the poems might be grouped, and she raised issues of copyright and financing the project.

In 1944, aged sixty-seven, Marion resigned as editor of the *RCM Magazine*. The post passed to Sir Percy Buck. She had been associated with the RCM for nearly fifty years, first as a student, then as a founder of the school Union and finally as editor of its magazine. But the fact that she gave up one job did not mean retirement. It simply gave her more time to focus on her Haydn research and writing, and to accept a position as editor of the *Proceedings* of the Royal Musical Association, an organization in which she had been active for many years.

Throughout the war years when travel was restricted, Marion was not able to visit Germany and Austria to conduct her Haydn research, so she relied upon what was available in Britain. On one occasion while searching for information at the University Library at Cambridge, she became so engrossed in her work that she experienced 'the sort of adventure that would have befallen Piglit [sic] in *Winnie the Pooh*'. She got locked in the library.[41] 'As the building covers 7½ acres I felt a very small animal indeed', she wrote to Kathleen Dale. 'It happened at lunch time. Quite without warning, the authorities issued the edict the Library was to begin shutting down from 1 till 2:15 now, just as it does (I now hear) in full term. So when I reached the main hall at 1½ minutes past one I found nothing but vast emptiness and a locked door.'[42] Marion took her bearings so she would not get lost and then set out to find if there were any staff in the building. After covering a portion of the seven and a half acres, she heard voices and followed them to the staff room, where amused employees let her out the back door of the Library.

By early 1945, with encouraging signs that peace was forthcoming, Marion looked forward to a productive year and the resumption of travel. On 16 April Florence Gurney died, ending the long relationship between these two very different women. Less than a month later, Britain celebrated Victory in Europe. Gerald Finzi, relieved of his duties in the Ministry of War Transport, returned to Ashmansworth eager to resume his work on Gurney's uncollected poetry, now typed, thanks to the efforts of Vaughan Williams. A third volume of Gurney's songs hung in limbo.

Marion was not feeling well. Her ongoing intestinal problems were aggravated by poor nutrition resulting from the food shortages that showed no sign of abating in the near future. Then, in the late spring, she faced a serious crisis that derailed all of her immediate plans and locked her in a cycle of uncertainty and anxiety. Her sister Stella suffered a major stroke that left her partially paralysed. Stella, who had always managed the Scott household, needed care twenty-four hours a day. Marion paid to have nurses on duty but aspects of Stella's basic care fell to Marion and her brother-in-law John, who was also in ill health. They had difficulty coping as domestic help was becoming increasingly difficult to obtain.

Throughout her life, Marion had never asked anyone for help with personal matters and could not bring herself to do so even when she was in desperate need of it. Her doctor stepped in. The situation in the Scott household was serious enough that he felt it imperative to write formally to authorities in an effort to alleviate some of her burden. He requested that she be given priority to obtain domestic help 'as the matter is urgent'. He explained that Marion was 'of very frail constitution and suffers from chronic abdominal trouble which prevents her from doing anything but the lightest domestic duties'.[43]

While Scott was struggling with her personal problems, Finzi contacted Edmund Blunden to involve him in the poetry project but little progress was made. Ivor Gurney remained an obscure figure although Kathleen Ferrier continued to perform his songs, and Elsie Suddaby began including them in her recitals. His poetic voice was silent. Ivor had slipped from public view. Finzi was frustrated.

Marion was overwhelmed and emotionally drained. The last thing she felt capable of doing was resurrecting her memories of Ivor at a time when her sister was critically ill. It was too much for her. Her main focus became her work on Haydn which she was able to pursue with the assistance of Kathleen Dale. Marion continued to publish regularly and added the popular *Radio Times* to the list of periodicals, newspapers and journals for which she wrote. Her articles stirred the interest of the general public and were 'designed to cast an anticipatory light on forthcoming performances [and] had a rare power of awakening expectation: not only by a luminous phrase remembered with gratitude years afterwards, but also by musical comments of the most acute and precise kind', observed musicologist Rosemary Hughes.[44] Marion began to contribute programme notes for concerts by the BBC Symphony Orchestra, the Hallé Orchestra and the Haydn Orchestra.

In the meantime, in 1948, Marion released more of Ivor's songs to the Finzis in preparation for the third Oxford University Press volume. However, it wasn't until late 1949 that she was willing or able to turn more of her attention to Gurney. 'I have just come through one of the hardest and saddest experiences of my life', she wrote to Alan Frank at OUP. 'My only remaining sister died three weeks ago [August 1949] after a long, cruel illness and her husband is so ill that I don't think he will long survive her.'[45] Stella had recovered enough from her stroke to make the long journey to her husband's native Australia where, to make matters even worse for Marion, she had died. Stella was sixty-eight years old. Marion was left completely alone in her advancing years. With the exception of her niece Audrey, everyone she was close to had died.[46]

Now in her seventies, Marion continued to work despite increasingly poor health. She had written several chapters of her book about Haydn but was giving priority to preparing the comprehensive catalogue of his music for the 1954 edition of *Grove's*. The forty-page compilation lists Haydn's compositions individually with a wealth of detailed information set out in columns: dates of composition, publication, first performances, the key, time signature, tempo indications, scoring, dedications, alternative versions, nicknames. Marion included a column of 'Remarks', adding up to a total length of 20 feet, in which she provided information about the 'locations of the autograph, statements of conflicting opinions upon the dating, numbering and authenticity of certain works, the occasion which gave rise to their composition or the special circumstances in which they were written, notes regarding Haydn's use of chronogram, and reprints of inscriptions he entered in his own catalogues', according to Kathleen Dale, who worked closely with Scott in the final stages of its preparation.[47] The Haydn Catalogue represented Scott at her best and as a woman who 'possessed the two attributes which go into the making of a great scholar – heroic thoroughness and creative imagination', observed Rosemary Hughes. 'She never stinted the laborious months of checking and rechecking edition after edition, either all wildly different or all apparently duplicates ... She never became so lost in the forest of facts that she could no longer see the wood for the trees – and that forest, as we know was a pathless jungle.' [48]

1951 opened on a sour note for Marion. She learned that Winifred Gurney was circulating 'completely false statements' about her, implying that she was 'withholding large sums of money' from her, Ronald and Dorothy that were due them from royalties, performing rights and sales of Ivor Gurney's published works.[49] Marion was furious, and wrote to Ronald to involve him in the matter. She reminded him that she was the court-appointed administrator of Gurney's affairs, an arrangement to which the Gurney siblings and their mother had consented. She mentioned the £143 owed her and made it clear that she had never been reimbursed. She let him know that all of the bank records were available should he feel it necessary to see them. She told him that she was willing to let that obligation remain unpaid 'otherwise it may be some years before we have sufficient accumulations in hand to meet the expenses of further publication'.[50] She informed him that she had already sanctioned the third volume of Gurney's songs.

Scott was firm, direct and all business. 'There is a separate banking account and I had been intending and hoping when I accumulated sufficient balances to be able to publish a further volume of his poems, and it would be a disappointment, and a matter of grief to me if I am prevented from doing so', she wrote. 'Had your Mother lived the copyright of such a publication would have been transferred to her and a scheme put on foot for perpetuating your brother's works ... I cannot think that your sister would seriously prefer to sacrifice the perpetuation of your brother's works for the sake of a few pounds ready cash.' [51]

She reminded Ronald also that 'not once, as far as I know, did [Winifred] or Dorothy visit Ivor during the fifteen years he was in the City of London Mental Hospital nor did she show the slightest interest in his work then, and it would seem that the interest has only awakened because she has heard that I have been receiving certain fees and royalties [from] his works'.[52]

An apologetic and distressed Ronald Gurney replied immediately. 'I cannot say I am surprised at [Winifred] – she has periodically spoken about any money there might be and I explained the facts and the unlikelihood of there being any.' [53] Although Ronald was aware that his sister had written to Marion, he did not know the contents of her letter, but 'expected trouble'. He regretted not keeping in closer contact with Scott about what he jokingly referred to as the accumulating 'fortune' so that he would have been better 'armed to shut Winifred up if she started in this manner'. Ronald assured

Marion that both he and Dorothy understood the arrangement and agreed with Scott that she should write to Winifred 'to demand a complete written withdrawal' of her statements.[54] He offered his 'complete' support, and told her that he would indeed come to London to meet with her to go over the bank accounts to ensure that there were no further misunderstandings on Winifred's part. Their meeting at the end of April concluded with lunch at Marion's home. Later Ronald made Winifred sign an agreement that all royalties be used to publish further editions of Ivor's work.

Gerald Finzi and Edmund Blunden, who had returned to England after serving two years with the United Kingdom Liaison Mission in Tokyo, finally managed to get together in the spring of 1951 to work on Gurney's poems. Blunden was revered in Japan, but upon returning to Britain he found himself skirting close to the edge of financial hardship. At the age of fifty-five, he had a young wife and three children under the age of five to support with his four-days-a-week job at *The Times Literary Supplement*. He and his family lived cramped together in a small four-room house at Virginia Water, not far from Windsor Forest. The five Blundens welcomed their retreat at Ashmansworth. After discussing Gurney and his poetry for a day, Finzi then isolated Blunden in his study so he could make his selections and write the introduction without distractions. 'He retired with all the material and with his trained eye and ear, his sympathy and the most intense concentration ... and got right inside the work', Gerald reported to Marion. 'I was glad that what started in the first instance as something of a duty forced upon him soon became an excitement and real interest.'[55]

Blunden had published collections of poetry by John Clare in 1920 and by Wilfred Owen in 1931. Finzi hoped that the interest generated in Clare and Owen by these editions would awaken similar interest in Gurney's poetry. He cautioned Marion: 'The present generation of poets is hostile to the Georgians (just as the Georgians were hostile to the nineties, and the nineties to the mid-Victorian and so on ad-infinitum) and I think [Blunden's] selection will not have covered much of [Gurney's] early work.'[56] As the project took shape and the search for publishers began, Finzi observed practically that 'we must remember the times are very much against the publication of such a volume, and without someone like Blunden as an intermediary there would be no hope at all.'[57]

Finzi touched upon the delicate subject of money, and suggested that the Gurney estate pay Blunden £25 for his week's labour 'but for heaven's sake don't let him know it has been suggested by me!'[58] The book was offered first to Sidgwick & Jackson, who had published *Severn and Somme* and *War's Embers*, but they would only consider publishing it if financial backing were available. Blunden hoped to interest the publisher Rupert Hart-Davis in the collection, but in the end Hutchinson agreed to bring the book out in 1954.[59]

After years of writing about others, Marion found herself in a reversal of roles when Joan Chissell, a young writer, arranged to interview her for the *Musical Times*. She had met Scott when she was a student at the RCM, and Marion had published some of her work in the college magazine. Marion invited her to tea at her Porchester Terrace home. 'She was a rather frail-looking, as the most exquisitely delicate piece of Dresden China, white-haired lady – very sensitive and soft-spoken but with the keenest imaginable intelligence, and passionately held convictions', Chissell recalled. 'She introduced me to the exotic habit of putting a lemon-slice in a cup of tea instead of the good old English milk. I thought there was something vaguely Russian in that. I stood in awe of so distinguished a lady, though no one could have been more encouraging and kind to the younger generation than she was.' [60] Chissell's profile of Marion appeared in the February 1951 issue of the *Musical Times*.

While no new editions of Gurney's poetry or music had been published for many years and his name was virtually unknown by the early 1950s, Scott, Finzi, members of Gurney's family, and various friends, including John Haines, were surprised when Don B. Ray, a young graduate student from the California State University at Long Beach some 6,000 miles away, began working on his study of Gurney's life and work. Ray had been searching for a subject for his master's thesis that combined both literary and musical elements when his department chairman, Pauline Alderman, suggested Gurney. His initial inquiries were met with scepticism by Finzi and caution by Marion Scott. Ray began his work at a time when many of the people who knew Gurney were still living. The material he gathered had immediacy and it provided information about aspects of Gurney's life, such as insights into the Gurney family, that might otherwise have been lost. Ray's enquiries prompted a flood of twenty-four 'long, rambling discursive letters' from Winifred Gurney and four 'opinionated' ones from Ronald Gurney.

Ray regarded the comments from the Gurneys with caution, and used them sparingly in his work. With the initial draft of his study completed, he sent it to Marion Scott and Gerald Finzi, who annotated it. Finzi had Edmund Blunden read it, and reported that he was 'impressed with the work' and 'in particular with the way [Ray] recaptured the war years which can hardly be understood by any of a younger generation as they were known by Gurney and Blunden himself'.[61] Ray delayed the completion of the biography and his degree requirements to begin his career as a film composer for a major American television network.[62] This spark of interest in Gurney was ultimately gratifying to both Scott and Finzi and encouraging to Blunden as his volume of Gurney's poetry moved closer to completion.

As 1951 drew to a close, Marion was forced to curtail her activities as her health deteriorated. She had published a new edition of Haydn's Quartet op. 1, no. 1 with Oxford University Press, contributed programme notes for orchestral performances of Haydn's music and had written a half-dozen articles for a variety of publications. Her scholarship remained precise and insightful. Her writing had lost none of its vitality and humour. She showed no diminishment of her great intellectual gift but she was growing weaker physically. She no longer had the energy to continue her duties as editor of the Royal Musical Association *Proceedings*, and resigned in 1952.

Marion felt ominous changes in her physical condition. She managed to write two important articles but, sensing that her time was limited, she knew she must devote herself exclusively to completing her Haydn Catalogue to meet the deadline for the 1954 *Grove's*. Then, in 1953, she was diagnosed with colon cancer. Nothing could be done. In her weakened state, she could no longer go to libraries in London and Cambridge to work with their Haydn collections. She relied upon Kathleen Dale to gather material for her. Working together, the two women completed the catalogue on time. 'If mine was the pen that wrote the titles of hundreds of folk-song arrangements, and the particulars of numerous instrumental pieces, Marion Scott's was the mind that directed the whole undertaking, and hers were the eyes that scrutinized every single entry in this exhaustive work, her invaluable legacy to the world of musical scholarship', Dale wrote.[63] 'I shall never cease to marvel that anyone so frail and exhausted as she was by then could nevertheless direct these intricate operations with so clear a mind, with such complete mastery of method, and with such undiminished zest for her work.'[64]

Recognition of Marion Scott's work began to come to her while she was still able to appreciate it. She was elected to Honorary Membership in the Royal Philharmonic Society and was nominated for election as Fellow of the Royal College of Music. She last appeared in public in July 1953 when she attended a reception at the Arts Council. Friends found her frail, but observed that 'she had lost none of her alertness of mind nor interest in fellow-musicians'.[65]

In her last months she showed great serenity and was relatively free of pain. She kept her telephone by her bed and insisted on talking with friends when they called. She was cheered by their visits and her bedroom was always alive with the colour and scent of fresh flowers from well-wishers. 'My parting sight was of her propped up in bed looking very pretty and mentally the Marion Scott we had always known', said her friend Dorothy Mortimer Harris.[66] As autumn deepened into winter and the sixteenth anniversary of Ivor Gurney's death on 26 December approached, Scott's decline seemed to mirror his. She grew desperately ill and in the early hours of Christmas Eve, Marion Scott died. She was seventy-six years old. Her remains were taken to Golders Green for cremation on 28 December.

Eschewing the traditional funeral service, Marion had planned her own memorial service featuring music, poetry and prayers. It was held on the afternoon of 22 January 1954 at St Michael's, Cornhill. Played before the service were Parry's *Elegy*, the same piece played at Ivor Gurney's funeral sixteen years earlier, and the Largo from Haydn's String Quartet in D major. The service opened with Walford Davies' *Requiem aeterna*, followed by a reading of Psalm 121 – 'I will lift up mine eyes' – a lesson from Revelations 21, verses 1–7, Parry's *Songs of Farewell* and a poem by John Gibson Lockhard:

> There is an old belief that on some solemn shore
> Beyond the sphere of grief, dear friends shall meet once more,
> Beyond the sphere of Time and Sin and Fate's control
> Serene in changeless prime of body and soul.

That creed I fain would keep, that hope I'll ne'er forego,
Eternal be the sleep, if not waken so.

At the conclusion of the service, the congregation stood while Mendelssohn's *Funeral March* filled the church.

Writing about her friend in the *Musical Times*, Kathleen Dale pondered Scott's diversity and her many contributions to music. '[A]n unswerving love for her art was the guiding principle of her long life', she wrote. 'Whether she will be best remembered for her invaluable research on Haydn and her ownership of a unique collection of early editions of his work; as the inspiration of still flourishing musical societies; as an acute and discerning critic; as the author of an exceptionally enlightening book on Beethoven; or as the individual chiefly responsible for preserving both the musical and literary output of the composer-poet Ivor Gurney, time alone will prove'.

Replying to a letter from her old RCM friend William Harris at a time when her health was failing, Marion was less assured about her achievements than her friends and colleagues. 'What you wrote about the work I have attempted to do for music touched me very much, and your kind, encouraging words are a great help to me. I do thank you, good friend for all these years. I shall always think of them now when I get assailed with despondency at all I should have liked to accomplish but came short of.' [67]

'This diary fragment in Marion Scott's handwriting I came across in our attic. It must have come with her papers concerning Ivor Gurney, which she left to my husband Gerald Finzi.'

Joy Finzi
Ashmansworth 1968

In the diary but set apart from other entries, Marion Scott had written a poem. It bore no title and no date.

> In time to come, when we have done with time,
> And the one tyrant, like a worn out toy
> Lies far below, impotent to destroy
> Or bring about our bliss, we two will climb
> Some sunny height of air, you chanting rhyme
> And well-contented songs, innocent as a boy,
> I by your side quite silent in pure joy.

NOTES

1 Richard Capell, 'Ivor Gurney – A Musician's Tragedy', *Daily Telegraph*, 28 December 1937, p. 13.

2 'Mr. Ivor Gurney – Poet and Musician', *The Times*, 28 December 1937, p. 14.

3 'Death of Gloucester-Born "Schubert"', *The Citizen*, 28 December 1937, p. 1.

4 'Ivor Gurney, Author of Song and Music', *New York Times*, p. 22.

5 The McKays, like the majority of families in the Greater Boston area, routinely subscribed to two different newspapers. the morning edition of one and the evening edition of a different one. It is very likely that Annie Drummond McKay read about Gurney's death.

6 GF to Howard Ferguson, 1 January 1938, GA.

7 Ibid.

8 Gurney told Scott that he used his 'Chant for Twenty-Third Psalm ... to steady himself when in fear in the trenches ...' (Note by Scott on manuscript of 'Chant for Psalm 23', GA).

9 'Mr. Ivor Gurney Buried, Moving Service at Twigworth', *The Citizen*, 1 January 1938, p. 6.

10 Ibid.

11 Curiously, less than four years after uttering his praise of Ivor Gurney, Alfred Cheesman told Ronald Gurney that Ivor was 'all wrong – no good – better dead; when he could not torment anyone any longer'. RG to DBR, 3 May 1951, GA.

12 Gurney's grave is at the foot of the grave of Herbert Howells' son, Michael.

13 MMS to GF, 4 January 1938, GA.

14 Soprano Nancy Evans, baritone Sydney Northcote and pianist Hubert Foss performed both volumes of the songs in a recital at the London offices of Oxford University Press to celebrate their publication.

15 Dutton have released the Nancy Evans (1915–2000) recordings in the *Singers to Remember* series under the title 'The Comely Mezzo', CDBP9723. The compact disc also features songs by Vaughan Williams, Warlock, Parry and Bliss.

16 The cellist in the Kutcher String Quartet was John Barbirolli, who became known as a conductor.

17 MMS, draft, MSC.

18 Ibid.

19 HH manuscript 'Ivor Gurney', BBC National broadcast 18 July 1938, quoted in Christopher Palmer, *Herbert Howells: A Centenary Celebration* (London: Thames Publishing, 1992), pp. 265–6. Howells' 1914 portrait of Ivor Gurney in his composition *Suite for Orchestra: The Bs* turned out to be remarkably prophetic. At the end of the movement, Howells suspends sound for a long stretch before returning to the music in a subdued but radiant burst of sound. The music parallels Gurney's fate, mirroring the silence that befell him during his asylum years, certainly something Howells could not have foreseen when he composed *The Bs*.

20 MMS to RG, 20 March 1951, GA.

21 Anonymous, *Glasgow Herald*, 2 November 1939.

22 Annie Prince Scott to her cousin 'Annie' in Salem, Massachusetts, 3 September 1938, S. Hardy Prince Collection, Beverly, Massachusetts.

23 Ibid.

24 Early Prince family tradition held that Priscilla Brewster, the *Mayflower* passenger, later married Thomas Prince [Prence], who had sailed to the New World on the ship *Good Fortune* soon after the *Mayflower*. This Thomas Prince was not from the same line as Mrs Scott's Prince ancestors. Prince family historian S. Hardy Prince corrected this misconception long after Marion had died.

25 Annie Scott to 'Annie', 3 September 1938.

26 Ibid.

27 Eugene Prince served the United States as a member of Army Intelligence before and during World War II. He did resurface after his exploits in Europe and returned to the US to live in Connecticut.

28 FG to MMS, 30 May 1926, GA.

29 FG to MMS, 10 March 1938, GA.

30 Kathleen Dale was born Kathleen Richards in London in 1895. She studied privately with York Bowen, Davies and with Benjamin Dale (1885–1943), whom she later married and

divorced. Dale studied Swedish language and literature at University College, London, and published a number of translations from that language and others, including works on music. She was Dame Ethel Smyth's musical executor and published a biography of Brahms in 1970. Her 'apprenticeship' with Marion Scott opened another career for her in musicology. She died in 1984.

31 In her *Grove* entry, Marion wrote that Gurney had been 'shell-shocked in the war' despite having been told otherwise by doctors. To have suffered because of war is more poignant and more heroic than to have suffered because one is ill, particularly at a time when mental illness carried so many stigmas. Marion Scott, ever the image-maker, knew this and believed that portraying Gurney as a shell-shock victim would be to his advantage. Thus the notion that Gurney's mental illness had been caused by the war took root and set the tone for how Gurney would be perceived in the future.

32 KD, 'Memories of Marion Scott', *Music and Letters*, vol. 35, no. 3 (July 1954), p. 236.

33 Ibid., p. 237.

34 MMS to GF, 30 August 1939, GA.

35 Karl Geiringer, 'Appreciations: Marion Scott', *RCM Magazine*, May 1954, p. 46. Not long after meeting Scott in London, Geiringer (1899–1989) emigrated to the United States, where he remained for the rest of his life.

36 MMS, 'London Itself', from her unpublished memoir, *The Home of All Our Mortal Dream*, MSC. Subsequent quotes are taken from this memoir.

37 KD, 'Commemoration of Marion Scott', in Society of Women Musicians, *Commemoration of Marion Scott* (programme book, 25–6 June 1954), p. 13.

38 Ibid., p. 239.

39 Ibid.

40 *Huddersfield Examiner*, 24 October 1942.

41 KD, 'Commemoration of Marion Scott', pp. 15–16.

42 Ibid.

43 Copy of letter from Dr G. E. Gange-Andrews dated 9 July 1945, MSC.

44 Rosemary Hughes, 'Marion Scott's Contribution to Scholarship', *RCM Magazine*, May 1954, p. 42.

45 MMS to Alan Frank, 20 September 1949, MSC.

46 Audrey Lovibond had married a Scotsman, Graham Priestman, a member of the Bach Choir who became Master at Oundle School. Audrey was a speech and drama coach who worked at Stratford. She was seriously injured in an automobile accident in the late 1980s and never fully recovered. She died in 1996.

47 KD, 'The Haydn Catalogue ... and an Unfinished Manuscript', *RCM Magazine*, May 1954.

48 Rosemary Hughes, 'Commemoration of Marion Scott', in Society of Women Musicians, *Commemoration of Marion Scott* (programme book, 25–6 June 1954), p. 19.

49 MMS to RG, 20 March 1951, MSC.

50 Ibid.

51 Ibid.

52 Ibid.

53 RG to MMS, 23 March 1951, MSC.

54 Ibid.

55 GF to MMS, 21 May 1951, MSC.

56 Ibid.

57 GF to MMS, 8 June 1951, MSC.

58 GF to MMS, 21 May 1951, MSC.

59 Rupert Hart-Davies was the son-in-law of poet-novelist Mary Borden, who ran her mobile hospital at the Front for four years during the Great War.

60 Joan Chissell (1919–2007) to the author (1998). At the time she interviewed Scott, Ms Chissell was the editor of the *RCM Magazine* and had published her biography of Robert Schumann in the Dent Music Masters series in 1948. Like Scott, Ms Chissell enjoyed a successful career as a respected music critic.

61 GF to MMS, 20 May 1951, GA.

62 Ray's work on Gurney was the basis for his recommendation to receive a scholarship to Cambridge which he won but did not pursue after he joined the CBS-TV Music Department in 1956. He was music supervisor and/or composer for a variety of popular American television series, including *G.E. Theater, Playhouse 90, The Twilight Zone, Rawhide, Gunsmoke, Wild Wild West, Gilligan's Island,* and *Hawaii Five-O*. He returned to his work on Gurney many years later, and in 1980 earned his master's degree from California State University at Long Beach. Copies of his thesis on Gurney are at the GA and the British Museum. Don Brandon Ray died on 16 April 2005 at the age of 78.

63 KD, 'The Haydn Catalogue ... and an Unfinished Manuscript.

64 Ibid., p. 240.

65 Rupert Erlebach, 'Appreciations: Marion Scott', *RCM Magazine* (May 1954).

66 Ibid., Dorothy Mortimer Harris.

67 MMS to William Harris, 14 January 1951, collection of Margaret Brockway.

Epilogue

*W*HEN MARION SCOTT'S NIECE Audrey Priestman arrived at 4 Rutland House on Marloes Road, London, a week after her aunt's death, she faced one of the most difficult and emotionally draining tasks of her life. Newly married at the age of forty-five and setting up house with her husband at Oundle, Audrey now had to sort through the accumulation of books, music, papers, files, notes, letters, mementos and family heirlooms that filled her aunt's flat. Marion and her sister Stella had reared Audrey as their daughter after Audrey's mother, Freda, had died shortly after her baby's birth. Audrey had lived with her father in the Scott household, and later, as an adult, had for a time shared Marion's home on Porchester Terrace. The two women were very close, and Audrey inherited the bulk of Marion's estate.[1]

Audrey and her husband, Graham, were overwhelmed by the volume of material Marion had amassed, particularly Ivor Gurney's manuscripts and letters. They had only two months to remove everything, because Marion's lease expired in March. Every time Mrs Priestman opened a drawer something connected with Ivor 'fell out of it', she explained to Gerald Finzi in a plea for him to come and retrieve the Gurney collection.[2] Audrey identified three major areas where he would find the Gurney papers: an oak chest in the passage, the top half of a green steel cabinet, and on metal racks in two halls. Marion had also deposited two boxes of Ivor's manuscripts at the Midland Bank, where they had to remain until her will went through probate. Audrey warned Finzi that he couldn't possibly sort through the huge collection in an afternoon, and told him that she was employing Marion's housekeeper, Kitty Walsh, for another month to open the flat for Finzi when Audrey could not be there. The task he faced was formidable and it was complicated by Marion's legal manœuvring.

For the better part of twenty-six years, Marion Scott had nurtured, protected and loved Ivor Gurney. For another sixteen years after his death, she protected his interests as Administrator of his estate. Matters were severely complicated by the fact that Ivor had been legally declared mentally incompetent at the young age of thirty-two, before he had made a will, and thus he died intestate. Through Scott's influence, both his mother Florence and his brother Ronald Gurney had renounced Letters of Administration for Ivor's estate, which were granted to Scott on 26 February 1938, two months after Ivor's death. In this manner, Scott gained legal control over his estate.

During Ivor's lifetime, Marion did not have any rights in his music, poetry, letters or other writings, although she had all of them in her possession. When Ivor was certified insane in 1922, his brother Ronald became Ivor's legal guardian, and as such had legal control over his possessions and decisions about his care, even though he nearly always deferred to Marion. Ronald Gurney's co-operation with Marion was certainly spurred in part by the fact that Marion was shouldering a large portion of the financial burden for Ivor's care. When Marion secured the Letters of Administration, she gained the authority and responsibility for ensuring distribution of Ivor's property to his rightful heirs in accordance with the applicable laws of succession. Ivor's mother Florence Gurney was his statutory heir.

As Administrator, Marion's legal obligation would have been to discharge Ivor's legitimate debts from his property before making distribution of the assets. All of Ivor's property, i.e. original compositions and poetry and royalties accruing, then fell under her jurisdiction for purposes of fulfilling the duties imposed by law on the Administrator. Gurney, of course, died insolvent. Because Marion Scott had personally paid for portions of Gurney's care and his funeral expenses, she was probably his only documented creditor.[3] She shrewdly used this debt to justify her continuing efforts to get Ivor's music performed and both his music and poetry published, ostensibly so that the royalties could be used to discharge the debt Ivor owed her. In reality it was forwarding her own desire to preserve Gurney's legacy of music and poetry.

Marion opened a separate bank account in which she placed the royalties from publications of Gurney's works and performances by the BBC. She let the royalties accumulate untouched. The debt to her was never discharged and she held the Letters of Administration until the day she died. Ivor's estate was still 'unadministered' even though Florence Gurney, the rightful heir, had died intestate in 1945. Ronald Gurney and his sisters, Winifred and Dorothy, succeeded Florence as the beneficiaries of Ivor's estate, and by law, Ronald would succeed Marion as Administrator of Ivor's estate when Marion died. Ronald Gurney was also the Administrator of his mother's estate.

Marion feared that Ivor's literary and musical legacy would be jeopardized as soon as the Letters of Administration passed to Ronald Gurney, who would then regain control of the legal rights to Ivor's creative work. She could not convey Letters of Administration through her will. However, in her will, dated 22 March 1951, she bequeathed to Gerald Finzi the still undischarged 'debt' Ivor Gurney owed her. She hoped that after her death, by continuing to keep alive the debt she was owed by the Gurneys, she would be able to ensure the co-operation of Ronald Gurney and his siblings with the Finzis in their efforts to continue the publication and performance of Ivor's works.

Marion had every reason to fear that Ivor's legacy might be destroyed or lost because of the hostility Ronald Gurney harboured towards his brother. She also feared that the Gurneys would keep the royalties for themselves and not put them towards more publications. In a flap about control of manuscripts in 1951, Marion resorted to reminding Ronald that not once, to her knowledge, did Winifred or Dorothy, his sisters, visit Ivor in the City Mental Hospital, and forcefully mentioned the amount of money she herself had paid to cover Ivor's hospital bills and living expenses from January 1932 to December 1937.

Marion died on 24 December 1953 and Ronald Gurney was granted

Letters of Administration for Ivor's estate on 5 April 1954. He retained them until his death in 1971. He, too, left part of the estate unadministered (i.e. literary works and accrued royalties), and the estate remains in the hands of trustees to this day.

When Audrey Priestman turned to Gerald Finzi for his help, Finzi feared that the already hostile Ronald would create trouble. He tried to smooth things over by laying the blame on Marion's failure to bring them all together to discuss arrangements for Ivor's manuscripts. Knowing that he had no legal grounds to continue Marion's ploy to maintain control of the manuscripts, Finzi tried to mollify Ronald. 'But in fairness to Miss Scott, it is my belief that she hadn't the least idea she was dying', he explained to Ronald, believing that she was suffering only from anaemia.[4] In reality, Marion knew her anaemia was caused by internal bleeding related to her cancer. She knew she was dying, which is one reason why she pushed so hard to complete her catalogue of Haydn's music for the 1954 edition of *Grove's Dictionary*.

After years of enduring what he regarded as interference and bullying from Ivor's upper-class, intellectual London friends, Ronald was in no mood to be placated. His resentment was in danger of boiling over. He was in charge now, and he made certain that everyone knew it. When he declared that 'all these London people breaking their necks trying to get him published' was 'useless' and that they were 'flogging a dead horse', Herbert Howells came to Ivor's defence. 'The "dead horse" you so sincerely believe is being uselessly flogged has, over many years, seemed to me to be one of the most vital minds in the whole page of English song', he wrote. 'If there is any possibility of more of the songs being published I hope their appearance in print will not be delayed.'[5] Howells took on the issue of Ivor's poetry as well, telling Ronald that he personally had been moved by the early verse and that 'minds better than mine have found in Ivor's poetry things you seem to miss in them.'[6]

Edmund Blunden's edition *Poems by Ivor Gurney: Principally selected from unpublished manuscripts* had just been issued by Hutchinson in 1954. With its appearance, Ronald seemed to soften and experience a flutter of pride in his brother. He inscribed a copy and gave it to the library at the King's School, where Ivor had studied during his Cathedral days. He baffled everyone when he sent a copy of Blunden's own book to Blunden at Christmas! However, his seemingly improved mood did not last for long. When Finzi attempted to secure publication of a fourth volume of Ivor's songs by Oxford University Press, Ronald refused to co-operate. Ivor's friends grew increasingly nervous, fearing that his disrespect and animosity towards Ivor, even in death, might lead him to destroy his brother's legacy or make it unavailable.

Vaughan Williams tried to purchase the manuscripts from Ronald, but Ronald ignored him for months. When he finally wrote to Vaughan Williams, he declared that Ivor's work was not of any importance and that his 'reputation was based on the efforts of a few friends'.[7] He had, after all, asked an expert who told him that Ivor's music was 'not popular'.[8] Vaughan Williams told Finzi that he thought the 'expert' was 'probably a dance-band musician or something of that sort.'[9] Ronald hinted that he might give the papers to the Gloucester Public Library, but nothing came of it. Then Gerald Finzi died on 27 September 1956, leaving his widow, Joy, to soothe Ronald and try to extricate the manuscripts from his control. Within eight months of her husband's death, Joy Finzi had managed to gain enough of Ronald Gurney's trust and co-operation that he allowed her to take Ivor's music manuscripts home with her to Ashmansworth. Further, he granted his permission for the publication of the fourth volume of his brother's songs by Oxford University Press.

The victory was hard-fought and one that required delicate diplomacy and deft negotiating skills to overcome Ronald's distrust and resentment toward anyone interested in advancing Ivor's reputation. However, by March 1959 Ronald had resumed his threatening pose, informing Joy Finzi that she had 'no standing' to have any say about Ivor's manuscripts, and that there would be 'no more publications of any sort – music or poems.'[10] Not one to be intimidated, Mrs Finzi shot back a reply reminding Ronald that he had promised to place the manuscripts in the Gloucester Public Library.

Nothing happened for another two months. Then Ronald agreed to the publication of ten songs, and indicated his willingness to pay any costs from Ivor's meagre estate. This was not necessary, however, because Howard Ferguson volunteered to edit the songs 'for love'. *Ivor Gurney: A Fourth Volume of Ten Songs* appeared towards the end of 1959. Around the same time Ronald Gurney made another important decision, acting on his promise to Joy Finzi. 'You will rejoice and your husband rest easier, to hear that today I handed over the Box complete, together with 4 published volumes of the O.U.P. and the 2 Carnegie Trust volumes, therein, to the Gloucester Reference Library on Permanent Loan', Ronald informed Mrs Finzi. He added that his loan also included 'most of the Poems.'[11]

The story does not end here. While Ronald did nothing to disturb the manuscripts once they were in the library, he continued to make life difficult for Mrs Finzi and others interested in Ivor's work. Instead of continuing to co-operate, he reverted to his March 1959 declaration – 'no more publications' – and he kept his word for the remainder of his life. In the process, he angered his sister Winifred, who understood the importance of Ivor's work and supported its publication.

Chatto & Windus expressed interest in publishing a new edition of Ivor's poetry, writing directly to Ronald: 'I believe you will have heard from Mrs Gerald Finzi that I and my colleagues would very much like to publish a selection of your brother's poems, chosen and introduced by Edmund Blunden and Leonard Clark ...'[12] Ronald received the news with an outpouring of rage because he felt that Mrs Finzi had tried to circumvent his control. '[I] would remind you that I warned you to your face that Chatto and Windus would have to speak to me first', he railed like a petulant child when he wrote to Mrs Finzi.[13] 'As usual ever since 1953 you have treated the whole business as if it was yours and you ignored my warning. I would remind you that I am my brother's administrator and I don't intend to let anyone usurp my position.' He warned Mrs Finzi to 'get off my back and cease to trouble me, or else I shall have to consider legal action.'[14] Still seething, he wasn't finished with her and instructed her to turn the page over. It read:

> On further consideration I think it would be just as well to put things straight now and [be] done with it. I intend for GOOD that the ONLY people that will ever authorise any future publications will be myself and my two sisters. Nothing will ever be done except when paid for entirely by the family.
>
> I am tired beyond anything at your remarks about money and your behaviour only seems to make it worse. NOW! as a final word to you I give you till the end of May to return to me all the copies that you illegally took of all my brother's poems – entirely without asking me. If you don't comply – I am going to court and if possible get damages out of you for keeping them back at Miss Scott's death. And if you don't comply, I will remove everything from the library till you do.[15]

Meanwhile the Gurney family dynamics came into full force, with misunderstandings and blame going around in circles among them. The 'terrible barrier' of 'obstinacy' and 'unbreakable control' that had divided the family in Winifred's youth had never been broken down.[16] It still formed a wedge that prevented Ivor's siblings from communicating rationally and calmly with one another.

Ronald had become unreasonable, controlling and obsessive in his role as the leader of his family, the keeper of his brother's legacy and the overseer of Ivor's slim income. He felt that others were trying to usurp his power and that no one knew better than he what was best for Ivor. Ronald was a proud man who was not going to take charity from anyone, especially those he perceived as his natural enemies in the war between the rich and the working classes. If there were to be any future publications, the family would pay for them as he had so harshly informed Mrs Finzi. Although he complained that the royalties were negligible, he did nothing to improve the situation. Instead he threw obstacles in the way of the very people capable of securing the publication of Ivor's work – Joy Finzi and Ralph Vaughan Williams. Ronald believed that their interest in Ivor was based on ulterior motives designed to take money away from him and his family. No one could make him believe otherwise.

Money was a driving force that fuelled Ronald Gurney's anger, bitterness and pride. He had spent years resenting the fact that the wealthy Marion Scott had taken an interest in his brother and had done so much for him. Ronald could not have been pleased when he learned that over the years Marion had also given his mother, Florence, considerable amounts of money – £5, £10, £15, £20 from time to time – none of which filtered down to him or to Winifred. Florence, always struggling, always feeling poor, had kept this gift of her friendship with Marion to herself. The amount 'horrified' Winifred, who assumed, rightly or wrongly, that Florence gave the money to her younger sister Dorothy. Even in death Marion Scott managed to upset the Gurneys.

Whenever Ronald visited Winifred he brought the estate account books to her to underscore how bad the financial situation was and how heavy a burden rested on his shoulders as the head of the family. He seemed to think that the royalties from Ivor's poetry and music should be enough to support the family. He even told Winifred that she ought to get a job doing private nursing. The idea was ludicrous. 'Me starting at nearly 82. Working'; she was incredulous.[17] Ronald backed off when Winifred began listing some of her ailments.

Even though she herself had caused problems in the early 1950s by spreading false rumours that Marion Scott was withholding large sums of money from the family, Winifred had mellowed. She realized the gravity of the situation and truly wanted what was best to preserve Ivor's legacy.

Ronald was so enraged by Joy Finzi's efforts that on one occasion when she went to visit him, he slammed the door in her face. He was furious that she had contacted the BBC about presenting Ivor's poems on the radio with Leonard Clark, a Gloucestershire poet, as the reader. Ronald claimed that 'the literary people at the BBC' had condemned both Clark and Mrs Finzi for going over his head to arrange a programme.[18] Upset and embarrassed by her brother's irrational behaviour, Winifred started to correspond with Joy Finzi in an effort to bring some calm to the deteriorating situation. 'I wanted to do something to help you and so I wrote to the BBC and sent your letter to them', she informed Mrs Finzi. 'I told them I had never felt that you or Mr. Clark had any ulterior motive in what you are trying to do other than what was in fairness to Ivor ... I have told him that if it wasn't for such as you Ivor would have been forgotten ...' Winifred thought it 'natural that Mr. Clark would want to be one of the first to read and give Ivor to the public. As a Gloucestershire poet one would expect it.'[19]

By communicating with Joy Finzi, Winifred was taking a big risk. She knew that Ronald would be furious if he thought that she was in any way betraying him by helping Joy Finzi or Clark, who also wanted to see a new edition of Ivor's verse in print. Ronald's visits upset Winifred but she was afraid to tell him to stay away. 'I do not think I can afford to keep him away. After all he is my only kith and kin if I need it', she explained to Joy Finzi.[20] Winifred was troubled by Ronald's wife Ethel and thought that she was responsible for her husband's difficult behaviour. She described Ethel as 'a wicked woman' and believed that it was Ethel who expected her to return to work at age eighty-two, not Ronald, whom she claimed was 'afraid' of his wife and that he 'was never like this before he married her.'[21]

Winifred attempted to reason with Ronald, partly to protect herself and partly to protect Ivor's legacy. She knew full well that the royalties from Ivor's work 'should have been banked and ploughed back into publishing. This I told Ronald and he now has to admit it.'[22] Apparently not all the money was administered in this way, exactly as Marion Scott had feared. Winifred took another bold step, telling Ronald that he must 'put things right' by changing his will to leave 'the equivalent amounting to the Royalties received'. She suggested that he move with speed because at his age and with his health 'anything could happen to him' including 'a "stroke" from worry [then] he would not be able to do a thing.'[23]

Winifred was afraid that if Ethel found out that Ronald might change his will and designate a sum of money to be left for Ivor's royalty fund instead of to her, she would stop him. 'He says he has the money but unless she dies before him he will do nothing and I shall certainly not get any of his money', Winifred observed. She wrote to the BBC suggesting that they 'get the publishing done' after Ronald's death. 'You see it is the only way out because Ethel need not know until it is too late for her to interfere.'[24]

The situation did not improve. Ronald grew increasingly tyrannical, paranoid and possessive. In a letter written to Joy Finzi on May 1970, he launched another threatening attack. 'I am not at all certain that you will have grasped the fact yesterday that there will not be another book of Ivor's within the copyright. That is definite and final.'[25] Not only was he determined to maintain his iron grip on Ivor's work, he seemed bent on alienating anyone who neglected to contact him first about Ivor's music or poetry. He even chastized the secretary of the Harrogate Festival, telling him that 'it is more decent behaviour to consult an administrator first. Not ignore him.' 'It is precisely this way of doing things that has completely alienated me from the whole business and this applies all the way round', he railed at Mrs Finzi.[26] What Ronald failed to comprehend was that he had made himself inaccessible. His mean-spirited attitude and unpredictability scared people off and forced them to work for Ivor through other routes, namely Joy Finzi.

Matters hung in an uncertain limbo until Ronald Gurney died eight months later on 21 January 1971, aged seventy-seven. He had survived Ivor by thirty-four years. Throughout those years he was unable to surrender the resentment he had harboured towards his older brother since childhood. With Ronald no longer in control of Ivor's work, the possibilities for its publication and performance improved.

Edmund Blunden, Leonard Clark and Chatto & Windus were able to go ahead with the publication of *Poems of Ivor Gurney, 1890–1937*, which appeared in 1973. The holders of the copyright for Ivor's poems were listed as Winifred Gurney, Dorothy Hayward (his younger sister) and Ethel Gurney.

Since 1973 Gurney's reputation has steadily grown as more scholars, writers, performers and the general public have discovered both his poetry and music. In 1976 Dr Charles W. Moore, an American musician, wrote the first extended biographical study of Gurney titled *Maker and Lover of Beauty: Ivor Gurney Poet and Songwriter*. It was based on his 1967 master's degree thesis at the University of Indiana, *The Solo Vocal Works of Ivor Gurney (1890–1937)*. The slim volume was published by Triad Press. In his introduction to the book, Herbert Howells praised Dr Moore's work for its 'fine directness and sober fact' and singled it out 'as one of the earliest signs of growing realisation of Gurney's claim upon our instructed attention and powers of assessment'. He predicted Dr Moore's work would have 'many successors.'[27] Prior to writing about Gurney, Dr Moore had made an important contribution to the cataloguing of Ivor's songs.

While in Gloucester he met with Ronald Gurney to discuss his work on Ivor. Ronald was then about seventy years old. He stood about 5 feet 10 inches tall and was 'quite lithe looking', with a full head of steel-grey hair. He looked 'much like Ivor in structure and had a light baritone voice that was just beginning to show signs of his age', Dr Moore recalled.[28] Upon his arrival, he was greeted by Ethel Gurney, 'a pleasant matronly lady'. The visit, including tea, a performance on guitar by his step-grandson, David, and cordial conversation, lasted four hours. Dr Moore said he encountered none of the difficulties experienced by others. When he left, he had secured Ronald's permission to microfilm whatever material he needed for his dissertation.

Ivor Gurney's upward climb had begun in earnest. In 1977 publisher John Bishop and musicologist Lewis Foreman produced the first major recording of Gurney's music and poetry for Pearl Records. This old vinyl LP remains the only recording to fuse both of Ivor's arts and features ten of his poems recited by Leonard Clark and eighteen of his songs sung by baritone Christopher Keyte and tenor David Johnston. Composer and writer Michael Hurd's critically acclaimed 1978 biography, *The Ordeal of Ivor Gurney*, brought the story of the man and his work to wider audiences and sparked a reassessment of his achievement that continues today. The following year, Oxford University Press published *Ivor Gurney: A Fifth Volume of Ten Songs* edited by Hurd. P. J. Kavanagh's *Collected Poems of Ivor Gurney* (1982 and republished in 2004) marked another milestone in Gurney scholarship, while Dr R. K. R. Thornton's volumes of Gurney's *War Letters* (1983) and *Collected Letters* (1991) brought readers into personal contact with Gurney's life, thoughts and work through his own words. Interest in Gurney accelerated after the 1990 centenary celebration of his birth held in his native city of Gloucester, the formation of the Ivor Gurney Society in 1995 (http://www.ivorgurney.org.uk) and the official Ivor Gurney website in 1998 (ivorgurney.net).

Ivor Gurney has journeyed a long way since the dark days of 1937 when he was dying in a London asylum and believed that he had been forgotten by the world outside. His place in music and literature is now secure. The tragedy is that he did not live to see it, nor did Marion Scott.

After her death in 1953, Scott's own character, achievements and genius were praised in tributes by her friends and colleagues. Obituaries of the influential and highly regarded Scott appeared in all the major British newspapers. *The Times* singled out her musicology as 'revealing a sensitive, discerning and inquiring mind (loath to accept anything at secondhand) ...'[29] In listing her achievements, the anonymous writer continued:

> The formation of the Society of Women Musicians in 1911, and, in 1930, the admission of women instrumentalists into the newly formed BBC Symphony Orchestra both testify to her tactful and quietly gracious yet at the same time resolute determination.[30]

Writing in *Music and Letters*, Kathleen Richards Dale recalled that 'in all the years I had known her she had habitually seemed a being apart, detached from the littleness of everyday life and utterly dedicated to her work'. But on rereading her 'precious' collection of Marion's letters, Dale realized that her friend expressed her deepest feelings and her inmost thoughts more readily by means of her pen than she did with the spoken word. In conversation she could sometimes be disconcertingly monosyllabic or very slow to warm to her subject. When asked for an opinion she would apparently weigh all the pros and cons leisurely in silence before committing herself to considering a reply. But when it came to putting pen to paper her thoughts seemed to flow with the greatest ease.[31]

Marion was a contemplative woman, one given to looking inward in order to see the larger significance of the multitude of events around her, both personal and professional. Silence was her refuge, her retreat, her inner sanctum from which she drew strength, inspiration, serenity and clarity of thought and vision. To Herbert Howells, who had known her for forty years, she was 'tranquil, cool-minded [and] ... ageless', a self-reliant woman whose 'sheer grit and will-power compensated for the lack of physical strength'. In his memorial to her, Howells observed

> Peace in her was the product of a watchful but freely-imposed discipline, and was enriched by a quick readiness to fight (but, again, under discipline) for any cause or person needing and deserving militant support ... she could be stubborn in defence of a line of conduct, a practical scheme, a policy, whenever these seemed good in her sight or satisfied an acute intelligence.[32]

On 25 and 26 June 1954 the Society of Women Musicians paid tribute to Marion Scott at a special Composers' Conference held in her honour at the Royal College of Music. The two-day event featured talks by her friends Kathleen Dale, Katharine Eggar, Hester Stansfeld Prior and Rosemary Hughes, who recalled her life and work. They were joined by Gerald Finzi, who discussed Marion as the 'Guardian of Genius (Ivor Gurney's Work)'. After all his years of frustration and seeming annoyance with Marion, Finzi came to recognize her as a 'formidable character ... [whose] energy seems hardly consistent with her slightness and fragility but one soon learned that beneath this exterior lay an iron will equal to a great heart'.[33] The Society of Women Musicians' tribute included two concerts, one featuring Haydn's String Quartet op. 54, no. 2 in C and a reading of Marion's poem 'A Song of Silence', and the second featuring Marion's song 'To Sleep' on a programme that included works by Elizabeth Maconchy, Madeline Dring, Elizabeth Poston and Margaret Hubicki, among others.

Then silence. Marion Scott became a footnote in twentieth-century music history where once she had been an eminent voice. Only her 1934 biography of Beethoven and her relationship with Ivor Gurney kept her name alive. She never pursued her own composition seriously after World War I. Her music manuscripts sit unheard in five large boxes at the Royal College of Music. She wrote little poetry after the war. Her poetic legacy rests on her one small, obscure volume, *Violin Verses*, published in 1905 and now a rare collector's item. She never completed her book on Haydn. She had only managed to draft three chapters before her death.

Music criticism, her primary occupation, is by its nature ephemeral. What she wrote one day became yesterday's news overnight. Yet when taken as a whole, this body of her work forms a singular history of British music spanning forty years, from about 1910 to about 1950. She was a prolific critic, at times attending five or more concerts a week and writing about them in addition to writing feature articles for a variety of newspapers and journals. She kept typed carbon copies of much of her writing, some of it now bound into six volumes housed at the RCM. She also employed a clipping service to scan numerous publications for articles by her or that mentioned her. Despite her excellent record keeping, it is impossible to account for every piece she published as they number well over a thousand.[34]

Marion Scott's legacy is intangible but nonetheless real and enduring. Like her pioneering American ancestors she blazed new paths for others to follow. The opportunities for women were few when Marion was young, a reality she was quick to grasp. Despite the odds against them, Marion and her contemporaries were determined to study music and aspired to roles more significant than teachers and composers of sentimental songs. Marion Scott led the way in breaking down the barriers that held women back.

When Marion entered the RCM in 1896, she was one of some 270 women enrolled in the college. At a time when it was rare for a woman to study composition, she became one of Charles Stanford's first female pupils. After college, Marion began opening doors for women by setting an example. A natural leader, she was not afraid to explore the unknown or to take risks. She first opened opportunities for women when she set out on her own to become a free-lance teacher and lecturer on the technical aspects of music, ranging from composition and theory to harmony and orchestration. In college she had been an early experimenter in composing music for voice and string quartet.

Later she broke tradition when she formed and led the Marion Scott String Quartet, composed of an equal number of men and woman. She became an early champion of contemporary British music and introduced it to new audiences via her string quartet and through other venues that she arranged and produced. By 1911 Scott was an authority on chamber music and a regular contributor to the Chamber Music Supplement of W. W. Cobbett's *The Music Student*. She had already taken the first steps toward opening the field of musicology to women with her 'cultured research' into her various lecture topics such as 'Folk Songs of Four Races – England, Scotland, Wales and Ireland', 'English Music: The Inheritance of the Past', and 'The Evolution of English Music'.[35] Each of these lectures reveals the depth and range of her intellect and her ability to work like an archaeologist, carefully and methodically peeling back layers of information to discover the source of an idea or to evolve her own original theories.

While Marion Scott had been earning part of her income as a writer since 1910, music criticism became her primary occupation from 1919 on. She was the first woman to write music criticism for an international daily newspaper, the *Christian Science Monitor*. In doing so, she opened yet another door for women. She was the first, and only, woman to write a biography of Beethoven. Her work on Haydn, particularly his chamber music, won her international acclaim.

Few people today realize how influential and powerful Marion Scott was during her lifetime. A significant force, she reshaped women's roles in classical music, promoted and championed the work of several generations of British composers and musicians, and brought men and women together for the common good of all in music. 'We may think of her as our tuning-fork, and test our pitch by hers', declared Katharine Eggar in summing up Marion Scott's life and contributions.[36]

After her death, Marion Scott's contributions as a music critic, scholar, writer, champion of twentieth-century music and authority on Haydn were eventually forgotten. Her final achievement, her catalogue of Haydn's music, appeared posthumously in the 1954 *Grove's Dictionary of Music and Musicians.*

Despite all of her achievements that educated, enlightened and informed others and provided opportunities for them, Marion Scott's name has lived most notably until now through her preservation of Ivor Gurney's creative legacy. For whatever reason – love, spiritual affinity – he fed her flame and his flame burned through her. Each sparked the other's genius and stoked it. The two formed an unlikely partnership that illuminated and enriched the musical and literary worlds in which they moved. Their names, as their lives, will be forever linked in the annals of history.

TO M.M.S.

O, if my wishes were my power,
You should be praised as were most fit,
Whose kindness cannot help but flower.

But since the fates have ordered it
Otherwise, then ere the hour
Of darkness deaden all my wit

I'll write: how all my art was poor,
My mind too thought-packed to acquit
My debt ... And only, "Thanks once more."

– Ivor Gurney's dedication of *War's Embers* to Marion Scott [37]

NOTES

1 At the time of her death, Marion Scott's wealth was a considerable £30,401 2s. 11d. That amount would be worth approximately £1.5 million today. She still possessed the Guadagnini violin her father had purchased for her when she was a teenager. She passed it to Audrey, who also received a Russian frosted silver service from St Petersburg and a watch once owned by Marie Antoinette. Marion gave her Haydn collection, including her editions of his works and a breast pin that belonged to him, to the Fitzwilliam Museum at Cambridge and bequeathed her music manuscripts and literary works to the RCM. She made a number of monetary bequests to friends, including £50 each to Herbert Howells and Kathleen Dale.

2 Audrey Priestman to GF, 12 January 1954, GA.

3 Ralph Vaughan Williams undoubtedly considered his contributions to Gurney's care as charity and did not feel as compelled as Marion Scott to pursue the matter once Gurney had died.

4 GF to RG, 27 February 1954, GA.

5 HH to RG, 4 November 1954, GA.

6 Ibid.

7 GF to Edmund Blunden, 2 August 1955, GA. In this letter Finzi repeated what Vaughan Williams had told him about Ronald.

8 Ibid.

9 GF to Edmund Blunden, 2 August 1955, GA.

10 RG to JF, 13 March 1959, GA. Joy Finzi (1907–91) was born Joy Black in Hampsted, the daughter of Ernest Black, a prosperous businessman, and Amy Whitehorn. Educated at Moira House in Eastbourne, where the family settled after her father's retirement, Joy was a multi-talented woman who was an artist, sculptor, poet and violinist. She married Gerald Finzi in 1933 and became the administrative force behind the organization of the Newbury String Players, founded by Gerald in 1940. She was one of the second violins. Both Gerald and Joy championed young musicians and composers, including Julian Bream and Kenneth Leighton, by providing them with engagements and performances of their compositions. In addition to preserving Gurney's work, the Finzis also played important roles in the preservation and cataloguing of the music of Sir Hubert Parry. After Finzi's death in 1956, Joy, along with her sons Christopher and Nigel, founded the Finzi Trust together with Howard Ferguson. Under the Trust's auspices most of Gerald's music was recorded, first with Lyrita and later by Hyperion, Chandos and EMI. A collection of Joy Finzi's portraits was published as *In That Place* (Marlborough: Libanus Press, 1987). Her portrait of Vaughan Williams is in the collection of the National Portrait Gallery in London. Joy wrote poetry and published two collections: *A Point of Departure*, with engravings by Richard Shirley Smith (Cambridge: Golden Head Press, 1967), and *Twelve Months of the Year*, with engravings by Simon Brett (Marlborough: Libanus Press, 1981).

11 RG to JF, 3 December 1959, GA.

12 Chatto & Windus to RG, 21 March 1967, GA. Although born in Guernsey, Leonard Clark (1905–81) was reared in the Forest of Dean in Gurney's Gloucestershire. Will Harvey encouraged his early interest in poetry. Trained as a teacher, Clark became an Inspector of Schools. In addition to his advocacy for poetry, he served as editor of *Longman's Poetry Library* and of *Chatto Poets for the Young*. He wrote verse, autobiography and edited a number of anthologies. Clark became one of Ivor Gurney's earliest and most committed champions.

13 RG to JF, 12 May 1967, GA.

14 Ibid.

15 Ibid.

16 WG to DBR, 25 May 1951, GA.

17 WG to JF, undated, GA.

18 Ibid.

19 Ibid.

20 Ibid.

21 Ibid.

22 Ibid.

23 Ibid.

24 Ibid.

25 RG to JF, 18 May 1970, GA.

26 Ibid.

27 HH, Introduction, Charles W. Moore, *Maker and Lover of Beauty: Ivor Gurney, Poet and Songwriter* (Rickmansworth: Triad Press, 1976).

28 Dr Charles W. Moore, conversation with the author 2005.

29 Unsigned, 'Miss Marion Scott', *The Times*, December 1953.

30 Ibid.

31 KD, 'Memories of Marion Scott', *Music and Letters*, vol. 35, no. 3 (July 1954), pp. 237–8.

32 HH, 'Marion Margaret Scott, 1877–1953', *Music and Letters*, vol. 35, no. 2 (April 1954), p. 134.

33 GF, 'Guardian of Genius (Ivor Gurney's Work)', in Society of Women Musicians, *Commemoration of Marion Scott* (programme book, 25–6 June 1954), p. 10.

34 For a selection of Marion Scott's writing, see Appendix 4. To read a selection of her reviews and articles, see http://www.musicweb-international.com/Scott/index.htm.

35 Anonymous article, 'Folk Songs of the Four Races', *The Queen*, 18 March 1911.

36 KE, 'Marion Scott as Founder of the Society of Women Musicians, in Society of Women Musicians, *Commemoration of Marion Scott* (programme book, 25–6 June 1954).

37 IG, dedication to Marion Scott, *War's Embers*, 1919.

Ivor Gurney's Published Music

Songs

Five Elizabethan Songs for Voice and Piano
(To Emily Hunt)
London: Boosey & Hawkes, 1920 [Note: Winthrop Rogers published individual editions of each song.]

> Orpheus (Shakespeare), Tears (John Fletcher), Under the Greenwood Tree (Shakespeare), Sleep (John Fletcher), Spring (Thomas Nashe)

Ludlow and Teme: Song-Cycle for Tenor Voice, String Quartet and Pianoforte
Words by A. E. Housman, Music by Ivor Gurney; Carnegie Collection of British Music *(To the memory of Margaret Hunt)*
London: Stainer & Bell, 1923

> When Smoke Stood up from Ludlow, Far in a Western Brookland, 'Tis Time, I Think, Ludlow Fair, On the Idle Hill of Summer, When I was One and Twenty, The Lent Lily

Lights Out
On poems by Edward Thomas *(To the 2/5th Gloucesters)*
London: Stainer & Bell, 1926

> The Penny Whistle, Scents, Bright Clouds, Lights Out, Will you Come?, The Trumpet

The Western Playland (and of Sorrow): A Song-Cycle for Baritone Voice, String Quartet and Pianoforte
Poems by A. E. Housman; Carnegie Collection of British Music
('To Hawthornden' [*Annie Nelson Drummond*])
London: Stainer & Bell, 1926

> Reveille, Loveliest of Trees, Golden Friends, Twice a Week, The Aspens, Is my Team Ploughing, The Far Country, March

A First Volume of Ten Songs
London: Oxford University Press, 1938

> The Singer (Edward Shanks), The Latmian Shepherd (Edward Shanks), Black Stitchel (Wilfrid Gibson), Down by the Salley Gardens (W. B. Yeats), All Night under the Moon (Wilfrid Gibson), Nine of the Clock ('John Doyle' [Robert Graves]), You are my Sky (J. C. Squire), Ha'nacker Mill (Hilaire Belloc), When Death to Either shall Come (Robert Bridges), Cathleen ni Houlihan (W. B. Yeats)

A Second Volume of Ten Songs
London: Oxford University Press, 1938

> The Scribe (Walter de la Mare), The Boat is Chafing (John Davidson), Bread and Cherries (Walter de la Mare), An Epitaph (Walter de la

Mare), Blaweary (Wilfrid Gibson), A Sword (Robin Flower), The Folly
of Being Comforted (W. B. Yeats), Hawk and Buckle ('John Doyle'
[Robert Graves]), Last Hours (John Freeman), and Epitaph in an Old
Mode (J. C. Squire)

A Third Volume of Ten Songs
London: Oxford University Press, 1952

Shepherd's Song (Ben Jonson), The Happy Tree (Gerald Gould),
The Cherry Trees (Edward Thomas), I shall ever be Maiden (Bliss
Carman), Ploughman Singing (John Clare), I Praise the Tender Flower
(Robert Bridges), Snow (Edward Thomas), Thou didst Delight mine
Eyes (Robert Bridges), The Ship (J. C. Squire), Goodnight to the
Meadow (Robert Graves)

A Fourth Volume of Ten Songs
Oxford, Oxford University Press, 1959

Even Such is Time (Walter Raleigh), Brown is my Love (Anon. 16th
century), Love Shakes my Soul (Bliss Carman), Most Holy Night
(Hilaire Belloc), To Violets (Robert Herrick), On the Downs (John
Masefield), A Piper (Seumas O'Sullivan), A Cradle Song (W. B. Yeats),
The Fiddler of Dooney (W. B. Yeats), In Flanders (F. W. Harvey)

A Fifth Volume of Ten Songs
Edited by Michael Hurd
London: Oxford University Press, 1979

By a Bierside (John Masefield), Desire in Spring (Francis Ledwidge),
Severn Meadows (Ivor Gurney), Song of Ciabhan (The Isle of Peace)
(Ethna Carbery), The Apple Orchard (Bliss Carman), The Cloths
of Heaven (W. B. Yeats), The Fields are Full (Edward Shanks), The
Night of Trafalgar (Thomas Hardy), The Twa Corbies (Anon. ballad),
Walking Song (F. W. Harvey)

Ludlow and Teme: A Song-Cycle to Poems of A. E. Housman for Tenor
and Piano (To the memory of Margaret Hunt); Introduction by Michael
Pilkington
London: Stainer & Bell, 1982

When Smoke Stood up from Ludlow, Far in a Western Brookland,
'Tis Time, I Think, Ludlow Fair, On the Idle Hill of Summer, When I
was One and Twenty, The Lent Lily

The Western Playland (and of Sorrow): A Song-Cycle to Poems of A. E.
Housman by Ivor Gurney for Baritone and Piano
(To Hawthornden [Annie Nelson Drummond]); Introduction by Michael
Pilkington
London: Stainer & Bell, 1982

Reveille, Loveliest of Trees, Golden Friends, Twice a Week,
The Aspens, Is my Team Ploughing, The Far Country, March

The Singer's Collection
  For High Voice and Piano; Edited by Alan Ridout; 2 volumes
  Bury St Edmunds, K. Mayhew, 1992

  Volume 1, Nine of the Clock ('John Doyle' [pseudonym for Robert Graves]), Hawk and Buckle ('John Doyle' [Robert Graves])

  Volume 2, Down by the Salley Gardens (W. B. Yeats), Bread and Cherries (Walter de la Mare)

20 Favourite Songs: Voice & Piano
  Oxford: Oxford University Press, 1997

  All Night under the Moon (W. W. Gibson), The Apple Orchard (Bliss Carman), Black Stitchel (Wilfrid Gibson), Bread and Cherries (Walter de la Mare), Brown is my Love (Anon., 16th century), The Cloths of Heaven (W. B. Yeats), Desire in Spring (Francis Ledwidge), Down by the Salley Gardens (W. B. Yeats), An Epitaph (Walter de la Mare), Even Such is Time (Walter Raleigh), The Fields are Full (Edward Shanks), I Praise the Tender Flower (Robert Bridges), Most Holy Night (Hilaire Belloc), A Piper (Seumas O'Sullivan), The Scribe (Walter de la Mare), Severn Meadows (Ivor Gurney), The Singer (Edward Shanks), Snow (Edward Thomas), To Violets (Robert Herrick), Walking Song (Cranham Woods, F. W. Harvey)

Eleven Gurney Songs
  Introduced by Michael Hurd
  London: Thames Publishing, 1998 (distributed by William Elkin Music Services, Station Road Industrial Estate, Salhouse, Norwich, nr13 6ns, United Kingdom)

  On your Midnight Pallet (A. E. Housman), Cock-Crow (Edward Thomas), Sowing (Edward Thomas), Since thou, O Fondest and Truest (Robert Bridges), Come, O Come my Life's Delight (Thomas Campion), The Bonnie Earl of Murray (Scots ballad), The County Mayo (Raftery, trans. James Stephens), West Sussex Drinking Song (Hilaire Belloc), Captain Stratton's Fancy (John Masefield), Edward, Edward (from Percy's *Reliques* 1765), Star-Talk (Robert Graves)

Seven Sappho Songs, for Soprano and Piano
  Sappho, poems translated by Bliss Carman; Edited and Introduced by Richard Carder, with a note on the poet by Michael Hurd
  London: Thames Publishing, 2000 (distributed by William Elkin Music Services, Station Road Industrial Estate, Salhouse, Norwich nr13 6ns, United Kingdom)

  Soft was the Wind, I shall be Ever Maiden, The Apple Orchard, Hesperus, Love Shakes my Soul, The Quiet Mist, Lonely Night

Individual Songs

The Bonnie Earl of Murray (Scots ballad) *(To Mrs Waterhouse)* (London: Winthrop Rogers, 1921)

Captain Stratton's Fancy (John Masefield) *(To F. W. Harvey, singer of this song in many prison camps)* (London: Stainer & Bell, 1920)

Carol of the Skiddaw Yowes (Edmund Casson) *(To J. W. Haines)* (London: Boosey & Hawkes, 1920)

Come, O Come my Life's Delight (Thomas Campion) *(To Frederick Saxty)* (London: Boosey & Hawkes, 1922)

Desire in Spring (Francis Ledwidge) (London: Oxford University Press, 1928) [first published in *The Chapbook II*, 1920]

The County Mayo (Raftery, trans. James Stephens) *(To Mrs [Margaret] Taylor)* (London: Winthrop Rogers, 1921)

Edward, Edward (Anon. ballad, Percy's *Reliques of English Poetry*) *(To A. H. Cheesman)* (London: Stainer & Bell, 1922)

The Fields are Full (Edward Shanks) (London: Oxford University Press, 1928)

I will Go with my Father A-Ploughing (Joseph Campbell) *(To Miss Marion Scott)* (London: Boosey & Hawkes, 1921)

Severn Meadows (Ivor Gurney) *(Written for Miss Dorothy Dawe [Dorothy Howells])* (London: Oxford University Press, 1928)

Since thou, O Fondest and Truest (Robert Bridges) *(To Robert Bridges)* (London: Boosey & Hawkes, 1921)

Sowing (Edward Thomas) *(To H. N. Howells)* (London: Stainer & Bell, 1925)

Star-Talk (Robert Graves) (London: Stainer & Bell, 1927)

The Twa Corbies: A Border Ballad *(To Sir Hubert Parry)* (London: Oxford University Press, 1928) [first published in *Music and Letters*, vol. 1, no. 2 (March 1920), pp. 171–5]

Walking Song (F. W. Harvey) (London: Oxford University Press 1928)

West Sussex Drinking Song (Hilaire Belloc) *(To F. W. Harvey, comrade to many in Captivity)* (London: Chappell, 1921)

Choral

The Trumpet, a setting of the poem by Edward Thomas for SATB [with orchestra], vocal score, ed. Philip Lancaster (Lichfield: Chosen Press, 2008)

Instrumental

Preludes and Nocturnes for solo Piano, ed. Jennifer Partridge (London: Thames Publishing, 2004)

Two Pieces for Violin & Piano (London: Oxford University Press, 1940)

    1. The Apple Orchard; 2. Scherzo

Five Western Watercolours for Piano (London: Oxford University Press, 1923)

Five Preludes for Piano (London: Winthrop Rogers, 1921)

    Prelude in F sharp major (dedicated to Sir Charles Stanford), Prelude in A minor (dedicated to Gerald James), Prelude in D flat (dedicated to Mrs Chapman), Prelude in F sharp (dedicated to Sydney Shimmin), Prelude in D (dedicated to 'Winnie' – Winifred Chapman)

Orchestral

War Elegy for Orchestra, Full Score, ed. Philip Lancaster and Ian Venables (Lichfield: Chosen Press, 2008).

Ivor Gurney's Published Writings

Poetry Collections published in Gurney's lifetime

Severn and Somme (London: Sidgwick & Jackson, 1917)

War's Embers and Other Verses (London: Sidgwick & Jackson, 1919)

Collections planned by Gurney but not published during his life

Ivor Gurney: Best Poems and The Book of Five Makings, ed. R. K. R. Thornton and George Walter (Ashington: MidNAG; Manchester: Carcanet, 1995)

Ivor Gurney: 80 Poems or So, ed. George Walter and R. K. R. Thornton (Ashington: MidNAG; Manchester: Carcanet, 1997)

Ivor Gurney: Rewards of Wonder: Poems of Cotswold, France, London, ed. George Walter (Ashington: MidNAG; Manchester: Carcanet, 2000)

Other Editions and Collections

Poems by Ivor Gurney: Principally selected from unpublished manuscripts, with a memoir by Edmund Blunden (London: Hutchinson, 1954)

Poems of Ivor Gurney, 1890–1937, with an Introduction by Edmund Blunden and a Bibliographical Note by Leonard Clark (London: Chatto & Windus, 1973)

Collected Poems of Ivor Gurney, chosen, edited and with an Introduction by P. J. Kavanagh (Oxford: Oxford University Press, 1982; reprinted, Manchester, Fyfield Books/Carcanet, 2004)

Ivor Gurney: Severn and Somme and War's Embers, Critical Edition, ed. R. K. R. Thornton (Ashington: MidNAG; Manchester: Carcanet, 1987)

Ivor Gurney: Selected Poems, selected and introduced by P. J. Kavanagh (Oxford: Oxford University Press, 1990)

Everyman's Poetry: Ivor Gurney, ed. George Walter (London: Everyman, 1996)

Ivor Gurney: Selected Poems, selected and introduced by P. J. Kavanagh (Oxford: Oxford University Press, 1997)

Correspondence

Stars in a Dark Night: The Letters of Ivor Gurney to the Chapman Family, ed. Anthony Boden with a foreword by Michael Hurd (Gloucester: Alan Sutton, 1986; revised and updated, 2004)

Ivor Gurney: Collected Letters, ed. R. K. R. Thornton (Ashington: MidNAG; Manchester: Carcanet, 1991)

War Letters: A Selection, ed. R. K. R. Thornton (Ashington: MidNAG; Manchester: Carcanet, 1983)

Essays

Ivor Gurney, 'Charles Villiers Stanford: By Some of His Pupils', *Music and Letters* 5 (1924), pp. 193–207

Ivor Gurney, 'Cotswold Plays, Six Plays by Florence Henrietta Darwin', Review, *The Times Literary Supplement*, 23 March 1922

Ivor Gurney, 'The Springs of Music', *Musical Quarterly*, vol. 8, no. 3 (July 1922), pp. 319–22

Anthologies: A Select List

Gurney's poetry appears in a number of anthologies, including the following:

The Muse in Arms: A Collection of War Poems, for the most part written in the field of action, by Seamen, Soldiers, and Flying men who are serving, or have served in the Great War, edited with an introduction by E. B. Osborn (London: John Murray, 1917): 'Strange Service', p. 14; 'To the Poet Before Battle', p. 30; 'To Certain Comrades', p. 130, and 'Aftermath', p. 152

Selections from Modern Poets, made by J. C. Squire (London: Martin Secker, 1921): 'To the Poet before Battle' and 'Song of Pain and Beauty', pp. 249–50

Second Selections from Modern Poets, Made by J. C. Squire (London: Martin Secker, 1924): 'Thoughts of New England', 'Smudgy Dawn', and 'Dawn', pp. 215–22

Georgian Poetry, Selected and introduced by James Reeves (Harmondsworth, Penguin Books, 1962): 'Townshend' and 'Robecq Again', pp. 113–14

Men Who March Away: Poems of the First World War, edited with an introduction by I. M. Parsons (London: Chatto & Windus, 1965): 'The Silent One', p. 60; 'The Bohemians', p. 76, and 'To His Love', p. 153

Poetry of the First World War, ed. Maurice Hussey (London: Longmans, Green & Co., 1967): 'Dirge for Two Striplings', 'Ypres', 'Picture of Two Veterans', and 'When I am Covered', pp. 154–7

A Certain World: A Commonplace Book, W. H. Auden (London: Faber & Faber, 1971): 'The High Hills', p. 105; 'Kilns', p. 209, and 'Larches', p. 218

The Faber Book of Poems and Places, edited with an introduction by Geoffrey Grigson (London: Faber & Faber, 1980), 'Dawns I Have Seen' and 'Elver Fishermen on the Severn: Two Gloucestershire Fragments', pp. 125–7

The following anthologies include Gurney's poems but do not feature any that were previously uncollected:

Poetry of the Great War: An Anthology, ed. Dominic Hibberd and John Onions (London: Macmillan, 1986)

The War Poets: The Lives and Writings of the 1914–1918 War Poets, Robert Giddings (London: Bloomsbury, 1988)

Lads: Love Poetry of the Trenches, ed. Martin Taylor (London: Constable, 1989)

Forest and Vale and High Blue Hill: Poems of Gloucestershire, the Cotswolds and Beyond, selected by Johnny Coppin (Moreton-in-Marsh: Windrush Press, 1991)

The Norton Anthology of English Literature, 6th edition, vol. 2 (New York: W. W. Norton & Co., 1993)

The Wordsworth Book of First World War Poetry, selected with an introduction and bibliography, by Marcus Clapham (Ware: Wordsworth Editions, 1995)

The Winter of the World: Poems of the First World War, ed. Dominic Hibberd and John Onions (London: Constable & Robinson, 2007)

Ivor Gurney – A Select Discography

Vocal Music

Ludlow and Teme, Andrew Kennedy, baritone, Simon Phillips, piano, Dante
Quartet; Signum 112 (2008)

> [also features Vaughan Williams, *On Wenlock Edge*]

Love's Voice – British Songs, Nathan Vale, tenor, Paul Plummer, piano; SOMM
SOMM063 (2007)

> On Wenlock Edge, Bread and Cherries, Down by the Salley Gardens,
> Hawk and Buckle [also features Venables, Ireland, Finzi]

Ludlow and Teme, James Gilchrist, tenor, Anna Tilbrook, piano, Fitzwilliam
String Quartet; Linn 296 (2007)

> [also features Vaughan Williams, Bliss, Warlock]

Severn and Somme, Roderick Williams, baritone, Susie Allan, piano; SOMM
SOMM057 (2006)

> On your Midnight Pallet, Dearest, when I am Dead, Edward, Edward,
> Dreams of the Sea, In Flanders, Severn Meadows, Dinny Hill, Captain
> Stratton's Fancy, Red Roses, Song of Silence, The White Cascade,
> The Folly of being Comforted, Desire in Spring, Walking Song, Lights
> Out, Black Stitchel, Western Sailors [also features Howells, Sanders,
> Wilson, Venables]

*War's Embers, A legacy of songs by composers who perished or suffered in World
War I*, Michael George, bass, Martyn Hill, tenor, Stephen Varcoe, baritone,
Clifford Benson, piano; Helios/Hyperion CDH55237 (2006; originally released
1988)

> The Twa Corbies, Black Stitchel, Blaweary, The Fiddler of Dooney,
> Goodnight to the Meadow, The Boat is Chafing, Cathleen ni Houlihan,
> Edward, Edward, The Night of Trafalgar, Thou Didst Delight my
> Eyes, To Violets, Last Hours [The 2006 reissue omits Orpheus, Tears,
> Under the Greenwood Tree, Sleep and Spring, which were on the
> original release.]

Songs by Finzi and his Friends, Stephen Roberts, baritone, Ian Partridge, tenor,
Clifford Benson, piano; Hyperion A66015 (reissued on CD 2003; originally
released 1981)

> Sleep, Down by the Salley Gardens, and Hawk and Buckle [also
> features Finzi, Milford, Farrar, and Gill]

Singers to Remember, 'The Comely Mezzo' Nancy Evans, Dutton CDBP9723 (2002;
reissue of Evans' 1938 Decca recordings)

> The Scribe, Nine of the Clock, All Night under the Moon, Blaweary,
> You are my Sky, The Latmian Shepherd

Severn Meadows, Paul Agnew, tenor, Julius Drake, piano; Hyperion 67243 (2001)

> Epitaph in Old Mode, You are my Sky, All Night under the Moon,

The Folly of Being Comforted, By a Bierside, Severn Meadows,
In Flanders, Even Such is time, Ha'nacker Mill, Bread and Cherries,
Most Holy Night, Desire in Spring, Nine of the Clock, A Cradle
Song, Orpheus, Tears, Under the Greenwood Tree, Sleep, Spring,
An Epitaph, The Fields are Full, Down by the Salley Gardens, The
Cloths of Heaven, The Singer, I will Go with my Father A-Ploughing

A Century of English Song, Volume 3, Sarah Leonard, soprano, Jonathan Veira,
baritone, Malcom Martineau, piano; SOMM SOMM224 (2001)

Snow, I shall be Ever Maiden, I will Go with my Father A-Ploughing,
A Cradle Song, Ploughman Singing, When Death to Either shall Come,
On the Downs, Sowing [also features Quilter and Warlock]

English Orchestral Songs, Christopher Maltman, baritone, BBC Scottish
Symphony Orchestra cond. Martyn Brabbins; Hyperion 67065 (1999)

In Flanders, By a Bierside, and from Five Elizabethan Songs: Under
the Greenwood Tree, Orpheus, Sleep, Spring [also features Parry,
Stanford and Finzi]

The English Songbook, Ian Bostridge, tenor, Julius Drake, piano; EMI Classics,
56830 (1999)

Sleep, I will Go with My Father A-Ploughing [also features traditional
songs, and songs by Vaughan Williams, Stanford, Quilter, Finzi,
Dunhill, Denis Browne, Somervell, Grainger, Parry, Delius, Warlock,
and Britten]

Songs from A. E. Housman's A Shropshire Lad, Graham Trew, baritone, Roger
Vignoles, piano, Coull String Quartet; Meridian CDE84185 (1989, 1997, and
1998)

Western Playland (including Reveille, Loveliest of Trees, Golden
Friends, Twice a Week, The Aspens, Is my Team Ploughing, The Far
Country, March) [also features Somervell, Butterworth, Moeran, and
Peel]

An Anthology of English Song, Janet Baker, contralto, Martin Isepp, piano; Saga
Classics EC 3340-2 (1996)

Sleep, I will Go with my Father A-Ploughing [also features Dunhill,
Vaughan Williams, Ireland, Head, Gibbs, Warlock, Howells, and Finzi]

Songs of Travel, Anthony Rolfe Johnson, tenor, David Willison, piano; IMP
Classics PCD 1065 (1993)

Down by the Salley Gardens, An Epitaph, Desire in Spring, Black
Stitchel [also features Butterworth, Ireland, Vaughan Williams and
Warlock]

A Shropshire Lad: Three Song Cycles to Poems by A. E. Housman, Adrian
Thompson, tenor, Stephen Varcoe, baritone, Iain Burnside, piano, Delmé
String Quartet; Hyperion CDA66385 (1990)

The Western Playland and *Ludlow and Teme* [also features Vaughan
Williams]

When I was One-and-Twenty: Butterworth & Gurney Songs, Benjamin Luxon,
baritone, David Willison, piano; Chandos CHAN8831 (1990)

Carol of the Skiddaw Yowes, The Apple Orchard, The Fields are

Full, The Twa Corbies, Severn Meadows, Desire in Spring, Ha'nacker
Mill, Down by the Salley Gardens, The Scribe, Hawk and Buckle On
the Downs, The Fiddler of Dooney, In Flanders, The Folly of Being
Comforted, I Praise the Tender Flower, Black Stitchel, An Epitaph,
By a Bierside, Cranham Woods, Sleep [also features Butterworth]

English Songs: Frederick Delius and Ivor Gurney, Ian Partridge, tenor, Jennifer
Partridge, piano; Etcetera KTC1063 (1989)

The Fields are Full, Severn Meadows, Desire in Spring, The Singer,
An Epitaph, The Folly of Being Comforted, Bread and Cherries, All
Night under the Moon, Down by the Salley Gardens, Snow, The
Cloths of Heaven, Brown is my Love [Also features Delius]

Orchestral and Instrumental Music

The Spirit of England, BBC Symphony Orchestra and Chorus, cond. David
Lloyd-Jones; Dutton Epoch CDLX7172

War Elegy [also features Elgar, Kelly, Parry, Elkington]

Trails of Creativity – Music From Between the Wars, 1918–1938, David Frühwirth,
violin, Henri Sigfridsson, piano; Avie AV0009 (2003)

Apple Orchard, Scherzo

Piano Music by Ivor Gurney and Howard Ferguson, Mark Bebbington, piano,
SOMM SOMM038 (2004)

Despair, Sehnsucht, Song of the Summer Woods, The Sea, Nocturne
in B, Nocturne in A flat, Preludes nos. 1–9

Poetry

David Goodland Reads the Poetry of Ivor Gurney, David Goodland, reader,
David Beames, narrator; Bright Tracks Production BT2 (1998; reissued on CD
2007)

70 poems presented in six parts: Severn Meadows, London Dawns,
A Bloody Mess, Strange Hells, Roped for the Fair, Bright Tracks

Songs on Lonely Roads: The Story of Ivor Gurney, performed by David Goodland
as Ivor Gurney, Johnny Coppin, and John Boswall, narrator; Gloucestershire:
Red Sky Records RSKC 110 (1990)

A musical drama of Gurney's life, including an adaptation of Walking
Song (Cranham Woods), a unique rendition of Captain Stratton's
Fancy, and songs by Coppin set to Gurney's poems: The Songs I Had,
After-glow, Fisherman of Newnham, Maismore, Under Robinswood,
Strange Service, Contrasts, Ballad of Three Spectres, Songs on Lonely
Roads, War Poet, The High Hills

Severn and Somme: Songs and Poems by Ivor Gurney, David Johnston, tenor,
Daphne Ibbott, piano, Christopher Keyte, baritone, Geoffrey Pratley, piano,
Leonard Clark, reader (programme notes by Leonard Clark); Pearl SHE 543
(1977).

You are my Sky, Black Stitchel, Epitaph in Old Mode, Hawk and
Buckle, Sleep, Severn Meadows, The Scribe, The Latmian Shepherd,
To Violets, Desire in Spring, Snow, In Flanders, Lights Out – The

Penny Whistle, Scents, Bright Clouds, Lights Out, Will you Come?
The Trumpet. Poems: Up There, February Dawn, Strange Service,
The Motets of William Byrd, Schubert, The Silent One, De Profundis,
Bach and the Sentry, I Would Not Rest, The Songs I Had.

Marion Scott's Writings – A Select List

This select list of Marion Scott's writings, organized chronologically, represents only a small fraction of the articles, essays, criticism and lectures that she wrote during a career that spanned more than forty years from 1909 until shortly before her death in 1953. It features examples of her writing on British music – composers, performers, the history, current musical events and contemporary performances in England. Marion Scott's writing appeared in the *Christian Science Monitor, Daily Telegraph, The Listener, Monthly Musical Record, Music and Letters, Music and Youth, Music Bulletin, Music Magazine, Music Review, Music Student, Musical Quarterly, Musical Times, The Observer, Radio Times, Royal College of Music Magazine* and *The Sackbut*.

In addition, Scott wrote programme notes for the BBC Symphony Orchestra, the Haydn Orchestra and for the Royal Philharmonic Society, delivered papers to the Musical Association (now the Royal Music Association), produced broadcasts for *Music Magazine*, and wrote entries for Cobbett's *Cyclopedic Survey of Chamber Music*, Cobbett's *Chamber Music Supplement*, and *Grove's Dictionary of Music and Musicians*.

Her 1934 biography of Beethoven is still available in used editions. Published under the J. M. Dent & Sons imprint as part of the Music Masters series, it was reprinted in 1937, 1940, 1944, 1949, 1951, 1956, 1960, 1965, 1968, 1974. She also published *Haydn's Opus One, Number One*, Oxford University Press, 1931; *The Band Book* by M. M. Scott ('Mary Margareta Scott'), Oxford University Press, 1937 (contains forty-one tunes for violins in unison with piano accompaniment), and in 1938, her brief study of Mendelssohn was added to the Novello series of *Biographies of Great Musicians*. Her book *History of British Music, 1848–1900* remains in manuscript.

'Chamber Music at the Royal College of Music', *Music Student*, May 1915

'The Chamber Music of Charles Wood', *Music Student*, January 1916

'The Royal College of Music: A Brief History', *Music Student*, March 1916

'The Chamber Music of William Sterndale Bennett, *Music Student*, October 1916

'Contemporary British War-Poetry, Music and Patriotism', *Musical Times*, 1 March 1917

'British Women as Instrumentalists', *Music Student*, May 1918

'Second Lieut. Ernest Bristowe Farrar' [obituary], *RCM Magazine*, vol. 15 (September 1918), p. 36

'Herbert Howells's Piano Quartet, An Appreciation', *Music Student*, November 1918

'British Music in the War Years, *Christian Science Monitor*, 8 February 1919

'The Orchestra in England', two parts, *Christian Science Monitor*, 22 March and 5 April 1919

'The Royal College of Music' [two parts, article illustrated with a pencil drawing of the college], *Christian Science Monitor*, 10 May and 17 May 1919

'English Society of Women Musicians', *Christian Science Monitor*, 7 June 1919

'A Young Composer of Promise' [profile of Herbert Howells, illustrated with pencil portrait of Howells], *Christian Science Monitor*, 14 June 1919

'The Gloucestershire Group' [three parts, the history of Gloucestershire and the composers and poets, including Gurney, Howells and F. W. Harvey, associated with it], *Christian Science Monitor*, 26 July, 2 August and 9 August 1919

'The Word Setting of a Song' [an essay on poetry and music], *Christian Science Monitor*, 29 August 1919

'A New Elgar 'Cello Concerto' [review of the première], *Christian Science Monitor*, 13 December 1919

'John Ireland and His Work' [profile of the composer], *Christian Science Monitor*, 3 January 1920

'British Violin Sonatas' [two parts], *Christian Science Monitor*, 17 January and 7 February 1920

'A Man of Large Endowments' [profile of Thomas Dunhill], *Christian Science Monitor*, 24 January 1920

'Cecil Sharp and Folk Song' [examines Sharp's role as a folk song collector], *Christian Science Monitor*, 2 April 1920

'British Music Society' [two parts – reportorial coverage of the organization's first National Congress and debates with a history], *Christian Science Monitor*, 12 June and 19 June 1920

'Poet's Touches' [features Gurney among others], *The Sackbut*, June 1920

'Folk-Song Gift to Herbert Howells' [feature article about music composed for Howells' wedding], *Christian Science Monitor*, 11 September 1920

'Herbert Howells, His "In Gloucestershire"' [feature on Howells' string quartet], *Christian Science Monitor*, 25 December 1920

'Programs by the English Singers' [review of Gurney's *Ludlow and Teme*], *Christian Science Monitor*, 25 December 1920

'Gustav Holst' [profile of the composer], *Christian Science Monitor*, 5 March 1921

'Adrian Boult: A Teacher of Conducting', *Christian Science Monitor*, 23 April 1921

'The Lutenist Song Writers: The English School', *Christian Science Monitor*, 21 May 1921

'Ralph Vaughan Williams' [profile in two parts], *Christian Science Monitor*, 17 December and 31 December 1921

'History of "The Boatswain's Mate" Is Told by Dame Ethel Smyth', *Christian Science Monitor*, 13 May 1922

'Walter Wilson Cobbett' [profile of Cobbett], *Christian Science Monitor*, 3 May 1923

'Sir Ernest Palmer, Noted Patron of British Music' [Palmer and the Patron's Fund], *Christian Science Monitor*, 16 June 1923

'William Byrd's Place in the History of Music', *Christian Science Monitor*, 21 July 1923

'Mr. Delius Discourses on His Music to Hassan' [interview with Delius], *Christian Science Monitor*, 27 October 1923

'Elizabethan Keyboard Music' [three-part series], *Christian Science Monitor*, 10 November, 22 December, 29 December 1923

'Introduction: Herbert Howells', *Music Bulletin*, May 1924

'A British Woman Conductor' [interview with Gwynne Kimpton], *Christian Science Monitor*, 21 June 1924

'Music in London' [review of Gerald Finzi's Violin Concerto], *Christian Science Monitor*, 17 January 1927

'Orchestra Conducting: An Unexplored Profession for Women', *Christian Science Monitor*, 3 January 1928

'A Dictionary of Chamber Music' [Cobbett], *Music and Letters*, vol. 10, no. 4 (October 1929), pp. 363–71

'All-England Folk Dance Festival', *Christian Science Monitor*, 1 February 1930

'Paul Hindemith: His Music and Its Characteristics' [the earliest discussion and analysis of his work in England], *Proceedings of the Royal Musical Association*, vol. 56 (1929–30), pp. 91–108 [paper given 15 April 1930]

'Haydn in England', *Musical Quarterly*, vol. 18, no. 2 (April 1932), pp. 260–73

'Maddalena Lombardini, Madame Syrmen', *Music and Letters*, vol. 14, no. 2 (1933), pp. 149–63

'Grand Old Concerts' [a personal account of the Crystal Palace concerts], *The Observer*, 12 June 1932

'London Concerts' [review of Finzi's *A Young Man's Exhortation*], *Musical Times*, January 1934

'Haydn's Opus Two and Opus Three', *Proceedings of the Royal Musical Association* [paper given 6 November 1934], vol. 61 (1934–5), pp. 1–19

'London Concerts' [review of Finzi's *Interlude*], *Musical Times*, May 1936

'Immanent Form', *Music and Letters*, vol. 17, no. 4 (October 1936), pp. 322–7

'Ivor Gurney: The Man', *Music and Letters*, vol. 19, no. 1 (January 1938), pp. 2–7

'Recollections of Ivor Gurney', *Monthly Musical Record*, vol. 68, no. 794 (February 1938), pp. 41–6

'Ivor Gurney' [obituary], *Royal College of Music Magazine*, March 1938

'In Memoriam: Ivor Gurney', *The Listener*, vol. 20, no. 596 (14 July 1938), p. 105

'Michael Tippett and his Music', *The Listener*, 8 April 1943

'Holst, Cotswold Man and Mystic', *The Listener*, 18 May 1944

'Some English Affinities and Associations of Haydn's Songs', *Music and Letters*, vol. 25, no. 1 (January 1944), pp. 1–12

Marion Scott's Unpublished Compositions – A Select List

Marion Scott's manuscripts are in the Royal College of Music, London.

Requiem – 'Under the wide and starry sky' (Robert Louis Stevenson)

Russian Folk Song Arrangements for the 1908 stage production of *The Song of Kalashnikoff*, translated from the Russian of Marcus Lermontov by Ethel Voynich

Chamber Music, including a piano trio and string quartet

Vocal Music

Nine songs from 'A Child's Garden of Verses' being a miniature suite for voice and piano – To Audrey

> 'Prologue, Happy Thought'
> 'Looking Forward'
> 'Whole Duty of Children'
> 'System'
> 'A Thought'
> 'Auntie's Skirts'
> 'Rain'
> 'Night'
> 'The Wind'

'To music' (Herrick) for contralto and string orchestra

'Falmouth Town' (adapted by W. E. Henley from an old ballad) for tenor and piano

'Rondel' (Bernard Weller) vocal with string quartet

'The idle life I lead' (R. Bridges) vocal with string quartet

'Sea Gipsy – I am fevered with the sunset' (Bliss Carman)

'Golden slumber kiss your eyes '(Thomas Dekker), contralto and piano

'The tide rises, the tide falls' (Longfellow)

'To Sleep' (Sir Phillip Sidney)

'The Hag' (Herrick)

'Hawke' (Henry Newbolt)

'In Early Spring' (Alice Meynell) with orchestra

'Song of the Night at Daybreak' (Meynell)

'Thoughts in Separation' (Meynell)

'A Norman Chansonette' (Austin Dobson)

'To Violets' (Herrick), vocal quartet

'For the Lord will not Fail His People', vocal quartet

'While I Watch the Yellow Wheat' (Gwenith Gwyn)

'Ophelia's Song' (Shakespeare)

'The Bells of Forrabury' (E. H. Tipple)

'The fighting Termeraire' (Henry Newbolt)

'The Fairies', part song SATB (William Allingham)

'Renouncement' (Meynell)

'Fair Phyllis' (Anon.)

Two songs of the Earl of Surrey: 'Rue on my life' and 'Lover's Chess' (Henry Howard)

'San Stefano' (Henry Newbolt)

'Hame, Hame, Hame', Scottish song for women's voices

'The Campbells are Coming', for women's voices

'Lullaby' (Christina Rossetti)

From 'Ecclesiastes' – Vanity of Vanities

'Ballad of Patrick Spens'

Psalm 94

Bibliography

Archives and Collections

Boston Public Library, Boston, Massachusetts

City of Boston, Office of Public Records, Boston, Massachusetts

Corporation of London Records Office, London, England

Greenbank Parish Church, Edinburgh, Scotland

Ivor Gurney Archive, Gloucester, England

Harvard University, Baker Library, Cambridge, Massachusetts

Library of Congress, Washington, DC

Royal College of Music, London, England

Prince Family Papers, S. Hardy Prince, Beverly, Massachusetts

Somerset House, London, England

West Lothian Council, Education and Cultural Services, Blackburn, West
Lothian, Scotland

Correspondence, interviews, etc.

Barnett, Janet, Edinburgh, Scotland, interview (June 2000)

Brockway, Margaret, Burford, England, interview, correspondence (2000–2002)

Carter, Peggy Ann McKay, California, interviews, correspondence (1990–2004)

Chissell, Joan, London, England, correspondence (1991, 1996, 1998)

Cook, Andrew, correspondence (2004)

Corbo, Dr Joseph, Arlington, Virginia, consultations (1994)

Ferguson, Howard, Cambridge, England, correspondence (November 1989)

Finzi, Christopher, Ashmansworth, England, correspondence (March 2001)

Finzi, Joy, Leckhampstead, England, interviews, correspondence (1984–9)

Goodland, David, Nailsworth, England, correspondence, conversations
(1995–2004)

Howells, Ursula, England, correspondence (March 1997)

Jamison, Dr Kay Redfield, Washington, DC, conversations (2002)

Jasiulko-Harden, Dr Evelyn, British Columbia, correspondence, conversations
(1998, 1999)

Johnson, Dr Harald, Scituate, Massachusetts, conversations (1990–6)

Munro, Mrs E. A., Edinburgh, interview (June 2000)

Officer, Adrian, correspondence (1991 and 2003)

Priestman, Audrey, Oundle, England, correspondence, conversations (1990–1)

Prince, S. Hardy, Beverly, Massachusetts, correspondence, conversations (1998–2005)

Ray, Don Brandon, California, correspondence (1998–2004)

Vaughan Williams, Ursula, London, correspondence (1991, 1995)

Watson, Isabella, Armadale, Scotland, interviews, correspondence (1990–8)

Publications

Aldrich, Mildred, *A Hilltop on the Marne* (Boston: Houghton Mifflin Co., 1915)

—— *On the Edge of the War Zone: From the Battle of the Marne to the Entrance of the Stars and Stripes* (Boston: Small Maynard & Co., 1917)

Anderson, Ronald, and Anne Koval, *James McNeill Whistler: Beyond the Myth* (New York: Carroll & Graf Publishers, 1995)

Babington, Anthony, *Shell Shock: A History of the Changing Attitudes To War Neurosis* (London: Leo Cooper, 1997)

Banfield, Stephen, *Sensibility and English Song: Critical Studies of the Early Twentieth Century* (Cambridge: Cambridge University Press, 1985)

—— *Gerald Finzi: An English Composer* (London: Faber & Faber, 1997)

Bannerjee, Jacqueline, 'Ivor Gurney's "Dark March" – Is It Really Over?', *English Studies: A Journal of English Language and Literature*, vol. 70, no. 2 (April 1989), pp. 115–31

Barnett, Robert, 'Arthur Benjamin: Australian Symphonist', *British Music Society Journal*, vol. 10 (1988), pp. 27–36

Barnett, T. Ratcliffe, *Scottish Pilgrimage in the Land of Lost Content* (Edinburgh: John Grant Booksellers, 1944)

Bass, Ellen, and Laura Davis, *The Courage to Heal: A Guide for Women Survivors of Child Sexual Abuse* (New York: Harper & Row, 1988)

Batchelor, George, *The Life and Legacy of G. I. Taylor* (Cambridge: Cambridge University Press, 1996)

Baylock, Maria Foltz, *Women Musicians in Early Twentieth-Century London: The String Players in the English Ensemble* (MM thesis: Southern Methodist University, Dallas, 1998)

Benjamin, Arthur, 'A Student in Kensington', *Music and Letters*, vol. 31, no. 3 (July 1950), pp. 196–207

Berquist, Laura, 'A Best Seller in Russia', *Look Magazine*, 8 July 1955, pp. 68–70

Blevins, Pamela, 'Marion Scott's American Heritage', *Ivor Gurney Society Journal*, vol. 11 (2005)

Boden, Anthony, *F. W. Harvey: Soldier, Poet* (Gloucester: Alan Sutton Publishing, 1988)

—— 'Ivor Gurney: Schizophrenic?', *Ivor Gurney Society Journal*, vol. 6 (2000) pp. 23–8

Borden, Mary, *The Forbidden Zone* (Garden City, NY: Doubleday, Doran, 1929)

Burtch, M. A., 'Ivor Gurney – A Revaluation', *Musical Times*, vol. 95, no. 1340 (1 October 1955), pp. 529–30

Cabot, Harriet Prince, 'The Early Years of William Ropes and Company in St. Petersburg', *American Neptune*, vol. 23, no. 2 (April 1963), pp. 131–9

Capell, Richard, 'Ivor Gurney – A Musician's Tragedy', *Daily Telegraph*, 28 December 1937, p. 13

—— 'Ivor Gurney: A Symposium of Poets and Musicians', *Daily Telegraph*, 18 December 1937, p. 13

Carder, Richard, 'Long Shadows Fall: A Study of Ivor Gurney's Songs to his Own Poems', *British Music Society Journal*, vol. 15 (1993), pp. 34–70

Carter, Leslie Stuart, 'A California Resident says Wellesley is tops', profile of James McKay, Annie Drummond's husband by their son-in-law, unknown newspaper (no date)

—— 'The Old Soldier', *New England Senior Citizen*, April 1978, p. 10

Chamberlain, Samuel, *A Stroll Through Historic Salem* (New York: Hastings House, 1969)

Chissell, Joan, 'Marion Scott', *Musical Times*, vol. 92, no. 1295 (February 1951), pp. 62–4

Christian Science Monitor, 1919–33 [Library of Congress, Arlington, Virginia Public Library]

Claridge, Gordon, Ruth Pryor, and Gwen Watkins, *Sounds from the Bell Jar: Ten Psychotic Authors* (Cambridge, MA: Malor Books, 1998)

Cook, Andrew, *Ace of Spies: The True Story of Sidney Reilly* (Stroud: Tempus, 2004)

Cooper, Jeff, 'Ivor Gurney and the Abercrombies', *Ivor Gurney Society Journal*, vol. 9 (2003)

Crichton, Paul, ' "A profound duplicity of life": Uses and misuses of "schizophrenia" in popular culture and professional diagnosis', *The Times Literary Supplement*, 31 March 2000, pp. 14–15

Dale, Kathleen, 'Marion Scott' [Obituary], *Musical Times*, vol. 95, no. 1332 (February 1954), p. 97

—— 'The Haydn Catalogue ... and an Unfinished Manuscript', *RCM Magazine*, vol. 50 (May 1954), p. 44

—— 'Marion Scott as Music Critic and Letter Writer', in Society of Women Musicians, *Commemoration of Marion Scott* (programme book, 25–6 June 1954), pp. 12–17

—— 'Memories of Marion Scott', *Music and Letters*, vol. 35, no. 3 (July 1954), pp. 236–40

Dally, Peter, *The Marriage of Heaven and Hell: Manic Depression and the Life of Virginia Woolf* (New York: St Martin's Press, 1999)

Daly, Donald R. (compiler), *The Trial of Sarah Osborne: Transcript from the Salem Witchcraft Trials of 1692* (Salem, MA: New England and Virginia Co., n.d.)

Desowitz, Robert S., *The Malaria Capers: More Tales of Parasites and People, Research and Reality* (New York: W. W. Norton & Co., 1991)

Dressler, John, *Gerald Finzi: A Bio-Bibliography* (Westport, CT, Greenwood Press, 1997)

Daubney, Brian Blyth (ed.), *Aspects of British Song: A Miscellany of Essays* (London: The British Music Society, 1992)

Eggar, Katharine, 'Marion Scott as Founder of the Society of Women Musicians', in Society of Women Musicians, *Commemoration of Marion Scott* (programme book, 25–6 June 1954), pp. 4–6

Ely, Penny, ' "A Combination of Don Quixote and D'Artagnon": John Haines on Ivor Gurney', *Ivor Gurney Society Journal*, vol. 1 (1995), pp. 59–68

Essex Institute Historical Collections (Salem, MA: Essex Institute, 1890)

Ferguson, Howard, and Michael Hurd (eds.), *Letters of Gerald Finzi and Howard Ferguson* (Woodbridge, Boydell & Brewer, 2001)

Finzi, Gerald, 'Guardian of Genius (Ivor Gurney's Work)', in Society of Women Musicians, *Commemoration of Marion Scott* (programme book, 25–6 June 1954), pp. 8–10

Freemantle, Anne, 'The Russian Best-Seller', *History Today*, vol. 25 no. 9 (September 1975), pp. 629–37

Fried, Stephen, 'Kay Jamison's Road to Life: Creative Tension', *Washington Post Magazine*, 16 April 1995, p. 11

Fussell, Paul, *The Great War and Modern Memory* (London: Oxford University Press, 1975)

Garlick, Barbara, 'At the Marge – Rereading Ivor Gurney', *Ivor Gurney Society Journal*, vol. 2 (1996), pp. 17–27

Gloucester Citizen, 'Death of Gloucester-Born "Schubert", Tragedy of Ivor Gurney's Unfulfilled Promise, War Sufferings that Vitiated Powers, Brilliant Poet and Musician', 28 December 1937, p. 1

—— 'Mr. Ivor Gurney Buried: Moving Service at Twigworth: Own Works Played', 1 January 1938, p. 6

Gosling, Nigel, *Leningrad: A Magical Evocation of an Historic City, Its Treasure and Traditions* (New York: E. P. Dutton & Co., 1965)

Grant, Joy, *Harold Monro and the Poetry Bookshop* (Berkeley: University of California Press, 1967)

Grove's Dictionary of Music and Musicians, 2nd edition, ed. J. A. Fuller Maitland (Philadelphia: Theodore Presser Co., 1926); 3rd edition, ed. H. C. Colles (New York, Macmillan Co., 1927); supplementary volume (New York: Macmillan Co., 1940)

Gurney, Ivor, *Severn and Somme* (London: Sidgwick & Jackson, 1917)

—— *War's Embers* (London: Sidgwick & Jackson, 1919)

—— 'Charles Villiers Stanford by Some of his Pupils', *Music and Letters*, vol. 5, no. 3 (July 1924)

—— *Poems of Ivor Gurney, 1890–1937*, with an introduction by Edmund Blunden (London: Chatto & Windus, 1973)

—— *Collected Poems*, ed. P. J. Kavanagh (Oxford: Oxford University Press, 1982, 1984)

—— *Stars in a Dark Night: The Letters of Ivor Gurney to the Chapman Family, 1914–1919*, ed. Anthony Boden (Gloucester: Alan Sutton Publishing, 1986)

—— *Severn and Somme and War's Embers*, ed. R. K. R. Thornton (Ashington: MidNAG; Manchester: Carcanet, 1987)

—— *Collected Letters*, ed. R. K. R. Thornton (Ashington: MidNAG; Manchester: Carcanet, 1991)

—— *Best Poems* and *The Book of Five Makings*, ed. R. K. R. Thornton and George Walter (Ashington: MidNAG; Manchester: Carcanet, 1995)

—— *Selected Poems*, ed. George Walter, Everyman's Poetry (London: J. M. Dent, 1996)

—— *80 Poems or So*, ed. George Walter and R. K. R. Thornton (Ashington: MidNAG; Manchester: Carcanet, 1997)

—— *Rewards of Wonder: Poems of Cotswold, France, London*, ed. George Walter (Ashington: MidNAG; Manchester: Carcanet, 2000)

Haines, John, 'An Hour with Books: Mr. Ivor Gurney, A Gloucestershire Poet', *Gloucester Journal*, 5 January 1935, p. 28

Harris, Joseph E., *Africans and Their History* (New York: New American Library, 1987)

Hassall, Christopher, *Edward Marsh, Patron of the Arts: A Biography* (London: Longmans, Green & Co., 1958)

Haywood, Richard Mowbray, *The Beginnings of Railway Development in Russia in the Reign of Nicholas I, 1835–1842* (Durham, NC: Duke University Press, 1969)

Hendrie, W. F., and D. A. D. Macleod, *The Bangour Story: A History of Bangour Village and General Hospitals* (Edinburgh: Mercat Press, 1991 and 1992)

Hibberd, Dominic, *Owen the Poet* (Basingstoke: Macmillan, 1986)

—— *Wilfred Owen: The Last Year, 1917–1918* (London: Constable & Co., 1992)

—— *Harold Monro: Poet of the New Age* (Basingstoke: Palgrave, 2001)

—— *Wilfred Owen: A New Biography* (London: Weidenfeld & Nicholson, 2002)

Holden, Wendy, *Shell Shock: The Psychological Impact of War* (London: Channel Four Books, 1998)

Howells, Herbert, 'Marion Margaret Scott: 1878 [*sic*]–1953', *Music and Letters*, vol. 35, no. 2 (April 1954), pp. 134–5

Hughes, Rosemary, 'Marion Scott's Contribution to Musical Scholarship', *RCM Magazine*, May 1954, pp. 39–43

—— 'Marion Scott as the Authority on Haydn', in Society of Women Musicians, *Commemoration of Marion Scott* (programme book, 25–6 June 1954), pp. 18–20

Hurd, Michael, *The Ordeal of Ivor Gurney* (Oxford: University Press, 1978)

Hynd-Brown, R., *Armadale: Past and Present* (Bathgate: Linlithgowshire Gazette, 1906)

Hynes, Samuel, *A War Imagined: The First World War and English Culture* (New York: Collier Books, 1990)

Jamison, Kay Redfield, *Touched with Fire: Manic-Depressive Illness and the Artistic Temperament* (New York: Free Press, 1993)

—— *An Unquiet Mind: A Memoir of Moods and Madness* (New York: Vintage Books, 1996)

—— 'Interview with Dr. Kay Redfield Jamison' [backstage at Lincoln Center New York], transcription (n.d.)

Jasiulko-Harden, Evelyn, 'Major George Washington Whistler, Railroad Engineer, in Russia, 1842–49', in *Ex oriente lux: mélanges offerts en hommage au professeur Jean Blankoff* (Brussels: Centre d'Études des Pays de l'Est, 1991), vol. 1

Journal of Society for Psychical Research, 'Obituary: Sydney Charles Scott' [signed J. G. P.], October 1936, pp. 270–7

Kelley's Directory, Bosham, 1899 and 1937 editions

Lamb, John Alexander (ed.), *The Fasti of the United Free Church of Scotland, 1900–1929* (Edinburgh: Oliver & Boyd, 1956)

Lunn, John E., and Ursula Vaughan Williams, *Ralph Vaughan Williams: A Pictorial Biography* (London: Oxford University Press, 1971)

MacHale, Desmond, *George Boole: His Life and Work* (Dublin: Boole Press, 1985)

Mackay, Donald G. M., *The Story of Greenbank* (Edinburgh: private publication, 1990)

Maine, Basil, *Behold These Daniels: Being Studies of Contemporary Music Critics* (London: H. & W. Brown, 1928)

Moore, Charles Willard, *The Solo Vocal Works of Ivor Gurney (1890–1937)* (DMA thesis: University of Indiana, 1967)

—— *Maker and Lover of Beauty: Ivor Gurney Poet and Songwriter*, introduction by Herbert Howells, illustrations by Richard Walker (Rickmansworth: Triad Press, 1976)

Mottram, R. H., *Journey to the Western Front: Twenty Years After* (London: G. Bell & Sons, 1936)

Music and Letters, vol. 19, no. 1 (January 1938), Symposium on Ivor Gurney's Life and Work, contributions by Harry Plunkett Greene, Marion M. Scott, Sir John Squire, Walter de la Mare, Edmund Blunden, R. Vaughan Williams, Herbert Howells, ed. Eric Blom

Music and Letters, 'Richard Capell – March 23rd, 1885 – June 21st, 1954', vol. 35 no. 4 (October 1954), pp. 277–86

The Music Student (1910–18)

National Institutes of Health, *Fact Sheet – Syphilis* (Bethesda, MD, 1998)

National Park Service, *Salem: Maritime Salem in the Age of Sail* (Washington, DC: US Department of the Interior, 1987)

Neumayr, Anton, *Music and Medicine: Haydn, Mozart, Beethoven, Schubert: Notes on Their Lives, Works and Medical Histories*, trans. Bruce Cooper Clarke (Bloomington, IL: Med-Ed Press, 1994)

New England Historical & Genealogical Register (Boston: Samuel G. Drake Publisher, 1851)

New York Times, 'W. M. Voynich Dies; Noted Bibliophile', 20 March 1930, p. 27

—— 'Ethel L. Voynich, Novelist, was 96', 29 July 1960, p. 25

Officer, Adrian, 'Harrogate and Ernest Farrar', *Finzi Trust Friends Newsletter*, vol. 14, no. 1 (Summer 1996), unpaginated

Ostwald, Peter, *Schumann: The Inner Voices of a Musical Genius* (Boston, MA: Northeastern University Press, 1985)

Owen, Rev. W., 'A Tribute' [to Canon Alfred Cheesman], *Twigworth and Longford St Matthew Parish Magazine*, July 1941

Owen, Wilfred, *Collected Letters*, ed. Harold Owen and John Bell (Oxford: Oxford University Press, 1967)

—— *The Poems of Wilfred Owen*, ed. Jon Stallworthy (New York: W. W. Norton & Co., 1986)

Palmer, Christopher, *Herbert Howells: A Study* (Sevenoaks: Novello, 1978)

—— *Herbert Howells: A Centenary Celebration* (London: Thames Publishing, 1992)

Perley, Sidney, *The History of Salem, Massachusetts* (Salem: Sidney Perley, 1926)

Pilkington, Michael, *Gurney, Ireland, Quilter and Warlock* (Bloomington: Indiana University Press, 1989)

Press, John, *Poets of World War I*, Writers and Their Work, vol. 280 (London: Longmans & Co., 1983)

Prideaux, Tom, and the Editors of Time-Life Books, *The World of Whistler, 1834–1903* (New York: Time-Life Books, 1970)

Pruys, Karl Hugo, *The Tiger's Tender Touch: The Erotic Life of Goethe*, trans. Kathleen Bunten (Carol Stream, Illinois: Quintessence Publishing Co., 1999)

Rattenbury, Arnold, 'How the sanity of poets can be edited away', *London Review of Books*, 14 October 1999, pp. 15–19

Ray, Don Brandon, *Ivor Gurney (1890–1937): His Life and Works* (MA dissertation: California State University at Long Beach, 1980)

Raymond, Edward S., and Eugene Prince, 'Whistler Had a Father Too', *My Country*, vol. 8, no. 2 ([My Country Society, Litchfield CT], May–June 1974)

Read, Mike, *Forever England: The Life of Rupert Brooke* (Edinburgh: Mainstream Publishing, 1997)

Reed, James, *The Border Ballads* (London: Athlone Press, 1973)

Reed College Quest, 'Arthur Benjamin, Esquire – Musician Extraordinaire', vol. 33, no. 14 (26 February 1945), p. 1

Robinson, Enders A., *The Devil Discovered: Salem Witchcraft, 1692* (New York: Hippocrene Books, 1991)

Royal College of Music Magazine, 'Appreciations: Marion Scott', Hester Stansfeld Prior, Beatrix Darnell, Karl Geiringer, Harold Darke, Dorothy Mortimer Harris, Rupert Erlebach (May 1954), pp. 45–7

Ross, Robert H., *The Georgian Revolt: Rise and Fall of a Political Ideal, 1910–1922* (Carbondale: Southern Illinois University Press, 1965)

Sandblom, Philip, *Creativity and Disease: How Illness Affects Literature, Art and Music* (London: Marion Boyars, 1997)

Saul, Norman E., *Distant Friends: The United States and Russia, 1763–1867* (Lawrence: University Press of Kansas, 1991)

Savage, James, *Genealogical Dictionary of the First Settlers of New England* (Baltimore: Genealogical Publishing Co., 1986)

Schwartz, Mark F. and Leigh Cohn (eds.), *Sexual Abuse and Eating Disorders* (New York: Brunner/Mazel, 1996)

Scott, Marion M., 'Contemporary British War Poetry, Music and Patriotism', *Musical Times*, vol. 58, no. 889 (1 March 1917), pp. 120–3

—— 'Ernest Farrar' [Obituary], *RCM Magazine*, vol. 15 (September 1918), p. 36

—— articles in *Christian Science Monitor* (1919–33)

—— *Beethoven* (London: J. M. Dent & Sons, 1934, 1940)

—— 'Ivor Gurney: The Man', *Music and Letters*, vol. 19, no. 1 (January 1938), pp. 2–7

—— 'Recollections of Ivor Gurney', *Monthly Musical Record*, vol. 68, no. 794 (February 1938), pp. 41–6

—— 'In Memoriam: Ivor Gurney', *The Listener*, vol. 20, no. 596 (14 July 1938), p. 105

Shephard, Ben, A *War of Nerves: Soldiers and Psychiatrists in the Twentieth Century* (Cambridge, MA: Harvard University Press, 2001)

Sirbaugh, Nora, *Ivor Gurney and his Vision of Gloucestershire in Music* (DMA thesis: Johns Hopkins University, 1994)

Small, Robert, *History of the Congregations of the United Presbyterian Church from 1733 to 1900* (Edinburgh: David M. Small, 1904)

Society of Women Musicians, *Commemoration of Marion Scott* [contributors, Kathleen Dale, Hester Stansfeld Prior, Gerald Finzi, Rosemary Hughes] (programme book, 25–6 June 1954)

Spicer, Paul, *Herbert Howells* (Bridgend: Seren, 1998)

Street, Sean, *The Dymock Poets* (Bridgend: Seren, 1994)

Taylor, Martin, 'Ivor Gurney: "Only the Wanderer"', *Imperial War Museum Review*, no. 2 (1987), pp. 98–105

Terr, Lenore, *Too Scared to Cry: Psychic Trauma in Childhood* (New York: Harper & Row, 1990)

Thomas, Helen, with Myfanwy Thomas, *Under Storm's Wing* (Manchester: Carcanet, 1988)

Thornton, R. K. R., 'New Howells–Gurney Papers', *Ivor Gurney Society Journal*, vol. 1 (1995), pp. 69–76

—— and George Walter, *Ivor Gurney: Towards a Bibliography* (Birmingham: Ivor Gurney Society and the School of English at the University of Birmingham, 1996)

Townsend, Frances, *The Laureate of Gloucestershire: The Life and Work of F. W. Harvey* (Bristol: Redcliffe Press, 1988)

Trethowan, W. H., 'Ivor Gurney's Mental Illness', *Music and Letters*, vol. 62, nos. 3–4 (July/October 1981), pp. 300–9

Vaughan Williams, Ursula, *R.V.W.: A Biography of Ralph Vaughan Williams* (Oxford: Oxford University Press, [1964] 1988)

Vital Records of Salem Massachusetts to the End of the Year 1848 (Salem, MA: Essex Institute, 1918)

Volkov, Solomon, *St Petersburg: A Cultural History*, trans. Antonina W. Bouis (New York: Free Press, 1995)

Walter, George, ' "My True Work Now", An Unpublished Ivor Gurney Letter', *Ivor Gurney Society Journal*, vol. 3 (1997), pp. 57–74

Webster, Donald, 'Ernest Bristow Farrar, 1885–1918', *Finzi Trust Friends Newsletter*, vol. 16, no. 1 (Summer 1998), unpaginated

Weintraub, Stanley, *Whistler: A Biography* (New York: Truman Talley Books, 1998)

Willner, Gerhard, 'Richard Capell in Egypt', *Music and Letters*, vol. 36 no. 3 (1955), p. 224–5

Winter, Denis, *Death's Men: Soldiers of the Great War* (Harmondsworth: Penguin, 1979)

Wolf, Paul, 'Mystery of How Illness Affected the Famous', *American Association for Clinical Chemistry, Conference Summary* (July 2000)

Youdell, Andrew, 'Storm Clouds: A Survey of the Film Music of Arthur Benjamin', *British Music Society Newsletter*, vol. 15 (1993)

Index

Abercrombie, Catherine, 86–7, 95, 96, 110, 113
Abercrombie, Lascelles, 41, 65, 86–7, 170–1, 183
Achurch, Janet, 45
Alderman, Pauline, 277
Aldrich, Mildred, 120, 128 n3
Alexander, Joan, 267
Alston, Audrey, 15
Anderson, W.E., 238
Arbós, Fernández, 8

Bach, C. P. E., 269
Bach, Johann Sebastian, 5, 34–5, 93–4, 102, 111, 122, 125, 143
Bache, Walter, 31
Baillie, Isobel, 266, 272
Bairstow, Ernest, 229
Bantock, Granville, 20
Barham, Minnie, 267
Barnett, T. Ratcliffe, 134–6, 139, 159, 146 n41
Barnett family, 134–5, 145 n21
Barnwood House, 208–12, 216
Barton, Marmaduke, 8
Bax, Arnold, 20
Beach, Amy, 87
Beethoven, Ludwig van, 102, 127, 143, 241, 254–7, 261, 293
Belloc, Hilaire, 40–1, 241
Beloved Vagabonds Club, 15
Benjamin, Arthur, 21–2, 25–7, 41, 66, 77, 81, 82 n20, 85, 139, 165–7, 180, 187, 190, 203, 206, 209, 242, 266
  meets IG, 22
  friendship with IG, 72, 75, 79, 155, 223–4, 246
  confidant of IG, 42, 79, 207–8
  opinion of IG, 75
Bennett, Fred, 94
Bennett, William Sterndale, 100
Bernard, Anthony, 190

Binyon, Laurence, 106
Bliss, Arthur, 27, 81, 100, 180, 184, 190
Blom, Eric, 259
Blunden, Edmund, 168, 189–91, 201, 258, 274, 276–7, 285–6, 289
Boole, Alicia, 43
Boole, Ethel Lilian, see Voynich, Ethel L.
Boole, George, 42–3
Boole, Lucy, 43
Boole, Margaret, see Taylor, Margaret ('Maggie')
Boole, Mary Everest, 42–3
Borden, Mary, 116, 120, 128 n4
Borrow, George, 95
Boughton, Rutland, 15
Boult, Adrian, 166
Bradford, Hugh, 191
Brewer, Herbert, 19–20, 57, 60–2
Brewster, Priscilla, 267
Bridge, Frank, 105, 168
Bridges, Robert, 111, 160, 168, 183, 191, 199, 200–1
Bright, Dora, 10, 21
British Broadcasting Corporation, 253, 266, 288–90
British Music Society, 191, 198
Brock, Arthur, 136
Brockway, Margaret Harris, 261
Brockway, Michael, 221 n17
Brooke, Rupert, 41, 87, 99, 140, 168, 185–6, 199
Browning, Robert, 64
Buck, Percy, 12, 273
Bucke, Richard M., 228, 236 n41
Bunning, James Burnstone, 215
Butterworth, George, 180, 199

Capell, Richard, 243, 251 n30, 264
Carey, Clive, 16
Carman, Bliss, 174
Carnegie Trust, 200, 229, 238, 286
Carter, Peggy Ann McKay, 235 n27

Chapman, Arthur, 88

Chapman, Catherine ('Kitty'), 88–9

Chapman, Edward, 88–9, 94–5, 158

Chapman, Marjorie ('Micky'), 88

Chapman, Matilda, 88, 106, 129, 183–4

Chapman, Winifred ('Winnie'), 88, 193

Chapman family, 88–9, 105–6, 173, 182

Cheesman, Alfred Hunter, 51, 54–6, 61–2, 68–9, 71, 74, 85, 96, 124, 171, 200, 264–5

Cheesman, Elizabeth Hunter, 55

Chissell, Joan, 276–7, 282 n60

Christian Science Monitor, 154, 167–8, 172, 174, 175 n13, 187–90, 223, 244, 257, 292

City of London Mental Hospital ('Stone House'), 210–2, 215–7, 222–34, 238–42, 275

Clare, John, 189, 276

Clark, Leonard, 286, 288, 290, 294 n12

Clarke, Rebecca, 17 n14

Cliffe, Frederic, 21

Closson, Ernest, 255

Cobbett, Walter W., 13, 17 n21, 292

Coleridge-Taylor, Samuel, 10, 20, 25–6

Corder, Frederick, 12

Crawshaw, Aubrey Aitken, 10

Cridland, Basil, 94–5, 265

Crockett, S. R., 71

Crystal Palace, 4–7, 9, 34

Curas, Jeanne, 155

Daily Telegraph, 243, 264, 268

Dale, Kathleen Richards, 243, 268–9, 271, 273, 275, 278–9, 280 n30, 290–1

Darke, Harold, 12, 16, 180

Davies, Fanny, 9, 173, 243–4, 251 n32, 268

Davies, W. H., 40–2, 86, 140, 168

Davies, Walford, 8–9, 12, 19, 34–5, 73, 106, 279

Davis, Randolph, 228–34, 237 n68, 238, 240

Dawe, Dorothy, *see* Howells, Dorothy

Day, Effie, 132–3

Daymond, Emily, 9–11, 17 n15

De la Mare, Walter, 41, 86, 93, 140, 168, 189, 191, 199, 202, 227, 258

Deavin, Charles, 57

Debussy, Claude, 21, 25

Delius, Frederick, 20

Doyle, Arthur Conan, 31–2

Dring, Madeline, 291

Drinkwater, John, 86, 168

Drummond, Annie Nelson (McKay), 134, 137–42, 144, 159, 182, 203, 226, 228, 235 n37, 238, 264

Drummond, Margaret, 226

Drummond family, 138

Dunhill, Thomas, 13, 21, 117, 119 n41, 126, 184, 188, 191

Dunn, Beatrice, 16

Dutton, Mary (IG's grandmother), 51

Eaton, Gertrude, 12, 218

Eaton, Sybil, 166, 173, 229

Eddy, Mary Baker, 167–8

Edinburgh War Hospital, 131–3, 155, 159, 215, 258

Egerton, Helen, 9

Eggar, Katharine, 12–14, 18 n28, 87–8, 291, 293

Elgar, Alice, 13

Elgar, Edward, 20, 23, 73, 84, 106, 265

Eliot, Thomas Stearns, 41

Elwes, Gervase, 105, 168, 189

Enesco, George, 20

Epstein, Jacob, 42

Evans, Nancy, 266

Evans, T., 136–7, 155

Fahey, John, 272–3

Fane, Valentine (Ivor Gurney pseudonym), 248

Farrar, Charles Druce, 15

Farrar, Ernest, 14–16, 114, 138, 190, 229
    Celtic Suite, 15, 18 n35

Ferguson, Howard, 260–1, 263 n42, 265, 286

Ferrier, Kathleen, 272, 274

Finzi, Gerald, 45, 62, 223, 228–9, 258–61, 264–5, 269, 272–4, 276–7, 279, 283–6, 291

Finzi, Joy, 261, 265, 272, 279, 286–9, 294 n10

Fogg, Eric, 191

Foss, Hubert, 261

Foulds, John, 18 n33

Frank, Alan, 274

Freeman, John, 86, 150, 156

Frost, Robert, 86–7, 156

Fuller, Sarah, 33

Gardiner, H. Balfour, 20

Gaye, Winifred (Eisenhardt), 44, 203

Geiringer, Karl, 269

George V, King, 259, 267

Georgian poetry, 41

German, Edward, 7

Gibbs, Armstrong, 189

Gibson, Wilfred, 41, 86–7, 189

Godding, Tim, 94

Godfrey, Herbert, 5

Godfrey, Louis, 12

Goossens, Eugene, 21

Grainger, Percy, 20

Graves, Robert, 183, 193 n17, 243

Greene, Harry Plunket, 258

Grenfell, Julian, 123

Grinke, Frederick, 267

Grove's Dictionary of Music and Musicians, 269, 274, 278, 293

Gurney, David (IG's father), 50–2, 54, 57, 63, 68, 141, 149, 152–3, 158, 160, 169, 171–2

Gurney, Dorothy (IG's sister), 51, 77, 141, 150, 153, 157–8, 160, 165, 275–6, 284, 287, 289

Gurney, Ethel (IG's sister-in-law), 203–4, 265, 288–90

Gurney, Florence (IG's mother, *née* Lugg), 50–4, 63, 68, 71, 73, 77, 153, 158, 204, 209, 225–8, 265–8, 275–7, 283–4, 287

Gurney, Ivor, 2, 3, 29, 30, 37, 38, 256, 271, 274, 277–8, 279, 291, 293

childhood/early years, 49–58

as composer, 16, 19, 22, 24, 26–7, 61, 69–70, 77, 79–82, 84–5, 87, 103–7, 112, 124–5, 136, 139, 142, 156, 166, 169, 170, 172–4, 181–4, 186, 188–92, 199–200, 202, 217, 228–9, 238–9, 243, 258–9, 260–1, 265–7, 272, 275, 277

contemporary trends, 20, 22, 40–2, 123, 181

death, 262

family, 50–4, 56–8; *see also* Gurney, David; Gurney, Dorothy; Gurney, Florence; Gurney, Ronald; Gurney, Winifred

education, 20, 57, 60–1

Royal College of Music, 16, 19–27, 66, 73–4, 84, 167, 171, 173, 175, 180–2, 186, 187, 192

scholarship to RCM, 2, 16–17

employment, 186–7

cinema pianist, 199

farm work/labourer, 160, 165, 171, 201

financial situation, 187, 189–90, 192, 199, 210

organist, 61–2, 73, 88–9, 173, 185, 187

tax clerk, 199–204

friendships, *see* Abercrombie, Catherine; Barnett, T. Ratcliffe; Benjamin, Arthur; Chapman family members; Cheesman, Alfred H. Haines, John W.; Harvey, F. W.; Howells, Herbert; Hunt, Emily; Hunt, Margaret; Scott, Marion M.; Shimmin, Sydney; Taylor, Maggie; Voynich, Ethel

and Gloucestershire, 19, 51, 56, 60, 62, 64, 70, 77–9

health & related themes, 72–3, 88–9, 102, 171, 241

Barnwood House, 208–12

bipolar illness, 26–7, 68, 70, 73, 77–82, 88–9, 122, 133, 140, 142–5, 148–52, 156–8, 170, 172, 175, 183–4, 185–6, 187, 192–3, 196, 202–4, 206–12, 215–20, 222–4, 229–34, 238–42, 259–60

(Gurney, Ivor, *continued*)
  (health & related themes, *continued*)
    City of London Mental Hospital
      (Stone House), 222–34, 238–42
    Christian Science healer, 239–40
    eating habits/digestive problems, 40,
      71–3, 84, 92, 121, 141, 158–9, 182,
      202, 203, 209, 217, 241–2, 260
    malaria, 218, 222
    nervous breakdown, 77–8, 79,
      142–45, 150–2
    suicide threats, 92, 149–50, 152, 203,
      209, 211, 216
    tuberculosis, 259–62
  legacy, 283–90
  letters, 290
  personal traits
    appearance, 16, 19, 22, 50, 60, 71–2,
      86, 122, 189, 203, 208, 245–6
    behaviour, 22, 42, 68–73, 82, 122,
      133–4, 139, 157–9, 173–4, 184, 186,
      199–200, 202–3, 239
    faith, 93–4
    humour, 106–7
    in society, 166, 173–4, 183, 189
    personality, 19, 21, 45, 50
    sexuality, 45–6, 74–6, 89, 114, 207
    temper, 24, 82, 202
  as poet, 40–42, 64, 78, 87, 99–101,
    103–4, 107, 110–2, 114–5, 117, 120–8,
    136, 139–41, 156, 160–1, 165–7, 169,
    170–5, 182–3, 191–2, 197, 200–1, 209,
    211, 223, 228, 238–9, 241–2, 248, 250,
    258–9, 265–6, 272, 274, 276–7
  tributes to, 264–7
  war service, 88, 89, 92–6, 99–108,
    110–18, 120–28
    alleged shell-shock, 150–2, 160, 216,
      264
    Armistice, 165
    discharge, 157
    Edinburgh War Hospital, 131–9
    gassed, 128
    Lord Derby's War Hospital, 144,
      148–50
    training, 92–5
    wounded, 121–23

women, 40, 45, 46
  Chapman, Catherine (Kitty),
    proposes marriage, 88–9
  Drummond, Annie Nelson, 137–42
  Hunt, Margaret, 68–71, 169–70
  Scott, Marion, 40, 45–7

Instrumental music
  The Apple Orchard, 265, 267
  In August, 70
  Nocturne in A flat, 69–70
  Nocturne in B major, 69–70
  Piano Preludes, 172
  Revery, 70
  Romance, 70
  Song of the Summer Woods, 70
  String Quartet in A minor, 79
  String Trio in G major, 79
  Violin Sonata (1918) 79, 161
  Violin Sonata in E flat major, 166, 170,
    172
  Wind in the Wood, 70

Orchestral music
  Coronation March, 182
  A Gloucestershire Rhapsody, 170, 181,
    182
  War Elegy, 182, 191

Songs
  All Night under the Moon, 266
  Black Stitchel, 191
  Blaweary, 191, 266
  The Boat is Chafing, 191
  By A Bierside, 103, 105–06, 117, 124,
    136, 173, 183, 188, 191
  Captain Stratton's Fancy (The Old
    Bold Mate), 87, 169, 182–3, 186
  Carol of the Skiddaw Yowes, 186
  Cathleen ni Houlihan, 170, 183
  The County Mayo, 156
  A Cradle Song, 191
  Desire in Spring, 166, 186
  Digging, 173
  An Epitaph, 191
  Epitaph on an Army of Mercenaries,
    166
  The Fields are Full, 191

(Gurney, Ivor, *continued*)

  (Songs, *continued*)

  Five Elizabethan Songs, 84, 85, 104, 186, 189

  The Folly of Being Comforted, 136, 139

  Goodnight to the Meadow, 191

  Halt of the Legion, 183

  Hawk and Buckle, 191

  The Horses, 169

  In Flanders, 169, 170, 173, 184, 191

  The Latmian Shepherd, 191, 266

  Lights Out, 191, 228, 238

  Loveliest of Trees, 182

  Ludlow and Teme, 182, 184, 190, 200, 272

  Most Holy Night, 191

  The Night at Trafalgar, 81

  Nine of the Clock, 191, 266

  O, happy wind, 166

  On the Downs, 183

  On Wenlock Edge, 125

  Only the Wanderer (Severn Meadows), 121, 184, 265

  Orpheus, 85

  The Penny Whistle, 156

  Sappho Songs, 172

  The Scribe, 166, 266

  Sleep, 85, 105, 170, 228–9, 265, 267

  Song of Silence, 142

  Sowing, 142

  Song of Solomon, 61

  Spring, 267

  Star Talk, 243

  Tears, 85

  To Violets, 191

  The Trumpet, 238

  The Twa Corbies, 17, 104, 186

  Under the Greenwood Tree, 85

  The Western Playland (and of Sorrow), 182, 190–1, 229, 238

  You are my sky, 266

  A Fourth Volume of Ten Songs, 286

  A Fifth Volume of Ten Songs, 290

Poetry

  Aberdonian, 172

  After Music, 104

Afterwards, 99

The Ballad of the Three Spectres, 120

The Battalion is Now on Rest, 114

To Certain Comrades, 103–4

The Crocus Ring, 170, 186

Dawn, 228

The Day of Victory, 165, 167

De Profundis, 156

Epitaph on a Young Child, 228

Equal Mistress, 186

The Estaminet, 114

Fire in the Dusk, 156

The Fire Kindled, 272

Firelight, 168

From the Window, 156

Girl's Song, 156

Hidden Tales, 156

High Street – Charing Cross, 174

The Hooligan, 186

Hospital Pictures – Ladies of Charity, 132

I Would not Rest, 242

In a Ward, 167, 186

Interval, 156

The Irish Sea, 41

It is near Toussaints, 228

La Gorgues, 114

Like Hebridean, 166

The Mangel-bury, 228

Migrants, 156

Of the Sea, 166

Omens, 156

On Rest, 114

The Peddlar's Song, 242

The Poets of My Country, 228

The Poplar, 156

The Retreat, 197

Robecq Again, 114

Sea Marge, 241

The Silent One, 228

Smudgy Dawn, 228

Snow, 228

Soft Rain, 242, 265

Solace of Men, 156

Song at Morning, 168

Song – I had a Girl's Fancies, 228

(Gurney, Ivor, *continued*)
  (Poetry, *continued*)
  Song (My Heart Makes Songs on
    Lonely Roads), 141
  Song of Pain and Beauty, xviii, 104, 117,
    197
  Sonnet to J. S. Bach's Memory, 265
  That County, 156
  Thoughts of New England, 228
  To An Unknown Lady, 115
  To F.W.H., 156
  To God, 209
  To M.M.S., 293
  To the Poet Before Battle, 99
  Toussaints, 156
  Twigworth Vicarage, 156
  The Volunteer, 167
  War Books, 228
  The Wind (by 'Valentine Fane'), 248
  Ypres, 104
  Ypres–Minsterworth, 156
Poetry collections
  The Book of Five Makings, 228
  Collected Poems of Ivor Gurney, 290
  Out of June and October, 272
  *Poems by Ivor Gurney: Principally
    Selected from unpublished
    manuscripts*, 285
  Poems of Ivor Gurney, 1890–1937, 289
  Rewards of Wonder, 228
  Severn & Somme, 99–100, 111, 117, 120,
    124–6, 139–41 (publication), 156,
    160–1, 167–8, 200, 276
  War's Embers, 156, 161, 167, 169, 170,
    172 (dedication to MMS), 174, 183,
    276
Asylum poetry collections
  The Book of Lives and Accusations, 228
  Dayspaces and Takings, 228
  Fatigues and Magnificences, 228
  La Flandre, and By-Norton, 228
  London seen Clear, 228
  Limestone, Ridge Clay, 228
  Memories of Honour, 228
  Pictures and Memories, 228
  Poems in Praise of Poets, 228

  *Poems of Gloucesters, Gloucester and
    of Virginia*, 228
  Poems to the States, 228
  Roman Gone East, 228
  *Six Poems of the North American
    States*, 228
  To Hawthornden, 228
Gurney, Marie (IG's aunt), 74, 200, 203
Gurney, Ronald (IG's brother) , 51–4,
  56–7, 62, 69, 72, 153, 167, 171–2, 192,
  203–4, 206–12, 218, 223–4, 233,
  265–8, 275–7, 283–90
Gurney, William (IG's grandfather), 52
Gurney, Winifred (IG's sister), 27 n2,
  47, 51–4, 56, 58, 61, 63, 72, 172, 265,
  275–7, 284, 286–9
Guthrie, Charles, 136

Haines, John, 41, 65, 84–7, 94, 96, 101,
  106, 123, 140, 150, 153, 156–60, 165–6,
  168–9, 171–4, 182–3, 187, 192, 200,
  203, 209, 265, 272, 277
Hall, Marion Amelia (Prince), 32
Hallé, Lady (Wilhelmina Norman-
  Neruda), 9
Halsted, Caroline Louisa, 55
Hamilton, William, 131
Handel, George Frederick, 5–6
Hardy, Thomas, 42, 80, 168, 238
Harper, Dr., 77, 211
Harris (lock-keeper), 77–8, 80
Harris, Dorothy Mortimer, 278
Harris, William H., 11–12, 16, 17 n16, 37,
  88, 260, 279
Harrison, May, 13
Harty, Hamilton, 173
Harvey, Bernard, 169
Harvey, Eric, 157, 169
Harvey, F. W. ('Will'), 41, 60, 69, 71, 73,
  78–80, 84–5, 96, 123–4, 137–8, 141,
  149–50, 152, 155, 165, 168, 170, 174,
  183–4, 192, 203, 206, 209, 265
  friendship with IG, 62–6, 74–6, 111–2,
  157, 160, 169, 200, 223–4
Harvey, Howard, 63
Harvey, Matilda, 63–4, 152
Hawkins, Mary (IG's grandmother), 52

Hay, Mrs, 230–3

Haydn, Franz Joseph, 241, 244–5, 255, 261, 269, 271, 273, 277–8, 285, 291, 293

Hedmondt, Charles, 6

Hensel, Fanny, 87

Heseltine, Philip (Peter Warlock), 188

Hindemith, Paul, 253–4, 255

Hislop, Gladys, 12

Hitler, Adolf, 269–71

Hodgson, William Noel, 103–4

Holmes, Sherlock, 31

Holst, Gustav, 10, 20, 26, 150, 243

Hopkins, Gerard Manley, 86, 200, 266

Horrocks, Amy, 21

Housman, A. E., 123, 140, 182, 191

Howard, Geoffrey, 103

Howells, Dorothy, 88, 123, 141, 170, 187, 189

Howells, Elizabeth, 21

Howells, Herbert, 42, 61, 74–5, 77, 79, 92, 94, 96, 102, 106, 111, 116–7, 126, 137–40, 144, 148, 160, 167–9, 172, 181, 185, 192, 200, 242, 255, 258, 265, 272

  appearance, 21–2, 64–5

  background, 19–20, 64–5

  meets Arthur Benjamin, 21–2, 24

  at Royal College of Music, 19, 21–2, 24, 26–7, 66, 80–1, 180

  friendship with IG, 27, 80–1, 88, 105, 141–2, 157–9, 170, 173–4, 184, 187, 223–5, 264, 266, 285, 289

  dedication of music to IG, 66

  rivalry with IG, 123–4

  and MMS, 38, 64–5, 100, 104–5, 149–50, 154–5, 161–2, 166, 184, 189, 198, 224–5, 259–60, 291

  and Stanford, 24, 26, 81

Howells, Michael, 259

Howells, Oliver, 64

Hubicki, Margaret, 291

Hughes, Rosemary, 257, 274–5, 291

Hummel, J. J., 244

Hunt, Emily, 50, 62, 68–9, 74, 79, 96, 114, 139, 153, 170–1, 174, 226, 258, 265

Hunt, Margaret, 50, 61–2, 68–71, 74, 79–80, 85, 89, 96, 114, 124, 139, 144, 149, 153, 160, 169–70

Hurd, Michael, 79, 193 n10, 290

International Exhibition for the Book Industry and Graphic Art, 87–8

Ireland, John, 26, 84, 174, 188

Ivor Gurney Society, 290

James, Ivor, 11

John, Augustus, 42

Kane, Sarah Anne, 192

Kavanagh, P. J., 290

Keay, Mrs John, 132

Kennedy, Joseph, 267

Kennedy-Fraser, Marjory, 87

Kerr, W. R. P. ('William'), 200–1, 206–8

Kinze, Herbert, 11

Kipling, Rudyard, 61

Korngold, Erich Wolfgang, 21

Kravchinski, Sergei ('Stepniak'), 43–4

Lawrence, D. H., 41

Lehmann, Liza, 13–14, 87

Letters of Administration, 266–7, 283–4, 285

Levetus, Jill and Daisy, 79

Lidderdale, H. M., 239–40

Lind, Jenny, 87

Listener, The, 265–6, 268

Liszt, Franz, 31

Lockhard, John Gibson, 278

Logan, Sinclair, 266

Lombardini, Maddalena (Mme Syrmen), 254

Longfellow, Henry Wadsworth, 64

Lord Derby's War Hospital, 144, 148–50, 156, 209

Lovibond, Audrey (MMS's niece, later Priestman), 9, 29–30, 38 n3, 104, 123, 168, 253, 267, 274, 283, 285

Lovibond, George Francis, 29

Lugg, William (IG's grandfather), 51

Mackenzie, M. Muir, 150–1, 160
Macleod, Fiona (William Sharp), 15
Maconchy, Elizabeth, 291
Mahler, Gustav, 21–2
Manns, Auguste, 6
Marsh, Edward, 41, 192, 199, 201
Mascagni, Pietro, 7
Masefield, John, 46, 87, 103, 106, 173, 182–3, 185, 188, 199
Mason, Olive, 16
Maturin, Sybil, 11
Mayflower, 267, 280 n24
McKay, James L., 203
Menges, Isolde, 265
Mendelssohn, Felix, 261, 279
Miles, Mrs Napier, 151
Miles, Philip Napier, 150–1, 160
Mill, John Stuart, 3
Milton, John, 93
Moberly, E. H., 7–8
Moberly's Ladies String Orchestra, 7–8
Monck, Agnes, 33
Monro, Harold, 41, 183, 189
Montagu, Olga, 166, 260
Moore, Charles W., 289–90
Moore, Lady Montgomery, 35
Morley, Charles, 11
Morris, R. O., 191
Mozart, Wolfgang Amadeus, 7, 142, 265
Muller, J. P., 84
Muse in Arms, The, 104, 117
Music and Letters, 14, 87, 88, 243–5, 254, 257–8, 259, 265, 290
Music Student, The, 13, 14, 87, 88, 292

Navarra, Dr, 230
Nesbitt, Cathleen, 186
Newman, Ernest, 255
Nicholls, Agnes, 13, 173
Nichols, Robert, 183
Nicholson, Mr and Mrs, 172
Nielson (sailor), 136–7

Osborn, E. B. (Edward Bolland), 104, 117
Owen, Wilfred, 116, 136, 189, 238, 276

Pankhurst, Emmeline, 3
Pankhurst, Richard, 3
Parratt, Walter, 10, 12
Parry, Hubert, 10–12, 19, 23, 73, 84, 149–50, 157, 181, 188, 190, 265, 279
Podmore, Frank, 31–2
Poldowski, Wieniawska ('Irena'), 21
Poston, Elizabeth, 291
Pound, Ezra, 40
Powell, Maud, 9
Priestman, Audrey Lovibond, *see* Lovibond, Audrey
Priestman, Graham, 283
Prince, Emily, 169
Prince, Eugene, 169, 267–8, 280 n27
Prince, George, 32–3
Prince family, 32–3, 39 n8
Prior, Hester Stansfeld, 250, 291
Pulitzer, Joseph, 167

Quilter, Roger, 84

Rachmaninoff, Sergei, 22
Radio Times, 274
Ravel, Maurice, 21, 25
Rawsthorne, Alan, 272
Ray, Don B., 277, 282 n62
RCM Magazine, 99, 117, 261, 265, 269, 271, 273
Reed, William, 73
Rheinberger, Joseph, 46
Richter, Hans, 6
Robinson, Dr, 258, 260
Rogers, Calista, 202
Rogers, Winthrop, 170, 186, 189, 202
Roland, Romain, 142
Rosenblum, Sigmund ('Sidney Reilly, Ace of Spies'), 44
Royal College of Music, 2–3, 7–12, 15–16, 19, 21, 23, 26–7, 29, 35, 61, 66, 70, 73–4, 77, 79, 81, 88, 102–5, 116, 123–4, 159, 165–7, 171–2, 175, 180–1, 187, 192, 211, 260–1, 264, 272, 276, 278–9, 292
Royal Musical Association, 253, 267, 269
Russian Free Press Fund, 43, 45

Sackbut, The, 188

Saint Petersburg, Russia, 30, 32–3, 43

Salem, Massachusetts, 32, 39 n8

Salmon, Thomas W., 151

Samuel, Harold, 173, 180

Sassoon, Siegfried, 113, 116

Scarlatti, Domenico, 269

Schoenberg, Arnold, 20–1, 22, 255, 272

Schrenk, Walter, 168

Schubert, Franz, 6, 16, 80

Schumann, Clara, 87

Schumann, Robert, 9, 143, 243

Scott, Annie (MMS's mother, *née* Prince), 3–4, 8, 10, 29–30, 32–3, 36–7, 45, 101, 123, 139, 149–50, 169, 187, 226, 259, 267, 269, 272

Scott, Cyril, 20

Scott, Edward (Sydney's brother), 30

Scott, Freda (MMS's sister, later Lovibond), 5, 29–30, 33, 35, 101

Scott, Herbert (Sydney's brother), 30

SCOTT, MARION MARGARET,
2, 19, 42, 72, 74, 75, 77, 79, 85, 88, 89, 92, 94, 95, 107, 110, 112, 120–5, 127–8, 133–9, 140–4, 165, 201–2

American heritage, 30, 32–3, 39 n8, 267, 292

birth, 3, 33

childhood, 4–8, 10, 33–5

education, 4–8, 23–4 30, 34–5
  RCM studies, 7–9, 292
  RCM Student Union, 10, 16, 29, 180, 261

family, 29–37, 169, 253, 259–60, 267–9, 272, 277, 283; *see also* Lovibond, Audrey; Scott, Annie; Scott, Freda; Scott, Stella; Scott, Sydney;

final years and death, 268–79

friendships, 38, 279; *see also* Eaton, Gertrude; Eggar, Katharine; Dale, Kathleen Richards; Davies, Fanny; Daymond, Emily; Vaughan Williams, Ralph; Voynich, Ethel

and Gurney family, 50–1, 152–3, 206–8, 212, 225–6, 266–8, 275–7, 283–5

and Ivor Gurney

concerns for IG, 50–1, 114–5, 143–4, 148–50, 152, 155, 198, 208, 211–2, 215, 218, 220, 230, 239–41, 245, 249

death of IG, 265–7

feelings for IG, 45–7, 48 n16, 114–5, 245–7, 256, 262, 265, 283

friendship with IG, 16, 29, 38, 40, 45–7, 77, 96–7, 105–6, 118, 172, 196–8, 201, 243–5, 245–50

guardian of IG's legacy, 104–5, 266–7, 275–6, 283–5

illness of IG, 50–1, 142–3, 148–58, 160–1, 187, 196, 206–12, 215–6, 218–20, 222–34, 238–41, 245–50, 257–9, 261–2

opinion of IG, 77, 85, 148, 154, 171, 190–2

partnership with IG, 99–108, 117, 122, 126–7, 160–1, 170–1, 174, 184, 198

health, 9, 46, 100–2, 122–3, 148, 160, 168, 219, 277–8

nervous breakdown, 218–20

personal traits

advocacy for social reform, 3–4, 8, 12–13, 37

appearance, 3, 46, 269, 277, 278, 291

character, 8, 10, 13, 16, 29, 30, 38, 102, 148, 161, 266–7, 269, 273, 275, 277, 279, 290–3

humour, 5–6, 38, 273

metaphysical beliefs, 7, 36, 103, 143, 198, 218–20, 222–3, 255–6

promotional skills, 3, 8, 10, 12–13, 168, 184, 188, 253

professional life

advocacy for contemporary music, 10–11, 14, 166, 184, 292–3

advocate for women, 4, 11, 253, *see also* Society of Women Musicians

assessment of achievements, 279, 290–3

Beethoven biography, 254–7

as composer, 9–10, 102, 291, 309–10

as critic, 154, 165, 167–9, 172, 174, 187–9, 190, 192, 206, 243–4, 272, 274, 291–2

as editor, *Proceedings*, 273, 177

(Scott, Marion Margaret, *continued*)
(professional life, *continued*)
as editor, *RCM Magazine*, 261, 271, 273
lecturer, 11, 253–4, 292
Marion Scott Quartet, 11, 38, 45, 292
music editions published, 245, 263 n45
as musicologist, 102, 244–5 (Haydn), 253–4 (Hindemith), 254 (Lombardini), 254–7 (Beethoven), 261, 277–8
as performer, 7–10, 31, 37, 45
as poet, 8, 34, 37, 116, 291
Society of Women Musicians, 12–14, 87, 188, 196, 253, 261, 271–2
as writer, 4–7, 11, 13, 14, 16 n2, 33–6, 87, 100, 102–4, 180, 188, 244, 257, 265–6, 268–9, 274, 277, 278, 291–3, 306–8
relationships
attitude towards men, 13, 46
Capell, Richard, 243
Farrar, Ernest, 14–16
jealousy, 37, 115, 138, 226
love affairs, 18 n35, 35, 229, 243
Russian heritage, 30, 32–3, 45, 169, 277
travel, 30, 87–8, 196–8, 218–20, 254
wealth, 32, 35, 207, 260, 293 n1
World War II, 269–72
youth, 35–37
Scott, Mercy (Sydney's mother), 30
Scott, Sydney (MMS's father), 3, 8, 10, 12, 29–33, 36–7, 101, 113, 123, 152–3, 168, 211, 226, 259–60, 269
Scott, Stella (MMS's sister), 5, 29–30, 33, 35, 46, 101, 123, 139, 161, 226, 253, 260, 267, 269–70, 272–4
Scott, William (Sydney's father), 30, 35
Scott-Moncrieff, Charles, 189, 195 n47, 199
Scriabin, Alexander, 174, 180
Shakespeare, William, 61, 95, 241
Shanks, Edward, 167, 174, 183, 189
Shanks, Phillis, 184
Sharp, Cecil, 184
Shostakovich, Dmitri, 271–2

Shelley, Percy Bysshe, 247
Shimmin, Mona, 127
Shimmin, Sydney, 45, 79, 93, 96, 102, 116, 123, 126–7, 144, 165, 174, 187, 218, 220, 223–4, 265
Sibelius, Jean, 22
Sidgwick, Frank, 201
Sidgwick & Jackson, 117, 123, 126–7, 156, 160, 201, 276
Soutar, James Grieg, 208
Smith, Adam, 134
Smith, Mabel Saumarez, 180
Smyth, Ethel, 13, 87
Society for Psychical Research, 31, 260
Society of Friends of Russian Freedom, 43–5
Society of Women Musicians, 12–14, 102–4, 116, 188, 244, 253, 268, 290–1
Somervell, Arthur, 24
Spitta, Philipp, 43
Stanford, Charles Villiers, 8–12, 19, 22–7, 66, 73, 81–2, 84, 124–5, 173, 181, 184, 199–200, 227–8, 292
Stanford, Geraldine, 125
Stanford, Guy, 125
Stanford, Jane ('Jenny') Wetton, 23
Steen, R. H., 218, 222
Stevenson, Robert Louis, 9, 136, 140
Strangways, A.H. Fox, 183, 191, 257–9
Strauss, Richard, 22–3
Stravinsky, Igor, 20–1
Squire, John C., 174, 189, 216, 250, 258
Squire, W. H. Haddon, 168
Subira, José, 168
Suddaby, Elsie, 228, 274
Swanwick, Helena, 115
Synge, John Millington, 22

Taylor, Colin, 105
Taylor, Edward, 44, 173
Taylor, Geoffrey, 45, 166
Taylor, Julian, 45
Taylor, Margaret ('Maggie'), 43, 45, 80, 85, 138–9, 141, 172–3, 226
Taylor, Mr, 105
Temple Church, 34–5
Terry, Harold C., 203, 207–8

Thalben-Ball, George, 166, 184, 189

Thomas, Edward, 86, 156, 168, 173, 238, 249, 266, 272

Thomas, Helen, 249–50

Thornton, R. K. R., 290

Tippett, Michael, 272

Tovey, Donald, 257

Townsend, Arthur, 209–12, 215

Tulloch, Esmé, 15

Turner, W. J., 183

Tyron, Winthrop P., 168

Underwood, Samuel, 60, 62

Van Dieren, Bernard, 168

Vaughan Williams, Adeline, 216–7, 226, 239, 242, 259

Vaughan Williams, Ralph, 20, 22, 24, 26, 60, 77, 84, 102, 105, 150, 182–3, 190, 201, 217, 226, 242, 255, 258, 265–6, 286

  teacher of IG, 181

  and music of IG, 261, 269, 273, 285, 287

  and poetry of IG, 272–3

  and illness of IG, 203, 206, 208–9, 216, 230–2, 266

Verne, Jules, 33

Viardot-Garcia, Pauline, 87

Victoria, Queen, 35–6, 259

Voynich, Ethel L. (Boole), 43, 79–80, 92–3, 95–6, 99, 106, 110, 114, 138–9, 141, 166, 175 n6, 179 n6, 226

Voynich, Wilfrid Michael, 42–5

Vuillermoz, Emil, 168

Wagner-Jauregg, Julius, 234 n2

Wagner, Richard, 25–6

Walsh, Kitty, 283

Warren, Francis Purcell, 155, 180

Wharton, Edith, 121

Wheatley, Tom (Mr & Mrs), 185

Whitehead, Miss, 63–4

Whitman, Walt, 240

Wilde, Oscar, 75, 95

William Ropes & Company, 32

Williams, Iolo Aneurin, 192

Williams, Tom Emlyn, 267

Wilson, Steuart, 183–5, 189–90, 265–6

Winkelmann, Emilie, 87

Winterbotham, Ernest, 266

Wolf, Hugo, 264

Wood, Charles, 19, 73

Wood, Henry, 20, 173–4

Wordsworth, William, 93

Wurm, Mary, 10

Yeats, William Butler, 22, 40, 81, 183